A History of England in Eight volumes
Founder Editor, Sir Charles Oman

Volume VI
ENGLAND UNDER THE HANOVERIANS

METHUEN'S
HISTORY OF MEDIEVAL AND MODERN EUROPE

ENGLAND UNDER THE HANOVERIANS

Sir Charles Grant Robertson

LONDON: METHUEN & CO LTD
NEW YORK: BARNES & NOBLE INC

First published February 23rd, 1911
Reprinted seventeen times
Reprinted 1958

16.3
CATALOGUE NO. (METHUEN) 3376/U

PRINTED IN GREAT BRITAIN

HL 3/13

INTRODUCTORY NOTE

BY THE GENERAL EDITOR

IN England, as in France and Germany, the main characteristic of the last fifty years, from the point of view of the student of history, has been that new material has been accumulating much faster than it can be assimilated or absorbed. The standard works of the 19th-century historians need to be revised, or even to be put aside as obsolete, in the light of the new information that is coming in so rapidly and in such vast bulk.

The series of which this volume forms a part is intended to do something towards meeting the demand for information brought up to date. Individual historians will not sit down, as once they were wont, to write twenty-volume works in the style of Hume or Lingard, embracing a dozen centuries of annals. It is not to be desired that they should—the writer who is most satisfactory in dealing with Anglo-Saxon antiquities is not likely to be the one who will best discuss the antecedents of the Reformation, or the constitutional history of the Stuart period. But something can be done by judicious co-operation. In the thirty-four years since the first volume of this series appeared in 1904, it would seem that the idea has justified itself, as the various sections have passed through many editions and revisions varying from six to seventeen.

Each is intended to give something more than a mere outline of one period of our national annals, but they have little space for controversy or the discussion of sources. There is, however, a bibliography annexed to most of the series, which will show the inquirer where information of the more special kind is to be sought. Moreover, a number of maps are to be found at the end of each volume which, as it is hoped, will make it unnecessary for the reader to be continually referring to large historical atlases—tomes which (as we must confess with regret) are not to be discovered in every private library.

The general editor and his collaborators have been touched lightly by the hand of time. All regret the too early decease of our colleague Henry Carless Davis, sometime Regius Professor of Modern History in this University, who wrote the second of the eight volumes of the series. He had several times revised his contribution. Most of us survivors continue to do the same from time to time, as the pen (or sometimes the spade) produces new sources of information. Naturally the spade is particularly active for the purveying of fresh material for the first of our volumes, and the pen (or the press) for the two last. Information must be kept up to date, whatever the epoch concerned, even though it is known that much undiscovered evidence may yet be forthcoming in the near future.

C. OMAN

OXFORD, 1st Jan., 1938

PREFACE

THE writer who endeavours to cover in a single volume of 500 pages the period of English history from 1714 to 1815 is confronted by an insoluble and continuous difficulty. The problem is not the selection of what he will insert, but of what he will omit. The original sources are so embarrassingly rich, the historical stage is so crowded with attractive or commanding personalities, the plot is so packed with episodes, and the story so interlaced with the evolution of the European state system that a writer, with space at his disposal double that of the present volume, would of necessity lay himself open to criticism on the score of arrangement, choice of subjects, and omissions. Every reader, or would-be reader, comes to the history of eighteenth century Great Britain with decided interests, preferences, and a scale of values ; and every writer working under exacting conditions of space is probably bound to disappoint more readers than he can satisfy, even if the treatment of what he has selected be adequate.

I cannot expect, therefore, that this volume has achieved the impossible ; and I fully recognise that, while selection has been an insuperable difficulty, I have too often been obliged to be brief when I would willingly

have been copious, to sacrifice much material I had
hoped to include, and to be silent on many points which
I would gladly have discussed. It has been my object
to treat the eighteenth century as a whole, to emphasise
as clearly as lay in my power what, on prolonged reflection, appear to be capital, characteristic, and important features, to be guided in the choice of topics and
principles by the century that preceded and the century
that followed, to present the period from 1714 to 1815
as a great chapter in a continuous but unfinished national evolution, and to touch lightly, or pass over, with
much regret, aspects, episodes, and details that, tested
by this standard, appear to be of secondary interest
and importance.

Briefly, it has been my endeavour to trace the
ordered development of an imperial, constitutional, and
industrial State, the foundations of which were laid
when George I. ascended the throne, and to show how
far the structure of that State had been modified or
advanced when Napoleon was overthrown in 1815.
The expansion of the British Empire, the consolidation
of Parliamentary government under a constitutional
monarchy, the transformation of the political and economic organisation of society by the agricultural and
industrial Revolution—to illustrate and explain these
three capital features of eighteenth century British
history has been my self-imposed task. Certain controversial points, a discussion of which would have
interrupted the narrative text, have been relegated to
appendices ; and in each case the evidence on which
conclusions are based is specifically indicated. Military
or naval history, in which the century is so rich, but
which can only be profitably handled or studied in

elaborate detail, has been summarised rather than expounded at length. But I have striven to connect the evolution of the constitution, the broad movement in thought and ideas and the working of the underlying economic forces with the central issues of political history proper. The Bibliography has been drawn up with a view of providing a student with the necessary and practical information both as to topics and features discussed in the text and to episodes handled lightly or omitted. I may, perhaps, be permitted to hope that the volume may prove helpful even to those who do not find in it all that they expect or need.

There remains the pleasant duty of thanking specifically some kind friends. M. Paul Mantoux, the well-known author of a brilliant study of the Industrial Revolution, *bien documenté*, put at my disposal the fruits of his researches which are embodied in the two maps illustrating the movement of population in the eighteenth century. With no less generosity Mr. Blaikie allowed me to adapt for my purposes the map, an indispensable piece of painstaking research, in his *Itinerary of Prince Charles Edward ;* and Professor Terry also permitted me to incorporate, if necessary, material embodied in his *The Last Jacobite Rising of 1745.* The map, therefore, at the end of the volume is due to these two experts. Mr. H. W. C. Davis, of Balliol College, undertook the thankless task of reading the proofs, and helped me with many criticisms and suggestions. To my editor, Professor Oman, I am similarly indebted, and I have drawn freely on his *History of the Peninsular War*, the completion of which is eagerly awaited by all serious students. But none of these gentlemen must be held responsible for the accuracy of statements, or for opinions expressed, in the text. My general debt to the standard secondary authorities will be obvious to all acquainted with the literature of the period ; but throughout I have aimed at independence of judgment, and, to the best of my ability and knowledge, at basing my conclusions on the original sources rather than on the secondary authorities, however authoritative.

C. G. R.

ALL SOULS COLLEGE, OXFORD,
November, 1910.

NOTE TO THE TENTH EDITION (1930)

SINCE this book was published in 1911, various additions of a piece-meal kind have been made to subsequent re-issues. The present edition is the result of a complete revision both of the text of the narrative, the Appendices, and the Bibliographies. The revision is based on the research work of many scholars since 1911, so as to bring the book up to date in every way. History, happily, can never be like mathematics, an exact science in which a conclusion is either exactly right or wholly wrong. Historical judgments will always be influenced by "values" to which different minds will attach a different qualitative scale. I have endeavoured to see that the facts have been accurately stated ; my conclusions from those facts, framed after prolonged reflection, must be left to the reader's judgment.

The main results of the revision will be found in the footnotes to the text, the Appendices, many of which are new and all of which have been revised, and in the Bibliography. The differences in the present text from that of 1911 could only be shown by a page to page collation.

I have been helped in the *improbus labor* of revision by many comments from teachers and readers ; and the Revised Edition will, I hope, be not less useful than I should like it to be.

C. G. R.

THE UNIVERSITY, BIRMINGHAM,
October, 1929.

CONTENTS

CHAPTER III

CHAPTER IV

THE REIGN OF GEORGE III

CHAPTER I

CHAPTER II

b

APPENDICES

NOTE.—*New* and not merely revised Appendices are marked with an asterisk.

TABLES

MAPS

ENGLAND
UNDER THE HANOVERIANS

INTRODUCTION

THE seventeenth century as a historical epoch in British history properly closes with 1714. The death of Anne, the last of the Stuart line, saw the end of the long struggle which began in 1603 with the peaceful accession of the first Stuart to the English throne. The equally peaceful accession of George I. meant much more than the introduction of a new dynasty. Thrice in the previous hundred years the form of government had been violently altered. One King had perished on the scaffold ; the founder of the Commonwealth had been branded as a usurping traitor; a second sovereign of the restored line had died in exile and his sons disinherited by penal statutes. In 1714 an Englishman of sixty years of age could recall the downfall of the military republic, the restoration of Charles II., alliance with France to destroy Holland, alliance with Holland to destroy France, the horrors of the Popish Plot, the struggle over the Exclusion Bill, the proscription of the Whigs, the campaign of Sedgemoor, the expulsion of James II., civil war in Ireland and Scotland, twenty years of war abroad, and the "last four years of Queen Anne". Foreign observers might well be justified in pronouncing the English people singularly fickle, unstable, turbulent, treacherous and vindictive. In reality the era of fierce travail was finished. Behind the welter of bloodshed, and warring creeds, a national State had been slowly built up, and the coming of the new German ruler triumphantly indicated the solidarity of its basis in the Revolution Settlement. George I.'s crown was the creation of law and national will ; the people he was invited to rule were in culture, institutions and principles of government indelibly stamped with the spirit and achievement of an intense and peculiar nationality. At Westminster, Edinburgh and Dublin the Protestant national State was linked with a Protestant national Church.

The legislative union of 1707 had converted the personal union of
the English and Scottish Crowns into the single dominion of Great
Britain.   And with 1714 set in a remarkable change.   Henceforward Europe may be rent asunder by political upheavals;
dynasties may come and go, forms of government be remade,
crumble and perish, and the streets of European capitals run with
the blood of revolution.   Great Britain alone is the exception.
Her sovereigns die in their beds and pass their sceptre undisputed
to their heirs ; the outward form of the constitution defined in 1689
and 1701 remains unaltered ; London, unlike Paris, Moscow, Berlin,
Vienna, Brussels, Rome, has never seen a foreign foe in possession ;
in the British calendar days of March, May, July, August and
December are not marked for national rejoicing or remorse.   Whatever verdict may be passed on the British people since 1714 they
must be acquitted of the charge that in constitutional matters
they are incurably turbulent, unstable and vindictive.   A single
formula—the expansion of Great Britain—conveniently sums up
the main results of the new epoch which begins with 1714 and
ends with Waterloo and the Congresses of Vienna.   And in this
expansion three features stand out in deep-cut relief—the growth
and consolidation of the empire, the organisation of the parliamentary State, the Industrial Revolution.   These three are triple
aspects of the evolution of a single national life.   They are concurrently worked out ; common formative causes combine to operate
in producing effects that are revealed concurrently in the political,
constitutional and economic spheres of State-development.   But
the student, anxious to compare broadly the contribution of the
eighteenth century to our national development with that of the
seventeenth and the nineteenth centuries, is entitled to disentangle
and to analyse these features separately, in order more accurately
to appreciate their intrinsic characteristics and import.

I. In 1714 the treaties of Utrecht mark a definite stage in the
expansion of the British Empire, whose groundwork was now
firmly laid.   Gibraltar and Minorca were stepping-stones to the
East; on the West coast of Africa trading settlements pointed to the
Cape and across the Atlantic to Jamaica and the British islands in
the West Indies.   In North America twelve colonies hold the
eastern littoral from the Penobscot River to South Carolina.   Farther
North, Acadia, Newfoundland, Rupert's Land and the Hudson Bay

Territory were a threat to, and threatened by, the growth and expansion of New France. In the Peninsula of Hindustan, Bombay, Calcutta and Madras marked the footholds of the East India Company. Will these results be retained? What structure can or will be built on these foundations? It is the problem of the new world, East and West, a problem of oceanic commerce and colonial development, whose full significance is not grasped until half the century has worn itself out in efforts to upset, and counter-efforts to maintain, the Treaties of Utrecht from which it starts. And then the imperial movement sets in with impressive force, so that by 1815 the answer to the questions of 1714 has been given with unmistakable emphasis. To the diplomatists of 1713 Great Britain is the paramount sea-power, to the diplomatists of 1814 she is also the paramount colonial Power. "The old colonial system" serves to remind us that before 1714 the empire and the imperial problem were fully recognised. To the men of the eighteenth century the problem in foreign policy is first and foremost a question of the relations of Great Britain to France and the kindred Bourbon States, Spain that flanks the Western Mediterranean and looks across the Atlantic to a jealously guarded commercial empire, the Two Sicilies, which are the creation of eighteenth-century diplomacy. From 1689-1815 for Great Britain seventy-seven years are years of war, and of these fifty-six are waged openly with France as a principal. The rivalry extends from Europe to the remote corners of the earth, and it is one not merely of arms, but of exploration, of commerce, of civilisation in its intellectual and social aspects, of political principles and systems of government. For France strikes with her civilisation and her national and racial ideals as well as with her ships and guns. Europe, it has been well said, was Bourbonised, before she was revolutionised, by France. From the unceasing struggle with the Bourbon, Great Britain passes inevitably to the titanic battle with Napoleon and the French Empire which "the heir of 1789" founded on the Bourbonised Europe of the *ancien régime*. In 1713 Great Britain had survived the collision with the monarchy of Louis XIV.; in 1815 she emerges victorious from the fight for existence with Napoleon; and the results are woven into the fabric of the British State and written on the map of the world.

II. In the evolution of the British Constitution the change

between 1714 and 1815 is superficially less striking perhaps, but none the less of permanent significance. In 1714 Great Britain alone of the leading European States had definitely committed herself to a constitutional monarchy, to parliamentary institutions, to representative government in principle by and on behalf of the governed. Defective as we, the heirs to-day of that system who have entered into and extended our heritage, may regard it, the capital fact remains that Englishmen in the seventeenth century had literally cut their national life from the broad currents of European State-development, and had bought with their blood and treasure the right to liberty under a limited monarchy. Nor can it escape a student's notice that before the men of our race entered on the critical period of imperial expansion they first settled beyond dispute the fundamentals of their home-government. In 1689 and 1701 they closed the long account with monarchy and Church, with Kings, soldiers and priests. The supremacy of the Constitutional Crown over all causes and all persons ecclesiastical as well as civil throughout its dominions—the supremacy of the civil over the military power—the supremacy of law as made by the Crown in Parliament—the supremacy of the Commons in taxation, the practical independence of the judiciary as the interpreter of the law, the responsibility of the executive agents of the Crown to the legislature—these and their corollaries are, in the language of the national settlement, "the birthright" of the people of England. No Englishman, Whig or Tory, was prepared to surrender them; they sum up with telling precision the fundamental difference between the British State of 1714 and the rival European States of that day. A triple duty was thereby imposed on the eighteenth century British citizen —to prove that his system would repay what it had cost to win— in the grinding strain of international competition to convince a sceptical and hostile Europe that, in Fox's noble phrase, liberty was order, that liberty was strength, and that liberty was also unity— to apply to the Britains growing up beyond the seas the same principles of freedom and self-government. In two of these tasks the facts supply an adequate verdict. Great Britain fought as a parliamentary State with the absolutist Bourbon Powers and the centralised military despotism of Napoleon, and though she was guilty of many mistakes, one blunder she persistently declined to make. Even in the darkest hours of national peril and disaster the belief of Englishmen in the superior efficacy of their free government remained unshaken. For us who can look back, their justification most truly lies not in Quebec, Minden, Salamanca, Trafalgar, Waterloo, but in the moral and spiritual elements built into our national life and our conception of citizenship by that noble national obstinacy of conviction—the faith of a people in its ideals and interpretation of life. And if the independence of the United States witnesses to a failure, the development of Cabinet government at home, the retention of Canada, and the establishment of British power in India by a parliamentary State, were instructive object-lessons for the nineteenth century.

III. The seventeenth century had made Great Britain and Holland "the two sea-powers"; England already was, in 1713, what Louis XIV. had called her, a nation of shopkeepers. But as yet her national economy is that of a trading not a manufacturing community; she is a commercial not an industrial State. As early as 1714, the influence of trade and the commercial classes on English policy, on government, and on institutions and social organisation is a characteristic emphasised by every foreign observer.[1] The Bank of England and the National Debt showed how commerce and wealth combined to be the motor forces and the armoury of a national policy. And the commercial aspects of the State found their most comprehensive and concrete political expression in the mercantilist system based on mercantilist economics. The chief aim of this system, dating from the Navigation Acts of 1651 and 1660, was to develop national power; its method, the tariff-book, may be economic but its objects are essentially political, derived from a conception of national well-being and imperial unity whose justification rested on the current definition and interpretation of wealth. It thus operates both as the cause and the effect of the seventeenth century ideal of nationalism. But if we compare 1815 with 1714 we see that a new Great Britain has been brought into existence. Manufacture on a large scale in specialised districts, capitalistic production, a series of mechanical inventions altering the methods,

---

[1] "These gentlemen [the merchants] . . . used in time past to come Cap in Hand to the office praying for relief, now the second word is, *You shall hear of it in another place*, meaning in Parliament. All this must be endured, and now in our turn we must bow and cringe to them" (Delafaye to Keene, Oct. 3rd, 1731. P.R.O., Spain, S.P.F., 109; cited by Temperley, *Royal Hist. Soc.*, 1909, 222).

scope and volume of trade, the scientific and extended utilisation
of the raw material, iron and coal, hidden in the soil; the trebling
of population and a redistribution of it on the map, the increasing
concentration of life in towns, comprehensive enclosures, scientific
agriculture, the break up of the mediæval village community, the
displacement of domestic industry, the dying out of the yeomanry,
and a new school and system of economics—these are the striking
features of the new Great Britain which justify the term "industrial revolution". The era of coal, iron, machinery, water-power,
factories, and the industrial proletariat has been reached. The
transition from mercantilism to the era of steam, electricity, and
industrial democracy has been accomplished. The centre of economic gravity in 1815 is now fixed in the heart of the district
bounded by a line from Glasgow to Edinburgh, and a diagonal
line from Bristol to the Wash. The seventeenth century wastes
are already the familiar Black Country of the nineteenth century.
We may pause to note further : (1) these striking changes are com-
pressed largely into the epoch between 1780 and 1815. Seldom
has an organised State passed through so complex and complete an
alteration of its economic life in so short a period ; (2) the change
begins in the era of the American war which dismembered the
Empire and culminates in the colossal strain of the Napoleonic
wars ; (3) it was in reality a political revolution, for it dislocated
the established distribution of political power ; (4) it was inevitably
accompanied by widespread and deep social suffering; it made
unemployment, pauperism, and the regulation of industry formidable national problems. By 1815, viewing the results as a whole,
the industrial primacy of Great Britain is established beyond
challenge. At that date she is in Europe the only industrial State
in the modern sense of the term, and her supremacy rests on three
qualities—the synthetised features of her industrial organisation,
the volume, character and range of her economic production, and
her maritime ascendancy.

The roughest analysis of these co-operative forces whose effects
are graven deep on the structure of our modern, imperial, constitutional, and industrial British State, thus suggests that it is unjust
and inaccurate to limit the proud title of empire-builder to a handful of admirals, generals, and statesmen. Hume, Burke, Bentham
and Adam Smith, Mansfield, Camden, Erskine and Eldon, Jethro

Tull, "Turnip" Townshend, Arthur Young, Bakewell and Coke of Norfolk, Arkwright, Boulton, Wedgwood and Watt, Wesley, Wilberforce, Clarkson, Romilly and Howard, even a profligate demagogue such as Wilkes, or the dissipated staymaker Tom Paine, have a right to share the mansions assigned by the proud gratitude of fellow-citizens to Walpole, Chatham, Pitt, Clive, Warren Hastings, Dorchester, Nelson, Wellington, Castlereagh, Canning, and Wellesley. Multiply or diminish the list, the names are only isolated voices expressing more or less eloquently the inarticulate aspirations of the national spirit, broken lights through which flash the unquenchable aspirations of millions of humble hearts, the reaching out of millions of groping hands for the undying ideal of a nation's life. In the valleys of the eighteenth century, so storm-ridden then, so dim to-day, the vanquished, too, speak of the sweat and dust of a nation's travail—Bolingbroke and Charles Edward, the Highlanders who perished at Culloden, the Irishmen of '98. Every parish churchyard, the forgotten graves under tropical suns, the oblivion of the blood-stained seas, hold unnumbered nameless men and women who before they died had responded to the magic of the dreams of the great dreamers, had given to their land and their people's future that small but costly sacrifice without the free gift of which they and their country would have been the poorer. The great empire-builder has been the British people. At the tribunal of history the chronicler is only the clerk of the court; the British people stand at the bar, and the British people, who come after, must judge. Mercy, truth, and justice alike demand that the verdict should be based, not upon the sum of what was accomplished, but upon the final value to the world of the ideals of national life that failure and success in the efforts of a century alike reveal.

The year 1714 opens a new chapter in the evolution of the State-system of modern Europe. From 1714-40 the elements of the political situation, particularly as they affect the foreign policy of Great Britain, combine and dissolve with kaleidoscopic suddenness, while the apparent reversal of the principles of the dominant party at London adds a further confusing element.

The last four years of Queen Anne had witnessed a bitter and dramatic struggle between the two historic parties in the British State. The contest at home turned largely on principles of foreign policy, and on the issue of that struggle, as was clearly grasped by Bolingbroke, Harley and Ormonde, by Marlborough, Godolphin, Sunderland and Stanhope, by Louis XIV. and Prince Eugène, depended the character of the future government of Great Britain. The Whigs, taught by their master William III., were determined to maintain the Balance of Power by breaking the Bourbon ascendancy in Europe of Louis XIV. From 1689 to the outbreak of the French Revolution this fear of the Bourbon dynasties (traceable even in the period of the *entente cordiale* from 1717-38) remained the most characteristic article of the Whig creed in foreign policy. The system of William III., completed by Marlborough and Godolphin, rested on an identity of political interest between three European centres—London, the Hague, Vienna; diplomatically it was expressed in a network of continental alliances, militarily by using British troops in co-operation with the armies of the grand alliance, navally by securing the command of the sea, financially by lavish subsidies to the anti-French allies. William III. and Marlborough thus secured the Revolution system at home, the balance of power in Flanders, and on the Rhine. Conversely, the Tories decided to sever Great Britain from costly and unnecessary continental entanglements, and to base her power on insular isolation made invincible by a supreme fleet. France was not the enemy to be annihilated, but a rival, an understanding with whom could secure European peace and the extension of our commerce.[1] The Bourbon hostility to the Revolution system and support to Jacobitism made this an audacious and difficult policy, but the Tory Ministry of 1710-14 carried it out. The treaties of Utrecht, negotiated under

---

[1] *Cf.* Sunderland's statement: "The strange whim . . . as if the Parliament was not to concern themselves in anything that happens" in Germany or the Continent, "and indeed this notion *is nothing but the old Tory one that England can subsist by itself, whatever becomes of the rest of Europe, which has been so justly exploded by the Wigs (sic) ever since the Revolution*" (*Hist. MS. Comm.*, Rep. xi., App. IV., p. 103): with these dicta from Bolingbroke : "*an island*, under one government, advantageously situated, rich in itself, richer by its commerce, *can have no necessity in the ordinary course of affairs to take up the policy of the Continent, to enter into the system of alliances* . . . or, in short, to act any other part than that of a friendly neighbour and a fair trader" (*Works*, ii., 191) : " We must remember we are not part of the Continent, but we must never forget that we are neighbours to it " (*op. cit.*, viii. 382), and Swift's *Conduct of the Allies, passim*.

fierce Whig criticism, gave peace to England and France, and withdrew Great Britain from the continental struggle. How the victories won by the Whig system secured the concession of tolerable terms, and how Bolingbroke's policy was mutilated by the rejection of the commercial treaty does not concern us here. It suffices that Bolingbroke's diplomacy accomplished two decisive results—peace with France and the acceptance by Louis XIV. of the Protestant succession as regulated by British law. Bolingbroke indeed intended to go much farther. A new system of alliance between Great Britain, the Bourbon Powers (France and Spain), and Savoy to compel the House of Austria and its allies (the former allies of Great Britain) to accept a European settlement satisfactory to this new coalition was already on foot at Whitehall. It is not necessary to discuss here whether this was also to be followed by upsetting the Protestant succession, and the establishment of the permanent supremacy of the Tory party by imposing Tory terms on the Jacobite claimant. Bolingbroke won his free hand too late, and the Queen's death on August 1st, 1714, left England in a singular position. At that moment she had not an ally in Europe. The policy of one great party had been reversed, the members of the Whig Grand Alliance alienated ; the Tories had so far secured only the bare neutrality of France. Outstanding questions—the expulsion of "the Pretender" from Lorraine, the demolition of the fortifications at Dunkirk, the treatment of the Catalans—had still to be regulated. Spain and the House of Austria were still at war ; the Barrier Treaty between England and Holland, by which the Dutch pledged themselves to garrison a line of fortresses between the new Austrian Netherlands and France at Austrian expense, and guaranteed the Protestant succession together with the grant of commercial privileges, had not been accepted by the Emperor. The political and economic relations of England to Spain, embittered by the transfer of Gibraltar and Minorca, were not properly defined, and the vital questions between Madrid and Vienna, involving the distribution of power in the Mediterranean were still unsolved. France, too, might repeat her conduct of 1701, and repudiate her acceptance of the Protestant succession. If the fateful Sunday of August 1st was followed by what has been called the greatest miracle in our history, the peaceful accession of George I., the uncertainty and confusion in the relations of the European States do not evaporate until the death of a more important world-figure, Louis XIV., on September 1st, 1715.

For two decades and more the maintenance or reversal of the Treaties of Utrecht dominate European and British diplomacy. Europe expected in 1714 that a Whig Ministry, restored under the Hanoverian sovereign to ascendancy, would return to the system of Marlborough and Godolphin and renew the war à outrance with France. Only in this way could the Grand Alliance be rebuilt and Britain and British allies exact retribution from the Ahab who troubled Israel. For twelve months England hovered on the edge of war. But the European chanceries had not penetrated the patriotic selfishness of Whig statesmanship. Foreign policy to the Whigs was not an end in itself but simply the means to a grand object, the maintenance of the revolution system. The annihilation of Bourbon ascendancy, the Balance of Power, the Whig watchwords, were primarily based not on European but on purely English needs, as interpreted by a great party. That the Whigs decided to uphold the treaties of 1713 may be a paradox of party government, but it was the facts not the Whigs that had changed. From 1714-42 the preservation of the Protestant succession and the Revolution system are as persistently pushed as previously from 1689-1710—but by a different method. Stanhope who made the French alliance of 1717, Walpole who strove to keep it intact, worked for the same party interpretation of a national ideal as William III., Somers, Marlborough, and Godolphin who fought to bleed France white. Nor did the decision rest with Great Britain alone. The sleepless disturber of the peace of Europe from 1715-40 is Spain, inspired by a woman, Elizabeth Farnese. The Treaties of Utrecht had placed the Bourbon Philip V. on the throne of a dismembered empire; they had restored the Pyrenees by forbidding the union of the French and Spanish Crowns; to the House of Austria they assigned the (Spanish) Netherlands, Milan, Naples, and Sardinia; to Savoy Sicily; to Great Britain Gibraltar, Minorca, and the Assiento concession in the South Seas. Spain had good reasons to work for a new settlement, and dynastic ambitions inflamed national resentment. A wife and a hassock, it was said, were all that the new King of Spain needed. The wife (she was his second) was provided in " the Termagant " from the House of Parma; the hassock was adequately represented by Cardinal Alberoni. Elizabeth Farnese shares with Caroline of Anspach, Maria Theresa, and Catherine II. the right to figure as one of the four great political women of the eighteenth century. Her dynastic ambitions convulsed Europe for thirty years and permanently moulded the destinies of the Bourbons and of Italy from her death until the final unification of the peninsula under the House of Savoy in 1870. In concert with the Queen of Spain, Alberoni desired to revive the glories of the humiliated Spanish Empire by extirpating the Austrian power in Italy. The future of "Baby Carlos" (the later Charles III.) and subsequently of "Baby Philip" (the later Duke of Parma), Elizabeth's two sons, was injured by the prior rights of Ferdinand (King of Spain, 1746), Philip's son by his first wife (Mary Louise of Savoy). They must be provided with appanages in Italy, partly from Austrian possessions (*e.g.* Sicily, which the Emperor proposed to gain by handing Sardinia to Savoy), partly from Tuscany and Parma, in which the ruling houses were on the point of extinction. Elizabeth therefore had the strongest of motives to upset the treaties and to challenge the claims of the Austrian Habsburgs in Central and Southern Italy. And Great Britain? Her statesmen, influenced by the powerful commercial classes, aimed at a balance of power in the Mediterranean, the security of Gibraltar and Minorca, and the extension of British trading privileges in the Spanish-American colonies. A new commercial treaty with Spain was one of the most pressing needs of the Ministry in 1714, and Stanhope summed up English sentiment in his remark, that a war with Spain would cost him his head, but that in twenty-four hours he could get Parliament to vote for a war with France. After Anne's death Anglo-Spanish relations developed in two phases: (1) from 1714-17 in which Alberoni endeavours to carry out his Italian policy by keeping Britain friendly or neutral; (2) 1717-38 in which Elizabeth, aided by Alberoni and Ripperda, actively opposes British power. Schemes to overthrow the Hanoverian dynasty, to recover Gibraltar and Minorca and build up anti-British coalitions have to be frustrated by counter-coalitions and the concerted coercion of Spain skilfully directed 1738 from St. James's until the Third Treaty of Vienna established a compromise. The war of 1739, however, brings the intrinsic contradiction between English and Spanish aims once more into 1740 the foreground, and with the death of Charles VI. Europe and

Great Britain enter on a train of events no longer essentially derived from the Treaties of Utrecht.

Nearer home the relations of "the two sea-powers"—Great Britain and the United Netherlands—provide a clearly marked link between the seventeenth and eighteenth centuries. The integrity and independence of Holland, an alliance based on reciprocal guarantees of the political systems of the two allies, the closing of the Scheldt, and a fortified barrier along the North-east frontier of France are prime objects of British policy. Both Whig and Tory were in agreement that the littoral of the Channel and the North Sea from Dunkirk to Rotterdam must be in the hands of a friendly Power, that France must be debarred from annexing "the Low Countries," that the modern Belgium should be a market for British goods leading to the commercial centres of Europe. Britain's interest in this command of the seas facing her vulnerable East and South-east coast, and her determination to prevent the control passing into hostile hands were inherited from the past, and are as clearly marked in the policy of the younger Pitt, Castlereagh, Canning and Palmerston (to go no farther), as in the policy of Elizabeth, Cromwell, and the Revolution Whigs. That this policy involved a continuous effort to frustrate the historic and ineradicable ambition of France to secure the "natural boundary" of the Rhine, and is vitally connected with the wider problem of sea-power and command of the oceanic routes to the East and West, is obvious. Whig statesmanship after 1702 proposed to effect the desired end by a closer concert with Vienna and the Hague, by making the Spanish Netherlands (Belgium) an Austrian buffer-State, by the Barrier Treaty and a commercial convention with the House of Austria. In 1714, however, the Emperor and Holland were almost at an open rupture, the Barrier had not been established, and the commercial treaty had still to be made. An essential preliminary therefore to a return to the Grand Alliance was a restoration of the solid anti-Bourbon League between London, the Hague, and Vienna. Could this be achieved without another great European war? In 1719, also, a tremendous struggle—the great Northern Question—independent in its origin and character of the War of the Spanish Succession, had long harassed European statesmen. The conspiracy of Russia, Denmark, and Saxony-Poland in 1698 to dismember the Swedish Empire of the Vasas had developed into a widespread

war in which the original anti-Swedish coalition had been joined by
Prussia-Brandenburg and Hanover, bent on stripping the heroic
and obstinate Charles XII. of his territories (Livonia, Pomerania,
Bremen and Verden), on the South and Eastern littoral of the
Baltic. English interests in the Baltic problem were considerable
and historic. The Eastern market supplied her with timber and
raw material (pitch, tar, hemp and flax), essential to her navy, and with
an outlet for manufactured goods ; her friendship with the Protestant Power at Stockholm was a century old. So far, despite inroads
on her commerce by Swedish privateers and increasingly strained
relations with the Government of Charles XII., Great Britain had
remained neutral. She desired peace, a balance of power in the
Baltic, and the open door for British trade. Suddenly in November,
1714, Charles XII. dramatically returned from his self-imposed and
mysterious exile at Bender and plunged into a hopeless defence of
Stralsund. Swedish ascendancy in the Baltic was in fact doomed.
What system was to take its place? The death of Anne brought
a new and embarrassing element into British policy, for the personal
union of the British Crown with the Hanoverian Electorate handcuffed Great Britain to a German State, already mortgaged in its
foreign policy. As Elector of Hanover, George I. was a member of
the anti-Swedish League, pledged to prosecute the Northern war October
and guaranteed as to his share of Swedish dismemberment with
the reversion of the Duchies of Bremen and Verden, so important
for rounding off the Guelph territories. Great Britain, too, had commercial grievances of her own to redress. George I., not unnaturally,
therefore desired to fulfil the treaty obligations of the Elector of
Hanover by employing the powerful naval and financial resources of
his British kingdom. Even without the pressure of his allies he saw
that English adherence to the anti-Swedish coalition must make
Sweden's defeat certain and rapid. But for the British Ministers
the problem was not so simple. The Hanoverian dynasty was new ;
if it became unpopular the Revolution system was seriously menaced
The danger of continued neutrality, of embarking in a war not of
England's making and not required by her true needs in the Baltic,
Sweden's refusal to grant satisfaction for legitimate grievances, the
clamour of the commercial classes for the protection of their ships
and goods, the importunity of the sovereign and his Hanoverian
advisers, ignorant of English sentiment and of the mystery of

ministerial responsibility, the deep-seated hostility in public opinion
to the dictation of a "wee, wee German lairdie," and continental
entanglements made the Northern problem a maze of conflicting
interests. Nor could a British Ministry forget that in the West and
South of Europe two black war-clouds threatened to envelop the
whole political horizon. And if the Whigs came back to power
at home they had still to establish a foreign ruler on a parliament-
made throne, to reconcile the nation to a new order and consolidate
the political organisation in accordance with the principles of the
Protestant succession, and the Revolution system and party-govern-
ment. It is as easy to underrate the very serious difficulties of the
Whig government as it is to exaggerate their ultimate success. "La
politique," it has been said by a master of state-craft, "est l'art de
s'accommoder aux circonstances et de tirer parti de tout, même de
ce qui deplâit." It is a priceless gift to statesmen to start from
settled and unshakeable convictions as to the destinies of the land
and people they are called upon to serve. In Whig eyes the creed
of a party summed up the ideals of Britain's future. On the
foundations of the Treaties of Utrecht Whig statesmen of the two
first Georges built up a system which made the soundness of their
principles of foreign policy essentially dependent on the needs of
the British nation at home as Whigs interpreted them. And if
Chatham departed from the methods of Walpole and Stanhope as
they in turn had departed from those of William III. and of the
Whig junto, he and they proved by so doing that they were true
sons and heirs of "the Revolution Whigs".

CHAPTER I

GEORGE I. AND THE ESTABLISHMENT OF HANOVERIAN RULE

ON Sunday, August 1st, 1714, Anne died and George I. was at once proclaimed King of Britain and Ireland without opposition, even in Scotland and Ireland, where the Jacobite Chancellor, Phipps, was promptly removed. Holland was ready to act on its treaty guarantee of the Protestant succession, and France as yet showed no sign of repudiating its pledged acceptance of the Hanoverian title. "The events of the five days last week," Swift wrote, "might furnish morals for another volume of Seneca." Atterbury may have asserted that he was ready to proclaim King James III. and VIII., and that the best cause in Europe was lost for want of spirit, but a Jacobite *coup d'état* was effectively checkmated by the suddenness of the Queen's fatal illness, the removal of Harley, the placing of the Lord Treasurer's staff in Shrewsbury's hands, and the vigour with which the great Whig peers intervened in the memorable council meeting. The law was clear: the Whigs had been watching for four years, they were organised, and in the hour of crisis the men and the measures were as ready as Bolingbroke was not. By the Act of Succession (6 Anne, c. 7) a Council of Regency, under the title of Lords Justices, consisting of the seven great officers of state, together with nominees of the lawful heir, were to administer the government until the new sovereign arrived. When the sealed packets were opened, eighteen peers, the most important of whom were the two archbishops, Shrewsbury, Halifax, Anglesea, Cowper, Townshend, Bolton, Devonshire, and Nottingham, with Addison as their secretary, were found to have been nominated. Neither Oxford (Harley), only deprived of office the previous Tuesday, nor Bolingbroke, who still held the Secretary's seals, was in the list. The council was predominantly, but not wholly, Whig. Notable omissions were Marlborough, Sunderland his son-in-law, Wharton, and Somers. Parliament met on

August 5th, and the oaths of allegiance to George I. and of abjuration from the Stuart claimant were duly taken by the members of both houses. A civil list of £700,000, the same sum that had been granted to Anne, was voted. Oxford was for the present ignored. But Bolingbroke, after the Queen's funeral, was ordered from Hanover to deliver up his seals of office, and his papers placed under lock and key. "His fortune turned rotten at the very moment it grew ripe." The grief of his soul, he wrote to Atterbury, was that he saw plainly the Tory party was gone. And he was right. George, delayed at Hanover by the requirements of the electoral administration, set foot for the second time on English soil at Greenwich on September 18th—the third sovereign in fifty-four years who had been summoned from abroad to occupy the English throne. The new King was in character as different from Charles II. and William III. as were the circumstances of 1714 from those of 1660 and 1688. Charles had symbolised to an enthusiastic people the restoration of the hereditary monarchy and the downfall of the military republic; William III. had been invited by the leaders of a party to deliver the constitution and the Established Church from absolutism and Roman Catholicism, and the Revolution Parliament had legalised the invitation by offering a Crown and supplying a statutory title; George's peaceful succession was at once the homage to, and the union of, hereditary (in the Protestant line alone) with parliamentary right. Born in 1660, the year of the restoration of the dynasty whose claims he now so effectively annulled, he was the son of the Electress Sophia and the great grandson, therefore, of James I. In 1698 he had succeeded to the Electorate and had seen military service under Sobieski at Vienna, at Neerwinden in 1693, while from 1707-9 as a member of the Grand Alliance, he had commanded an imperial army on the Upper Rhine. His coldness, said the witty Elizabeth Charlotte of Orleans, would freeze his surroundings. German to the core, passionately devoted to Herrenhausen and his beloved Hanover, a Lutheran by creed, he was a brusque, heartless, cruel, avaricious mean, sensual, punctilious, and masterful man, and he had grown up in a provincial court where the ruler's wish was law. His abilities were mediocre, his manners not without a certain stiff dignity, but wholly unattractive. If, in Shippen's memorable phrase, he was as little acquainted with the forms and usages of

Aug. 24

Aug. 28

Parliament as with the language of his new subjects, he had reached an age when men of his type can neither forget nor learn.   As a Protestant member of the Grand Alliance he had contributed 12,000 men to the great war with France ; conviction and interest made him a firm supporter of the foreign policy of William III. and of the Whigs.   The reversal of that policy in 1710 he regarded as a fatal and insulting breach by Great Britain of solemn treaty obligations.   Since 1710 the Elector, encouraged by continuous Whig teaching, had come to believe that to the Whigs he owed his throne, and that England's home affairs quite as much as her foreign policy required a government based on Whig principles.   A King made and kept on the throne by a party must necessarily become the King of that party.   George was, therefore, reluctantly prepared to assign, when he was compelled, internal administration to Whig hands.   What else, indeed, could h e do ?   Whig principles and objects in this land of foreign speech and strange institutions coincided by a Leibnitzian pre-established harmony with his dynastic interests.   To alienate in the critical September of 1714 the organised group of able, experienced, and loyal men who had frustrated Bolingbroke in the hour of victory was impossible.   The Whigs understood English politics if George did not, and they left no alternative between surrender and defiance.   George in surrendering had still to learn, as William III. had learned, that if the Tories were the opponents of his Majesty's title the Whigs were no less the opponents of his Majesty's prerogative.   A parliamentary title meant parliamentary government ; parliamentary government must become party government under which the sovereign's powers would be syndicated amongst his responsible Ministers.   George's accession, in fact, emphasised by his antecedents and his personal characteristics, was more than a triumph for the principles of 1689 and 1701.   In the logic of facts it made explicit what was previously only implicit in the nature of the Revolution Settlement.

No royal consort accompanied the new King.   George in 1682 had married his cousin Sophia Dorothea of Celle, and the unhappy union twelve years later was broken by the mysterious death of the Electress's lover, the Swedish Count Königsmarck.[1]   Promptly 1694

---

[1] Brother to Aurora von Königsmarck, whom Voltaire called the most beautiful woman of two centuries, the mistress of Augustus, " The Physically Strong," and by him the mother of the Maréchal de Saxe, the victor of Fontenoy.

divorced, the miserable woman, who might have been Queen of Great Britain and Ireland, was shut up in a virtual state prison at Ahlden, and in prison, as her unforgiving and tyrannical husband intended, she died, the world forgetting, by the world forgot.[1] The shame of this sordid scandal was to repeat itself with wearisome iteration in the quarrels of fathers and sons, and of mothers with their children in the domestic chronicle of the electoral and royal dynasty. Nor were the morals of the first two Hanoverians calculated to compensate for their foreign extraction and unfamiliar ways.   Two greedy and ill-favoured favourites were a poor substitute for an honest queen—if such were to be had.   The lean Countess of Schulenburg, created Duchess of Kendal, and the fat Countess of Kilmansegge, created Countess of Darlington, not unjustly became " the Maypole" and " the Elephant" of English satire.   The Schulenburg, by her insatiable appetite for intrigue and plunder, played a backstairs part with a zeal that prompted Walpole's remark " that she would at any time have sold her influence with the King for a shilling advance to the best bidder ".   Such conventionally-respectable Court life as English society deigned to grace was provided by the heir to the throne, George Augustus, the son of the unhappy prisoner of Ahlden, in whose innocence, with credit to his feelings if not to his judgment of evidence, he believed to the last. Created Prince of Wales in 1714, he revived a title virtually dormant since 1649, though from 1688-1701 it had been formally retained by the Prince " across the water," who now in 1714 was called by Jacobites James III. and VIII. or the Chevalier St. George, and by Whigs the (Old) Pretender.   The Princess of Wales, Caroline of Anspach-Brandenburg, both as Princess and Queen, was destined by her intellectual gifts, her political insight and her broad-minded friendships, to be the most remarkable woman in the history of two reigns.   The King's first task was to appoint Ministers. Archbishop Tenison, who was included in the Cabinet, won from George the remark that he liked him better than all the rest of the Court for he was the only one who came to ask for nothing.   The Ministry when completed contained Halifax as First Lord of the Treasury, Cowper as Chancellor, Nottingham as Lord President, Townshend and Stanhope as Secretaries of State.   Sunderland became Lord-Lieutenant of Ireland, Marlborough was reinstated as

[1] See Appendix I.

Commander-in-Chief and Master of the Ordnance ; Robert Walpole,
Townshend's brother-in-law, to whom shrewd observers already
ascribed a dominating influence, was only Paymaster, but next year
he was appointed First Lord of the Treasury and Chancellor of the
Exchequer.   The aged Somers was a member of the Cabinet without office.   Hanoverian affairs were reserved for the able junto of
Germans, Bothmer, Bernstorff, Robethon, and Görz, who had worked
hard to secure their master's Crown, and on whose knowledge and
advice in foreign affairs George I., with good reason, relied.   Of
the English Ministers an inner group of three—Stanhope, Townshend and Marlborough—with Bothmer and Bernstorff, practically
decided policy.   But after 1716 Marlborough's influence vanished,
and Stanhope shared with Townshend the preponderating influence
in the closet.   With the exception of Nottingham, who lost office in
1716, the new Administration was selected from the Whigs, in whose
eyes the authors of the Treaties of Utrecht were traitors to the true
interests of their country.   Convinced that Bolingbroke and his
colleagues, by methods discreditable, if not plainly treasonable, had
plotted to overthrow the Protestant succession, the Whigs were
determined to teach their opponents that the principles of the
Revolution Settlement were beyond the power of any group of politicians to tamper with or betray.   The crisis of the succession was
not yet surmounted.   If the action of the Whigs seems vindictive it
was salutary and decisive, and, under the accepted conventions of
political life, inevitable.   The Tory party had yet to learn how to
blend Jacobitism as a sentimental creed for the private conscience
with public acceptance of the principles of Church and State laid
down in the Bill of Rights and the Act of Settlement.   The conduct of the Tory leaders, Bolingbroke, Oxford, Ormonde, Strafford,
was suspiciously sinister, and it was at the political leaders that the
Whigs with sound strategy struck.   For the time the memory of
Sacheverell saved Atterbury and the other Jacobite divines.   After
George had been crowned with all the solemn ritual of the old hereditary monarchy Parliament six months after the demise of the
sovereign was, as required by law, dissolved.   The elections took Jan. 5,
place amidst strong excitement ; a Jacobite reaction had inevitably 1715
followed the strain of the crisis in August, and riots, revealing
the latent feeling in many centres, occurred, particularly in the
Midland counties.   Aided by a royal proclamation and by an ill-

judged manifesto issued by "the Pretender," the Whigs obtained
a decisive majority in the new Parliament that met on March
17th. The address, explicitly framed against the authors of the
Treaties of Utrecht, was a Whig declaration of war. A secret committee was appointed to examine the papers of the late Ministry,
and its report, for which Walpole was chiefly responsible, was a
masterpiece of party tactics. Though it did not furnish, as was
hoped, clear legal proof of treason, it inflamed the pent-up bitterness
amongst the Whigs. But Bolingbroke had already lost his head
before his enemies could take it off. On April 6th he committed the
most serious of the many serious blunders of his life when, disguised
as a valet, he fled to France, shortly to enter openly "the Pretender's" service. His flight relieved the Ministry of the difficulty
of proving that as Anne's Secretary he had been guilty of treason,
while it effectually completed his ruin. The popular Ormonde,
"the star of danger," fled in August, also to take service in the
Stuart cause. " Farewell, Duke, without a Dukedom," Oxford remarked at parting. " Farewell, Earl," retorted Ormonde, " without a head." Oxford and Strafford stood their ground and were
formally impeached. Against Bolingbroke and Ormonde acts of
attainder were passed. From the chaos of recrimination caused by
these measures two points emerge. The Whigs emphasised the doctrine of ministerial responsibility. They refused to admit the late
Queen's authority as an adequate reason for exonerating her Ministers from liability, and thereby the precedent laid down in Danby's
case was made good. It was not to be forgotten. Walpole, who
encouraged the demand of the Commons for condign chastisement,
already foreshadowed the principle which later as a minister he was
to enforce. In the interests of the Protestant succession and of the
Whigs, its avowed champions, the Tories must be branded as disloyal
Jacobites and politically broken. The Tories, unfortunately for
themselves, were justifying the soundness of such tactics, and the
plausibility of the indictment. For the moment they were disunited, discredited, and leaderless. Shippen, Bromley, Wyndham,
in the Commons ; Anglesea, Trevor, Harcourt, in the Lords, were
feeble substitutes for the brilliant Bolingbroke, the experienced Oxford, and Ormonde, the toast of squire, parson, and the daughters
of the manors. Jacobite lawlessness provided an excellent reason in
the same session for strengthening the executive by "the Riot

Act" (1 Geo. I., st. 2, c. 5), which made it a felony for a rioter to refuse to obey the command of lawful authority to disperse. It is noticeable that both this act and the Septennial Act of next year, which originated in the troubles of the Hanoverian succession, remained on the Statute Book until 1911, when the Parliament Act became law.

With no less firmness of purpose the Whig Ministry had begun to handle the problems of foreign policy. . A change began at once under the Lords Justices. Bolingbroke's schemes were dropped. The demolition of the fortifications at Dunkirk (as provided by the treaties) and the expulsion of the Pretender from Lorraine were actively pressed. It was a foregone conclusion that the new Ministry would return to the system of 1710. If the Emperor could be persuaded to accept the Barrier Treaty of 1713 two advantages would follow, the reconciliation of the House of Austria to the United Netherlands, the imperial guarantee of the Hanoverian throne, the latter of cardinal importance to a country at that moment without allies whose relations with France were exceedingly critical. Fortunately for the Whigs, Stanhope and Marlborough had previously earned the gratitude of the Emperor, Charles VI., by their military and political achievements, and Stanhope now commenced his notable work in diplomacy by a personal mission to Vienna which convinced Europe that the Whigs October would not shrink from renewing the war with France. British efforts were primarily concentrated on the Barrier Treaty, and after a year of tedious negotiations Dutch and Austrians were cajoled into agreement and the Barrier question settled. That the barrier Nov. 15, thus set up would prove worthless against a resolute France was 1715 happily not made clear until 1743. Meanwhile Great Britain had secured the commercial privileges she desired, the North-east frontier of France was apparently barred and the agreement of Holland and the House of Austria might be made the basis of an effective alliance between the Emperor and George I. It was the first and a welcome Whig success. Concurrent negotiations had been proceeding with Spain to amend the unsatisfactory commercial treaty of 1713 and to assist in settling the claims of Charles VI. (who persisted in regarding himself as the true King of Spain) and those of Philip V. who refused to admit the validity of Habsburg rights to the former Spanish possessions in Italy. Alberoni agreed to a fresh commercial treaty, though the advantages it promised

were subsequently made nugatory by the reluctance of the Spanish
Government to act up to its word.   In reality both the British
and Spanish Ministers were playing an insincere game of bluff, because neither had penetrated the ulterior objects which each Power
had in view.   Alberoni for the present was willing to speak Stanhope
fair and make illusory commercial concessions on paper until his
recuperative measures had provided the means to defy Great
Britain, if necessary, and to expel the Habsburg intruder from his
ill-gotten gains in Italy.   Stanhope had no intention of sacrificing
a renewal of the historic and valuable alliance with the Emperor to
a speculative *entente* with the Bourbons at Madrid.   As regards
the North, Hanover had secured a Prussian guarantee of the cession
of Bremen and Verden and a renewed Danish guarantee to the
same effect.   As Elector, therefore, George was doubly committed
to the war on Sweden.   Under the provocation of a Swedish pri-
vateering ordinance, a violation of the rights of neutrals which
Townshend said "no treaty, law, nor reason could justify," and
the pressure of the commercial classes and of the Court, the British
Ministers consented to ask for a parliamentary vote and to send
Admiral Norris to the Baltic with a fleet.   But to the indignation
of his continental allies the King of Great Britain was not permitted formally to declare war, and the ships avowedly sailed only
to protect British trade.   The dangerous dualism between England
and Hanover was thus correctly, if somewhat hypocritically, maintained, and George received his first unpleasant lesson in the doctrine that British Ministers could not forget their responsibility to
a Parliament which was impeaching the Tory leaders, despite the
undeniable fact that their acts had been endorsed with the full approval of the late sovereign.   Nevertheless George profited by the
refusal of his English advisers to commit themselves to the aims of
the allies.   The presence of the British fleet co-operating with the
Danish ships enabled the Anti-Swedish League to achieve a decisive stroke.   The capture of Rügen, the fall of Stralsund and
Wismar deprived Charles XII. of his last foothold on German
soil.   The adamantine obstinacy of the Swedish King in refusing
to make concessions to Great Britain which might have secured
the friendship of Ministry, Parliament, and people had practically
ensured Bremen and Verden for the Elector of Hanover.   But the
Northern Question was by no means settled yet.   The death of

Louis XIV. had altered the whole European situation, notably in Sept. 1 three directions.   By making the Regent Orléans the next heir 1715 (under the Treaties of Utrecht) to the sickly boy who now became King as Louis XV. it severed the union between Madrid and Paris ; it cut the ground from under the Jacobites' feet at the precise moment when help from France might have proved decisive; it made the maintenance of the Treaties of Utrecht as necessary to the Regent in Paris as to the Whigs and Hanoverians at St. James. The way was open for a new system, but before the Whigs could utilise it the home Government was embroiled in a rebellion.

A rising had been simmering on both sides of the Channel for some time.   Scotland naturally offered the best prospects of success. The geographical configuration of the country, the clan system, and the adherence of many of the most influential chiefs to the Stuart dynasty, sharpened by the jealousy of Argyll and the Campbells, would probably win the Highlands.   South of the Tay and East of the Grampians the Episcopalian gentry and clergy were almost wholly Jacobite.   The memory of the Darien fiasco still smouldered.   The legislative union and the subsequent legislation were very unpopular, and the cry of Scottish independence under a national King of Scottish blood appealed to many Whig and Presbyterian hearts outside the Jacobite fold.   Had a Scottish rising against the domination of England been properly prepared and judiciously timed with effective English risings in the northern and western counties, " the Fifteen" might have been the first chapter of a bloody struggle for a throne, and, as in 1689 and 1701, led up to a European Armageddon, once more to determine the fundamental principles of the British State.   The military weakness of the Whig Government, the estrangement of the continental Powers, the growing disillusionment in England with regard to the new dynasty, and the widespread resentment of the Church and the Tory landed gentry at Whig tyranny and vindictiveness offered a splendid opportunity to unquenchable sentiment, resolute skill and organisation.   But against stupidity even Divine Right and the White Rose fight in vain.   "The Fifteen" was hopeless from the outset, nor was its pitiful tragedy illumined as it was thirty years later by the imperishable romance which can touch even hearts convinced that the better side won.   Wodrow's comment : " The providence of Scotland's God has been adorable at this juncture," tersely sums up the effect of

Louis XIV.'s death. Babbling women, dreaming priests among the refugees, ignorance, treachery, jealousy, divided counsels and imbecile leadership damned the cause even more effectively than the poverty of the Pretender, the abstention of France, the power of the British fleet, and Whig vigour at headquarters. James's noble loyalty to his religion chilled the Lowlands, the parochial clergy and gentry of England. But Berwick, Bolingbroke, Mar, and Forster cannot be exonerated from the chief responsibility for the disaster. Misled by advices from England, the Chevalier had authorised a rising in August. He countermanded it, but the letter either was disobeyed or never reached its destination. Order—counter-order—disorder. On September 6th the Earl of Mar, popularly known as "Bobbing John," raised the standard at Kirkmichael on the Braes of Mar, and James VIII. was proclaimed at Aberdeen, Dunkeld, Dundee, and Inverness. The English Administration was well served by Stair, the Ambassador at Paris, and by spies. The Habeas Corpus Act was suspended; Lansdowne and Wyndham were arrested together with other known Jacobites in the midland and western towns ; 6000 Dutch troops were summoned from Holland. Ormonde's expedition, betrayed to the Government, found the West neither ready nor willing to be ready, and the leader was derisively compared to the picture of the soldier "with his heart where his head should be, and no head at all ". Instead of Marlborough, Argyle, whose knowledge of Scotland was as conspicuous as his loyalty, was given the command against Mar. In October a handful of Catholic gentry under Forster and Derwentwater, amateurs in rebellion and war, had ridden out in Northumberland, and Kenmure with Nithsdale, Wintoun and Carnwath, independently rose at Moffat. The two little bands, who met with feeble support, joined hands at Rothbury. Islay, Argyll's brother, using Inveraray and Dumbarton Castles, effectively checked the Jacobite clans in the West. Farther North, Lochiel's efforts were bridled by Fort William, while the loyalty of the disloyal and memorable Simon Fraser, Lord Lovat, was a fresh blow to the success of the Cause. Mar, whose force at Perth had swollen to some 12,000 men, and who might have pounced on Edinburgh and made a union with Forster and Kenmure, threw away weeks in laborious idleness. At last a small detachment under Mackintosh crossed the Forth, and, frustrated by Argyle at Edinburgh, thanks to Mar's amazing folly, joined Forster at Kelso. Thence, the eastern route being blocked at Newcastle, they sealed their fate by crossing the border to the West with Manchester as their objective. "You will take them," Marlborough said, putting his finger on the map at Preston, "there"; and at Preston, place of ill omen for the Stuart arms, they were taken. Drifting rather than marching, "courting and feasting" most of the way from Hawick by Carlisle, Penrith, Kendal and Lancaster, they were finally penned at Preston by General Wills, advancing from Wigan, and General Carpenter from the North. After some fierce barricade fighting on November 12th, the force capitulated next day at discretion. The quixotic travesty of civil war by a mob of foxhunters had found no support save from the more dare-devil of the Catholic gentry and Mackintosh's Highlanders. The English rebellion was at an end.

On the same fatal November 13th, Inverness fell to George I., and Mar had stumbled on, rather than brought Argyll's force to, an engagement at Sheriffmuir. The conflict was a confused scuffle on both sides in which the Highlanders gave the regulars a taste of their quality. Well might Gordon of Glenbucket make his famous remark, "Oh, for an hour of Dundee!" though Dundee or Montrose would have swept the Hanoverian army out of existence at least a month earlier. Mar by retreating proclaimed his real defeat. His army, spared by Argyll's dilatory tactics, rent by divisions and jealousies, and soon to be driven back on the hungry North, was doomed. And just as the cause had received its *coup de grace* James, who had escaped from Lorraine, lingered at St. Malo, and then evaded the British frigates, landed at Peterhead. His arrival Dec. 22 was an act of homage to an obstinate honour. This melancholy young man, who shares with Charles II. alone of his race the gift of seeing things as they really were, was not the sensual bigot, faithless to friend and foe, that Jacobite scandal and Whig tradition have conspired to picture. A prince, the victim of his inheritance, of a sane but profound pessimism, born of unbroken misfortune, the pawn of incapable and selfish conspirators and foolish dreamers, he was condemned to expiate the sins of his forefathers, and to be traduced after he was dead. He deserves our pity, for if his chilling manner and misinterpreted silence were a sore disillusionment to the Highland chiefs and the romantic hearts of Jacobite women, in an age of spiritual bankruptcy, he refused to the end to sell his soul and

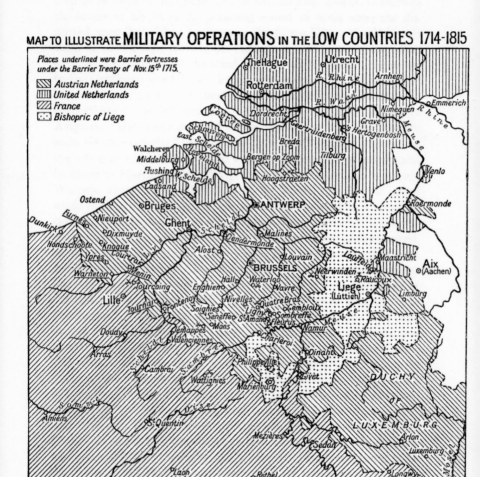

MAP TO ILLUSTRATE **MILITARY OPERATIONS** IN THE **LOW COUNTRIES** 1714-1815

Places underlined were Barrier Fortresses under the Barrier Treaty of Nov. 15th 1715.

- Austrian Netherlands
- United Netherlands
- France
- Bishopric of Liege

B.V. Darbishire, Oxford, 1910

English 10 0 10 20 30 40 50 Miles

of this and of subsequent Parliaments from three to seven years. Whig advocates urged on general grounds that the bill would diminish bribery and secure the authority of the representative chamber; Opposition critics denounced it as an unconstitutional and purely partisan measure, the offspring and the parent of corruption, fatal to freedom and subversive of the rights of the electors. Unconstitutional in the sense of illegal the Septennial Act certainly was not. How far urgent political necessity, of which the legislature without reference to the electoral body is the sole judge, can entitle a representative body elected for a limited period to prolong its own existence is a nice question in political jurisprudence to which very different answers will be given. Englishmen had as good reason to fear a standing Parliament as a standing army. But the Whig Government (as the preamble to the bill asserts), probably rightly, believed that a general election "when a restless and Popish faction are designing and endeavouring to renew their plots" would endanger the stability of the Revolution System. Foreign policy too required continuity of policy and the permanence of a Government in which foreign Powers could trust. In the critical condition of affairs at home and abroad the Septennial Act had its origin and must find, if anywhere, its justification. Somers, a true friend to constitutional liberty (who died in May), warmly supported it. His view that it would help to emancipate the Commons both from the Crown and the Lords was confirmed later by the experienced judgment of Onslow, the greatest of eighteenth century Speakers. The act, though intended to be temporary, remained unrepealed until 1911, and tested by its consequences, not fully foreseen at the time, it is an important codicil to the great formative statutes of the Revolution era, whose principles it markedly helped to rivet in the law and custom of the Constitution. For the moment it set the seal on the Whig triumph; the young Hanoverian dynasty and the Hanoverian-British State had survived the sharp distemper of rebellion and civil war. Sceptical foreign Governments could now believe that the new dynasty would rest where it was. With the crushing of the Jacobite rising and the passing of the Septennial Act the real political supremacy of the Whigs began and remained unimpaired until it was broken by the Hanoverian monarchy it had created and preserved.

Whig diplomacy now aimed at securing a political alliance with both Holland and the Emperor. Was this to take the form of a triple union or two separate arrangements which could be cemented later into a single agreement? To Charles VI. a British fleet in the Mediterranean was no less essential than a British fleet in the Baltic was to the Anti-Swedish Coalition. When English Ministers protested that at Vienna more time was wasted in haggling over a single point than it took to equip a squadron at Portsmouth, the Austrians retorted that at London they asked in an hour more than the Emperor could consent to in a whole year. George desired an imperial guarantee of his throne and the ratification of the cession of Bremen and Verden; Charles VI. required the coercion of Spain into accepting his terms. After wearisome negotiations Whig diplomacy concluded two separate treaties, a formal alliance with Holland, a formal alliance with the Emperor. In each case the contracting parties guaranteed their respective possessions with a pledge of armed assistance against attack. The isolation of Great Britain was thereby brought to an end, the Hanoverian dynasty was shored up with solid support, and the old understanding with the Hague and Vienna renewed. This fresh success was the effective prelude to a new and startling departure in Whig diplomacy.

Feb. 17,
1716
June 5

The King's first visit to Hanover marked the growing sense of security. His Ministers, Townshend in particular, reluctantly consented to procure the repeal of the clause in the Act of Settlement which forbade the sovereign leaving England without the consent of Parliament. But George was insistent. "I believe," Peterborough drily remarked, "the King has quite forgotten the misfortune that befell himself and his family on August 1, 1714." In his absence the Prince of Wales, as guardian and lieutenant of the realm, acted as Regent; Stanhope accompanied the King, Townshend remained as chief adviser in London. The existence of two centres of political authority, Hampton Court and Herrenhausen, was fatal to Whig unity. The brusque Townshend had incurred George's enmity, fomented by the intrigues of Bothmer, Robethon, and the Duchess of Kendal, whose influence and rapacity he thwarted. Sunderland, chafing at his subordinate position, was jealous of his power. The estrangement, at first personal, soon involved principles of policy, and next year led to an open schism.

The credit of the alliance with France, which shortly amazed

Europe, belongs mainly to Stanhope and the Abbé Dubois, "goat-faced Cardinal, ugliest of created souls, Archbishop of Cambrai by the favour of Beelzebub". Dubois had met Stanhope at Hanover in August, and by October 11th the treaty had been drafted. This decisive stroke was much facilitated by the presence of George and Stanhope abroad, but its conclusion was hindered by opposition in the Cabinet. Townshend's insistence on the participation of Holland increased the growing breach between himself and his master, supported by Stanhope, Sunderland, and the other Hanoverian Ministers. On November 28th the treaty was signed, and the inclu-Jan. 4, sion of Holland consummated the famous Triple Alliance—a Tory 1717 conception grafted on to the solid stock of the old Whig system. Great Britain and France solemnly guaranteed the clauses in the treaties by which the Protestant succession in England and the renunciation of Philip V.'s claims to the French Crown were regulated Minor clauses pledged France to secure the expulsion of the Pretender from Avignon and to demolish the fortifications of Mardyck. The story that the Regent Orléans and his mother kissed the ratified treaty picturesquely epitomises its importance to their ambitions. For neither Europe nor the Regent could divine that the sickly Louis XV. would see two Kings of Spain and two of Great Britain into their graves, and by his policy and debauchery ruin the monarchy for Bourbon and Orleanist alike. But the Anglo-French alliance did much more than secure George on his throne. Stanhope was quick to see that the union of the two Powers whose rivalry had convulsed Europe could be slowly forged into an instrument, irresistible if judiciously used, to settle the problems arising from the treaties whose maintenance it guaranteed, and might make Hanoverian Great Britain the predominant influence in the councils of Europe. Two storm-centres—the Baltic and the Mediterranean—menaced the continental horizon, and events were working to blend them into one. In 1716 a stronger fleet, with Norris again in command, had been sent to the Baltic. But under the pressure of conflicting interests the anti-Swedish coalition was rapidly dissolving. The ambitions and power of Peter the Great combined Great Britain, Hanover, and Denmark, in opposition to the concert of Russia and Prussia. George and Peter each desired to get a separate peace with Sweden in order to checkmate the objects of the other, but neither defeat nor the exhaustion of Sweden moved Charles XII. to satisfy

British claims, or to cede an inch of territory, or a stone of his fortresses to his victorious foes.   The English Ministry was importuned to secure Bremen and Verden by force, and to checkmate the growing supremacy of Russia in the Baltic by compelling Peter to withdraw his troops from Mecklenburg.   Townshend stood out for preferring Swedish inroads on English commerce to a war with Sweden and Russia too.   Great Britain, therefore, continued its attitude of a correct neutrality, and after much ink had been wasted on paper the Czar's withdrawal of his troops from Mecklenburg averted the crisis for the moment.   A new phase opened with the sudden rise to influence with Charles XII. of Görtz, a knight of diplomatic industry, gifted with ability, insight and courage.   The Anglo-French alliance deprived Sweden of France's benevolent friendship, and Görtz now played with an ambitious plan to reconcile his master with Peter, defeat the coalition by their united forces, and overthrow George at London, the Regent at Paris by Jacobite and Bourbon plots.   Ever since Anne's death the help of the great soldier, Charles XII., had been a Jacobite dream, and through Gyllenborg, the Swedish Ambassador at London, Görtz entered into close relations with the Jacobites in England.   Money was what he wanted above all, and money might be wheedled out of Jacobite purses for purely Swedish needs by lending an ear to Jacobite schemes.   For it is more than doubtful whether Görtz entertained seriously the proposed union of the foreign forces without and the Jacobite forces within against the reigning dynasty.   But the plot—if it was a plot—was betrayed.   The Whig Government did not hesitate to arrest Gyllenborg, while the publication of his papers explained, if it did not justify, the daring breach of an ambassador's rights.[1] Görtz at the same time was arrested by the Dutch, though he was shortly released.   The Government was well informed of what was afoot, and it struck at the plotters when it knew not so much that the plot was ripe, as that an exposure of the intrigue would powerfully influence public opinion, and weaken the dangerous parliamentary opposition to its policy in the Baltic.   And this it certainly did. The revelation of the "plot" and the publication of the incriminating documentary matter caused no little excitement in London ; it

Jan. 29, 1717

---

[1] Similarly in 1718 the French Government arrested Porto Carrero, the Spanish Ambassador, on the occasion of the Cellamare conspiracy ; and in 1726 Philip V. had Ripperda seized in the house of Stanhope, the British Ambassador at Madrid.

staved off a parliamentary defeat, yet the demand for parliamentary supplies brought to a head the dissensions in the Ministry.

Townshend had already been transferred to the lord-lieutenancy Dec., of Ireland, but in April the vote of credit against Sweden was 1716 supported so lukewarmly by Walpole and Townshend's followers that the lord-lieutenant was dismissed, whereupon Walpole with Devonshire, Methuen, Orford, and Pulteney marked their resentment by resigning. Walpole's ability and influence with the Commons were so conspicuous that the King begged him to remain. No fewer than ten times were the seals placed upon the table, but in the end George, not Walpole, yielded, and the Ministry was reconstructed. Stanhope became First Lord of the Treasury, Sunderland and Addison Secretaries of State, and from now till his death Stanhope's supremacy in foreign policy was assured.[1] The split in the Whig party rejoiced the dashed Jacobite spirits, and was important. Aggravated by personal feeling, the quarrels raised questions of policy, as well as the right of the sovereign to choose his Ministers unfettered by party or parliamentary dictation. And behind Walpole's resignation lay the principle, which later he was to enforce, that ministerial responsibility implied ministerial unity on the vital public questions of the day. Tories and Jacobites detected in the party quarrel and the discreditable squabble of the King with the Prince of Wales over the restricted powers of the Regent, a welcome proof of the decay of the Whigs and the failure of the dynasty. Atterbury's correspondence shows that the strenuous opposition of the ex-Ministers to the measures of their former colleagues was read as the writing on the wall. No view could have been more mistaken. Walpole and Townshend were as sound on the Revolution System as Stanhope and Sunderland. The rupture in reality strengthened rather than weakened the Whig supremacy. It provided salutary Whig criticism of Whig measures ; it gave Stanhope a free hand to complete his diplomatic work, and when a financial maelstrom engulfed the country, leaders of ability and experience and unimpeachable Whiggism were at hand to replace the discredited Whig Ministry, reorganise the demoralised party, and continue the Whig predominance. The next four years are crowded

---

[1] In 1718 Sunderland became First Lord of the Treasury, Aislabie Chancellor of the Exchequer, and Stanhope (to control foreign affairs more effectively) Secretary of State, with James Craggs as his colleague.

with important events, and Stanhope's hands were fully occupied with foreign affairs.   The failure of Görtz's first "plot" had not scotched the zeal and fertility of resource in this subtle and cool-headed intriguer, and the storm-centre in the South shortly burst In August, 1717, Alberoni and Elizabeth Farnese threw off their masks and challenged their foes.   The treaties of 1716 and 1717 had opened Alberoni's eyes to the real aims of Great Britain.   Probably he would have preferred to wait until the army and fleet of Spain were in a better state, but the arrest in Italy of a Spanish inquisitor by the Austrian Government fired national resentment and forced his hand.   England was engaged in the Baltic ; the military forces of the Emperor were locked up in the Turkish war, and in France the Legitimists had found a leader in the Duke of Maine, aided by the strong sentiment of Bourbon solidarity and the unpopularity in the ruling class of the Anglo-French Alliance, To prevent its exchange for Sicily, a Spanish army was flung into Sardinia, but, unfortunately for Alberoni, ten days before Eugène had captured Belgrade.   The Emperor promptly claimed from Great Britain the assistance due under the treaty of 1716.   But the Ministry hesitated.   In marked contrast to 1739 a war with Spain was unpopular, and the Baltic situation threatened also to issue in an equally unpopular war.   Charles XII. and Görtz had come into touch, through the Jacobites, with Alberoni in the South.   The common enemy to both was the Anglo-French union. The overthrowal of the Hanoverian dynasty would free Sweden from the coalition, unite France and Spain, and make the latter more than a match for the Emperor entangled in the East.   Behind the curtain of official diplomacy was spun a network of ambitious and menacing schemes.   The reconciliation of Charles XII. with Peter the Great was to be followed by risings in Scotland and England, aided by the victor of Narva and Clissow, with 10,000 of the unconquerable Blue Boys of Sweden.   Porto Carrero and Cellamare and the Spanish party at Paris were to overthrow the Regent Orlèans and the English alliance.   But Stanhope was not idle.   English diplomacy was strenuously employed to mediate a peace between the Emperor and the Turks.   Dubois, under pressure from London, agreed to a joint mediation based on the exchange of Sicily for Sardinia, and the reversion of the succession in Tuscany and Parma to Don Carlos, Elizabeth Farnese's elder son.   Alberoni rejected the offer, though England went so far as to hold out a prospect of restoring Gibraltar. The Turks and Prince Ragotski of Transylvania were encouraged to hamper the Emperor : Cellamare's conspiracy grew, and Ormonde and the two Keiths were selected for risings in the West of Scotland and England. Charles XII., who was attacking the Norwegian fortress of Frederikshall, was to clinch its fate by joining in an invasion of England from the East. So at least Alberoni and the industrious Jacobite agents hoped, and the British Government feared, not without a very clear perception of the advantage the menace gave them in manipulating public opinion and coercing a critical legislature. But it is more than doubtful whether the scheme went beyond paper plans, and verbal assurances capable of very different interpretations. The evidence is wholly against the conclusion (believed at the time) that Charles XII. either in 1716 or 1718 consented to be the general of a Jacobite rising in England. Yet never had the Jacobite hopes risen so high as in this critical summer of 1718. But fortune, treachery, and the British fleet were against them, and the issue for Great Britain lay on the water. Stanhope now was determined to bring about a quadruple alliance with France, Holland, and the Emperor. On June 4th, Byng sailed for the Mediterranean, and the same month Stanhope intervened in person at Paris, and after a sharp struggle won the Regent from the Spanish party. On August 20th the Quadruple Alliance was signed in London.[1] Though bitterly criticised by Walpole, Shippen, and Wyndham, it was a notable victory for British and Hanoverian diplomacy. For if Stanhope by tact and decision secured the wavering Regent, the conversion of the Emperor was mainly the work of Bothmer and Bernstorff.

Already on August 11th, Byng had destroyed the Spanish fleet off Cape Passaro [2] and the Spanish army was locked up in Sicily— a signal illustration of the influence of sea-power. Eleven days earlier, thanks largely to the skill of the British envoy, Sir R. Sutton, the Emperor had made peace with the Turks at Passa-

---

[1] The terms ran on the lines of the foiled mediation. Don Carlos was to succeed to Tuscany, Parma, and Piacenza, separated from the Spanish Crown ; the Emperor and Spain were to renounce their respective claims on each other's territories ; Sicily was to be exchanged for Sardinia. If heirs in the direct line failed the Spanish Crown had the reversion of the succession in Savoy.

[2] See Appendix II.

a

rovitz and the victors of Belgrade were thus free to act against
Spain.

Stanhope, after a visit to Madrid, was convinced that peace would
come only when Alberoni had been dismissed. Philip V. must
therefore be coerced. The Jacobite plots were ruined by treachery,
mismanagement and fate. The bullet which on December 1st killed
Charles XII. in the trenches at Frederikshall was followed by the
betrayal and crushing of the Cellamare conspiracy at Paris. On December 17th Great Britain, and on January 3rd France, declared war
on Spain. The fear of a combination of Sweden, Spain, and Russia,
aided by the Jacobites against the Revolution dynasty and settlement, silenced for the time the parliamentary critics. On March 3rd
Görtz, deprived of his one protector, the late king, and detested by
the Swedish aristocracy, after the mockery of a trial was judicially
murdered at Stockholm. When Ormonde's expedition, delayed week
after week in the Spanish dockyards, finally sailed from Cadiz on
March 7th, Stair and Dubois knew more about it than Ormonde
himself. Norris waiting off the Lizard was not, however, to have
the honour of rivalling Byng. The unfortunate pawn, the Chevalier,
once again was brought by the desperate gamblers too late into
the game. When James, who had escaped from Rome, reached
Corunna on April 17th, he learned that not for the first nor the last
time in his career a storm had ruined the stroke.[1] Ten days earlier
the two Keiths with Tullibardine and Lord George Murray had
shipped from Havre with a handful of Spanish troops, and April 13th
found them stranded at Loch Alsh. With tragic irony June 10th,
the birthday of the prince whose cause they represented, saw the
little force, swollen by about 1000 Highlanders, "shamefully dispersed" by General Wightman at Glenshiel. It was a wretched
commencement of the careers of James Keith, the Field-Marshal of
Frederick the Great, and of George Murray, destined to fight for
the White Rose at Preston Pans, Falkirk, and Culloden. On August 14th, the unfortunate James left Spain to marry Clementina
Sobieski, the girl of sixteen whom Charles Wogan, in an evil hour

1719

March 29
March 19

Sept. 5

---

[1] Ormonde henceforward followed the example of Berwick and Bolingbroke and
abandoned the cause of the White Rose. His brother, Lord Arran, was permitted to
repurchase his forfeited estates. At Avignon in 1745, the most promising year for
Jacobitism, Ormonde closed a singularly adventurous career, in which he had twice
been attainted (in 1689 by James II., in 1715 by the Whigs).

of romance for bridegroom, bride, and the Cause, had stolen for his master, and conducted through the snows of the spring from her captivity at Innsbrück to share a " Pretender's " crown.

The French victories in Spain and Cobham's expedition to Vigo (in which the father of the author of *Tristram Shandy* served) compelled Philip V. to yield, and in December, 1719, Alberoni was dismissed. Grimaldi, who took his place in May, 1720, accepted the terms of the Quadruple Alliance. The Treaty of Madrid, comprising the commercial treaties of 1713, 1715, and 1716, established a defensive alliance between France, Spain, and Great Britain, and relegated outstanding questions to a congress at Cambrai. The Alberoni phase of Anglo-Spanish relations was closed. If Spain had met with a severe check Elizabeth's dynastic aims had been partially recognised. The next well-defined phase was to turn on the relations of Spain with the Emperor, and the dynastic appetite of " the Termagant" encouraged by her success. There still remained the great Northern Problem. With the accession of Ulrica Eleanora to the Swedish throne, and the political revolution that destroyed the royal absolutism, the astonishing resistance of the exhausted Swedish nation collapsed. The best that Sweden could hope for was to purchase peace either from Great Britain or from Russia and to resist the demands of her other foes. Stanhope's diplomatic work elsewhere had secured the co-operation of France and neutralised for a time imperial jealousy. Great Britain now aimed at the restoration of a peace which would satisfy Hanoverian, Danish, and Prussian claims ; at checkmating a Russian supremacy in the Baltic and leaving Sweden sufficiently strong to withstand in the future Russian expansion. These objects were only partially realised, but Stanhope's difficulties were insuperable. Public opinion at home could be easily inflamed by the cry of Hanoverianism in the Cabinet and royal closet ; the concert with France and the Emperor had to be maintained ; the conflicting greeds of the claimants for the spoil defied all efforts at reconciliation. The idea of a general offensive league against the Tsar broke down ; yet war alone would coerce Peter, and neither Stanhope nor Parliament was prepared to plunge England into a war with Russia for benefits to be shared by Hanover, Prussia, and Denmark. Prussia too adhered to the Tsar. In 1719 Carteret, who had made the brilliant *début* of a brilliant career by a defence of Ministerial policy in the House of Lords, was sent to Stockholm. Norris with

June, 1721

1721-31

his fleet was ordered "to give countenance to Lord Carteret's negotiations," and from that date a sheaf of conventions and treaties, after long hagglings and no little chicanery in Stanhope's diplomacy, was slowly vamped together. Carteret made peace between Sweden and Great Britain; Prussia was detached after much difficulty and some dishonesty from the Russian alliance and her terms with Sweden settled; finally Denmark and Sweden were brought into a sullen acquiescence of terms that satisfied neither. The hope that the Russian fleet might be provoked into a conflict with Norris and destroyed was disappointed. The First and Second Treaties of Stockholm and the Treaty of Frederiksborg assigned Bremen and Verden to Hanover; Stettin and Pomerania, as far as the Peene, to Prussia; restored Stralsund, Rügen, and Wismar to Sweden, and permitted Denmark to retain the Duchy of Schleswig. Money payments from Great Britain and Sweden salved these concessions. The Tsar alone remained obdurate, and though England endeavoured to help her new Swedish ally's attempts to form a great anti-Russian coalition, by subsidies, and the sending of a fleet, Peter bided his time. Stanhope's death, the financial crash at home, and British hostility to war with Russia, finally forced Sweden to make the peace of Nystad, which by the cession of Livonia, Ingria, and Carelia, established Russia as the predominant Power in the Baltic. A great chapter in European history was ended. Sweden sank from the first-rate rank to which she had been raised by the Vasas to comparative insignificance, and British influence in the Baltic steadily waned before the wonderful expansion of the empire of the Tsars and the rise of Prussia under the Hohenzollerns. The ultimate failure of British Ministers to maintain a Scandinavian barrier cannot be attributed to the Hanoverian bias in their policy. Such English interests as could be secured by diplomacy alone were on the whole gained. The insane obstinacy of Charles XII., and worse, the continuous and incurable disunion of the Scandinavian peoples, ruined the great fabric of Gustavus Adolphus. For Great Britain the need of the Baltic exports declined with the fostered growth of raw material in her American colonies. After 1721 British policy concentrated on more vital political and commercial interests elsewhere which compensated for the decay of prestige and power in the Northern Sea. But despite these considerations the victory of Peter the Great was a virtual checkmate to the policy of

Jan. 21,
1720
Oct. 20

1721

George I. The King's ambition had been first to secure Bremen and
Verden and then to crush the new Russian Power. In this he
completely failed.

By 1721 England at home had been shaken by an economic
convulsion, and the administration had passed into other hands.
On leaving office Walpole in particular did not scruple to utilise
the Tory party led by Wyndham and Shippen against the Whig
Administration. Foreign policy was severely criticised, the Jacobite
charge of peculation against Cadogan supported, the Mutiny Act
of 1718 denounced, and by use of a technical point of privilege
Oxford's impeachment dropped. Oxford received a pardon and is ₁₇₁₇
the last example of a purely political impeachment—the transition
from the legal to the moral responsibility of Ministers, from the
criminal liability of a politician arraigned by political foes for political blunders to lose his head to the political liability to lose his
office. The lenient temper of the Government was illustrated by
pardons to the rebels of 1715, and the proposals to repeal the Schism
Act and to modify the Test and Corporation Acts. Walpole, who
had previously described the Schism Act as worthy of Julian the
Apostate, now allied with Anglican Toryism to resist concessions to
the Nonconformists. The Schism Act indeed was repealed, but by
so narrow a majority that the idea of further relief to classes whose
loyalty, apart from equity and justice, deserved Whig gratitude
was abandoned. In these various actions it is impossible to acquit
Walpole from the charge of ambition, faction, and bigotry. But
now on the Peerage Bill he vindicated his right to be regarded as
the true exponent of progressive Whiggism. By this Ministerial
measure it was proposed that the existing number of the Peers
should not be enlarged beyond six. Peerages lapsing from failure
of issue male could, however, be replaced. The scheme was mainly
Sunderland's, who feared the unlimited power of the peer-creating
prerogative when it fell to the Prince of Wales, the mainstay of the
Opposition of the day. By a statutory restriction of the royal prerogative the Whig supremacy in the House of Lords would be
permanently assured. The King's hatred of his son was stronger than
his love of his prerogative ; the sixteen Scottish peers were won over
by making them hereditary Lords of Parliament, and the idea of turning the House of Lords into a close college and an unalterable caste,
entrenched in the Statute Book, appealed to the social pride and

political ambitions of the existing members of the Upper House. When the bill, passed by the Peers, came down to the Lower House, Walpole seized the opportunity to discredit its ministerial authors. On the threshold of a career which was to make the Commons the centre of political authority, he exposed in a masterly speech the sinister and inevitable consequences of the measure. The Lower would in all conflicts with the Upper House arm the peers with a statutory veto irreversible by the Crown, Commons, or the electorate, and alterable only by a law which there would be no legal means to compel the Peers to accept. "There would be no arriving at honour," he summed up, "but through the winding-sheet of a decrepit lord, or the grave of an extinct noble family." The bill was rejected and the contemporary theory of ministerial relations to the legislature is aptly illustrated by the fact that Ministers did not resign, while Walpole and Townshend accepted office as Paymaster and Lord President respectively under the men they had just signally defeated. Walpole had as yet no seat in the Cabinet nor a real voice in determining policy, but with the bursting of the "South Sea Bubble" his hour had at last struck.

The South Sea Scheme originated in a sincere desire to deal with a problem, regarded as pressing by politicians and publicists of both parties—the growing burden of the National Debt. That the scheme culminated in widespread disaster was due partly to fallacious finance, but chiefly to one of the inexplicable cyclones of speculation which sweep over nations and which in Law's similar proposals devastated France at the same time. In 1711 Harley had formed the South Sea Company by funding £10,000,000 of floating debt, assigning it to the stockholders as the Company's capital and securing the interest by duties and commercial privileges. By 1719 the Company's stock sold at a premium. In 1714 the National Debt amounted to £54,145,363, a large part of which was unfunded, and the annual charge was about £3,351,358, in an average budget of £10,000,000. Many politicians, failing to understand the resources out of which both debt and revenue had grown, saw in these figures impending national bankruptcy. In 1717 Walpole's Sinking Fund authorised the borrowing of money at the lowest market rate to redeem debt, and ear-marked the savings on the redemption operations for the further reduction of the outstanding dead-weight of debt. The South Sea Act of 1720 was a proposal to combine the advantages of the Sinking Fund with the machinery of the Joint-Stock Company. The directors of the South Sea Company outbid their financial rivals and agreed to convert into stock annuities to the amount of £30,981,712 (at 5 per cent. until 1727 and 4 per cent. after that date), and to make the annuities redeemable. They also offered to pay a sum equivalent to £7,500,000 for the bargain and to circulate gratis £1,000,000 in exchequer bills at 3 per cent. In return the Company was to be remunerated for its management expenses of the debt taken over and to have the monopoly of the South Sea trade. The Government in fact had made far too favourable a bargain, but despite Walpole's criticism Parliament accepted the scheme. Success required that the public should be tempted to subscribe by an inflation of the Company's shares, and that the Company from its trade profits should pay a dividend adequate to the premium on the shares. Thanks to artificial manipulation, wild rumours as to Spain granting gold and silver districts in Peru, the amount of capital available for investment, and the gambling fever that now gripped every class, issues of South Sea stock were eagerly absorbed at rising prices. By the end of May £100 stock stood at £890. Change Alley became a roaring Hell-porch of insane or dishonest speculators. The most transparent impostures were daily floated. Proposals to transmute quicksilver, make wheels of perpetual motion, found hospitals for bastard children or import Spanish jackasses for unspecified purposes to unsuitable regions found ready investors. Even "a company for carrying on an undertaking of great advantage, but nobody to know what it is" obtained 1000 subscriptions. South Sea Stock touched its highest price, £1060, on June 25th. But the action of the Company in prosecuting illegal frauds on the market probably precipitated the inevitable crash. On September 21st South Sea stock had fallen to £150. The failures of banks unable to realise, and of sound business concerns unable to meet their creditors because their debtors were ruined, followed on the bursting of the innumerable quacks. Many men and women were reduced to beggary ; every class in the community suffered heavily. Jacobite correspondence shows that, apart from the economic panic and havoc, " the heaven-sent " catastrophe might be used by deft intriguers to focus the universal cry for vengeance on the foreign dynasty and its corrupt and incompetent advisers. This danger became more serious when Aislabie, the Chancellor of the Exchequer, and the two Craggs were found guilty of being bribed into connivance at the worst features of the scheme. By general consent but one man, Walpole, "who could convert stones into gold" could save the situation. And Walpole proved equal to the task. Resisting the demand for retribution and instantaneous relief he saw that a financier's first duty was to re-establish public credit and make a permanent settlement. Confiscation of the Company's property as a sop to bankrupt sufferers would only ruin the Company and stain a fresh financial panic with State-sanctioned injustice. The private property of the directors, however, to the sum of £2,000,000 was distributed to shareholders; the Company was relieved of £7,000,000 it had undertaken to pay Government, and by a redivision of the capital every holder of £100 stock received 33 per cent. By 1741 both the interest and the total of the capitalised annuities taken over from the National Debt were successfully reduced. Of the inculpated Ministers Aislabie was ex-pelled the House of Commons; the elder Craggs committed suicide, and his son died of small-pox before the inquiry was over. Sunder-land was acquitted, but public opinion made his resignation necessary, and his death followed in 1722. Stanhope, of whose innocence there was no question, was so affected by a bitter attack from the

Feb. 1721 Duke of Wharton that he was struck with apoplexy and died. His death marks the close of a well-defined phase of the Whig supremacy. As a statesman Stanhope has received scant justice in our text-books. A Whig of the Whigs, he had given proofs of his abilities both military and civil previously to 1714, and his capture

1708 of Minorca was in 1717 fitly associated with the title of his peer-age. No man after George's accession worked harder to make the Revolution System and the new dynasty a success. But his chief claim to national gratitude will rest securely on his achievements as a Minister of Foreign Affairs. Insight, tact, patience, decision, and fertility of resource were his gifts, and he devoted them to the service of his country. As a diplomatist he did not stick at trifles nor was overburdened by scruples. But even in these respects he will compare favourably with the men whom it was his business and his duty to defeat or to win. In 1714 he found Great Britain isolated, discredited, and vacillating in the principles of her policy. He left her in 1721 powerful, respected, and the centre of the

European system. The more closely these seven years of crisis are studied by the light of the copious evidence now available, the more convincing is the conclusion that the difficulties imposed tests of the highest statesmanship, and that in most of the successful solutions the originative and driving force came from London. And Stanhope's most signal achievement, which he handed on to his successors, was the French alliance and the masterly adaptation of it to the needs of Great Britain. By it the Jacobites were stale if not checkmated. From 1719-43 the Jacobite danger was never really serious ; and the crisis of 1744 proves what would have happened more than once in these twenty-five years if there had been no French alliance. As employed by Stanhope and Walpole, the concert of France and England was a powerful instrument for peace, and peace was priceless to the statesmen whose duty it was to reconcile a nation exhausted by long wars to the Hanoverian dynasty and the Revolution System. The prestige of French diplomacy aided British efforts in every disturbed quarter of Europe. Equally important was the severance of Spain from France. Strategically as well as politically and commercially France and Spain were Great Britain's most natural and formidable adversaries. Sooner or later she was bound to enter on a prolonged struggle with both. The Anglo-French alliance crippled Spain, France's future ally, and deferred the long duel with France until England's dynasty and financial credit were secured, her American colonies developed and her own resources quadrupled. On the sea, the French Government came to rely on the British fleet, with the desirable result for England that her fleet was adequately maintained while that of the French declined. The fleet indeed was Britain's most persuasive diplomatist. Unfortunately a navy that a Foreign Office converts into an international police force tends to lose its grip on the science of war. The ineffectiveness of our fleet, 1743-48, was probably due in part to the mildew bred by the long non-existence of a serious competitor. On the whole, however, it is not surprising that French historians of weight should be disposed to place the treaty of 1717, which demonstrably worked with greater benefit for Great Britain than for France, in the same category as the Austro-French Treaty of 1757. But such criticism only serves to emphasise in British eyes the patriotic insight of the statesman who originated, and of those who strove and knew how to maintain it, as the cardinal principles of a sound Whig foreign policy.

Marlborough's death in 1722 left no successor on whom his mantle could fall. In the titanic struggle with Louis XIV. the marvellous versatility of his genius made him the most conspicuous figure in Europe. After 1714 his career, as previously, was tainted with duplicity and avarice, and since 1717 he had hardly been more than the shadow of a splendid name. The greatest soldier our country had yet, or perhaps has ever, produced, he carried with him to the grave a great tradition. Not until the Peninsular War did Great Britain, though she sorely needed both, find a chief and a military instrument of the quality that Marlborough provided.

The way was now open to Walpole, whose primacy in the Commons had been completed by his period of Opposition. In April, 1721, he was appointed First Lord of the Treasury and Chancellor of the Exchequer, while Townshend became Secretary of State with Carteret as his colleague. Walpole's long tenure of power, without a parallel save in the Ministry of the younger Pitt, gives the next twenty years a character of their own. "I parted with him once," said George I., "against my inclination, and I will never part with him again." By birth, taste, and fortune, Robert Walpole belonged to the country gentry. Born in 1676, two years earlier than his rival, Henry St. John, his political career exemplified the apologue of the idle and the industrious apprentice. And at the accession of George I. he was already a notable figure. Gifted with robust health and great powers of work, he had steadily pushed his way to the front by his sincere and intelligent devotion to Whig principles, his solid abilities, his discerning penetration of men and affairs, and his intuition of his country's needs. These qualities he retained to the end, and they stamped his administration. Hervey, who knew him well, said that no man was ever blessed with a clearer head, a truer or quicker judgment, or a sharper insight into mankind, and his conduct from first to last confirms the verdict. His character and personality have perhaps little on the surface that attracts, much that repels. He was neither a brilliant orator nor a cultivated spirit, save in his love of good pictures. His tastes, habits, and morals were those of the squire of his day. For a man who could bet with Pulteney over a classical quotation, he cared little, if at all, for good literature. It is said that he always opened first the report from his head gamekeeper. He drank deeply, hunted hard, swore, talked coarsely, kept at least one mistress, none of which things shocked Hanoverian England. He was ready to provide for his sons with pensions and sinecures at the expense of the State ; he did not scruple to bribe men and women who were willing to be bribed. He was intensely ambitious, loved power, and was intolerant of opposition. But no man cared less for the frippery and trappings of success ; when we remember the ethics of his world and his unique opportunities for plunder and self-advancement we may well be astonished at his moderation. What distinguishes him from his political rivals and places him in the first division of the first class of our statesmen is not his gifts as a debater, nor as a financier, nor even his supremacy in the House of Commons—remarkable as these are—but the political sense and intuition which differentiate genius from mere ability in statesmanship. Starting from the axiomatic premiss that an Englishman's duty was to maintain the Protestant Succession and Revolution System, and convert them into instruments of national efficiency and prosperity, Walpole regarded public affairs as serious business. A Minister's function was to administer ; men in the long run at home and abroad were governed by " interest " ; the nation must have a policy that would pay national dividends. In the power to lead a party, create a practical programme and carry it out under a parliamentary *régime*—a task that requires a combination of the highest political qualities—Walpole has few equals and no superiors. By exercising the functions of a Prime Minister, by the development of the Cabinet system, and the organisation of party government through the House of Commons as the centre of authority, he permanently moulded the machinery of government. He maintained his control in the teeth of unscrupulous opposition for twenty years ; he was called upon to solve both at home and abroad problems the complexity and difficulty of which the evidence now at a student's disposal fully reveals ; he was matched against critics of brilliance and ability—Townshend, Carteret, Chesterfield, Pulteney, Wyndham, Bolingbroke, and the elder Pitt—and in nine cases out of ten when Walpole and they differed Walpole was right and they were wrong. His opponents ascribed his success to his extraordinary luck. But good fortune in statesmanship is only another name for the proper use of opportunities. The solid qualities that inspire the confidence of a sovereign and of a representative legislature may be brilliantly displayed, but they are not to be acquired haphazard, in the royal closet or on the floor of the House of Commons.

The Ministry of Walpole in the strict sense perhaps is more correctly dated from 1730 than from 1721. The Administration that replaced Stanhope and Sunderland was a business partnership of Townshend and Walpole, in which the chief control of foreign affairs fell to the Secretary of State. Walpole was sufficiently occupied with finance and "the King's business" in the Commons to be content to leave his brother-in-law for the time a separate sphere of power. But no one understood better that neither an efficient business firm nor an efficient Cabinet can have two chiefs, and in the clash of character and the issues of public policy a trial of strength between these two masterful men was sooner or later inevitable. The unseemly squabbles of the Court provided public opinion with scandal and Ministers with no little worry. George I. regulated his family life with the despotism of a military martinet. In 1718 the judges had declared in his favour that the King was guardian of his grandchildren, and could, even against their father's wishes, veto their marriages. A quarrel at the baptism of the eldest son of the Prince of Wales, and a threat to fight a duel with the Duke of Newcastle, led to the Prince and his family being ordered from St. James, and all who visited the heir to the Crown were forbidden to appear at Court. In 1720 Walpole with Cowper's help succeeded in patching up a reconciliation, and Leicester House, the residence of the Prince and Princess of Wales, whose relations [1] with the King continued to be strained, became the centre of the political Opposition. Walpole, however, had divined the ability and influence of the Princess ; for the time he riveted his grip on the Court by using the venal power of the Duchess of Kendal, "as much Queen of England as ever woman was" ; but he did not forget that an alliance with Caroline would one day justify the pains to secure it. With equal truth and wit Chesterfield remarked later that the easiest way to disgust the nation with "the Pretender" would be to make him Elector of Hanover.

---

[1] George I. actually sounded two Lord Chancellors (Cowper and Parker) as to the feasibility of disinheriting the Prince from the Electoral Succession in Hanover. And in 1727 a paper was found in which apparently it was suggested to the King that the Prince should be kidnapped and carried off to America.

The Jacobite "Plot" of 1720-21 presented the familiar combination of farcical and serious elements. Goring, a Sussex baronet, Kelly, Atterbury's secretary, and a gang of smugglers, "a hellish crew," known as "the Waltham Blacks," were mixed up in a wild-cat scheme to seize the Tower, the Bank of England, and the King, and raise a popular insurrection which was apparently to be helped by an invading force led by Ormonde and Dillon. Dubois got wind of the vapourings of these comic opera conspirators, and warned his Ministerial allies in London. The Duke of Norfolk, Lords Orrery, North, and Arran (Ormonde's brother) were implicated. Correspondence was intercepted, and Atterbury was imprisoned in the Tower. The affair with all its incoherent ramifications and its atmosphere of treachery caused a great deal of excited talking. Walpole and the Government took it more seriously than it deserved. The Habeas Corpus Act was suspended for a whole year, the longest period on record ; sharp measures were meted out to Roman Catholics and Non-Jurors. An example was made of Atterbury, Dean of Westminster, Bishop of Rochester, and a friend of many of the literary lights of Anne's reign : Pope, Swift, Prior, Gay, Arbuthnot, and South. Since 1717 the Dean, the most prominent of the High Church party, had been in communication with the Jacobite leaders. His arrest stirred clerical fanaticism, but despite an able defence by the Whig Lord Cowper, he was condemned by bill of attainder, deprived of his offices and banished. Already an old man, he died abroad in 1732, one more heart broken in a hopeless cause. As the last of a long list of political attainders, Atterbury's case is memorable ; but it also serves to illustrate the severity with which Walpole was prepared to treat those in high places who were foolish enough to dabble in treason.[1]

Both Ireland and Scotland were sources of trouble. Swift, indeed, showed again how a literary genius by an hour's work in his study could make three kingdoms drunk. There was no mint in Ireland, which had a great need of small coins. In 1722 a patent to issue a new copper currency had been granted to the Duchess of

---

[1] Mar was believed to have been instrumental in betraying "the plot". On Mar's guilt or carelessness, see A. Lang, *History of Scotland*, iv., 336-42. Mr. Lang says : "I could not give a verdict of 'guilty' against Mar"; and on the whole question of Atterbury's intrigues, Canon Beeching's *Atterbury* (London, 1909), pp. 251-307.

Kendal who sold it to Wood, an English merchant.   Irish public opinion, exasperated by the recent act, further limiting the Constitution (6 Geo. I., c. 5) believed that a greedy mistress and the hack of a Ministry had combined to drain the country of its small stock of gold and silver, and leave it at the mercy of debased copper coins.   And Wood's threat "to pour the coinage down the throats of the people," only stiffened the universal determination to boycott the new issue absolutely.   Swift, in his *Drapier's Letters*, lashed public excitement into the verge of rebellion.   In the memorable Fourth Letter he indicted the whole system of English power in Ireland, and by arguments leading up to the triumphant conclusion, "government without the consent of the governed is the very definition of slavery," effectively unwhigged the Whigs.   It was useless for authority aided by Isaac Newton to demonstrate that the coinage was free from the defects alleged.   Warned by the Irish Primate Boulter that the growing opposition would produce a formidable union of Papists, Jacobites, and Whigs, the Ministry compensated Wood and cancelled the patent.   Nine years later in the Excise Scheme, fifteen years later in the Spanish War, Walpole was taught the same unmistakable lesson that once sentiment, however ignorant or unjust, has mastered a nation, appeals to reason and facts are useless.

1725

A firm attitude was more successful in quelling the trouble in Scotland caused by a change in the malt tax.   Under Anne it had been agreed that Scotland was to be exempt from the tax until the war was over.   In 1714 fear of strengthening the anti-union feeling made the tax a dead letter, and instead, in 1724, an additional sixpence was laid on each barrel of beer, while the bounty on exported grain was removed.   The general indignation was skilfully fanned by the Jacobites, and the Ministry compromised by placing a tax of threepence a bushel on malt, just half the amount of the English tax.   A riot in Glasgow was suppressed by Wade's troops, but in Edinburgh the brewers refused to brew.   Duncan Forbes, famous later as the President of the Court of Session, urged firmness on the Government.   An Act of Sederunt accordingly required the breweries to be kept going, and after a public meeting the brewers decided to obey.   Walpole, like George III. later, did not forget defaulters.   Roxburgh, the Secretary of State who had supported Carteret in the Cabinet, and Craigie, the Lord Advocate, were both

1725

dismissed. Islay, the brother of Argyle, though not made Secretary, stepped into Roxburgh's place, and with his brother's help and that of Forbes, promoted Advocate General, successfully kept Scotland quiet until the Porteous Riots.   1737

In foreign policy Townshend and Walpole had inherited the French alliance, as well as the congress at Cambray which was to secure for the Emperor the terms agreed upon by the Treaty of Madrid. By 1723, owing to the deaths of the Regent Orléans and of Dubois, French policy was no longer in the hands of the authors of the *Entente*, and had fallen to the incompetent Duke of Bourbon, "the one-eyed ruffian," ruled by his mistress, the Marquise de Prie, who was the tool of the Paris financiers, Duverney. Townshend's co-Secretary was Carteret, brimful of ideas, masterful, and above all anxious to complete his diplomatic work in the North, by checkmating Russian ascendancy in the Baltic. Carteret would have sent a fleet to coerce the Tsar, but the Swedish aristocracy preferred to come to terms with Russia, and Townshend's pacific 1724 policy of non-intervention won the day. The Anglo-French understanding alone prevented France from adding to the Tsar's supremacy by a renewal of the Franco-Russian alliance. Carteret, unfortunately for himself, sought to strengthen his position by Court influence rather than by solid political connections, and a sordid family intrigue gave Walpole the opportunity to assert his control. Two royal mistresses, the Countess of Darlington and the Countess of Platen, were scheming to marry the daughter of the latter and the niece of the former to the Comte de St. Florentin, whose father, the Marquis de la Vrillière, was for his compliance to be rewarded with a dukedom. The King, our ambassador, Luke Schaub, Bernstorff and Bothmer, even Bolingbroke, were all concerned, and Carteret took their side. The affair became a trial of strength in the Cabinet, but the deaths of Orléans and Dubois ruined the project. Walpole's brother, "old Horace," replaced Schaub at Paris, and Carteret was transferred to the viceroyalty of Ireland. The young Duke of Newcastle, an adherent of Walpole's, received Carteret's seals. Walpole, in fact, had not merely showed that he would not tolerate insubordination. He had extended his right to direct into the sphere of foreign policy.

The Congress at Cambray, "most inane of human congresses and memorable on that account if no other," spent two years in "eat-ing, drinking, and other civilities," and in settling minutiæ of diplomatic etiquette and red-tape. It was not formally opened until January 26th, 1724, and by October it was at a standstill. The Emperor had proved as irritable as usual over the investiture of Don Carlos and the introduction of the Spanish garrisons into the Italia*. ports, but by 1723 the investiture had been obtained. More serious trouble was brewing elsewhere than at Cambray. Charles VI., who had no sons, had begun in earnest the great "shadow-hunt" for "the imperial bit of sheepskin"—the Pragmatic Sanction, first promulgated in 1713 (which secured the succession of his elder daughter, Maria Theresa, to the hereditary dominions of the Habsburg House). The European ratification of this arrangement was now the prime object of Austrian diplomacy. By granting a charter to the Imperial and Royal East India Company of Ostend the Emperor roused English and Dutch jealousy in its most sensitive quarter. The idea of promoting Belgian commerce by such a chartered company dated as far back as 1714 and John Ker of Kersland, a Scottish adventurer, and John Colebrooke, "a perfect master of the art of stock-jobbing," played a part in its promotion. By 1720 Belgian ships were already competing in the monopoly of the Eastern trade, and factories had been set up at Coblom (coast of Coromandel) and Canton, to the anger of the Dutch and English traders. The menace was no idle one. The venture was profitable, and, under Imperial protection, bid fair to inflict serious loss on its long-established rivals. In 1723 the English House of Commons declared the scheme antagonistic to British interests, and English subjects were forbidden to subscribe for the Company's shares. The commercial classes, thoroughly roused, called on the Government "to destroy this cockatrice whilst still young". No Whig Government, even if it had wished, which it did not, could resist such pressure. But the matter shortly was connected with larger issues. Spain, pressing for the enforcement of the terms of the Madrid Treaty, offered the sole mediation between herself and the Emperor to Great Britain. The Ministry, aware that acceptance would practically involve a breach of the French Alliance, declined, and Bourbon's peremptory action in breaking off the proposed dynastic marriage between the Courts of Madrid and Paris brought about an open rupture between France and Spain. Elizabeth Farnese, tired of waiting, and furious at the insulting return of the Infanta, Maria

Dec. 19, 1722

Mar. 1725

Victoria from Paris, had come under the influence of Ripperda, "the man with great views rather than with great parts". Europe was startled by the new policy embodied in the Treaty of Vienna. April 30 Ripperda aimed in this triumphant *coup de théâtre* at creating by inter-marriages of the two dynasties a close union between Madrid and Vienna, the establishment of Don Carlos with a Habsburg bride in Italy, the recovery of Gibraltar and Minorca from Great Britain, and a supremacy in Europe for the allies. Spain guaranteed the Pragmatic Sanction and opened her colonial ports to ships bearing the certificates of the Ostend Company's directors. The British Ministry, not without reason, suspected that support of the Pretender would be one of the weapons of the new allies. The menace to British trade, both in the West and East Indies, and the menace to the Protestant succession, secured enthusiastic assent from Parliament and public opinion to a vigorous policy. Townshend, with France as an ally, was eager to build up a counter-European system, and in September the treaty of Hanover—an alliance with Prussia—was a reply to Ripperda's challenge. It was in vain that the new Opposition organ, *The Craftsman*, denounced the unpatriotic Hanoverianism of the Ministry, continental subsidies, and the sham bogey of Jacobitism. Parliament was convinced that the Treaty of Vienna was "calculated for the entire destruction of British trade," and implied the loss of Gibraltar and the subsequent restoration of the Stuarts. With French and Dutch support England was determined to kill the Ostend Company and force a settlement on both Spain and the Emperor. Diplomatic activities on both sides were feverishly employed to procure allies. The Emperor, by the treaty of Wusterhausen, detached Prussia in 1726, secured Russia, and in the Second Treaty of Vienna committed himself to recovering by force, if necessary, Gibraltar and Minorca, and to a dismemberment of France. Townshend, on the other hand, had won over the Dutch, Denmark, the Landgrave of Hesse, and Portugal. By the fitting out of three fleets England in 1726 showed that she was in earnest, and it looked as if a great European war must follow from the division of Europe into two well-defined confederations. In April Hozier's squadron was despatched to blockade Porto Bello and to seize the Spanish treasure fleet. Opinion in the British Cabinet, however, was seriously divided. Townshend throughout desired to break with the Emperor and use the confederation to compel him by force to give way. Walpole, averse from continental engagements, was reluctant to go to war with Spain. It was clear that the hostile alliance could only be dissolved by offering acceptable terms either to Vienna or Madrid. A breach with the Emperor was a serious departure from established Whig traditions, from which a strong party in the Cabinet dissented. The accession to power at Paris of the peace-loving Cardinal Fleury, anxious to prevent war between France and Spain, turned the scale in favour of an attempt to deal first with Charles VI. Madrid and Vienna were already quarrelling.

May 14 Ripperda, unable to secure from the Emperor the execution of the terms of his treaty, was dismissed, and his revelation of the secret articles in the Vienna Treaties further inflamed British indignation, while it broke up the artificial and ill-mated union. Two more British fleets—one to the Baltic to protect Denmark from a Russo-Swedish attack, another to the Mediterranean to check a possible Jacobite invasion—were sent to sea. Charles and his ambassador, Palm, very nearly brought about a war. Palm throughout had supplied the Opposition with ammunition for their attacks, but his

Mar. 2,   publication of a memorial " to the whole nation," traversing the
1727   statements in the King's speech, was justly resented as an impertinent interference on the part of a foreign Power in British home government. Supported by a parliamentary address, the Ministry ordered Palm out of the country, and military preparations continued on

Jan., 1727 both sides. With Spain, Great Britain already was formally at war,
Feb 22 and the siege of Gibraltar began. Fleury worked hard for peace.
Feb. 27 Preliminaries to be offered to the Emperor were agreed upon, and were presented on May 2nd, with an ultimatum that war would follow

May 31 their non-acceptance. The Emperor consented ; his desertion left Spain isolated, unable to take Gibraltar, and with her trade harassed by British ships. A fortnight later the Spanish ambassador at Vienna consented to sign the articles. The reign of George I. thus closed with the prospect of a definitive settlement in sight.

This chapter of foreign policy emphasises instructively the value of the French alliance, the power of France and Great Britain acting in concert, the devotion of the Emperor to the Pragmatic Sanction, the extreme difficulty of severing France from Spain, and the strength of Elizabeth Farnese's dynastic ambitions. Great Britain, however, emerged with renewed power. Her fleets and her subsidies were decisive factors in the final issue. The importance of commerce and the pressure of the commercial classes are revealed in her strenuous hostility to the Ostend Company, her grip on Gibraltar, and the hostility to a Spanish war which must strain to breaking point the Anglo-French understanding, damage trade, and lead up to a European imbroglio menacing to the stability of the Revolution System. The Ministry had worked for peace, so essential to light taxation and commercial prosperity, but they were not prepared to purchase it at any price. No less important for the future, a widening divergence between the views of Walpole and of Townshend had been disclosed. On the cardinal point—a policy to strengthen the Protestant dynasty—they were at one. But Walpole regarded with increasing distrust the methods and objects of his colleague's European diplomacy. The preliminaries of May 31st were in reality a victory for Walpole. The political difference between the brothers-in-law was accentuated, as had been the case in the Ministerial split of 1717, by personal elements. Walpole having secured a virtual supremacy in home affairs was bent on having the like in foreign policy. Townshend was not the man to brook control in a sphere that he regarded as peculiarly his own. The struggle too cut deeper. Cabinet unity and efficiency required, as the logic of its development slowly proved, that Ministers must agree on political principles, which in practice must come to mean the principles of the most influential chief. A departmental division of public affairs and administration into water-tight compartments, the individual independence of Ministers, must be fatal to an effective system of parliamentary and party government. The evolution of a Prime Minister was inevitable and desirable. And the place would be automatically taken by the Minister who could make himself indispensable to his Sovereign and Parliament, and whose insight and ability would teach him how to build and maintain a Ministry based on parliamentary support, and its capacity to promote national interest, as interpreted by a majority of the nation's representatives. Apart from the impeachment and condemnation of Lord Macclesfield, the Lord Chancellor, in 1725, for financial irregularities, the most important event in these years had been the return of Bolingbroke. Pardoned in 1723, he had met Atterbury on his way to exile. "We are exchanged," had been the dean's concise comment; and in 1725 Bolingbroke, thanks to unwearied efforts on his behalf, assisted by a handsome *douceur* to the Duchess of Kendal, was permitted to recover his landed estates. Walpole, who had agreed to this with the greatest reluctance, refused all suggestions of a coalition; nor would he even allow him to take his seat in the Upper House.

Bolingbroke, who settled at Dawley, where his new home became a notable centre of literary and political celebrities, now set to work to organise a new Opposition out of the reorganised Tories and the discontented Whigs. Jacobitism was a dying, if not a dead, political creed. The marriage of James Edward and the birth of Charles Edward, aided by the South Sea crash, had galvanised the party into new and disastrous activities. But the unhappy marriage, the scandal about Mar, the struggle between Mar's party and the Hays, and the unreasonable and childish conduct of "Queen" Clementina, rent the exiled Court across the water with the bitterest, meanest, and most absurd strifes. The growing solidarity and success of Walpole's Ministry and the patent hostility of the nation to any dynastic change further discredited the cause. Its former leaders had either, like Bolingbroke himself, found salvation by laudable submission, were in impotent exile like Atterbury and Ormonde, or were dead. Bolingbroke saw that an Opposition could not be created out of an anachronistic theology (in which he had never believed), the help of "honest" Shippen, and the reactionary political philosophy and decaying dogmas of an Oxford hopelessly out of touch with the intellectual and moral life of the nation. Twice it was to be his task to create a virile, united, and progressive Tory party ; twice he was to have the instrument, forged with such care and brilliance, broken in his hands. *The Craftsman* became the organ for educating both the new party and his and Walpole's masters—Parliament and the electorate. And the polish of its pages and the unscrupulous venom of its epigrams has, as with the Letters of Junius, cast on it the shadow of an immortality that its message little justified. Of an enduring criticism of life in its political expression the student will find virtually nothing in *The Craftsman*. And Bolingbroke, too, like Mirabeau later, was damned by his past—*les fautes de sa jeunesse*. The ambrosial nights of the wits at Dawley appealed as little to the rectories and manor-houses as they did to the Dissenting chapels, to the seats of the great Whig territorials, and to Lombard Street.

"Bagatelles, Bagatelles," as George I. said of Bolingbroke's

1720

in 1714
and in
1735
1726-36

schemes. But in proclaiming that they would fight neither with small nor with great, save only with Robert Walpole, the confederates were practically right. "Sir Blue-String," Leicester, Villiers, Empson, Dudley, Wolsey, Catiline, Sejanus, Harlequin, Mac-Heath, Bob Booty are some of the denominations under which they gibbeted with misplaced erudition and unwearying malignity the chief of the government. Corruption—"the bottomless pocket of Robin"—is the one unfailing charge, and the traditional belief in the magnitude and profligacy of Walpole's bribery is largely an illustration of the truth that in politics unproved and reiterated assertion will in time become its own evidence.[1] The lies of a literary artist who makes himself readable become the proofs of historical and political critics whom no one troubles to read. Continuous indictment of foreign policy, the identification of Hanoverianism and Whiggism, the iniquity of standing armies, "the Gothic wisdom which made our Parliament annual," the need of Pension and Place Bills, the destruction of party—such are the main elements of the new creed. W. Pulteney, Akenside's Curio, "who bellows for liberty to-day and roars for power to-morrow," was the most important of the new recruits. He had been left out of the reconstructed Ministry in 1721, and by 1725 his political quarrel with Walpole had become acute. As leader of the Opposition, Pulteney founded with Bolingbroke's help the "Patriots'" party, which included Shippen, Gower, Bathurst, Wyndham, Mar, Marchmont, Bromley, and in the next reign was reinforced by Carteret, Chesterfield, and other Whig rebels, and later still by the Boy Patriots. The common bond between its various members was antagonism to Walpole; its weak points lay in the real difference of political creed between its two wings and its lack of a constructive programme truly calculated to satisfy the correctly interpreted needs of the nation's political life. Shippen, as 1742 showed, had divined the character of his associates when he said: "Robin and I are two honest men; he is for King George and I for King James, but those men in the long cravats only want places under one or the other". The men in the long cravats (including Bolingbroke), who drank to each other's epigrams at Dawley, knew in their heart of hearts that they only wanted Walpole's place. Walpole had virtually lost the two most brilliant of the younger Whigs, Carteret in 1724 (though he remained a nominal adherent until 1730), and

[1] See Appendix XXI.

Philip Stanhope, who became Lord Chesterfield in 1726, the year after his refusal of the revived Order of the Bath had marked his quarrel with the Government. But in 1724 began the long tenure of office of the Duke of Newcastle and his matchless and indefatigable efforts in season and out of season to create a Pelham battalion. In [the same year his brother, Henry Pelham, the trusted subordinate of his Chief, who taught him the art of parliamentary management and ministerial leadership, was appointed Secretary at War. Financial capacity proved to be one of Henry Pelham's gifts, and in finance Walpole had already justified his reputation. The first function of a Chancellor of the Exchequer is to provide with a minimum of dislocation the revenue required both for ordinary and extraordinary occasions. The ways and means in the strain of 1726-27 had been provided with ease. In 1727 the interest at which the State borrowed was successfully lowered from 5 to 4 per cent., thereby effecting a saving of £377,381. If it is true that Walpole frequently raided his own sinking fund, established in 1717, either by diverting to current revenue the surplus or by using it as collateral security, or by employing it to keep the land tax at one shilling, the Chancellor would have replied that political quite as much as financial reasons enter into budgets. Reduced taxation, avoidance of deficits, or recourse to fresh loans are frequently as sound methods for increasing a nation's assets and taxable capacity as direct diminution of its capital liabilities. To steal by the adjustment of taxation the support of the landed gentry from the Opposition was a legitimate political object. If through finance the nation as a whole became reconciled to the new *régime* the result was as beneficial, if not as brilliant, as a column of figures proving the amount of dead-weight of debt paid off. Indirectly and in a variety of ways Walpole showed himself an enlightened mercantilist, anxious to redeem the pledge in the King's Speech of 1721 : " to make the exportation of our own manufactures and the importation of the commodities used in the manufacturing of them as practicable and as easy as may be ". In 1721 and 1724 the book of rates was much simplified : in 1723 the customs were put under one commission. From 1722-25 the powers of revenue officers were increased to check smuggling and increase revenue. Export duties were taken off manufactures, import duties either removed or lowered. Bounties to colonial-grown hemp, to the whale-fishery, to silk goods, mark the desire to cut new channels or deepen the existing ones of trade.   In 1724 there is a distinct anticipation of the famous excise scheme when inland duties were laid on tea, coffee, and cocoanuts, and the system of bonded warehousing introduced.   The promotion of the prosperity of the mercantile marine as the necessary basis of a powerful navy and the index of a flourishing foreign trade looms largely in Walpole's policy.   And the energy with which he made the destruction of the Ostend East India Company a political object tells its own tale.   There is indeed some reason to believe that Walpole more readily acquiesced in Townshend's foreign policy because its success would involve the abandonment by Charles VI. of that project.

But before further progress could be made apoplexy had struck down George I. at Osnabrück.   His death was a sad blow to Bolingbroke, since the heir to the throne was no friend of his.   How it would affect Walpole and the European situation had yet to be seen.   It cannot be said that the King was sincerely regretted by any one in Great Britain, even by the Duchess of Kendal, to whose appetite for plunder his death would administer a quietus.   Yet George had not been unsuccessful.   He had been fortunate to find and to keep Ministers of commanding ability whose loyalty to their country and the institutions that the monarchy represented was greater than their respect and affection for the Sovereign.   The much decried connection with Hanover cannot be proved to have worked detrimentally to British prosperity.   George as naturally exaggerated, as did his Ministers underrate, the importance of the Electorate; but it would be difficult to single out an example in which it could be conclusively shown that British interests were deliberately sacrificed to Hanoverian selfishness.   And in 1717 and in 1726 Hanoverian influence and ability were of material advantage in helping to secure important British ends.   Through Hanover and its ruler England was kept in touch with the live currents of central European politics, severance from which would in the long run have been damaging to our national life and our political development and position.   The social inconveniences and excrescences of the German Court, on which contemporary opinion so readily fastened, were a small price to pay for a throne resting on the principles of the Revolution System.   If Anne, James II. and Charles II. prove anything, it is at least arguable that a Stuart

Court in 1714 would not have been more moral and elevated, less amenable to backstairs intrigue and the corrupt competition of men and women who were courtiers first and last than the Hanoverian St. James. If the English Church suffered under the political Erastianism and theological latitudinarianism of the wicked Whigs and their Lutheran Parliament-made King it, is more than doubtful whether the substitution of Atterbury for Wake, of Bolingbroke for Walpole would have promoted tolerance, spirituality, and love of truth. The new spirit needed in the English Church was not to be found in the lawn sleeves of the lords spiritual nor in the country rectories and the universities. In 1727 it had not yet found expression in "The Serious Call," and was still dormant in the Rectory of Epworth and the derided band of "Methodists" at Lincoln and Christchurch in the University of Oxford.

George I. could die happy for one fact alone. The father had been the only person in Great Britain prepared to dispute the title of the son, George II., to the throne.

NOTE.—The most recent authority, particularly on foreign policy, for the Walpole period is P. Vaucher, *Robert Walpole et la politique de Fleury* (1924), based on an exhaustive study of the MS. sources in Paris and London and with an admirable bibliography ; see also W. Michael, *Englische Geschichte im* 18 *Jahrhundert*, vol. ii. (1920) (a continuation of the history, given on p. 518) ; *Cambridge History of British Foreign Policy* (1922), vol. i.   Introduction by Sir A. W. Ward, pp. 1-143.   L. G. Wickham Legge, *Matthew Prior* (1920), is important for the years 1713-15 ; J. F. Chance, *The Alliance of Hanover* (British Foreign Policy in last year of George I.) ; F. L. Edwards, *James, First Earl Stanhope* (1926).

CHAPTER 11

GEORGE II (1727-1760)

THE MINISTRY OF WALPOLE 1727-1742

WALPOLE killed two horses in order to tell the new King the news from Osnabrück, and for his reward was directed to apply to Sir Spencer Compton, Speaker of the House of Commons, and Treasurer to the Prince of Wales, "a plodding, heavy fellow with great application and no talents, his only knowledge, forms and precedents ". The general belief was that Walpole's power was gone. Compton's reception was crowded while Walpole's was deserted. But the new favourite had offended the Queen by paying court to the Countess of Suffolk, the King's mistress, while Walpole's prudence and insight had enlisted the Queen's approval. When it appeared that Compton had been obliged to engage Walpole's help in drawing up the King's Speech, and that Walpole was ready to add £130,000 to the civil list with a jointure of £100,000 for the Queen, the tables were turned. The change was picturesquely announced at Leicester House. "There," Caroline remarked, singling out Lady Walpole from the crowd, "I see a friend," with the result that, as the happy lady put it on retiring, " I might have walked upon their heads ". Walpole's offer was not a mere bribe to retain the powers for which he was so well fitted. George I.'s civil list of £700,000 was inadequate to meet the growing expenditure, and the additional sum was opposed only by Shippen. The Administration remained practically unchanged. Walpole, whom the King had once dubbed a rogue and a rascal, was First Lord and Chancellor of the Exchequer ; Newcastle "the impertinent fool," and Townshend "the choleric blockhead," were joint Secretaries. Compton had the sense to recognise his lack of fitness to be Prime Minister. As Lord Wilmington he became Paymaster-General and then Privy Seal of the Council. Within the Cabinet, policy was directed by an inner group, "the select lords" (Walpole Townshend and Newcastle, Wilmington, the Lord Chancellor, King, and the Lord President, Lord Trevor).

The new King, born in 1683, and the son of the miserable prisoner of Ahlden, was a dry, irascible, punctiliously punctual man with the passion for routine of a military martinet. Personally brave, interested in the red-tape of the army, he had fought at Oudenarde, and, at Dettingen, was to be the last British Sovereign to command a force in the field. From 1718 his Court as Prince of Wales had been the centre of domestic and political opposition to his father, an example of filial conduct not lost on his own son. Walpole's judgment of him [1] scarcely does justice to his qualities. Since 1714 he had been steadily trained in English ways, and had adapted himself with some success to a strange political atmosphere. No less devoted than his father to Hanover and Hanoverian interests, a firm believer in his prerogative, he was obstinate though he generally recognised when it was necessary to give way. His confidence was difficult to win, but once won his loyalty was sincere and enduring. His relations with Walpole, Carteret, Henry Pelham, Newcastle, and Pitt exemplify the strong and weak sides in his character. Above all he relied, though he would stoutly have denied it, on the judgment of those whom he trusted, and preferred unconsciously to be guided. Throughout his reign he was always under the influence of a personality stronger than his own. The sharp-sighted men and women who divined that he could not be bullied but could be led by tact were those who enjoyed both the royal confidence and real power.

The most notable of these for the first ten years was the Queen. Walpole's political career was largely occupied with endeavouring to checkmate the schemes of one royal and headstrong woman, Elizabeth Farnese, and with maintaining his alliance with another, Caroline of Brandenburg-Anspach. Born in the same year as the King, she had "scorned an empire for religion's sake" when she refused the hand of the Archduke who became the Emperor Charles VI. But as Burnet says, "her pious firmness was not to go unrequited even in this life," for in 1705 she married her cousin, to become in due course Queen of Great Britain. Her intellectual tastes were

1683

1727

---

[1] " He thinks he is devilish stout, but if I know anything of him he is with all his personal bravery as arrant a political coward as ever wore a crown."

wide, if not very deep. She was the third woman of the Welfenhaus who corresponded with Leibnitz and would know the why of a why. In her grotto at Richmond she placed the busts of Woolaston, Locke, and Clarke. Latitudinarian in theology, she favoured Whiston, Tindal, Hoadly, Butler, Secker, Sherlock, and Berkeley, and was the patron of Sterne, Gay, Tickell, Arbuthnot, and Handel. Her domestic life was very unhappy. With her eldest son she quarrelled bitterly more than once, and her political supremacy at Court was only maintained by close study of and obedience to the King's foibles, and by alternately conniving at and encouraging the infidelities of an exasperating husband. If in Caroline a coarseness of fibre and conduct, lack of heart and cynical tolerance of the intolerable, jar on us, we may remember what as a woman, wife, and queen, she was called on to endure, and that she pursued her duty with unfaltering courage and cheerfulness to the end. Walpole pronounced her to have a greater political capacity than any woman he had ever met (and he was a severe critic of women who interfered in politics) and she proved it by her industry, insight, and forbearance. To the Minister whom she had practically selected she was a tower of strength, and their unbroken friendship and mutual respect reflect equal credit on both.

John, Baron Hervey, the "Sporus" of Pope's savage "Epistle to Arbuthnot," whose memoirs give a vivid, entertaining, and heightened picture of Caroline's Court, was, next to Walpole, the Queen's most trusted adviser. Henrietta Howard, married to the Earl of Suffolk, had been the reigning beauty of Leicester House, and down to 1734, when she retired from Court, was the *maîtresse en titre* of the King. After Caroline's death the Countess of Walmoden took the place both of the Countess of Suffolk and of the Queen. But during Walpole's tenure of power none of the "chargeable" ladies whom his majesty was pleased to dishonour with his affections can be reckoned as a serious political force.

The traditional hostility of the heir to the throne was fully maintained by George II.'s son, Frederick Louis, created Prince of Wales in 1729. Born in 1707, the young prince, who had the literary tastes of a precocious fop, rapidly developed into a libertine. The *Histoire du Prince Titi*, inspired if not written by himself, was a caricature ₁₇₃₅ of his father and mother, and his support of Buononcini against Handel was one of the least harmful examples of his cultivated

perversity. His continuous connection with and patronage of the
Opposition was a political fact of importance. His father's constant
condemnations of him as a puppy, fool and rascal, and his mother's
amazing verdict,[1] require considerable discounting; but it is difficult to understand Bolingbroke's reason for selecting him in *The
Idea of a Patriot King* to be the prince who could " distinguish
the voice of his people from the clamours of a faction," " break
the spirit of faction," and effect " the union of his people ". Had
Frederick been called to the throne, which fortunately he was not,
he would probably have thrown over the *habitués* and allies of Norfolk House with as little scruple as his debauched grandson threw
over the Whigs in 1810. A prince who, in 1745, when Charles
Edward had reached Derby, was found playing blindman's buff with
the pages added no doubt considerably to the gaiety of the world
of Courts and political scandal, but was scarcely entitled even to the
confidence of hungry office-seekers out of place.

The thirty-three years of George II.'s reign cover an important
epoch in our national development, the first clearly marked phase of
which ends with the fall of Walpole in 1742. In many respects the
year 1740 more accurately indicates the dividing line. The war
with Spain, the death of the Emperor Charles VI., the accession of
Frederick the Great, and the Silesian war, which is the unmistakable
commencement of the long duel for supremacy in Germany between
the house of Hohenzollern and the house of Habsburg, ring up the
curtain on a revolution in the State-system in Europe. For Great
Britain the same year brings her once again into sharp collision with
the Bourbon Powers. The struggle for colonial, commercial, and
naval supremacy will become the struggle for empire. It is to be a
struggle chiefly with France. From 1740-56 the true meaning of
the war and the futile peace that follows are concealed. But with
the Diplomatic Revolution in 1756 the world stage is cleared and the
issues are fairly joined. Though George II. died in the fifth of the
momentous seven years of war, it was tolerably clear that decisive
victory in this first round of the struggle for empire lay with
Great Britain. At home after Walpole's fall the development is
tedious, confused, and perplexing—a period of second-rate men for
the most part, of rapid changes and complicated political intrigues.

---

[1] " My dear first-born is the greatest ass and the greatest liar and the greatest *ca-
naille* and the greatest beast in the whole world, and I heartily wish he were out of it."

The unity and character that Walpole and his system impress on the first great phase are but faintly traceable in the leadership of Henry Pelham, illuminated by one imperishable gleam of romance, 1743-54 the tragedy of the Young Pretender and the White Rose, as irrelevant to the working out of the central theme in the drama, as it is picturesque and appealing. The rise of Pitt to a unique dictatorship is emphasised, the crumbling away of the Whig party concealed, by the magnitude and importance of the events outside the narrow world of St. Stephens. The future of Great Britain was being moulded more decisively at Sans Souci, on the St. Lawrence, the coast of Coromandel, and the Ganges ; as well as in the economic evolution at home that paved the way for the Industrial Revolution.

" There are few difficulties that cannot be surmounted," Walpole said, " if properly and resolutely engaged in."   The remark, characteristic of the man and his methods, is peculiarly applicable to his foreign policy. At the death of George I. a settlement of the European difficulties was possible, but not yet made. The convention of the Pardo, signed by Elizabeth Farnese, " after a rage," and with March 6 the home-truth that the English were never content, partly cleared 1728 the situation for the congress to meet at Soissons. But there were disquieting elements in the situation. A *rapprochement* between France and Spain, the growing independence of France towards Great Britain, were signs that the alliance was wearing thin and required tactful handling and a wary eye on the European horizon. The Emperor had still to be converted or coerced into acquiescence, despite the acceptance of his preliminaries. It was clear that Elizabeth would fight to the last for her dynastic policy, and that the commercial relations of Spain and Great Britain were the crucial matter. The Cabinet was divided. Townshend and (old) Horace Walpole (at Paris) desired to come to terms with Spain, even by ceeding Gibraltar, and thus coerce the Emperor. Walpole and New castle preferred overtures to the emperor and thus isolate Spain. In an offer to guarantee the Pragmatic Sanction they held a trump card. At the same time Walpole was extremely reluctant to renew the war with Spain and strain the Anglo-French alliance to the breaking-point. The Congress of Soissons meanwhile proved futile. June 14 William Stanhope, formerly an ambassador at Madrid, was sent to Spain on a special mission. Townshend's policy had won the day, Nov. 9

and the Treaty of Seville, to which the Dutch acceded, with French co-operation, promised redress for commercial grievances, the restoration of the commercial *status quo* in America, and of the privileges granted in 1713 and 1716, pledged France and England to the introduction of Spanish instead of neutral garrisons into the Tuscan fortresses, and (by a secret article), if war followed with the Emperor, the regulation by treaty of European questions. The Gibraltar difficulty was thus brushed aside, French support had been retained and Great Britain, if she could make the treaty operative, was in a favourable position to deal with the Emperor.

The Emperor's reply to the treaty was to refuse his consent to its terms, unless the allies guaranteed the Pragmatic Sanction. In the case of refusal he was prepared to prevent by force the introduction of Spanish garrisons into Italy. A year went by in idle negotiations, plans of campaign, and proposals by Great Britain for a joint military stroke on Sicily to bring the Emperor to reason—all of which the French diplomatists did their best to postpone or nullify. Spain in disgust, in November, 1730, declared that in consequence of the failure to execute the Seville Treaty she would no longer be bound by it. Great Britain therefore decided to come to terms with the Emperor. The resignation of Townshend had removed the most weighty member of the opposition in the Cabinet to this step. And despite the delays caused by Hanoverian demands in connection with the imperial investiture of Bremen and Verden and the administration of Mecklenburg, Robinson, on March 16, 1731, concluded the (second) Treaty of Vienna. In return for a guarantee of the Pragmatic Sanction (voidable if the Archduchess Maria Theresa married a Bourbon prince) the Emperor consented to the introduction of the Spanish garrisons, the suspension of the Ostend Company, and a new commercial tariff for the Austrian Netherlands. Commercial considerations had been an important element in the protracted discussions, and Robinson wrote that the Austrians complained he "had sucked them to the very blood". The suspension of the Ostend Company (in reality an abolition though the more politic term was employed) "the original cause of all the jumble" was not the least of the gains of the treaty which once more made the Emperor formally Britain's ally. By June, Spain had been brought to renew the Treaty of Seville, and after the usual haggling and recriminations, Don Carlos in 1732 was

May 15,
1730

solemnly escorted by a Spanish and British fleet across the Mediterranean and installed in Tuscany.

It is not easy to strike the balance in the complicated transactions thus briefly summarised. Certain points are obvious. Great Britain had succeeded in bringing both Spain and the Emperor to a settlement. She had saved Gibraltar, recovered her commercial concessions and killed the Ostend Company.[1] Throughout her diplomacy had worked hard to avoid war, and to dissolve the dangerous union of Charles VI. and Elizabeth Farnese, to keep Spain and France apart, to preserve the alliance with France and not to sacrifice the traditional friendship with Vienna. On the face of it she had succeeded in these objects. The Opposition critics who denounced in the Ministerial policy the predominant influence of Hanover really selected the weakest and most untenable line of attack. "I see my affairs," growled George II., "are on that foot that I must yield in everything." A close study of the negotiations does not support the conclusion that the Treaty of Vienna of 1731 was detrimentally affected by Electoral bias. On the contrary what British Ministers demanded on behalf of British interests was wrung from the Habsburgs, while Robinson was expressly authorised to sign even if he failed to secure imperial assent to Hanoverian demands. In a word Britain's wishes were, those of the Elector of Hanover were not, fully granted. Walpole, however, had paid a price for his document. The guarantee of the Pragmatic Sanction was a serious mortgage on British policy for the future, justifiable if it is agreed that the Emperor's alliance could not have been obtained without it and that that alliance was worth the price paid. Did the alliance necessarily involve an inevitable rupture with France? Experienced diplomatists like Townshend and (old) Horace Walpole feared such a result, and preferred the understanding with France to the dubious advantages of the imperial alliance. It is unquestionable that the tone of the French Foreign Office had been far from cordial, and some historical writers would date the termination of the Anglo-French *entente* as early as 1732. Events and national ten-

---

[1] The Company was not formally dissolved until 1793. Pitt's opinion later is worth reading : The suppression was " a demand we had no right to make nor was it our interest to insist upon it ". But it is very doubtful whether he would have expressed himself thus in 1731.

dencies which no diplomatist could control were steadily driving France and Great Britain apart. From 1731 colonial and trading difficulties with both the Bourbon Powers begin to crop up. On April 9th, 1731, Captain Jenkins of *The Rebecca* lost his historic ear,[1] and though the complaint was duly recorded and forgotten, the world was to hear more of Captain Jenkins and to verify Pulteney's prophecy "that his story would raise volunteers". Jacobite intrigues and Dunkirk, facts of a sinister hue, were sticking in men's memories, and the plain truth that the Franco-British alliance no longer was a necessity to France, that despite Fleury's smooth words the younger school in France chafed at the bondage to England, was not lost on Walpole and Newcastle. Nevertheless Walpole rightly clung to the *entente* he had inherited from Stanhope. His secret service fund kept him uncommonly well informed about the unending web of intrigue and the secret aspirations in foreign chanceries; he declined to believe that friendship with Vienna necessarily meant the loss of France, while if the worst happened the Emperor had already been secured in advance. The future for Great Britain would turn mainly on two points—her relations with the Bourbon Powers, and, above all, Spain, for with Spain France would in the last result act; and secondly on the capacity of Ministers to keep Great Britain out of all continental intrigues where her interests were not directly and manifestly concerned. The installation of Don Carlos had been a triumph for Elizabeth Farnese and the dynastic ambitions of the Bourbons. It affected the distribution of power in the Mediterranean and created a suitable base for an extension of the Spanish Bourbon claims. But the negotiations had shown that without British help Don Carlos would have won his appanage only at the cost of a great war. The maintenance of British sea power and the strengthening of her financial and commercial resources were the most effective means of neutralising what Spain had gained. Peace, and no one knew it better than Walpole, would do more for Great Britain than for any other European Power. It was his duty and interest to secure it, for he was now master in his own Cabinet.

Townshend's retirement in 1730 was brought about by a combination of causes. Strong differences on foreign policy, on parliamentary tactics, on patronage, and the assured position of Walpole

[1] See Appendix III.

in the royal closet, were aggravated by personal friction. A violent altercation at Mrs. Selwyn's was followed by his resignation. Virtually defeated on the issue of foreign affairs, Townshend was not the man to carry out a programme of which he disapproved. The firm had become Walpole and Townshend, and he declined to carry on business on those terms. But with singular dignity and self-restraint he equally declined to follow the example of Carteret, Chesterfield, Roxburgh, and other notable Whigs, and join the opposition to his brother-in-law. He gave up public life, retired to Rainham in Norfolk, and as "Turnip Townshend" by his experiments in agriculture made himself one of the pioneers of the new scientific farming. This service to his country was not an unfit close to a distinguished career which had begun with helping to make the legislative union with Scotland. Honourable, high-minded and liberal, he had shown himself to be one of the most energetic and progressive of the Whig leaders who established the Whig supremacy. As Secretary of State, his work was characterised by great industry, acumen, boldness of conception, and vigour. With the Cabinet and the Queen against him, he tacitly admitted that there was not room in a Ministry for both Walpole and himself; but he left a gap which was not adequately filled by William Stanhope, to whom the Treaty of Seville had brought the title of Baron Harrington. For Stanhope as Secretary for the Northern Department failed to justify the reputation he had won as a diplomatist. The firm was now Walpole alone, and the first true premiership in our political annals may be said to date most accurately from 1730.

A fresh and serious complication in Europe speedily tested the Minister's mastery of the situation at home and abroad. The death in 1733 of Augustus, the Physically Strong, Elector of Saxony and King of Poland, reopened the succession to the Polish throne. The Emperor and Russia supported the late King's son Augustus, the Morally Weak, while the French candidate was Stanislaus Leczynski, ex-King of Poland, whose daughter was the wife of Louis XV. Russian and Saxon troops put Augustus upon the throne, but France, joined by Spain and Savoy, made the election a trial of strength between Bourbon and Habsburg in Europe, and attacked the Emperor. The Austrians could be driven out of Italy, the kingdom of Naples won for Don Carlos, whose Duchy of Parma

5

would then be available for his brother Don Philip. The issues on the surface seemed to repeat those of the previous great wars—the prevention of a Bourbon supremacy in Europe. Plainly Great Britain could only intervene on one side, the imperial. Her troops, her subsidies, and her fleets would turn the scale. Pressure of every kind was put upon Walpole. But despite the imperial defeats, the arguments of the Court, the martial ardour of George II., the national desire to prevent a Bourbon triumph, the attacks of the Opposition and the party in the Cabinet, to whom the Whig traditions of support to Vienna were as the laws of Medes and Persians, England was kept out of the war. Walpole saw that the Polish succession to Great Britain was not worth the bones of a grenadier of the First Foot Guards. "Madam," he said to the Queen, "there are 50,000 men slain in Europe this year, and not one Englishman." War was costly; taxation crippled trade and was unpopular. Openly to take the imperial side meant sooner or later a breach with France and Spain. And Walpole knew, what Opposition critics did not, that Paris and Madrid had drifted into a secret alliance. Keene at Madrid, thanks to paid treachery, had Feb. 1734 sent to Newcastle, almost before the ink was dry, an accurate draft of the First Family Compact of 1733, though Walpole could not confute his critics by revealing it in debate. The maintenance of the Anglo-French *entente* alone could prevent the Bourbon solidarity, now written out on paper, from maturing into an effective anti-British coalition. The right policy was to keep our powder dry, the Cabinet cool, and throw the whole weight of our diplomacy into restoring peace and safeguarding British interests in the final settlement.

In the domestic annals of the dynasty a minor matter had absorbed a vast amount of ink, energy, and fruitless scheming—the famous "double-marriage" project.[1] Chesterfield in 1728 had successfully arranged the marriage of the Princess Royal to William IV. of the Orange House, thereby renewing the connection between the British and Dutch royal families. Sophia Dorothea, George II.'s sister and Queen of Prussia, earnestly desired to unite Prussia and Great Britain by a double wedding. The Crown Prince (afterwards Frederick the Great) was to marry the Princess Amelia, while his sister Wilhelmina, known to history as the Margravine of Bay-

[1] See Appendix IV.

reuth and the witty authoress of remarkable memoirs, was to become
the Princess of Wales. Difficulties both personal and political barred
the way. The jealousy of Prussia and Hanover was of long standing : King Frederick William I. and King George II. revealed
in phrases characteristic of both that they were on the worst of
terms. The bondage of Prussia to Vienna, so dexterously maintained by Grumbkow and Seckendorff at Berlin, had long thwarted
the German policy of Hanover. The marriage project appealed to
George II. and his Hanoverian advisers, backed by his sister's ambitions, as a means of destroying Grumbkow's power, detaching Prussia
from Vienna, and bringing it into the Hanoverian sphere of influence.
Hotham at Berlin succeeded in arranging a single marriage, that of
the Prince of Wales and the Princess Wilhelmina, but the English
Court would have the double marriage or nothing. And when the
domestic intriguers learned that every effort to shake, by fair means
or foul, the position of Grumbkow only stiffened the aversion of
Frederick William from the Crown Prince's marriage to a British
princess, and that Prussia, represented by the tyrannical drill-
sergeant who laid the basis of the army and State of Frederick the
Great, was not to be weaned from his infatuation for the House
of Austria, Wilhelmina's marriage with the Prince of Wales was
promptly dropped. The Crown Prince was reserved to make
another woman unhappy, and the Prince of Wales, bereft of his
Wilhelmina, was married in 1736 to Augusta of Saxe-Gotha. It
is easy to speculate on the possibilities in Queen Sophia Dorothea's
motherly ambitions. At no time in his career would a wife have
influenced the policy of Frederick the Great. But Wilhelmina
might well have been happier at St. James's, even with the Prince
of Wales, than at Berlin and Bayreuth. Great Britain would not
at a critical juncture have lost Pitt, and she might, to her advantage, have never heard of Bute.

The year of the Polish war is also memorable for a sharp Ministerial rebuff. The Pension Bill of Sandys, nicknamed " the motion
maker " from his energy in bringing resolutions before the Lower
House, was an unsuccessful effort in 1730 to deal with an admitted
evil, the number of members whose dependence on the Ministry was
secured by salaries on the Civil List. The real remedy was not the
exclusion of placemen, but the suppression of places and a more complete control, appropriation, and audit of the Civil List by Parliament.

Next year the most effective of the Opposition leaders, Pulteney, who was in the thick of the bitter pamphlet war and the intrigues whose object was to procure Walpole's dismissal, had fought a duel with Hervey, and so incensed the King that he struck his name from the roll of Privy Councillors. Pulteney was to have his revenge when Walpole submitted his notable excise scheme. In 1732 the excise on salt had been reimposed and the land tax reduced to one shilling. Walpole now proposed to extend the excise system, begun in 1724, to tobacco and wine. His object was to increase the revenue while lowering the duty, check smuggling and frauds, both on the trade and the revenue, and make London the free port of the world. With the savings thus made he desired to keep the land tax at one shilling or abolish it altogether. The Opposition at once saw their chance, and by a skilful combination of exaggerations, appeals to sentiment and plain untruths lashed the country into rage and panic. The Budget they announced was the prologue to a general excise, " that plan of arbitrary power " ; the Constitution was to be sacrificed to the prevention of frauds in the revenue ; excises were in every country badges of slavery ; the increase of revenue would augment the arbitrary power of the Crown, subject every free citizen to an unlimited inquisition, and enable a corrupt Minister to control elections by his hirelings from the custom house and debauch the House of Commons by a bloated patronage fund. Placards representing the excise vampire sucking the blood of the populace were widely circulated. " No slavery, no excise, no wooden shoes," became the motto of the day. Petitions poured in from all quarters and riots broke out. In vain it was pointed out that brewers and maltsters already lived under an excise and were not slaves in wooden shoes, that the additional increase in revenue officers would be exactly 126, that the profits would be strictly appropriated to the public expenditure and would not go to the Crown, that warehouses alone would be liable to official inspection without a warrant. The second reading of the Bill was carried by a majority only of thirty-six. Lord Scarborough, consulted by the Queen, replied that he could answer for his regiment against the Pretender, but not against the opponents of the excise. Walpole, of whom the King said truly that he had more spirit than any man he ever knew, summoned a meeting of his supporters and decided that " this dance could no further go ". He would never be the Minister to impose taxes at the expense of blood. The pro-

March 14, 1733

posal was therefore dropped. It is clear that it was not defeated on its merits. Long after, it met with the approval of Adam Smith, and was carried out in an extended form and to the great benefit of trade and the revenue by the younger Pitt. It is practically certain that its adoption in 1733 would have been followed by the advantages claimed for it by its author. But the Opposition neither understood nor wished to understand the scheme; and the combination of personal hatred and faction playing upon credulous ignorance was all the more deplorable because it succeeded. Walpole assured the House of Commons that he " was not so mad as ever to engage again in anything that looked like an excise ". The bonfires, feasting, and healths to Bolingbroke and James III. which had disgraced London and Oxford when the scheme was abandoned convinced him that political duty to the dynasty was superior to economic benefit to the national revenue. But his hand fell heavily on the Whig malcontents who had abetted the disgraceful conspiracy against the Bill and himself. The Ministerial party " had been put to their stumps," and the restoration of discipline was imperative. The Duke of Bolton and Lord Clinton were removed from their Lord-Lieutenancies; Cobham and Bolton lost the colonelcies of their regiments; Montrose was deprived of the Great Seal, and Lord Stair of the Vice-Admiralship, of Scotland. Stair had also drawn from the Queen a delightful retort. His opposition was a matter of conscience, he said. " Ah, my lord," Caroline replied, " do not talk to me of conscience, *vous me faites évanouir.*" Most distinguished of them all, Chesterfield, who had been reconciled to Walpole, was now deprived of the Lord Stewardship he had accepted in 1730, and promptly rejoined the Opposition. These various dismissals are often alleged as proofs of Walpole's insatiable jealousy and vindictiveness. But if a Minister with a parliamentary majority and the confidence of the Crown had not taught his subordinates that disaffection is punishable by loss of office, Cabinet and parliamentary government would never have been established. Walpole had neither the misplaced charity nor political pusillanimity of Newcastle in 1754.[1] To have passed over the congenial

---

[1] " I do not care," George II. said to Newcastle, " for the Opposition if all my servants act together. But if they thwart one another then it will be another case." The case for collective unanimity and responsibility and its importance in the evolution of parliamentary government could not be more pithily put. Newcastle, who

disloyalty of high-placed peers was to place a premium on mischievous intrigues and a penalty on loyal service. A Ministry in Walpole's eyes was not a group of independent office holders voting as their interest or ambition dictated, but a union of the Crown's servants chosen from a party because they could unite in common action on a common policy for the benefit of their country. The dismissal of military officers opens up a different line of argument. In 1734 the Opposition unsuccessfully attempted by bill to prevent for the future such means of expressing the Crown's displeasure. The question was again raised under George III. But so long as the Crown regarded the army as a sphere of prerogative withdrawn from parliamentary control, and colonelcies of regiments were granted as political rewards, and military officers on the active list claimed the right, as Pitt did when a Cornet of Horse, to take part in controversial politics, no satisfactory remedy was possible. Even to-day it is not easy to draw a line between military and political considerations. The modern elimination of the army from politics implies on the part of Crown, Ministers, and the public constitutional conventions and a practice which in 1733 were neither accepted nor in existence.

The failure of the excise scheme damped effectively bold financial reform. In 1737 Walpole defeated Barnard's scheme for the redemption of the old and new South Sea Annuities, interesting constitutionally as the proposal of a private member. The scheme was very unpopular with the moneyed men and the stockholders, and Walpole objected to it on that ground and also because it would prevent the application of the Sinking Fund to current expenses. On principle he preferred to appropriate from that fund rather than to raise new loans or additional taxation. And throughout the years 1730-40 the national finances were constantly balanced only by such appropriations. The policy of postponing the reduction of debt by avoiding the necessary taxation when national expenditure increases is more often determined by political than financial considerations. Walpole saw that the steady increase in national resources made the burden of the National Debt much less serious than it was popularly held to be. Low taxation provided him with the means of meeting a sudden strain without serious

forgot the lesson from 1733-41, was taught its value later by Henry Fox, Murray and Pitt, 1754-56.

discontent, and he aimed above all at reconciling the classes on whom the bulk of the taxation must fall to the Hanoverian government. It is questionable whether a more heroic policy of continuous amortisation of capital liabilities by extended taxation would have commended itself to Parliament, and it was with a Parliament in which money and commerce were influentially represented that as a practical politician he had to deal. At any rate the war scares of 1731, 1734, 1735, and 1738, and the war expenditure from 1739-41, were met with singularly small additions to the debt. By ingenious arrangements he paid his way. Despite the diversion of moneys from the Sinking Fund the National Debt was nearly £9,000,000 less when he resigned than when he took office, and he left the public finances on a sound footing and the nation in a position to meet far more serious demands on its taxable wealth than he had permitted himself to make. The wisdom and insight of one of his many remarks deserves recording afresh. To a suggestion for imposing taxation on the colonies he replied that as he had Old England against him he had no wish to have New England also. He would leave it to a successor who had more courage and cared less for commerce than he did.[1]

In the general election of 1734 the Opposition more than held their own, and the new Parliament brought to the Opposition two promising recruits, William Pitt, member for the family pocket borough of Old Sarum, and George, afterwards Lord, Lyttelton. With Richard Grenville, afterwards Lord Temple, these two formed the nucleus of the "Boy Patriots," known as "the Cobham cousinhood" or "Cobham's cubs" from their leader and relative Lord Cobham. Fresh blood was sorely needed, as there had been a split in the Opposition. Pulteney, like Walpole, found Carteret and Chesterfield difficult political allies, and Bolingbroke and himself had quarrelled. A great assault led by Wyndham, and skilfully organised by Bolingbroke to combine the two Opposition wings of Tories and malcontent Whigs, had failed. The denunciation of the standing army March 13, 1734

[1] The Financial Act 7 Geo. II., c. 12, is a notable constitutional departure. It provided £1,200,000 from the Sinking Fund and a vote of credit, by which the Crown was empowered to raise at discretion any sum of money necessary for augmenting the sea and land forces, i.e. it empowered the King to contract debts unspecified in amount, and spend money not specifically appropriated. Walpole used it three times, in 1739, 1740, and in 1741, and a total of £1,000,000 was borrowed under the powers conferred.

and the demand for the repeal of the Septennial Act were defeated by 247-184 votes. Bolingbroke now practically threw up the

1733 game. With the publication of his *Dissertation on Parties,* the most finished exposition of his latter-day political creed, and the continuance of a Ministerial majority in the new Parliament, he withdrew to the Continent, convinced that "some schemes then on the

1735 loom made him one too many, even to his most intimate friends".

1736 The next year, however, showed that the Opposition could push the invincible "sole minister" hard. The Prince of Wales had stepped into Bolingbroke's place as chief of the Opposition staff. Pitt's maiden speech was made in moving the address of congratulation to the Prince on his marriage, for which the King proposed to allow him £50,000 a year from the Civil List. Frederick, however, thought himself entitled to a separate establishment and a fixed income specifically provided by Parliament. Walpole persuaded the King much against his will to meet the Prince by making the paternal allowance a fixed grant with a jointure for the Princess. But the Prince's advisers were determined to demand £100,000, and grasped the opportunity of inflicting a parliamentary rebuff on the King and of effecting a permanent breach between the heir to the throne and the all-powerful "Grand Vizier". The Prince's reply to his father's offer, that the matter must be settled by Parliament, threw George into a passion in which both Frederick and Walpole were bitterly reproached, the one for being a puppy and a blockhead, the other for suggesting indulgence to such a rascally fool. Pulteney moved the grant in the Commons, Carteret in the Lords. Both were rejected. "If ever," Walpole said in his vivid way, "any man in any cause fought dagger out of sheath I did that day". Intrigues at Court and mutiny in the Cabinet made the issue doubtful. Newcastle in particular wished to come to terms with Carteret. "Your grace," Walpole said, "must choose between him and me. I have said it to your betters and I will stick to it." The Minister was saved by the action of Wyndham, who with forty-four of the Tory country gentlemen walked out without voting rather than co-operate in further payments to the German rulers. But Walpole having won, characteristically kept the King to his bargain, when he would have punished the rebellious son by withdrawing the concession offered. The young Pitt, whose speech founded the hostility of the King to himself, so disadvantageous to both, was marked out by being deprived of his cornetcy. "We must muzzle this terrible cornet of horse,"[1] had been Walpole's remark. But the time was coming when more than a muzzle was needed for the ambitious young orator. The political quarrel between the Sovereign and the heir to the throne was followed by a domestic scandal. Prince and Princess had continued to live under the same roof as the King and Queen, but suddenly one night at Hampton Court the Princess, on the point of her confinement, was hurried by her husband into a chaise and in the pains of labour driven at full gallop to the empty Palace of St. James, and there an hour after her arrival her first child was born. The King, not unnaturally, was furious. The infant was in the direct succession to the Crown, and, apart from the danger to the mother's life and the insult to the King and Queen implied in the act, the custom of the constitution required official confirmation of the birth of a royal child. Frederick was ordered to leave the Court; the guards were taken away from his door; foreign Ministers were warned and the Court forbidden to hold intercourse with Norfolk House, which had been lent to the Prince of Wales. When presently Prince and Princess moved to Carlton House, this became the centre of the Opposition, and it was in this demoralising atmosphere of family scandals and political *tracasseries*, of petticoat politics and backstair intrigues, that the future George III. was born and brought up.

Two years earlier Scotland had again thrust itself on the 1738 notice of the Government by an affair, immortalised, if necessarily somewhat manipulated by the novelist's art, in Scott's *Heart of Midlothian*. Two smugglers, Robertson and Wilson, sentenced to death for robbing a custom house, made an attempt to escape from the Tolbooth Church where they had been brought to hear their last sermon. Robertson succeeded, while Wilson failed in getting away. At Wilson's execution Lieutenant Porteous in command of the town guard, fearing an organised effort to rescue the condemned prisoner, ordered his men to fire on the crowd, was tried and sentenced to death. The Queen in the absence of the King reprieved him for six weeks in order that discrepancies

---

[1] A cornetcy not in the Royal Horse Guards, "The Blues," as generally stated, but in the Second or Cobham's Horse (now the First or King's Dragoon Guards).

in the evidence at the trial might be examined. On the night of September 8th, 1736, a crowd, carefully organised, stormed the Tolbooth Prison, and, with a rope duly paid for, hanged Porteous on a dyer's pole in the Grassmarket. The rioters then quietly dispersed, committing no other outrage. There seems little doubt that the magistrates, aware how incensed popular feeling was against Porteous, acted with culpable negligence both on the night of the murder and subsequently by their failure to bring the ringleaders to justice. The murder itself had probably no political significance beyond illustrating the sympathy of the populace with smugglers, the detestation of the English custom-house system, and the determination to forestall a pardon for a man by whose orders the hateful minions of the law had shed blood. The Queen and Walpole resented strongly the affront to authority, and a bill was introduced to revise the city charter, abolish the town guard, and disable the Provost from holding any civil employment in Great Britain. Scottish sentiment was further exasperated by the summoning of three of the Scottish judges to London to be examined at the bar of the House of Lords. Argyll [1] voiced the national resentment at the severity of the penalties proposed, which in deference to the strenuous opposition both of English and Scottish members of Parliament were considerably reduced. Unpopular as the English government unquestionably was in Scotland, the whole affair furnishes proof of the helplessness of the Jacobite cause. The Jacobites had no share in the lawless acts of the mob, nor were they in a position to turn the fierce popular sentiment to their advantage. Twenty years earlier the standard of James III. would probably have been hoisted at the Tolbooth Cross as a reply to Whig insults and Hanoverian tyranny.

1737   In this year of conflict the death of the Queen inflicted an irreparable loss on Crown and Minister. Caroline had long suffered from an internal infirmity, the true nature of which she concealed from her physicians. A wrong course of treatment was followed, and when the real character of the malady was discovered it was too late. "Tant mieux," was her calm comment, revealing much, when she was informed that final release from pain was at hand.

---

[1] The frequently quoted remark of the Queen that she would make Scotland a hunting ground, and Argyll's retort that in that case he would retire to his native country to make ready his hounds, rest on very untrustworthy evidence.

She quietly urged the King to marry again. "Non, non," he replied, "j'aurai des maîtresses." "Ah, mon Dieu!" the Queen answered, "cela n'empêche pas." She forgave her eldest son, but refused to see him, and after commending the kingdom and her house to Walpole, and her "good Sir Robert" to the King, met her end with the courage that was not the least of her gifts. To Walpole the loss was even more serious than to George II. And it came at a time when events both at home and abroad with increasing exigency called for insight, patience, and self-restraint.

Had the Queen's life been spared another year, she would have seen the conclusion of Walpole's elaborate diplomatic efforts to restore the peace of Europe, broken by the Polish Succession War. The situation on the Continent was critical. If the imperial candidate had secured the Polish throne, French victories on the Rhine strengthened the determination of Fleury to justify his policy of intervention by compensation for France at the expense of the Empire. The combined Spanish and Savoy forces had overrun Naples, and Don Carlos had been crowned as Charles III. The Emperor was insisting on the re-establishment of the *status quo*, while Elizabeth Farnese, flushed with victory, was bent on confirming Don Carlos as King of the Two Sicilies, and transferring his Duchy of Parma to his brother Don Philip. The close understanding between the Bourbon Powers and the success of their arms made their demands difficult to resist, unless the military balance was altered by the active intervention of Great Britain on the imperial side. A British fleet in the Mediterranean, the Hanoverian contingent stiffened by British troops, financial subsidies, possibly Dutch co-operation also brought about by British pressure, would make a substantial difference in the situation. The obligations of the Treaty of Vienna made the policy of Great Britain delicate and embarrassing. A strong party in the Cabinet sided with the 1731 stronger feeling of the Court to aid the Empire, give France a sharp lesson, and checkmate Bourbon ambitions. The crowning offer to George II. of the command of the imperial forces on the Rhine appealed to his Electoral pride as much as to his confidence in his own generalship. Caroline said truly enough of the combinations that divided Europe that they put her in mind of the South Sea Scheme. Everybody went into it knowing it was all a cheat, still hoping to get something out of it. Everybody meant to make his own fortune and be sharp enough to scramble out, leaving the others deeper in the lurch. Walpole slowly converted Court and Cabinet to the view that the interests of Great Britain and of Europe would be best served not by prolonging the war or extending the sphere of its operations, but by patching up a compromise which could be forced on each of the combatants. By October, 1735, preliminaries were submitted only to be rejected, but Walpole believed in the principle of "pegging away". Great Britain's position was in reality a strong one. Refusal to aid the Emperor made his continued resistance impossible. A guarantee of the Pragmatic Sanction from France would go a long way to salve the loss of Naples. Versailles and Madrid feared that either might come to terms with the Emperor at the expense of the other. The despatch of a British fleet to the Tagus to support Portugal in a quarrel with Spain was a timely hint that British forbearance was not inexhaustible. The historic alliance enabled direct pressure to be brought on France. And throughout, the severance of France from Spain was the keynote of Walpole's plan. By the use of every diplomatic device, by bluster, cajolery, and sops, and the gradual exhaustion of the combatants, definite terms were at last laid down by the Third Treaty of Vienna. An elaborate territorial juggle satisfied, so far as they were capable of being satisfied, the signatories to the treaty. France withdrew her Polish candidate, guaranteed the Pragmatic Sanction, and was awarded the reversion of Lorraine, assigned as compensation to Stanislas Leczynski, and on his death to be incorporated in the French kingdom. The Kingdom of the Two Sicilies fell to Don Carlos. Francis, Duke of Lorraine, who in 1736 had married Maria Theresa, was transferred to the Duchy of Tuscany. Savoy was given a rectification of frontier, which added Novara and Tortona to her territory, while Parma and Piacenza and Milan were confirmed as imperial fiefs. Great Britain asked for and received nothing ; she had played with pertinacity the part of the honest broker, and as proof of her good faith repeated her guarantee of the Pragmatic Sanction. The success of the negotiations cannot be credited to Walpole without considerable reservations. If he had worked hard for peace and prevented an unjustifiable expenditure of British treasure and lives, the King and his Hanoverian advisers had ably co-operated in the final stages. Bolingbroke's comment, endorsed by the leaders of the

1738

Opposition, was not amiss when he said that if English Ministers had a hand in the peace they had more sense than he thought ; if they had no hand in it they had better luck than they deserved. Alberoni's previous criticism of the Utrecht Treaty, that it pared and cut countries like Dutch cheeses, is applicable to this as to many of the great European settlements before and since 1738. And if the principle of the balance of power was artificial, it was in many respects when expressed in the diplomatic idiom of dynastic ambition capable of producing results as durable as treaties based on the previous principle of religion or the modern one of nationality. The incorporation of Lorraine into France, Fleury's best title to gratitude from his nation, lasted for 130 years, as did the Bourbon dynasty at Naples, and the connection between Tuscany and the Habsburg House in Vienna. The splendid pertinacity of Elizabeth Farnese had once more reaped a rich reward. In two particulars the arrangements were ominous for the future—the Western Mediterranean was steadily tending to become a Bourbon lake ; the cutting away of a rich province from the empire was a serious dislocation of the imperial fabric. Walpole's defence that France had seized and kept Lorraine in every war corresponded with plain facts, but did not really meet the argument that it was directly against the interest of Great Britain to assist France in realising step by step the policy of those "natural frontiers," the Rhine and the Alps, which harmonised dynastic with national aspirations. Yet it would be unfair to blame Walpole for the subsequent failure of the chief European guarantors of the Pragmatic Sanction to keep their faith with Maria Theresa. The Third Treaty of Vienna did not give Europe peace ; mainly because those who negotiated it exaggerated the value of diplomatic pledges, and would not or could not foresee that the Pragmatic Sanction would not by itself solve the problem which the death of Charles VI. must raise ; still less, that the Emperor's death would coincide with the accession of Frederick the Great in Prussia, and would be preceded by a war between Great Britain and Spain which sapped the system on which British foreign policy had for a quarter of a century been based.

The causes of that war were strikingly varied. Their cumulative force is rich in political instruction.[1] By the Treaty of 1729

[1] See Appendix III.

the commercial relations between Great Britain and Spain were confirmed. Since 1713 Great Britain had enjoyed the right to supply the Spanish colonies with negro slaves (*assiento de negros*) and to send annually one ship to trade at Cartagena or Portobello (*navio de permiso*). Under the cover of the slave trade and this annual vessel, a commerce, technically illegal, had grown up; for with the connivance of the Spanish dealers the English merchant, freed from the prohibitive Spanish tariff, undersold the Spanish importer. The business was profitable and British traders came to regard the illegitimate extension of trading rights as legitimised by prescription. To enforce the treaties and prevent an increasing evasion of the protected colonial trade, the Spanish coast-guard fleet was reorganised, while the Spanish authorities pushed to extreme limits the right of search against British vessels suspected of smuggling. If the British trader was guilty of defying the Spanish commercial code, the Spaniard was guilty of harsh acts of violence and retaliation. Walpole desired to settle the claims for redress and counter-claims for damages by direct agreement between the Governments at London and Madrid. There was more at issue than the trade disputes which came with disquieting vehemence and frequency from the Spanish Main. Our quarrel with one great Bourbon Power, Spain, might, probably would, strain to the breaking-point our relations with another, France, and a conflict with the united Bourbon States involved the whole future of the British colonial possessions across the seas. The Opposition saw their opportunity, and now resumed with vigour the advocacy of the national case against Spain. England rang with the tales of atrocities "enough to fire the coldest," and Captain Jenkins at the bar of the House of Commons retold his story with the famous comment, that in the hour of outrage and impotence he had commended his soul to God and his cause to his country—a sentence worthy of Junius or Bolingbroke, which we may be sure a rough sea captain did not frame without assistance. The Convention of the Pardo (Jan. 14, N.S.) was a sincere effort of both Governments to eliminate the causes of the dispute and pave the way for a complete understanding—perhaps even a treaty of alliance between Great Britain and Spain. And the provision of £95,000 by the Spanish Government as compensation implicitly recognised the damage inflicted on British traders by arbitrary seizures. But it had one

fatal omission—the right of search was not abandoned—though on
this point as on the others in the controversy it would appear that
Spain had in the argument a stronger case, both in law and facts,
than a factious Opposition and an ignorant public opinion would
admit. And Walpole knew it. The Convention was denounced by
Pitt, in a speech which established his oratorical reputation, as March 5
"insecure, unsatisfactory, dishonourable, and a stipulation for
national ignominy". More ominous still, Pitt contended that "it
was a suspension of the first law of Nature—self-preservation and
self-defence," and rested the British case on rights "from God and
Nature"—that double-edged argument of illimitable potency, appealed to again in 1776 and in 1789. Alike in 1739, 1776, and in
1789 these title-deeds of "a Natural" humanity converted into
national ideals and rooted in the politician's interpretation of history
and philosophy, were to be baptised in torrents of blood. After
a stiff debate the Convention was approved by the House of Commons, and the Opposition, led by Wyndham, seceded to mark its
condemnation of the Minister's treachery; a foolish *coup de théâtre*
which has never succeeded in our political life and which was not
devised but condemned by Bolingbroke, who at least knew the
temper of the House of Commons. But it became clear that no
Convention which did not secure a categorical renunciation of the
right of search would satisfy the inflamed temper of the nation.
The Prince of Wales appeared in the streets and shouted for
revenge; Argyll joined the Opposition and was dismissed from his
offices; within the Cabinet, Newcastle, who in 1755 thirsted to
make Byng a scapegoat, was cowed by the popular clamour, and
was ready as ever "to yield to the times," to sacrifice his chief, if
need be, and to stoop to any diplomatic dishonesty that would
satisfy the public. In vain the Prime Minister strove to bring
his colleagues and his countrymen to reason. For behind the
critical relations of Spain and Great Britain he knew lay critical
relations in Europe. The Family Compact of 1733 would unite
Versailles and Madrid and a war with Spain would sooner or later
involve war with France; war with France was the destruction of
our system of policy. Assistance from the Emperor, the German
Princes, Holland, and Sweden was not to be expected. It is
doubtful whether the fear of a Bourbon coalition was justifiable;
it is certain that it profoundly influenced the Cabinet. On March

10th Newcastle sent counter-orders to the Mediterranean fleet, a distinct step towards war. The expectation that Spain, under these circumstances, could abandon the right of search was absurd. The South Sea Company, whose affairs had been most mischievously blended with the diplomatic issues, declined to pay what was due to the Spanish King or to substantiate its counter-claim by the production of accounts. The Spanish Government by a counter-refusal to pay the £95,000 stipulated in the Convention, provided a technical *casus belli*. The powerful mercantile classes, national sentiment, and Newcastle fought against Walpole and peace. War "threatened little bloodshed and promised victories more solid than glory". A war with Spain was "a war of plunder". Walpole yielded to Court, Cabinet, the trading interests and the Opposition. "It is your war," he said to Newcastle, "and I wish you joy of it,"— Newcastle "whose name was perfidy". On October 19th the British ultimatum was rejected and war declared. "They are ringing the bells," Walpole remarked. "They will soon be wringing their hands."

His retention of office, which made him an unwilling accomplice in a war of which he disapproved, can be explained but certainly needs explanation. The political custom of 1739 did not require a Minister to resign because he failed to have his own way on a definite issue of policy. Provided that he still enjoyed his Sovereign's confidence and could carry on the King's business in the legislature he was entitled, almost bound by duty, to remain in the service of the Crown. The authority and peculiar primacy of the modern Prime Minister were not yet accepted conventions. Walpole had not lost the confidence of George II., nor had he been defeated in either House. He had simply declined to press his policy against his colleagues and the nation, which to a certainty had there been a general election would have endorsed the demand for war. The King's appeal not to desert him, a natural reluctance to surrender power to a group whose chief object was not so much the defeat of his policy as the proscription of himself, confidence in his own capacity to avert more blunders, fortified his desire to remain. Nevertheless it was a grave and regrettable error. He was not fitted to carry on a war in whose justice and expediency he rightly disbelieved. Resignation would have made him the most formidable of critics; when the incompetence of his successors had been proved it might have brought him back with renewed prestige to the service of Crown and country ; it would have been a homage to conscience, and in any case a dignified close to a great career. His retention of office was not due simply to lust of power, but no act of his life contributed more fatally towards making the accusation plausible.

We have Burke's authority [1] for the statement that later many of the fanatical critics of 1739 did not "in the least defend the measure or attempt to justify their conduct ". Pitt lived to recant handsomely his views as to the right of search and to regret his opposition to the policy of "that wise and excellent Minister".[2] None the less, both Great Britain and Europe stood on the threshold of a new epoch, and the Spanish war emphasises the rise of a new and inarticulate feeling in the nation which Pitt and the Opposition voiced if they selected an illegitimate opportunity for proclaiming the fact. With the logical irony of national evolution that inarticulate feeling was largely the result of Walpole's success in giving Great Britain twenty years of peace, prosperity, and economy. The expansion of British trade was fettered by the colonial policy and colonial monopoly of the Bourbon Powers. The development of the British settlements in North America brought her into conflict with Spanish Florida in the South, with the French in the North. Diplomacy and conventions could only postpone, not avert the day when the maritime, political, and colonial issues that were implicit in the Spanish question of 1739 must bring Great Britain into collision both in the East and the West with rivals whose political strength centred in Europe. The broad gravamen of Pitt's indictment both now and later rested on a statesman's intuition that the British nation, as an imperial Power, must either assert its right to expand beyond the limits prescribed in the parchments of the chanceries or perish. Pitt, the representative of the new and younger England, felt that in 1739 the facts had completely altered. He demanded, and in vain, for ten years a new interpretation of England's interest, a new system, a new attitude on the part of Ministers, and a new method which would provide an adequate synthesis between policy and national ambition. He was ignorant, hot-headed,

---

[1] *Works*, viii., 147; see also p. 116.
[2] *Letters of Sarah Lennox*, i., 55 n.

factious; in details he betrayed his inexperience; but his central conviction was sound; in the pith of his demand he was right, and both in his faults and in his aspirations he came to be the champion of all that was best in the spirit of the British nation. To assert so much is not equivalent to asserting that sound statesmanship demanded in 1739 a direct challenge to the Bourbon Powers. How long it would have been possible, had war with Spain been averted, to have maintained after 1740 the *entente* of 1717 with France, the original reasons for whose existence were now worn out, it is idle to argue. The die was cast in 1739. The system of Stanhope and Walpole was broken when the nation plunged Walpole into war. And the death of Charles VI. created a wholly new situation for Europe. On October 28th the Tsarina Anne of Russia died. On December 16th Frederick the Great who had succeeded in the same year to the army and bureaucratic autocracy created by his father, invaded Silesia to wrest that province from Maria Theresa. Frederick's act was a cynical violation of the Pragmatic Sanction which Prussia had guaranteed. On September 29th Anson had sailed from Portsmouth on the memorable three years' voyage round the world which proclaimed the newly awakened determination of Great Britain to assert her sea power in the Pacific. Two hard questions at once confronted the new Europe: was the new Emperor to be from the friends or foes of the House of Habsburg? would the Bourbon States follow Prusia and repudiate solemn treaty obligations, or Great Britain and observe the Pragmatic Sanction? The Spanish war proved a bitter disappointment. Vernon delighted the buccaneering spirit at home by destroying the defences of Porto Bello, but the great expedition against Cartagena ended in disaster. Delay in despatching it, the death of its original commander, Cathcart, defective equipment, quarrels between the admiral, Vernon, and the general, Wentworth, imbecile tactics and slowness and the deadly climate, justified the criticism "that the general ought to hang the guides, and the King ought to hang the general". It was abandoned and followed by a failure on Santiago de Cuba and a final failure on Portobello. A vast expenditure of life and money had been thrown away to no purpose. The military fiasco in the West Indies damned the Government at the time when it most needed support.

The sands of Walpole's Ministry were running out. **Four**

Oct. 28

Nov. 21,
1739
Nov., 1740

May 7,
1741
May, 1742

millions in 1739 were voted for the war, though the irresponsible levity of the Opposition was exemplified in the fact that twice in this year they pressed their annual motion for the reduction of the standing army. " Sir Robert," Pulteney wrote with contempt for his own reputation as a statesman, " will have an army, will not have a war and cannot have a peace." A Place Bill was only defeated by the significant majority of sixteen. Next year Wyndham died. " What a star has our Minister ! " Bolingbroke exclaimed. But the death of Wyndham, a courageous and sincere opponent of Whig supremacy, in reality signified little. The stars in their courses were fighting against, not for, Walpole. Leicester House under the Prince of Wales was the centre of the Opposition in which Pitt became more and more prominent. Walpole's wonderful physical powers were collapsing ; the Cabinet seethed with intrigue and treachery ; Hardwicke and Newcastle supported King and Court, who desired to add a war on the Continent to a war with Spain. The justifiable criticisms on the conduct of the campaign against Spain culminated in a combined assault, led by Carteret in the Lords, by Sandys in the Commons, for the dismissal of the Minister.[1] Both motions were thrown out ; in the Lords by 108-59, in the Commons by 290-106, a majority swollen by the refusal of Shippen and his group to vote. The general election in May went heavily against Walpole. The Prince of Wales and Lord Falmouth turned the Cornish boroughs ; in Scotland Argyll's powerful influence was thrown on the Opposition side. When the new Parliament met in December the Ministry were faced by an exultant coalition of Jacobite and Hanoverian Tories, rebel Whigs, and Frederickites. The early letters of the greatest of eighteenth century letter-writers, Horace Walpole, tell the story of the fierce fight to oust his father from the Councils of the Crown. Pulteney's motion for a secret committee to inquire into the conduct of the Administration was defeated only by three votes, though both sides

Feb. 14 and Nov. 28

Feb. 13, 1741

[1] The significant terms of the Lords' Protest deserve verbatim quotation : " We are persuaded that a sole, or even a first, Minister is an officer unknown to the laws of Britain, inconsistent with the Constitution of this country, and destructive of liberty in any government whatsoever ; and it plainly appears to us that Sir R. Walpole has, for many years, acted as such by taking upon himself the chief, if not the sole, direction of affairs in the different branches of the administration " (Rogers, *Protests of the Lords*, ii., 10). The Protest according to Lord Trevor was drafted by Bolingbroke (Coxe's *Walpole*, 3, 564).

polled the sick and the dying; Ministers failed to carry their Chairman of Committee, and on the Chippenham election petition the Scottish and Cornish vote turned the scale and the Opposition had a majority of sixteen. Divisions on election petitions were recognised trials of party strength. Walpole, a martyr to stone, and broken physically, had met the continued attacks "with a great and undaunted spirit and a tranquillity more than human"; but he was convinced now that for the head of a Cabinet rent by dissension it was impossible to carry on the King's business in defiance of a virtual vote of no confidence by the representative Chamber. On February 9th he became Earl of Orford and ceased to be a Minister of the Crown. "The reign of Sir Robert" was over. He left the House of Commons "sure that no other Minister would ever be able to stand so long as he had done, twenty years," and he was right. Newcastle was a Secretary of State continuously for thirty-

three years, a State career unparalleled in our political annals ; but not until the younger Pitt did a Minister enjoy the confidence of sovereign, legislature, and nation, or an enduring supremacy in the Cabinet equivalent to that asserted and maintained by Walpole.

It is strikingly characteristic both of the man and his system that he refused to yield to the Opposition until he had been plainly defeated, not in the closet, but in Parliament. He had still the confidence of George II. and a majority in the Lords, but he had lost the trust of the Commons. The Chippenham vote was a personal censure. A reconstruction of the Administration under his leadership would simply have transferred the struggle from St. Stephen's to the Cockpit at Whitehall. Walpole had too great a mastery of the secrets of political efficiency under parliamentary conditions to believe that the shuffling jugglery of place-hunters and managers could make a tesselated mosaic of discordant pieces anything but a tesselated mosaic. Unlike Newcastle, but like Chatham, he was not prepared indefinitely to accept responsibility for the measures of whose principles and objects he disapproved, nor to lead an independent horde of departmental colleagues by whom he would be continuously outvoted. Walpole stood for a definite and intelligible system both in home administration and foreign policy. His fall was the fall of that system. New men, new problems, a new national temper, a changed European situation sharply mark off the last twenty years of George II.'s reign from the age of Walpole. But the essential features of his work as a statesman endured. They provided the basis on which his successors could build with assured success. Modern criticism can easily emphasise the great Minister's defects. Throughout he exaggerated the efficacy of diplomacy : "the rage of negotiating" fastened on by contemporary opponents, particularly in later years, blinded him, though not alone of European masters of state-craft, to the deep and rising currents of national life. In common with most British statesmen both in the eighteenth and nineteenth centuries he failed to see that a scientific organisation of the military resources of the kingdom was as essential as a well-filled treasury to a policy of peace and economy. He was not fitted to conduct a great war. Neither tattered drums and colours in our cathedrals, a swollen national debt, new imperial provinces on the map, nor an impressive list of legislative enactments enshrine his memory for generations that only by an effort can reconstruct the problems and the needs of the Great Britain which he patiently studied and overcame. The perils of a Stuart restoration, the transition from monarchical to parliamentary government and the evolution of the Premiership, the Cabinet, and the party system can only be pieced together painfully to prove the share of a commanding political genius in their construction. In the closet, in finance, in foreign policy, in the management of trade, and on the unseen foundations of national and imperial prosperity and power, Walpole accomplished much. Statesmen may fairly claim to be judged not merely by the successes they achieve, but by the dangers they avert. Estimated by this test, Walpole has an indisputable place amongst the master-makers of modern Great Britain. Intensely English both in his strength and his weakness, he was the last of the true Revolution Whigs, of the men who overthrew the monarchy and system of the Stuarts, and substituted for it a gigantic experiment in self-government. The twenty years of dull, plodding, but gifted statesmanship and administration under Walpole put the coping-stone on the fabric of 1688. In 1742 the Revolution State had taken an impregnable place in the State systems of modern Europe.

NOTE.—See the authorities cited on p. 56 : and add : Sir R. Lodge, *Great Britain and Prussia in the Eighteenth Century* (1922).

CHAPTER III

THE STRUGGLE FOR EMPIRE

§ 1. THE WAR OF THE AUSTRIAN SUCCESSION, 1740-1748

W HO was to succeed Walpole ? In the confusion that ensued three points were tolerably clear ; a Cabinet dominated by a single leader was impossible, because no one at the moment desired the continuance of a " sole or Premier Minister," and there was no one with the qualities, the character, or the authority capable of playing the part; it was impossible to satisfy all the claims of all the claimants for office in the heterogeneous coalition ; the majority of the existing Ministers welcomed the sacrifice of their chief, but resisted the sacrifice of themselves. Horace Walpole, fresh from Rome, said that the maze of intrigue reminded him of nothing so much as the cardinals in a conclave electing a Pope. But in 1742 at St. James no one desired a Pontiff, though all hungered for a share in a syndicated tiara. Newcastle and Hardwicke anxiously negotiated with Carteret and Pulteney. Walpole, too, " had left his tongue in the Commons," and his advice was both asked for and acted upon. That Carteret failed to become First Lord of the Treasury and Pulteney took an earldom was largely the fallen Minister's work. " I have turned the key of the closet on him," he said of Pulteney. " Here we are, my lord," was his greeting to his rival, " the two most insignificant fellows in the kingdom," which was truer of the first Earl of Bath than of the first Earl of Orford. Pulteney in fact lost his head in the crisis. He had made his position by that tongue which Walpole said he feared more than another man's sword, but in the House of Lords he had an alien audience and no party. He redeemed his pledge that he would not take office by entering the Cabinet without a portfolio, and he had no opportunity of showing administrative skill ; with his failure to force on the new Ministry an adequate contingent of his personal followers his career after 1742 " was a wretched tissue of disappointed hopes ". The nominal head of the Broad-bottom [1] Administration was Lord Wilmington, on whose dull mediocrity, as in 1727, a brief greatness was thrust a second time. Newcastle retained his Secretaryship, Hardwicke the Chancellorship, Henry Pelham the Paymaster-Generalship. Sandys, " who thought he could make out the revenue and the House of Commons " (in both of which he failed), became Chancellor of the Exchequer. The one admission of importance was Carteret. To make room for him Harrington exchanged his Secretary's Seals for the Lord Presidentship. The omissions were numerous and significant. Chesterfield was left out. Of the young men, " the silver-tongued " Murray, the contemporary of Henry Fox and Pitt at the University of Oxford, who had at once on his entry into Parliament justified his great reputation at the bar, became Solicitor-General ; Henry Fox was too stout a Walpoleite 1742 to receive anything ; Cobham was made a Field-Marshal, but his " cubs " the " Boy Patriots," Pitt, Lyttelton, George Grenville, were left to growl and bark outside the doors of office. Nor was the Bottom of the Administration broad enough to admit the strict Tory element. Argyll, pacified with the chief command in Scotland and the Master-Generalship of the Ordnance, demanded in vain recognition of the Tory allies, and in a huff at the refusal resigned his offices. The new Ministry in fact was as bitter a disappointment to Leicester House as to Bolingbroke. The dream of a national union, dissolving party connections and combining the talents of all in disinterested service of the Crown and country, vanished in thin air as soon as it became a serious question of offices and places, of Whigs and Tories, of carrying on the business of an obstinate and prosaic King in a workaday House of Commons. In the witty phrase with which, in the happier hours of irresponsible Opposition, Pulteney had attacked Walpole's Sinking Fund, " the promised philosopher's stone " that was to make England patriotic, pure, independent of Crown and Ministerial corruption, " ended in some little thing for curing the itch ". A modest Place Bill

---

[1] " One now hears of nothing but the broad bottom ; it is the reigning cant word and means the taking all parties or people indifferently into the Ministry " (H. Walpole to Mann, February 18th, 1742).

was carried, but the other heroic remedies for an England ruined by Walpole—the repeal of the Septennial Act, the abolition of the standing army in time of peace, the surrender of the Secret Service Fund, the extinction of the National Debt, the reduction of taxation and the rigorous exclusion of all pensioners and placemen—were quickly dropped. The plain truth was that these things were as necessary to the intriguing gentlemen to keep themselves in office as they had been to the Minister they had turned out. But one matter could not be wholly burked—the demand for the exposure and punishment of the monster of political and financial iniquity, who for so long had defied the Opposition and manipulated Crown and Legislature. Against Walpole articles of impeachment were drafted, but the evidence that would convict the fallen Minister of treason was difficult to find, and a triumphant acquittal after a brilliant defence might bring Walpole back to power. A Bill of Pains and Penalties, by which a fair trial might be avoided, even if it got through the Commons, would certainly be rejected by the Upper House, to which Lord Orford now belonged. It was fairly clear that the clamour for Walpole's head had been only a clamour for his place, and the clamour was now satisfied. Ministers were not anxious to reforge an instrument which a year or two hence a victorious Opposition could use for a like purpose against the new occupants of the Treasury Bench. Recourse was therefore had to a Secret Committee of twenty-one (nineteen of whom were Walpole's avowed foes) to scavenge in the dust heaps of the past ten years and publish to a horrified nation a damning indictment. But again the evidence was not forthcoming, probably because it did not exist. Scrope, the Treasury official who had confidential knowledge and might have revealed to whom payments had been made and (perhaps) for what, wisely and stoutly refused to lay bare secrets which might have affected members of Parliament, and certainly would have affected the organised intelligence department of our Foreign Office. To aid the baffled committee a bill was brought in providing an indemnity to all who would reveal damaging information, but it was riddled with criticism by Hardwicke, and on the advice of Carteret, who had some sense of justice and of humour, this device for intimidating the honest and rewarding the dishonest was summarily rejected. The Committee soon became an object of ridicule, and its report proved a fiasco.[1] Burke's later judgment that Walpole governed 1790 "by party attachments" has the authority of Walpole's own explicit and repeated statements. "The charge," Burke proceeds, "of systematic corruption is less applicable to him perhaps than to any Minister who ever served the Crown for so great a length of time." Certainly the politicians of 1742—Pitt alone excepted— were not those who could thank God that they were not as the fallen Minister. And in the collapse of the retributive measures one more decisive step was taken towards substituting for impeachment deprivation of office as the penalty for failure to retain the confidence of the representative Chamber of the Legislature.

The crucial question of the hour was foreign policy. George II. Nov. 29 had announced his intention to maintain his treaty pledge as re- 1740 gards the Pragmatic Sanction, and Walpole had obtained from Parliament a vote for an armed force, and a subsidy for Maria Theresa, whose cause was popular in Great Britain. But with the succession to the hereditary dominions of the House of Austria, threatened by Frederick, was bound up the succession to the Imperial Crown. As a woman Maria Theresa was debarred from election, but her husband, Francis of Lorraine, was not. The most formidable candidate for the Imperial Crown was the Elector of Bavaria, who had never accepted the Pragmatic Sanction, and was a candidate also for the Austrian heritage. Another claimant was the King of Spain. If the Pragmatic Sanction was observed one great object of Maria Theresa was automatically gained ; but the imperial election necessarily involved securing the votes of the German Electors, of whom George II. was one. Behind the Elector of Bavaria and the King of Spain might be found the Bourbon Monarchy at Paris, anxious to weaken the traditional Habsburg foe. Frederick's invasion of Silesia was a deliberate attack on the integrity of the Austrian dominions, and Frederick was an Elector to the Imperial Crown. Did Britain's treaty pledge and national interests require her to plunge into a continental war in order to protect Maria Theresa's rights, and further the Hanoverian policy of securing for Germany an Emperor whom marriage had made a

---

[1] The charges and evidence adduced by the committee are analysed at length and with critical acumen by Coxe in his *Walpole*, i., 719-64. See also Lord Morley's *Walpole*, pp. 121-9; Anson, *Law and Custom of the Constitution*, vol. ii., part i., p. 107 n., and see also Appendix XXI.

Habsburg? Clearly, if a French ally ousted Maria Theresa from Vienna and won the Imperial Crown, Europe would be confronted by a resurrection of the dreaded Bourbon ascendency led by France, which it was the traditional policy of the Whigs to defeat. Was the Government to accept the logic of the Spanish war and enter on a life-and-death struggle with France? But Walpole, who had seen in 1739 one-half of his system of foreign policy shattered, struggled hard against sacrificing the other half. He did not share the Hanoverian and Austrian envenomed hostility to Prussia; he distrusted the policy of continental engagements, the end of which could not be seen. To come out into the open against France destroyed all hope of dividing the Bourbon Powers and of controlling the policy of Maria Theresa. The Austrian Ministers clearly grasped that as long as Walpole was in office the renewal of the Grand Alliance and the identification of Great Britain with the House of Habsburg, for which they were working, could not be expected.[1] They were, therefore, as eager for his fall as Carteret and Pulteney. Meanwhile our Ministers saw that Berlin was the key to the position. If Frederick could be kept from a French alliance, and reconciled to Maria Theresa, diplomacy might settle the imbroglio without a general European war. Negotiations were begun for a Grand Alliance (Holland, Russia, Austria, Saxony, and Great Britain) against Prussia. But bitter was Austria's disillusionment when George II. announced his readiness to mediate between Frederick and Maria Theresa. The King of Prussia was willing, if Silesia were ceded, to support Maria Theresa and vote for Francis to be Emperor. British Ministers therefore urged the acceptance of these terms. But the Austrian Court, deceived by Fleury's pacific language, foolishly rejected them. The Franco-Prussian alliance of June 4th was a second bitter disillusionment; in August two French armies crossed the Rhine to support the claims of the Elector of Bavaria; the Treaty of Nymphenburg, which detached Saxony from the Habsburg to the Bavarian cause, revealed the objects of French policy—the dismemberment of the Austrian dominions, the election of an Emperor under French control. If Walpole's dwindling authority was proved by George's journey to Hanover against his Ministers' wishes, the hasty declara-

March,
1741
April 10

Sept. 19

---

[1] See especially the evidence for this from the Austrian archives in Pribram, *Oesterr. Staatsverträge, England*, i., 551-53.

tion of Hanover's neutrality, made behind the back of the British Sept. 27
Cabinet, which roused both Ministerial and popular indignation,
was a fresh blow to Austrian hopes.   Our diplomacy still strove to
reconcile Vienna with Berlin, and the secret Convention of Klein-
Schnellendorf, under which Frederick checked his military opera- Oct. 9
tions, was due to English pressure.   Maria Theresa had appealed
to the loyalty of Hungary with triumphant success, although the
election of the Elector of Bavaria as Emperor with the title of Jan. 24,
Charles VII. was a severe set-back to Austrian ambitions.   At this 1792
point Walpole resigned.   The Broad Bottom Administration inherited a problem in foreign policy which called for great courage,
decision, and a wide and deep insight into the confusing elements
of a complicated situation.   Above all, it was essential to frame a
clear view of the true interests of Great Britain, and to settle the
first principles of our political and military action.   But here the
new Ministers failed.   The War of the Austrian Succession, so far
as Great Britain was concerned, is a dreary record of conflicting
principles, half-pursued, involving a vast expenditure of life and
treasure with small or no results.   The Cabinet, no doubt, was
divided by internal strife, clogged by the Hanoverianism of the
Crown and the inadequacy of British military resources.   For the
next fifteen years Great Britain paid a heavy price for the starvation of her standing army, her neglect of the science of war, her
criminal failure to organise a reserve in the form of a national
militia.   No nation can divorce policy from war without disastrous
consequences in both spheres, and the War of the Austrian Succession shows how a series of attempts to combine principles radically
opposed vitiates strategy, and mars even sound strokes of executive
action.   Too often the strokes were as ill-devised as the principles
underlying them were confused and imperfectly conceived.

For the first two years interest centres on Carteret.   His knowledge of European politics and acquaintance with the German
language (rare in his contemporaries) made him very acceptable to
the King ; his previous advocacy of Maria Theresa's cause acceptable to Vienna.   His diplomatic experience and brilliant
gifts of intellect and oratory especially fitted him to realise his
ambition of controlling the foreign policy of his country.   A Whig
by birth, culture, and sympathy, Carteret approached the problem
with the traditional attitude and measures of the old Revolution

Whigs. "I always," he said, "traverse the views of France in place or out of place; for France will ruin this nation if it can." As the architect of a grander Grand Alliance, Carteret aimed at repeating the work of William III. The Bourbon ascendency was to be smashed on the Continent by continental methods. The union of London, the Hague, Vienna, with the lesser German States, in securing which Hanoverian influence would be useful, could be concentrated by the diplomacy which was his joy and his finest gift into an irresistible instrument for humbling France. But at the outset four assumptions may be noted in this wide conception. (1) Carteret must get and keep a free hand over Court, colleagues, and Parliament; (2) the objects of the Viennese Court must be broadly identifiable with the true interests of Great Britain; (3) the issues between Great Britain and France must really be capable of being settled in Flanders, the Rhine, Silesia—on continental battlefields as the result of continental measures; (4) the military executive must be equal to the diplomatic plan and to the political ideas underlying both. The Grand Alliance had found its Marlborough and rested on a united Whig party at home. Carteret had to deal with the Pelhams, Hardwicke, and Newcastle; he had to reckon with Pitt, with Maria Theresa, and above all with Frederick the Great. And outside Europe there had grown up a new world. Louis XV. had entered the war not as a principal but as the auxiliary of Charles VII.; Great Britain now entered it as the auxiliary of Maria Theresa. A large subsidy to the Queen of Hungary was voted; Savoy was detached to co-operate with Austria in Italy against Spain; 16,000 Hanoverians and 6000 Hessians were hired to bring a British force in the Low Countries up to 30,000. In 1742 Mathews drove Spanish galleys into St. Tropez and burned them despite the neutrality of France; at Naples, Commander Martin gave Charles III. one hour by the watch to withdraw his contingent from joining the Spaniards in North Italy. Charles III. submitted, but never forgot the humiliating coercion of the naval "tyrant". The relentless pressure of our diplomacy compelled Maria Theresa June 11 to accept the Preliminaries of Breslau, confirmed by the Treaty of July 28 Berlin by which Frederick gained Silesia, threw over his allies, and withdrew from the war. In consequence the French retreated from Jan., 1743 Prague and relieved Maria Theresa from the grip of her foes in Bohemia. Carteret and his colleagues had made a brilliant start.

The moment for a sharp blow at France had come. Had the
advice of Stair, appointed to the command in Flanders, been taken,
the Anglo-Hanoverian force would have struck at the weakly defended north-east frontier, with Paris as the objective. But the
delay of the Hanoverian contingent, fear of such bold strategy, the
fiction that we were not directly at war with France, the desire at
Vienna to use "the Pragmatic Army" for Austrian objects in
Germany, caused the winter of 1742 and the spring of 1743 to be
wasted. Despite Frederick's protests the army advanced towards
Mainz to find the French now ready on the Meuse and the Moselle.
When the King joined it on June 16th Stair's force was cut off
from Franconia in the East and Hanau in the West, though the
fault was not Stair's. De Noailles had secured the bridges on the
river below and above the British forces and as soon as lack of supplies compelled them to retreat on Hanau, he prepared to crush
them. The battle, however, that ensued at Dettingen, the last in June 19
which a British King commanded in person, resulted in a French
defeat, thanks to the rashness and disobedience of De Grammont,
who abandoned his strong position and engaged the whole Anglo-
Hanoverian army before De Noailles' enveloping movements were
completed. By pushing on at once to Hanau, George had the good
fortune to extricate his army from almost certain disaster and to enable Handel to celebrate a royal victory in his "Dettingen Te Deum".
Stair, who had urged a vigorous pursuit, resigned a few month later,
disgusted at being repeatedly overruled. As the French army in
Bavaria had been defeated and fallen back on Alsace, De Noailles
retreated also. George then advanced to Worms where a convention of neutrality between Charles VII. and Maria Theresa brought
operations to a standstill. Spain too had been severely checked in
Italy by the Austro-Sardinian victory at Campo Santo and the co-
operation of the British fleet; the Electoral territories of Charles
VII. were in Austrian possession, and the hour of the diplomatists
had come. The danger points were really three. France, smart-
ing under her failure, meditated shifting the theatre of her main
operations in order to strike Great Britain out of the coalition
by combining a campaign in Flanders with a Jacobite invasion
of Great Britain; Maria Theresa refused to regard the loss of
Silesia as irrevocable, and desired at least adequate compensation
on the Rhine; Frederick was determined not to imperil the future

of Prussia by permitting unchallenged a renewal of an undisputed Habsburg supremacy in Germany. Carteret's position was hampered by the jealousy of his colleagues and the strong anti-Hanoverian feeling both in the Cabinet, Parliament, and public opinion. In July Wilmington had died. Carteret favoured Bath's (Pulteney's) ambition to succeed him, but the Pelham group aided by Lord Orford's influence placed Henry Pelham at the head of the administration.[1]

In complete agreement with George, Carteret was busily engaged in an elaborate scheme (the Preliminaries of Hanau) for securing his imperial title and Bavarian territories to Charles VII., while he waived all claims on the House of Austria, and the French abandoned all fortified posts within the Empire. His colleagues sympathised with the popular desire for war (in alliance with Vienna) with France, but they declined to provide Chesterfield and Pitt with new arguments for denouncing the curse of Hanoverianism and to demand in Parliament a subsidy for a Bavarian Emperor in order that the Elector of Hanover might pose as the Dictator of the Empire. The Treaty of Worms, which substituted a great league (England, Holland, Austria, Saxony, Sardinia) for the rejected scheme, was only carried in Cabinet after violent recriminations. The treaty drew severe criticism from the Opposition. On the brink of a war with France, Great Britain added Sardinia to her subsidy list, prolonged the subsidy to Austria, and pledged herself to territorial guarantees, which might be interpreted to include the recovery of Silesia and the lost possessions in Italy. On March 15th, 1744, France declared war on Great Britain and on Austria; Frederick replied to the Treaty of Worms by the union of Frankfort in support of the Emperor, by renewing his alliance with France, by seizing East Frisia, long coveted by Hanover, by marching into Bohemia, and thus commencing the Second Silesian War. The responsibility for this renewal of the general European struggle cannot be shifted from the British Cabinet. Austria was dependent on British subsidies and Hanoverian contingents for the realisation of her policy. A policy which pinned down the Viennese Court to frank acceptance of the Treaty of Berlin and the recogni-

Marginal dates: July 7-Aug. 1   Sept. 7   April 14   May   June   August

[1] "You have taken post," Orford wrote, "and will be able to maintain it. . . . Broad Bottom cannot be made for anything that has a zest of Hanover. Whig it with all opponents that will parley, but 'ware Tory."

tion of Charles VII. as the basis of a settlement would have separated France from Prussia, British from Austrian and Hanoverian interests in Germany, and left England free to concentrate every man, gun, and penny on the maritime and colonial struggle with France. Carteret's original policy was preferable to the compromise which satisfied the Cabinet. But it ignored the imperial issues at stake beyond the seas, and his influence with the King and passion for wide-flung continental combinations deflected British resources from vitally British ends. The Treaty of Worms to be successful, moreover, imposed on the Cabinet the task of organising and conducting under the conditions of a coalition a great war, for which events soon showed they had not the capacity. In the Mediterranean the indecisive action of February 22nd off Toulon, where the combined French and Spanish fleets might have been crushed, though it brought out Captain Hawke, proved the mismanagement of Admirals Matthews and Lestock and the inefficiency of our tactics. The cashiering of Matthews was a poor compensation for the escape of the enemy to Carthagena and Alicante. In Flanders the inadequacy of our force, the sluggishness of the Dutch, the jealousy of the Austrians left Marshal Wade, a cautious commander at best, helpless against the superior French army under a general of genius, Marshal Saxe. The French secured the line of the Lys as a basis for more serious efforts next year. Austrian operations in Alsace were nullified by Frederick's invasion of Bohemia, and Bavaria was abandoned to the Emperor. Though Frederick was compelled to retreat from Prague the French crossed the Rhine, captured Freiburg and overran Bavaria; in Italy the Austrians were defeated at Velletri; but the Sardinians, aided by the British fleet, foiled the French at Coni, and compelled them to recross the Alps. The end of a year memorable for a futile expenditure of human life and treasure saw a reconstruction of the Cabinet. Carteret, who had become Earl Granville, supported alone by the influence of the Crown, insisted on controlling foreign policy, for which his colleagues were required to find the money in Parliament and share the unpopularity of his demands. To the request for his favourite Minister's dismissal, the King, aided for the first and last time by the Prince of Wales, offered a stout resistance. The question raised political and constitutional issues of capital importance. Orford had broken silence in the Lords in the spring by a powerful speech emphasising the dangers to the Revolution Settlement in the continental policy of the Secretary of State. A dying man, he now hurried up to London, and Carteret's retirement was largely due to his intervention. It was the last service rendered to the dynasty by Robert Walpole. His prediction that a breach with the Bourbon Powers would involve the reopening of the dynastic question at home had been verified this year, and was to be more strikingly fulfilled in the year of his death. The Pelhams carried out their master's counsel of silencing the Opposition by giving office to its most prominent members. Harrington succeeded Carteret as Secretary, Chesterfield became Lord-Lieutenant of Ireland ; the Tory Lord Gower was made Privy Seal, the Duke of Bedford, head of " the Bloomsbury gang," and conspicuous for his opposition to Walpole, was put at the head of the Admiralty. Even Sir John Cotton, a professed Jacobite, was gratified by a place at Court. Minor posts were found for Lyttelton and George Grenville. The " Patriots " party was thus largely reconciled with the Administration. Pitt alone was passed over. Given to understand that royal resentment at his denunciation of Hanoverianism forbade his being offered office, he was obliged to wait, and in the meanwhile be gratified with the recognition of his allies and the removal of " the execrable sole Minister," who " had drunk of the potion described in poetic fiction which made men forget their country ". George sullenly accepted these changes, enforced by a veiled constitutional lecture from Hardwicke on behalf of the Cabinet. " Ministers, sir," wound up the Chancellor, " are only your instruments of government." " Ministers," was the royal retort, " are the King in this country." And eighteen months later George II. was to receive a still sharper lesson in the power of Ministerial solidarity. Carteret's fall invites a comment. He left St. James laughing, we are told. Neither the extent of his political knowledge, the versatility and energy of his diplomacy, the polish and refinement of his culture, which made his personality so attractive then and since, had availed him. Yet it was not his *bravura* levity of tone, his arrogant and dictatorial nature, nor his self-indulgence which branded him as the *âme damnée* first of Walpole's and then of the Broad-Bottom Administration. Pitt was quite as arrogant, perhaps a more difficult, colleague. It would be unjust to deny to Carteret the proud patriotism of the cultivated aristocrat, a burning ambition to achieve for his country an ascendency in the

Nov. 24, 1744

March, 1745

councils of Europe, a remarkable knowledge of and interest in the politics and temper of the Continent. His contempt for popular opinion, his reliance on the power of the Crown, his neglect of the machinery of parliamentary government, reveal the instructive secret of his failure. Had he, as was well said by a contemporary, studied Parliament more and Demosthenes less he might have been a successful Prime Minister. *La haute politique* was his self-chosen province. In the upper sphere of government, Pitt, who denounced him more savagely than any other critic, judged him to be without an equal. But he never seems to have grasped the meaning of ministerial responsibility and the multiplex unseen but vital relations between Ministers and a representative House of Commons under the conditions of party and parliamentary government. Under an absolutist sovereign he would probably have won fame and wrought enduring results. In the England of his day he was a century too late. Statesmen who fail to understand their countrymen or their age are invariably punished by being themselves misunderstood. Carteret challenged the right of a system of growing self-government to work out its own salvation by its own methods. The system revenged itself by breaking his power and strengthening its authority by his defeat.

To all appearances, however, the reconstruction of the Ministry was not followed by a marked change in foreign policy. The war with France stamped 1745 as one of the most critical years in our annals, and the gravity of the situation at home and abroad made it clear that for Great Britain the question now was not one of principles and systems but of her capacity to maintain her independence and save the balance of power by an honourable peace. The Treaty of Warsaw confirmed and extended the alliance with Austria, Jan. 8. Saxony, and Holland, and the subsidies this year reached the 1745 enormous sum of £1,178,753. A great effort in the Low Countries was organised under the chief command of the Duke of Cumberland. But Marshal Saxe was the first in the field and invested Tournay. April 30 Against the allied force advancing to its relief Saxe took up a strong position, stretching from the Scheldt on his right across Fontenoy to the woods of Barri on his left. Though the battle of Fontenoy resulted in a French victory, the frontal attack of the British and Hanoverians, unsupported by the Dutch or Austrians, May 11 across an open plain, commanded by artillery, into the heart of the

7

centre and left of the French, must remain one of the most astonishing achievements of infantry on record, and a source of undying pride to the regiments which are entitled to bear the bloodstained name of Fontenoy on their colours. Cumberland perforce retired and Tournay surrendered—the beginning of a disastrous campaign for which inferiority in numbers, defective generalship, the weakness of the Dutch and quarrels with the Austrians, were jointly responsible. Ath, Ostend, Bruges, Oudenarde, and Ghent fell to the French, and the allies were able to do little more than cover Antwerp and Brussels. The brilliant capture of Louisburg in Cape

June Breton Island, "the one real stroke done upon France this year," was a partial set-off against this failure. But the outbreak of the Jacobite rising at home was the finishing blow. To man the army in Flanders the garrisons in Great Britain had been dangerously depleted. Now in order to cope with the Highland clans, for which reserves that did not exist should have sufficed, the situation in Flanders was seriously imperilled by the withdrawal of the British Commander-in-Chief and practically the whole of his force. The

July 25 landing of Charles Edward at Loch-na-Uamh thus dramatically shifted the centre of interest to a plain issue in the United Kingdom.

Until 1740 Jacobitism had given little trouble. Indeed had Duncan Forbes' scheme in 1738 for raising five Highland regiments been adopted, it might have made "the Forty-five" impossible; certainly an adequate military force distributed at the strategic centres would have crushed at the outset the romantic but mad fling for a throne of Charles Edward. But the Government did nothing, and events created the opportunity for which the young Stuart Prince (born 1722) hungered. The dreams of the faithful few had long centred on this brown-eyed, vigorous and attractive young man "with the bloom of a lass". Charles believed in his star and himself. He saw the Whigs quarrelling, the Hanoverianism of George II. provoking widespread discontent, Britain embroiled in a continental war and her scanty military resources mortgaged. As early as 1741 the chief Jacobite agents, Macgregor of Balhaldy and Lord Sempill, aided by Murray of Broughton, were actively negotiating with Cardinal Fleury. To France, on the brink of war with England, the Jacobite Pretender was an effective instrument for a counterstroke which would "contain" Great Britain and might revolutionise her dynasty and system of policy. After Fleury's

death Maurepas continued the intrigue ; and though Louis XV. acted 1743
with characteristic secrecy and tortuous caution, serious preparations
were put in hand. The information given with confidence and
minuteness of detail in the memorials laid before the French
Government is the familiar medley of self-deception, crude exaggeration, and reliance on paper calculations of fortune and the future.
The plan adopted apparently was to dispense with a formal declaration of war and to cover with the fleet from Brest a surprise invasion
under Marshal Saxe launched from Dunkirk. History repeated itself.
The hesitations and delays of the French executive, the unwilling-
ness of the English Jacobites to rise before the French regiments
had landed, the quarrels, ignorance, and disunion of the Jacobite
leaders on both sides of the Channel and of the Tweed postponed
the stroke until the British Ministry were ready to frustrate it.
Once again a Protestant and parliamentary gale devastated the
Brest ships and wrecked the transports at Dunkirk.   Norris, too, March 6
was prowling in the Channel for his prey, and the French promptly and 7,
abandoned an expedition doomed to failure if it had started.   Charles 1744
Edward had escaped from Rome and reached Paris in February.
Influenced by a small group, mainly of Irish adventurers, and against
the wishes of his father, lucidly pessimistic as ever, he was determined
" to win or to lose all," and to get into Scotland even if accompanied
only by a single footman.   After sixteen months of scheming, and
stimulated by the victory at Fontenoy, Charles slipped out of Nantes
in a small privateer, and after landing at Eriskay (the tiny island July 2,
south of Uist where, as every true Jacobite knows, he planted a pink 1745
convolvulus which still grows there and will grow nowhere else) set
foot on the mainland at Borrodale in Moidart.   On August 19th July 25
the standard of the White Rose was raised at Glenfinnan at the head
of Loch Shiel.   He had already been joined by Lochiel and the
Camerons, Glengarry, Keppoch, Clanranald, and the Appin Stuarts.
Amongst his other supporters were the famous-infamous Murray of
Broughton, and the aged Tullibardine.   The English Government,
though taken by surprise, had already placed a reward of £30,000
on Charles's head—an intrinsically disgraceful and contemptible proceeding because it showed a ridiculous ignorance of Highland sentiment ; the Lord President Forbes hurried to Inverness to organise
the Whig clans, and prevent Simon Lovat and the Frasers from
joining the Cause ; while Sir John Cope with not more than 3000

men, new and raw regiments, was ordered to march northwards. Charles planned to surprise and destroy his force at the Pass of Corryarrack, but Cope turned off at Dalwhinnie and took Wade's

road to Inverness. Charles slipped round him, reached Blair-Athole and then occupied Perth. Joined there by the Duke of Perth, Lord George Murray, and some 200 Robertsons of Struan, he crossed the Forth at the Fords of Frew, skirted Stirling, routed Gardiner's dragoons at Coltbridge ("the Canter of Coltbridge"), and after a feeble show of resistance by the city authorities, entered Edin-

burgh. Though the Castle still held out for King George, the Stuart King was proclaimed the same day at the Cross, and the young Prince slept that night at Holyrood, the palace of his ancestors. The gamble for a throne had developed into a challenge to the Hanoverian dynasty and civil war.

Cope meanwhile transhipped his force from Aberdeen by sea to
Dunbar, and Charles advanced to meet him as he marched by the coast road to Edinburgh. Cope, near Prestonpans, shifted his front from west to east with the sea and Edinburgh behind him, and his face protected, as he believed, by an impassable morass, which he did not guard by sentinels. He had some 2400 men with six small guns. On the night of September 20th Charles and his men, numbering about 2500, found a passage across the morass and flung themselves on Cope's regulars at dawn. The "battle" was finished in about six minutes. The dragoons on the wings at the first rush of the Highlanders "fled like rabbits"; the infantry with exposed flanks found bayonets useless against broadsword and target, and were swept away. Cope escaped with the cavalry to Berwick, having lost his army; the Highlanders dropped perhaps 100 killed and wounded. The moral effect of Prestonpans was prodigious.

What was to be the next step? The victory did not, as had fondly been hoped, secure the political support of Scotland nor bring out the Jacobites in England. The British fleet prevented the French Government, involved in Flanders and on the Rhine, from sending anything but doles of money, guns, and a few officers. But the home Government demanded from the Dutch the Treaty contingent of 6000 men, and recalled Cumberland and his army. Clearly, Charles must either cross the Tweed and galvanise English Jacobitism into life before the Whigs had completed their military preparations, or await an organised attack in Scotland. He chose the former, and, in deference to the advice of Lord George Murray, decided to turn Wade's force at Newcastle by taking the Western route. To deceive Wade as to the route of the invaders, one column marched by Peebles and Moffat, the other under Charles himself by Lauder and Kelso, and on November 9th they united at Carlisle, which surrendered. Manchester was reached on Novem- Nov. 15 ber 29th, but the results so far were dispiriting. The invaders scarcely numbered more than 5000; neither English gentry, burghers, nor peasants came forward; North Wales under Sir Watkin Wynn, South Wales under the Duke of Beaufort and the " gentlemen of the Cycle," were perhaps ready to rise at a nod; yet Cumberland was lying between Tamworth and Newcastle-under-Lyme; Wade reinforced could cut the communications with the North, and a camp of the guards and trained bands to guard London was being formed at Finchley. But the capital was Charles's objective. By a skilful feint his army in forced marches got past Cumberland, and reached Derby on December 4th. In the race to the South, Cumberland, now at Stafford with his cavalry horses worn out, could be outstripped by the superior marching power of the Highlanders. The camp at Finchley alone barred the way. The news reached London on December 6th, and the panic added the name of Black Friday to our calendar. The Bank was reduced to paying in sixpences. It was also a Black Friday in the calendar of the White Rose. For while London was a prey to consternation the Cameron pibrochs were already sounding not the advance on Finchley but—retreat. Charles, with the greatest reluctance, had yielded to the unanimous advice of his officers, and by December 12th his army was back at Preston, heading northwards. The military reasons for the retreat are plausible, but not absolutely convincing. With Wade and Cumberland behind them, a reverse meant ruin to the Jacobite forces. Five thousand men in the heart of an apathetic country, cut off from their base, could not achieve the impossible. Scotland could at least be secured. Further advance was a gambler's throw. But Charles was a gambler who could only win all by risking all. Another Prestonpans on the heights of Hampstead would have given him the capital, might have brought in the French Government and led to a general rising in England and Wales. To-day no one can be dogmatic on what might have been. Charles's instinct was sound, and had he failed his fate would have been no worse than the disaster that awaited him and his Highlanders in the spring of 1746. It is certain that as soon as Derby was left behind the prince's heart was broken, and the belief in the Cause and its inspiring leader which had brought the clans from the Grampians to the centre of England was irretrievably shattered. From Derby to Culloden is a record of a forlorn hope struggling against superior organisation and resources, of noble gallantry marred by cabals, jealousies, blunders and despair.

The honours of the retreat belong to Lord George Murray, who commanded the rear-guard, for Charles who in the advance had won the enthusiasm of the Highlanders by wearing kilt and tartan, and sharing their hardships, was now guilty of a sullen slackness. Cumberland pressed the pursuit, but Murray's coolness and dexterity at Clifton Moor, south of Penrith, checked the English dragoons. At Carlisle against his advice a small garrison was foolishly left which promptly surrendered to Cumberland, who occupied the town ten days later. The Esk was safely crossed and Glasgow reached; a wonderful march from Edinburgh to Glasgow *via* Derby in no more than fifty-six days on eighteenth century roads. Cumberland returned to deal with the expected French invasion and the command fell to Hawley, a fair soldier and ferocious disciplinarian, "with no small bias to the brutal". Charles, after joining with the Northern force collected in his absence, which brought his numbers up to some 9000 men, proceeded to besiege Stirling.[1] Hawley's force coming to its relief was met on Falkirk Muir, but the nature of the ground, a high slope cut by ravines, darkness and a storm of rain, prevented a complete victory, and Hawley made an orderly retreat, leaving 500 killed and wounded on the field. The Highland loss was about forty; and as Hawley's army included at least one regiment that had fought well at Fontenoy, it is not unfair to infer what Charles's men in the flush of an unchecked advance might

In the margin:

Dec. 19

Dec. 26

Jan. 3
Jan. 17

---

[1] It was at Bannockburn House at this time that the Prince made the acquaintance of Miss Clementina Walkinshaw (daughter of John Walkinshaw of Barronsfield), the blonde beauty with gold hair and blue eyes whom Alan Fairford (in *Redgauntlet*) saw at Fair Ladies. She followed the Prince to France and lived with him from 1749 to 1760, but it is pure conjecture that she became his mistress as early as 1746. Separated from the Prince in 1760, she died in 1792.

have done at Finchley. It was the last conspicuous success. Cumberland hurried North, determined to reorganise his army and prove that regulars could face and beat the Highlanders, whom he regarded with hatred and contempt. Lord George Murray and the chiefs urged the necessity of abandoning the siege of Stirling, and once again Charles sullenly complied.

On February 1st the retreat on Inverness was begun. The reasons for this retirement on the lean North are obscure and conflicting. Since the unhappy decision at Derby jealousies, divided counsels, lack of accurate intelligence had ruined the confidence of Charles in his followers and of his followers in the Prince. In a vigorous offensive, as Falkirk re-proved, lay the sole chance of success, while Cumberland now was given the time he needed to restore the moral of his troops and introduce new tactics. Two small successes preceded the inevitable and final disaster. Loudon from Inverness attempted to seize Charles at Moy Castle, but a handful of Highlanders struck panic in his men (the Rout of Moy, February 10th), and Charles occupied Inverness. Fort Augustus was then captured, but the strokes against Fort William and Blair Castle failed. Murray's operations between Blair-Atholl and Inverness were quite masterly, but they were futile. Cumberland was at Aberdeen on February 27th and at Nairn on April 14th. Desertion and lack of supplies had reduced Charles's force to 5000 half-starved men; nevertheless it was decided to try a night surprise on the Duke's camp. It failed, and Charles, against Murray's wishes, insisted on giving battle on Culloden Moor. Cumberland's army, with eighteen guns, was 9000 strong, well-fed and confident of victory. The Highlanders were half their number, exhausted by the night-march, and starving. A quarrel between the Macdonalds and the Athollmen as to the place of honour on the right added a further disadvantage to the Jacobite host fighting on open ground against troops specially trained to meet their methods of attack. Cumberland ran no risks. He drew up his army in three lines, the second in square formation to stop a rush if the first were broken. Galled by the artillery, the Highland right and centre under Murray charged and partially broke the first line, only to be enfiladed by musketry and grape, and the centre gave way. The Macdonalds on the left were prevented from closing by the artillery and the death of Keppoch, their leader. A dragoon charge on both flanks, despite the splendid gallantry of the Highland right, crumpled up the lines of the clansmen. In half an hour the battle was decided. Charles "was led off the field by those about him"; and as no rendezvous had been settled, the task of rallying the decimated forces fell to Murray, who succeeded in collecting about 1200 men at Ruthven. Culloden ended the rising.

April 26 Charles fled first to Lovat's house of Gortaleg, thence to the Castle of Glengarry; thence he escaped from Borrodale in a boat and commenced the wonderful wanderings which have immortalised the name of Flora Macdonald. The loyalty and devotion of the Highlanders to the hunted fugitive, in whose cause they had ruined themselves, would only be vulgarised by praise. To the men and women who kept the Prince's secret, chivalry and duty were one and the same thing. After five months of adventures and escapes, Charles, on September 20th, sailed for France with Lochiel from Loch-na-Uamh at Borrodale in Moidart, the precise place where he had landed in 1745; and Jacobitism as a serious political cause in British history ceased to exist. From that day until his death in 1788 the career of Charles Edward is a pitiful record of deterioration, of a man broken in fortune, character, and hopes, over whose life it is kindest to draw a veil.

It would be better for the fame of the conquerors could the crushing of the Rebellion have ended with April 16th, 1746. The completeness of the victory and the strength of the victors offered a golden opportunity to the mercy which can bring the richest rewards of constructive statesmanship. The important Act of 1747 (commonly called Hardwicke's), abolishing the feudal jurisdictions and social system of the clans and their chiefs, was a necessary and a wise step.[1] The vesting of the forfeited estates in the Crown, due mainly to the advice of President Forbes, was also a sound measure. But the Disarming Act, though cruelly enforced, was not effective, and the Act which proscribed the wearing of the Highland dress rested on the absurd assumption that the kilt, and not its wearers, had swept away the breeches at Killiecrankie, Prestonpans, and Falkirk. But the failure of the Government to combine with Hardwicke's Act the diversion of the military energies of the

---

[1] Cumberland was really right when he wrote: "If we had destroyed every man, such is the soil, rebellion would sprout again *should a new system of government not be found out*".

clansmen, by the formation of Highland regiments and a generous economic treatment of a poor semi-civilised country, delayed for a generation the absorption of the Highlands into the administrative and social system of Scotland. The execution of Lords Balmerino and Kilmarnock, of the rank and file taken in arms, was excusable, but a serious mistake. No one can regret that Lovat ended on the scaffold a career of matchless duplicity and villainy. Most will regret that a traitor as selfish as Lovat, and far more mean, Murray of Broughton, by turning King's evidence, lived to inherit a baronetcy. But the *régime* of vengeance was as stupid as it was cruel. The burning of villages and of crops, the shooting of prisoners in cold blood, the torture and floggings of men and women, the deliberate encouragement of tribal hatred by letting loose the loyal clans on the vanquished,—these and similar atrocities carried out by Cumberland's orders or with his connivance, cannot be condoned. "Butcher Cumberland" he was called by contemporaries, and Butcher Cumberland he will and must remain. The carnival of terrorism that he authorised did not exorcise the spirit of the Highlanders; it invested Jacobitism with the halo of martyrdom, and indelibly stained the fame of a soldier to whose courage and skill in an hour of failure and national peril the Hanoverian dynasty and Government were deeply indebted. Nor did the work of the Lord President, Duncan Forbes, whose energy, loyalty, and prudent advice did so much to keep Scotland for George II., ever receive the recognition it deserved. He had the courage to protest against the methods of Cumberland and his minions, and his death in 1747 marks the beginning of a new Scotland which as much as any man he had helped to inaugurate.[1]

The Jacobite rising had coincided with decisive changes in the European situation. The Emperor Charles VII. died and his son, Jan. 20, the new Elector of Bavaria, by the Treaty of Füssen came to 1745 terms with Maria Theresa. He agreed to accept the Pragmatic Sanction, withdraw from the war, and vote for Francis in the forthcoming imperial election. In return the validity of his father's imperial title was recognised and the Bavarian territories restored. To the disappointment of the French, one great object of Habsburg

---

[1] Cumberland spoke of him as "that old woman who talked to me of humanity" —quite in keeping with another memorable remark: "The laws of the country, my lord. I'll make a brigadier give laws, by God!"

policy was secured by Francis of Lorraine's election to the imperial
crown. But the other, the recovery of Silesia, was as far off as
ever. Frederick's victories at Friedberg, on the Sohr and at
Kesselsdorf, and his occupation of Dresden, led up to the Treaty
of Dresden which ended the second Silesian war and confirmed the
Prussian annexation of Silesia. The French victories at the
Netherlands, and defeat of the Sardinians at Bassignano, only
strengthened Frederick in his cool determination to be guided by
his own interests alone, and in the pressure of British diplomacy
at Vienna he had an ally, anxious to limit the war to a plain
struggle with France. But until July, 1746, Great Britain was not
in a position to give material support to Charles of Lorraine and
the Austrians in the Netherlands, and by that time the French had
taken Brussels, Antwerp, and Mons. The arrival of Ligonier and a
British contingent failed to stem the French advance. Namur
fell and Saxe inflicted a severe defeat on the allies at Raucoux
which ended the campaign for the year. Had the six British
battalions uselessly employed in a diversion to the coast of Brittany,
which ended in a discreditable failure, been sent to stiffen Ligonier's
force in Flanders, or to India, where Madras had been lost, they
might have achieved some valuable results. The Ministry, however, seemed more bent on defeating the King than their enemies,
and here their success was decisive.

The Pelhams desired to consolidate their administration by
offering office to Pitt. George, whose aversion from Pitt had not
cooled, aided by Granville's advice outside the Cabinet and Bath's
within it, stubbornly refused to give way. Whereupon, when
affairs in Scotland were still highly critical, the Pelham group resigned. The King promptly had recourse to Granville and Bath
who set about forming an administration. But "they had forgotten
one little point, which was to secure a majority in both houses".
The parliamentary solidarity of the Pelhams reinforced by the
Cobham group threatened the embryo Ministry with certain defeat.
In vain offices were offered in every quarter. The wits said that it
was not safe to walk the streets at night for fear of being pressed
for the Cabinet. The new Ministry flourished in the morning,
grew green at noon, and in the evening it was cut down and forgotten. Granville and Bath begged to be excused, and the Pelhams
resumed their places. Pitt became Vice-Treasurer of Ireland and

was shortly transferred to the Paymastership of the Forces. Created
a Privy Councillor "as yet he had no seat in the Cabinet". But he
had earned his promotion by his resolute support of the administration since Granville's fall. It is significant that he owed his place 1744
to that strength of the Whig oligarchy and their party organisation which the orator to the end loved to denounce. At the
same time Chesterfield succeeded Harrington as Secretary of State ;
and Henry Fox, the rival in debating power of Murray and Pitt,
became Secretary at War. George might well be alarmed and
embittered. For the first time a collective resignation had enforced two principles. Obviously no Ministry without the support of
a majority in the legislature could carry on public business, but
George had challenged the claim of his confidential servants to
dictate how the royal prerogative of appointment should be exercised, and he had been obliged to ask Ministers whom he had
practically dismissed to come back on their own terms, bringing with them a colleague highly distasteful to the Sovereign.
In Almon's words a constitutional King "must take into his
service those who have the greatest influence among his subjects".
The Pelhams too had not resigned merely to secure Pitt's inclu-
sion, but to prevent recourse to irresponsible politicians outside
the definite group of the Crown's recognised advisers. When
Harrington remarked that those who dictate in private should be
employed in public he protested, as did Burke later, against the
competition of a camarilla of King's Friends with the Cabinet, and
indicated (unconsciously perhaps) the relations between Sovereign
and Ministers indispensable for adapting the Cabinet to become
an effective organ of parliamentary government. But it would
be premature to see in Pelham's success a surrender of the
government-making power by the Crown to the House of Commons.
The part played by Parliament was purely passive. The Pelhams
were not a committee of a majority freely elected by independent
electors to an independent legislature. The creators rather than
the creation of a majority they had simply proved what a united
Ministry could do when it rested on the organised control of the
Lower House. The corollaries and consequences of this were
reserved for a later generation to work out and adopt.

In 1747 the victor of Culloden returned to Flanders, but the
hard-fought battle of Lauffeld, in which British cavalry and in- June 21

fantry acquitted themselves with signal distinction, was followed
by Cumberland's retreat, and though Maestricht was saved, Bergen-
op-Zoom fell to the French. Next spring Saxe, who saw that
"peace lay within the walls of Maestricht," laid siege to the fortress.
But the French suffered severely at sea. Hawke crushed one squadron off Cape Finisterre, and part of the enemy which escaped to
the West Indies was captured there ; Anson defeated another squadron off Belleisle. French maritime commerce was hard hit, and
after 1747 " the French flag did not appear at sea ". Yet Ministers
failed to utilise the offensive to the full. An expedition up the St.
Lawrence was delayed and finally countermanded. By 1748 the
nation was thoroughly sick of the war. Chesterfield's unwearied
advocacy of peace was strengthened by the lavish expenditure on
subsidies, the failure in the Low Countries, and the growing divergence in the objects of the allies. The French, beaten at sea, driven
from Italy, deserted by Prussia, and weakened by the accession of
1747   Ferdinand VI. in Spain, were ready to discuss terms. The prelim-
April 30   inaries, arranged without waiting for Austrian or Spanish consent,
Oct. 18   matured into the definitive Treaty of Aix-la-Chapelle, which was
subsequently joined by the Viennese Court after a formal and
public protest against the sacrifices imposed by its ally on the
House of Austria. Mutual restoration of conquests, with some
modifications, was the broad result. Spain confirmed the Assiento
and trading rights ; Madras was exchanged for Louisburg ; the
sea fortifications of Dunkirk were to be demolished ; the Austrian
Netherlands were evacuated by the French ; Silesia was assigned to
Prussia, Parma to Don Philip ; Francis was acknowledged Emperor,
and the Pragmatic Sanction guaranteed. Pitt's view that the peace
" was absolutely necessary for our well-being " can hardly be gain-
said, but Bismarck's description of the convention of Gastein, that it
"papered over the cracks," is eminently applicable. The Peace
registered important results on the Continent—the new power of
Prussia and the genius of Frederick the Great, the loss of Silesia, the
decadence of Holland, the extension of Bourbon power in Italy, the
resources available to the House of Austria within its hereditary
dominions. Ten years had profoundly modified the grouping and
interrelation of the Continental States. The Europe of 1748 was
very different from the Europe of the Third Treaty of Vienna
(1738); but the treaty indicated rather than solved the problems

which these changes had thrust upon statesmen. And for Great Britain in particular the crucial issues between the Bourbon powers and herself were left unsettled. Englishmen had good reason to be dissatisfied with the conduct and results of the war. "We were beat," said Bolingbroke, truly enough, "on every spot in which my Lord Marlborough had conquered." The burden of the national debt had been doubled ; our military weakness and lack of organisation had been conspicuous ; our naval efforts pointed to ineffective tactics and confused strategy. "The Government at sea," said a great Elizabethan, "hardly suffereth a head without exquisite experience." Great Britain had not adequately applied the offensive force that co-ordinated direction of, and strategical insight into, sea-power could have given her. And between the lines of the treaty could be read still more disquieting conclusions. The right of search, which had plunged us into war with Spain, was significantly ignored ; the door to the new markets was still locked. Of our claims—"as from God and Nature"—there was not a word. The Bourbon Courts of Paris, Madrid, Naples, and Parma dominated the Western Mediterranean, and the littoral of the Atlantic that looked across the ocean to the colonies beyond. The French plan to found an empire in India was neither frustrated, limited, nor accepted ; the ragged boundaries of Acadia were not defined ; Louisburg was restored to guard the St. Lawrence and menace the New England settlements ; there was nothing to check French schemes of expansion on the Mississippi and the Ohio, nor any attempt to stake out legitimate spheres of influence. The Dutch Alliance and the Barrier had proved worthless ; the Austrian Netherlands had been overrun and could be overrun again, and a prime object of British policy—the retention of "Belgium" in friendly hands—checkmated. The alliance with the House of Austria had proved costly and inadequate ; it had been maintained with increasing recriminations on both sides, and the peace was as unsatisfactory to Vienna as it was to Great Britain. Pitt's and Chesterfield's fierce criticisms had ascribed British failure to Hanoverianism, to the shrivelling of the imperial Crown under the Elector's cap, to the dependence of this country on a despicable German Elector. If Pitt meant that George II.'s Hanoverian bias was the main cause of the squandering of British lives and money to no purpose he was unjust both to George II. and to Carteret. But

Pitt's insistence on *English* measures must be interpreted more broadly. He was really indicting the inherent vices of the traditional system of foreign policy as understood by "the continental" school of Whigs, rather than the accidental vices of the men who worked that system. He was insisting that the true question was not, "for what is Great Britain fighting?" but, "for what *ought* Great Britain to fight?" The destinies of the British people turned on her imperial future; her interests were fundamentally colonial, maritime, commercial; their development lay, not in the blood-sodden fields of Flanders and Lombardy, the valleys of the Rhine and the Bohemian passes, but outside Europe, on the coast of Coromandel, in Bengal, in the hinterlands of the Alleghanies, and the vast basin of the Mississippi, where its headwaters reached out to the Great Lakes and the St. Lawrence. These were English objects, and they required English measures to keep them English. But if the criticisms of Pitt, imperfectly acquainted with the diplomatic factors of the Continent and inflated by rhetoric, were to be followed there must be a reconstruction of the system and a new scheme of political and imperial values, as well as a reconsideration of the objects of our foreign relations. The War of the Austrian Succession had ushered in a new age, and in Pitt was the incarnation of the awakened spirit and the consciousness of unsatisfied minds moving in Great Britain. But the new age and the new spirit had not yet moulded the principles that still dominated the mandarins of the Cockpit at Whitehall and the legislature at St. Stephen's. The Peace of Aix-la-Chapelle proclaimed for those who had eyes to see and ears to hear that the traditional system, the synthesis of principles and methods of William III. and Marlborough, of Stanhope, Walpole, Carteret, and Newcastle and Hardwicke was worn out. But old systems die hard, especially when they are consecrated by success in the past and are enshrined in the ends of organised parties. Great Britain was conscious of her failure, and she ascribed it to the men rather than to their principles. There was no clear warning how similar failure in the future could be averted. Pitt alone, perhaps—and Pitt was now silenced by office and the cessation of the strain brought by the peace—had concluded that a new system was urgently needed, and a new system implied new men touched to the gravity of the imperial problem in all its bearings, and gifted with the courage and constructive power to frame new measures. Before

ten years were out that new system did come and justify itself beyond expectation; for it started from a revolution in the State formation of Europe and it placed the British Empire in a new setting.
But the transition from the school of Carteret, Hardwicke, and
Newcastle to the gospel of Pitt was brought about more by the
inexorable pressure of the forces in Europe and the new world than
by a conscious conversion of the Whig leaders and the nation of
1748. The interest of the eight years that intervene between the
Peace of Aix-la-Chapelle and the Seven Years' War centres in the
nature and consequences of this process of evolution.

§ 2. The Diplomatic Revolution, 1748-1756. The Seven Years' War, 1750-1760

The war had brought to the front the imperial question.   In
the West Indies, in America, in India, British possessions were
menaced.   In America the Treaty of Utrecht had given Great
Britain Newfoundland, Hudson's Bay, and Acadia.   The British
settlements occupied the littoral eastwards of the Alleghany
Mountains; to the north was New France or Canada, to the south 1669 87
Spain, to the west a vast unexplored hinterland.   French exploration under La Salle had laid the basis of a claim by the French
Crown to all the lands called Louisiana, watered by the Mississippi;
and the idea of a great North American dominion from sea to sea,
from the Gulf of Mexico and the mouth of the Mississippi to the
mouth of the St. Lawrence and the Atlantic seaboard, linked up by 1718
the Ohio and the Great Lakes, steadily grew.   New Orleans pointed 1731·42
the way.   Verendrye carried on the work of penetrating to the main
lines of communication which would effectively encircle the British
settlement.   Acadia meanwhile was not delimited.   What were "the
ancient boundaries" of the treaty?   Nova Scotia alone? or did they
include the modern New Brunswick and part of Maine to the south?
The French relied on keeping the loyalty of the Acadians and
fortifying Louisburg in the Isle Royale.   Then in 1744 came open
war.   Colonial sentiment was determined Acadia should not fall
back to the French.   Thanks to William Shirley, Governor of Massachusetts, and with the aid of a naval squadron under Warren,
Louisburg, "the Dunkirk of North America," "the pride and
terror of these Northern seas," capitulated.   "Good Lord," said a
New England pastor, "we have so much to thank Thee for that

time will be too short and we must leave it to eternity." But the
conquest of Canada was abandoned and a French counterstroke
failed in 1746. Frontier raids went on till the end of the war,
when Louisburg, to the disgust of the colonials, was restored to
France. It was clear that the struggle for supremacy between the
French and British peoples, between the French and British systems
of colonisation, had only begun. Whatever might happen in
Europe, La Salle's dream of a great North American Empire was
more than a dream to French brains at Quebec and Montreal; the
policy of peaceful penetration would be pushed, whatever Versailles
might say. To the British colonies, rapidly growing in population
and wealth, it was a matter of life and death to secure the right to
expand westwards uncontrolled by political foes and a rival
civilisation. The French population of Canada was a handful
compared with the million and a half of British colonists. If North
America became French it would be because France, not Canada,
was superior to Great Britain in Europe and in the strategic area
across the ocean. The issue for the British colonists therefore lay
primarily upon the water. If the communications between Quebec
and Brest were cut, Canada might remain French, but the vastly
superior numbers of the British colonists would keep North America
south of the Great Lakes for the British Empire. The capture of
Louisburg, Anson's defeat, off Finisterre, of the French squadron

1747

destined for Canada, revealed the capacity of sea-power both to
menace the existence of the French and to provide the British
colonies with the means to achieve their own salvation. But
neither continental campaigns nor continental alliances which made
the mainland of Europe the strategic centre of our efforts would
solve the imperial problem. And the old strategy, false because it
was the outcome of a worn-out system of policy, if persisted in
might easily end in an imperial disaster, beyond repair.

The same plain moral could be drawn from the situation in
India. In 1702 the two rival companies trading to the East Indies
had been amalgamated. The English were now established at three
presidential centres, Madras, Bombay, Fort William (Calcutta), with
auxiliary factories at Surat and Patna. These three centres broadly
provided three possible spheres of commerce and political influence,
the Carnatic, the Mahratta area, and the Ganges basin and Bengal.
The French, who had replaced the Dutch as our leading rival

were similarly established at three main points, Pondicherry, Chandernagore, and Mahé. In 1707 the break up of the Mogul Empire, consequent on the death of Aurangzib, led to the formation of the chief political areas with which the French and the British in the eighteenth century would have to deal—the Deccan and the Carnatic, the Mahratta confederacy, 1720-50 (the successors of Sivaji— the Peishwa, Sindhia, Holkar, and Gaikwar), the kingdoms of Bengal and Oudh with Rajputana lying beyond. The real struggle for supremacy in India between the representatives of European States begins in the Carnatic in 1741, when Dupleix was governor of Pondicherry. Thanks to his genius and organising power the French in India as in North America were first in the field with clearly conceived principles and a plan. Dupleix saw that Europeans could create for themselves a political lever by judicious and decisive interference in the rivalries of the native rulers and states, that native troops under European officers and discipline could be made a potent instrument for building up organised spheres of influence. Furthermore, if the English could be ousted a commercial and political monopoly must fall to those who ousted them. It therefore was the duty and the interest of the French first to crush the British company and then to expel the English and thus lay the foundations of a great French Empire. The French started with the great advantage of possessing in Mauritius outside the Indian peninsula a naval station, strategically situated to provide the government in Europe with means for supporting offensively and defensively the efforts in the East. What Louisburg was to the St. Lawrence, Mauritius could be to the Carnatic. In 1746, with the aid of La Bourdonnais from Mauritius, Madras was captured. Though the attack on Fort St. David failed (thanks to Stringer 1748 Lawrence and Boscawen's fleet) the counter-attack on Pondicherry had been repulsed. And the peace of 1748 gave Madras back to the East India Company. But the struggle would not end with this drawn game. Dupleix was a man of genius ; his diplomatic ability in dealing with the natives, and his defeat of the Nawab's 1746 troops by trained sepoys, had brought great prestige to the French. His partial success proved that his interpretation and methods were sound and that a higher degree of combination and perseverance would bring more substantial rewards. As in North America, the gravity of the position for the British Company lay in their rivals'

8

scientific grasp of the problem as a whole, the extent and character of their ambitions, and the skill with which their methods could be applied. Would the English be able to pit against the French equal ability and superior resources? Clearly, as in North America, the purely local effort could not be decisive. The command of the sea must be settled by the home governments, and the command of the sea would decide the fate of the French and British in India. True, the mastery of the Carnatic or Bengal would not necessarily fall to the power that controlled the Atlantic and the Mediterranean; but, as between European rivals for that mastery, the power that could prevent reinforcements of ships, men, and money reaching India and provide a superiority of force in the Bay of Bengal or the Indian Ocean could prevent any European country from disputing its right to establish itself in India. The character and ability of the men on the spot must then decide whether and how a European dominion could be built on the ruins of the Mogul Empire.

The eight years that precede the outbreak of the war for Empire are great years in India and North America and in Europe, but they are not great in English political life. The plain lessons enforced by the peace of 1748 were not grasped by the men at home, absorbed in domestic politics and the complicated and repellent intrigues for place and power. Some useful work in finance and legislation was accomplished, but for the most part the age of the Pelhams is a record of neglected opportunities and misused resources. The Empire evaded irreparable disaster by the fortunate accident that the Court of Versailles was still more completely corroded by intrigue, quite as incompetent to interpret the true interests of its subjects, and quite as ignorant of the essential facts. And in Great Britain the morale of the country was sound; it had not been sapped by a profligate and extravagant despot, a corrupt and persecuting Church, or a functionless, atrophied, and demoralised aristocracy. In 1763, as in 1870, France paid the price that is sternly exacted from nations devoid of the strength to endure their self-made vices, or to provide remedies for them. The blunders of her diplomacy were significant rather of a bankruptcy of character than of a famine of ability in the ruling class. The three first-rate men she produced, Dupleix, Montcalm, and Choiseul, were not permitted to save her. But the tale is different at Vienna and Berlin. With

1748 Kaunitz, pronounced by Frederick the Great to be so frivol-
ous in his tastes, so profound in his judgments, began the work
which prolonged the rule of the Austrian Habsburgs into the
twentieth century.   And in Maria Theresa, Kaunitz had a royal
collaborator who was a noble woman, as free as any eighteenth
century ruler from the vices and defects of her age.   The contrast
between the courts of St. James and Versailles and the court of
Berlin is dramatically complete.   Lethargy, pessimism, blurred
vision, are set in clear-cut antithesis against Argus-eyed vigilance
and sleepless energy.   Frederick was indeed earning the honour of
being, as he asked to be, the first servant of his kingdom ; by his
genius for self-sacrifice he created the historic mission of the House
of Hohenzollern.   That Prussia preserved her independence against
the coalition of Bourbon, Habsburg, and Romanov, and came to
be one of the capital formative forces of the modern European
world, was largely the work of the wonderful eleven years crowded 1745-56
with the scientific reforms, and inspired by the passionless patriotism, of her King.   Frederick the Great is not a lovable character,
perhaps, but his gospel, first forced on himself, proclaimed the creed
of knowledge, self-denial, and national discipline.   He presents a
rare combination of high statesmanship with military and administrative abilities of the first order.   He enriched Europe with a
new and much-needed conception of kingship, the absolutism of
the enlightened and royal expert, with a new ideal of national life
expressed in a new type of State.   That these were a challenge,
then and since, to the ideals of liberty, law, and self-government,
which Englishmen after their own fashion were struggling to realise
for Great Britain, should not blind us to their intrinsic value nor
to the comprehensive contribution that the Hohenzollern State,
moulded by Frederick the Great, has added to the science of
government and the civilisation of Europe.

From 1748-54 the Ministry under Henry Pelham enjoyed
comparative quiet.   Henry Pelham's main achievement was in
finance.   The credit of Great Britain was so good and the available supply of capital seeking investment so abundant that the
burden of the National Debt was considerably reduced by a consolidation scheme.   In 1750 the interest on fifty-four and a half
millions of debt was reduced (to $3\frac{1}{2}$ per cent. up to 1757, and
to 3 per cent. after that date).   The total saving amounted to

rather more than a quarter of a million per annum up to 1757, and
to rather more than half a million afterwards. Next year nine
separate loans were formed into a consolidated stock at 3 per
cent. The success of the proposal was seen in the rise of the three
per cent. stock to 106½. Thus within three years of a long war,
which had crippled most European States, Great Britain proved
that she could reduce her financial obligations and compel her
creditors to accept a lowered rate of remuneration. Policy was
chiefly controlled by an inner group of three, Pelham himself, his
brother, Newcastle, and Hardwicke. To Newcastle, besides foreign
affairs, fell the acceptable task of organising, within and without
Parliament, the party which kept the Ministry in power. And
Newcastle's energy (recorded in nearly six hundred MS. volumes)
in arranging patronage and places, in carrying on a vast correspondence on every conceivable subject, from the high issues of imperial
policy to the most pettifogging details of the party machine, in
registering every whisper and confiding every fear to paper, has
stamped on him the character of the brainless busybody, always in
the way and always out of it, which with all his defects is unjust
to his real if second-rate abilities and his genuine devotion to the
public service. So long as Henry Pelham lived the changes and
events were singularly unimportant at home. Pitt accepted the
administration. If in 1751, " being ten years older, he had considered public affairs more coolly," he formally abandoned the views
expressed in 1739 on the right of search,[1] he also permitted himself
the luxury of voting with Lyttelton against the reduction of seamen
from ten to eight thousand men, on the ground apparently that
" the fleet was our standing army ". In 1751 the deaths of the
Prince of Wales and of Bolingbroke broke the political power of
the Leicester House party. The intimacy of Bute with the dowager
Princess of Wales, and that lady's desire to counterbalance the
predominant influence of the King's mistress, Lady Yarmouth, by
continuing the Leicester House tradition, were significant for the
future. But so long as the Pelhams kept the talents of the Whigs
comfortably provided in the ministerial coach, Egmont, Lee, Cotton,
and Bubb Doddington, who were the foremost of the Leicester
House opposition, were not formidable.

The removal of the Prince of Wales, however, enhanced the

[1] Parl. Hist., xiv., 798-803, and *cf.* Hist. MSS. Comm. Rept., x., App. i., 212-21.

importance of the Duke of Cumberland, who already had his
"group" of which Henry Fox was the ablest, most unscrupulous,
and most ambitious member. Newcastle also, long bent on getting
rid of "the Bloomsbury gang," succeeded in 1751 in displacing the
Duke of Bedford, and the Earl of Sandwich, personally profligate,
and a mediocre head of the admiralty. These two henceforward were
reckoned in the Cumberland party, which also included Albemarle
and Hanbury Williams. Holdernesse succeeded Bedford as Secretary
of State, and Granville came back to the Cabinet as Lord President, holding the office until his death in 1763. The Reform of
the Calendar introduced by Chesterfield, and Hardwicke's Marriage 1751
Act were useful legislative reforms ; [1] the foundation of the British 1753
Museum by Henry Pelham is also notable, but the repeal of the Act 1753
permitting the naturalisation of the Jews passed in the previous
session was not unfairly described by Temple as due " to disaffection
clothed in superstition ". Fox had shown his debating power in his
criticisms of the Regency Bill of 1751 ; and his strenuous opposition
to the Marriage Act, sometimes held to be the one example of con-
scientious conviction in his career apart from his determination to
make a fortune and win a peerage, cost him Hardwicke's friendship.

When Henry Pelham died in 1754 the King might well exclaim 1754
" Now I shall have no more peace ". Pelham, like Liverpool later,
without commanding personality or ability, had the gift of keeping
together under his leadership colleagues of very diverse characters
and conflicting ambitions. The selection of his successor was left
to the Cabinet by George II., and by judicious and persevering
management Newcastle engineered his own nomination. The Duke,
who was the one colleague whom his late brother had never satisfied,
succeeded to the First Lordship of the Treasury. He had three
marked qualifications for the post, an unrivalled official experience
of public business, a disciplined corps of Parliamentary janissaries,
the devoted friendship of Hardwicke, a great lawyer with a sane
judgment in political affairs. But Newcastle could not be in the
Commons ; his jealousy of his colleagues in the royal closet
and cabinet amounted to a disease ; and he was determined to reserve all patronage and control of the governmental machinery in his
own hands. A lieutenant in the Lower House was indispensable.
There were three and only three men who could adequately fill the

[1] See p. 191.

place, Murray, Fox, and Pitt. Murray's ambitions were legal. A powerful debater and a fine intellect, he aimed at high judicial office. Unpopular as a Scotchman, of dubious Whiggism, and on bad terms with Hardwicke, he now became Attorney-General. Fox, whom the political world regarded as the possible head of a Ministry, had been reconciled to Newcastle's promotion by an understanding that he was to be made Secretary of State; but though ready to waive the management of the Secret Service Fund "further than was necessary to enable him to speak to members without appearing ridiculous," he discovered that Newcastle intended him to be a complete cipher, and, indignant at the breach of faith, refused to accept the seals. This unnecessary affront to a man of great ability, who neither forgave nor forgot grievances, was Newcastle's first serious blunder. Legge, who had marked ability for finance, but was not comparable to Murray, Fox, and Pitt as a debater, became Chancellor of the Exchequer, while Thomas Robinson, a second-rate diplomatist whose principles in foreign policy commended him to the King, and who was willing to play the docile understudy to Newcastle, was given the seals refused by Fox, and required to lead the House of Commons. George Grenville was made Treasurer of the Navy; Lyttelton, Cofferer of the Household. Pitt was passed over, *i.e.* he remained Paymaster-General. Newcastle and Hardwicke elaborately explained that the strength of the King's hostility was an insuperable bar to his promotion, and that by giving office to three of his "connection" (Legge, Grenville, and Lyttelton) they had done their best to meet his views, and Pitt was obliged to accept the explanation.[1] For eight years he had worked as a supporter of the Pelhams; he was conscious of his powers, and this "painful and too visible humiliation" was a bitter mortification. Yet the general election showed how little the personal rivalries of the narrow political world affected the constituencies. If the evidence can be trusted, there was no lack of bribery and corruption, but only forty-two seats were contested and the Administration obtained a solid majority. George with Robinson as Secretary perhaps felt "himself in the very Elysium of Herrenhausen," but Newcastle speedily discovered that it was easier

---

[1] "The weight," Pitt wrote, "of immovable royal displeasure is a load too great to move under; it must crush any man; it has sunk and broke me. I succumb and wish for nothing but a decent and innocent retreat" (*Chatham Cor.* i., 105).

to vamp up an Administration than to carry it on. The ministerial rank and file might be willing to vote as they were told, yet "a Minister in the closet for the House of Commons" was required, and with subsidy treaties ahead and foreign affairs daily growing more critical, policy required defence more than votes. It is characteristic of Newcastle's "system" which made the House "an assembly of atoms," and the prevailing political conventions that Fox, the Secretary at War, and Pitt, the Paymaster-General, openly defied their chief. Fox, with Cumberland's powerful influence with the King behind him, and Pitt, who had begun to renew his suspended connection with Leicester House (where the Princess of Wales under Bute's direction desired to be a thorn in the flesh of the King's advisers and to checkmate Cumberland) informally allied to flout and jeer. The unhappy Robinson, "the jackboot to lead us" of Pitt's contemptuous phrase, was made ridiculous, and Murray was severely handled, "else we should sit only to register the edicts of one too powerful a subject." The King, whose aversion from Pitt was strengthened by this cool mutiny, would have dismissed him, but Newcastle instead, after many palpitations, decided to surrender to Windsor Lodge. Fox was brought into the Cabinet, Dec. 12, but, "with no special power or confidence outside the Ministers," 1754 shortly was made one of the Lord Justices, and eleven months later took Robinson's place as Secretary of State, Robinson returning to the Mastership of the Wardrobe with a pension. The Dukes of Marlborough and Rutland, two other members of the Cumberland group, were given the Privy Seal and Lord Stewardship respectively. Overtures to Pitt failed. He demanded "an office of execution as well as of advice," "with habitual, frequent, familiar access to the Crown" (the very idea of which put Newcastle in a paroxysm of panic) and as the First Lord wanted "lieutenants," not "generals." Pitt curiously enough was permitted to continue to trumpet his sedition. Newcastle had made his second great blunder. True he had separated Fox from Pitt—after May, 1755, the quarrel between them was an open one—but he had allied with the man who must now "either be First Minister or ruined," a politician who, as events proved, would keep the recent bargain just so long as he judged it served his interests. The famous comparison of the coalition to the junction of the Rhone and the Saône was as felicitous as it was true. Chesterfield's comment too hit the mark. Newcastle, he said, had turned every one else out and now he had turned himself out. On Fox's part it was a blunder also. He showed himself a fine party organiser and a good administrator. But office gave him too little power to control policy in accordance with his and Cumberland's ideas, too much to escape responsibility for the disasters that wrecked the Administration. By union with Pitt, some patience, and more tact, he could have dictated his own terms and formed a strong Fox-Pitt Ministry. In Parliament, however, at first things went well. Despite Legge's revolt and growing public resentment, Fox with Newcastle's organisation secured the defeat of the amendment to the address (condemning the subsidy treaties to Russia and Hesse) by 311 votes to 105. Newcastle's charity or cowardice had reached its limit. The quarrelsome Legge, Pitt himself, and George Grenville were dismissed. The rift in "the Cousinhood" was made final by the acceptance of the Chancellorship of the Exchequer by Lyttelton, "who stumbled over millions and strode pompously over farthings".

Between Pitt and the Ministry there could now be no truce. His indictment of their continental system cut down to the quick of the imperial problem. Ministers as men might be competent, but their system and measures were in his view the root of the mischief. Pitt's immortal declaration later to the Duke of Devonshire: "I can save this country and no one else can," sums up his unshakable conviction that, unless there was a radical revolution in the principles and methods and objects of ministerial action, "within two years his majesty will not be able to sleep in St. James for the cries of a bankrupt people". And by November, 1755, the imperial problem could no longer be burked. In India, Dupleix had pushed with great skill his plan of operations. By December, 1749, Dupleix's two candidates—Chanda Sahib to the throne of the Carnatic, Muzaffar Jang to the Nizamship of the Deccan—held the field, and on the latter's death the French nominee, Salabat Jang, succeeded. French influence threatened to control the native States south of the Deccan. But precisely at the critical hour an Englishman of genius, Robert Clive, came forward. Born in 1725, the son of an impoverished country squire, he had as a boy been "out of measure addicted to fighting"—a taste to be gratified pretty fully in manhood. In 1744 he went out to Madras as a writer in the Company's service, and twice, in a sullen despair, made

attempts on his own life. In 1746 as a prisoner he had been
paraded at Pondicherry, and had shown great courage under Boscawen in the attack on Pondicherry and the attack on Devikota. 1748
He now made a diversion to relieve the siege of Trichinopoly by
seizing Arcot and holding it triumphantly against Chanda Sahib's Aug. 31-
forces. The moral effect was immense, and the brilliant defence of Nov. 15
Arcot has been generally held to be the turning-point in the
development of British power in India. It was followed by a
victory at Arni, the recapture of Conjeveram, another victory at
Kaveripauk, and the destruction of Dupleix Fatihabad. Clive and
Stringer Lawrence then relieved Trichinopoly, and the surrender of
Chanda Sahib's forces and the assassination of Chanda Sahib himself left the British nominee, Mohammed Ali, undisputed Nawab of
the Carnatic. Two years later Dupleix was recalled, a memorable
act of stupidity and ingratitude, for neither Versailles nor the
directors of the French Company understood his greatness nor how
much he had accomplished for France. The Governors of Madras
and Pondicherry meanwhile had agreed for the time being to ab-
stain from interference in the affairs of the native States. But
the struggle was far from being over. Bussy, the able French officer
who had assisted Dupleix, and who saw that the French might still
succeed, had since 1751 made himself supreme at the Court of
Salabat Jang at Haidarabad. In the coming war in Europe a
blow for Empire might yet be struck. Clive had in 1753 returned
to England and attempted to enter home politics. But the
defender of Arcot was destined not to enter on the scuffle for place
and power at St. Stephen's, but to become the architect of an
Empire in the East. His excursion into politics swallowed up his
savings, and Britain's good fortune provided that he should be un-
seated on petition for St. Michael's in Cornwall.[1] Accordingly, he 1768
was ready to go back to India, where work that no one could do so
well as himself awaited him.

The situation in America was far more unfavourable. The
French had been pursuing their plan of securing the line of the
Ohio, in order to connect Louisiana with the Great Lakes and
Canada, and in 1749 Céleron de Bienville's mission showed that
they were in earnest. The formation of a British Ohio Company as

[1] One of the successful candidates was Simon Luttrell, the father of the famous
and successful candidate against Wilkes in the Middlesex election.

a counter-stroke was spoilt by the mutual jealousy of Virginia and Pennsylvania, and in 1752 the French proceeded to attack the Miamis, on the Miami River, who traded with the British and sided with them. Next year the French planted two forts, one at Presque Isle (the modern Erie), the other Fort Le Boeuf, on the Alleghany River, thus commanding the sources of the Ohio and securing the connection through Lake Erie with the French centres in Canada. Thence it would be the next step to push down the Alleghany and Monongahela Rivers and by a chain of forts block Virginia and Pennsylvania from spreading west of the Alleghany Mountains. Dinwiddy, the governor of Virginia, was alive to the danger. In November he selected George Washington, who first steps into history as the representative of the imperial claims of the British Crown, to warn the French that they were intruding on a hinterland claimed for the British flag. Following Washington a detachment was despatched to build a rival fort at the junction of the Mononga-hela and Alleghany; but the French overpowered the colonists and established in its place Fort Duquesne, which was intended to hold the ground for Louis XV. Washington, established at Fort

1754 Necessity in the Alleghanies, was attacked and obliged to surrender, while the French returned, conscious that they had driven their rivals back behind the mountains to the east.

Nova Scotia had been as great a cause of anxiety as the Ohio valley. Louisburg, restored to France by the treaty of 1748, had been refortified more strongly than ever; partly to be a counterpoise, partly to help in maintaining British control of Nova Scotia, the town of Halifax, named after the President of the Board of Trade,

1749 was directly founded by the home Government and provided with colonists, financed from Imperial funds. From 1748-51 a boundary commission appointed to settle the long-disputed question of the delimitation of Nova Scotia wrangled and haggled at Paris to little or no purpose. The French established themselves at Fort Beau-séjour on the mainland, and under the guidance of Le Loutre, the Vicar-General of Acadia (Nova Scotia), aimed at seducing the Acadians, who were British subjects, from their political allegiance. Fort Lawrence, on the Eastern side, was accordingly built to pro-tect the British territory. By 1754 the situation had become in-tolerable. The French and their Indians utilised every opportunity to harass the British authorities and to prevent the Acadians from settling down as peaceable British citizens. The English governors were obliged to prohibit them from emigrating to the French colonies, and it was clear that if opportunity occurred the French meant to oust the British from the territory ceded in 1713.

In that momentous year 1754, under imperial inspiration, a conference was held at Albany, in which Franklin put forward a scheme of colonial federation. On its failure to secure colonial assent, Dinwiddy perceived that if the French menace was to be averted, and the future development of the British settlements safeguarded, direct help from the home Government was indispensable. He therefore appealed to Newcastle's Ministry. The need was primarily colonial and local, but it raised far-reaching issues of Imperial and European policy. Under the pressure of the Cumberland group, and Cumberland himself, the home Ministry decided to send out General Braddock, a " Cumberland man," with two regiments, whose duty was to win back the Monongahela valley and penetrate to the Ohio; and in January, 1755, the reinforcement sailed from Cork. The Governments at Versailles and St. James were at peace, and Newcastle's ministry claimed that they were entitled to aid British subjects in the defence of British territory and colonial frontiers. This soothing fiction, not out of harmony with prevailing ideas as to the relations of rival colonies to rival mother-countries, could only work if, first, the French Government did not reply by a similar stroke with a similar plausible plea, and, secondly, if the British Ministry did really mean to do no more than they said. It broke down completely because neither British nor French in North America would acquiesce in a restoration of the *status quo*, even if that had been a possible solution, which, given the natural forces of French and British expansion, it was not. The French quite legitimately meant to pen the British into the coast-line ; the British quite as legitimately knew there could be no peace until at least the enveloping chain of French forts in the Ohio basin was severed and disarmed. Able and vigorous heads in the British colonies—Shirley, Johnson, Dinwiddy, Franklin—with colonial sentiment behind them, were convinced that the French power must be broken in the north as well as in the west. Able and vigorous heads at home, with national sentiment on their side, had come to the same conclusion. Cumberland and his group, of whom Henry Fox was now a Cabinet Minister, desired to expel the French neck and crop, and on strategic, political, and commercial grounds to make the war in America, so plainly inevitable. a purely maritime and colonial struggle.   In the autumn of 1754 Braddock's expedition came to the war party in the Cabinet as a convenient opportunity to advance their policy and force the hands of the Newcastle group.   When in the spring of 1755 the French Government prepared to reply by despatching a fleet of eighteen vessels and 3000 troops, and a new Governor of Canada, De Vaudreuil, the strictly colonial struggle merged into the wider and complicated problem of the relations of France to Great Britain, and the offensive and defensive powers of the two European States, as members of the European system.   The issues were joined in America.   They might be resolved by diplomacy or by force.   But in either case the result would not be determined solely by the local factors outside Europe.   France and Great Britain had European allies, obligations, ambitions, and vulnerable points.   Diplomacy and war cannot be separated into water-tight compartments.   For England the imperial issue was primarily and ultimately a problem that went to the heart of her system of foreign relations in Europe.

The Peace of Aix-la-Chapelle had bequeathed two European problems—the struggle between Hohenzollern and Habsburg, symbolised in the struggle for Silesia ; the duel between France and Great Britain—and two well-defined groupings of the leading Powers.   France and Prussia were united by a treaty of alliance, which would expire in March, 1756.   In opposition to them was the historic connection of Great Britain, Holland, and the House of Austria.   The equally historic enmity of Bourbon and Habsburg had been once more exemplified by the War of the Austrian Succession.   Maria Theresa and Frederick were primarily interested in the Silesian question, Great Britain and France in colonial and extra-European questions.   But the existing diplomatic agreements, resting on defensive alliances and reciprocal guarantees, involved France indirectly in the Silesian, the House of Austria indirectly in Britain's colonial complications.   A colonial war which made France the aggressor in Europe of Great Britain would bring the Empress in on the side of England.   Outside these Powers, Russia had broken with France, hated Prussia, and was friendly to Vienna and London.   It could, therefore, by judicious diplomacy under the existing conditions, be made available against the Bourbon system.

But the development of natural tendencies very soon pointed, so far as London and Vienna were concerned, to a readjustment of Austro-British relations.   Maria Theresa smarted under the losses of 1748 ; she was convinced that Frederick, not Louis XV., was the irreconcilable and dangerous foe, and she felt that England was a selfish ally who had deserted her in the end as well as forced her throughout the previous war to a line of action humiliating, dishonourable, and costly.   In short, as Kaunitz and others saw, a reform of Austrian policy was as desirable as a reform of the Austrian machinery of government.   Kaunitz had already urged the importance of securing the neutrality or friendship of France ; and though when he went to Paris as ambassador in 1750 the advice was academic, it rested on the sound principle that the Empress's engagements should be determined by purely Austrian interests.   Kaunitz did not desire to dissolve the traditional connection with England, but, by weaning France from Prussia, to isolate the latter.   To recover Silesia and re-establish the Habsburg hegemony in Germany—this was his ambition and Maria Theresa's also.   There was nothing necessarily or pointedly anti-British in such objects.   But Kaunitz forgot that Great Britain, too, was thoroughly dissatisfied with the results of the Austrian alliance.   Her interests were peace in Europe, the balance of power, and the expansion of her colonial and commercial empire.   France was the enemy.   But against France, Austrian aid had proved a disappointment.   Recriminations, suspicion, mistrust, tension had marred the co-operation of the allies.   Continental engagements, Hanoverianism, subsidies leading to the conquest of Flanders by Saxe, stank in the nostrils of the British public. British statesmen felt, as Frederick said of his ally's (France's) efforts, that they might as well have been made on the Scamander.   They expected Austrian troops, if financed from Parliament, to cover Hanover and protect the Netherlands.   What was Silesia to them or they to Silesia ?   In short, a clear divergence between the vital interests of both States was now apparent which did not necessarily involve a dissolution of the alliance, but eminently called on both sides for a redefinition of the terms and objects of the partnership.

Unfortunately the British Ministers in power failed in the essentials of their task.   Conscious that their country's differences with France were drifting into war, they did not see that a struggle also between Maria Theresa and Frederick could not be indefinitely postponed. Clogged by Whig traditions, they assumed that the Austrian alliance would hold good, and that if they manœuvred aptly so as to be the attacked, not the aggressors, in Europe, Austrian forces would, as of old, defend the Netherlands and withstand the French on the Rhine. They made no serious effort to remove by diplomacy at headquarters the colonial difficulties. Worse still, with the plain moral of the late war before them, they made no attempt to reorganise the military and naval forces of the empire or repair the patent defects in the military machine. From 1748-51 Newcastle dabbled in a grandiose German scheme of buying the election of Joseph (II.) as King of the Romans by subsidies to Bavaria and Saxony, and thereby proving the identity of British and Austrian objects on the Continent. Yet how deep-rooted the British aversion from the subsidy system really was came out in 1755 as soon as a colonial war appeared certain. Peace had obliterated in Newcastle and his colleagues the lessons of Carteret's fall and Pitt's gospel of *English* measures. And until 1755 the preacher was silent. He accepted the Bavarian and Saxon subsidies without a murmur. And France was equally quiescent— in Europe. But (it was not lost on the lynx-eyed toiler at Berlin) the Austrian point of view was altering, her objective taking shape. Kaunitz in 1753 became Chancellor. The Treaty of Aranjuez with Spain guaranteed the *status quo* in Italy. Russia was notoriously hostile to Prussia. Saxony could be won. The league against Frederick was already in the making, and if France could only be detached the doom of Prussia might be sealed. Differences with Great Britain, over the Barrier Treaty and commercial privileges in the Netherlands, strengthened the Empress's interpretation of British policy and her reluctance to be embroiled in the Franco-British struggle which would deflect her forces from the vital issue with Prussia.

By despatching Braddock, ministers had taken a serious step. Mirepoix, the French ambassador in London, was engaged in endeavouring to maintain the peace, but while Newcastle was sending casks of beer and his humble duty to Madame de Pompadour, Fox, Granville, and the war party got the upper hand and his April 21 Government had taken a still more serious step. Boscawen was despatched on April 29th with instructions to stop and capture the French squadron conveying Vaudreuil and the French reinforcements to Quebec. The French ultimatum claiming the whole of the Acadian territory was rejected, and another fleet under Hawke was in preparation. Newcastle's absurd idea apparently was " to strike such a blow upon French trade as would make the whole kingdom cry out against war," as if a proud and undefeated nation such as the French would crumple up because in time of peace two or three hard blows were treacherously struck without warning. War was now inevitable, and Ministers, firmly convinced that Great Britain could not cope single-handed with France, pushed on their diplomatic negotiations. The day before Boscawen sailed, George, in agony for Hanover, defied his Cabinet and left for the Continent, where very shortly an Anglo-Hessian Convention was arranged ; while lavish bribery at St. Petersburg secured the Tsarina's promise to protect Hanover by attacking Prussia if Frederick moved. It only remained to clinch a settlement with Vienna, and the ministerial plan of a great defensive ring of alliances against France, which would pass into an offensive confederation, if France moved.

But the plan collapsed. To the British demands for 25,000 men, and the protection of Hanover and the Netherlands, the Viennese Court replied with an angry despatch and an offer of 10,000 alone. There must be a new commercial treaty, and England must June 12 be responsible for the defence of the Netherlands. From this virtual ultimatum it was clear that Austria declined to make her quarrel with Frederick subsidiary to the maritime struggle with France, and that Great Britain, by refusing these terms, declined to commit herself to extensive German operations for Austrian objects. Boscawen, too, failed to cut off Vaudreuil. He captured two small June 9 vessels, the *Alcide* and *Lys*, and the rest escaped. In plain words, England incurred all the odium of the stroke and none of the advantages. Braddock's expedition too ended in disaster. The rough martinet, brave as a lion, trained in the pipe-clay tactics which might succeed at Fontenoy or Roucoux, was a child in backwood fighting. Badly supported by Virginia and Pennsylvania in his march against Fort Duquesne he was entrapped on the Monongahela by the French and Indians, himself killed, and his forces cut to pieces. In the rout, as Washington put it, you might as well have tried to stop the wild bears of the mountains. "Another time," Braddock murmured before he died, " we shall know better how to deal with them." Washington, with 1500 Virginian militia, was left to face a terrible frontier war. Shirley's advance against Ontario succeeded only in garrisoning the important post of Oswego ; while Johnson, advancing against Ticonderoga and Crown Point after repelling an attack in which Dieskau was taken prisoner, contented himself with establishing two forts, Fort Edward on the Hudson, Fort William Henry on Lake George. The French base at Ticonderoga for an advance southwards was thus left intact. In Acadia alone a decisive step had been made. Beauséjour was captured and renamed Fort Cumberland, and the territory on both sides of the isthmus passed into British hands. To complete the stroke the Acadians were now deported, a cruel but essential part of the colonial policy of breaking the French power in North America. The deportation, depicted with a poet's pathos in " Evangeline," and also a poet's disregard of the whole truth, can only be defended on the ground that half-measures had hitherto failed, and that nations at bay in a struggle for supremacy, into which warring creeds of religion and race enter, will be driven to subordinate mercy to security.

July 22   Mirepoix' recall proclaimed the open rupture between France and Great Britain. Hawke's fleet, which Newcastle had wished to use against French trade ("vexing your neighbour," as Granville put it, "for a little muck"), had put to sea with contradictory instructions which " bound it to a violation of peace and were a travesty of war ". If the result was a sweeping up of French commerce by the end of the year it did nothing to solve the pressing strategic and diplomatic problem. England must now come to terms with France or fight it out. But a settlement which would involve reparation for the " piratical " acts of Boscawen and Hawke and acceptance of the French claims in America was impossible. Such terms could not have been enforced on the colonists, and the suggestion of surrender, in the temper of the nation, would have hurled the Ministry from power. Ministers were aware that a continental system was becoming more and more unpopular.[1] But in their straits they procured the ratification of the Anglo-Hessian Convention, and pressed the conclusion of the Anglo-Russian Treaty. The Dutch had practically declined to move, so that continental support was a greater necessity than ever.

[1] " Sea-war, no continent, no subsidy is the universal cry " (*Newcastle Papers*, July 25th, B. M. Add. MS. 32,857).

When in November the treaties were triumphantly carried in Parliament, Pitt, Legge, and Grenville had been dismissed, and Fox was Secretary of State, the situation had further cleared. Austrian overtures to France had resulted in secret conferences at Paris. At Paris, as at London, it was understood that Spain Sept. meant to remain neutral. Frederick was still the French ally. What a stroke it would be to detach the Empress from George II.! But the vanity of Louis XV., the Pompadour's influence, and the incompetence of French diplomacy were no match for the Austrians, who had clear ideas of what they wanted—the security of the Netherlands and the isolation of Frederick.

Frederick, "toujours en vedette," was rightly convinced that a great conspiracy was on foot. Austria (with Saxony) in the South, Russia in the East were his two formidable foes. He did not intend, as regards France, to be like the ruler of Wallachia under the Porte, obliged to make war the moment he received orders. The struggle on the St. Lawrence and the Ohio was for Prussia only another futile scuffle of Greeks and Trojans on the Scamander. When, therefore, Frederick learned that Great Britain was willing to suggest neutrality for Germany he was quite willing to listen. But the Anglo-Russian treaty submitted for his perusal was a sharp disappointment. In its amended form the subsidised Russian troops were not to be employed in Hanover or the Low Countries. The Tsarina intended them to attack Prussia alone, as had been also the intention of Great Britain in the spring. None the less Frederick promptly acceded to the Convention of Westminster, by which in an Anglo- Jan. 16, French war Germany was to remain neutral. Although the Low 1756 Countries were explicitly excepted, the Convention was popular in England, for it seemed to protect Hanover without involving British troops and money. Pitt, however, with a strange ignorance of what he was himself to do, regarded it as an additional German millstone round the Ministers' necks, and asserted that he would not have signed it for all the five great places of those whose signatures were on the document. Probably neither Newcastle nor Frederick intended it as a breach of the traditional groupings of the Powers. Yet its effect was decisive. Hanbury Williams had concealed the Convention from the Russian Court until the Anglo-Russian treaty was ratified, but in her anger at British duplicity the Tsarina declared her readiness to march 80,000 men into the April

9

field to recover Silesia for the Empress. It swept France into Kaunitz's net. The French ambassador, De Nivernais, sent culpably late to Berlin, and still more culpably kept waiting for his instruc-

March tions, failed to renew the French alliance with Berlin. At Ver-sailles, Frederick's action was interpreted as a breach of faith. The conferences of the autumn of 1755 rapidly matured into a formal agreement between Vienna and Versailles. Yet neither France nor Austria were quite ready to attack their former allies. Maria Theresa was honourably reluctant to become an open foe of

May 1, Great Britain. The first treaty of Versailles was therefore purely
1756 defensive. Yet Newcastle could say with truth that "the long-established system of alliances was now dissolved". Two events only were required to consummate the diplomatic revolution, and

May they came quickly. Great Britain and France declared war. Frederick, unable to obtain anything but evasive replies to his

Aug. 29 peremptory questions at Vienna, marched into Saxony. "Adieu, monsieur de la timide politique," had been his remark to his Minister Podewils. His action provided the Empress with the *casus foederis*. The Austrians must have the help of France. The Franco-British, Austro-Prussian issues which might have been kept distinct were now practically blended. The same war would decide whether Prussia was to be dismembered, whether France or Great Britain was to be the dominant Power in North America and Hindostan.

The honours of the Diplomatic Revolution fall to Vienna and Berlin. Frederick had been preparing for eleven years, and with characteristic vigour and insight he used diplomacy and war as twin instruments. Rightly convinced that his ruin was planned [1] he preferred to have time on his side and strike before his foes were ready. Unquestionably the Treaty of Versailles was a great diplo-matic triumph for the cool and patient Kaunitz. France was now going to fight for Austrian ambitions—to assist in restoring a Habs-burg hegemony in Central Europe. Since 1748 the French share in events convict her King and her Ministers of every blunder a Govern-ment can make—vacillation, uncertainty, blindness, negligence, and rash decision. The fatal Austrian alliance and the results that fol-lowed from it damned the Bourbon Monarchy until the Revolution

---

[1] Kaunitz wrote: "with God's help we will bring so many enemies on the back of the insolent King of Prussia that he must succumb".

of 1789 swept it away. The verdict on the British Cabinet can scarcely be less severe. It permitted events in America to develop without resolute efforts either to remove causes that must issue in war, or to provide for the inevitable consequences if they did. Their diplomacy failed to penetrate the real designs of the Viennese Court, and they lost the Austrian alliance because, as Napoleon said of his generals, they made a picture and assumed it corresponded with facts. The neutrality of Spain was a piece of luck they scarcely deserved. They drifted into the Convention of Westminster, (which in the summer of 1755 was no part of a seriously prepared policy,) and they entered into engagements with Russia and Prussia, which were contradictory and illusory. In the autumn of 1754, when Braddock's expedition was deliberately planned, they had ample time to prepare.[1] But when the time came the fleet was not adequate for the task imposed on it, the garrisons at Gibraltar and Minorca and elsewhere were depleted, without stores, proper artillery or ammunition. The army in Great Britain was hopelessly inadequate.[2] The Ministry were waiting for the wind "to blow them mercenaries from Europe," and the whisper of an invading fleet at Brest threw the Government into a panic which deranged the strategy of the first campaign with disastrous results. Pitt said with truth, "If he saw a child driving a go-cart close to the edge of a precipice with May 11, 1756 the precious freight of an old King and his family, he was bound to take the reins out of such hands". The responsibility for this pitiable state of things must fall mainly on the Newcastle-Hardwicke group. Cumberland and Fox—the war party of 1754—urged decisive and vigorous action. But Fox after his admission to the Cabinet was "scarcely suffered to give an opinion". The Newcastle papers make it clear that the Cabinet was rarely consulted. Control was in the hands of "the inner clique," "the conciliabulum," as Granville called it, in which Fox was only one voice. Had he been wise he would have resigned before 1755 was out, and let the "go-cart" rush to ruin. It has been said that the experts did not warn Newcastle. But it is notable that Ligonier, the most experienced military chief in Great Britain, had been ousted from the

[1] "As no natural enemy should be trusted, I hope the King's Ministers will not neglect the little time that is left for preparation" (Cumberland to Newcastle, February 11th, 1755, B.M. Add. MS. 32,852).

[2] "There is not in all the west and north a single soldier" (H. Fox, Torrens, *Hist. of Cabinets*, 2, 273).

Master-Generalship of the Ordnance to suit Newcastle's shuffling of the party cards. And if Anson, Hardwicke's silent son-in-law, held his tongue he was either culpably silent or culpably incompetent. Ably as he redeemed his reputation under Pitt, he seems to have been affected from 1754 to 1756 by the *lues Newcastliana*, the creeping party paralysis. Finally, the Ministry wholly misunderstood the temper of the nation. Fox throughout his career despised public opinion. Not an aristocrat by birth, he had an oligarch's contempt for "the mob," and throughout he regarded Pitt's reliance on support outside the narrow circle of the represented as a demagogue's appeal to the ignorant crowd. Newcastle seemed to think that popular agitation could be appeased by shaking the ministerial kaleidoscope into a new pattern but composed of the same pieces. Leadership was a synonym for party management and Cabinet reconstruction. He was soon to be rudely undeceived.

Had the Court of Versailles been governed by a Frederick, had even Versailles and Madrid been united, 1756 might have been a year of irreparable disaster for England. But it was serious enough. By early spring the Ministry had worked first themselves and then the country into a panic over the possibilities of invasion, so that when in March the King announced that the contingent of Hessian troops had been sent for, an address from Lords and Commons expressed a preference for Hanoverians, and, despite Pitt's indignant protests against this unnecessary substitute for the efficient use of native resources, both Hessians and Hanoverians were brought over to guard English hearths. Pitt's counterscheme of recruiting and reorganising the national militia, which he explained in a speech masterly for its insight into principles and grasp of detail, was rejected in the House of Lords, on the advice of Newcastle, Granville, and Hardwicke, on the ground that it would breed a military spirit in a commercial nation. At last, on April 7th, the ill-fated Byng was despatched with ten ships and some reinforcements to the Mediterranean. Two days later La Galissonnière, with twelve ships and 16,000 troops under Richelieu, left Toulon to attack Minorca. Blakeney, the Governor, now past eighty, was obliged by lack of officers and men to retire into Fort St. Philip, commanding Port Mahon. By May 8th, when the home Government decided to reinforce Byng, Blakeney was already under siege. On May 19th Byng fought an indecisive action off Minorca, and, judging his fleet

unequal to re-engage a superior enemy, left Minorca to its fate, in
order to defend Gibraltar, which was in no fit state for repelling
attack. On June 28th the garrison surrendered, and a howl of
fierce indignation went up which centred on the admiral to whose
"cowardice" the loss of the key of the Western Mediterranean was
ascribed. The Government had already sent out Hawke "with the
little cargo of courage" to supersede Byng; Newcastle went about
saying, "Oh, indeed, he shall be tried immediately, he shall be hanged
directly," and his colleagues were quite ready to make the admiral the
scapegoat for their sins. Court-martialled and sentenced to death
for neglecting to do the utmost to save the situation, Byng was
shot on March 14th, 1757, in Voltaire's famous phrase, "to encourage the others".[1] Pitt generously endeavoured to save him,
but in spite of numerous petitions for pardon the King was obdurate. To Pitt's representations that the Commons would welcome a
pardon George made one of his most celebrated remarks. "You
have taught me," he said, "to look for the sense of my subjects
elsewhere than in the House of Commons." Anson resolutely held
his tongue, Fox fought in the House of Commons to have the
sentence carried out, and Newcastle's janissaries steadily voted to
cover up the responsibility of the Ministers. The personal aspect
of the matter is far from creditable to the political chiefs. The
popular temper was well shown in a handbill: "Hang Byng or look
to your King," and Ministers gladly "diverted" resentment on to a
man who, at worst, was guilty of handling his squadron badly in
difficult circumstances. Byng was no coward, and he was expressly
acquitted of cowardice. The higher political direction, such as it
was, had brought about the disaster. Ministers left Minorca unfit
to defend itself; they despatched too weak a fleet; they selected
the wrong man, and they sent him too late.[2] Under the pressure
of the shipping trade, the necessity of covering the escort of the
Hessians, the fear of invasion, the unpreparedness of the dockyards, Anson, who must be regarded as mainly responsible for the
disposition of the ships available, weakened Byng's squadron in
order to keep an unnecessarily strong fleet in the Channel. It

[1] See Appendix XVI.
[2] The Newcastle Papers show that as early as December, 1755, Cumberland
suggested reinforcements for Minorca. On February 3rd, and again on February
25th, the Government had explicit information as to the objective of the expedition
at Toulon. On March 7th Fox pressed for aid. Byng sailed a month later!

may be that the French threat of invasion was genuine (after Minorca it was given up, which suggests it was a ruse to divert the fleet from the Mediterranean); but why, with two years' notice given by themselves, the Cabinet had not enough ships ready to secure both the Channel and the Mediterranean admits of only Pitt's answer : " Ministers had provoked before they could defend, and neglected after provocation ".

Pitt,
May 11,
1756

Equally bad news came from America, where Loudoun had been sent to supersede Shirley, and Abercromby to command until Loudoun's arrival.   Shirley had planned attacks on Forts Frontenac and Niagara and on Crown Point.   Loudoun, a tactless commander of mediocre abilities, found his troops inadequate, the preparations disorganised, and irritating obstacles in the jealousy and inexperience of the colonial levies and officers.   Abandoning the attack on Niagara, Loudoun focussed his main effort on Crown Point and Ticonderoga.

Aug. 10

But he was frustrated by Montcalm, who had been permitted by our Admiralty to get out to Canada in the spring, and now pounced on Oswego and compelled it to surrender.   Retiring on Ticonderoga, Montcalm made himself too strong for Loudoun to dislodge, and the British effort ended with nothing more than the strengthening of the defences of Fort Edward.   The loss of Oswego was serious. " The barrier of the Six Nations " and " the curb of the power of the French," it cut the line of French communications, and was a gateway to the West and to the Indian trade.   Its capture was a tribute to Montcalm's rapidity and decision, and completed the work begun in the Ohio valley the year before.   Added to the news of June, that Calcutta had been captured by Suraj-ud-Daulah, it deepened the consternation in England and sealed the fate of the Ministry, which had also to contend with difficulties at home.

May 25

Sir Dudley Ryder, Chief Justice of the King's Bench, died, and Murray not only insisted on succeeding him but on having a peerage as well (Baron Mansfield), so that a prominent supporter was lost in the Commons.   On June 4th the future George III. came of age, and the question of a separate establishment occasioned much intrigue and negotiation.   The King desired to free the young prince from his mother's influence, but in the end Leicester House got its way ; Bute was made Groom of the Stole, which consolidated his power, and the new Court became a recognised centre of the new

Oct. 4

Tory opposition.   Fox, who had supported the prince's claims,

thereby not improving his position with Newcastle and the King,
now "put the knife to his colleagues' throats" by insisting on Oct. 13
resigning. His position in the Cabinet satisfied neither his political
ambitions nor his thirst for wealth. Probably, too, he had never
forgiven Newcastle's desertion of Walpole, and was not sorry "to
repay good Lord Orford's score".[1] Lady Yarmouth's intervention
failed to shake his decision, and Newcastle recognised that to carry
on with Fox and Pitt against him was impossible. A last appeal
to Pitt, through Hardwicke, met with "an absolute, final negative". Oct. 19
Newcastle therefore resigned, refusing a pension, after being con- Nov. 13
tinuously in office since 1724, and was followed by Fox, Hardwicke, Nov. 13
and Lyttelton, who took a peerage. Granville, to whom Newcastle
had previously offered the headship of the Government, with Hardwicke and himself as his chief colleagues, had bluntly replied that
" I will be hanged a little before I take your place rather than a
little after". Although the King was convinced that Pitt "would
not do his business," it was clear that the new Administration must
include him. Pitt, moreover, intimated emphatically that he
would not serve with Fox, but the Ministry formed by the Duke of
Devonshire, with Pitt as Secretary for the Southern Department,
was not the complete reconstruction that his speeches had demanded. His brother-in-law, Temple, succeeded Anson at the
Admiralty ; Legge became Chancellor of the Exchequer ; George
Grenville Treasurer of the Navy. But against this little group of
the cousinhood " Granville, Gower, and Holdernesse kept their
places, while Bedford, the new Viceroy of Ireland, belonged to the
Cumberland party. It is remarkable that Pitt now gave up the
Newcastle "pocket seat" at Aldborough, which he had kept during
his period of open opposition to its patron ; still more remarkable
that he did not anticipate the action of his son twenty-seven years
later, and endeavour to make himself independent by an appeal to
the constituencies. There are in the manuscript sources for the
period suggestive indications that the Newcastle Whigs feared a
dissolution. Public feeling was so strongly moved by the failures of
Newcastle's Administration, and Pitt was so evidently the marked
man of the hour, that 1757 might have been a precedent for
1784, and the political world might have learned of "Fox's martyrs"

[1] Hanbury Williams, October 28th. B. M. Stowe MS., 283.

two years before William Pitt the Younger was born. Six months showed that the nation, even without a general election, insisted on giving a mandate to the new Secretary of State. But of the arts of political organisation and party tactics the elder Pitt was as ignorant as the younger was a master.

The Devonshire-Pitt Administration was not in office long enough to prove a success. In the tedious inquiry into the Minorca fiasco Pitt played a passive part. Forty years earlier it certainly would have led to an impeachment, but the Newcastle party under Fox's able leadership were glad to construe the new Minister's indifference as a further precedent that political failure was (as Newcastle at least agreed) adequately punished by deprivation of office. The result was sarcastically summed up in Horace Walpole's sentence. "To their great astonishment the late Cabinet is not thanked parliamentarily for having lost Minorca". The Government started with vigorous measures. Supply was taken for £8,355,000, a million more than in the previous year. The army and navy were augmented and eight battalions were sent to America. The Militia Bill was introduced and passed. Highland regiments were formed by enlisting 2000 men for the American service—a fine vindication of the Secretary's claim in opposition that Great Britain could provide as many and better soldiers than German princelings. Nor did Pitt fail to "find room in his virtue for Hanover". The proposed vote of £200,000 for the Electorate was carried unanimously, and co-operation with Frederick by an army under Cumberland was planned. Critics might with justice repeat Granville's remark, "Pitt used to call me a madman, but I am not half so mad as he is"; but the nation was quick to feel the new spirit blowing life into the dead bones of the executive. It did not ask for consistency but for leadership; it wanted not politicians but a statesman. Yet statesmen obliged to work under representative institutions must have loyal colleagues, the confidence of the Crown, and a majority. The Pitt-Devonshire Ministry in reality had, in Chesterfield's phrase, as many enemies as the King of Prussia. The floor of the rickety structure was strewed with gunpowder and the roof covered with thatch. Devonshire was perfectly loyal, but Pitt was never an easy colleague to work with. Temple's temper was the curse of himself and the Cabinet into which Pitt's devotion brought him. The support of Leicester

House and the Tories [1] alarmed the orthodox Whigs, who longed
to be back in office. The King resented having had Pitt forced on
him, and Cumberland on the eve of leaving for the continental campaign declined to serve under the Secretary of State.   On March
8th the King ordered Fox, in consultation with Cumberland, to
frame a new Administration, and before Fox could do it Cumberland procured Temple's and Pitt's dismissal. Legge and George April 5
Grenville then resigned, and for two months and a half Great and 6
Britain was without an Administration.   In the carnival of intrigue and Ministry-making that followed (no less than six different combinations were tried and broke down) several points became clear, and ultimately facilitated the coalition of Pitt and
Newcastle.   Public opinion insisted that Pitt must have what he
would alone accept, a position of virtually supreme control. The
"rain of gold boxes," when he resigned, was a warning to his rivals
and a mandate to himself. Newcastle's power with the great Whig
territorials and his solid phalanx of followers made his friendship
or neutrality essential. And with Newcastle went Hardwicke.
Bute and Leicester House could not be ignored. The King was
old.   And Bute, who wished to support Pitt, could keep the
Dowager Princess and the Prince of Wales quiet, for his day must
come, perhaps soon.   Fox had definitely decided to sacrifice his
political ambitions. He had had more than enough of high office
without power; he would not be at the beck and call of Newcastle,
or of Pitt, who would either damn him again by their failure or rob
him of the credit if they succeeded. As he could not be Prime
Minister, he would at least be rich. He stipulated with the King
for the Paymaster's office, (which as the war promised to be long
and lavish in its expenditure meant to a skilful financier vast sums,)
and he would take it from the King and from no one else. That meant
that men might come and go but at the receipt of subsidies he
would remain until some fresh service brought him a peerage. And
Henry Fox won what he desired, the Pay office, without a seat in
the Cabinet. He also earned, which did not trouble him at all, the
contempt both of the honest and the dishonest. For Englishmen,

[1] " Mr. Pitt is accused of a coalition with the Tories ; and it is certain that he
has become the Cocoa Tree toast " (Lyttelton). " This new Administration has the
Tories and nothing but the Tories to support them " (Digby to Lord Digby,
H.M.C., 8 Rept., App., 4, 223).

with whom spirit will cloak a multitude of sins, will always despise a craven surrender of great abilities and justifiable ambitions to the lust for lucre. The gold amassed in these years of national glory completed Henry Fox's moral ruin, and ruined, so far as anything could ruin, the career and character of his father's idol, Charles James Fox.

The gods, hard facts, and Chesterfield now brought Pitt and Newcastle together. Pitt consented to borrow the Duke's majority and to permit his grace to make bishops and tide-waiters, and flutter in reams of manuscript through the labyrinthine back stairs that led to the Council chamber where the Secretary of State toiled to save and extend an Empire. Newcastle took the Treasury, Legge went back to the Exchequer, Hardwicke to the Chancellorship, Anson to the Admiralty. Temple, whom the King insisted should not have a place that involved constant attendance in the closet, became Privy Seal. Granville and Holdernesse kept their offices. It was a coalition, and a strong one, for it included all the important front-bench chiefs. England, Beaconsfield said, does not love coalitions. But she was to adore this one, the most triumphantly successful Ministry in our annals.

Until the winter of 1756 Pitt had been given little opportunity to prove capacity for administration or constructive statesmanship. He had impressed himself on the House of Commons and public opinion chiefly by three qualities : his remarkable oratory, his courage and vehemence as a critic, his indifference to the material rewards of success. When he became Paymaster, for example, he had renounced on principle the lucrative perquisites and percentages of the post, and this though he was a poor man.[1] Although he always claimed to be a Whig of the Revolution school his political career had largely rested on a small family connection, dating from the Boy Patriots of 1735, and he had made no serious effort to build up a distinct party, with an independent programme, under his own leadership. Many of his utterances were strongly tinged with Bolingbroke's ideas, which identified party with faction and aimed at breaking up the prevailing system and machinery. To the end of his life he remained outside the official circle of the

---

[1] Dr. von Ruville's interpretation of Pitt's conduct as having been twice detrimentally influenced by a legacy, the Duchess of Marlborough's and Sir W. Pynsent's, is purely hypothetical, and at variance with other well-established facts.

great Whig aristocrats and their parliamentary connection.   As a
critic he had been unsparing in denunciation, and in notable instances (his treatment of Walpole, Carteret, and Hanoverianism)
had shown himself ignorant, prejudiced, and unjust.   The violence
of these attacks, corresponding to well-defined phases in his career,
had demonstrably hindered his advance, inspired his contemporaries
with mistrust, and the Crown with justifiable resentment.   Pitt's
ambitions were high, his confidence in his own powers unlimited,
his determination to obtain office obvious.   But the political world,
which saw him near at hand, could not forget the sudden transformation of the savage guerrilla leader of 1738-43 into the
silent and docile supporter of the Pelhams, his equally sudden re- 1744-54
appearance on the warpath when disappointed after Henry Pelham's
death, his strange omission to warn the country until the autumn
of 1755, contrasted with his personal attacks on Newcastle and
Murray, the vehemence of his denunciation of the subsidy system,
and the ease with which he quietly swallowed his criticisms of
the convention of Westminster and Hanoverianism, followed by
his own lavish support of the war on the Continent.   His close
connection with Leicester House from 1736-44 had been snapped
for ten years, and was resumed because, it was not unnaturally said,
he wanted tools to break Newcastle as he had tried to break Walpole
and Carteret, in order to get their offices and then carry out their
policy.   It is not surprising that many who knew him well and had
been under the wand of the enchanter now and later (Walpole,
Newcastle, Hardwicke, Granville, Fox, Horace Walpole, Shelburne,
Burke, George Grenville), were in despair at his vagaries of judgment and temper.   Indeed Pitt himself provided ample material
for the portrait of an able adventurer, cursed with a domineering
and capricious nature, of a colleague hyper-sensitive about his
own feelings, callous to the feelings of others, a theatrical *poseur*,
intoxicated by the exuberance of his own rhetoric.

It must be admitted that Pitt's surrender to, and treatment of,
Newcastle are difficult to explain away, and that his political services
were marred throughout the reigns of George II. and George III. by
grave and avoidable errors of judgment which singularly crippled
his power for good.   His deference to Temple was fatal more than
once.   Most serious of all, Pitt never seems to have assimilated into
his political philosophy the vitalising secret (which Burke strove to

teach his generation) that under the conditions of parliamentary self-government the deliberate association of public men for public ends is not a trick but a duty, that party is not faction, but the realisation of that duty, and that without the charity that hopeth all things, endureth all things, statesmen who have the gift of prophecy and speak with the tongues of angels will be but sounding brass and tinkling cymbals. Pitt's strange neglect of the machinery at his hand put him at the mercy of Newcastle; it made him first the tool and then the victim of George III. The public, however, judged him more accurately than the politicians. Qualities greater than his courage, his passionate love of liberty, his unshakable attachment to the cardinal tenets of the Revolution creed—a Protestant and constitutional Crown realising with the co-operation of a free people the union of freedom with law— appealed to their imagination, and touched all that was best in the nation. Pitt shared with Carteret, who, he said, had no equal in the upper sphere of government, the prerogative of moving in the high and intoxicating atmosphere of great subjects, great Empires, great characters, and effulgent ideas. His genius was inspired by a profound belief in the mission and destinies of his race and country, and in the categorical imperative of national and imperial duty. "I will" implied "I can". To a generation enervated by the selfish rivalries of politics, and cowed[1] by repeated failure, he preached a new imperial gospel, and in unforgettable words gave voice to the inarticulate aspirations of a people's heart. Momentous as were his achievements, unquestionable as is his greatness as a War Minister, Pitt's claim on the gratitude of Great Britain rests on the surer foundation of a noble imperialism. He did not make the Empire; but he saved it in the hours of a great peril from the sinister coalition of Bourbon and Habsburg, because failure to retain and extend what our forefathers had won was treason to the ideals of the British State. This conception of its task was a more enduring gift to his generation than the victories by which he achieved it. The Empire stood for the priceless qualities in a nation's life which had made his England great in the past, and which alone

---

[1] "Whoever is in or whoever is out, I am sure we are undone both at home and abroad. I never saw so dreadful a prospect" (Chesterfield, *Works*, 4, 198). "The time has come for England to slip her own cables and float away into some unknown ocean" (H. Walpole, Sept. 3rd, 1757).

could justify her ambitions to be a world-power and keep her great in the future.

The Seven Years' War blended into one two great issues, the future of British power outside Europe, the future of the Frederician State in Prussia. By estimating what defeat would have involved — the dismemberment of Prussia, a Bourbon-Habsburg supremacy in Europe, the establishment of the French on the St. Lawrence, the Ohio and the Mississippi, rivalry if not dominance of the French in India, supremacy of the French in the West Indies and the Gulf of Mexico—we can measure more precisely both what was averted and what was won. The alliance of Great Britain and Prussia linked in a common purpose two very different types of States ; and, if the religious element was subsidiary, it remains substantially true that the main protagonists on the one side were Protestant and progressive and on the other Catholic and reactionary. Prussia represented on the continent enlightened monarchical absolutism, essentially national, against the effete centralisation of the Bourbon autocracy and the dynastic non-national empire of the Habsburgs. The magnitude and extent of the operations were as striking as the apparent inequality of the combatants. The population of Prussia may be reckoned at five, that of Great Britain and her colonies at not more than twelve, millions, while the numbers of France and her allies have been calculated at a hundred millions. Both in Europe and outside it the war was a test of systems, and the parliamentary government of Great Britain on the whole survived the strain as successfully as the military absolutism of the Hohenzollern monarchy.

When the Pitt-Newcastle Ministry was finally formed, the second Treaty of Versailles had committed France to an annual subsidy, the pay of 10,000 German troops and a French army Feb. 1757 of 105,000 men. The great European League was completed by the Treaty of St. Petersburg, which brought in the Tsarina with 80,000 men, by the Treaty of Stockholm, which added Sweden and 20,000, and by the adhesion of Bavaria and the Elector Palatine. For Great Britain the campaign on the continent was not July 26 promising. Cumberland, pitted with 40,000 against D'Estrées with 80,000 troops, was worsted at Hastenbeck, and retreated upon Stade, thus abandoning the Electorate. In terror for Hanover, George, behind the back of his Ministers, and in his capacity as

Sept. 8 Elector, ordered negotiations to be opened.   Counter orders were sent too late, and the humiliating Convention of Klosterseven imposed neutrality on the Hanoverian army.   George threw all the blame on his son, who returned to England to be greeted with the remark: "Here comes my son, who has ruined me and disgraced himself".   The convention was subsequently repudiated, on the technical ground that the French had violated its terms, and that Great Britain was not bound by the Elector's obligations.   Pitt, with courageous magnanimity, defended Cumberland's action, and showed that war in Germany and support to Prussia were part of his strategic scheme.   He proposed to take the Electoral army into

Sept.-Oct. British pay and utilise it to guard the western flank of our ally. Meanwhile a diversion against Rochefort, under Hawke and Mordaunt, proved a failure, and the expedition returned, having accomplished nothing, to the nation's indignation.   The officers were exonerated on inquiry, the attack being pronounced impracticable, which was not pleasant for Pitt.

Nor had the operations in America gone as Pitt desired.   A French attempt to surprise Fort William Henry in the spring failed, and Loudoun decided to concentrate his chief effort on

June 20 Louisburg.   The co-operating fleet under Holborne was delayed, and Loudoun started without it, only to learn that Louisburg was strongly garrisoned and reinforced by a fleet as strong as Holborne's.

Nov. 1 The enterprise was abandoned and Holborne's ships were shattered by a storm off Cape Breton, while on the mainland Montcalm, collecting 7000 to 8000 men, surrounded Fort William Henry. Colonel Webb at Fort Edward was too weak to come to its rescue, and after six days' siege the fort surrendered.   By the terms of the capitulation the garrison was to be escorted to Fort Edward, but the French Indians broke out of hand, and despite Montcalm's efforts butchered some fifty and carried off two hundred more of the prisoners.   The French then wound up their victorious campaign by a raid on the German Flats, a district between the headwaters of the Mohawk and Schenectady Rivers inhabited by colonists from the Palatinate.   The moral of events was obvious. The British required abler commanders, and much stronger assistance from the mother country and the colonies.   The blockade of the French coasts was not effective.   Two squadrons had sailed for Canada, D'Aché got away for India and Kersaint for the West

Indies.   Until we could bring a superiority of force to bear on the
strategic area in North America and prevent the reinforcements
from reaching Canada the French power could not be broken.   And
Frederick's campaign emphasised the pressing need for strategic
science in the higher direction and for a more strenuous use of every May 6
available resource.   After a victory at Prague, Frederick had been June 20
beaten at Kollin and abandoned Bohemia.   In East Prussia his Aug. 20
forces were defeated at Gross-Jägerndorff, and Breslau the capital of
Silesia fell to the Austrians.   Cumberland's failure had exposed
his western flank.   Men in England began to think with Chesterfield
" that neither we, nor our ally, can carry it on three months longer,"
when there followed suddenly Frederick's two most classic victories. Nov. 5
At Rosbach he routed the French and Imperial army.   Hurrying Dec. 5
back to Silesia, he inflicted at Leuthen an equally damaging defeat
on the Austrians.   Prussia was more than saved for the year and
the menace of the coalition averted.

Happily for both Prussia and Great Britain the lessons of 1757
were turned to good account.   War on the grand scale was planned,
and Pitt's despatches show how carefully the scheme had been
studied, officers selected, and the details of the organisation worked
out.   A vote for more than eleven millions was taken and the main
blow was to be struck in America, " to eat up the French ".   Loudoun
was recalled and the attack on Louisburg was entrusted to Amherst
with 12,000 men.   Wolfe, picked after his service at Rochefort, was
to be one of Amherst's brigadiers, and Boscawen, " old Dreadnought,"
was to co-operate with a powerful fleet.   Abercromby with Lord
Howe was simultaneously to move up the line of Lake George
against Ticonderoga, while a third force under Forbes advanced April 11
against Fort Duquesne.   A subsidy convention of £670,000 was
concluded with Frederick, while Great Britain also agreed to maintain 55,000 men to operate on the Elbe and the Weser, the command being given with Frederick's consent to Prince Ferdinand of
Brunswick.   Equally important blockading squadrons were detached to seal up the French ports, and a reserve force of ships and
14,000 men was concentrated at the Isle of Wight.

By June 8th the Louisburg expedition had made a landing,
and ten days later the siege began.   It lasted until July 27th,
when the fortress capitulated.   Île St. Jean was reduced, and had
Wolfe, " who shone extremely," had his way the original intention

of striking the same year at Quebec would have been carried out.
But the stubborn defence of Louisburg had saved the Canadian
capital for that year.   Amherst preferred to reinforce Abercromby,
who had failed against Ticonderoga.   In the advance from Albany,
Howe, described by Wolfe " as the very best officer in the King's
July 8   service," had been killed in a reconnoitring skirmish, and Aber-
cromby's stupid frontal attack on the fort, where Montcalm had
concentrated his forces, was repulsed with serious loss.   Whereupon
Aug. 27   the British expedition fell back on the southern end of Lake
Sept.   George.   Bradstreet had succeeded in capturing Fort Frontenac ;
Nov.   and Forbes, despite a reverse to his advance party, pushed on, only
to find that Fort Duquesne had been evacuated and burnt by the
French.   Next year a British fort took its place, to which the name
of Fort Pitt was given—a name kept alive to-day in the roaring
furnaces and forest of chimneys of Pittsburg.

The tide in America had turned.   If for lack " of a little
soldiership and a little patience " the central assault had failed, the
French were struck hard on both flanks.   The maritime provinces
and the guard of the St. Lawrence had fallen to the British.
Superiority in the numbers, organisation, and determination of her
foes placed Canada on the defensive.   Montcalm was now left to
himself.   The absorption of France in the continental war and the
English command of the sea, together with the lavish support from
Great Britain, must in the end focus the struggle in the heart of
the French colony.   Pitt was learning from events.   For generals
Nov.   who blundered Great Britain had no use, and Abercromby was
Feb. 15   recalled.   Ferdinand, however, had justified his appointment.   By
June 23   skilful operations he drove the French back behind the Aller and
Aug. 21   then across the Rhine.   At Crefeld he won a signal victory.   His
purely German army was now reinforced by a British contingent of
six squadrons of cavalry and six infantry battalions, under the
Duke of Marlborough.   Their despatch showed that the Ministry
fully recognised the importance of enabling Ferdinand to act as a
true containing force, to work in concert with Frederick and protect Hanover, Brunswick, and Hesse, if possible, against the army of
the Rhine under Contades and the army of the Main under Soubise.
By the end of 1758 Ferdinand occupied a line from Münster to
Paderborn.   Earlier in the year the Spithead force, under Marlborough and Lord George Sackville, had been employed against

the French coast, but St. Malo proved too strong and the expedi- May 20
tion returned, having accomplished little but the burning of mer-
chantmen and privateers. It was resumed under Bligh. The docks Aug. 1
at Cherbourg were destroyed and a landing made in the Bay of St.
Lunaire. But the landed troops were driven to retreat, suffered a
loss of 750 killed and wounded, and then were withdrawn by the
fleet. The tale of captures was completed by the surrender of
Fort Louis on the Senegal River and of the Island of Goree, which April 30
practically deprived France of her West African settlements. The Dec. 29
year had been one of increasing difficulty for Frederick. The
bloody battle of Zorndorf had checked the Russian advance in the Aug. 25
east, but a defeat by the Austrians at Hochkirch was a serious
blow. Subsequently the Austrians were compelled to evacuate Oct. 14
Saxony, but with every year Frederick was at a greater disadvantage. The superb army with which he had begun the war was
being rapidly decimated ; his enemies were rapidly making up lee-
way in skill and organisation, and their resources in men were far
superior to those of Prussia, already exhausted by the drain of three
campaigns. Nothing but the King's indomitable tenacity and military genius could hope to save his State from destruction.

In Pitt he had an ally after his own heart. Great Britain
recognised, as Frederick did, that after long travail she had at last
produced a man. The country had shaken off the enervating and
hysterical despair so conspicuous in 1756. Pitt had inspired every
class with his own unconquerable spirit ; he had won at last the
complete support of the King. "Give me your confidence, sir," he
had said to George, "and I will deserve it". "Deserve my confidence, and you shall have it," replied the King, and they both kept
their word. By 1758 Pitt was virtually a dictator. Newcastle
sparred and grumbled, but for the most part kept his fears, suspicions, and humiliations to paper.[1] Bute was troublesome more
than once ; Fox held his tongue and amassed money. The House
of Commons listened and voted.[2]

Pitt's system and conduct of the war are peculiarly interesting Dec. 25,
                                                                1758
[1] "The Duke of Newcastle and Pitt jog on like man and wife, seldom agreeing,
often quarrelling, but by a mutual interest upon the whole, not parting" (Chesterfield).

[2] "You would as soon hear 'No' from an old maid as from the House of Commons" (Walpole, Dec. 25th, 1758). "Mr. Pitt declares only what he would have
them do, and they do it nemine contradicente" (Chesterfield, Corr. 3, 1247).

10

as those of a Minister working under parliamentary conditions and a constitutional monarchy. But if his success was exceptional, the circumstances were still more exceptional. No other Minister in the modern epoch has come into power under such a unique conjunction of party forces. There was no organised Opposition. The coalition included and silenced all the front bench chiefs; it had the advantage of Newcastle's unrivalled experience, and control of the party machine; Leicester House, so long an element of embarrassment to the Crown, accepted the Secretary of State. In India, Britain's good fortune provided her with a great genius in Clive, whose achievements converted a subsidiary phase of the war into the operations that laid the basis of an imperial structure. Nor has any British Minister, before or since Pitt, waged a great war in alliance with a single military absolutism directed by a single brain, and that a brain of genius in soldiership, diplomacy, and administration. Frederick the Great was his own Commander-in-Chief, and his own Foreign Minister. Compared with the difficulties of William III. and Marlborough, of the younger Pitt, Castlereagh, and Wellington or Aberdeen, the disadvantages of a coalition both at home and in Europe were thus for Pitt and Frederick the Great reduced to a minimum. For four years Pitt gathered into his own hands the higher military direction and the central control of the machinery of the British State. The technical constitutional forms were, Pitt prided himself on the fact, strictly observed. The orders were the orders of the Crown through its customary and lawful organs. The King acted on advice, to the grounds and nature of which he was a party. An inner Committee of the Privy Council, virtually a Committee of Imperial Defence (Hardwicke, Newcastle, Devonshire, and Pitt, afforced by Anson, Ligonier, or any other expert required), discussed and decided, while the wider issues of diplomatic business were submitted to the full Cabinet; but in the determination both of the principles, methods, and objects of the operations, Pitt's supremacy was unquestioned. He availed himself freely of advice from those most competent to offer it; Anson and Ligonier were permanent naval and military chiefs of the staff, and the executive agents, such as Hawke, Saunders, Boscawen, were consulted, but the strategic initiative, the political higher direction, he unified in his own office. He demanded and retained the entire correspondence with the naval

and military commanders; from his pen came both the instructions and the covering despatches that regulated the business
in hand.   The civil authorities, working on parallel lines, were
organised and directed by Pitt.   Naturally much latitude had to
be given to individual action, but the general scheme arranged at
headquarters co-ordinated its results to a uniform purpose.   Hence
it came about that in practice Admiralty, Horse Guards, and
Ordnance Board, commanders and subordinates looked to Pitt.
They were responsible for executive action to him, as he was for
the central control.   Equally remarkable is Pitt's mastery of detail.
His despatches are singularly copious in the range, scope, and minuteness of the provisions made, and the toil represented by these records
will always remain as a wonderful achievement of work by one man.
And through the dead and dusty files gleams the spirit which left
an ineffaceable impression of demonic power on Pitt's generation.
If ever we are tempted to believe that empires can be made and
campaigns won, not by nights and days of sacred toil but by oratory
and epigram, the documents of Pitt's Ministry will dispel the pernicious superstition.   They are a fit complement to the *Politische
Correspondenz* of Frederick the Great.

As an organiser of victory Pitt has no superior in British history.   In the higher direction his strategic conception is marked
by clearness, decision, and grasp.   At first sight, the campaigns of
1757-60 seem to justify the criticism that, while he condemned
Carteret and the Pelhams for a wasteful and futile indulgence in
continental schemes, no one spent more, or on a more extended
scale, in continental operations than himself.   The millions spent
on the Prussian subsidy and on maintaining Ferdinand's army are
striking compared with the dole to Russia and Hesse and Hanover,
the denunciation of which brought about his dismissal in 1755.
But Pitt's "system" rested on a sharp distinction between continental measures as an end in themselves and as a means to an end.
For him, in the first three years, the strategic centre was North
America, the strategic object the crushing of the French in a
limited area.   The problem, therefore, was how to bring a superiority of force to bear on that limited area, for he acted on Nelson's
principles that numbers alone could annihilate.   The command of
the sea covering the concentration of a superior force could ensure
victory and the political result desired—the expulsion of the

French.   But this result would be barren if the Bourbon-Habsburg
alliance achieved as decisive results in Europe as the British in
North America.   No one grasped more clearly than Pitt, (his policy
towards Spain is an additional proof,) that Great Britain was not
fighting with France alone, but with a Bourbon-Romanov-Habsburg
coalition.   To defeat France was only half the battle; a France
beaten in North America but in alliance with a victorious coalition
in Europe meant the isolation of Great Britain and the total
destruction of the balance of power in Europe, without which the
British Empire as a State system could not exist.   Anne and
Maria Theresa must be beaten as well as Louis XV.; and if Spain
made common cause with this sinister conspiracy, Spain must be
beaten too.   Tactically, Canada was not won in Germany but in
North America—at Louisburg, Quebec, and Montreal.   But it is
neither correct nor just to represent the Prussian War as a comparatively unimportant element in Pitt's strategic conception.
Without Rossbach and Leuthen, Crefeld and Minden must have
been impossible.   The capture of Quebec would have been a poor
set-off to the loss of Hanover, the dismemberment of Prussia,
Flanders in Austrian hands, and a hostile Bourbon sovereign at
Madrid.   Pitt saw plainly that Frederick's failure would mean that
Great Britain also had failed in the strategic objects for which, he
held, she was as an imperial Power bound to fight.   And precisely as
he perceived this, and as Frederick's capacity to execute his share
diminished, so did Pitt's efforts extend.   The Hanoverian army of
observation is transformed into a containing force; it is stiffened
with British troops, the purpose of which is to relieve the pressure
on Prussia.   Correctly interpreted, therefore, Pitt's famous phrase
implies that Canada may have been won in Canada, but it will be
kept, and only kept, in Germany.   To desert Frederick was worse
than ingratitude or treachery—it was fatal to the true interests of
Great Britain.   Hence his insistence in the diplomatic negotiations
that a separate peace with France, which did not also secure the
status quo ante in Germany, would rob that peace of half its value.
The change in the character of the war, noticeable after 1759,
which drove France into the necessity of recovering elsewhere and
by other means what she had lost across the seas, was therefore
promptly met by Pitt.   The soundness of his strategy and tactics
were justified by this very change.   The new military and diplo-

matic problem was complicated by irrelevant but disturbing elements at home. But the completeness of the victory in North America gave him the means of decisive intervention on the Continent; and his plan for the Spanish War, even in inferior hands, revealed his grip on the new strategic situation. Had George II. lived till 1763 it is almost certain that the answer to Choiseul and Grimaldi would have been given not merely at Martinique, Havana, and Manila, but by another Minden, in which the victors of Quebec would have played their part.

The feature of Pitt's strategy and tactics most vulnerable to criticism is the expeditions against the French coast, deliberately planned to relieve the pressure on Frederick and Ferdinand, and to employ the army as " a sword of the fleet ". Fox wittily condemned them as breaking windows with guineas, and some experts since Pitt's day have seen in these eccentric raids a flaw in the strategic scheme which locked up at great cost forces that might have been employed more effectively elsewhere. But the place and use of eccentric diversions are a highly controversial part of modern military science, on which the layman may well hesitate to be dogmatic. And it is worth noting that Pitt's " error " was shared by Frederick the Great and Anson (strategic experts not lightly to be set aside), and that the effect even of ineffective diversions on the spirit and temper of our nation in the war is very remarkable.

The next year—1759—was the year of victory. A triple plan of 1759 attack on Canada had been planned to bring about a converging advance on Montreal and Quebec. For the main effort up the St. Lawrence, Saunders was selected to command the fleet and Wolfe (with Guy Carleton as his quartermaster-general) the army. In the choice of this young general of thirty-three, a sandy-haired, chinless man, from youth a victim to gravel, Pitt showed courage and insight. Wolfe's previous career marked him out as an officer of inextinguishable spirit and fertility of resource, who had patiently studied the science of his profession, and whose last campaign set the seal on his reputation. Amherst was to co-operate on land by striking north after capturing Ticonderoga and Crown Point, while Prideaux, marching by way of Oswego, was to secure Fort Niagara and close in from the west. At sea the grip on the French ports was tightened; Boscawen off Toulon, Hawke off Brest, and Rodney in the Channel were intended to deal with the hostile fleets.

The triple plan was not a complete success. The difficulties of the concerted operations had been underestimated, and the forces were not adequate to carry through in the allotted time so sweeping an enveloping movement. Amherst, on whom the burden of organising the preparations both for himself and Wolfe fell, found Ticonderoga and Crown Point abandoned, but was able to do little more than master Lake Champlain. By July 8th Prideaux had reached Niagara; and after his death his successor, Johnson, routed

July 24   a relieving force and the fort surrendered. The French line of communication with Louisiana by the Ohio was then cut; and Montcalm's detachment of Levis to defend Montreal, necessitated by Amherst's and Johnson's operations, was of signal advantage to Wolfe and Saunders, whose splendid co-operation exemplified what fleet and army could do under the right leaders working together.[1] "The prevailing toast" in the expedition, "British colours on every port, fort, and garrison in America," finely expresses the spirit which Pitt's genius had inspired. Despite the bad luck which

May   prevented Durell from intercepting a French squadron that ran safely up to Quebec, Saunders' seamanship had by June 26th accomplished the dangerous task of bringing his fleet of battleships up the St. Lawrence to the Isle of Orleans. But for two months Montcalm's defence of an impregnable position baffled all Wolfe's

July 31   efforts. A desperate attack on the Beauport lines partly spoiled by the ardour of the grenadiers, who got out of hand, ended in a costly repulse. Wolfe's health broke down, and it was not until the dis-

Sept. 8   covery of the track up the face of the Anse du Foulon and the audacious transport of his army across the river on the immortal night of September 12th, and thence up to the Plains of Abraham that Wolfe succeeded in forcing Montcalm's position and compelled him to fight in the open. By this stroke of genius, executed to perfection, the failure which had threatened the whole expedition developed, as by magic, into a brilliant *coup de théâtre;* and in the battle of September 13th the fire-discipline of our infantry swept the French into rout. On September 18th, Quebec surrendered to Townshend and Saunders. Wolfe's victory had practically given

---

[1] Mr. Beckles Wilson, however, *Fortnightly Review*, March, 1910, cites important passages from an unpublished and recently discovered diary of Wolfe's, tending to prove that the co-operation of Wolfe and Saunders was not as harmonious as is generally represented. See note p. 159.

Canada to Great Britain. Fate decreed that neither the victor
nor the vanquished general should survive. But both Wolfe and
Montcalm could "die in peace". Montcalm was a type of the
best of France; he had done everything that a brave and capable
soldier could to save Canada, and in the imperishable renown that
Wolfe deservedly won, Saunders and the British fleet have full right
to share.[1] For Quebec was won as much by the British navy as by
the British army.

On the Continent, Minden had fitly prepared the way. De Aug. 1
Broglie had replaced Soubise, and Contades' plan aimed at concentrating a superior force against Ferdinand and forcing him back on
the line of the Weser. By July 10th Broglie secured Minden,
while Contades secured Cassel, Lippstadt, and Münster, so that the
French had now 60,000 men against 45,000 led by Ferdinand. By
able tactics, however, the commander of the Anglo-Hanoverian
army succeeded in enticing the French into the plain of Minden
and forcing a battle upon them, which ended in a much-needed
success. The battle was as remarkable as that at Fontenoy for the
splendid advance of the British and Hanoverian infantry across
open ground against a cross artillery fire and three lines of cavalry.
"Never were so many boots and saddles seen on a battlefield as
opposite to the English and Hanoverian guards." But the deplorable conduct of Lord George Sackville, who ignored orders four
times repeated, kept his cavalry at the decisive moment out of action,
and by his cowardice or perversity, or both, prevented the French
from being annihilated. Sackville was justly condemned by court-
martial and declared unfit to serve under the Crown. Unfortunately
he was a favourite at Leicester House, and his subsequent career
made his rehabilitation by George III. an unpardonable blunder,
and justified the universal reprobation of his conduct at Minden.
Although the French evacuated Cassel, lost Marburg, and were
defeated at Fulda, Ferdinand's operations were crippled by the
necessity of detaching 12,000 men to Frederick's assistance; and at
the end of 1759 the armies occupied practically the same ground as
at the beginning of the year. The Prussian King had been hard
pressed; his defeat at Kunersdorf and the surrender of Finck Aug. 12

---

[1] It is notable that two of the greatest of French and British maritime explorers
took part in the campaign—Bougainville as Montcalm's lieutenant, Cook as the
master of the *Centurion* in Saunders' fleet.

at Maxen, were serious disasters. The repulse of the French invasion of Hanover probably alone saved him from destruction.

On the blue water two decisive fleet-actions tightened the grip of sea power, offensively used on the strategic theatre of the war.

Aug. 19
Nov. 20
Rodney's bombardment of Havre had proved futile, but Boscawen's crushing of the Toulon squadron off Lagos was followed by Hawke's pursuit of the Brest fleet, after months of weary watching, into Quiberon Bay. Neither the storm nor the danger of the coast stayed Hawke, whose relentless determination and fine seamanship were rewarded by the signal loss inflicted on Conflans' command. If the Brest ships were not completely wiped out as a result of the action, the French fleet ceased to be an offensive force. The war had also extended to the West Indies. The plan of seizing Martinique was abandoned, but, thanks to Barrington and Clavering, Guadeloupe and Marie Galante were captured and kept—a brilliant bit of work, particularly creditable to the skill of the soldiers.

1760
Pitt's efforts for the next year were planned on a still larger scale. A sum of nearly sixteen millions was voted without opposition ; reinforcements were sent to Ferdinand in Germany, bringing up the British contingent to 20,000 men ; Amherst resumed the plan which made Montreal the objective of an enveloping combination. Great Britain, in fact, had some 190,000 men in her pay (100,000 on the British, 12,000 on the Irish, establishment, 20,000 embodied militia, and 55,000 Germans) ; and Pitt's policy of preserving Hanover and maintaining Frederick by continental operations until the subjugation of Canada was completed, is clearly revealed.

In Germany the Minister's hope of another decisive victory was not fulfilled. Ferdinand was seriously outnumbered by the French, whose two armies were nearly double the 80,000 men at his disposal. The struggle centred chiefly in Hesse and Waldeck. A
July 10
July 31
defeat at Korbach was followed by a victory at Marburg. But the raid on Wesel was unsuccessful, and culminated in a reverse at
Oct. 10
Klosterkampen and the retreat of the allies from the Rhine. The French maintained their hold on Hesse, and Ferdinand could at
June 22
best only expect to prevent their invasion of Westphalia. For Frederick it was a chequered year too. The reverse at Landshut was made good by a success at Liegnitz ; and after a temporary
Dec.
occupation of Berlin by his foes, the campaign closed with a bloody victory over Daun at Torgau.

In Canada, Murray had been left to defend Quebec in complete isolation. With the spring Levis and Vaudreuil made a desperate effort to retake the city; and on April 27th Murray, provoked into taking the initiative, was defeated in an action outside the walls. Until the dramatic arrival of a frigate, the forerunner of a relieving May 9 British squadron, his position in the beleaguered city, with a decimated garrison and exhausted stores, was critical. The triple movement—Murray from Quebec, Amherst from Oswego and thence down the St. Lawrence, Haviland from Ticonderoga—for the capture of Montreal could now be pushed with vigour. Amherst's genius for organisation was ably supported by the energy and skill of the column commanders, and punctually to the moment, all difficulties surmounted, the three leaders joined hands outside the doomed town. There was nothing for Vaudreuil and Levis but to accept Sept. 6 the inevitable, and on September 8th the capitulation was signed which ended the French power in Canada and transferred a new colony to the British Crown. To Amherst in particular this crowning mercy was mainly due. The concerted operations of 1760, with their triumphant conclusion, stand on record as " one of the most perfect and astonishing bits of work which the annals of British warfare can show ".

Choiseul's plan of averting the final disaster in America by an invasion of England had been effectually frustrated by Boscawen's and Hawke's victories of the year before; but in the autumn of 1759 the possibilities of the defensive had been neatly illustrated. Thurot had slipped out of Dunkirk, and after wintering in Norway, now appeared off the western coast of Scotland. On February 21st he pounced on Carrickfergus, but eight days later he ran into the vessels despatched to intercept him; Thurot himself was killed and his three ships captured. The contrast between 1757 when Britain cowered at the prospect of invasion, and 1760 when the French effort fizzled out in " a smart display of cruiser control," is certainly striking. The confidence of the country rested securely, as well it might, on the strategic science which had established and maintained the command of the sea. Lagos and Quiberon made invasion by evasion little better than a mad raid, to which there could only be one end. And with Canada now conquered, forces were about to be set free whose employment might alter the whole character of the struggle for empire.

Equally remarkable results had been achieved in the chief areas
in which the struggle for supremacy in India was fought out. The
contest in the Carnatic was virtually an open duel between the
English and the French, using the quarrels of rival pretenders
within the native dynasties as the weapons of attack ; whereas in
Bengal the British were brought into collision with a native power
with which the French were not directly concerned. Between the
Carnatic and Bengal stood Bussy at Haidarabad, controlling the
Circars, with an excellent chance of intervening decisively in either
sphere. But the real connecting link between Madras and Calcutta
is Clive, whose iron nerve and strategic eye for the issues at stake
were worth more than a squadron of ships and several regiments
of men.

On his return to the East in 1756 Clive found that the agreement between the Governors of Madras and Pondicherry prevented
as yet direct hostilities between the English and the French ; but
after suppressing, with the aid of Admiral Watson, a pirate stronghold on the west coast at Gheriah he was sent to Calcutta, where
July 21 Suraj-ud-Daulah, the new Nawab of Bengal had captured Fort
William and inflicted on his European prisoners the atrocity of
" the Black Hole, wherein the greater part of them perished
by suffocation in the narrow prison into which they had been
thrust ". Clive and Watson arrived on December 15th, and next
month the Nawab was driven back from Calcutta. To prevent the
March 23 co-operation of the French with the Nawab's forces, Chandernagar
was captured, and Clive then entered on a negotiation through a
secret agent named Omichund with Mir Jafar, the Nawab's Commander-in-Chief, the object of which was to displace Suraj-ud-
Daulah as the ruler of Bengal and substitute a British nominee in
the person of Mir Jafar himself. It was the policy of Dupleix
applied in a new sphere, but unhappily, as far as Clive was concerned, stained by an act which was both a crime and a blunder.
In order to secure Omichund's full support Clive, with the connivance of the Council, stooped to forge Admiral Watson's signature
to a document defining the rewards for Omichund's services.
The real document, containing the agreement by which Clive and
the Council intended to be bound, omitted these clauses. The
treachery succeeded. Omichund, who might have revealed the
scheme in which Mir Jafar was so deeply implicated, believed in the

good faith of the forged signature and held his tongue. Clive June 23, then advanced to defeat the Nawab in the field, and at Plassey, 1757 with splendid audacity, risked all on a single stroke. The Nawab's army was routed. Suraj-ud-Daulah himself was murdered shortly June 27 after and Mir Jafar proclaimed in his place. Omichund was then simply thrown over. It was Clive's first and last act of treachery to native or European, but it cannot be condoned even by the gravity of the situation that tempted him, still less by the apparent success with which the deception was rewarded. Plassey marks one of the epochs in the history of British India ; it not only made Clive, through Mir Jafar, the ruler of Bengal, but laid the foundation of British political supremacy in the Ganges basin. The next two and a half years showed that the victor was gifted with a personality and administrative powers as remarkable as his genius for command. In Southern India Lally had been forced by the appearance of a British squadron off Karikal to abandon the siege of Tanjore. Summoning Bussy and his troops from Haidarabad he attacked Madras—the last offensive movement of the French in Feb., 1759 that quarter—but Kempenfeldt's squadron broke up the siege. Clive, in the north-east, meanwhile, grasped the situation, and sent Colonel Forde to the Circars to secure the communications between April, 1759 Bengal and the Carnatic ; and the capture of Masulipatam transferred the Nawab from a French to a British alliance. In his own immediate sphere Clive, by another brilliant and audacious stroke, had tightened his grip on the territories under British influence. Rejecting Mir Jafar's advice to come to terms with the Nawab of Oudh and the Shahzada, the heir of the Great Mogul, whose forces beleaguered Patna, Clive, by a forced march, relieved the European garrison, scattered the Nawab's forces, and once more proved that the offensive, controlled by genius, was the true policy. The autumn of the same year saw British ascendency further strengthened by the reduction of the Dutch settlement at Chinsurah and the capture of seven of their ships. In their jealousy of the growing British power, the Dutch had entered on an intrigue with Mir Jafar and had seized British vessels ; but Clive, the greater portion of whose fortune was in the hands of the Dutch East India Company, did not hesitate to use the opportunity to ruin, in the interests of his country, the one European rival that remained. His decisive action compelled the Dutch to pay compensation for their aggression and to limit their troops to a military police for their commercial station.

Recognising the critical character of the struggle in the Carnatic where Pocock's fleet had fought an indecisive action with the French under D'Aché, Clive despatched Colonel Eyre Coote to command the British troops.   What Plassey had achieved for the

Jan. 21, 1760   north the victory at Wandewash over Lally now achieved for the south.   Unlike Plassey, this battle was one directly between French

Oct.   and English, and Coote followed it up by investing Pondicherry on land, while Steevens, who had succeeded Pocock, blockaded it

Jan. 1761   by sea.   Its surrender was primarily due to Steevens' obstinacy and skill.   The French fleet under D'Aché, fearing an attack from Europe on their base at Mauritius, (an attack contemplated by Pitt but diverted to Belle Isle,) were obliged to leave Pondicherry to its fate, and its capitulation was a triumph for the seamanship of the British admiral.   Not without reason have naval experts held that Steevens' unprecedented feat of keeping the sea through the terrible cyclone season on that exposed coast must rank as one of the greatest feats of our sailors in the Seven Years' War, comparable to Hawke's great winter blockade off Brest.   And there is a dramatic fitness in the fact that the fall of the chief station of the French in India should be brought about by the indirect operation of Pitt's wide-flung strategy, and the direct offensive of fleet and army working in harmonious combination.   If Clive had failed to persuade Pitt that an Empire in India, such as few in 1760 dreamed of, could be won, if only he would consent to divert troops and ships from the West to the East Indies, it remains true that the final victory of the British could not have been secured without continuous support from home.   The steady reinforcement of the British squadron in 1758 and 1759, and the despatch of two British regiments, turned the scale.   And our sea-power was asserted at precisely the moment when the land campaign had entered on a critical stage.   Yet this patent fact need not detract from the services rendered by Pocock, Forde, Eyre Coote, and Clive himself. To the latter, "the heaven-born general," Pitt paid a tribute fully

Feb., 1760   deserved.   Clive had left Calcutta before the last blow was struck. His work in India was not yet over.[1]   But in Hindostan no less

---

[1] In a striking letter to Pitt, Clive urged the extension of the British conquest and the resumption of the direct authority of the Crown over the areas acquired.   He

decisively than in North America the French schemes had been completely checkmated; and if the much abused title of "Empire builder" belongs by right to any man it belongs to Clive, whose peerage, tardily granted in 1762, emphasised achievements as remarkable for the rapidity and insight with which they were accomplished as for the new epoch they opened for the British race in the East.

Interest at home now centred on the diplomatic situation. In 1759 the accession of Charles III. (King of Naples) to the throne of Spain had substituted for the peaceful Ferdinand VI. a sovereign, hostile at heart to Great Britain, whose policy was based on the solidarity of the Bourbon dynasties and a desire to prevent a settlement detrimental in Europe and the New World to Spanish and Bourbon power. The loss of Canada and West Indian Islands by France involved in Spanish eyes a serious displacement of the colonial balance of power; and Spain had, moreover, special grievances of her own against Great Britain—the alleged attacks of English privateers on Spanish ships, the illegal cutting of logwood in Honduras by English traders, and the maintenance of Spanish rights in the Newfoundland fisheries. A desire to end the war was growing with the combatants, and Spain was ready to offer her mediation. But these "dapplings for peace" came to nothing as yet. If France was ready to discuss a separate negotiation with Great Britain, both Maria Theresa and her Russian ally were averse from the idea of a general congress. Pitt made it clear that Prussia must be included in any separate arrangement made by Great Britain with France, and the tentative proposals broke down because Maria Theresa still hoped, by a continuance of the war on the Continent, to force Frederick into considerable cessions of territory. Henceforward Spain is the chief cause of Pitt's diplomatic May, 1760 anxiety; the reorganisation of her resources, the revival of her claims, the close connection between the Courts at Paris and Madrid, were additional elements of danger; and from the first the Minister grasped the new phase into which the war was necessarily

also suggested that, if the British administration were consolidated under a single Governor-General, the central seat of power should be in Bengal, the youngest of the company's settlements. His influence and knowledge were mainly responsible for the terms with regard to the French settlements in the treaty of 1763. In all these directions he proved his mastery of the conditions of the imperial problem of India passing—a struggle not for supremacy in America but one to compel France and her allies to acknowledge that in Europe their coalition had been as decisively defeated as the French in North America and India.   Hence Pitt's determination at the outset, first, to indicate that Great Britain would not surrender her colonial conquests ; secondly, that Frederick's cause was identical with her own.   Already in 1759 the expedition to Belle Isle was under consideration ; its capture would be a valuable piece when the diplomatic chess-board was set up, and it would give our fleet a convenient base for separating the French and Spanish navies, as well as place it astride the main routes from Western Europe across the Atlantic.   With victory Pitt's views of the scope and object of the war were inevitably extending.   Martinique, and perhaps Mauritius might be wrested from France, and the Bourbon power " beaten not to her knees but laid upon her back ".   The action of Spain confirmed the suspicion that she was ready to make common cause with France rather than see the kindred Bourbon dynasty capitulate to Great Britain.   In the autumn Fuentes presented a peremptory memorial on the Spanish grievances, and intimated that the document had already been communicated to the Paris Foreign Office. Sept. 20 Pitt's reply not merely rejected the Spanish claims on the Newfoundland fisheries and asserted the British right to cut timber in Honduras, but laid down in unmistakable language that the previous communication to the French Court was a breach of diplomatic conventions ; and that Great Britain would not tolerate the intervention of a third party (Spain) in matters which solely concerned herself and France.

At this critical point, while the ultimate success of Pitt's policy turned on tightening the war pressure on France, in order to Oct. 25 strengthen his diplomatic position, the sudden death of George II. altered the whole situation at home.   The old King had been spared to see his kingdom triumphant in a great war, and had learned under the charm of victory to forget the resentment and distrust that he had so long felt for Pitt.   While George II. was King the masterful Minister could rely on the Royal support in the Cabinet ; and if that support was essential to Pitt's system of conducting the war, it was doubly so for the conclusion of a satisfactory peace.   Fortune dealt no more cruel blow to Great Britain than in removing a Sovereign with forty years' knowledge of public affairs and taught by bitter experience the duty of acquiescence in the political conditions of a constitutional monarchy. George II. was neither a good man nor a great King. But he could appreciate both good and great men. He was never the victim of charlatans in character or intellect, and he knew when to yield. Hanoverian England learned to value his sound qualities more truly when the Crown passed to a young man, ignorant, obstinate, and eager to govern as well as to reign

NOTE.—On Clive see the standard Life by G. W. Forrest, 2 vols. (1918); on Canada, Wolfe and the campaigns, G. M. Wrong, *The Fall of Canada* (1913) and the authorities there cited; and the same author's *Rise and Fall of New France* (2 vols. 1928); on Foreign Policy consult R. Lodge, *Great Britain and Prussia in the Eighteenth Century* (Ford Lectures), and his articles in *Eng. Hist. Review* for Oct., 1923, July and Oct., 1928, April, 1929; for the Naval side of the War (1739-48) Sir H. W. Richmond, *The Navy in the War of the Austrian Succession* (3 vols. 1925). Prof. W. T. Waugh's recent *Life of Wolfe* is well worth consulting (1929).

CHAPTER IV

HANOVERIAN ENGLAND (1714-1760)

IN 1714 the foundation and fundamental principles of the Protestant, parliamentary, constitutional State as defined by the Bill of Rights and the Act of Settlement were firmly laid down. The Whig theory of 1688—the contractual origin of civil society, the forfeiture of the Crown on the violation of that contract, the tenure of a parliamentary throne and the regulation of the succession on statutory conditions, the compulsory membership of the Sovereign in the Protestant State Church as by law established, the practical independence of the judiciary and the supremacy of Parliament in legislation, taxation, and administration—had originated in a Revolution and involved the repudiation of the counter-theory and principles of the Divine Right Monarchy. With 1714 a new and instructive chapter of constitutional development opens. Between 1714 and 1760 important changes can be traced—the position of the monarchy, the extension of Parliament's authority, the extension of the party system, the evolution of the Cabinet and of the Prime Minister, and the working of the administrative machine—which in their totality give the epoch a character of its own, but they are the result of the logic of political facts and ideals for the most part, and not of statutory enactment or abstract theories of political science. The vitalising and enduring achievements in constitutional progress are not revealed in the scanty record of the legislation of the period. After 1714 there is a distinct cessation in the renovation of the structure of the State by great formative statutes. Even the Septennial Act, important as it is, involved no new principles or theory. It is the inevitable outcome of principles already operative and an instrument to an end already defined. This period 1714-1760 synchronises with the domination of that great party which by 1714 had riveted the Revolution system into

the historic fabric of the Constitution. The Septennial Act in-
augurates the true political supremacy of the Whigs. From 1688-
1714 we observe the gradual triumph of Whig principles ; two years
of uncertainty and then in 1716 follows the triumph of the Whig
party. As indicated elsewhere, the ability of the Whig leaders, the
strength of their organisation resting on a social solidarity, the
fixity of their purpose, the possession of a theoretical creed and a
practical programme were reinforced by good fortune and the mistakes of their opponents.

Bolingbroke was at bottom responsible for George's accession
as the nominee of a party, and Bolingbroke's policy turned a Tory
victory in 1710 under Anne into an irretrievable Tory disaster in
1714. We can mark definite phases in the Whig supremacy—the
Sunderland-Stanhope, the " Robinocracy " of Walpole, the Pelhams,
the Pitt-Newcastle coalition—but through them run common and
typical features which largely determine the trend and results of
constitutional progress. The Koran of Whiggism is the verbally
inspired Bill of Rights and Act of Settlement, with their explicit
implications. The Law of the Whig dispensation is the Law of
the land and Locke is the prophet. Orthodox Whig doctrine, so
far as it professes to be a creed of political philosophy, starts from,
and ends in, the Lockian social compact, of government by consent
of the governed, expressing itself in a Lockian harmony and balance
of conflicting powers. Hanoverian Whiggism, though intellectually
reinforced by Montesquieu's *Esprit des Lois*, "which taught
Englishmen to take a pride in their (balanced) Constitution" (the
lesson was hardly necessary [1]), leaves its mark not so much as a creed 1726
of political science, but rather as a practical way of political life ;
it is based on a series of attempts which start from principles beyond
dispute and seek largely through compromise to realise a workaday
reconciliation of the liberty of the subject with administrative
stability, of economic prosperity with political power at home and
expansion abroad. In opposition to the court, the Church and the
squirearchy, the Whigs pressed into their party system three broad
and distinct elements—the territorial aristocracy, the commercial
hierarchs (trade, banking, the city, the "moneyed men" of an expand-

---

[1] " We are the greatest country in the world ; our climate is the most agreeable
to live in ; our Englishmen are the stoutest and best men in the world " (Defoe,
The Compleat Englishman, i., 369).

11

ing commercial State), and the Nonconformists. These respective classes broadly corresponded to definable strata in the society of the time. The combined interests of these groups, progressive but exclusive, inspired policy and the Whig interpretation of national well-being. Hence the necessity of " control " and " balance " in order to reduce and cool the friction of the machinery, central and local, of government, and to thwart the predominance of any single class. The direction inevitably fell to the great families whose power rested on their historic share in the Revolution, their intuitive aptitude for government, their social status, their wealth and territorial influence, their majority in the Upper, and their indirect control of the Lower, Chamber. Aristocratic, even oligarchic in temper, the Revolution families stood for popular principles, government in accordance with the national will as expressed in lawfully established organs (but which they could powerfully influence). They crystallised into a socially privileged caste which was roughly the result of the existing social and economic organisation. Fear of the Crown and prerogative was their guiding maxim. But with the accession of the House of Brunswick statutory checks on prerogative are no longer their main object. The Whigs are the core and flower of the social world and are transformed into the Court party ; they disarm the legal prerogative of the monarchy by transferring its exercise to Ministers (chosen from their own ranks) responsible to Parliament, and by utilising plastic conventions to conceal the transfer. The growth and application of these conventions, framed by a fine intuition and experience—party Government, ministerial responsibility, the Cabinet system—solved a problem of great difficulty and complexity and are the great contribution of the golden age of Whiggism. The Revolution monarchy, for all its limitations, inherited from statute and common law and custom an undisputed supremacy in the executive and a wide discretionary authority ; it had yet to be reconciled with the legal authority and growing ambitions of Parliament. And when the Whigs had demonstrated the practicability and flexibility of these conventions, as well as their necessity, they had indicated how the monarchical principle could be harmonised with parliamentary supremacy, and executive efficiency with responsibility to representative institutions. Their work was then done.

In the accomplishment of this task Whig " rule " has been

charged with three great faults. The Whigs were, it is commonly said, corrupt. Despite their parliamentary majority they failed to extirpate patent abuses and to give England the essentials of a really liberal Government—religious toleration, a free Press, a popular suffrage, a really representative legislature, a scientific and humane criminal code. Parliamentary government, it is often argued, was the outcome of a series of happy accidents, and the Whig principles of 1689 were not a correct diagnosis of the problems left unsolved by the Revolution. The indictment is partly true. But the character and extent of Whig corruption has been greatly exaggerated; it consisted in applying the influence of the Crown and the patronage of the Executive to sustain the balance between the monarchy and the popular element. Without some such transitional phase there must have followed in 1714 either a further statutory reduction of the Crown's prerogative or a relapse to the pre-Revolution monarchy; in other words, a fresh structural renovation or a counter-revolution. The indispensable condition of drastic progressive reforms (for which England in 1714 was not intellectually or socially prepared) was a Government whose principles and practice were accepted by the whole nation. But in 1714 the Revolution state was still only the creation of a powerful and enlightened minority. Legitimate in law, it had yet to be legitimised by usage and sentiment. By 1760 this transition has been satisfactorily brought about; and if Cabinet and party government were not foreseen in 1689 and 1700, their establishment put the coping-stone to the Revolution scheme, government by and through Parliament. The Whig supremacy, with all its defects, was an inevitable and beneficial stage in the long journey from 1689 to 1910. Under the domination of a proud, patriotic, and enlightened aristocracy, England proved to Europe the success of a gigantic constitutional experiment. The Whigs added an unwritten code to the letter of the law; and their success destroyed automatically the reasons for their own supremacy.

Toryism, on the other hand, in 1714, was rent asunder. Allegiance to the national Church collided with allegiance to a fallen dynasty; and the triumphant Tory party of 1710-13 entered on its forty years' wandering in the wilderness. After ten years of futile and spasmodic opposition it found a Joshua in Henry St. John, under whose leadership the creed of Filmer, Rochester, Sacheverell and Atterbury, and the October Club, was transformed into the creed of Wyndham and Marchmont, and finally of Johnson, Gibbon, and the younger Pitt. Bolingbroke, as a loyal subject of George II., proved indeed to be a far more dangerous foe to Whiggism than the Minister of Anne and the half-hearted rebel of 1715. He accepted the structure of the Revolution state and the conventional theory of a balance of powers ; he purged his party of its anachronistic belief in divine right ; by ceaseless denunciation of corruption he associated " party " with " faction," and he legitimised opposition by allying it with the heir to the parliamentary throne and with the rebel Whigs.[1] The new Toryism identified the interest of the truly national state with the legal authority of an ideally intelligent and patriotic kingship, freed from caste selfishness and the bigotry of faction, blending all parties into one great union to achieve national ends by national means. Though Bolingbroke did not perceive it, at his death the promised land was near. He had captured the future sovereign and armed him with a plan of campaign ; outside the strongholds of Whig monopoly he had rallied the army which emerged as " The King's Friends " ; and he had vamped up for both a stock of ideas, tricked out in the trappings of the fashionable philosophy of the *Salons*, which could easily be applied as a panacea for misinterpreted defects, and still more easily mistaken for a progressive political faith. Aided by the social revolution in operation since 1714, by the reconciliation of the squirearchy and the Church to the House of Brunswick, and by the disintegration of the Whig party, the Toryism of Bolingbroke in 1760 opens a new chapter in its own history and in that of Great Britain.

The Revolution settlement had laid down what the Crown must be and what it could not do ; it had said very little as to what the Crown could or ought to do. It left the prerogative, except where expressly limited, unimpaired and the discretionary powers of the Sovereign, as head of the Executive and the necessary participant in every act of government, undefined. After 1714 there

---

[1] " All experience convinces me that ninety men out of a hundred, when they talk of forming principles mean no more than embracing parties " (Chesterfield, *Works*, i., 109). " Every administration is a system of conduct : opposition, therefore, should be a system of conduct likewise, an opposite, but an independent system " (Bolingbroke, *Works*, vii., 59).

is a slow change in the character of the Crown and its attitude towards its functions which ushers in the modernisation of the Monarchy. With Anne perished the indefinable prestige and atmosphere of the Divine Right Sovereign. George I. and II. were in name kings by the Grace of God; in fact they existed by Act of Parliament and (more important) by the goodwill of the Whig party. They might threaten to retire to Hanover, but they might not find it so easy to come back. The hereditary quarrel between the King and his legal heir secured in a remarkable way the allegiance of the Opposition to the continuity of the dynasty, although it diminished the respect of the nation. Unnoticed, the Whigs enmeshed the legal prerogative of initiation in a network of indirect checks, the breaking of which would lead to a breach of the law. It is significant that after Anne the Sovereign ceased to attend debates in the House of Lords; and when George I. ceased also to sit in the Cabinet he made a far-reaching surrender to the solidarity of the ministerial system. The necessary approval by Parliament of every important act in home and foreign policy and the jealous scrutiny of the Crown's intentions, suspect because the King was avowedly German by blood, training, and interest, fostered a geometrically increasing progress in the limitation of the sphere and objects of the royal will. The royal veto on parliamentary legislation was tacitly dropped, though in relation to colonial assemblies it was carefully retained and exercised. The evolution of ministerial responsibility, the growth of administrative business, and the expansion of the code of conventions, materially strengthened the steady transition to the status of official royalty.

Yet it would be a serious mistake to place the Hanoverian monarchy in the same category as the Victorian. The closer one studies the inner working of the mechanism of government the more convincing become the proofs of the reality and ubiquity of the power of the Crown in the person of the wearer of it. George I. and II. took a deep interest in European politics. Their knowledge made them formidable critics, their bias obstinate advocates. In foreign policy their assent, as the documents show, was essential and not easily gained. The judicial decision of 1718 made the King an absolutist in his own family. Despite the Mutiny Act the army was a jealously guarded preserve of an autocratic prerogative. "This province," George II. said, "I will keep to myself from your scoun-

drels of the House of Commons." In the disposition of the Civil
List the royal will, uncontrolled by specific appropriation or effective
audit, was supreme. The Crown lands and the hereditary revenues
of the heir to the throne gave both to King and Prince of Wales
powerful parliamentary and territorial influence. The careers of
Walpole and of Carteret prove how invaluable, those of Bolingbroke and Pitt how damaging, to political success the Sovereign's
personal likes and dislikes could be. Queen Caroline and the Countess of Yarmouth are witnesses to the same conclusion. Indeed the
Whig domination of the Court and society, by intensifying the
personal issues in political life, and by multiplying the opportunities
for social intrigue, provided an ample field for the exercise of a varied
patronage. Scotland and Ireland swelled the tale. Ribands and
stars, pensions, peerages, colonelcies of regiments, boroughs and
places, from the important offices in the Ministry and the Household
to sinecures in the civil establishment and tide-waiterships in Ire
land, were distributed according to the royal pleasure. The Diary
of Lady Cowper, the Memoirs of Hervey, the Letters of Chesterfield
and Horace Walpole, the Calendar of Treasury Papers, and the
vast Newcastle Correspondence, enable us to understand how Whig
fear of the powers of the Crown even in the hands of foreign
Sovereigns, personally unimpressive, was no idle shibboleth. Thanks
to the unwearied organisation of the great Whig managers, such
as Newcastle and Islay, these innumerable resources were marshalled,
on the whole, to promote Whig ascendency, and to make the Cabinet
and the House of Commons the working centre of government ; and
it is worth noting that under an equally unwearied (but royal)
manager, George III., the same resources kept the Opposition at
bay for twenty years and finally broke up the Whig party.

The Upper Chamber of the Legislature had not yet assumed its
familiar modern form. Composed of hereditary lay peers, and the
official spiritual peers, and the sixteen representatives of the Scottish
peerage added in 1707, it numbered at the accession of George I.
one hundred and seventy-eight members, of whom twelve were
minors. Previously to 1688 there had been considerable additions,
as there were after 1783 ; but in 1760 its numbers (one hundred and
seventy-four) were practically the same as in 1714, showing that the
new creations made by George I. and George II. were substantially
balanced by the steady and natural extinction of existing peerages.
Nor was the Whig jealousy of the royal prerogative of creating

peers, exemplified in the abortive Peerage Bill of 1719, wholly due
to the exclusiveness of a privileged social caste. The power of the
Crown to create peers lavishly at the bidding of a Ministry in a
minority, seen in the famous twelve creations made to secure the
acceptance of the Treaties of Utrecht, had been fiercely resented.
This right was, not without reason, regarded as liable to abuse
and provocative of retaliation—a power which might be employed
recklessly to undermine the character of the House and endanger
its constitutional privileges. The dominant theory of a balance
of powers found its expression in the desirability of maintaining
the House of Lords in practical independence alike of the Crown
and the representative Chamber. The newer senatorial theory on
which the younger Pitt seems to have acted in his wholesale additions—the representation in the Upper Chamber of political and
intellectual eminence, and of the great industrial capitalists—was
not yet an accepted political practice; nor did social and economic
conditions and political exigencies as yet furnish powerful arguments in its favour. The peers represented personally a historic
estate—the temporal peerage together with their spiritual brethren.
Under George I. and II. they continued to be a great Council of
the Crown, whose members were invested by law, usage, and the
characteristics of national development with defined rights and
duties. Their legal privileges, freedom of debate, the right of
free criticism and advice, were bound up with their position as
hereditary Councillors. Minorities could find influential expression;
and the established custom of Protests provided for a personal and
permanent record in the Journals of the House of reasoned dissent
from the collective action and views of the majority. These Protests of Dissentient Peers in the eighteenth century (good examples
are those on the Mutiny Bill, the Middlesex Election, the Regency
Bill) are often weighty contributions to the fund of political ideas
as well as a valuable source of information to the historical student.
The right of initiating and amending taxation had been practically
surrendered; the claim to reject money Bills was not urged; but
the Upper Chamber regarded itself in legislation and discussion
as a co-ordinate part of the Legislature, and not merely a revising
body. True that, already in 1711 a Ministry, with a majority in
the Commons, had disregarded a double vote of no-confidence by
the House of Lords. But after 1714 the remarkable harmony

between the two Chambers on the fundamental issues of policy prevented the precedent from being decisive. For the rejection of ministerial bills by either House was not in the practice of the day considered to require the resignation of their authors. But it was already quite clear that support by the House of Lords alone would not enable a Government to go on. The preponderance of peers in the Ministries of the time is striking. In the Cabinets of 1737 and 1740, of which we have official lists, fourteen out of sixteen, and eleven out of fourteen members, respectively, are peers, and this percentage is characteristic of the century as a whole. The House of Lords, in short, was an organic representation of property, social power, and office. In practice it broadly represented the dominant Whig aristocracy; and its powers and dignity were enhanced by its judicial pre-eminence as the Supreme Court of Appeal for the United Kingdom and Ireland, and by its function to decide on impeachments preferred by the Commons, though from 1725-60 we have no important example of this method of punishing an unpopular Minister.[1]

The record (from 1714-60) of the House of Commons does not offer the picturesque drama of the seventeenth century. Hence the Hanoverian Lower House is often represented either as the mere mirror of a stagnant Whiggism or the demoralised accomplice of a corrupt oligarchy, distinguished alone by its classic orators—Walpole, Pulteney, Wyndham, Murray, Fox, Pitt—speaking within jealously closed doors to an audience whose votes were already determined. In reality these fifty years permanently build up the English type of State, of which government by the regular meeting of a representative body is the most striking feature. In the form and structure of the Lower House there is little change. After the large additions by the Stuart monarchy and the legislative union with Scotland, the next large influx does not come till 1801. Ninety-four members in 1714 represent the English counties, 415 the boroughs, four the universities, while Scotland sends thirty county and fifteen burgh members. The county suffrage is the forty-shilling freehold qualification of 1430; but in the boroughs the qualification defies scientific analysis, though a rough fourfold classification can be made out, based on the Scot and Lot, the Burgage, the Corporation, and the Freeman franchise. The extension of the Burgh franchise was finally closed by the Last Determination Act of 1729, and the next

---

[1] Consult A. S. Turberville, *The House of Lords in the Eighteenth Century* (1927), particularly Chs. V.-X. and Appendix XIV.

change, a sweeping one, is delayed until 1832. By 1714 the Commons are able to utilise the fruits of the continuous struggle of the preceding century. The fundamental privileges—freedom of speech, a co-ordinate share in legislation, freedom from arrest (except for treason, felony, or breach of the peace), the right to impeach peers and commoners, the settlement of contested elections, parliamentary taxation—are no longer in danger from the Crown or its executive servants, and several rest on a statutory guarantee. The prerogative of the Crown to summon or extend the duration of Parliament is regulated by the Septennial Act, a model example of the legal sovereignty of Parliament. The House italicises these privileges by additions essential to its self-defined functions and ambitions. The exclusive right to originate and determine the incidence of taxation, asserted against the peers in 1678, is not questioned in the eighteenth century. The right to exclude strangers and prohibit the publication of debates, corollaries to freedom of speech, are expressed in Standing Orders, defended in 1738 by Pulteney against his colleague in Opposition, Wyndham, with the significant argument that publication "looks like making members accountable without doors for what they do within". Hence the claim "that to print or publish any books or libels reflecting upon the proceedings of the House of Commons or any member thereof for or relating to his service therein" is a breach of privilege punishable by the House ; and enforced as it was (e.g. in the case of *Mist's Journal* and others) virtually amounted to a special censor- 1721 ship of the Press. With this naturally was involved the right to punish its own members for breaches of discipline. In the case of Alexander Murray the judge held that the law courts were not 1751 required to question the validity of a return to a writ of Habeas Corpus, stating that a prisoner was committed for contempt on a warrant issued by the Speaker. But essential as these privileges were to the maintenance of the dignity and efficiency of the House of Commons, they were subsidiary to the grand end, the power to control the Executive. And for this purpose a formidable instrument had been created in the code of Parliamentary Procedure, a body of parliamentary "law," enforced by the Lower House in its long struggle with the Crown and the Executive.

Parliamentary procedure is not, as we are tempted to regard it at first, a mosaic of technical antiquities, nor an interesting compendium of rules of the oldest national debating assembly in modern Europe. It is one of the weapons forged by the representatives of a practical nation, by which they have conquered the problem of making popular government workable and efficient. And these rules, amended and strengthened by continuous experience, have become the model for the legislatures given to our self-governing colonies as well as for those founded by European States in open imitation. Already by 1714 the characteristic features of legislative procedure—questions, petitions, divisions, amendments, the functions of the Speaker, the Grand Committee of Supply and of Ways and Means—have been established. Based on the equality of all members, they provide the ordered methods of free and jealous criticism. The majority decides, but after every opportunity has been given to the minority to express its views. Members of the Government as such have no special precedence; they are simply representatives of a group of voters with the common rights of such. Indeed a servant of the Crown by his position provokes a rigorous scrutiny. He cannot retaliate except by argument if he is attacked, nor can he reverse elsewhere a refusal of his proposals. His fellow-members can be persuaded by superior argument or special information; they cannot and will not be coerced by an authority extrinsic to themselves.

The Hanoverian House of Commons drives the results of this system home. First they secure and improve the rules. Under 1728-61 the guidance of an able Speaker, Arthur Onslow, parliamentary procedure is solidified, a noble and conservative tradition built up, the political ethos completed. Secondly, they employ the code to enforce Ministerial responsibility in policy, finance, administration, legislation. In a word the Minister who most freely invites the advice and support of the House will be the Minister it most freely trusts. Thirdly they elaborate the application of the system to all money grants. Finance, not legislation, is the chief function of Ministers. The rules which provide the fullest consideration for the amount, character, and incidence of the burden imposed on the taxpayer enforce a control from which there is no escape. In 1713 a Standing Order prohibits the discussion of any demand for public funds, except on the recommendation of the Crown through its authorised agents. Ministers are thus indirectly ordered to make themselves responsible for all the financial proposals of the

State. The specific procedure—Committee of Supply and of Ways and Means, with Ministerial explanation and Opposition criticism, embodiment of the Committee's conclusions in legislative forms and its proper stages, appropriation to defined purposes—show how the Budget is the main work of the session and how every step in the process is safeguarded to secure control. From 1689 the expansion of Great Britain, involving a continuous increase in expenditure and votes of supply, has to be financed. From 1688 the army and navy are the great spending departments. Directly, the forces of the Crown are in this way controlled, indirectly, and more important, policy is reviewed, reversed, or approved; and with each year the handcuffs on the arms of the Executive are provided with locks whose keys are in the custody of Parliament. The Chancellor of the Exchequer is virtually promoted to the first rank, for unless he can secure a majority Government is helpless. Year by year the political centre shifts more surely to the floor of the House of Commons. A Walpole, a Pelham, and a Pitt, in whom a majority believe, stand in marked contrast to a Carteret in whom they do not. True, the civil list is not yet included in this annual revision and this national audit. But presently royal and departmental debt, the growth in the civil needs of the State will compel the Crown to ask for more money and then the procedure, proved to be so efficacious, will be extended to regulate and appropriate this reserve of royal policy also. A distinction will be gradually drawn between expenditure on the apparatus of the monarchy and expenditure on the civil and public administration of the State, between national and purely royal finance; and the distinction will be emphasised by the assertion of complete Ministerial responsibility for everything that clearly belongs to the State as a national unit.

We may note further that this extensive control is secured largely by indirect means. Annual Parliaments become a necessity because the Commons will only vote supplies for a year. And, thanks to the Revolution legislation, the power of Parliament can only be destroyed by a *coup d'état*. But to be efficient Parliament itself must be guided, advised, and managed. The direction falls inevitably to the group of responsible Ministers who, under the rules, are expected to provide the main business of the session and determine the chief topics for debate. Ministers also, to carry out the will of the Commons, require a permanent not a haphazard majority. Disciplined supporters are a party; and the system by which they work evolves as party government. It is the age of the great managers—Walpole who sees the advantage of a trades union to promote "the King's business" and of a united policy, and boycotts the non-unionists as "blacklegs"; Newcastle and Islay who create cats with ninety tails. And so under the Hanoverians, the Patronage Secretary and the Junior Lords of the Treasury become the party whips, salaried by the Legislature in the name of the whole nation to do the work of a party majority. The settlement of contested elections inevitably becomes trials of party strength. Failure to carry your candidate will count two votes on a division to your opponents, and will indicate to the leaders the rise and fall in the political barometer. Conversely behind *The Craftsman* Bolingbroke strives not unsuccessfully to organise against His Majesty's Government, His Majesty's (or rather His Majesty's heir's) Opposition with a counter-programme, and uses parliamentary procedure as its weapons of attack. His ambition now is not to engineer a counter-revolution but to get and to keep office. The Toryism of 1710-13, fought under a transparent mask and with ropes round its neck for a fallen system and a proscribed dynasty; the Opposition from 1725-42 and afterwards only desires to make a clean sweep of the monarchy's confidential staff. The game is a great because a national one; the rules are becoming rigid and the rival teams born and trained in the same social system learn to play, as it behoves citizens who are gentlemen to play.

We have passed from the spirit and methods of the seventeenth century, when it was a life-and-death struggle for fundamental principles, to the first chapter of the modern era. Three defects of this parliamentary machine are important for the future : (1) The Commons do not represent adequately the constituencies, the constituencies do not represent the nation. The anomalous and moth-eaten suffrage law excluded large classes from the franchise, both in the counties and boroughs. The distribution of seats in the latter, as the electoral map shows, rested too often on the arbitrary creations of the Crown in the past, or on an economic organisation no longer corresponding to that of England even in 1714. Sarum was already a sheep-walk, Dunwich half under the sea, Droitwich an abandoned salt-pit. A handful of Cornish fishing villages, each returning two members, could out-vote the representatives of the capital, the centre of the nation's finance and trade. Towns that modern trade had created had no recognition in the allotment of seats. The property qualifications, the political and religious disabilities, witnessed to a political theory and ideals that every year became more difficult to defend on political theory or expediency. (2) The restricted franchise and low ethical standards facilitated corruption and manipulation. Seats were bought and sold, and the patrons of these nomination boroughs could aid in creating an artificial representation of opinion that existed only in a financial transaction. More than two hundred office-holders were said to sit in the Parliaments of George II. Chesterfield remarked of the "Court" or "Treasury" boroughs that their electors would "obey were the person named the minister's footman". The Scottish representatives notoriously received "wages," and were controlled by the Administration of the day; and we have noted above how the varied resources of Crown influence could keep together a majority. The strength of the Pelham connection, the methods by which Henry Fox carried the Peace of 1763, are sinister facts beyond dispute. Yet Walpole, in the plenitude of his powers, had to abandon his Excise Bill, and later failed to avert war with Spain and to keep himself in office. The Tammany Hall genius of Newcastle could not save his Ministry in 1756. Pitt, who had no wealth and scorned party connections, enjoyed for four years a parliamentary dictatorship unequalled before or since. Neither wealth nor ability nor lack of scruple could make Henry Fox Prime Minister.

Parliament also endeavoured to check a recognised evil by Place Bills, such as that of 1742, which disqualified the holders of various Crown appointments from sitting in the Commons. But the remedy was timidly applied. It was not until an economic revolution and the slow growth of political theory made the electoral system and its abuses an intolerable anachronism that the reform of Parliament became a pressing public necessity. (3) This conclusion was clinched by the results on Parliament itself of the constitutional progress made under the Hanoverians. The Lower House enforced the responsibility of Ministers, but became itself irresponsible. It could ignore public opinion, save when profoundly stirred, partly because that very public opinion to be salutary and effective required to be organised, to be provided with adequate organs of expression, protected by the law and custom of the Constitution. We touch here on the intimate and necessary connection between the efficiency of a representative Legislature and the social and political system that it represents. The abuses of the one are correlative to the abuses in the other. The growth of political intelligence and the success of Whig rule were needed as an indispensable preliminary to the changes wrought by the great economic upheaval. By 1760 a new England is coming into being. The House of Commons, stereotyped in its form, clinging to the letter and misinterpreting the spirit of the law, after 1760 is forced into sharp collision with the new forces. The tinkering alterations in the details, not in the principles of the structure, are seen to be inadequate, then irrelevant; and gradually as the century winds to a close political controversy returns to first principles. The cause of parliamentary reform, which half a century earlier had started with modest demands for the removal of patent anomalies and abuses in an accepted system and a time-honoured state structure, was by 1792 in reality a revolutionary programme. It involved an assault on the system itself, and a remodelling of the existing social and economic organisation, and not merely the reconstruction of the parliamentary machine. But the stage of development already reached in Great Britain in 1792, and the true nature of the issues, were first concealed and then arrested by the outbreak of the French Revolution and the smoke of the European conflagration that followed. The English party of reform were inevitably but falsely confused with the revolutionists of 1789, with whose principles and ends they had little or nothing in common. After twenty-three years of war and suffering Great Britain found herself once more at peace. And the State that had strained moral and material resources to the uttermost, in order to keep the French Revolution at bay, startled Europe by proceeding shortly to carry out a long-postponed and inevitable revolution of its own. In that revolution the great Reform Bill of 1832, fundamental and imposing as it must always remain, is neither the first nor the last article of the programme. The revolutionary Whigs of 1832 were the explicit executors of the ideals implicitly formulated in 1792.

In this constitutional development the theory of Executive responsibility rested on three broad implications. The Crown is the

Executive, conveying its will and pleasure to authoritative agents, whom it appoints and dismisses. These authoritative agents are primarily responsible to the Crown for the execution of the business assigned to them by law and custom, while Parliament asserts slowly also a joint responsibility to itself. But neither theory nor practice have as yet defined with precision the fluctuating and ragged boundary line between these two conflicting spheres of responsibility. Parliament, however, does not claim then nor since to appoint the Executive agents of the Crown. It can only aim at securing that on the whole they shall work in accordance with the wishes of the Legislature. Thirdly, law and custom, with increasing stringency of form and detail, prescribe the procedure of Executive action. The Crown and its authorised agents are bound by the law of the land. Nor can the Crown in its Executive capacity act without advice. For every Executive act the agent, authorised by law or custom, is technically held responsible. The Executive, therefore is the body of Crown servants who through various organs carry on the administrative work of the State, and translate into the necessary action the commands of the Crown, as law and custom from time to time prescribe.

These Crown servants fall roughly into three groups—the great officers of the Royal Household, the heads of organised departments to which a definite sphere of administration has come to be assigned, the Privy Council and its committees. The importance of the first slowly diminishes, and the diminution is significant. After 1714 the chief officers—the Lord Steward, the Lord Chamberlain, the Master of the Horse, the Treasurer and Controller of the Household—are regarded as political, *i.e.* they change with the Administration. The first three named continue to be Cabinet appointments, and occasionally such offices as those of Groom of the Stole, Captain of the Band of Pensioners also bring their holders into the Cabinet. But they are held less and less by politicians of the first rank. Shrewsbury, under Anne, is the last statesman of eminence who held the Chamberlainship. This change is partly due to the increasing importance of the strictly departmental chiefs and partly to the increasing distinction between the purely Court and the Governmental aspects of the monarchy, already noted. The offices which belong to the personal life of the Sovereign lose their administrative importance and become honorary and social. By 1714 a group of the modern heads of organised departments is clearly recognisable. The functions of the Lord President of the Council are bound up with the Privy Council, but the Lord Chancellor, the Lord Lieutenant of Ireland, the First Commissioner or Lord of the Admiralty, the First Lord of the Treasury, the two Secretaries of State are all posts of the first rank and invariably in the Cabinet.

The Secretaries are the authorised organs of the Royal will; their combined duties, apportioned according to a geographical division, cover both foreign and home affairs. The Secretary for the Northern Department dealt with the northern powers, that for the Southern with the other foreign States, with Ireland, the colonies, and the home sphere. In practice, the Lord Lieutenant, with the Irish Executive and the Committees of the British Privy Council, relieved the Southern Secretary of much of his purely domestic work. But the Secretarial division was illogical and inconvenient, " as if," in the classic simile, "two coachmen were on the mail box, one holding the right and the other the left rein". The Secretaries are Executive officers, invariably regarded as amongst the chief members of the Ministry, while the increase and political importance of their work prepare the way for the decisive change in 1782 which is the foundation of the modern Secretariat. From 1707-46 a third Secretary, for Scotland, was, with one short interval, in existence.

In the dramatic crisis of Anne's last days the historic office of Lord High Treasurer was filled for the last time when the white staff was assigned to Shrewsbury. After his resignation, in October, 1714, the post became a constitutional antiquity, and henceforward the Treasury was continuously kept in commission. In the development of the Treasury Board three features of interest are prominent: (1) The position of First Lord is associated with the titular presidency of the Ministry; (2) the rise of the Chancellor of the Exchequer; and (3) the growth of the Treasury Department as the central organ of State administration. As regards the first, the long Ministry of Walpole, 1721-42, is the decisive epoch. The evolution of the Chancellor of the Exchequer from the position of a subordinate to that of an equal with the great Executive officers epitomises the expansion of a commercial State and the collateral growth of parliamentary government. By degrees the Chancellor becomes the specialised officer, whose function is to explain and defend in terms of finance Ministerial policy and to provide, with parliamentary approval, the revenue essential to its execution. " A man," as Burke said of Walpole, " will do more with figures of arithmetic than figures of rhetoric." And behind the Chancellor necessarily grow his administrative staff and department. Every advance in the area and reality of parliamentary control indirectly involves an advance in the supervision of the Exchequer over the finance of the whole State. But between 1714 and 1760 the position of the modern Treasury is foreshadowed rather than realised. The organised expert staff, the comprehensive financial revision of all estimates and expenditure, the Chancellor, responsible for a complete Budget and a collective fiscal policy, are still a long way off. The Hanoverian Treasury is not much more than an expanding book-keeping establishment, which issues and accounts for public money appropriated by parliamentary authority. There is as yet no Consolidated Fund. Expenditure is met by separate taxes, assigned to separate votes, charged on separate items, and kept in a separate series of accounts, whose complexity and interlacing baffle those who, both then and to-day, would seek for a single balance-sheet of the nation's revenue and expenditure. The Treasury, in short, acts as a State trustee, whose duty is to see that these various moneys are paid into, and out from, the separate statutory reservoirs, as the law has determined. The control over expenditure is severely limited. There are no Civil List Estimates. The Admiralty frames its own Estimates, and deals directly with the Privy Council and the House of Commons. And though the Treasury exercises some revision of army expenditure, its powers are weak and contested, and the system of audit intermittent and inadequate. For its executive work the original Treasury Board, presided over until 1760 by the King, met four times a week. The administrative reorganisation was to come in the next reign. Meanwhile the demands of Parliament for control, the gradual separation of royal from State expenditure, the increase in the debts of various executive Departments, and the swelling cost of financing the expansion of the Empire paved the way for drastic changes, to be noted later.

In 1708 the office of Lord High Admiral was put in commission, but the Hanoverian Admiralty differed from the modern Board : (1) it had not the complete management of all naval business, for part was done by the Navy Board and the Victualling Board, while the Treasurer of the Navy had a separate office ; (2) the First Commissioner was not necessarily a civilian. The power and independence of the Admiralty, which wielded a general control over the policy of the navy, are striking facts in the administrative *régime*, to be accounted for by the national recognition of the supreme importance of their duties. To Parliament and the country the fleet meant the frontier of Great Britain, the prosperity of sea-borne

1743   trade, the first line of offence and defence. The cases of *Rex v.*
1776   *Broadfoot* and *Rex v. Tubbs*, ratifying the power of impressment, show that public sensitiveness as to encroachments on the liberty of the subject, and the royal devotion to a shrinking and syndicated prerogative, which hindered so fatally the co-ordination of the administrative machinery and the efficiency of the military forces of the Crown, were far less operative in the case of the navy. The Executive of the army remained split up into a conflicting medley of jurisdictions. A unified central War Office did not exist. The nation did not cease to fear, and had not learned to trust, in the army—a necessary evil and a modern innovation entirely lacking the historic prestige and atmosphere of the navy ; public opinion, both within and without Parliament, oscillated between recurrent epidemics of panic—the dread of absolutism, and the loss of civil liberty, to be brought about by a hireling standing army, and the dread of "popery and wooden shoes" imposed by the successful invasion of foreign foes from over seas. The Crown, too, was opposed to the supremacy of the civil power in military affairs, and resisted the harmonisation of the prerogative over the army with the claims of ministerial and parliamentary control. As late as 1757 Newcastle opposed the Militia Bill, on the ground that it would breed a military spirit in an industrial and agricultural people ; and the echoes of this fear, dating from Cromwell's *régime*, still reverberate to-day.

Thus it came about that the King, as Commander-in-Chief, ruled at the Horse Guards. The channel of his pleasure was the Secretary at (not for) War, defined by Pulteney in 1717 "as a ministerial, not a constitutional officer, bound to issue orders according to the King's directions". Not till 1783 was his anomalous position reconstructed on the basis of an acknowledged parliamentary responsibility. The Paymaster of the Forces dealt with the Treasury Board, and all moneys, including foreign subsidies, voted by Parliament passed through his hands. In times of war the balances were always large, and the Paymaster, besides taking commissions on the totals, treated them as belonging to himself until they were paid over, often a matter of decades. Some of Henry Fox's accounts for the Seven Years' War were not finally closed until 1774. The commissariat was managed by the Treasury ; while the Ordnance Board, presided over by the Master General of the Ordnance, an office held by the chief military leaders of the day, which generally carried with it Cabinet rank, provided armament and stores both for the army and navy, with a separate parliamentary vote and a separate parliamentary responsibility. Briefly, the administrative work of the army exemplifies the recent origin of a permanent force and the piecemeal character of the machinery created to meet a need reluctantly admitted. The theoretical supremacy of the civil power and of the Legislature was secured by the annual Mutiny Act, which legalised for times of peace and within the Kingdom alone the existence of military courts and a special code of military law. Outside the Kingdom the rule of the army rested on prerogative ; and at home, in military administration, the Crown was virtually supreme. Parliament, in fact, by legalising and paying for a standing army, provided the Crown with one of its most undisputed spheres of discretionary authority. The prevailing theory of neutralising menaces to the Constitution by checks and balances was partly responsible for the illogical overlapping of the spheres of the various executive organs. Costly and cumulative experience proved that concentration in a unified War Office, under a single responsible Ministerial head, was the only sound method for securing a national force under national control. The eighteenth century system thwarted effective parliamentary supervision, fostered political and social intrigue, financial waste, and Executive inefficiency, with military and political results graven deep in our national history. And it left to the future a problem both in law and administration, which it required more than a century of effort, opposition, unfulfilled prophecies, and military failures, partially to solve.

The Post Office was already a department providing the Government with revenue. In 1710 a Postmaster-General had been created by Letters Patent. The office, usually held by two joint Postmasters, and disqualified by the Place Bill of Anne from being 1705 represented in Parliament, was not treated as political and the statutory disability was not removed until 1867.

The third great branch of the Executive was concentrated in the Privy Council, whose Lord President ranked with the highest officers of State. The gradual atrophy of its consultative functions, and the transference of its judicial work to other bodies, left its executive powers unimpaired ; and three aspects of these call for notice : (1) The regular attendance of the Sovereign at Council meetings, though not at Committees of Council, assisted the devolution of business. In the eighteenth century the modern custom developed that, when duties are assigned by statute to these Committees, the presence of the Sovereign may also be dispensed with. (2) The Council remained the formal body on whose advice the royal pleasure, by orders and proclamations, in numerous matters of administration, is conveyed. Under statutory authority, or as custom prescribed, these took effect without parliamentary or other intervention. In sum, they amounted to a quasi-legislative and effective executive power, important both in their character and comprehensiveness. But for the most part they simply initiated or ratified the necessary departmental action. (3) The Standing or temporary *ad hoc* Committees dealt with assigned branches of executive business, *e.g.* Foreign Affairs, Ireland, the Colonies. These Committees provided the nuclei out of which in time the modern specialised departments have grown. By 1660 the Secretariat had practically absorbed Foreign Affairs. In 1695 the Board of Trade and Plantations, which lasted till 1782, was set up to take over the work of a Special Committee. In 1784 the composition of the newly constituted Board of Trade shows how in theory it is properly a Committee of the Privy Council. Colonial affairs had already passed to a Secretary of State. Other great modern departments have a similar origin. Their growth has been dependent on several elements, which illustrate the historic features of the Council. The importance of some specific sphere of administration first calls into existence a temporary, then a Standing, Committee, to prepare and sift business for the Council ; which Committee in turn is transformed by Statute or Order in Council into an Executive department, in turn practically to become an independent organisation under its own chief. The modern development of permanent expert staffs, working under specified conditions as a branch of the State, gradually takes root, and is the foundation of the Civil Service. The original functions of the Council in administration, however, were partly consultative, *i.e.* with determining principles of policy. The comprehensive sphere of the Council's work unified the business of the State and brought it under the central control of the Crown's legally authorised ministers and advisers. Uniformity in action was thus attainable. But the growth of administrative work on the one side necessitated, as seen above, the creation of specially organised departments in the place of Committees. On the other, the gradual reservation of the right to determine policy to a group of Ministers—the Cabinet—took the place of the previous connection between the consultative and executive functions of the Council. The Privy Council in the eighteenth century dwindles before these two clearly marked developments into its modern position of an organ whose advice and consent are required by law and custom to initiate or complete a series of acts whose policy has been determined, and whose executive action will be carried out, elsewhere. But in securing the legal aspects of Ministerial responsibility the Council had a historic importance. Ministers, by custom Privy Councillors, belonged to a body known to the law whose share in executive action was susceptible of legal investigation. A politician can be impeached *quâ* Privy Councillor, but not *quâ* member of the Cabinet.

Here again, however, the decay of the process of impeachment for acts of policy follows the alteration in the council's functions. The Privy Councillor's responsibility could be enforced by depriving him of his head. The Cabinet Minister is punished by depriving him of his office. The change is partly the cause, partly the effect, of the growth of the Cabinet; and is profoundly influenced by the slow revolution in political ideas and the interpretation of political ends. Similarly, the absence in the Hanoverian England of many departments to-day considered essential is not merely a proof of the complex social and economic differences that distinguish a nascent from a developed Empire, a commercial and agricultural community from the highly differentiated organism of the modern industrial State. True, the existence of these organised and statutory creations—the Treasury, Home, Indian, Colonial, and War Offices, the Boards of Local Government, Trade, Public Works, Agriculture, and Education—can be primarily attributed to the imperious pressure of a continuous political and economic expansion. But they also represent a fundamental revolution in the methods and objects of administration, in the functions and ends of government, in the conception of citizenship. Behind the battlemented citadels of the modern Executive lie principles, dormant or undreamed of by Hanoverian England, that have passed from the philosopher's study and the scientist's laboratory into the commonplaces of political and civic life.

From 1688-1760 the movement in political thought in England was languid, compared with the feverish epochs that precede and follow. So far as English minds were active they were occupied with the problems commonly summarised under the name of the Deist Controversy, with metaphysics (Hume and Berkeley, Hutcheson and Butler), or with the ornamental frippery of thought that educated circles under the spell of the diluted optimism of Leibnitz and the shallow elegance of Bolingbroke mistook for philosophical science. Englishmen too were absorbed in securing the Revolution system at home and abroad and in pegging out the hinterlands of Empire. But under George III. we note the renascence of an intellectual activity of the first order, led by three of the masters, Adam Smith, Burke, and Bentham, whose writings leavened the best minds of two generations; and into the seventy years after 1760 are crammed the American Revolution, the Industrial Revolution, the French Revolution, the career of Napoleon, the Irish Revolution and the Legislative Union of the British and Irish Parliaments, the British conquest of India, and the triumph of Parliamentary Reform. In the classic epoch of Whig rule the fear of the Crown and the Executive retarded the extension of the functions of the State both in theory and practice. The modern Englishman has learned to endure taxation; he desires a strong Executive because his economic and political needs are complex, and because he knows that the Executive must work in harmony with the national will. If to-day there is tyranny, it is that of a majority over a minority. His eighteenth century ancestor had behind him fifty years of civil war and successful or thwarted *coups d'état*. His needs were simple and he wanted to be let alone. He feared the tyranny of a minority over a majority. The first condition of political advance therefore lay in the reconciliation of the rights of the Executive with the control of an independent legislature, and with the liberties of the subject under a free Constitution. The Cabinet, in Bagehot's phrase, was to become the hyphen between Executive and Legislature; and by 1760 the buckles of the band were being slowly hammered into a workable form.

The modern Cabinet is not the Executive, though it is the motive power of the Executive; it is not even the Ministry in the strict sense of the term, for it does not include all the Ministerial heads of Executive departments. It is a group of the Crown's confidential servants including all the important holders of office. So long as these retain the confidence of Parliament and of their Sovereign they have a monopoly right to advise as to the exercise of the prerogative of the Crown and on the principles and details of policy. The head of the Cabinet is the Prime Minister, who is selected by the Crown, but who with its approval selects his colleagues; and this Prime Minister is the main channel of communication between the Crown and the Cabinet as well as the Minister who enjoys the greatest influence both in the royal closet and in the country. Individually, the heads of the great Executive departments are responsible for the business and acts of their several bureaux; collectively, the Cabinet is responsible for the policy of the Empire. In practice it is virtually a committee of the party which for the time has a majority in the Legislature and the members of the committee who represent that party hold homogeneous views on the important issues of the politics of the day. So long as they command the support of a majority of the Representative Chamber as expressed in its votes or by the results of a general election, they will continue to hold office. The Cabinet, therefore, is the chief feature of a system, based not on statute law, but on customs, conventions, and convenience, whose *raison d'être* is to harmonise the exercise of the legal prerogatives of the Crown with the broad principle of Ministerial responsibility and with the powers and rights of a representative Legislature. It secures that the Sovereign through his authorised agents will govern in accordance with law and the national will. And apart from the special marks of the institution—the sole right of the Ministers who compose it to advise, collective responsibility for that advice, and its administrative results, the accepted position of the Prime Minister—it is tolerably clear that it implies a theory of parliamentary control accepted by Crown and people, a system of party organisation, discipline and

government, and the existence of constitutional machinery by which
the national will can be intelligibly and forcibly expressed. Parliament must not only represent adequately the constituencies, but
the constituencies through the electoral system must adequately
represent the nation. No less clearly it presupposes a theory and
a practice on the part of the Crown in the discharge of its functions
which together sum up the attributes of a Constitutional Monarchy
in the strict modern sense. Hence until these fundamental implications are generally accepted it is futile to look for the modern
Cabinet. In other words, in the eighteenth century only an ap-
proximation to the system can be expected, though we can trace
the gradual piecing together of the features that characterise the
later development.

The foundations were laid before 1714. (1) The prerogative
of the Crown in notable directions had been limited and defined
by two great statutes, the Bill of Rights and the Act of Settlement. Custom, almost more binding than statute, was stringently
fettering the Sovereign by prescribing formalities and procedure
for every expression of the royal pleasure. These formalities ensured that the Crown must act upon advice, and that for that
advice a Minister or group of Ministers will be politically responsible. Generally, the new atmosphere created by the Revolution
of 1688 completes this process; "according to the fundamental
Constitution of this Kingdom," said Rochester in 1711, "Ministers
are accountable for all". (2) Parliament though it could not
dictate policy nor the choice of Ministers, could and did veto the
action of the Executive. Its financial power made annual sessions
and its continuous approval of policy a necessity. Even if it did
not veto, it could and did most effectively harass unpopular or
incompetent Crown servants in the performance of their duties. As
the cases of Clarendon, Danby, Somers showed, by impeachment it
could indirectly remove Ministers regarded as impossible. And
the Act of Settlement showed that Parliament could and would
close the loopholes of evasion revealed by experience. In fine, William III. and Anne found it more and more convenient to govern
in accordance with the wishes of Parliament, distasteful as it might be
to their own views of policy or their conceptions of their prerogative.
(3) Since 1689 the system of defined and organised parties had
made great strides. Under Anne we see a continuous struggle

between two parties, led by able and authoritative leaders, whose programmes on the issues of foreign and domestic policy made Whig and Tory intelligible distinctions alike on the floor of Parliament and in the country.

Contemporary evidence establishes the fact that the political world was already familiar with the term "Cabinet," as a "Council of the Crown," distinct alike from the Privy Council or its committees, and applicable broadly to a group of Ministers holding high offices on confidential relations with the Sovereign, and defined by Lord Keeper Guildford as "those few great officers and courtiers . . . who had the direction of most transactions of Government foreign and domestic". In the reigns of William and Anne this body emerges with growing clearness as to its composition and functions. Its development from the time of Charles II. onwards had been attacked as unconstitutional. Both Whig and Tory critics, equally determined to secure Ministerial responsibility, saw in this nascent "Cabinet" an innovation which threatened to undermine the recognised position of the legal Privy Council. By changing the onus of responsibility, ascertainable and enforceable by process of law, to an undefined responsibility of an undefined group incapable of legal proof, the constitutional party felt it might destroy Ministerial responsibility altogether. For thirty years, however, the experiments in reconstructing the Privy Council and enforcing by Statute (as in the Act of Settlement) the legal accountability of Privy Councillors ended in failure. The attempted separation of Executive and Legislature in the Act of Settlement, which was part of the same policy, had to be repealed. The authors of the policy, in fact, did not diagnose the problem correctly, and therefore prescribed the wrong remedy. But their failure was helpful, because it convinced the men who worked the governmental machine that the reconciliation of Executive and Legislature could not be achieved by statutory means nor through existing constitutional machinery. It left the way open for further tentative experiments on different lines, but with the same grand object in view—control by Parliament and the rule of Law. By 1714 a Cabinet, then, is in existence, though not explicitly defined nor generally accepted. Its members have not acquired a monopoly-right of advice, nor are they collectively responsible. The choice of the Crown as to its confidential servants is but vaguely limited. The

Sovereign still governs through Ministers; Ministers do not yet govern through the Crown. The watershed, however, has been reached.

The fifty years of unbroken Whig supremacy add new features and rivet the system into the machinery of parliamentary government. (1) As already noted, the character of the Monarchy alters. It is demonstrable that whatever may be the share in, and influence on, government of George I. and II., they are not those of William and Anne, still less those of Charles II. (2) The Whigs are a party with a definite creed. They familiarise Parliament and the nation with the idea of a Ministry whose first function is to secure the realisation of a party programme; they create the atmosphere and the habit of thought essential to the Cabinet's existence. (3) The withdrawal of the Sovereign from presiding at Cabinet meetings weakened the initiation of the Crown and enormously strengthened the independence of Ministers; it makes the existence of a Prime Minister possible, and paves the way for collective responsibility. (4) The management of Parliament for the execution of "the King's business" becomes indispensable. The Ministers who can manage it are the Ministers whom the Crown must practically choose. (5) The nature of Ministerial responsibility is more clearly understood. The Crown's servants will not face Parliament unless the policy they expound is their own, and not that of others. (6) The Cabinet is more closely connected with the Executive departments of Government. The ornamental offices drop out; the true Executive chiefs come in. Parliament desires to control the Executive; the control is found to be most efficient when the group of advisers is intimately connected with the main organs of the Administration.

In this evolution the long Ministry of Walpole is, as in other directions, the most decisive epoch. Walpole's character and gifts, the circumstances which kept him in power, made a happy conspiracy. With a strong will, the determination to be senior partner in the Government firm, a patient and penetrating judgment of men, women, and affairs, a great power of work, he made himself indispensable to the Crown because he could manage Parliament better than any of his contemporaries. He was the leader of a well-drilled party; his policy was a party policy. He courted the verdicts of Parliament; and if he owed much of his

influence and success to his two royal masters, he owed more to the
House of Commons.   With justice, then, he has been called the
first Prime Minister.   Although he himself repudiated the accusation
of his critics, that he was assuming the powers of a " prime vizier,"
the unconstitutional position of " sole Minister," he asserted in the
Cabinet much of the pre-eminence and control which the modern
Premier enjoys.   After the resignation of Townshend he had the
chief direction of policy, foreign, domestic, and financial.   If it is
true that he was never called upon explicitly to form his own Cabinet
or directly nominate his colleagues, his power both of including
and excluding was considerable.   There were sharp struggles in his
Cabinet for predominance, and he had ambitious rivals (familiar features even in the Victorian Cabinets) ; but he compelled dissentients
either to yield or to resign.   Before his day there were prominent
leaders, yet Walpole first seems to have taught Crown, Parliament,
and colleagues the difference between pre-eminence and primacy.
The lesson was new, and in teaching it he not unnaturally aroused
opposition and no little personal bitterness.   The difference between
the Cabinet system proper and the departmental system is vital.
In the latter the Crown is the connecting link and the motor force
in policy ; it is based on the equal right of every Minister to advise,
coupled with his responsibility solely for the executive action of
his own department.   In the former, Ministers are co-ordinated
through the Prime Minister, and the necessary consequence is collective responsibility.   Walpole broadly aimed at a monopoly-right
of advice, i.e. he refused to tolerate the Sovereign seeking advice
from unauthorised councillors.   But he was not long enough in
power to effect collective responsibility.   " A Minister must be a
very pitiful fellow," he said, " if he did not turn out those who
pretended to meddle with the civil government ; and he would
leave that advice as a legacy to those who would follow him."
When he finally resigned it was because he had lost, not the confidence of the Crown, but the confidence of Parliament.   But his
long tenure of power had habituated George II. to a Ministerial
system far in advance of that in existence under Anne, or even his
father ; and, what is equally important, he had inoculated the leaders
on the Treasury and Front Opposition Bench with the essential
doctrines of Ministerial rights, duties, and privileges.

During the next twenty years the advance is necessarily not so rapid. Political practice in 1742 had virtually caught up political theory, whereas in 1721 it conspicuously lagged behind it. The position of Prime Minister, too, implies a peculiar combination of personal qualities; and neither Henry Pelham nor Newcastle nor Pitt possessed them in the same degree as Walpole. Pitt's supremacy, too, in his great Administration was exceptional, and due to exceptional circumstances. Secondly, the strong party colour was fading. The weaker is party the weaker will be the cohesion of an institution based upon party. The "Broad-bottom Administration" attempted to fuse discordant elements and broke down. Carteret was got rid of; and till 1754 Henry Pelham anticipated the part played by Liverpool from 1812-27. His successor, Newcastle, essayed the same rôle but failed. The House of Commons refused to be led by a nonentity nominated by an over-mighty subject in the House of Lords. The importance of the Lower House is strikingly exemplified in the coercion of Newcastle by Fox and Pitt.

But we note four interesting points in these twenty years: (1) The Pelham Ministry in 1746, by a collective resignation, forced the Crown to admit Pitt to office. Their success was due to their retention of a parliamentary majority and to their collective action. The Crown found itself unable either to form a rival Administration or to secure for it parliamentary support. George II., in two years, was thus compelled by Ministerial action to part with Carteret, whom he trusted, and to accept Pitt, whom he distrusted. (2) The continuation of an "inner" and "outer" Cabinet, between the titular and the real possessors of power. The nominal Cabinets numbered from fifteen to twenty, but within them existed a smaller group of Ministers who really decided policy. (3) Not merely the absence of collective responsibility, but the assertion by individual Ministers of their right to speak and vote against Governmental proposals without prejudicing their official position. This not unnaturally was also claimed by subordinates, e.g. by Pitt, when in 1754 and 1755 he denounced, though he was Paymaster, Newcastle's policy. Walpole had refused to tolerate such breaches of discipline. In 1733 he promptly punished by dismissal those who had openly opposed his Excise Bill. But Newcastle's endurance of Pitt's defiant mutiny gives the student a high opinion of his Christian charity and a low one of his political courage. (4) Pitt's career taught Crown and Ministers the importance in hours of national crises of public opinion as a factor in parliamentary government. Pitt himself was both a binding and a disintegrating force. His studied contempt for the party system and his appeal to national union were reinforced by Bolingbroke's previous political theories and continuous attacks on the monopolistic Whig *régime*. Pitt's genius for voicing the inarticulate demands of his countrymen proved the irresistible strength of the statesman who can win a nation's confidence. The Government-making power in 1756 and 1757 was not Parliament nor the Crown, but the public opinion of Great Britain.[1]

Briefly, to sum up, by 1760 the Cabinet is established in the sense of a group of Ministers who decide policy, are individually responsible and dependent on Parliamentary support. In selection the Crown is limited by their influence in Parliament and by their capacity to agree on a common course of action, and their readiness not to pursue political differences to open revolt. The leader of the Government, to whom the title of Prime or Premier Minister was frequently assigned, enjoyed a pre-eminence which varied with the confidence that he could win from the Crown, the quality of his own gifts and character, and his personal and political relations with his colleagues and his party. These results, however, were not due to any definite theory, and are not expressed in legislation or Orders in Council. The Cabinet was technically unknown to the law, and its development had not altered the legal powers of Crown, Privy Council, and Parliament, as Blackstone's *Commentaries* show. It rested on plastic conventions, and it was the outcome of fluctuating custom and convenience. Burke's *Causes of the Present Discontent* is the first attempt to state its nature in the precise terms of the political publicist. The Cabinet had in fact reached a stage when it had to reckon with counter-forces whose growth can already be detected : (1) The monopoly of the great Whig families had bred a belief (mainly in their own hearts) in their divine right to compose and direct the Government. Grafton's *Autobiography* shows how they claimed the right virtually to transfer the selection of the Prime Minister from the Crown to themselves, as well as the nomination of that Prime Minister's colleagues. (2) Many of the old Whigs, such as Hardwicke, considered that the advance towards "demo-

[1] See Appendix XIV.

cracy" had gone far enough.[1]   Henry Fox attacked Pitt because he "encouraged the mob to think themselves the Government," and his autobiographical memoir attributes to the House of Commons a desire, unprecedented and dangerous, to compel the Sovereign to nominate the Ministers of their, not his, choice.   (3) The revived Tory party looked to a resumption by the Crown of its usurped powers in order to break the monopoly of the Whigs and give their opponents a share in the Ministerial direction of policy.   (4) The Cabinet had advanced because the Crown had reluctantly accepted the Whig domination and the syndication of its prerogative amongst a group of Ministers who, with the aid of Parliament, could make any other Ministry impossible.   But if a new Sovereign, relying on the revived strength of the monarchical principle and the desire to "unite by breaking all parties," insisted on asserting his legal rights to govern as well as reign, and used his great powers of corruption and influence against, not in favour of, Ministers, there would be a revival of the theory and practice of departmental government under the personal direction and responsibility of the Sovereign.   The first twenty years of the reign of George III. witnessed such a deliberate policy on the part of the Crown; and they form the critical epoch of the history of the Cabinet.

The important legislation of the period is singularly scanty; the most pressing needs of Great Britain at home and abroad were not to be solved by statutory enactment, but by patient administration or foreign policy.   Nor was a legislative programme regarded as one of the chief duties of statesmanship, nor did rejection of his legislative proposals involve a Minister's resignation. The defeat of the Peerage Bill, the virtual defeat of the Excise Bill, at most lowered the political and moral prestige of the Governments concerned.   And it was part of the deliberate policy of Walpole to avoid raising unnecessary party strife.   For this reason he declined, in spite of the advocacy of Hoadley and Kennet, to repeal the Test and Corporation Acts, though after 1727 an annual Act of Indemnity protected those who had technically violated the law. Otherwise, the statutory progress of the principles of toleration was almost *nil*.   Stanhope had succeeded in repealing the Occasional

1719

---

[1] "The scale of power in this Government has long been growing heavier on the democratic side. . . . What I contend for is to preserve a limited monarchy entire, and nothing can do that but to preserve the counterpoise " (Hardwicke in 1752).

Conformity and Schism Acts; Jews and Quakers were exempted 1718
from Hardwicke's Marriage Act, but the Act permitting the natur- 1752
alisation of Jews occasioned such a violent outbreak of bigotry
that it was repealed next year. One welcome advance however was
made in 1736 when the statutes against witchcraft were repealed and
prosecutions for that offence forbidden. Astronomical science, too,
found tardy acceptance in Macclesfield's Bill, promoted by Chesterfield, for substituting the Gregorian for the Julian Calendar. In
order to rectify the accumulated error due to the use of the old style
eleven days between September 2nd and 14th were suppressed, which 1752
gave rise to the popular cry of "Give us back our eleven days!"
Henceforward the legal year was to begin on January 1st instead
of March 25th. The change met with the fierce opposition of
ignorance and invincible prejudice. "The style it was changed to
popery." And the subsequent death of Bradley, the Astronomer
Royal, who had worked out the calculations, was attributed to his
alleged profane interference with the dates of the saints' festivals.
"Hardwicke's Marriage Act" was an important social reform, long
overdue. No court existed which could grant a divorce, *i.e.* dissolve a marriage legally contracted, and the grave scandals arising
from the ease with which men and women, often under age, could
be duped into the indissoluble union of marriage were notorious.
The parsons of the Fleet in particular drove a lucrative trade,
responsible for a vast amount of fraud, misery, and immorality in
all classes of the population. Under the Act of 1753, henceforth, marriages could only be celebrated publicly by a properly
qualified minister of the Established Church in a lawful place of
worship. Due notice by the publication of banns, or by special
licence, the certified consent of parents or guardians where the
parties were under age, and the proper keeping of records formally
witnessed, were made compulsory. Otherwise the marriage was
null and void, and the person celebrating it punishable by transportation. Though the Act imposed a fresh disability on Nonconformists it was successful in exterminating the evil of Fleet
marriages; and by implicitly enforcing the principle that marriage
was a civil contract, in the conditions and maintenance of which the
State was primarily interested, it paved the way for further legislation and the subsequent legalisation of civil marriages, *i.e.* those in
which there is no ecclesiastical ceremony. Bitterly attacked in the

Commons (notably by Henry Fox, who had made one of the famous clandestine marriages of the day), as an unwarrantable invasion of the liberty of the subject, it also was held to violate feminine delicacy by prescribing public weddings—" the most shocking thing," Miss Burney asserted, " in the whole world ".   The Royal Family was expressly exempted from its clauses and its operation did not extend to Scotland.   Hardwicke thus created " Gretna Green " and gave back to runaway couples and the historical novelist adequate compensation and the colour of romance for the facilities so drastically abolished.

1737   Somewhat earlier the famous Playhouse Bill had legalised afresh the principle of a censorship of the drama, by forbidding the production of plays unless a copy had been submitted to the Lord Chamberlain fourteen days before, and his licence for the production obtained.   Actors, too, unless licensed by the same authority, were to fall into the category of rogues and vagabonds.   Undoubtedly this legislation was political, and was aimed at plays in which the Throne or Government were held up to the abuse that masqueraded as criticism.   It illustrates the maxim laid down in 1704 from the judicial bench that any speaking or writing calculated to bring the established Government into contempt was a libel and punishable as such.   Published writings could be dealt with in the courts, but plays technically not published presented a difficulty for which the Act endeavoured to find a solution.   Chesterfield, in a brilliant speech, unsuccessfully opposed its enactment as a resurrection of the Press censorship, abandoned in 1695, as a new and more hateful " excise office " and a felon's fetter on the art of the dramatist and the judgment of the public.   Both the principle and the results of the licensing restraint evoked two centuries of controversial literature ; but the censorship of the drama has so far survived every effort to abolish it.

In the sphere of constitutional law, apart from the Act of 1736 which provided that pleadings in the courts should be in English and not in French or Latin, the Riot Act of 1715 and the Militia Act are important measures.   The former strengthened the hands of local authority by making it a felony for rioters to refuse to disperse at the command of a magistrate ; it checked judicial extension of the treason-law by removing local riots from its operation, and it left the common law powers of the

Executive as regards the maintenance of law and order unimpaired. The Militia Act, due largely to Pitt, reorganised a national force which had been suffered to fall into neglect. Starting from the accepted historical principle that all free subjects of the Crown 1757 were bound to maintain peace in their respective districts and to assist in protecting the kingdom from danger, the Act (1) vested the appointment of the permanent staff together with a veto on the selection of officers in the Crown ; (2) the quota for each county was defined and the choice made determinable by ballot ; (3) it placed the Militia during training under the Mutiny Act and articles of war (but not extending to "loss of life or limb") ; (4) it empowered the Crown, provided Parliament was informed, to call out the Militia in case of invasion or rebellion and place it under the officers of the regular army. The Act thus aimed at recruiting the Militia as a second line of defence without weakening its popularity as the national force or severing its connection with the historic features of English local government. Until the remodelling of the force in the latter half of the nineteenth century the Act remained the basis of the home military system ; though the stress of war changed what was intended as a reserve for defence into a feeding reservoir for the regular army.

The Act of Settlement, by making tenure of judicial office dependent on "good behaviour," and not on the pleasure of the Sovereign, had established the practical independence of the Bench. The power of the Crown to secure an interpretation of the law favourable to its claims had thus been removed ; and this famous clause, combined with Bushell's case, which established the immunity of the jury from punishment for its verdicts, provided the 1673 nation with a system of justice with whose decisions it was beyond the power of the Executive seriously to tamper. Montesquieu, however, and others following his suggestion, who saw in the Revolution Constitution the theoretical "separation of Powers," missed two essential characteristics of the position of the English Judiciary. The Crown remained the fountain of justice, and to its initiative the judges continued to owe their appointment. Apart from the difficult question whether, in a case of flagrant misconduct, the Crown, without waiting for an address from Parliament, could or could not cancel the patent of appointment, Parliament is statutorily invested with the right, by address, to compel the Sovereign

13

to remove a judge. In plain words, just as with the Executive so
with the Judiciary—the Legislature is the ultimate authority linked
by its power to intervene effectively under circumstances of which it
is constituted the sole interpreter. But the statutory independence
of the judges was completed in 1760, on the initiative of George III.
himself, by the Act which secured that judicial commissions should
not determine on the death of the Sovereign who had appointed
them, and which removed from the Civil List and assigned to a
permanent charge that portion of their salaries hitherto paid from
it. After 1701 the part that the Law Courts play in the evolution
of the Constitution is governed by two distinct elements: (1) They
are in principle the law-interpreting organs to whose decisions the
nation can with confidence appeal. Their function in cases of dispute is to make the law of the land prevail; to consummate that
reign of law which foreign and home critics agree in regarding as
one of the most notable features of the modern British Constitution.
But law-interpreting bodies insensibly and of necessity become law-
making bodies. Subject to the sovereign power of Parliament to
alter the law, judicial decisions cumulatively tend to become additions to the law, though they claim only to be interpretations of it.
And cases such as *Rex v. Tubbs, Entinck v. Carrington, Stockdale v.
Hansard*, and the numerous decisions on the law of libel in the
eighteenth century, illustrate how much "judge-made law" can
broaden or diminish, without legislative intervention, the liberty of
the subject and modify or alter the relations between the Executive
and the ordinary citizen ; (2) the decisions of the courts from epoch
to epoch exemplify the subtle influence on the judges of contemporary or anachronistic constitutional and philosophical principles
and the connection between law and public opinion. The eighteenth-
century citizen compared with to-day enjoyed a very limited right
of free criticism and free speech. The criminality of a libel (until
Fox's Act in 1792) was determined, not by the jury, but by the
judge, and even judges such as Holt, who defended (1701) popular
rights against the tyranny of the House of Commons, started from
a theory of the functions of Government and the relations of the
State to its members directly antithetical to the modern conception
of the liberty of the Press and the right to criticise the established
Executive. The revolt of isolated judges, such as Camden (1765),
aided by an increasing force of public opinion against the principles

of State action enforced by the courts, is part of the revolution in
the theory of the State's functions, which was bound up with a new
conception of civic liberty and with a demand for its recognition in
the general law of the land.

The survey so far has been of a sound organism developing on
healthy lines, but the constitutional, political, and economic relations
of the United Kingdom of Great Britain with Ireland, provide a
depressing study in morbid anatomy.   If Whig policy and Whig
ascendency are seen at their worst in the treatment of Ireland, it
is only fair to add that the responsibility must be shared by the
whole English people.   Ireland, in fact, in English eyes, after 1688,
threatened the Revolution system with a quadruple danger—racial,
political, religious, and economic.   Its geographical position forbade
its being ignored or left to work out its salvation or its ruin without English intervention.   Its previous history and the prevailing
conditions demanded a policy clearly defined and unflinchingly applied both as to ends and means.   And in 1714 statesmen and the
average citizen in England continued to view Ireland with the
strange mixture of fear and contempt noticeable in 1641 and 1689.
Three-fourths, perhaps four-fifths of the population were alien in
race, were Roman Catholics, pledged to a creed proscribed by the
British Legislature, which of necessity made the Irish Roman
Catholic an irreconcilable rebel to the Protestant Constitution of
Great Britain.   The reign of William III. had shown that the
majority of Irishmen by mere force of numbers might furnish
the fallen dynasty of the Stuarts with a most formidable weapon
for destroying, in alliance with Roman Catholic France, the settlement laid down in 1689 and ratified in 1713 after a vast expenditure
of blood and treasure.   Economically, Ireland must always be a more
dangerous competitor than the colonies and plantations to the
mercantile and agrarian interests of the powerful classes in England,
whose union and whose prosperity were the mainsprings of Whig
solidarity and the basis of the Revolution State.   The machinery
of government at Dublin, with its separate Executive and bi-
cameral Legislature, and the necessary apparatus for taxation,
legislation, and administration could be easily transformed into the
organs of a hostile independence.   The true English interest was
only represented by a small minority of alien administrators whose
existence as the representatives of English religion, culture, and

independence depended unconditionally on British support. The
Whigs, too, obsessed by dread of the Monarchy, feared that the
Crown's resources in Ireland, and the utilisation of Irish revenues,
if permitted to slip beyond the control of the British Parliament,
might be employed to make the British Sovereign not merely independent of, but positively dangerous to, English liberties. These
dangers were aggravated by seven centuries of governmental experiments and failures and chronic rebellions against them, by a
social and agrarian organisation which Englishmen neither understood nor wished to understand, whose history was a dreary epitome
of social war blackened by savage reprisals, confiscations, counter-
reprisals and counter-confiscations. Since the days of Henry II.
and of John this terrible Irish question had baffled kings, statesmen,
and people, both at Dublin and Westminster. And in 1714 the
complexity of the conflicting interests made it a trackless labyrinth.

It would be unreasonable, as well as impossible, to expect Whig
or Tory in 1714 to apply to the most difficult problem that British
statesmanship was called on to solve, modern principles of economics,
toleration, public purity, even of Christian charity and racial sympathy. Whig and Tory did not wish to throw over for Ireland's
sake the principles of civil and ecclesiastical government they had
successfully forged for themselves in England. They were saturated
with economic selfishness ; to relax the grip of the mercantile system
threatened economic paralysis and financial bankruptcy. They had
no racial sympathy, and they were convinced that the loss of civil
and political rights was the merited penalty of an ineradicable devotion to a superstitious and dangerous religion, and of the perversity
of an inferior, debased, and conquered race. English statesmen were
possessed by one fixed idea. To maintain the absolute supremacy
of the English Cabinet over the Irish Executive and Legislature
was a plain duty which admitted of no argument. To act otherwise
was overt treason to the Revolution system and English freedom.
For it was the devil's choice of evils. Better some injustice, even to
Protestant interests in Ireland, than certain civil and social war,
fomented by foreign foes and the imperilling of the whole fabric of
1689. The policy of relentless repression succeeded, indeed, so well
that modern historical critics are tempted to add to the long charge-
sheet against the Whigs the belief that the menace from Ireland
was no menace at all ; or as Chesterfield wittily put it, that the

beautiful Miss Ambrose was the only dangerous Papist he had found in Ireland. It would be fairer to admit that the danger was a real one, and that the safety of the English State was purchased at the cost of valuable elements of Irish national life. The true indictment against Whig statesmanship is not that it insisted on Ireland being welded somehow into the Revolution State of the United Kingdom; nor that it failed to achieve the impossible by abolishing in the hours of crisis civil and religious disabilities, by endowing the Roman Catholic Church, and reconstructing the vicious land system; but that its policy was false to the principles of Whiggism, and that it grievously neglected the duties of a national trustee.

Ireland in 1714 was a poor, backward, and hostile country for the most part, degraded and rent asunder by racial, political, and social enmities for which the Whigs were not responsible. The task of statesmanship was to lay the foundations of unity, prosperity, and loyalty to the system to which necessity required Ireland must belong. Time, knowledge, and insight were the essential conditions of success. The Whigs were given the first. They had forty-five years of peace in Ireland, and they wasted them. English Ministers long after 1760 remained woefully ignorant of the unhappy island at their door; and their ignorance was fortified by the prejudicial counsels of their advisers on the spot. Worst of all, Whig policy was a policy of anachronisms aggravated by despair. The apparatus of self-government, which might have been slowly adapted to teach that loyalty was profitable and that Irish interests were indissolubly bound up with English, shrivelled into the engine of a corrupt bureaucracy. In the end the Whig system failed to retain even the support of the minority in whose behalf it was so remorselessly worked. Two luminous sentences of Grattan's reveal the heart of the problem : " The Irish Protestant can never be free until the Irish Catholic has ceased to be a slave " ; " The question is whether we shall remain a Protestant settlement or become an Irish nation ". The movement and programme of reform in Ireland was mainly the achievement of Irish and Protestant leaders, to whom British statesmen had revealed the fatal secret that England could be bullied but not argued into justice and generosity. Two words sum up the Irish tragedy. The remedy for each of the debasing maladies from which Ireland suffered, was invariably applied, if applied at all, "too late". For States as for individuals remedies that are "too late" invariably avenge themselves on the incompetent physician by aggravating the disease which in an earlier stage they could have cured. The eighteenth century handed on to the nineteenth, in the case of Ireland, an unsolved imperial problem and the damning heritage of a century of lost opportunities. The failure is the more tragic because at bottom it is a failure of the British race, finding an instructive parallel in the loss of the American colonies, and brilliant contrasts in Scotland, Canada, and British India.

Fitzgibbon later epitomised aptly the essence of the Whig system : "The only security that can exist for national concurrence is a permanent and commanding influence of the English Executive, or, rather, of the English Cabinet, in the councils of Ireland". And this principle found complete expression in the four great instruments by which Ireland in 1714 was manacled and misgoverned — the executive machinery, the Anglican Church, the penal code, and the commercial restrictions. The Crown was represented by the Lord Lieutenant—a great political officer, usually in the English Cabinet, who with his Chief Secretary and Privy Council constituted the central Government. In the periodic absences of the Lord Lieutenant the Lords Justices exercised a complete control. The Parliament consisted of two Houses as in Great Britain, though the English Privy Council was "in reality the second branch of the Legislature". The powers of Parliament were limited by important restrictions and by the defects of the Lower Chamber. Roman Catholics were debarred from sitting; and the Test Act indirectly excluded Nonconformists, who could not belong to the borough corporations, which were largely the electoral bodies. In 1727 Roman Catholics were formally deprived of the franchise. The Irish constituencies were a demoralising parody of the representative principle. Of the 300 members of the Lower House it was calculated that 176 were the nominees of individual patrons, and that 53 peers nominated to 123 seats, while the bishops constituted about half of the working majority in the House of Lords. The hereditary revenues were vested perpetually in the Crown, so that the power of the purse was effectively clipped, since in 1714 the Legislature could not initiate a money Bill. Legislation was supervised by the English Privy

Council; and the Irish Parliament could only originate heads of Bills for that Council, which could alter or reject them; while a Bill laid before the Irish House, as amended by the English Council, could not be altered, but only accepted or rejected. In 1719 a British statute (6 Geo. I. c. 5) added to Poynings' Law (1495) by affirming the right of the British Parliament at Westminster to legislate for Ireland over the heads of the Irish representatives. In administration the object of the Government was simply to create and keep in the Irish Parliament a majority obedient to its will. The Viceroy, the Chief Secretary, and the Lord Chancellor were invariably English, as were the Primate and many of the Bishops. The Government rested frankly on corruption, chiefly by means of Government patronage and the nominee boroughs. Serving the Crown and sharing the spoils now came to be synonymous terms. So long as "The Castle" was prepared to keep its alliance with "The Undertakers"—the leaders from the great Irish families of the landed oligarchy—a majority could always be bought; and this with the ample powers provided by the law enabled the Administration to carry out the will of the dominant English Cabinet.

In this system the functions of the Anglican Church were as much political as religious. "A true Irish bishop," said Boulter, "has nothing more to do than to eat, drink, grow fat, rich, and die"; and the main maxim of the rulers was "to get as many English on the bench here as can be decently sent hither". The Episcopal Church in Ireland was not even the Church of a united Protestant minority, though it was largely paid for by tithes exacted alike from the Roman Catholic and the Protestant Nonconformist; and it discharged the debt by copying the rich absentee landlords and so consistently neglecting its duties that it generally forgot it had any to perform, even to its own members. With some welcome exceptions, its annals reveal, in addition to the evils inevitable in an exotic institution in an alien soil, the same abuses that flourished in England—nepotism and absenteeism, pluralism, administrative paralysis, and spiritual lethargy. But in England these were the defects of a national establishment; in Ireland they were the characteristics of the chapel in the conquerors' citadel. The ecclesiastical penal code, avowedly directed against the Roman Catholic population, "the common enemy," proclaimed, in the words of a responsible historian, not the persecution of a sect, but the degradation of a nation. By depriving Catholics of all share in civil and political life, by forbidding the inter-marriage of Catholics and Protestants, by proscribing all Catholic education and religious worship, and by imposing severe restrictions as to the tenure, inheritance, and acquisition of land and property, the code aimed at, and succeeded in being, a disruptive and demoralising social and religious force. The laws, it was said in 1759, did not presume a Papist to exist in the kingdom, nor could they breathe without the connivance of the Government. But neither the letter nor the spirit of this terrible creation of Protestant bigotry, panic, and selfishness were, or could be, completely enforced. The code was a failure, because the Roman Catholic was neither converted nor extirpated ; on the contrary, he continued to increase in a greater ratio than the Protestant. But in two respects its effects were calamitous and far-reaching. The maintenance of the code was on the one side confused with the membership of Ireland in the dominions of the British Crown ; on the other, its final repeal by the inexorable logic of facts came to be identified with Irish freedom from the English yoke. For in this way the sins of the fathers are visited tenfold on the children. By keeping the Roman Catholic peasantry and their priests in subjection, poverty, and ignorance, it created an agrarian and social menace far more formidable, disruptive, and lasting than the political danger of Catholicism ever had been.

The commercial laws complete the picture. Economic was the counterpart to political and religious subordination. In principle Ireland was treated as a dependency, with the maximum of burdens and the minimum of favours that the colonial system allowed. Her harbours and her traders were excluded from all imperial trade. Her farmers were prohibited from exporting, her capitalists from manufacturing, wool. The natural products of the soil—live stock, butter, and cheese—were not allowed to be imported into England. In a word, Ireland was statutorily forbidden to compete either with the British shipper, the British manufacturer, or the British farmer ; and if after 1743 some support was given to flax and the linen industry at Belfast, it was poor compensation for the deliberate destruction of budding manufactures and the drying up of rich natural resources. Smuggling, jobbing, pauperism and emigration, and the sacrifice of the English in Ireland to the English at home, were the least of the evil consequences that dogged the working of the penal and commercial code. Poisoning the wells of national effort invariably proves more costly to the poisoner than the poisoned. When English politicians justly complained of the lawlessness, corruption, thriftlessness, and ingratitude of the Irish of all classes, which sterilised for two centuries the belated efforts at reform, they forgot that gratitude, economy, and respect for law can be destroyed, but not created, by Acts of Parliament; and that these qualities the mutilated and stunted national life of Hanoverian Ireland was neither encouraged to win from the Government nor was permitted to produce of itself.

The *Annesley case* in 1719 led to the enactment of the famous 6 Geo. I., c. 5, by which the British House of Lords was made the final Court of Appeal from the Irish courts, and appellate jurisdiction was emphatically denied to the Irish Upper House—an Act which completed the subjection of the Irish to the British Legislature. In 1751 and 1753 came a sharp struggle over an Appropriation Bill, earmarking a portion of the surplus of the national revenue to the reduction of the national debt. Though the Bill as amended by the English Privy Council was rejected and the surplus applied by royal prerogative, Kildare, Malone, and Boyle had taken a leading part in defeating the Executive; and the Irish House of Commons saw for the first time an organised Opposition and a cleavage between the English Ministers and the chiefs of the great Irish families. The incident, intrinsically unimportant, was full of significance for the future. Since 1714 slow but steady progress can be detected in the conditions of the country. After 1746 the position of the Catholics demonstrably improved. The economic recovery led to an equilibrium in the national finances. In the capital particularly a growing political life was making itself felt, most notably in the rise of a middle class fired by nationalist ambitions. Some conspicuous names redeem the period—Swift, Berkeley, Hutcheson (till 1729), Archbishop Synge, and Molyneux, the famous pamphleteer of 1698 who had claimed complete legislative autonomy for Ireland. Of the Viceroys, Carteret and Chesterfield maintained their reputations won elsewhere, but Bedford was the first to support a relaxation of the penal code. Two Primates 1757 figure prominently in the Administration, Boulter, by whose influence the Roman Catholics were disfranchised and whose policy aimed at the strenuous maintenance of English ascendency ; Stone, a notable pluralist but thoroughly capable, whose character has been assailed on public and private grounds, but whose leanings towards toleration indicate the new views in the hierarchy of politics. The abuses of the administrative system provided the material for a programme and a movement that slowly gathered strength. Ireland had no Septennial Act, no Habeas Corpus Act, no Annual Mutiny Act, no national militia ; the judges were appointed "during pleasure" ; the pension list and Governmental patronage corrupted and demoralised every class of Protestant. Toleration and religious equality, the removal of civil disabilities, emancipation from the commercial restrictions and from the legislative and administrative control of the British Parliament and Privy Council, and the reform of the Irish House of Commons and the electoral system, were the necessary preliminaries to creating a sane, clean, and rigorous national life. Apart from these, the question of tithes and the whole agrarian economy cried out for reconstruction. It is significant that the demand for a legislative union with Great Britain, put forward in 1703 and rejected, had so completely died away that in 1759 the rumour that such a union was in contemplation produced a fierce riot in Dublin. The next generation was to prove that there had grown up in Ireland leaders and followers both Protestant and Catholic who desired to grapple seriously with the constitutional, religious, and social evils that under George I. and II. throttled material and moral progress.

The most picturesque events of Scottish history—the resistance to Walpole's fiscal policy, the Porteous riots and "the '45" belong to the political history of Great Britain. There were still two Scotlands. Until 1760 the Highlands, *i.e.* the area occupied by the Highland clans, remained a separate country in manners, morals, and (until 1746) in its feudalised tribal government. Wade's roads and the formation of the Black Watch, the "red" garrisons at Fort Augustus, Fort William, and Fort George were an assault on the barrier which the Disarming Act, the Abolition of the Hereditary Jurisdictions, the Commission of the Forfeited Estates, and the enlistment of the Highland regiments, completed far more effectively than Cumberland's dragonnades. South of the Tay and east of the Grampians, Lowland Scotland had not yet realised the

1740

dowry secured by the Legislative Union. The triumphant vindication of that masterpiece of Whig statesmanship had yet to come. Down to 1746 the cry "Repeal the Union" made the national patriots and the oppressed Episcopalian clergy the most influential recruiters for the Jacobite cause. The English Government had been stung too often by the Scottish thistle to desire to control its growth; and Scotland was left mainly to Scottish rulers acquainted with Scottish ways and sentiment. Argyll and Islay anticipated Dundas in the extent of their influence and corruption; and if Scotland had surrendered its historic Legislature to forty-five representatives and sixteen peers at Westminster who were ready to sell their votes to the party managers of English affairs, she retained all the necessary organs for developing at home her own hard-bitten nationality. Scotland had a national system of law and courts, a Bench and Bar steeped in Scottish pride and independence, national schools, a national literature. Above all she had a national Church whose General Assembly largely compensated for the empty Parliament House at Edinburgh. The ecclesiastical chronicle may be neither very edifying nor intelligible, unless studied in minute detail. Yet the fierce protests against Episcopalianism and lay patronage, the logomachies over dogma, the continuous cellular formation of Dissident communities, such as the Reformed or Cameronian Church and the Original Secession, witness to a moral and intellectual vitality and to the influence of religion on public and private life, which lay bare the secrets of Scottish success and Scottish character. As Lowlander and Highlander proved, races that can fight for their convictions, even mistaken convictions, are the races to whom the future belongs.

As yet Scotland was still desperately poor and backward. But the standard of comfort and refinement in the gentry and middle class was steadily rising. In two directions the marvellous transformation of the last half of the eighteenth century was already foreshadowed. The lairds, particularly in the Lothians and Ayrshire, were turning their attention seriously to improvements in their estates, in farming and agriculture. In the North, at Ferintosh in Ross-shire, had been laid the foundations of the Scottish whisky distilleries by the family of Duncan Forbes, to whom both Scotland and England in so many ways were indebted. In the West, Glasgow had been practically created by the Union of 1707. By 1760 it was a shipping and commercial centre, capable of competing successfully with Liverpool and Bristol in the colonial and foreign trade. A linen manufacture already flourished and Bargarran thread was destined to make Paisley famous. Scottish banking, which supplied the Scottish people with capital of their own saving, had entered on its career of financial prosperity with the Bank of Scotland (1695), the Royal Bank (1727), and the Linen Bank (1746). The wealth in iron and coal underground was waiting to be discovered; Lanarkshire and the basin of the Clyde were ready to be transformed into an industrial centre second to none. The next generation was to see the Industrial Revolution and with it the development of the Scotland of modern times.

The same characteristics, somewhat more strongly emphasised, are revealed in the economic life of England. Defoe's travels in 1724 and 1725 point to a general diffusion of comfort and prosperity, though the shifting of population and industry to the North and Midlands, and the concentration in towns, are not yet typical features. The reigns of the two first Georges are a period of quiet preparation for the volcanic upheaval that set in from 1770 onwards. Of the staple industries the woollen trade continued to expand satisfactorily; and the Methuen Treaty of 1703 gave a great impetus by throwing open Portugal to British manufactures. Some new industries such as silk weaving had taken root, but manufactures generally were marking time. They had reached their limits under existing conditions; the advance of the future was to come from a series of mechanical discoveries. The growth of English wealth was chiefly derived from her commerce, the profits of an expanding shipping and the capacity to satisfy the home and foreign markets nursed by the mercantile system. After 1689, Parliament replaces the Crown in Council as the judge of economic interests; and one of its main functions is to regulate industry according to the prevailing criteria. The Legislature aimed at maintaining a favourable balance of trade as a test of progress and profit and an index of the good and bad in the nation's economic life; under Walpole and his successors it stimulated commerce by bounties and prohibited competition by tariffs; it aimed at providing cheap and plentiful raw material and promoting the export of manufactured articles; it regulated at home the quality and supply of material, the processes of the worker, the terms of employment. Politics

and economics are closely linked.   France being the enemy, French
trade must be scotched or killed.

   Bolingbroke's failure to carry the Commercial Treaty of 1713
was due as much to political opposition as to economic fears of its 1714-1760
results.   It is the era of parliamentary paternalism, striving to be
enlightened, meeting with but moderate success.   The bounties and
tariffs congested trade into parliament-made channels; the over-
loaded book of rates was costly in collection, concealed the true
incidence and amount of taxation, and fostered smuggling, jobbery,
and corruption.   Every student of the inner life of eighteenth century
politics must be impressed with the amenability of the Legislature
to the selfish pressure of jealous trades, and the debasing effects of
this on private and public morality.   Agriculture, on the whole,
prospered.   The epoch, indeed, has been called the golden age of the
agricultural labour.   Since 1689 a bounty for the export of corn when
above forty-eight shillings stimulated production; and England was
not only able to feed her own population but to send corn abroad.
The British farmer was protected from Irish competition; and even
Whig political theory supported the promotion of the interests of
a Tory squirearchy.   The most formidable foe to prosperity was the
system in vogue.   Though enclosure proceeded steadily, three-fifths
of the country were still under the open-field system with its extravagance in ploughing, its ignorance and neglect of scientific
methods, its extensive cultivation and its rigid conservatism.   Two
brilliant pioneers, however, had pointed the way to new methods
and ideas.   Jethro Tull, at Mount Prosperous in Berkshire, Townshend, at Rainham in Norfolk, introduced the turnip, and taught
the advantages of proper drilling and manuring, the treatment of
soils, a more scientific rotation of crops, and the value of artificial
grasses.   Progress in agricultural knowledge was largely due to the
big landlords, "the spirited cultivators" of Arthur Young—men
of enterprise and business capacity, desirous of large profits, who
showed the opening for capital judiciously applied on an adequate
scale to farming.   But the advance as yet was local, accidental and
halting.   Not until the medieval rural economy and the self-con-
tained co-operative village community had been broken up under
the inexorable forces of the Industrial Revolution was the transition,
and then with much suffering, effected.

   But in agriculture and industry the advent of the capitalist *régime* is foreshadowed. As yet the common type of organisation, though not without exception in both spheres, is the domestic, in which the workman owns his material and apparatus and sells the product of his labour.   To the cottier spinning or weaving may be a by-industry ; to the village artisan subsistence-farming is a by-occupation.   Higher in the scale the yeoman is a freeholder ; the master-weaver is the owner of his homeshop and looms.   In many trades the domestic and the capitalist system (in which the capitalist is the employer, owning the materials and the machinery, and paying the workmen by wages) existed side by side.   The change from one to the other is slow and imperceptible.   But the steady growth of capital, the profits from its organised application and business skill in an extended sphere, both in farming and industry, are making the competition between the two types of economic organisation more and more unequal.   The Bank of England, the rise of joint-stock companies, the expansion of foreign trade, facilitated the accumulation and profitable investment of capital.   The continuous complaints, notably of Davenant and Defoe, as to the increase in Stock Exchange gambling, the South Sea Bubble, and the ease with which Great Britain borrowed for and met the interest on a mounting National Debt, prove the steady growth and diffusion of available capital.

As yet the unequal distribution of wealth was not a social menace.   The problem of poor-law relief was simply quiescent. Against the fact that the cost had fallen from £819,000 in 1698 to £689,000 in 1750 must be set the conclusion that this had been attained by a remorseless application of the Caroline Settlement Law, and the fortunate absence of pronounced economic changes or strain.   Adam Smith's terrible dictum that no poor man could reach forty years of age without suffering oppression under the Settlement Acts at some time or another tells its own tale.   An Act of 1722 permitted the erection of proper workhouses and the provision of relief in these alone ; and Hay's Bill of 1736 proposed to make workhouses general, group them into unions, and provide guardians elected from the gentry to supervise the overseers—thereby anticipating some of the reforms of 1834.   The landed interest stupidly feared a general poor rate, worked up a general panic, as with Walpole's Excise Bill, and procured the rejection of the measure. Hanoverian England tided over its poor-law difficulties.   But two decades of economic crisis were more than enough to reveal the blots inherent in the system—the prevalence of out-door relief, the multiplication of parochial areas and overlapping of jurisdictions, the omnipotence of the justices, the tyranny, wastefulness, and jobbery of the overseers, the absence of central control, and the ignorance of sound principles in social and financial science. And by 1800 the Elizabethan system had really collapsed.

The annals of the Church of England are memorable for two prominent features : (1) The volume and vigour of theological literature ; (2) the rise and marvellous progress of Wesleyanism. The Bangorian Controversy, occasioned by Bishop Hoadly's *Pre-* 1716 *servative against the Principles of the Non-Jurors* and his sermon on " The Nature of the Kingdom or Church of Christ," which were censured by the Lower House of Convocation, and the Deist and Trinitarian Controversies, caused a vast amount of ink to flow and brought out a number of prominent writers : William Law (who lives as the author of the *Serious Call*), Waterland, Sherlock, Samuel Clarke, Warburton, Berkeley, and Butler, Antony Collins and Matthew Tindal, who so much enjoyed making "the clergy mad ". Butler's *Analogy of Religion* and Berkeley's philosophical work are permanent treasure-trove from the vast and dusty scrap-heap that sleeps undisturbed to-day in the lumber shelves of college libraries. The contrast between this literary fury and the aphasia and apathy of the English Church as regards its spiritual duties is striking. The general contempt for the persons and morals of the clergy, found in contemporary literature, is justified in the numerous charges of the bishops, pathetic in their tone of querulous acquiescence and despair. The neglect of parochial work, the spiritual stagnation, nepotism, absenteeism, pluralism, are facts beyond dispute. But when leaders such as Butler were content to combine a bishopric with a deanery and a clerkship of the closet, or (as Secker) a bishopric with a deanery, it is not surprising that the starved and imperfectly educated parochial clergy did well if they reached the standard of Parson Adams. There were, of course, some notable exceptions : Walker of Truro, " a Methodist before Methodism," Adam of Winteringham, Grimshaw of Haworth, Berridge of Everton, William Romaine. Nor can the blame be shifted to the tepid Erastianism of Walpole, the latitudinarianism of Queen Caroline and the wicked Whigs. It is true that the continuous prorogation of Convocation after 1717 for 135 years deprived the Church of a central organ and a representative life, but the Tories after 1770 must equally share the responsibility with the Whigs therefor. The rise of Wesleyanism, Evangelicalism, and Tractarianism show that spiritual and intellectual vigour could flourish in the absence of Convocation. Nor is 1714 a hard-and-fast line. Under the clerically-minded Anne the same defects are equally noticeable. The parochial clergy, by clinging to the worn-out creed of Filmer and Sacheverell, cut themselves off from the main current of national life, and proved their deplorable lack of insight into the needs of their generation. The work that England cried for in vain from its official spiritual pastors, and what great leaders could do, were proclaimed by John and Charles Wesley; and in their careers lies the severest condemnation of the Church under George II.

The mistress of the rectory of Epworth, in the fens of Lincolnshire, it has been justly said, was " the true founder of Wesleyanism ". To that mistress, their mother, the wife of Samuel Wesley the elder, her famous sons, John and Charles, owed, as so many other great men, the training, character, and moral inspiration which are the finest gift of a noble woman to her nation. John, born in 1703, graduated from Christchurch in 1724, and from 1729-35 was a fellow and tutor of Lincoln; Charles, four years his junior, became a student of Christchurch in 1726. In 1729 both brothers joined with a few of their contemporaries in a strict rule of study and religious observance, which earned for the group the nickname of "Methodists". Wesleyanism in one sense was an Oxford movement, begun at Oxford, led by Oxford men bred in the classic citadel of the Anglican Church, which a century earlier had bowed to the personality and ideals of Laud, and a century later came under the spell of John Newman and John Keble. But while Laudianism and Tractarianism grew naturally out of Oxford studies and leavened two generations of academic and religious thought, as did the Evangelical movement at Cambridge, the Methodism that founded the Wesleyan body owed nothing to Oxford teaching and left no legacy to the University whose intellectual decrepitude and moral paralysis justly incurred the damning contempt of the greatest of English historians, Gibbon. So far as Wesleyanism had a spiritual genealogy it is to be traced in the perennial appeal of the writings of Thomas à Kempis, Jeremy Taylor, William Law, and the Moravian, Peter Böhler. It was not a new creed ; its power was not purchased by the scholar's laborious search for truth ; it was a summons to the heart not to the head, a call to a new life, a warning to flee from the wrath to come, a categorical imperative to the individual as a moral unit in communion with the unseen. Needed sorely enough but unheeded by Oxford common rooms, it found its readiest hearers in the neglected village, mine, and slum.

Historic Methodism dates from the return of John Wesley from Georgia in 1738. For nine years the man had passed through the fires of a great spiritual struggle, without which no great religious leader has ever climbed to the awful conviction of a divine mission. His "conversion" followed ; and in 1739 began the wonderful course of field-preaching which only ended with his death in 1791. The same year saw the establishment of the United Society and the Foundry in Moorfields. In 1740 Wesley broke with the Moravian body and formally renounced Calvinism ; and in 1743 " the rules " for the United Societies, which remain practically unaltered to-day, were drawn up. By 1791 he had laid down the broad lines of an organisation which numbered 60,000 members in Great Britain; he had visited Ireland forty-two times, Scotland frequently, and his pleading voice had been heard throughout the length and breadth of England. The movement was powerfully aided by his brother Charles, despite sharp differences, both personal and religious, and at first by George Whitefield, the leader of the Calvinistic Methodists. Charles Wesley was a prolific hymn-writer, actually composing more than 4000 hymns, some dozen of which rank with the best inspired work of any Church. Whitefield, a preacher more than equal in persuasive eloquence to Wesley himself, was supported by the Countess of Huntingdon, an original "converted" member of the first Methodist Society and the founder of "Lady Huntingdon's Connection". Unhappily, the quarrel over "free grace" between Wesley and Whitefield, after 1749, defied all reconciliation, and the two men parted company for ever.

The Wesleyan Church was thus the creation of John Wesley, whose health and personal vigour would be incredible if not established beyond question. "I do not remember," he said of himself,

14

" to have felt lowness of spirits for a quarter of an hour since I was born." The personal ascendency noticeable at Oxford remained unshaken till his death; and it made him the self-constituted and accepted autocrat of a mighty spiritual organisation. Great as a preacher, he was greater as an organiser and leader of men. His gifts for command stamp him as probably the most striking of eighteenth-century figures, and leave him in the select division of the first class of the great leaders of all ages. It is easy to-day to point out defects; to dub him an intolerant and superstitious fanatic, a hard and self-centred character; to belittle the value of enthusiasm and pronounce his life's work "heat without light". Wesleyanism had little charm for most cultivated minds. The powerful brain of Hume brushed it aside as irrelevant; to the *salon*-sated curiosity of Horace Walpole it seemed the spiritual antics of a rhetorical *poseur*. It produced no enduring literature. Nevertheless, John Wesley's movement merits the abused epithet of "epoch-making". Methodism and the French Revolution are the two most tremendous phenomena of the century. Wesley swept the dead air with an irresistible cleansing ozone. To thousands of men and women his preaching and gospel revealed a new heaven and a new earth; it brought religion into soulless lives and reconstituted it as a comforter, an inspiration, and a judge. No one was too poor, too humble, too degraded to be born again and share in the privilege of divine grace, to serve the one Master, Christ, and to attain to the blessed fruition of God's peace. Aloof alike from politics and the speculations of the schools, Wesley wrestled with the evils of his day and proclaimed the infinite power of a Christian faith based on personal conviction, eternally renewed from within, to battle with sin, misery, and vice in all its forms. The social service that he accomplished was not the least of his triumphs. For Methodism, as has been pointed out by a great critic, diverted into religious channels a vast volume of social discontent which in France swelled the tides that submerged Church and State in 1789. At a time when Bishop Butler asserted that Christianity was "wearing out of the minds of men," Wesley kept the English people Christian and shamed the Church that closed her pulpits to him into imitating his spirit if not his methods. No historian will venture to stake out the limits of movements whose most vivifying force works in the silence of the religious life of masses of men and women. But it is certain that into the moral fibre of the English people, even in the classes most anxious to repudiate the debt, were woven new strands by the abiding influence of Methodism. Wesley's Society survived, and is a living force to-day. In the organised millions of the Methodist Churches amongst the English-speaking race in all lands has been built up the fittest monument to the greatness and achievements of John Wesley.

Beyond the limits of Great Britain, for those who had eyes to see, the American question already existed in 1760. With the foundation of Georgia in 1732 by General Oglethorpe, the mystic number of thirteen colonies was now complete. Oglethorpe had been chairman of the Parliamentary Committee on Debtors' Prisons; and the new settlement was intended to be a refuge for paupers and a barrier in the South against Spanish aggression. The founder succeeded in maintaining the colony against Spain; but his prohibition of rum and negro slavery, and difficulties with the Wesleys and Whitefield, made Georgia not merely the youngest but also the weakest of the British settlements. By 1714 the constitutional development of the other twelve colonies was practically complete; and henceforward their administrative and economic relations with Great Britain was the main question.

Broadly, each colony had a constitution roughly modelled on that of the Mother Country; and the inhabitants by race, tradition, and institution were saturated with the political principles and ideals of self-governing Englishmen. Connecticut and Rhode Island were chartered colonies with extensive rights of self-government: Maryland and Pennsylvania were proprietary, i.e. the government was vested in the representatives of the original proprietors, subject to special intervention of the Crown. In the remaining eight (New Hampshire, Massachusetts, New York, Delaware, New Jersey, Virginia, and the two Carolinas) the Executive was in the hands of the Crown, and exercised through a governor and council, while internal legislation and taxation were assigned to a representative assembly. The Crown retained and exercised a prerogative of veto, the right to nominate the governor and judiciary, and to control the policy of the colonies in their relation to each other and in imperial affairs. The expenses of administration were met by local taxation. Except in Maryland, Virginia, and North Carolina, the governor and judges were paid by annual grants. The

Home Government desired to make the Executive independent by securing a permanent appropriation, but was worsted in a sharp struggle with Massachusetts ; and after 1735 in most of the colonies the Assemblies steadily declined to surrender the control over the Executive, and the necessity of annual sessions which temporary grants ensured. The colonists thus were habituated to the practice of representative, though not responsible, government, to self-taxation, and to a general autonomy which the wholesome and studied neglect and ignorance of the imperial authorities, and their refusal to push their demands, strengthened with each decade. The supremacy of the Imperial Parliament in legislation was tacitly acquiesced in ; but even if the royal veto and judicial appeals to the Crown in Council be included, direct interference from home, apart from trade regulations, was spasmodic and slight. The

1696 Board of Trade and Plantations had been intended to act as a central organ in colonial affairs, but it was not an Executive authority. It collected and digested information ; Executive action remained with a Secretary of State or the Privy Council. Responsibility was thus divided and the imperial machinery dislocated. War alone brought the colonies into continuous connection with the home Government, and war was an abnormal state of things. The normal life in times of peace was suffered to develop unimpeached except by chronic official criticism and abortive official suggestions. The steady volume of colonial papers that came to London was read and docketed, and answered. They form an encyclopædic serial on the affairs and growth of the thirteen settlements ; but Cabinet Ministers and members of Parliament were ignorant of their contents, and they resulted in a meagre driblet of effective Executive action. The aphorism that George Grenville lost Great Britain her colonies, because he really read and acted on official despatches, is better substantiated by modern documentary research than most historical epigrams.

Colonial trade was strictly regulated by a code of statutes made at Westminster as part of a comprehensive imperial polity. The essence and ideal of " the old colonial system " was to maintain a self-sufficing Empire of customers by controlling production and consumption in the interests of the whole Empire. Its object was not so much to secure a favourable balance of trade or to raise revenue, (though there were useful subsidiary consequences and

tests of prosperity,) as to weld the dominions of the Crown into a
carefully co-ordinated national State and through the reaction of
economic legislation to mould the institutions and life of its members in harmony with that ideal.   The Navigation Act of 1660,
with its later prolific emendations, accordingly "enumerated" the
articles that the colonies were obliged to export to no other country
than Great Britain ; and it provided that the trade must be carried
on in British (or colonial) ships manned by British (or colonial) crews.
It is now generally agreed that the system was also part of the
theory of imperial defence and was not devised nor enforced solely
to enrich the home at the expense of the colonial producer and
consumer.   By elaborate schedules of tariffs, bounties, preferences,
and drawbacks, the monopoly of imperial trade was divided between
colonies and mother country, from which the foreigner was effectively
ruled out.   Sacrifice on both sides to the common weal was an implied statutory duty.   If the colonial manufacture of hats, woollen
goods, hardware, or manufactured articles generally was crippled in
the interest of Great Britain, the home citizen could smoke only
colonial tobacco, and consume colonial coffee, sugar, and rice ; substantial preferences were given to colonial lumber, hemp, raw silk,
naval stores, iron and copper ore, beaver skins, spirits, and molasses.
True, the Molasses Act of 1733 prohibited a lucrative colonial trade
with foreign ports ; but in 1730 rice, and in 1739 sugar, could be
exported direct to other than British ports south of Cape Finisterre.

The measure of the political and economic success, the comparative loss and gain of this policy are still matters of controversy on
which even with the help of much patient research most scholars
would shrink from a dogmatic verdict.   The system clearly involved
the principle of indirect taxation imposed by the imperial Legislature ; Adam Smith, its most exhaustive and influential critic, admitted that it was more liberal than that of any other European
country ; it is demonstrable that the colonies grew rapidly in
wealth, trade, and population, and that down to 1765 serious ob-
jection was not taken to the commercial restrictions.   It is even
arguable (though doubtful) that under a different system colonial
prosperity would not have been more highly developed.   But it
is equally clear that the system was artificial, the product of conditions which since 1660 had greatly altered ; it was neither quickly
nor easily readjusted, and was neither completely developed nor

rigorously enforced.   It involved considerable smuggling and evasion both of provincial and imperial laws, which debased the respect
both for colonial law and imperial authority.   It locked up capital
in congested channels, and gave a dangerous preponderance in
profit to the British merchant.   The balance of trade was steadily
against the colonial, who could only meet it by profits made in an
illegal trade with foreign settlements ; and it acted as a continuous
drain on the coin and bullion of the colonies.   The system confused
the idea of settlement with that of possession ; and there is much
indirect evidence that the economic dependence of the colonies on
Great Britain chilled rather than fostered imperial sentiment and
weakened political solidarity.

By 1760 the necessity of a fiscal reconstruction on wholly different principles is apparent.   The colonies were not a single economic
unit with a common economic interest.   The latent contradiction
between the principles and practice of colonial autonomy and the
commercial code more than once had already come to light.   The
Sovereign British Parliament was neither a scientific, nor a well-
informed, nor an impartial judge of interests, intrinsically conflicting and selfish, and the colonial view was not directly represented
in it.   But could fiscal reconstruction be carried out without
shattering the whole imperial fabric ?   That fabric as an effective
machinery for administration and defence was partly worn out,
mostly non-existent.   Competent observers had repeatedly exposed
its defects, and placed on record ideas, duly pigeon-holed in London, for its amendment.   Pownall dreamed of " a great commercial
marine," " a great commercial dominion," a real imperial *Zollverein*,
in place of the rusty, loosely-jointed, decentralised organisation he
had a share in working ; Franklin and Shirley desired federation
and parliamentary union for the separate colonial units ; Dinwiddy
urged direct imperial taxation to solve the financial difficulty and
teach imperial duty.   But Ministers at home, who were slowly
abandoning the belief that men can be taxed into prosperity, could
not as yet bring themselves to believe that Englishmen could be
taxed into loyalty.   A memorable congress at Albany, in 1754,
formulated a plan for colonial union, but it was rejected by the
separate assemblies.   The colonies proved once and again that
"they were a rope of sand, loose and unconnected," " one in
promises to pay, thirteen when performance was due ".   The great

war of 1756 italicised these conclusions.   British officers and statesmen were irritated by the disunion, reluctance, and miserliness of
the colonial assemblies ; British criticism and condescension annoyed
the ultra-sensitive colonial.   Pitt sternly rebuked and endeavoured
to check the persistence of the colonial trader who smuggled stores
and rations (at vast profit to his unpatriotic pocket) to the advantage of the common enemy.   The conquest of Canada removed the
strongest argument for imperial protection, but did not destroy the
menace from the Indian or the hope of revenge at Paris and Madrid.
Thus every factor in 1760 combined to create a situation demand-
ing on both sides sympathy, knowledge, tact, and, most difficult of
all, a common political end and outlook.   The temporary causes of
friction were trumpery, but behind them and aggravated by the
success of the war lay the fundamental problem of imperial government and unity.   The chaotic administrative, fiscal, and military
organisation had broken down in 1756; a treaty of peace and a
return to the *status quo* would not fill in the cracks.   How were
the weakness of the imperial Executive, the parochial outlook of
the colonial assemblies, the jealous particularism, the financial obstacles to be amended or removed ?

The logic of the principles hitherto prevailing was easy to draw
—enforce the sovereignty of the imperial Parliament, tighten up
the imperial tie, strengthen the central Executive, bring the colonial Legislatures to a sense of their shortcomings, and work the
commercial code up to the hilt—in a word, make the letter of
mercantilist imperialism correspond with the theory.   But two
generations of colonial growth ran dead against such logic.   Of
sentimental loyalty to the British Crown there was in the colonies
plenty ; but the duty of self-sacrificing loyalty to the Empire, as
represented by the British Parliament and the British Cabinet,
was neither recognized nor acted upon.   The constitutional rights
long enjoyed, the resentment at imperial interference, an expanding
political and commercial life, the unbridged estranging ocean, made
for extended not restricted powers of self-government.   We can see
now, though it was not seen in America or England then, that the
old colonial system by 1760 had crumbled away under the dissolvent action of forces created and fed by itself.   All the economic
and intellectual currents, running stronger each year, in the life of
the Empire, were working against, not for, its continuance.   The

colonist had unconsciously grown into the American.   Just because
he could not get rid of his English blood, his English traditions,
and his English ambitions, he was stretching out towards a freer,
wider life ; and he would reach it in the same illogical but effective
way that his forefathers had done in Great Britain.   He had not
yet learned to express his needs in articulate language ; but it only
required a false stroke of policy to fire him into speech and action.
The true task for British statesmenship was not to underpin a
tottering and cramping structure, but with faith in the binding
cement of a common liberty and common ideals realised through
different methods, to rebuild for the new Empire to come.   Between a fundamental reconstruction and colonial independence
there could be no halfway house for a race true to its political
heritage ; and it was in the best interests of the political and moral
future of the whole English-speaking peoples that the Time-Spirit
had so decreed.

NOTE.—For recent research and results on the topics discussed in this
chapter, see the following Appendices : XIV., XX., and XXI.   On the
" Hanoverian " Church of England, N. Sykes' *Life of Edmund Gibson* (1927),
is indispensable.   P. C. Yorke, *Life of Lord Hardwicke*, 3 vols., 1913, throws
a mass of light on the Walpole-Newcastle period.

THE REIGN OF GEORGE III

CHAPTER I

THE NEW MONARCHY (1760 - 1770)

GEORGE III., born in 1738, was now in his twenty-third year. His accession in the middle of a victorious war and aided by the steady growth of monarchical sentiment in the nation was hailed with enthusiasm. Born and bred in England, he was free from his grandfather's damning devotion to Hanover, (the wits said he could not find the Electorate in the map,) and could rightly claim "to glory in the name of Britain," while the demoralisation of Prince Charles Edward and the decay of Jacobitism made his hereditary and parliamentary title popular in the best sense. His youth, sincere piety, and attachment to Protestantism, his high standard of kingly duty, simple tastes and unblemished morals, his national pride and patriotic convictions appealed, as such qualities in a prince always will, to the loyalty of all classes in the State. That throughout a reign of exceptional length which began and ended with the two most critical phases of the titanic duel between Great Britain and France, George III. retained the affections and devotion of his subjects was largely due to the hold that his private life and domestic virtues had on English men and women. A nation convinced of the necessity and value of monarchical government readily and not unjustifiably condoned the political errors of the Sovereign, errors set in sharp relief against the moral and political vices of the heir to the throne and his brothers. And contemporaries with few exceptions were not able to measure accurately the grave consequences of the King's superstitions and prejudices. Like his granddaughter, George III. mirrored many of the most striking

qualities of the middle class—courage, sense of duty, decorum in
family life, pride of race, insular patriotism and ingrained conservatism.   He also shared their bigoted Protestantism, that intellectual indifference that so easily stiffens into hostility to ideas, and
a narrow and self-satisfied mental and moral outlook.   Sympathy,
the first condition of statesmanship, he lacked as completely as he
lacked charity.   The fuller air, the larger light which great characters, great principles, the formative forces of new life in a people
must find or be stifled were rigorously shut out from the earth on
which the King worked and the heaven for which he hoped alike
for himself and his subjects.   In the mediocre mind or the sub-
servient political hack—a Bute, a North, a Sackville, a Thurlow,
an Addington—he was happy to discover his most congenial ally
and instrument.   With the exception of Warren Hastings, to
whom the caprice of party prejudices made the King for once
generous and just, it is questionable whether George III. understood or wished to understand the great men and the causes for which
they stood that made his reign memorable, despite the disintegration of the empire for which the Sovereign was more responsible
than any one else.   Chatham and Burke, Grattan and Fox were as
much beyond his narrow vision as were Wilberforce, Adam Smith,
Bentham, Gibbon, Malthus, Wordsworth, Coleridge, and Sheridan.
Even in the younger Pitt, as the proposals for Roman Catholic
emancipation and the abolition of the Slave Trade showed, the
finer issues to which that proud spirit could be so finely touched
were hidden from his master, who only saw in him the indispensable
dyke between the throne and the hateful flood of opposition rebels,
and the bulwark of a perishing social order against anarchy and
revolution.   His education, "in which the mother and the nursery
had always prevailed " had unhappily not improved a character by
nature stubborn, resentful, and parsimonious.   Nourished in the
atmosphere of the women of the bedchamber and pages of the
backstairs of an opposition Court, his head stuffed full of obsolete
ideas of the prerogatives of the Crown, and of his mother's injunc-
tions "to be a King," he had grown to manhood, foolishly secluded
from bracing contact with the world of statesmen and high affairs,
and dominated by the influence of the Dowager-Princess of Wales, an
ambitious, intriguing, petty-minded, and disappointed woman.   It
is not surprising that in 1760 the young Prince was, as he confesses

in his correspondence, ignorant both of men and public business. Hard work, bitter necessity, and dogged ambition in time supplied him with adequate rule-of-thumb knowledge ; but to the last George remained obstinate, ungrateful, vindictive, and resentful of all opposition, obsessed by his own views, and capable of any meanness, trickery, or intrigue to achieve the ends he had framed for himself.

Since 1756 his chief adviser had been his Groom of the Stole, the Earl of Bute, who zealously co-operated in saturating his pupil with Bolingbroke's *Idea of a Patriot King*, enforced by the black-letter legalism of Blackstone's as yet unpublished *Commentaries*. Bolingbroke thus came to teach the same pleasing lesson as Johnson's comfortable maxim that the devil was the first Whig. Bute certainly was not the Machiavellian arch-conspirator of popular satire against the liberties and institutions of Great Britain. But he was a royal favourite, whose Scottish birth and close intimacy with the dowager-princess exposed him to coarse invective and damaging insinuations. His intentions were excellent, his ambitions lofty. Handsome, pompous, and conceited, " he would have made an admirable ambassador in any Court where there was nothing to do ". But he was cursed from the outset by third-rate abilities, vanity, total lack of real administrative experience, and the pathetic persistence with which he mistook aptitude in intrigue for political insight and statesmanship. With a young and opinionated sovereign, a great war on hand and a critical international situation requiring consummate skill and tact, the advent to power of this untrained amateur was a serious public misfortune.

The note of coming discord was struck at once. Pitt was obliged to insist on the description of the war in the first royal speech being altered from " bloody and expensive " to " expensive but just and necessary "; but though Bute as yet declined the King's offer to make him Secretary of State his admission to the Privy Council and the Cabinet, and George's plain hint " that my Lord Bute will tell you my thoughts at large," were profoundly significant. Two not unimportant measures marked the commencement of the reign. For the first time the Sovereign surrendered the hereditary revenues of the Crown in England, and in return was voted a Civil List of £800,000. Although the sources of royal income from Scotland, Ireland, and the Duchies of Cornwall and Lancaster were not affected by this statutory arrangement, the surrender and the legislative vote register a further stage in the extension of Parliamentary control over the expenditure of the Sovereign.   On the recommendation of the Crown, the statutory

March 3, 1761 independence of the judges was beneficially extended.   Henceforward (1 Geo. III., c. 1) judicial commissions were not to be terminated, as previously, by the demise of the Crown, and adequate salaries were assigned to the judges.   In the autumn of the same year, as arranged by the Princess-Dowager and Bute, alarmed at the King's attachment to the lovely Lady Sarah Lennox,[1] George

Sept. 8 was married to Princess Charlotte of Mecklenburg-Strelitz, and the

Sept. 22 royal coronation followed the marriage.   The Queen was as richly blessed as her husband with the domestic virtues, and proved a loyal and submissive consort, though her married life was much embittered by the undutiful conduct of several of her sons and, later, by the incurable insanity of the King.

The appearance at Court of Tory peers, and the appointment of six Tory Grooms of the Bedchamber, together with a remarkable pamphlet, *Seasonable Doubts from an Honest Man* (by John Douglas, subsequently Bishop of Salisbury), correctly indicated the inauguration of a "new system".   The conversion of the Tories, it was argued, into loyal supporters of the Revolution dynasty made their continued proscription unjustifiable.   With their help government by the Sovereign could now take the place of government based on connection, party, and the corrupt usurpation of the rights of the Crown by a handful of territorial families leagued together to keep the King in bondage.   Restore to the Crown its proper place, harmonise the exercise of the prerogative with the unquestioned theory of the constitution and the letter of the law, and you would dissolve the elaborate apparatus of corruption, influence, and control by which "a confederacy of Ministers" dictated to the nation, in the name of the King, the policy of a selfish

---

[1] Previously to 1760 George was said (on slender evidence) to have fallen in love with the beautiful Quakeress, Hannah Lightfoot.   The romance of Lady Sarah (daughter of the Duke of Richmond and sister-in-law of Henry Fox) can be read in her *Letters* (ed. Stavordale) and Walpole's *Memoirs of George III*.   It may be doubted whether a broken leg really prevented her from becoming Queen.   She lived to marry (1) Sir C. Bunbury, who was compelled to divorce her; and (2) G. Napier, her three eldest sons by whom were famous for their personal beauty and achievements, *viz.* Sir Charles, the conqueror of Scinde ; Sir William, the historian of the Peninsular War ; and General Sir G. Napier.

oligarchical caste. An independent Sovereign, framing his own policy, choosing and directing his Executive servants, irrespective of party, and dispensing his own patronage, would extirpate corruption at its source, and restore to the Legislature its long-lost independence. In brief, the programme and system of George III. had in their favour a plausible analysis of constitutional theory, a widespread dissatisfaction with prevailing methods and abuses, (the great Minister, Pitt, was notoriously averse from government by party or connection,) and the disorganisation of the Whigs, who had split up into a cluster of cliques, united only by a belief in the divine-right monopoly of office vested in "the Revolution families". The broadening conception of a national State, fostered by the triumphs of the war and new-born visions of empire, strengthened also the vague desire that a rehabilitated and national monarchy should employ the powers entrusted to it to work out a more complete expression of nascent national ideals.

Unhappily, the new policy, as interpreted by George III., failed to distinguish between the inevitable and beneficial results of the growth of parliamentary government and the accidental defects of the Whig *régime*. The hiatus between the letter of the law, as expounded by a lawyer such as Blackstone, and the accepted conventions which reconciled theory with the requirements of free government, was real, if concealed. George's ambition to restore the personal share of the Sovereign in the exercise of the prerogative could not be achieved by simply substituting the Crown for a dozen Whig peers; nor could the King, without violently straining the letter of the law, take the place of "the confederacy of usurping Ministers". An "independent Parliament" must prove to be absolutely incompatible with "an independent Crown". The Cabinet, in truth, was merely the central piece of machinery by which Parliament, through Ministerial responsibility to the Legislature, had tightened its comprehensive grip on the royal prerogative. For legislation, finance, administration, policy, a parliamentary majority was now indispensable. A Sovereign, legally irresponsible, and imposing his own measures on a group of departmental Ministerial servants, could only carry on the King's government either by accepting (as before) the will of the majority expressed through its trusted representatives or by enslaving and debauching Parliament to his will. The inevitable result of George's experi-

ment was the organization of the system of " the King's Friends,"
i.e. a body of members, created by influence and induced by corruption to vote always and only for the King's measures, even against
the King's Ministers.   In a word, the King's finger would be found
to be thicker than the loins of the Whigs.   The demoralising aggravation of the evils of the previous *régime*, the dislocation of
machinery, the fostering of faction and the fatal identification of
national policy with the interest of a single individual, disagree-
ment with whom was "desertion" and opposition to whom was
"sedition," were not the least deplorable results revealed by the
first twenty years of the reign.

Two advantages, however, indirectly accrued. The successful
rout of the Whigs proved to be only the first phase of a struggle
which in the end created, under Rockingham's leadership and
Burke's inspiration, a more scientific synthesis of constitutional
principles.   Burke's *Thoughts on the Causes of the Present Discontent* was a noble vindication of parliamentary and Cabinet
government and a searching reply to the flimsy philosophy of
Bolingbroke and Douglas.   To the " King's Friends " was opposed
party, the union of public men for public ends, and the indispensable organ of parliamentary sovereignty; with "influence, dead
and rotten as prerogative," was contrasted the power of Ministers,
responsible to the Legislature that represented the national will;
in place of the departmental system was set a Cabinet, bonded by
collective solidarity on the fundamental issues of the day.   The
débâcle of the royal policy in the American War gave the victory to
the new Whiggism.   But fortune ultimately decided that the
younger Pitt, the son of "the trumpet of sedition," should reap
the fruits of twenty years of Whig Opposition, and base a new,
constructive, and truer Toryism on the sound foundations of party
discipline and creeds, and on the Cabinet and the authority and
office of the Prime Minister as the most effective instruments for
harmonising the national will with the prerogative of the nation's
Sovereign.

The gradual introduction of the King's system required first
and foremost a satisfactory peace. The growing conviction in the
nation that peace could now be obtained on honourable terms was
strengthened by Maudit's pamphlet, *Considerations on the German War*, which, under circumstances broadly resembling those of

1710, influenced public opinion almost as profoundly as Swift's *Conduct of the Allies*. The writer argued that England's interest demanded an exclusively colonial and naval war, and emphasised the ruinous cost of subsidising Frederick, and the futility of fighting France for German ends on the continent. His criticisms of Pitt's methods and the "Continentalists" were italicised by the supplies voted for 1761 (£19,616,119—an advance of four millions), the alarming increase in the National Debt, and the exhausting demands for men. To Bute, opposed on principle to the German War, peace was the first step towards ending Pitt's and the Whig war, and shattering the power which the conduct of military operations gave to the great War Minister and his political allies. The successes of 1761 considerably strengthened the peace-party. Frederick had lost Schweidnitz and most of Silesia; his eastern border was open to Russian attack; and he was only saved from disaster by the timely death of the Tsarina and the accession of Jan. 5, Peter III., as ardent in his friendship to Prussia as Elizabeth had 1762 been irreconcilable in her enmity. In Western Germany, Ferdinand drove the French out of Hesse, defeated at Vellinghausen the July 15 combined armies of Broglie and Soubise, to the success of which the British contingent under Granby again signally contributed. The French, however, retained Cassel, and a renewed invasion of Hanover was certain for next year. Across the seas Dominica was captured, while, nearer home, the Mauritius expedition was diverted against Belle Isle. The first attempt failed, but Keppel and Hodgson, under Pitt's directions, persisted, and on June 7th the garrison capitulated, and the British flag triumphantly floated over French soil close to the French coast.

The general election at the end of March was remarkable for the amount and extent of corruption in the constituencies. Thanks to the new policy of employing the resources and patronage of the Crown for royal ends, the nucleus of a prerogative party was created, consisting of members pledged to the Court and not to the Whigs. So far Bute had skilfully supported Pitt against his colleagues, whose jealousy of "the dictator" played further into the favourite's hands. At the request of the Whigs, Holdernesse was now pensioned, Bute became Secretary of State, Barrington replaced Legge March 12 as Chancellor of the Exchequer, and George Grenville was brought into the Cabinet. Newcastle, however, soon found, to his intense

chagrin, how he had been duped. He had alienated Pitt, while
Bute steadily withdrew the patronage which alone made office
endurable, and used it against him. The conundrum debated by
the wits whether the King would employ Newcastle, Scotch (Bute),
or Pitt coal rapidly became a crisis in foreign policy and in the
Council Chamber.

Bute had already, through Viri and Solar, the Sardinian Ministers at London and Paris, begun secret overtures to France.
With the despatch of Hans Stanley to Paris, and De Bussy to
London, direct dealings between Pitt and Choiseul were opened.
To the French proposals of July 15th, Pitt replied with an ulti-
Aug. 15 matum granting limited fishing rights in Newfoundland, requiring the restoration of Frederick's territories in French occupation,
and reserving the power to help our Prussian ally if war continued
on the Continent. He had already peremptorily rejected the
memorial on the Spanish claims, presented with the French draft,
as " wholly inadmissible," and haughtily intimated that future
attempts to blend the Spanish and French claims would be regarded as an unfriendly act. Despatches from Lord Bristol, our ambassador at Madrid, and intercepted letters of Fuentes and Grimaldi,
the Spanish ambassadors at Paris and London, convinced Pitt that
Choiseul was insincere and was planning further mischief. The
suspicion was quite correct. The Third Family Compact, linking
the Bourbon Courts of Paris, Madrid, Naples, and Parma, with
hostile intentions against Great Britain, had been signed on the
same day that Pitt compelled a reluctant Cabinet to accept his
ultimatum. A series of no less than twelve Cabinet meetings
culminated in the critical day of October 2nd, when Pitt demanded
instant war with Spain, on the plain ground that the intercepted
papers showed that Charles III. intended to join with France. The
Cabinet, sceptical as to the prediction, clinging to the resources of
diplomacy, and convinced by the experts that our army and fleet
Oct. 5   did not justify provocation of so formidable a coalition, refused the
demand. Pitt, supported by Temple alone, at once resigned, de-
clining " to continue without having the direction ".[1] His popularity, dashed for a moment by his acceptance of a pension of
£3000 for three lives and a peerage for his wife—unsolicited honours,
inadequate to his imperishable services to his country—rose higher

[1] See Appendix V.

than ever; and his superb self-restraint, under misinterpretation and envenomed invective, in refraining from trying to overthrow the Ministry, marks the zenith of his career. His resignation was a public calamity. It played Choiseul's game to a nicety; it deprived the Administration of the one great master of the higher leading; it estranged Pitt from the old Whigs when a strong Opposition was essential; it convinced Frederick that his betrayal was at hand, and it left the self-willed King, the inexperienced Bute, and the headstrong Bedford to manipulate the situation as they pleased. At the same time the sons of Zeruiah were too strong to permit Pitt to secure the peace he regarded as indispensable. If resignation marked his isolation and failure, it saved his reputation from being tarnished with the sins and blunders of the royalist tools.

Egremont succeeded Pitt, Bedford replaced Temple, and George Grenville became leader in the Commons. Pitt's prediction was shortly justified to the hilt. The safe return of the Spanish Dec. 25 treasure ships and the publication of the Family Compact necessi- Jan. 2, tated a declaration of war. Charles III. had thus gained three 1762 valuable months and England had lost her invaluable War Minister. Newcastle, subjected to continued affronts and alarmed by the determination of the Cabinet to stop Frederick's subsidy and with- May 25 draw our troops from the Continent, at last resigned. The Duke's political character has received unduly hard measure; but his resignation and refusal to accept either pension or reward for services extending over nearly forty years of public life were a worthy close to a career of exceptional industry. His abilities were second rate; his defects easily lent themselves to exaggeration and ridicule; but in the single-hearted devotion of his life and fortune to the Hanoverian dynasty and the Revolution State he is a typical example of the best of the Whig aristocracy. The Ministry could now be further reconstructed on "King's Friend" lines. Bute became First Lord of the Treasury, Grenville, Secretary of State, while Anson (who had died) was succeeded by Lord Halifax; and a still poorer exchange was effected when Sir F. Dashwood, the owner of the famous-infamous Medmenham Abbey, an incompetent libertine who "blundered over pounds and strode pompously over farthings" was appointed Chancellor of the Exchequer.

The progress of the war helped Bute beyond his deserts.

15

July 10   Catherine had succeeded her murdered husband, Peter; but despite her neutrality, Frederick, by delaying the departure of the Russian army, whose neutrality was not yet known, virtually recovered
July 21   Silesia by the last of his great victories, Burkersdorf. A month
June 24   earlier, Ferdinand had defeated the French at Wilhelmsthal; and after complicated manœuvres, brilliantly repulsed, at Brücken
Sept. 21   Mühle, the French attempt to relieve the blockade of Cassel. With
Nov. 1   its fall the Hanoverian war ended. The invasion of our ally, Portugal, by Spanish forces was also repulsed by the despatch of a British contingent under the Count of Lippe-Bückeburg and General Burgoyne, who won a brief reputation that was destroyed later by the disaster at Saratoga. On the seas, England struck hard at both Bourbon Powers. Rodney and Monckton captured
Feb.   Martinique, while Grenada, St. Lucia, St. Vincent were also taken. Anson's last service was to send the Cuban expedition under Pocock and Albemarle unexpectedly through the dangerous
June 5   Bahama Channel, with the result that Havana was surprised. Albemarle's generalship was unfortunately not equal to Pocock's seamanship; and not until August 12th, after a hideous and unnecessary waste of life, Fort Moro and the city surrendered. "Havana stopped Grimaldi's cackle." The blow to Spanish prestige, commerce and wealth, and the lessons of organised sea power and amphibious war, were driven home by the storming of Manila in the Philippines, summarily effected by an expedition from Madras under Cornish and Draper. Truly enough it was the star of Pitt that had conquered at Martinique, Cuba, and in the Pacific.

Bute had it in his power to put Crown and Cabinet in a position of unassailable strength by making a great and honourable peace. It was not to be. The refusal to continue the Prussian subsidy, clumsy overtures to Austria behind Prussia's back (which met with a humiliating rebuff), and secret negotiations (through Viri and Solar) with France revealed the Minister's incompetence. Frederick, with characteristic cynicism developed his separate understanding with Russia and intrigued to bring about Bute's downfall, an exasperating interference in our home politics which provided Bute and Bedford with their strongest arguments for scuttling the Prussian ship. Amidst increasing signs of unpopularity on all hands, Bedford was sent as special envoy to Paris. The fear of Pitt's return coerced Bute, the fear of worse disasters coerced Choiseul who coerced

Grimaldi; and the preliminaries were signed at Fontainebleau. Nov. 3
Ministers, alarmed by Pitt's scathing criticism and their own unpopularity, appealed through the young Lord Shelburne to Henry
Fox to save them. "We must," said the King, "call in bad men
to govern bad men." The Paymaster, in return for a peerage,
entered the Cabinet and became the King's representative in the
Commons. With cold-blooded efficiency and unflinching corruption he promptly set to work to break once and for all the Opposition led by Newcastle, Hardwicke, Devonshire, and Pitt, once his
colleagues, but whom he had neither forgiven nor forgotten.
"Now my son is King of England," the Princess-Dowager cried
when the terms of the peace were carried in the Commons by 319
votes to 65 and in the Lords without a division. The victory was
a triumph for Fox, the King, and the resources of the prerogative;
but it was a sinister prelude to the policy of substituting "purity
and patriotism" for the selfish corruption of the Whig oligarchy.
Fox now went "to the general rout". Devonshire, whose name
had already been struck off the Privy Council Roll by the King's
own hand, was stripped of his Lord-Lieutenancy, as were Rockingham and Grafton of theirs. A vindictive expulsion of Whig placemen high and low completed the claims of Fox on the King's
gratitude, which he deserved but failed to win. On February 10th,
1763, the Peace of Paris was signed, and five days later the Treaty
of Hubertusburg between Prussia and the House of Austria ended
the Seven Years' War.

The unpopularity of Dashwood's budget clinched Bute's desire
to escape from the odium of his position. A war loan raised on
costly terms was corruptly distributed amongst the supporters of
Government; and a new excise on cider provoked riots in the cider
counties. Thoroughly disillusioned, Bute resigned on April 7th.
If he had repeated Bolingbroke's achievement of 1710 of breaking
up an apparently all-powerful administration, he had also made
himself the most hated Minister since Strafford's day. The first
phase of the reign of George III. was closed.

By the treaties of 1763 France ceded to Great Britain Canada,
Nova Scotia and Cape Breton, restored Minorca, and acquiesced in
the retention of Grenada, St. Vincent, Dominica, Tobago, and
Senegal. She also agreed to evacuate Hanoverian, Hessian, and
Prussian territories, and to dismantle Dunkirk. England withdrew

her troops from Germany, restored Belle Isle, Guadeloupe, Marie-
galante, Martinique, St. Lucia and Goree, as well as the French
commercial stations in India, and the fishing rights (with St. Pierre
and Miquelon) in Newfoundland.   Spain ceded Florida and the logwood rights in Honduras, receiving back Havana and Manila.
France transferred Louisiana, as compensation for Florida, to Spain.
For Portugal and Prussia the *status quo* as before the war was re-
established.

These terms register a notable landmark in the development of
two great States. Prussia emerged exhausted but undiminished ; and
this simple fact proclaimed the decisive defeat of the great coalition
to undo the work of the Hohenzollerns, and the rise to the first
rank in the European system of the Frederician kingdom, a power
with a future of immeasurable significance.   For Great Britain
the Seven Years' War gave a new definition to her imperial structure,
character and outlook.   Striking as are her gains, the moral of
the struggle is still more striking.   She had fought the Bourbon-
Habsburg combination with three weapons—finance (the National
Debt leapt from £72,000,000 to £132,000,000), conjoint sea and
military power, nationality that drew its sustaining strength from
free institutions.   But the unbribed judgment of public opinion
agreed that the terms were not adequate to the victories and sacrifices of the war.   Bute's diplomacy, indeed, is beyond defence.   He
negotiated as if Choiseul was the friend, Frederick, Pitt, and the
Whigs the enemies of England.   The interest of the Crown, not
of the Empire, was the dominating consideration.   The real glory
rests with Pitt who had placed Great Britain beyond the power of
amateurish incompetence to rob her of considerable reward ; to a
less degree with Grenville, Halifax, Granville, and Egremont, who
fought in the Cabinet against Bute and Bedford's incomprehensible
haste to buy peace at any price.   Martinique, Havana, and the
West Indian Islands were surrendered for inferior gains or no compensation at all.   With criminal recklessness Manila was flung
away ; not even the ransom bills of the inhabitants were honoured
by the Spanish Government.   Prussia, it is true, was not "betrayed," for the integrity of the kingdom was purchased by costly
British concessions; but the stupid and unnecessary alienation of
Frederick merits the severest condemnation.   If Bute had rightly
refused to bleed France white—a policy alike in 1709, 1762 and

1814 neither wise nor practicable—he had done nothing to reduce, and much to aggravate, the hostility of French, Spaniards, and Austrians ; he had poisoned the political atmosphere at home and abroad with distrust of the sincerity and methods of the British Crown, and he had thrown away the friendship of the one ally we possessed. Twenty years later the fruits of these fatal months of the favourite's supremacy were reaped to the full. As it was, Bute in April left office on the morrow of the most triumphant war we had ever waged, discredited and detested, and his country isolated and hated.

The supreme lessons of the Peace pointed forward. If Pitt and Clive had saved the future of British expansion in North America and India, scarcely more than the bases of the new Empire were laid. The task of healing the material exhaustion and of political architecture and scientific consolidation, inspired by a sane interpretation of the new needs, was the inevitable heritage of success. We can see now that in 1763 Great Britain and Europe stood on the threshold of an epoch that rings with the imperious challenge of new ideas and aspirations, but one in which the familiar political and economic strata were shifting and crumbling rapidly. Walpole's *Castle of Otranto*, Percy's *Reliques*, Chatterton's Poems, Goldsmith's *Vicar of Wakefield*, are the stray swallows of a spring to dawn in our literature ; they are followed in 1768 by Sterne's *Sentimental Journey*, the year that saw the Royal Academy founded, in the golden age of Reynolds and Gainsborough and Romney ; and in 1775, which saw the first blood shed by kinsmen at Lexington, comes Sheridan's *Rivals* preceded by Goldsmith's *She Stoops to Conquer*, two years before. The Stamp Act, and Watt's steam engine make 1765 memorable, while the Industrial Revolution dates from Hargreave's spinning jenny. In 1768 James Cook started on the ten years of heroic exploration [1] that added a new world to redress the balance so grievously upset for Great Britain by American independence. In the sphere of thought the age is richest of all : Rousseau's *Social Contract*, whose final editions were bound with the skins of the French aristocracy, precedes Blackstone's *Commentaries :* Burke's *Thoughts on the Causes of the Present Discon-*

(marginal dates: 1764, 1765, 1766, 1770, 1762, 1765)

---

[1] James Cook's ideal is best summed up in his own words : " I . . . had ambition not only to go farther than any man had been before ; but as far as it was possible for man to go " : see Appendix XVIII.

tents lead up to the Annus Mirabilis of 1776—the year of the Declaration of Independence, of Adam Smith's *Wealth of Nations*, of the first volume of Gibbon's *Decline and Fall*, of Bentham's *Fragment on Government*, of the *Common Sense* of a dissipated and revolutionary stay-maker, Tom Paine.

Three aspects of the new problems were of immediate importance: (1) imperial administration and finance, essentially a question of imperial defence; (2) foreign policy, based on the new grouping and interests of the European States which upset the traditional conceptions of the balance of power; (3) domestic— how to adjust the working of parliamentary government to the new policy of the Crown.

With 1763 we enter on a period of continuous Ministerial failure, culminating in a supreme disaster, the disruption of the Empire. But if history can teach one lesson, it is that disasters are never inevitable. They are always the result of blunders that need not have been committed, of omissions which might have been made good. One plain moral, as so often in our annals, was in 1763 forgotten or ignored—the home truths of a great war. By 1778 our navy was inadequate for its functions; and nothing had been done to remove the patent danger to an imperial country, vulnerable in every quarter of the globe, of relying on an army and military system improvised in the hour of need. The responsibility for the lack of military organisation in 1775 lies on the Crown and its advisers, Tory and Whig alike; and it was the nation that connived at their blunders which suffered justly merited punishment.

George Grenville now took Bute's place as head of the Government, combining it with the Chancellorship of the Exchequer; Dashwood going to the Lords with a peerage. Grenville's independence and protests against the continuance of Bute's influence "behind the curtain," and the unpopularity and weakness of the Ministry, shortly necessitated a further reconstruction. Three points emerge in these wearisome negotiations: the determination of the King to escape from a Cabinet based on solid party obligations; the jealousies in the groups of the Whig Opposition; the desire of the leaders to suppress the unconstitutional influence of the ex-Minister, Bute. Bedford (with whom Pitt refused to serve) finally consented to become President of the Council, with Grenville as leader in the Commons, while the Earl of Sandwich became Halifax's colleague as Secretary of State. Shelburne was replaced at the Board of Trade by Hillsborough, and now joined the small group that followed Pitt.

The Government had meanwhile come into sharp collision with one of its many virulent critics—John Wilkes[1]—and raised the first of a memorable series of issues connected with the name of a skilful and profligate demagogue. Wilkes was member for Aylesbury. In the famous No. 45 of his paper, *The North Briton*, phrases in the speech from the Throne on the Peace of 1763 were described as false. The King, ignoring accepted conventions of ministerial responsibility, ordered the writer's prosecution, on the ground that the criticism was a personal insult to the Sovereign. Halifax accordingly issued a general warrant for searching, arresting, and seizing persons and papers, not specifically named, but suspected of being connected with the alleged libel; and under it some fifty persons, including Wilkes, were arrested and their papers seized. On a writ of Habeas Corpus, Wilkes, who pleaded his privilege as member of Parliament, was set at liberty amidst vociferous demonstrations of public approval. Temple, whose money and brains were freely used to support insolent attacks on the Crown and its Ministers, was now as Lord-Lieutenant ordered by the King to deprive Wilkes of his colonelcy in the Bucks Militia; and on transmitting the order with a compliment to the offender was himself dismissed from the Privy Council and his Lord-Lieutenancy. Ministers promptly sought for parliamentary support. In the Lords the prosecution of Wilkes was demanded, and his arrest ordered on the singular plea that as the author of an obscene parody of Pope's *Essay on Man*, entitled *An Essay on Woman* (dedicated to Sandwich, but not published), with notes parodied on those of Bishop Warburton to Pope's poem, he had committed a breach of privilege. Sandwich's advocacy of the cause of decency and morality at once struck the public as a piece of ridiculous and treacherous hypocrisy; for the Secretary of State was a notorious libertine and formerly a fellow-member with Wilkes of the debauchee Medmenham brotherhood. The apt application of a quotation from the " Beggar's Opera " fixed on Sandwich the name of " Jemmy Twitcher ".

In the Commons a large majority voted: first, that No. 45 was

[1] See Appendix XVII.

a false and seditious libel, then (concurred in by the Lords) that privilege of Parliament did not extend to such libels, and, thirdly, that No. 45 should be burned publicly by the common hangman. The Opposition attempt to pronounce general warrants illegal was defeated, but only by a small majority (234-218). Wilkes, seriously wounded in a duel, had retired to Paris, and was now expelled the House. Having failed to present himself for sentence in the King's Bench for reprinting the famous No. 45, he was outlawed. Crown and Ministers had apparently won a victory, emphasised by lavish prosecutions of various printers and by the dismissal from their military appointments of three members of the Commons—Conway, A'Court, and Barré—who had voted against the Government. It is significant of the temper of the House that this characteristic refusal of the King "to forget defaulters" did not evoke the resentment stirred by the similar dismissals in 1733 and 1735. Still more significant was the widening breach between Parliament and public opinion. Wilkes' popularity was not a mere craze of the mob. The crowds which threw jackboots, Scotch bonnets, and petticoats, symbols of the hated Bute and the King's mother, on to bonfires, or cheered a bookseller driving to the pillory in a coach numbered 45 expressed much more than detestation of Scottish favourites and their high-placed patrons. "Popularity," Burke well said, "was to be rendered if not directly penal at least highly dangerous." There was, in truth, an end to Ministerial responsibility if the speech from the Throne was the personal declaration of an irresponsible Sovereign, enforcing his own interpretation of libel by general warrants. The expulsion of Wilkes by the Commons was admittedly within the powers of the House; but both Pitt and the seventeen protesting peers pointed to the danger of relying on parliamentary resolutions "applied *ex post facto* to a particular case and used to justify a judicial decision, contrary to law and usage". The action of the majority, in fact, recklessly prejudged a matter awaiting the proper investigation of the Courts, and was vindictive in its haste and unjust in its procedure. Such methods, if persisted in, might involve a dangerous collision between the Legislature and the Law Courts. And presently a series of decisions put a new complexion on the acts of the Executive. In *Wilkes v. Wood* £800 damages were given against the Under-Secretary of State; confirmed six years later when Wilkes' suit against Halifax brought him £4000 damages ; in *Leach v. Money*, 1765 the printer of the *North Briton* obtained £400 for the execution of the warrant ; finally, in *Entick v. Carrington*, Lord Camden condemned general warrants as illegal, and demolished the argument of State necessity and *droit administratif*, " because the common law does not know that kind of reasoning ". Camden's judgment reaffirmed the principle, essential to the liberty of the subject, that the highest office in the State will not protect the holder from the consequences of breaking the law ; and that the Courts will provide adequate remedies and damages for rights violated by the Executive. The judicial extirpation of general warrants from the armoury of Government was not the least of the results that our Press and individual liberty owed to the courage and obstinacy of Wilkes. But in 1766 neither King, Parliament, nor mob had heard the last of the outlaw.

Concurrently in the sphere of imperial administration George Grenville had unwittingly precipitated a still more serious collision between the Legislature and public opinion across the Atlantic. If the importance of events in history is measured by their consequences, the Stamp Act of 1765 and the summoning of the Estates-General in 1789 are the two greatest events of the eighteenth century. Grenville's famous measure was the outcome of a grinding necessity. The late war had been essentially " a colony war " ; it had laid on the mother country a burden of debt and administrative expenditure, cruelly crippling her exhausted resources. The serious Indian invasion of Virginia in 1763, and the fear of French insurrection in Canada made a force for the internal defence of the colonies essential. Grenville accordingly proposed to maintain in America a permanent establishment of 10,000 men, and to meet one-third of the cost (about £100,000) by stamp duties imposed by the imperial Parliament on all written agreements having legal validity in the colonies. " It is just and necessary," ran the preamble " that a revenue be raised in your Majesty's dominions in America for defraying the expenses of defending, protecting, and securing the same." The Act was, therefore, one item of a policy whose object was to eliminate the defects in imperial finance, administration, and defence, revealed and aggravated by the war. The imperial authorities already were enforcing the Navigation Laws more stringently, so as to increase the Customs revenue by checking

smuggling and suppressing contraband trade. At the same time
April, 1765 the port dues were revised and a new molasses duty (1764) imposed.
The Mutiny Act, too, was extended to America, laying on the
colonies the provision of quarters and necessaries for the troops. On
March 22nd the Stamp Act (to come into force on November 1st)
after a languid debate received the royal assent. Grenville had
explained his plan a year previously; but, in order to give opportunities for alternative suggestions from the colonies, deferred, with
more kindliness than statesmanship, its execution for twelve months.

In the furious controversy provoked by this ill-fated scheme
certain points are clear. To represent it as a cold-blooded attempt
to exploit the colonies for the benefit of the home taxpayer, and to
filch from the colonial subjects of the Crown rights long enjoyed,
and to reduce them to a slavish and impoverished subjection, is a
legend exploded by none more effectively than by American historical scholars. The equity of the proposed contribution to imperial defence is admitted. The colonies were flourishing ; the share
demanded was trifling compared with the burden borne by Great
Britain. Not one penny was to be expended elsewhere than in
America or for plain colonial needs. But unquestionably in method, if not in principle, the policy was new, perhaps unprecedented.
The plan of direct taxation had been repeatedly recommended by
experienced colonial authorities as the only practical method for
securing a just colonial contribution to imperial needs. The late
war emphasised the indifference of the colonies to their duties, and
the extreme difficulty, if not impossibility, of uniting thirteen
jealous and short-sighted provincial assemblies in agreement as to
allotment or the punctual payment of their rateable proportions.
Neither Grenville nor the colonial agents anticipated the strength
or the reasons of the fierce opposition to the proposal, which
surprised both the mother country and probably the colonials
themselves.

Already the stringent execution of the Navigation Laws, the
new molasses duty, and the employment of the royal navy in
suppressing contraband trade were very unpopular. Although in
1761 the legality of " writs of assistance " had been in vain disputed by Otis, it has been well said of his speech that " the child
Independence was born on that occasion ". The extension and
enforcement of Admiralty jurisdiction were denounced as an abuse

of authority, tending to the subversion of the common law rights and liberties of the colonists. The ungrounded suspicion that the English Episcopal system would shortly be planted in America was a further irritant to inflamed colonial sentiment. The Stamp Act at once kindled into a blaze all the smouldering embers of discontent. Under the leadership of Samuel Adams in Massachusetts, of Patrick Henry in Virginia, protests against taxation without repre- Nov. 7 sentation were passed ; and a Congress of nine colonies at New York submitted joint grievances to King, Lords, and Commons. Riots in Boston, New York, Rhode Island, and Connecticut made it impossible to execute the Act. The weakness of the Executive, one of the most conspicuous defects of the imperial system, was thus glaringly revealed. With the constitutional agitation, stiffened by mob violence, came retaliation. Associations sprang up to boycott British imports and substitute colonial goods until the Act was withdrawn.

The gravity of the issues involved was not yet fully appreciated on either side of the Atlantic. The Stamp Act was the logical result, as Franklin saw, of the failure of the Albany Congress of 1754. It was not merely perverse legal pedantry nor a blind lust of predominance that found in the imperial Parliament the only possible sovereign and unifying authority for the empire. To question the right to legislate for, and to bind the trade of, the empire as a whole was to impugn the nature of sovereignty and to shatter imperial unity by snapping its one uniting bond. It was held to be impossible to draw a valid distinction, in theory or practice, between the legislative and taxative functions or to separate the direct internal taxation of the stamp duties from the indirect and external taxation of the Customs, the legality of which was unquestioned.[1] In brief, that the imperial Parliament had the legal right claimed for it is now generally conceded by the most competent British and American authorities.

The strength of the colonial Opposition lay in a subtle blending of principles, hallowed by usage, with inextinguishable dreams of

[1] " The English Statute-book furnishes many instances in which the legislative power of Parliament over the colonies was exercised so as to make regulations completely internal, and in no instance that is recollected was their authority openly controverted " (Marshall (perhaps the highest legal American authority), *Washington*, 2, 84). See Appendix XX.

the political future of the Colonies. " No taxation without representation " was both a working hypothesis and a potent ideal of
liberty. Pitt's view that the power of the purse was inherent
in a representative body, that to deny it was to ignore the nature
of taxation and to annihilate the basis of self-government, that to
resist taxation imposed without the consent of the taxed was both
a right and a duty, drew its inspiration from immortal struggles for
liberty at home, and appealed to the ineradicable English instinct
for freedom and self-government. If lawyers could not distinguish
between the legislative and taxative functions, Englishmen had
done so in the past and must do so in the future if they wished to
remain free. Like Walpole, Pitt had resisted the temptation to
override by direct internal taxes the most important function of
the colonial assemblies. And to the colonist there was a vital
difference between taxation of the home citizen by a Legislature in which he was, imperfectly perhaps, represented, and
taxation of the colonists by a Legislature 3000 miles away
in which the colonies were not represented at all. For the
Colonist, also, submission to such taxation was a surrender of the
one master principle by which colonial development could achieve
in time the responsible self-government won by its means in the
mother country. It was not idle rhetoric, therefore, to call that
surrender treason to the future of the colonies. In brief, the logic
of English history and colonial sentiment contradicted the logic of
imperial unity and legal theory. And the clash of warring constitutional principles had already sounded a challenge more pregnant still in its illimitable consequences. Camden in this country,
Henry, Otis, Adams, in America appealed from the Cæsar of man-
made positive law in the Statute-book to the eternal decrees of
humanity, as such. The essential interdependence of taxation and
representation was proclaimed in the last resort as a law of nature.
The authority of Parliament, the obedience of subjects, were
boldly claimed to be limited by the natural rights of the colonists
as men. As in 1789, so in 1776, theories of natural rights inherent and inalienable in man as such and superior to all others
which they necessarily condition and define, may be met by
counter-theories of a like character, but the only effective answer
is shot and shell, the only effective vindication is a successful
revolution.

Unhappily the logic and superficial reasonableness of Grenville's measures are no justification of its statesmanship. As an act of policy the stamp duties deservedly stand condemned. Burke's profound aversion from arguments in politics deduced from the naked "metaphysical rights" of the schools was sound; his distinction between intellectual acquiescence in an abstract legality and the expediency of exercising it was a criticism of Ministerial methods that cut to the quick of the problem, though it failed to disentangle the underlying factors that governed the situation. The imperial fabric required not readjustment but reconstruction. Grenville's aims ignored the disagreeable truth that the old colonial system had broken down before the resistance to the Stamp Act revealed the collapse. To tighten the imperial tie and rivet more strongly the obsolescent bonds of a worn-out mercantilism ran directly counter to the forces underlying the economic and constitutional expansion of the colonies. The attempt was certain to be resisted and resistance spelt worse than defeat—disruption and disintegration. The blunder of direct taxation, avoided by Walpole in 1730, became therefore a crime in 1765. Worst of all, the mischief wrought was irreparable. A claim had been deliberately asserted and as deliberately repudiated. The imperial Parliament was defied and its authority was now at issue. By the same arguments that denied the power to tax directly, the power directly to legislate or to bind trade would be questioned and resisted. What was to be the next step? Surrender to resistance and shatter the whole imperial fabric? Maintain the rights by force? A remedy more disastrous than the disease it could not cure. And in the background lurked the spectre of independence. True, the weight of evidence supports Franklin's assertion that in 1765 independence was not the avowed goal of the colonial champions. But the opposed ideals of colonial autonomy and British authority, the absence of a true imperial sentiment in America, the embittered and democratic atmosphere of the New England settlements, had at once thrown to the front chiefs, able, unscrupulous, ambitious, determined to pare down to a minimum imperial control. Material economic interests silently and swiftly gave a selfish substance to the demand for complete freedom. The cry for independence would not be stifled if the colonists were once convinced that "the tyranny anticipated not the tyranny inflicted" was the real danger. On public leaders at home lay now the burden of averting such a tragic conclusion.

The friction between the King and "the Triumvirate" increased. George III. wished to control his Ministers, the Ministers wished to control the King. And the constitutional lectures of his advisers caused the King to say that he would rather see the devil than George Grenville in his Cabinet. The King's illness and some symptoms of his later insanity made provision for a regency desirable. Legislation was proposed by the Ministers, restricting the regency to the Queen and the members of the royal family. Bedford, in order to strike at Bute's influence, prevented, before the bill was read in the Lords, the name of the Princess-Dowager from being included ; and the King, persuaded that otherwise the measure would not pass the Commons, was tricked into accepting the exclusion. But an amendment, inserting the name of the Princess, was at once carried in the Commons ; and the King suffered the mortification, first, of consenting to a slur on his mother, and then to its removal being forced on the Ministry, apparently against the wishes of the Crown. Such underhand tactics justified the King in choosing a new Administration. The Duke of Cumberland, whose relations with the great Whig families had always been intimate, now approached Pitt at the King's instigation. But Pitt refused to act without Temple, and Temple was obdurate. The Triumvirate triumphantly imposed fresh concessions on their master. The King was compelled to give a pledge that he would never again consult Bute and to break his word to Bute's brother in a matter of patronage. Appeal was again made to Pitt, and again Temple's obduracy prevented him from accepting.

July 16, 1766   Cumberland now fell back on the great Whig families, and George with ill-concealed reluctance consented to the formation of a Ministry under the Marquis of Rockingham, which included the Duke of Grafton and Conway as Joint Secretaries, Dowdeswell as Chancellor of the Exchequer, Newcastle as Privy Seal, and a group of the King's nominees, Henley, Egmont, and Barrington. The weakness of the coalition was obvious. The witty and fickle Charles Townshend, the spoilt favourite of the House of Commons, who had replaced Lord Holland (Henry Fox) as Paymaster, described it with truth as "a lutestring Administration fit only for summer wear". The King withheld his confidence, which meant that the Court party were directly encouraged to undermine the Oct. 31 position of the Ministers in the Commons. Cumberland's death deprived the Cabinet of a staunch friend, while the Whigs them- selves were more imposing in name and social prestige than in ability, industry, and experience. To Rockingham belongs the credit of bringing his secretary, Edmund Burke, into Parliament; but though he had sound judgment and the gift of political friendships, Rockingham was not a leader and was useless as a speaker. The partiality of his friend, Horace Walpole, failed to convince the world or Conway himself that he was at best anything more than an amiable and second-rate politician. Grafton, by far the ablest of the three, gave to the turf and his mistresses (of whom one, Nancy Parsons, thanks to Reynolds and Junius, won a flash of immortality) the hours and the gifts which in politics might have achieved an enduring reputation. Crown, Ministers, 1765-1770 and public alike recognised that the fate of the Administration lay with Pitt. And unfortunately Pitt's acts at this critical epoch re- quire a charity of judgment which repeated attacks of severe gout cannot wholly justify. In yielding to Temple's obstinate perversity Pitt was guilty of a grave error. Though importuned he declined to serve with Rockingham and Newcastle; nor would he give the Ministry, anxious to carry out his wishes, generous support. It was in his power to unite the Whigs under his leadership on broad principles of reform and he threw the chance away. His mysterious aloofness, dictatorial temper, and shortsighted identification of party connection for public ends with oligarchical faction wrecked the Rockingham Ministry. It separated Pitt from men whose political creed was at bottom the same as his own; it vetoed the future organisation of a strong Opposition, and it left Pitt himself without a party, at the mercy of the King, of the King's Friends, and the Grenville and Bedford groups.

During its brief tenure of power the Ministry endeavoured to undo some of the mischief. The cider tax was repealed; general warrants were condemned by parliamentary resolution. But the American question pressed for decisive action. The mercantile interests, hard hit by the colonial boycott, clamoured for the repeal of the Stamp Act. Pitt in a great speech supported the demand. At the same time he asserted the right to legislate and to bind colonial trade. Ministers, however ready to repeal as a measure of

policy were not united on the legal point—the right to tax as well
as to legislate. They had to reckon with the avowed determination of the Opposition and the Court party to resist repeal, and
with the intrigues of George III. The King assented to his
Ministers' policy, while behind their backs he privately encouraged
the King's Friends to resist the Ministerial measures. The Cabinet
compromised by proposing repeal of the Stamp Act and accom-
panying it with a declaratory bill asserting the right both to tax
and to legislate. Both were successfully carried, in spite of the
opposition of Pitt and Camden to the declaratory statement. The
temporary effect on America was excellent. The repeal was received with loud demonstrations of approval and protestations of
loyalty ; and it appeared as if the storm clouds had dissolved as
quickly as they had arisen. But the Ministerial policy was a mistake and a signal proof of weakness. The Cabinet had a choice of
two straightforward alternatives—to maintain the rights claimed,
restore the impugned dignity of Parliament and the Executive and
enforce the Stamp Act—or to repeal the Act and renounce frankly
the claim to direct internal taxation. The first required great
courage and men of determination ; and in the face of Pitt's opposition and mercantile pressure would have been difficult but not
impossible. But it was dead against the convictions of the Whig
group in the Cabinet. Unconditional repeal would have secured
Pitt's whole-hearted support, and would have been a real message of
peace and goodwill to America. It would have cut away the ground
from any further attempt at direct taxation, and provided time for
opinion on both sides to ripen into an understanding on the scope
and incidence of indirect taxation. The commercial grievances of
the colonists were bound to become a pressing matter before long ;
but time and economic forces were on the side of a gradual modification, if the problem was not first aggravated by embittered feelings.
But the Ministerial policy evaded the difficulties by a dangerous
compromise. It surrendered with one hand what it studiously
reserved with the other. It admitted the victory of defiance, while
it asserted that the right was against those who resisted. Such a
concession was neither graceful nor dignified nor sincere. Nor was
it statesmanship. In reality it settled nothing but the success of
the agitation, and it was naturally taken at its face value in
America. The reluctance with which compensation was voted to

the sufferers from colonial riots was profoundly significant. The
plain truth seems to be that Ministers could not have carried anything but the compromise. In that case they would have done
better for themselves and the empire had they insisted on repeal
and renunciation, and made it clear to the King that unless they
had the confidence of the Crown, and the support of the King's
Friends, they would resign. Rockingham's and Conway's tolerance
of the King's dishonest tactics encouraged royal duplicity and confirmed the impression that they preferred office to their convictions.
The whole episode is instructive, because it reveals the crude desire
for coercion in the Opposition, the real sentiments of the King who
was already, though not recognised, the most formidable opponent
of the colonists, and the fatal division of opinion amongst the
Whigs themselves. The chaos of views amongst public men was
reflected in the temper of the nation, injured by the economic loss,
indignant at the defiance of law and order, puzzled by Pitt's exclusion from office, and anxious to patch up a quarrel on the rights
and wrongs of which it could not make up its mind.

The Rockingham Ministry slowly broke in pieces, sapped first
by Grafton's, then by Northington's resignations. Pitt, again
appealed to by the King, threw over Temple, and delighted the
public by agreeing to form an Administration. He came in with
high ambitions to justify the confidence of the nation in a stable
Ministry under the greatest of living statesmen. The colonial ghost
seemed to be laid; but Ireland, India, finance and foreign policy,
and the strained relations of Crown, Cabinet, and Parliament called
for firmness, insight, and continuity of policy. But his Administration was a failure. The allotment of posts justified Burke's
description,[1] Conway (Secretary of State), Saunders (Admiralty),
and Townshend (Chancellor of the Exchequer), were taken over
from the Rockingham Ministry; Grafton (First Lord of the Treasury), Camden (Lord Chancellor), and Shelburne (Secretary of State),
were "Pittites"; Northington (Lord President) adhered to the

---

[1] " He made an Administration so checkered and speckled; he put together a
piece of joinery so crossly indented and whimsically dovetailed; a cabinet so vari-
ously inlaid; such a piece of diversified mosaic; such a tesselated pavement without
cement; here a bit of black stone and there a bit of white; patriots and courtiers,
King's friends and republicans, Whigs and Tories, treacherous friends and open
enemies, that it was indeed a very curious show, but utterly unsafe to touch and
unsure to stand upon " (Speech on American taxation, April 1774).

16

King— when the King's interests coincided with his own. Temple
remained outside, with ample means and inclination for mischief.
Pitt himself damaged his reputation for independence by accepting
a peerage as Earl of Chatham ; and his removal to the Upper House
left a vacancy badly filled by Conway and Townshend, cursed by
an irresponsible thirst for popularity.   Even before he was finally
prostrated by gout, Pitt's dictatorial arrogance and reserve confirmed the verdict of all who sat with him in Council that a genius
could be his own worst enemy.   The assumption that he was the
King's Minister, called as in 1756 " to defend the closet against
every contending faction," ignored the fact that 1766 was not
1756, and that George III. was not George II.   Without the support of the collective co-operation of colleagues united by a common
creed a King's Minister must either become the King's tool or the
King's enemy, fighting alone a hopeless battle.   Chatham misinterpreted the King as fatally as he misinterpreted the working of the
parliamentary system.   It was not in his power to convert George
III. to his views.   But it was in his power to leaven the old and the
new Whiggism with his inspiring imperialism, his passion for freedom and reform, his contempt for the ignoble vulgarity of the
party huckster. Rockingham, Conway, Grafton, Shelburne, Burke,
Camden, craved a leader.   In Chatham, for all their despair at his
exasperating defects of temper and judgment, they recognised the
master.   And it was Chatham who failed them.

    The Prime Minister's high-handed dismissal of Lord Edgecumbe
from the Treasurership of the Household caused a breach with the
Rockingham group, the chief members of which, with the exception
of Conway, promptly resigned.   Their places were filled from the
Court party.   In order to deal with a scarcity of corn, due to bad
harvests, Ministers exceeded their legal powers by an Order in
Council prohibiting exportation.   Corn riots had broken out, and
it was necessary to quiet public fears.   Chatham's defence on the
ground of necessity expressed the bare truth ; but it was a peculiar
pleasure to the fine intellect of the Tory Mansfield to unwhig his
rival Camden for boasting that the prohibition was at most " a forty
days' tyranny ".

    In the sphere of foreign policy Chatham had hoped to in-
augurate a new system.   He viewed with profound anxiety the
dangerous isolation of Great Britain. The Family Compact of

1761 had closely united the Bourbon Courts; and, under Choiseul
at Paris and Grimaldi at Madrid, Spain and France were pursuing common ends—the humiliation of England and the recovery
of lost prestige and possessions.   The re-organisation of their
fleets, the removal of defects in administrative machinery revealed by the war, went on steadily.   The Austro-French alliance
of 1756 was another danger; and in 1765 the association in Government of the ambitious Joseph II. with his mother Maria Theresa,
opened a new epoch in the aims of the House of Habsburg-Lorraine.
Governed by his essentially Whig dread of Bourbon supremacy,
Chatham desired an anti-Bourbon system.   This could only be
found by a cordial understanding with Russia and Prussia, which,
by including Holland and the Scandinavian States, would control
the Baltic and the Levant as well as Central and Northern Europe.
To Frederick therefore Chatham turned; for the intimate relations
between Berlin and St. Petersburg would secure Russia, if Prussia
consented.   But Frederick still nourished his resentment at Bute's
" perfidy ".   Nor would he risk the interests of Prussia on the
uncertainty of a Chatham to-day and another Bute to-morrow.
Frederick's attention was focussed, moreover, on the East.   He did
not fear the Bourbon Powers, but he had a wholesome respect for
Catherine and Joseph II.   To secure the one and checkmate the
other was his ambition.   Poland was his Naboth's vineyard and it
was Catherine's also.   He therefore coldly declined to consider
the scheme of a comprehensive anti-Bourbon league.   Had Great
Britain retained the alliance of Prussia in 1763 it might have been
made the basis now of a system which would have prevented the
nullity of Great Britain in European affairs for the next twenty
years.   But the blunders of the past and the incompetence to come
made the Bourbon intervention, if a suitable opportunity arose,
both safe and certain.   Before Chatham could work out for Ireland
and India the plans in contemplation, he was prostrated by gout, Feb., 1767
which for two years clouded his intellect and practically removed
him from politics.   Grafton, now nominally chief, from indolence
and absorption in the turf, Euripides and Nancy Parsons, allowed
the Cabinet to degenerate into a debating syndicate, in which the
majority had their way and the minority shrugged their shoulders
and protested on paper for the benefit of posterity.   The one man
who knew his own mind and worked hard was George III.   The

ascendency he had established by 1770 was the honestly won triumph of a personality, narrow but sincere, and of a system coherent in principle and method over the parody of both.

After overtures to the Rockingham group had failed Grafton joined forces with the " Bloomsbury gang," the followers of Bedford, of all the groups the most opposed both to his own views and those of Chatham.   Gower became President of Council, Weymouth replaced Conway, (who remained in the Cabinet to the satisfaction of Horace Walpole alone,) and a third Secretaryship of State for the Colonies was created for Hillsborough.   This infusion was a fresh source of division, though it provided the King with zealous allies. Ministers now slipped or were pushed into a series of false steps and blunders.   Townshend's proposal to continue the land tax at four shillings had been defeated by a coalition of the Rockingham and Grenville groups, the first defeat of a Minister on a money bill since 1688 ; but, unabashed, the Chancellor kept his boast that he would raise a revenue in America to pay for the troops, and recklessly ripped open the half-healed wound of colonial taxation.   In addition to the rigorous enforcement of the trade regulations, duties were imposed on glass, paper, paints, and tea, and the receipts strictly appropriated to American purposes.   Having thus accomplished the easy task of translating the Declaratory Act into practice, and apparently impaling the colonists on the dilemma, either of resisting a customs duty or of paying money not imposed for the benefit of trade but for revenue, Townshend died.   Humorous to the last, he left to his successor the duty of seeing that the colonists found a satisfactory answer to the conundrum.   The colonial reply was what Ministers should have anticipated.   The new taxes were denounced as a plain violation of the spirit and practice of the trade regulations, already sufficiently galling, as a fresh encroachment on the rights of self-taxation, and a proof that the imperial Parliament intended to snatch a treacherous acquiescence in its contested legal powers.   Dickinson's " Farmer's Letters " voiced the colonial protests ; and Samuel Adams found growing support in his efforts to unite the colonies in combined action.   The Massachusetts Assembly took the lead.   It refused to withdraw a circular letter issued by Adams ; the law and the imperial Executive were openly defied.

The division in the Cabinet was fatal to the success of any

policy. The Bedford group, with the King behind them, were for
the maintenance of the taxes and coercion if necessary. Grafton
Camden, Granby, and Conway were for repeal. North (who had
succeeded Townshend) was for total repeal, but gave way to the
King, and consented to the compromise of the majority—the repeal,
save of the duty on tea. And so the Ministers retained both their
conflicting convictions and their offices. Bernard, the unpopular
Governor of Massachusetts, was replaced by Hutchinson, and half
the troops sent to overawe Boston were withdrawn. Bernard put
his finger on the blot in the Ministerial policy. Unless the imperial Executive was vigorously supported it was folly to threaten
coercion which came to nothing. Such weakness only made the
Government abettors in the defiance of the law. Either the
principles laid down in the Declaratory Act must be enforced or
the relations between colonies and mother country must be drastically revised. Had the King in 1768 dismissed Grafton, and deliberately maintained the right to tax at the point of the bayonet
against total repeal and renunciation of the right, the royal policy
might have succeeded; but coercion and conciliation were alike
damned by the vacillation of the next eight years. A regimen of
periodic purges blended with palliatives was not statesmanship but
political quackery.

By 1768 the Administration had become Grafton's in name.
Chatham resigned, and he was followed by Shelburne. Weymouth
and Rochford now became joint Secretaries of State. The general Oct.
election of this year, notable for the increase in corruption and the
increased support to the King's Friends, was still more notable for a
renewed collision with Wilkes. Having been defeated for the City
of London, he was triumphantly returned for Middlesex. His
reappearance in politics roused all the former enthusiasm and
violence; and when he surrendered to his outlawry a great mob
on May 10th, the day of the meeting of Parliament, demanded
his release from prison in order to attend the House. Weymouth,
with the King's consent, had prepared to use military force, and in
St. George's Fields the troops fired and killed several of the vast
crowd. Wilkes, whose outlawry was reversed on technical grounds,
had been condemned to twenty-two months' imprisonment; he
published Weymouth's letter to the magistrates, which he called a
"bloody scroll," and charged him with planning a "massacre".

Undeterred by previous experience, the Commons voted Wilkes's
remarks a seditious libel, and expelled him on the ground that his
former conduct rendered him unfit to serve. Twice Wilkes was re-
elected and twice the House quashed the election. The third time
a Ministerial candidate was found in Colonel Luttrell, (brother to
Mrs. Horton who married the Duke of Cumberland), but he only
received 296 votes to 1143 recorded for Wilkes. Nevertheless the
Commons with magnificent effrontery resolved that Luttrell "ought
to have been returned," and declared him the duly elected member
for Middlesex.

The gravity of this extraordinary decision far exceeded that
in the North Briton affair. The Commons had the right to expel
a member on grounds of unfitness, of which they must be the sole
judge. By law and custom they were the sole authority for deciding disputed elections. But both these privileges rested on the
assumption that they would be exercised in accordance with law,
and to vindicate the dignity of the House as a representative body,
and not to indulge the capricious spleen of a temporary majority.
By expelling Wilkes for acts for which he had already been
punished, the Commons were acting vindictively. And now, by
the resolution of a single chamber, they had created an incapacity
unknown to the statute book ; and they had deprived an undisputed
majority of the electors for Middlesex of a freehold right, secured
by the law, while they had awarded the seat to a candidate with
an undisputed minority of votes. This intolerable usurpation by
a single chamber of legislative power for party purposes, and the
cynical violation of legal rights was, as the protest of the peers
pointed out in an unanswerable indictment, an assertion of a dispensing power and the subversion of representative government unprecedented and indefensible in law or policy. In vain Grenville
and Burke in the Commons, Chatham, Rockingham, and the Opposition in the Lords, fought for sanity and legality against the wishes
of the King and his submissive majority. "Wilkes and liberty!"
was no longer the cry of a demagogue with a grievance. It became the watch-word of all who valued constitutional government,
and who saw what would follow if the King's victory was not challenged until it was reversed. The widening breach between the
nation and an irresponsible Crown, supported by an irresponsible
Parliament, threatened to develop into a situation from which a

coup d'état or a revolutionary reform would be the only way of escape. The acts and temper of the King and the Ministerial majority were a sinister comment on their attitude towards the general problem of government which was not lost on the American colonies. It was dawning on ardent minds on both sides of the Atlantic that the trusteeship of the heritage of self-government had fallen to the constitutional Opposition, who had a common interest in decisively defeating the policy that menaced the future even more than the present.

The ferment and violence engendered by the Middlesex election found their bitterest expression in the famous letters of the anonymous "Junius". Like the Man in the Iron Mask, Junius has become one of the unsolved riddles of history;[1] and the mystery of the author's identity, coupled with his peculiar and intimate knowledge, added spice and weight to his envenomed and polished invective. The lapses in taste and savage personalities of the letters add to, rather than detract from, their value as historical documents, for they reproduce the dust and dirt of the brief age of Grafton. In the heat without light of Junius's indictments still glow the ashes of dead and forgotten quarrels. But while Junius was nailing the men he hated to a perishing pillory, the issues between Crown and Opposition were stated in the *Thoughts on the Causes of the Present Discontent*; and Burke at once carried the controversy into those bracing and purifying uplands of literature and political philosophy which are a permanent school of states- 1770 men.

At the commencement of 1770 Camden, who had weakly bowed to the majority in the Cabinet, was encouraged by Chatham's fierce attack on the Ministry openly to declare against his colleagues, and was dismissed. The Great Seal was offered to Charles Yorke, son Jan. 17 of Lord Hardwicke, who accepted; and then, overcome by remorse and the reproaches of his friends, died, it was thought by his own hand. Grafton, filled with misgivings at his isolated position and Jan. 20 a policy opposed to his convictions, was driven to resign, and Con- Jan. 27 way and Granby retired with him. Lord North became First Lord of the Treasury, retaining also the Chancellorship of the Exchequer; the Great Seal was put in commission, Mansfield presiding over the Upper House; while a new Ministerial recruit was found in Thurlow,

[1] See Appendix VI.

whose robust and coarse intellect and high views on prerogative made him acceptable to the King.

The reconstruction of the Administration beneficially cleared the situation and opened a new phase. By 1770 the King's tactics of pegging away had been rewarded by a steady consolidation of Toryism, *i.e.* of the classes opposed in sentiment to change, disgusted at the violence of the left wing in the Opposition, at home and in America, and rallying to a strong Crown, controlling policy and the Executive. George's hold on influential sections of the public had grown as his grip on the machinery of administration tightened. The action of the majority in Parliament cannot be explained as simply the result of corruption, powerful and many-sided as that was. It would be unjust to represent the King as imposing a detested *régime* on an unwilling nation. The significant vote in 1769 of half a million of money, without inquiry, to pay the debts of the Civil List (mainly incurred in swelling the corrupt influence of the Crown) corroborates inferences derivable from many sources, as to the temper of large classes. The vote was a deplorable surrender of parliamentary control, vainly protested against by the Whig leaders. Yet Mansfield, Thurlow, Weymouth, Holland, North, Gower, Sandwich, Samuel Johnson represent points of view defensible in principle and endorsed at the time perhaps by a majority in the country. No little of the contradictions in the acts of such men as Shelburne, Grafton, Conway, even of Chatham himself, were due to an ill-concealed respect for the claims of the prerogative in the government of the empire.

Political creeds from 1763-1793 were floundering in a disintegrating flux. Until 1770 the Whig families fought against what they denounced, not always justifiably, as innovations in practice and custom. Toryism, growing under the leadership of the Crown, took the offensive and pinned the old Whigs to the defensive. The Grafton Ministry roughly marks the date when the Opposition was reluctantly driven to a counter-offensive. This involved an embarrassing alliance with the nascent radicalism, which was beginning to demand not a return to an impossible *status quo*, but far-reaching reforms, and a structural renovation of principles, law, and machinery, with corresponding conventions to secure these in practice. Parliament, the Press, the suffrage, Church and State, taxation, corruption, Ministerial responsibility and the connection of the Executive with the Legislature were fitted by degrees into the expanding programme. The adoption of a vigorous offensive along the whole line also involved the sloughing off of much that was characteristic of the old Whiggism; and, still more distasteful, a complete reconsideration by the great territorials as a class of their creed and attitude. The necessary synthesis of the old and the new was made more difficult by the series of crises in national policy and the break-up of the economic and industrial organisation of society. But for the thirteen years after 1770 the Crown and its supporters are being pinned down in turn to the defensive. George fought to maintain what he had won, the Opposition to wrest supremacy from him and substitute a different theory and a wholly different policy which would extirpate from law and custom "the system of George III.". The Toryism of 1770-83 came to be reactionary just because it was conservative. It was blind to the new needs; it refused to recognise that revolution would be the result of persistence in the principles of the King. Violence begot counter-violence; the leaders on both sides doubled and redoubled their opponents' declarations. Hence the monarchy by 1783 was on a lee shore with a revolutionary gale blowing; but it was Pitt, not George III., who weathered the storm with success more enduring than the opposition to the fierce hurricanes of the French Revolution epoch. Pitt in 1783 once again made Toryism a progressive creed.

The deepening distrust of the aims and methods of the Crown in powerful intellects and influential sections was the most disquieting feature of the situation in 1770. Nations, many of whose best minds and characters are driven to defy and defeat the convictions of a majority of their countrymen, are on the eve of disaster. By 1770 one great reputation had been established where so many had been marred. In 1766 Burke made his first speech in Parliament on the colonial problem. On American, Indian, domestic, and foreign questions his trenchant exposition was stamped with the wealth of ideas, grasp of principles, and passionate energy that characterised every utterance of his pen and tongue till his death. Unhappily, defects of manner, temper, taste, and judgment prevented his influence on Parliament and public opinion from equalling (until the French Revolution epoch) the quality of his work as a writer, speaker, and political thinker. But on the circle, fit though few, of his intimates his influence was profound and permanent. Garrick, Johnson, Goldsmith, Reynolds were as much in his debt as the Opposition leaders. Like Adam Smith, Burke was a master for the best minds of two generations. No one owed more to him than Charles James Fox, the third son of Lord Holland, who had entered Parliament as a minor in 1768. Until 1774 the young Fox revelled in " the wander years " of reactionary Whiggism. As yet he was simply a typical example of the gifted and dissipated young aristocrats to whom politics was a game that might be as exciting as gambling away a fortune or making love to fashionable *demi-mondaines*. It was the American question of the next thirteen years that brought Fox and the Whigs into open revolt, and unmistakably set the battle in array between the system of George III. and the system of the Opposition. The careers of Burke, the inspired apostle of the old, of Fox destined to be the champion of the new, Whigs, illustrate most aptly the forces and ideals that underlay the disintegration and renovation of the Whig party.

NOTE.—The six volumes of the Hon. Sir J. W. Fortescue's Correspondence of George III. are indispensable on the period from 1760-1783 and should be compared with the *Letters of Horace Walpole* (16 vols. Edited by Paget Toynbee).

CHAPTER II

THE DISRUPTION OF THE EMPIRE

§ 1. THE MINISTRY OF LORD NORTH : 1770-1778

THE King had now an Administration [1] in which the personal
ascendency of the Crown attained its zenith. Lord North,
its nominal head, was a man of high character, wit, and knowledge,
whose parliamentary gifts made him a popular and skilful leader of
the Lower House. His daughter said with truth that one of his
grooms " was the only man who could put papa in a passion " ; and if
charm and a sweet equability were the sum of statesmanship, North
possessed the quality in a remarkable degree. His loyalty to his
master was stronger than his industry, will, or convictions ; and
with misgivings only too accurately realised, he permitted his
judgment to be overruled by the indomitable pertinacity and fixed
ideas of the King, who coupled the appeal of friendship with the
principle that to fail " in my service " was " disloyal desertion ".
It is notable that the essential features of the Hanoverian
Cabinet system virtually vanished. North steadily repudiated the
title of Prime Minister. He was simply the chief responsible agent
of " the King's business " in Parliament. The other Ministers,
similarly, were executive instruments, selected by the Sovereign to
carry out that Sovereign's policy as the forms of law and custom
required. The departmental system was complete ; and such solid-

---

[1] The main Ministerial changes can be briefly summarised: Henry Bathurst
(Lord Apsley) was Lord Chancellor, 1771-78, and succeeded Gower as Lord President in 1779: Thurlow became Lord Chancellor in 1778 ; Grafton was Lord Privy
Seal 1771-75, but, by his own request, was not summoned to Cabinet meetings ;
Sandwich succeeded Hawke at the Admiralty in 1771. The Secretariat was frequently rearranged. Suffolk held the Southern Department, 1771-79 ; the Northern
was filled by Rochford until 1775, by Weymouth till 1779 ; the Colonial by Hillsborough till 1772, by Dartmouth till 1775, by Lord G. Germain (Sackville) until 1782.
Townshend was Master-General of the Ordnance from 1772.

arity as the Ministry enjoyed rested on the union imposed from above and accepted by the Cabinet. The real Prime Minister was George III., who would have gained nothing that he did not already possess by presiding at Cabinet meetings or defending Ministerial policy in the House of Lords. The policy, the party, and the management were under the royal control; the King was Commander-in-Chief and Chief of the Staff in one. The correspondence of George III. with Lord North, corroborated by many other sources, reveals the inner history of this instructive experiment. The King not merely mastered the work of the Executive departments, laid down and approved every step, but also investigated parliamentary proceedings with a lynx eye, and arranged the patronage down to the humblest and most trumpery details. Through Richard Rigby (Paymaster, 1768-84), who rivalled Lord Holland's achievements by leaving "nearly half a million of public money," George "managed" the solid phalanx of the King's Friends; through the Secret Service, Pension Fund, and the Civil List he bought votes and debauched the constituencies. He both resented and resisted every attempt (such as Grenville's statute in 1770 to transfer the decision in disputed elections from a party decision of the whole House to a Select Committee) to purify corrupt practices and to free Parliament from the grip of "influence," or the efforts to audit, inquire into, and control the expenditure of the Civil List. It is a sinister fact that, despite the debt extinguished in 1768, a further debt of £618,000 had to be paid off in 1777 out of public taxes, and in 1782 there was a further deficit of £296,000. Yet in 1777 the Civil List had been increased to £900,000, while the Speaker, Sir Fletcher Norton, was thanked by the House for expressing a hope that this liberal grant would be wisely spent—virtually a censure on the Crown. The General Election Bill of 1781 staggered even George III. The nation, indeed, was forbidden to question the prerogative of the Crown to demoralise the Legislature, and coerced into paying obediently for its own demoralisation.

It is also significant that the period from 1765 to 1784 was marked, more particularly in the society of the capital, by an increasing laxity of tone and conduct. Immorality, gambling, dissipation, and extravagance were never so rife nor so cynically condoned as in the days of Grafton, Wilkes, Sandwich, and the

American War.   It was the age of the apotheosis of the fashionable courtesan and of the dice-box.   Howe's winter quarters at
Philadelphia, which preceded Burgoyne's surrender at Saratoga,
reveal the same story as the pamphlets, memoirs, and the Press ;
and if the King himself was free from the vices of aristocratic
society, many of his agents and the effects of his system helped to
sap the principles of public and private life.   The cynical maxim
that you must call in bad men and utilise bad machinery to govern
bad men and defeat bad machinery only proved once again that the
vicious sophists who "take the world as they find it" leave both
the world and themselves worse than when they came into it.   The
King's system had in theory aimed at destroying faction and extirpating corruption.   Its failure in both respects was conspicuous.
Contemporary observers noted that party spirit, increasing since
1765, was at its height between 1770 and 1782, and that it poisoned
both the navy and the army.   The evidence makes it impossible to
exonerate the King from the chief share in fostering the bitterness
and extending the area of political animosities.   For the wholesome interplay of organised parties George III. strove to substitute
the unconditional submission of political leaders to his will and
policy.   He was prepared to treat all opposition with the vindictive
severity meted out to Wilkes.   The most painful and petty-
minded passages in the King's letters are those in which he condemns his critics and condones his allies.   And to describe Chatham,
to whom the King owed a glorious peace, and who strove to save
the continent that his genius had won for an imperial Crown, as
"a trumpet of sedition," was as graceless as it was gratuitous and
untrue.   Just because the King was the King, the baneful influence
of the royal closet on the narrow world of contemporary politics
was aggravated.   In the agony of a great conflict *pro aris et focis*,
as Chatham said, the Opposition leaders too often perhaps forgot
moderation of language.   But they can plead that, like Pym and
Eliot, they fought with the King of Israel and with him alone.

On the success or failure of his measures now turned the destinies of the Empire and the fate of the King's system.   That system,
indeed, was paved with the best intentions.   To George III. every
credit must be allowed for the sincerity of his convictions and his
wish to do nothing but what law and custom, as he interpreted them,
entitled.   He appreciated more justly than his Ministers the gravity

of the issues. And he fully recognised after 1770 that his ideals of government and empire were at stake. But from the outset two essential conditions of success were lacking. A George III. who was a Frederick the Great, or who could find and understand a Strafford, might have succeeded. But George was not Frederick, and in the Ministry of North there was no Minister fit to tie Strafford's shoe-latchet. Fortune, not the King or North, provided the man, Warren Hastings, who saved India. The second-rate intellect of the Sovereign was happily-unhappily mated with the second-rate intellect of his servants. And the King failed to grasp that his system perforce deprived him of the service of the best minds and characters at his disposal ; for the best minds and characters refused to surrender their intellectual independence to an inferior dictator. They either rebelled or were driven into opposition. Hence the vital difference between North and the younger Pitt lies in the refusal of the latter to serve on the conditions accepted with meek reluctance by the former. Indeed, had Pitt, which is inconceivable, consented to North's uneasy servitude, his period of office would have been as sterile and unfortunate as was North's. The King of a constitutional nation who deliberately ostracises the best minds from the service of the State demands an incalculable sacrifice which both Crown and nation will have to pay.

At home and abroad the King was rewarded at first with apparent success. The Opposition in vain endeavoured to rescind and condemn the proceedings in the Middlesex election. The violence of the City party, led by Beckford and Sawbridge and approved by Chatham, who had definitely declared himself for a parliamentary reform by drastic change, widened the breach between the Rockingham party and Chatham's smaller following. Chatham desired to force a dissolution on the King; but he was not supported by the Moderates, and the King was prepared to resist to the last. The presentation of an impertinently worded petition by the Livery of the City led to a severe rebuke from the Crown ; and further efforts of the same kind only heightened the contrast between the dignity of the King and the arrogant vehemence of the demagogues. The Rockinghams were right in their assumption that the victory of constitutional principles was not to be won by the tactics of the street nor by the abuse that stained

Junius's vulgar "Letter to the King". Apart from the success of Grenville's bill, transferring the decision in disputed elections to a Select Committee, the Opposition steadily lost ground in public opinion, while the King's firmness and North's parliamentary skill consolidated the Ministerial party.

On two other points issues of far-reaching importance were 1770 raised. In *Almon's case* Mansfield had laid it down that in libel suits the function of the jury was simply to decide on the fact of publication and not to pronounce on the character of the writing, which was a matter of law and belonged to the judge. Mansfield's ruling, though probably in accordance with the received doctrine of the courts, was contested by Camden and other high authorities. It conflicted with the growing demand for a free Press and extended liberty of public criticism, which desired to wrest from the Bench the claim to interpret the law of libel. But the Opposition quarrelled on the method of upsetting Mansfield's ruling, which in any case the dominant majorities in both Houses would have been strong enough to maintain, as they now did decisively. The second controversy illustrates the same principles. In spite of warnings from the Opposition, the Commons decided to enforce their standing 1771 order forbidding the publication of debates. The arrest of one of the printers, Miller, brought the House into conflict with the Lord Mayor Crosby and Aldermen Wilkes and Oliver, who released the printer and held the arresting messenger to bail. Wilkes was spoiling for another fight, but this time he was denied, for the Commons had tasted of his quality once too often. But Crosby and Oliver, who were members of Parliament, were committed to the Tower, where they were visited by the Opposition leaders; and on their release they were welcomed in the City as martyrs of a despotic tyranny. Their cause triumphed in fact if not in principle. For though the Commons retained the standing order, fear of further collision with public opinion induced them to allow the publication of debates to go unpunished. A notable step had thus been taken towards making Parliament more amenable to criticism and to public opinion as expressed through the medium of the Press. The King, as usual, had strongly supported the ministerial policy in both struggles; and the enactment of the Royal Marriage Bill 1772 was a welcome addition to his prerogative and the *patria potestas* of the Crown. By it, all descendants of George II. under twenty-five years of age (save princesses marrying into foreign houses) were required to have the consent of the Sovereign as a condition to a valid marriage.   Members of the royal family above that age, to whose marriage the Crown had refused its consent, were entitled to marry, provided that a year's notice was given to the Privy Council, and that Parliament in the interval did not by address protest against the proposed marriage.   The Bill was only carried after strenuous opposition, one of the champions of which was Charles Fox, who now repeated his father's opposition to Hard-wicke's Marriage Act.   It was the turning point in Fox's career; and it laid the basis of the personal and public enmity of the King to himself; for George was the last man to act on the maxim so finely illustrated by Fox himself—*amicitiæ sempiternæ, inimicitiæ placabiles*.   His final dismissal from office gave to the Opposition Feb., 1774 their greatest parliamentary orator and to the cause of Whiggism the most lovable and inspiring of eighteenth century leaders.

In foreign affairs two disputes had attracted considerable atten-tion.   In 1769 Grafton's Ministry had weakly first opposed and then acquiesced in the annexation of Corsica by France.   The Corsicans, relying on British sympathy and the sending of arms to aid them in their revolt against their masters, the Genoese, stood out.   But the Ministry refused to resist the French, and Corsica, sold by Genoa to France, was annexed.   Choiseul at Paris and Grimaldi at Madrid were determined to humble Great Britain a second time.   The Spaniards, to whom the French had trans-ferred the eastern of the Falkland Islands, laid claim to the western island, which had been occupied by England in 1765; and in the winter of 1769-70 forcibly took possession of it.   Both the claim and its assertion were wholly unjustifiable; but Grim-aldi, relying on the Family Compact, the reorganisation of the French and Spanish fleets, and the domestic divisions of British parties at home, thought he could extort our submission.   He was deceived.   North's Ministry prepared for war; and the dismissal of Choiseul by Louis XV. left the French Ministry no option but to disavow the action and to restore the island.   The King and North acted with creditable energy, and scored a success in a matter of little importance, save that the damaged prestige of the British Government was repaired.   In one respect the result was unfortunate.   It strengthened the assumption that the British

fleet was in a satisfactory state (which it was not), and that, in
the King's phrase, "a little spirit" would check the hostile intentions of the Bourbon Powers. Choiseul's fall had certainly
removed a dangerous foe ; but his place was shortly taken by
Vergennes, the ablest perhaps of French Foreign Ministers in the
century. The Bourbon Powers bided their time. The moral of
the war preparations as to the defects of our naval organisation
and the deficiency in the number and quality of our capital ships
and seamen was neglected.

The First Partition of Poland of 1772—a serious alteration in
the balance of power, and a grave violation of the public law of
Europe—exemplified the greed of the Eastern monarchies and the
cynical victory of combined piracy and force. Great Britain,
unable to remonstrate with any advantage, wisely on the whole
refrained from publishing her impotence to the world. The argument that an increase in the strength of the partitioning powers
tended to diminish the influence of the Bourbon coalition would
have had some weight had England been able to rely on the
political support of Prussia and Russia. But Frederick's indifference, which veiled positive hostility, was as complete as in 1765.
And the value of Catherine's smooth words and gratitude for
British help to her fleet in her war with the Turks was illustrated
later by the part she took in forming against us, at the height of
our difficulties, in the American War, the Armed Neutrality of the
North. The continued isolation of Great Britain was dangerous
and disquieting. But the grouping and policy of the European
States made it difficult for mediocre statesmen to remove it. And
the obvious moral that isolation necessitated an increased efficiency
in our military and naval resources was ignored by those responsible.
In the wider issues of imperial and foreign policy North and his
colleagues forgot the past, and were unwilling to learn from the
present. The true test of their statesmanship was found in the
rapid and critical development of the American question.

North had carried, equally against those who wished the reten- March 6,
tion or the repeal of all the taxes proposed by Townshend, resolu- 1770
tions that rescinded the recent duties, save that on tea, which was
retained on principle as a concrete illustration of the right laid down
in the Declaratory Act. The irritation in the colonies was steadily
increasing, and defiance of the law and the Executive were more

17

and more widespread. The cruel and lawless persecution of all suspected of being loyalists or "Tories" by the "Whigs" or Opposition,
now virtually Separatists, was a further proof of the impotence of
the imperial authorities. The so-called "Boston massacre," (afterwards so unjustifiably misrepresented by the anti-British party,)
in which three of a crowd were shot dead and five wounded by
the soldiers, who for months had been subjected to every provocation and insult, inflamed sentiment on both sides. But the
acquittal of officers and men after a studiously fair trial showed
that justice could still be obtained. The deliberate burning of the
June, 1773 *Gaspee*, employed in putting down smuggling, was an overt act of
rebellion which was made more serious by the complete failure of
the commission sent to procure the punishment of the offenders.
Dec. 16 It was followed by an organised attack in Boston Harbour on
the cargoes of the East India Company's ships, from which the tea
was defiantly pitched into the sea. The boycotting of other con-
signments at Charleston was insignificant compared with the bravado of the "Boston tea party". Ministers at home, unless they
were prepared to condone these and many other local triumphs
over the attempts to enforce the tax, and the contempt for imperial law and authority, had an unanswerable case for energetic
action. And, as so often, a personal incident once more illustrated
the truth of Aristotle's profound generalisation that the causes of
revolution are always great, but the occasions that bring them to
the birth may be trumpery. Franklin had privately obtained
letters of Hutchinson the Governor, and Oliver the Deputy-Gov-
ernor, the communication of which to Adams in Massachusetts
and their subsequent publication further exasperated public opinion
and led to a petition from the Assembly for the removal of their
authors. The petition was heard by a committee of the Privy
Council before which Franklin, as agent of the colony, appeared.
The methods by which he had obtained, and the use he had made
of, the letters is wholly indefensible. But Wedderburn's violent
attack on him and the indecency with which the tribunal showed
their approval of his coarse invective were positively criminal.
The proceedings of January 29th, 1774, turned the ablest colonial
representative, who hitherto had believed in the possibility of a
compromise and the maintenance of the imperial connection, into
an irreconcilable foe. Franklin kept the resolve made, while he

listened unmoved to Wedderburn and the laughter of the councillors. The plain brown suit that he wore that day was folded up and next worn when he put his signature to the treaty that ratified the independence of the thirteen colonies.

The Government now determined to crush the centre of disaffection by penal legislation. Four measures were proposed and carried. These were: (1) The closing of Boston Harbour and the transference of the government to Salem ; (2) the cancelling of the Massachusetts charter and the remodelling of its democratic machinery ; (3) the powers given to remove trials for capital offences in Massachusetts to Great Britain ; (4) provisions for the quartering of troops. At the same time Hutchinson was replaced in the governorship by General Gage, who was also made commander of the military forces. Neither North's nor Dartmouth's hearts were in this policy of legislative coercion. It expressed the views of the King, and the majority in the Cabinet and Parliament, and was a grave mistake in principle and method. Colonial disaffection was not to be disarmed or crushed by legislation which shattered the basis of self-government and confirmed the indictment of the Opposition leaders that Crown and Parliament, unless resisted, would enslave the colonies. It made Massachusetts the martyr of the common cause, and, so far from isolating her, cemented the cohesion of colonial resistance. It did not deal with the true lesson of the crisis—the hopeless weakness of the Executive. It did not admit nor try to solve any of the grievances festering under the discontent, irritation, and lawlessness. Had Ministers publicly asserted that they were prepared to consider those grievances sympathetically and find a remedy, but that law and order must first be restored ; and had they promptly despatched in the spring of 1774 a force adequate to show that they meant what they said, they would have had the support of moderate opinion on both sides of the Atlantic. But to deny the existence of grievances was blindness ; to enforce law by reviving obsolete statutes and imposing disfranchisement was to destroy all confidence in the justice of the law ; and to leave the Executive in Massachusetts and elsewhere still weak was to threaten a determined adversary with an unloaded revolver.

A welcome contrast to this parody of statecraft was afforded by the Quebec Act of the same year. Happily Ministers enjoyed the advice, experience, and intuition of a true soldier and statesman,

Sir Guy Carleton (Lord Dorchester), who had governed Canada from 1766 to 1770; and they had the sense to frame their measure on the lines he recommended as suitable to the peculiar features of the province. The Act extended the boundaries of Canada to the Mississippi and the Ohio; it guaranteed freedom of worship to the Roman Catholics, who constituted nine-tenths of the population, and secured the Roman Church tithe and dues from its members; government was vested in the Governor and a Legislative Council nominated by the Crown; the right of taxation was retained for the imperial Parliament; the English criminal law was introduced, but civil cases were to be decided according to the old French law. Chatham's opposition, particularly to the toleration of the Roman Catholics, was one of the most regrettable acts of his public life. And the King deserves great credit for overcoming his own ultra-montane Protestantism and supporting the Bill; but it is singular that he failed to see the justice of the demand for similar recognition by his Roman Catholic subjects in Ireland. The Act gave great offence in the American colonies, where its principles were attacked as a further proof of the menacing policy of the home Government. But it was fully justified by its results. If it did not at once make the Canadians loyal and prosperous, it brought from the British Government the gifts of justice and religious freedom, and in the great struggle now at hand the Canadians remained true to their new foster-mother country. As an instrument in the evolution of the Canadian nation and institutions, the Quebec Act was not the least of the great services rendered to the Empire by Carleton.

Sept. 5   The Continental Congress, at which delegates from twelve colonies (*i.e.* all save Georgia) met at Philadelphia, was the real answer to Ministerial policy. The discussion clearly illustrated the division of opinion—Tory, Whig, and Moderate—but as in the French Revolution an energetic minority, skilfully led and with strong convictions, were able to force their decisions through. The Congress condemned the penal legislation, approved resistance by force and counter-coercion by a rigid boycott of exports and imports—in a word, declared for no surrender on the colonial, and complete surrender on the imperial, side. The predominance of the Separatists, under the leadership of Samuel and John Adams, was as significant as the growing consciousness of the colonists that they

could, if need be, work out their own salvation without the help of
the imperial connection and Executive.   These two plain facts
were serious arguments against the well-meant conciliation proposals of Chatham, North, and Burke.   Chatham's Bill might have Feb. 1,
succeeded if its author had been called to power with *carte blanche* 1775
to use his draft scheme as the basis of a great treaty of reconciliation.   North's "olive branch" resolutions were damned by the
source whence they sprang—the Government that had just declared
Massachusetts to be in rebellion, and was despatching reinforcements
to Boston.   An olive wreath clumsily twined round the handle of
a sword was as distasteful to the colonists as to the King's Friends.
Not even Burke's majestic eloquence could convince the reasonable March 22
that in 1775 a return to the *status quo* of 1763 was possible.   The
general election of 1774 had increased the Ministerial majority.
Public opinion, ignorant of the true elements of the situation, and
incensed, not without reason, at the defiance in word and deed of
law, was convinced that coercion was necessary and would be easy
—an opinion, encouraged and shared by more than one Minister—
which made surrender impossible.   Gage at Boston, faced by strenuous military preparations in the northern colonies, was pleading for
more troops.   The man on the spot recognised that he must be
ready to meet, not disorder or insurrection, but civil war and revolution.   And at Lexington, on April 19th, the first blood in an open
encounter was shed.   The troops sent to prevent military stores
at Concord falling into the hands of the colonists accomplished
their task under fire and had to fight their way back to Boston,
which they only reached after losing some two hundred and fifty,
killed, wounded, and missing.   The colonial casualties were probably
under a hundred.   Alike the fact, the character, and the results
of this encounter were a military and political lesson of the first
order.

The true indictment of the measures so far pursued rests on
their failure to achieve two essentials of statesmanship which are
also essentials of the higher command in war.   These are recognition of facts as they are, not as they may be distorted in an imaginary picture, and a definite conception of the situation that a
given policy will mould out of those facts.   From the first, to avert
civil war was the plainest of plain duties, incumbent not on the
colonists but the home Government.   Civil war at once wrecked

the existing imperial organisation. It made the creation of a new structure out of the ruins of the old not impossible but excessively difficult. In 1770 there seem to have been three possible policies. A frank avowal that the problem was insoluble, followed by a free concession of virtual independence. This was courageously advocated by Dean Tucker in 1776. It must be dismissed as impracticable, because its supporters on either side of the Atlantic would not have filled a hackney coach. Secondly, the policy of the clean slate—unconditional redress of all colonial grievances, fiscal, commercial, administrative, and legislative. But two different sets of facts obstructed its successful realisation. The Opposition and the colonists were not agreed either as to the amount to be cleared off the slate or what was to be written on it, when once the legislative sponge had made it clean; while the Ministerialists supported by public opinion were convinced that the cleaning of the slate robbed what could be written on it of all value. Thirdly, the uncompromising assertion of defied imperial authority to be followed by a generous and sympathetic reconstruction of the imperial fabric. The insolent and corrosive lawlessness of the colonists, we may agree, in their own interests as well as those of Great Britain, called for the wholesome lesson that anarchy and outrage are not, and never can be, the nursery of true self-government. Unhappily by unconditional submission George III. and his advisers meant unconditional acceptance of the obsolete theory and cramping practices of the Declaratory and Navigation Acts, which were the deep-seated cause of colonial alienation. Nor was unconditional surrender in 1775 a return to 1765; it was the triumph of a policy, principles, and mental temper which would have been as fatal to the colonial future as the unconditional acceptance of the Ministerial action in the Middlesex election would have been to self-government in Great Britain. Military subjugation created a new problem; it did not solve the old one. The Washingtons and the Chathams, not the Adamses and the Tom Paines, proved that everything could be done in America with bayonets properly used, except to sit upon them. Military subjugation as an end in itself, not as a preliminary to a policy of reconstruction shattered the empire from top to bottom more disastrously than any grant or extortion of independence could do. The supposition that three millions of British subjects, who shared in our blood and constitutional heritage, could be permanently compelled to accept just so much freedom as the imperial Government was disposed to grant was sheer insanity; and the advocates of such a policy were traitors to the future of their race. Hence the tragedy of the colonial civil war lay in a cruel dilemma. The morrow of victory could not be trusted to the victors, for in the King's system were the seeds of stagnation, atrophy, and death. Military failure involved the disintegration of the empire, and the destruction of a great ideal in a struggle whose bitter passions could never be wholly quenched.

The skirmish at Lexington had shifted the colonial question from the council chamber of the statesmen to the field of the soldiers. Ministers had now to face three problems: first, purely military, —how could colonial resistance be most effectively and speedily crushed? Second, a problem in foreign policy, linked, as policy must be, with war—how could the civil conflict in America be isolated and kept isolated? Third, what was to follow success or failure in war? War always is a remorseless test of national machinery and character, and civil war is the most severe form of the test. However we may apportion the blame, it is clear that under the strain the King's system and the Ministry of North hopelessly failed. The difficulties of the task were considerable, and they were aggravated by bad luck, too often a smooth synonym for missed or misused opportunities. Ireland, under eloquent, able, and determined leaders, exploited the impotence of the British Executive to challenge with irresistible force the accumulated misgovernment of the Whig *régime*; in India a formidable combination of native powers united to destroy British authority and expel the English from the peninsula; at home the nominal Prime Minister doubted the wisdom of his policy and his own capacity to carry it out; the Cabinet was not united, and it was faced by an obstinate and capable Opposition representing influential classes of the population. The purely military problem presented a theatre of war 3000 miles away, in a vast area of differing physical and climatic features, imperfectly known at headquarters. Concerted operations were handicapped by long delays in communications, and the serious obstacles to transport and supplies.

Yet the King and North started with enormous advantages. Rockingham probably expressed the truth when he asserted that the Government was supported by a majority "of all ranks, professions, and occupations". If in Ireland the governmental policy was favoured only by a small minority, the overwhelming Ministerial predominance in Parliament represented at the outset the views of England and Scotland. The Opposition in 1775 could only reckon on a handful of peers, a minority in the mercantile classes, and the Dissenters; whereas the aristocracy, the Church (and the bulk of the Methodists, including Wesley), the landed gentry, the universities and the professions cordially sided with the policy of coercion. The loyalists in America, if badly organised, were numerous; Canada resisted all invitations to rebel. In wealth, therefore, numbers, prestige and organisation, the superiority of the British Government in 1775 was unquestionable. The colonists had neither an army nor a fleet; the Ministry had both. The military difficulties were not as great as those overcome by Chatham, nor was Great Britain as yet coping with a great military European Power. She had the initiative in the offensive and the unimpeded selection, through her fleet, of the line and objective of attack. For practically three years she had an absolutely free hand, and a strategic area already defined, in which a superiority of force could be concentrated at will. It was in her power to make the military struggle, in Swift's phrase, one between six armed footpads and an unarmed man in his shirt. Had the Ministry known their business the colonists could have been beaten to their knees before Europe intervened.

The alteration of the whole character of the struggle by the intervention of France in 1778 was due to the blunder piled on blunder for which from 1770 onwards the Government was responsible. In the face of ascertainable facts as to the increase and improved organisation of the French and Spanish navies, the number of our ships and seamen had been let down; and the lax and corrupt Administration of Sandwich at the Admiralty rotted our dockyards and demoralised the spirit of our men. In equipment, numbers, organisation, the fleet was inadequate even for the task of 1775. The army was still more deficient in every respect. The establishment was dangerously low for piping times of peace, and the machinery to cope with the inevitable wastage of war did not exist even on paper. After 1775 it was easier to vote the money and the numbers required than to find the men. But Lexington

was not a bolt from the blue. For five years the Ministry had
steadily provoked a civil war; and they now relied on carrying it
on with the imperfect machinery, corroded by the jobbery and
favouritism that flourished under the fattening sunshine of the
King's system. Once again, and not for the last time, Great
Britain learned that for able brains to improvise organisation in the
stress of war means grave peril, but that for the incompetent it
spells disaster.

Nor was it enough to have an imperious King, a submissive
Cabinet, and a crushing and docile majority in Parliament.
Ministers neither commanded success nor studied to deserve it.
With the weakness of mediocrity they overrated their own capacity
and resources, as foolishly as they underrated those of the enemy.
The fatal divorce of policy from war was revealed with damning
clearness in the sphere of our foreign relations, where the optimistic
blindness of those responsible would be incredible were it not
established by facts. In 1775 the hostility of the Bourbon Powers,
and the isolation of Great Britain, were beyond denial. The intervention of France was anticipated by Chatham in 1774; but despite repeated warnings, based on explicit information from the
Opposition, no serious effort was made to avert it by diplomacy or
to frustrate it by adequate preparation in advance. Truly the
immortal gods must have cared much for English liberty, and little
for the British Empire, when they thus drove mad those whom they
willed to destroy.

Vicious strategy, faulty and fumbling tactics, a bad choice of
commanders, vacillation as to methods and objective, reliance on
German mercenaries, were the inevitable results of this rooted incapacity to understand the plain moral of the situation. The
higher direction so superbly wielded by Chatham in the Seven
Years', so far as it existed, was syndicated between the King, North,
an amiable, lazy, and half-hearted parliamentary manager, Germain — the Lord George Sackville of Minden—who had been declared by a court-martial unfit to serve the Crown in any military
capacity, and Sandwich, a lax libertine called on to do the duty of
an Anson, a Spencer, or a St. Vincent, and who the King in 1780
admitted " was no use in his department ".

Yet Horace Walpole's phrase, " the name of the Opposition is
anarchy," was already true in 1775. The leaders, Rockingham,

Richmond, Grafton, Chatham, Shelburne, in the Lords ; Conway, Burke, Dunning, and Charles Fox, in the Commons, were agreed in attacking the Ministry, in thwarting their measures, and in emphasising with invective every failure and minimising every success. Their sympathies were wholly with the colonial resistance to a policy they held to be subversive of every valuable constitutional principle ; the victory of the King they regarded as fatal to the cause they championed at home. So strongly did many of the Whigs abhor the course on which their country was embarked that Grafton cut himself adrift from the Government, and many, including Chatham's son, refused to serve in the war. Such acts, and the language used, inevitably made the Opposition very unpopular. To the average sensual man, " My country, right or wrong," is almost an axiom of political conduct. It was difficult for such to understand, impossible to agree with, those who regretted the successes of " our " troops, and applauded the victories of the colonists. Yet it is hardly reasonable to argue that as soon as blood was shed it was the duty of the Opposition leaders to suppress their convictions, and refrain from exposing the nature and consequences of blunders for which Crown and Cabinet were responsible. Men forgot then and since that the war down to 1778 was not between the Empire and a foreign foe. It was as much a civil war as the contest in 1643 between Royalist and Parliamentarian—between two opposed systems and ideals of political life. And to Chatham, Burke, and Fox the struggle in the field was the same struggle that was being fought out on the floor at St. Stephen's. It was the duty of the Opposition in 1775, as it was Chatham's in 1755, to leave no stone unturned that would sweep out of power the men, and destroy before it was too late the system of government and measures, intrinsically pernicious, that infallibly were driving Great Britain to Niagara. The defect of the Opposition was not the violence of their language, (the young Pitt when he entered Parliament in 1781 assailed the Ministry in phrases as fierce as those of Fox,) nor their admirable courage in "instructing the Throne in the language of truth," but their failure to unite and to realise that after 1775 the colonists were no longer agitators with an unanswerable case, but men in arms who would secure independence unless they were first beaten decisively in the field. The successful impeachment of North and his colleagues might have been very wholesome for Great Britain, but it would not have solved the American problem. Every interest required that after Lexington coercion by force should be as sharp and short as possible. It was in 1775 the affair of the generals and the admirals, and the quicker they did their work the better. The turn of the statesman would come when Great Britain was in a position to discuss terms that the Americans recognised they must accept. And it was for the Opposition then to be ready with a thought-out plan, and to see that the settlement was generous and in accordance with the principles of self-government. But the Congress of Philadelphia had already made it plain that until imperial authority had been vindicated or unless independence was made the basis of negotiation, to parley or haggle or hold your hand was waste of time, as well as a serious military and political mistake. When Fox and Burke denied that the colonists were aiming at separation they were beating the air ; when Grafton and Richmond urged conciliation in vague terms they were academic theorists ; Chatham's assertion that Great Britain could not conquer America was irreconcilable with his assertion that he would never grant independence. One section of the Opposition clung to Chatham's view that the imperial Parliament could bind trade but not impose direct taxation ; another section was ready to yield everything, even independence, rather than that coercion should be successful. An Opposition that could not place an arguable alternative, as comprehensible as the Ministerial policy, before the public, was condemned to a sterile unpopularity and the melancholy satisfaction of seeing its worst forebodings realised. Already in 1775 Horace Walpole predicted with truth the result of the war.

The events of the first three years of the war point to a serious misconception of the character of the resistance, the inadequacy of the resources employed, and the incompetence of the generals in the higher qualities of command. The map shows that, with the undisputed control of the sea, a force operating from the loyalist stronghold of New York, on the lines of the Hudson, and a force co-operating from Montreal *via* Lakes Champlain and George, reinforced by a brisk offensive from the coast (Boston), would have gripped the centre of disaffection, the New England colonies, in a vice and broken the back of opposition, thus enabling the enveloping forces to shift on to the line of the Delaware and

complete the reduction of New York and New Jersey. A decisive blow at the commencement would have exercised an immense
moral effect; and the effective separation of the New England
colonies from Pennsylvania, Virginia, Maryland, and the South
might have brought matters to the stage when constructive statesmanship could have ended the quarrel. Rapidity of action, concert
of fleet and army, and adequate numbers were the essentials; and
the imperial forces failed conspicuously in all three. While
Generals Howe, Clinton, and Burgoyne were on their way to
support Gage, the Americans had grasped the importance of the
line of the Hudson, and under Benedict Arnold and Ethan Allen
surprised Ticonderoga and Crown Point. The Continental Con-
May 10   gress met at Philadelphia in the name of " The United Colonies,"
rejected North's conciliatory proposals, and appointed the hero of
the struggle for independence to chief command. The character
and ability of George Washington were worth two army corps to
his cause. Tired as we may be of hearing Aristides called the
just, the more closely George Washington's career is studied the
more convincingly does it compel homage. No success could spoil
his sound judgment, no adversity shake his indomitable will. His
firm belief in, and noble devotion to, the justice of resistance were
an inspiration to himself and thousands of his countrymen. He
was not a great soldier. In pure intellect he was inferior to
Alexander Hamilton, in statesmanship to Abraham Lincoln; but
when the balance is struck he stands in the history of the United
States with these two alone as one of the three master-builders to
whom the American Republic owes most. In the readiness of
such a man to sacrifice everything to save the land of his birth
from degradation lies the severest condemnation of the policy of
George III.

Gage committed his first blunder when he flung the forces which
he had allowed to be penned in at Boston in a frontal attack on
June 16   Bunker's Hill. The heights were won after a desperate struggle,
with a loss of 40 per cent. of the men employed; but the colonists, whose losses were a half of the British, had given Gage a lesson
in tactics and proved that they were neither cowards nor a rabble
of rebels. Farther north the defenceless state of Canada was a
grave danger. Montgomery, who had been charged with its invasion, secured Chamblée and St. John's; and on the surrender of

Montreal Carleton was called on to defend Quebec against the bold adventurer, Arnold, who, reinforced from Cambridge, had marched by the Kennebec and Chaudière Rivers to Point Levi. But the united forces of Montgomery and Arnold failed to carry Quebec by a desperate assault in the darkness of a snowy night, and the Dec. 31 former was killed. Next spring, when the Canadians had rejected every invitation to join the colonial rebellion, Carleton, slightly reinforced, routed and drove the invaders back on Crown Point. June, 1776 Canada, indeed, was saved by his skill and energy.

Gage was wisely recalled in the autumn, but his successor at Boston, Howe, was no less slack. The winter was passed in doing nothing (except that Falmouth was burnt, a stroke of futile vindictiveness). Howe calmly permitted Washington to occupy Dorchester Heights, which commanded the town, and was thus March 17 compelled to evacuate Boston, both a moral and a military success 1776 for the Americans. The King, at his wits' end for men, remembered Hanover and took 2000 Hanoverians into pay, to set free the garrisons at Gibraltar and Minorca, while arrangements were made to hire at an exorbitant price nearly 20,000 German mercenaries from three princely brokers in human flesh—the rulers of Brunswick, Hesse Cassel, and Waldeck. This desperate transaction justly exasperated Chatham and the colonists. The purchase and employment of foreigners in a civil war was a damning revelation of the King's principles, and of the straits to which the machinery of imperial defence had been brought. The Opposition contested unsuccessfully the legality of the recourse to Hanoverians and the embodiment of the militia. The diminution of the Irish army, already below its statutory establishment of 12,000, by 4000 drafted for war service, was another proof of the dearth of men ; and in this case reduced the Irish Executive to impotence, and left the island defenceless. Twenty-eight thousand men were voted for the navy, 55,000 for the army, and the deficit on the budget was covered by a loan. In the teeth of fierce criticism North carried a bill prohibiting Nov. 20 intercourse with the Americans, but empowering the Crown, through Commissioners, to restore to the privileges of peace any district prepared to submit. Admiral Lord Howe, "Black Dick," and his brother the general were appointed Commissioners under the Act. Their mission was a complete failure. To Howe's overtures the reply was a curt refusal to negotiate on any terms but independence.

And on July 4th the Congress at Philadelphia issued the famous Declaration of Independence, by which the thirteen colonies publicly renounced their allegiance and proclaimed the birth of a new and free political community—the United States. As a statement of grievances the Declaration contained nothing new ; its crude rhetoric gave heightened colour to the doctrine of natural rights on which its political theory was based. To the military situation it added simply the element of precise certainty. But, like the cannonade of Valmy in 1792, it heralded the opening of a new age and a new world. And it placed the colonies in a position to invite the recognition and support of foreign Powers.

The military folly of desultory tapping and pecking at the coast continued. A diversion to rally the loyalists of the South ended in a rout ; and the fleet and reinforcements on their way to Howe at Halifax turned aside for a stroke at Charleston, which ended in a useless bombardment by the ships and withdrawal. Howe, July 3 having seized Staten Island, drove the enemy with considerable July 26-27 loss from Long Island and occupied New York, an excellent base, Sept. 14 which ought to have been seized a year earlier. Washington's troops were broken and dispirited, and only the incomprehensible refusal of the British generals to push their success home saved him from a disastrous reverse. As it was, Washington was driven behind the Delaware, Clinton overran New Jersey, and Howe was in a position to secure Philadelphia, from which Congress had already fled to Baltimore. Instead he held his hand, went into winter quarters, and spread out his forces on an extended line. Washington saw his chance, pulled his disheartened men together, Dec. 25 pounced on Trenton, cutting the garrison to pieces, routed two regiments at Princeton, and cleared West Jersey. Howe was now confined to New York and Rhode Island, where he remained idle until next June. The intended co-operation from Canada had broken down. Carleton only succeeded in destroying Arnold's flotilla on Lake Champlain and securing Crown Point. When the command for the next campaign was transferred to Burgoyne, Carleton promptly resigned his governorship.

An elaborate plan had been framed for isolating the New England colonies. Burgoyne, from Canada, was to march down the lake line to the Upper Hudson and effect a junction with Howe, who would then be able to turn with overwhelming force on

the enemy west of the Delaware.   The success of the plan turned
on Burgoyne's capacity to make his march to time, and on Howe's
ability to contain the enemy first and prevent them from interfer-
ing with Burgoyne, and then make the arranged junction.   Howe's
misconception of the situation, and lack of precise instructions from
Germain ruined the scheme.[1]   Howe seems to have been bent
on capturing Philadelphia.   After a demonstration on land he
shipped his force to the mouth of the Delaware and thence to
Chesapeake Bay.   At Brandy-Wine Creek, he defeated Washington, Sept. 11
and Congress again fled from Philadelphia, which Howe then oc- Sept. 27
cupied.   Washington attacked a second time at Germanstown, and Oct. 4
was decisively beaten ; whereupon he led his shattered forces into
winter quarters at Valley Forge, where the disorganised colonial
army must have gone to pieces but for the unconquerable determination of their commander.   Washington's plight was a poor
compensation for the disaster that ended Burgoyne's operations.
Starting in June he secured Ticonderoga, Fort Anne, and Fort
Edward, whence at every step he found the enemy gathering in
superior numbers.   Burgoyne struggled on, deserted by his Indians,
yet hoping to get into touch, as ordered, with the main army
under Howe, which was now comfortably quartered at Philadelphia.
So far from containing the Americans, Howe had been contained
by them.   Clinton at New York did what he could by way of
diversion ; but Howe had withdrawn 4000 of his men, and at
last Burgoyne, completely surrounded, surrendered at Saratoga to Oct. 17
General Gates.   Burgoyne himself was allowed to return to England ; but the convention by which the troops were to be re-
embarked, under promise not to serve again, was shamefully
broken by Congress.   It seems clear that the disaster, the moral
and political results of which were far-reaching, need never have
happened had Howe not wasted the spring in idleness, and then
pursued a plan of his own which made co-operation with the
Northern force impossible.   Howe's resignation relieved the army Oct. 22
of a commander whose heart had never been in the business, and
whose misinterpretation of his duties had wrought irreparable
mischief.

At home, the Opposition in 1776, discouraged by their failure,

---

[1] For confirmation of this see *Eng. Hist. Rev.*, April, 1910, p. 315, and Fitzmaurice's *Shelburne*, i., 358, and see Appendix XV.

had seceded for a time from Parliament—an act which only increased their unpopularity. In the spring of 1777, Chatham, after
two years of illness, reappeared, and in vain pressed for "uncon-
May 30 ditional redress" of the colonial grievances. He warned Ministers
against the danger of French intervention, and appealed for national resistance to the Bourbon menace. Fox, fresh from Paris,
had already emphasised the fact that Silas Deane sent over before,
and Adams and Franklin after, the Declaration of Independence,
were negotiating with Vergennes. The American envoys, received
with enthusiasm in the French *salons*, had so far received little real
help, save for a few volunteers, such as the young Lafayette, some
stores, doles of cash, and harbourage for privateers who preyed successfully on British trade. But Vergennes now saw that Saratoga was the
opportunity for which Bourbon diplomacy had long waited. While
Chatham was again pleading with all his eloquence for the withdrawal of our troops from America, in order that we might grant
everything but independence, and concentrate on the inevitable
struggle with France; while Ministers deluded Parliament and
themselves with the official and friendly disclaimers of the French
Dec., 1777 Government, the preliminaries of an offensive alliance were already
concluded; and the definitive treaty rapidly followed. It provided
Feb., 1778 that, in the event of war between France and England, no peace
was to be made without the consent of the contracting parties, nor
until the independence of the United States was guaranteed. It
March 13 was shortly notified to Great Britain; and though Spain held aloof
for twelve months, the open hostility of the Bourbon Powers, predicted by the Opposition as a certain consequence of the "King's
War," was now an accomplished fact. If we could not conquer
the Americans alone, what prospect was there of subduing them
when supported by the armies, fleets, and resources of France?
"The game," to apply Washington's description of his position
two years earlier, "was pretty well played out."

§ 2. THE STRUGGLE FOR EMPIRE, 1778–1782.

With the spring of 1778 Great Britain entered upon a struggle
for empire for which she was singularly ill-equipped, and which left
her humiliated, disillusioned, and exhausted. The intervention of
France altered the whole character of the war. The Government

was no longer able to focus its military resources on the American theatre of operations. Home defence, imperial garrisons, the West and East Indies at once called for reinforcement and protection. A depleted establishment, no systematic reserves, and greater needs summed up the position. Hence in America, where Saratoga had virtually lost the northern colonies, the struggle tended to shift from the middle, and to be centred on the southern, States. The wide distribution and vulnerability of the possessions of the Crown thus imposed on the higher direction a complex strategical problem. The hostility of European States such as Prussia, and of potential belligerents such as Spain and the Dutch, were an additional embarrassing factor. Four important elements in this problem made themselves felt before long. France, not, as in the Seven Years' War, hampered by a continental war, was able to concentrate on the sea and the struggle across the seas. Spain joined in after twelve months, and not, as in 1761, at the end of a fight already decided. The resources of the American colonists, greater than those of Canada, more united, and inspired by a nascent nationalism, were flung into the scale against us. Ireland was ripe for a revolt against the " old colonial system ". The protection of a wide-flung seaborne trade, on the safety of which the taxable capacity of the nation largely depended, cut across the purely military task of assuming the offensive. The fundamental condition of success, therefore, lay in naval power and the command of the sea. Washington's often-quoted remark that the navy " would have a casting vote " in the contest applied with truth, not merely to the local theatre of the fight for independence, but to the wide-world battle for empire. The sea was the lines of communication for every imperial possession. To be robbed of the command meant certain defeat in America, the imperilling of our hold on Canada and all our other dependencies, and the severing or mutilation of the great vascular system of commerce from the heart of the empire.

Great Britain was geographically placed on the internal strategic lines. But already her financial resources were pledged to the hilt. Heavy taxation at home, the loss of American trade, the plundering of privateers made borrowing necessary but costly. Loans of six millions in 1778, seven in 1779, twelve in 1780, tell their tale. The American War added in all £114,000,000 to the National Debt. The jobbery, corruption, and inefficiency of the

18

Administration in finance became a serious and demoralising scandal. If for no other reason, economic sanity, political purity, and financial stability required the system of "patriotic kingship" to be swept away. The navy, too, was inadequate for the doubled strain that war with France at once entailed. Even on paper it was defective in numbers and *personnel*. France had eighty ships of the line and 60,000 seamen ; behind her stood Spain with sixty ships. Great Britain professed to have 119, but Sandwich's Administration with difficulty got only about one-half of these to sea. That three admirals—Howe, Keppel, and Parker—in turn resigned their commands in disgust is the most telling comment on the condition to which our first and only line of defence had been reduced. Criticism, as the Opposition discovered, was useless. The King's mercenaries voted obediently as their royal chief demanded. These glaring defects were aggravated by the continued incompetence of the central direction, whose measures showed the results of a vicious strategy executed with inferior forces.   Three capital mistakes were committed.   Despite the lessons of the Seven Years' War the French (D'Estaing, April 15th, 1778 ; D'Orvilliers, June 3rd, 1779; De Grasse, March, 1781) were permitted to leave their harbours unopposed for the West. The key of the naval position was primarily in Europe; and, as Howe pointed out, "the fate of the West Indies, perhaps the whole fortune of the war might (ought to ?) have been decided in the Bay of Biscay" Secondly, the distribution of the forces at our disposal was not arranged so as to concentrate for the offensive in a strategic area selected for its importance and to secure in it a clear superiority. Ministers with defective resources aimed at equality at every point, and thereby imperilled every operation. The failure to provide a decisive superiority at the vital point was responsible for the disaster at Yorktown. Thirdly, the co-operation of the military and naval arms was loose. Too late the truth was grasped that "no land force could act decisively unless accompanied by a maritime superiority ". In the dry-rot at headquarters lay the seat of the mischief. A Chatham would have obtained the best from a Howe, a Rodney, and a Hood. But the admirals were expected by a Sandwich to achieve what he had made impossible.

The renewal of the duel with France brought out a new spirit in the nation. Public sentiment, disillusioned by the purely

American War, responded to the challenge from the ancient and irreconcilable foe. The best Whig opinion, dominated by its ingrained fear of Bourbon supremacy, recognised that with France it was not a battle of constitutional principles, but a struggle for empire. Chatham, Rockingham, and Fox agreed in the duty of taking up the challenge and fighting with France to a finish. But the Whig leaders were fatally divided as to the methods. Chatham desired to grant everything to the colonists but independence. The Rockinghams urged that we should sever the alliance of France and the colonists by a grant of independence, and then concentrate with free hands on the Bourbon Powers. The arguments for this policy were also felt in the Cabinet. The colonial armies were crippled; their organisation was disheartened by impending bankruptcy, and weakened by factious intrigue. Judged by the results, it would have been wiser to have limited at once the American operations to a purely naval war, sealed up the colonial coasts, and strained every nerve to inflict as rapidly as possible a damaging defeat on the French navy. The moral effect on Spain and the material effect on America of French reverses at the outset would have been considerable.

Be that as it may, public opinion correctly felt that a strong Ministry was needed, and looked to Chatham to provide it. North himself desired to resign. Chatham made it clear that he would only accept office with a new Cabinet and a new system. But the King was inexorable. He was fighting now for his own system; to stoop to the Opposition he would never consent. If Chatham would adopt the royal policy, he would with reluctance allow him office. And so North, backed by the Ministerial phalanx, with a weary heart agreed to go on. One last futile concession he wrung, to the dismay of his majority, from his implacable master. Bills were carried offering everything short of independence, and the commissioners were appointed to treat with Congress on these terms. When they arrived in June the answer was—nothing but independence. It was Chatham's policy—conciliate in order to crush France—and Chatham alone could have made it succeed. Had the man whose prestige was greater than that of the Crown been given *carte blanche* twelve months earlier and come into power with a new system implying the obliteration of the blunders of the past, he might have wrought the miracle. And the terror of his genius might have paralysed France. But Congress did not trust George III., and Vergennes with good reason did not fear North. Before the commissioners set foot in America, Chatham was dead. He appeared for the last time in the House of Lords to answer April 7 the Duke of Richmond's motion for recognising American independence; but before he could complete a faltering reply he was carried a dying man from the House. On his death he was voted May 11 a public funeral in Westminster Abbey; his debts were paid and a pension attached to his earldom. Four peers to their shame protested against these expressions of public pride and remorse; and it would be well if the passage in the King's letter to North on the same subject could be erased from the annals of our Monarch,. The monument at the northern end of the Valhalla of our mighty dead does more than record a nation's gratitude for an inspiring life and an empire saved by "the great Commoner"; it enshrines the imperishable ideal and secret of Chatham's imperialism—free institutions and self-government by a free and self-governing people.

Nothing now but success could save the King and the King's system. The negotiations with Chatham had confirmed the Opposition in their conviction that a complete change of men and measures could alone break the influence of the Crown by which a divided Ministry was kept in office. Burke's teaching was bearing fruit. It was essential to defeat the King, and by a new system, explicitly made the basis of a new Ministry, to prevent the recurrence of the old. The next four years saw two important changes. The Opposition leaders gradually united. Chatham's death and the course of events brought Shelburne, Camden, and Grafton into line with Rockingham, Fox, Richmond, and Lord John Cavendish. But the union owed more to the cement of disaster than to fundamental convictions as to future policy. Concurrently, the popularity of the Ministry steadily waned. The resignation of Gower, who passed to the Opposition in 1779, was significant. But the power of the Crown, and the indomitable will of the King, were convincingly illustrated in the maintenance of the struggle for four years against military failure, maladministration, and a "Prime Minister" pleading to be relieved of a task he had disliked from the first.

The full effects of the French Alliance were not felt immediately. During 1778 Clinton, who had succeeded Howe, withdrew from Philadelphia to New York. D'Estaing had arrived with a fleet;

but a joint Franco-American attack on Rhode Island failed, mainly owing to Admiral Howe's skilful seamanship; and D'Estaing disgusted his allies by leaving for the West Indies. An expedition sent by Clinton to Georgia successfully established its hold in the South; and with reinforcements, drawn also from Clinton's army, Barrington captured St. Lucia, and compelled D'Estaing to fall back on Dec. 29 Martinique. In home waters Keppel fought an indecisive action with D'Orvilliers off Ushant, and laid the blame on Sir Hugh Palliser, one of the Lords of the Admiralty, and his third in command. The quarrel became a party affair with the sympathy of the crowd entirely on Keppel's side. Both officers were acquitted by court-martial; but Palliser's acquittal led to his house being attacked, and Keppel followed Howe's example in refusing to serve under the existing Ministry. The Government had also to face the fierce exculpatory criticisms of Generals Howe and Burgoyne, who had joined the Opposition in the Commons. The extent to which party passion had invaded all classes may be seen in the King's personal efforts to prevent Keppel in 1780 being re-elected for Windsor, while the little Duke of Gloucester was whipped and sent supperless to bed for wearing Keppel's colours.

Next year brought Spain into the struggle (Franco-Spanish Alliance, April 12; Declaration of War, June 16), which increased the difficulty of maintaining the command of the sea. The Spaniards at once invested Gibraltar. For three years Sir George Eliott, whose dogged determination and rugged soldierly face live for ever in Reynolds's superb masterpiece in the National Gallery, defended the fortress, and deservedly won his peerage as Lord Heathfield of Gibraltar. A combined French and Spanish armada evaded Hardy's fleet, and for thirty days held the mastery of the Channel. Fortunately, neither at home nor elsewhere, did the hostile squadrons push their offensive. D'Estaing in the West Indies contented himself with the capture of St. Vincent and Grenada, and then returned to the American coast, where British ships were effectively distressing the American seaports and shipping. The British grip on Georgia was not relaxed; and it was clear that the war on land had developed into a fight for the southern colonies, in which the command of the sea would be all-important.

The critical year, 1780, opened well. Rodney, on his way to the chief command in the West Indies, defeated a Spanish fleet off

April 16

May 12

Aug. 16

Cape St. Vincent and successfully got his convoys into Gibraltar and Minorca, the former of which was hard pressed. Off Dominica only the failure of his subordinates to understand his signals prevented him from winning a crushing victory over De Guichen. As it was, the engagement was indecisive, and Rodney in the autumn joined the base at New York with half his fleet. Clinton had struck a sharp blow in the South by taking the bulk of his forces to South Carolina, where the siege of Charleston ended with the surrender of its general, Lincoln, and some 5000 prisoners, while Cornwallis reduced the colony. Against these successes the allies could only place the skilfully-planned capture of the East and West India merchant fleets off the Azores, which were triumphantly carried into Cadiz. The loss to our commerce was estimated at over £2,000,000. Round New York a stalemate had been reached. Rochambeau had arrived from France with 6000 men and seven ships of the line. The American forces occupied Rhode Island, and contained a British force in New York, but a temporary naval superiority enabled our fleet to blockade the French squadron in Newport, the failure to destroy which was a grave blunder on Rodney's part, and contributed to the disaster of next year.

Gates, the victor of Saratoga, had been sent to the South; but Cornwallis and Rawdon routed him near Camden, and the energy of Colonel Tarleton, the inventor of mounted infantry of the modern type, dispersed a subsidiary colonial force. Cornwallis now pushed into North Carolina; but the defeat and death at King's Mountain of one of his subordinates, Ferguson, who had raised a large force of loyalists, prevented him from executing his plan of joining hands with a division of Clinton's at Chesapeake Bay. The defeat of Gates, the rival of Washington, and the treachery and desertion of Arnold [1] greatly depressed the Americans, who were in sore straits

---

[1] Arnold's treachery unhappily involved an episode which, however, had no effect on the course of the war. Major Andrè, Clinton's adjutant-general, a young and brave officer, carried on the negotiations with Arnold, who was ready to betray the important post of West Point to the British. Andrè, unfortunately, was persuaded in the course of a prolonged interview to enter in ignorance the American lines; and on his return, dressed as a civilian, was arrested with papers from Arnold on his person arranging for the betrayal of the post. Despite Clinton's efforts to save him after he had been condemned by court-martial, Washington refused the young soldier's request to be shot and insisted on his being hanged as a spy. The contrast between

for money by the end of the year, and very dissatisfied also with their French allies. But the impolitic severity of Cornwallis and Rawdon in the Carolinas to the "rebels" weakened their military hold, and the guerilla character of the war rendered the British grip only effective where it was exerted in force.

The autumn of the year added yet another European enemy—the Dutch—to our foes. This disagreeable rupture was brought about by a series of causes, kindred in origin and character. The continuous supply of stores and contraband to our enemies, the armed opposition to our claimed right of search, help to harassing privateers, the discovery in a captured American vessel of a proposal for an alliance between the United Netherlands and the United States, and the reluctance of the Dutch Government to disavow and discontinue their hostile proceedings, enabled the Ministry to force the Republic into war. "The bullying and oppressive conduct" of North's Administration, as Harris (afterwards Lord Malmesbury), called it,[1] dissolved the connection between Holland and Great Britain, roused intense exasperation in the Dutch, and was responsible for difficulties that harassed British policy as late as 1801. The "Armed Neutrality of the North," which had come into existence in the spring, was another proof of the hostility of March, Europe. Induced by Russia, the signatories (Denmark, Sweden, 1780 Prussia, and the Emperor) asserted that they would maintain for neutrals certain principles,[2] largely accepted since, but which at the time menaced our desperate efforts to maintain the control of the seas. Combined with the critical condition of the situation in India and Ireland, Great Britain entered on the year 1781 with the maritime power of Europe openly or covertly arrayed against her.

Cornwallis was pushing his campaign in the South. Though Tarleton was defeated at Cowpens, Cornwallis won a Pyrrhic victory Jan. 17

the fate of the unsuccessful traitor Arnold, who made a timely escape and was rewarded with the rank of brigadier-general in the British Army, and that of André heightened the natural but unjust indignation of British opinion at Washington's conduct. But the verdict of the court-martial was based on proved facts; and Washington's decision, stern but necessary, was in accord with the recognised laws of civilised warfare.

[1] See Addenda, *Dropmore Papers*, vol. iii., and Introd. to vol. vi., pp. xix-xx.

[2] These were that the flag covered the trade, *i.e.* that neutral ships made neutral cargoes; that neutrals had a right to sail unmolested from and to the ports of belligerents; that nothing was contraband of war except as specified by treaty; that a blockade to be respected must be effective.

March 15 over Greene, who had replaced Gates, at Guildford Courthouse, and now marched north, made a junction with Arnold in Virginia, and overran that colony. Rawdon was left to face Greene, and

April 25 gained a dubious success at Hobkirk's Hill; but his forces in the autumn (Rawdon having gone home), after another drawn engage-

Sept. 8 ment at Eutaw Springs, were driven back on Charleston. Clinton, who disapproved of Cornwallis's northward march, feared a joint Franco-American attack on New York, and directed Cornwallis to retire on Yorktown, where he would have access to the sea. Washington and Rochambeau having deceived Clinton by a feint at New York, joined Lafayette in Virginia, and the united forces

Sept. 4 blocked Cornwallis on land. At this point we lost the command of the sea. Rodney had opened the campaign in the West Indies

Feb. 3 by capturing the enormously rich Dutch island of St. Eustatius. Defective combinations and inferiority of numbers at home allowed De Grasse to leave Brest with a powerful fleet, and the French admiral picked up more ships at Martinique, took Tobago, and then

Aug. sailed for American waters. Rodney returned to England; and Hood followed the French to America, where he missed his junction with Graves at Cape Henry and joined him at Sandy Hook. De

Sept. 5 Grasse, in superior force, met the combined fleet, and after an inde- cisive action [1] compelled it to fall back on New York to refit. With the seven blockaded ships at Newport which Rodney had failed to destroy the previous year, the French fleet was raised to thirty-six, a marked superiority to the British numbers, and it now blockaded Yorktown from the sea. The French navy had given the casting vote. Cornwallis, after gallant efforts to extricate himself, was compelled to capitulate with all the honours of war. Clinton,

Oct. 19 naval reinforcements having arrived, set out too late to relieve him, and was obliged to return to New York.

The decisive disaster at Yorktown did not complete the failures

Oct. 25 of the year. St. Eustatius was retaken; and at home, though Gibraltar was again relieved and Eliott held out against a furi- ous bombardment, a combined Franco-Spanish fleet reasserted its mastery in the Channel, the English fleet, inferior in numbers, not venturing to bring it to the issue of a battle. A combined

Feb., 1882 expedition invested Minorca, which surrendered; and Parker, after

Aug. 5 fighting a bull-dog engagement with the Dutch off the Dogger

[1] See Appendix VII.

Bank, resigned, in disgust at the Admiralty's action in sending him
to sea with insufficient and ill-equipped ships.   A French raid on
Jersey, however, was successfully repelled by the gallantry of Major
Pierson.

Since 1778 the Opposition, by votes of censure and demands for
inquiry into the misconduct of the war and the financial mismanagement, had pressed their attacks.   North was more anxious than
ever to resign ; but two, if not three, negotiations to reconstruct the
Ministry broke down.   The King, dissatisfied with the divisions and
incompetence of his departmental agents, was ready to draft Shelburne and others into the Cabinet, but they were to come in on the
King's terms.   Largely owing to Grafton, the two wings of the
Opposition held together and demanded the displacement *en bloc*
of the existing Administration, and the formation of a new one on
a new basis with a different policy.   But to the defeat of his system
and the victory of the hated Whigs the King refused to consent.
The Opposition, now united in a common determination to diminish 1779
the power of the Crown, carried the contest from the walls of a
Parliament where they were steadily outvoted into the country.
Parliamentary reform, economic reform, the independence of the
House of Commons became their watchwords ; agitation by public
meetings and the strenuous public discussion of the evils throttling
the represented and debauching the representative were their
methods.

The crisis of the war marks an epoch in the history of parlia- 1780
mentary government by this open reference to public opinion ; and
from that year the movement for parliamentary reform assumed a
new character.   The great Yorkshire Petition, presented by Sir G.
Savile, demanded the extirpation of the extravagant emoluments
and corrupt sinecures which increased the demoralising influence of
the Crown.   Twenty-three counties, the centre of the forty-shilling
freehold vote, and many large towns sent similar petitions.   Associations were formed to drive the programme home.   Burke in Feb. 11,
Parliament advocated economic reform in a speech of eloquence, 1780
wit, and solid argument, which constituted an unanswerable indictment.   Fox fired the electors of the great constituency of Westminster by a demand for annual Parliaments and one hundred new
county members ; Richmond pleaded in the Lords for manhood
suffrage and equal electoral districts : Dunning startled the House

of Commons by carrying his motion that "the influence of the Crown has increased, is increasing, and ought to be diminished". But more than eloquence and logic were required. Burke's bill was destroyed in committee ; and the adoption of Dunning's motion was little better than an academic pleasantry to the King's Friends. Another side of English feeling and life was displayed in the Gordon Riots. Savile's bill, relieving Roman Catholics, produced under the leadership of Lord George Gordon,[1] a crack-brained and fanatical Protestant, a disgraceful carnival of anarchy aggravated by

Jan. 4-8 religious intolerance. For four days London was in the hands of the mob; chapels, shops, breweries and distilleries were sacked, and prisons opened, while fires raged. The firmness of the King, who, with the courage that never forsook him, took the responsibility of ordering the military to act, at last crushed the rioters. These four days furnish an instructive comment on the savage forces of disorder that seethed below the surface of the eighteenth century metropolis, and on the absence of an efficient police system for the protection of life and property. The general election, in which corruption played its usual part, had little effect on the relative strength of parties. Burke paid for his courage in advocating Irish toleration and free trade by the loss of his seat at Bristol, but two important new recruits were added to the Opposition—Sheridan, who was to equal as an orator his established reputation as a dramatist, and who joined Fox's group, and William Pitt, Chatham's second son, and now in his twenty-second year. Pitt attached himself to Shelburne, and made his mark at once by his finished power of speaking and his vehement invectives against the war.

The disastrous year, 1781, turned public opinion steadily against the Government. Yorktown convinced North that the "continental war" in America could not go on, though the King was anxious to fight with the Americans and the Opposition to the last. The fall of Minorca and the loss of St. Kitts and Nevis

Feb., 1782 (despite Hood's brilliant manœuvres to save the island), pulled down the Ministerial majority. Jamaica was threatened, but was

April 12 saved by Rodney's masterly victory off Les Saintes, in which the manœuvre of breaking the line was successfully carried out.[2] De

---

[1] Lord George subsequently became a Jew; was imprisoned for libels on Marie Antoinette (1788) and died, mad, in Newgate in 1793.

[2] See Appendix VII.

Grasse lost eight ships and might have lost a dozen more if Rodney, as Hood wished, had followed up his attack. The news of this signal triumph of seamanship restored the tarnished prestige of our arms, but came too late to benefit the tottering Administration. Germain withdrew from the Cabinet to enter the Upper House as Viscount Sackville, and on March 20 North resigned.

The King was in the greatest distress, "my heart truly tore in pieces". Surrender to the Whigs was a bitter personal humiliation. It meant the reversal of his policy and system of government, and the acceptance of Ministers whose principles of public action he abominated. But there was no way of escape. Shelburne and Gower in turn declined to form a new Administration. Rockingham therefore for the second time became Prime Minister, in a Cabinet composed from the two chief groups of the united Opposition. Keppel (the Admiralty), Lord John Cavendish (Chancellor of the Exchequer), Richmond (Master of the Ordnance), Fox (Foreign Secretary), represented the Rockinghams ; Shelburne (Home Secretary), Camden (President of the Council), Conway (Commander-in-Chief), Dunning, now Lord Ashburton (Chancellor of the Duchy of Lancaster), and Grafton (Privy Seal), were drawn from the other wing. Thurlow, as Lord Chancellor, represented the King. Burke became Paymaster-General, and Pitt surprised friends and foes alike by refusing to accept anything but a Cabinet post. It is noticeable that the third secretaryship was dropped, while the duties of the historic Secretariat were rearranged on a more logical basis—foreign affairs falling to Fox, home, Irish, and colonial to Shelburne. This redistribution of functions, from which the modern Home and Foreign Secretaries of State are derived, was not effected by statute. It was quietly carried out by instructions from Fox, as Secretary of State, conveying the pleasure of the Crown to its representatives abroad—a method which illustrates the origin and character of the Secretariat as the responsible organ for conveying the will of the Crown in accordance with the law and custom of the constitution.

The Whigs had gained the upper hand through the blunders of their opponents, rather than by their political statesmanship. They had now to prove their capacity to deal with the difficult legacy bequeathed by North's Ministry. They had wrung from the King a reluctant consent, but they had neither the confidence nor the goodwill of the Crown.   And George III. was waiting his chance to profit by every false step, every division in their ranks. The sixteen years since Rockingham's first Administration had supplied the King with the knowledge and the skill of a first-rate political tactician ; they had stiffened his obstinacy, narrowed his narrow point of view, deepened his self-confidence, and sharpened his passion for intrigue To George III. ends always justified means, and never more so than in the next two years.   From March 20th, 1782, when North so basely "deserted" him, to March 25th, 1784, he wrestled with Apollyon.   From the first the struggle was with Fox.   Fox was everything that the King detested—a Whig by birth, the son of a bad (but very useful) man, a leader who could have no principles because he had ratted from prerogative to "licence," the friend and ally of the profligate heir to the throne, and proved it by being a libertine and a gambler himself,—facts which strangely galled the master who had accepted Grafton, Rigby, and Sandwich.   But had Fox remained in political grace, it is more than probable that little would have been heard from the King of his gaming and dissipation.   For it was not with the aristocratic gambler that the King fought from 1775 to 1806, but with the principles of the "unprincipled" leader.   No one understood better than the King, except Fox himself, the nature and consequences of the political creed that Fox desired to enforce ; and between Fox and George III. there could be no compromise, because from 1782 onwards neither desired to give, nor ask for, quarter.

In addition to the making of peace, Irish and Indian affairs had developed through a series of crises into a condition that demanded immediate attention.   Until 1767 the most notable feature in Ireland had been the organisation in Munster and Leinster of the secret society of the "Whiteboys," which led to a number of outrages, mainly agrarian in origin, and intimately connected with the enclosure of commons and the payment of tithe.   But with the appointment of Lord Townshend as Viceroy in 1767 the Ministry inaugurated a policy similar in aim to that pursued in England, viz. to break the political monopoly of the Whigs, "The Undertakers ".   The result was to throw the powerful "Undertakers" into the arms of the constitutional Opposition under Henry Flood, and to precipitate a collision between the Govern-

1762

ment and the Reformers.   Townshend succeeded in securing the
augmentation of the Irish military establishment from 12,000 to
15,000, while the Octennial Act limited the duration of Parliament
to eight years.   But the Viceroy's protest against the rejection of 1769
a money bill, prepared by the British Privy Council, as a breach
of the constitutional practice, brought the question of taxation by
the representative Legislature to the forefront.   Only by increased
corruption did the Viceroy manage to maintain a Governmental
majority; and Townshend's recall in 1772 was hailed with joy, for
he had made himself as unpopular personally as he was politically.
Harcourt, the next Viceroy, continued and extended the system of
his predecessor.   The Civil List and the Pension List were doubled
—eloquent testimony to the Parliamentary straits of the Executive.
And the growth of debt and annual deficits led to a proposal for a
tax of 10 per cent. on the rents of absentee landlords.   The fierce
opposition that this caused in England, particularly amongst the
Whigs, induced North to have the bill rejected.   In 1775 Flood
joined the Government; but his place as leader of the Opposition
was taken by Henry Grattan, who was brought in for the pocket
borough of Charlemont, and whose superb oratory and political
judgment made him the ablest and most formidable leader of Irish
opinion in the eighteenth century.

From 1775 Grattan and the patriotic Earl of Charlemont
engineered the Reform movement.   Grattan's ascendency synchron-
ised with the outbreak of the American War.   The colonial demand for self-taxation appealed to the Irish Reformers, striving to
obtain the financial independence of their own Legislature.   And
Chatham in 1767 had condemned the claim of the Imperial Parliament to tax British subjects in Ireland with no less emphasis
than he condemned the Stamp Act.   The colonial struggle had
the sympathy of a majority of Irishmen, and the effects of the war
wrought commercial ruin in Ireland.   For the colonial market was
the chief depot of Irish exports, while the withdrawal of Irish
garrisons, the depredations of French and American privateers, and
the absence of a militia, exposed an impoverished country to invasion without the means to resist.   By 1778 the economic distress
was severe, and the Exchequer virtually bankrupt.   The demand
for economic freedom and legislative independence was in any case
bound to become serious, but England's needs were Ireland's oppor-

tunity. Under Grattan's and Charlemont's leadership the Reformers concentrated on "a free trade" as the only method for saving Ireland from ruin; and the formation of the United Volunteers, caused by the intervention of France in the war, provided an instrument for coercing the British Executive. The country was perfectly loyal, but it was captured by the Reformers, who taught the English Ministry the consequences of "that thing called a nation" which had grown up on Irish soil. "England," as Hussey Burgh said, "had sown her laws in dragon's teeth, and they had sprung up in armed men." In 1780 the first great breach in the system of 1688 was made—by freedom of trade. The export of wool, woollens, glass, and glass manufactures, and participation in the colonial trade on the basis of equality in customs and taxes were granted. At the same time Dissenters were relieved from the sacramental test, and a third moderate Catholic Relief Bill was passed. The Volunteers, Grattan said, were the "charter of the Irish nation"; and the next step was to secure free trade by extorting legislative independence. The Volunteer movement grew amazingly. In 1782 they numbered 80,000 men; and a helpless Government saw with increasing dismay this force turned into a great political instrument. Flood, "after seven years of eclipse," rejoined the Reformers, and Grattan summed up Irish grievances in a pregnant sentence— a foreign Legislature, a foreign judicature, a legislative Privy Council, a perpetual army. The Viceroy informed his colleagues that the independence of the Legislature had become the creed of the kingdom. A month before North resigned the great Volunteer convention at Dungannon endorsed the demands of Charlemont, Grattan, and Flood for the repeal of Poynings' Law and 6 George I., c. 5, a limitation of the Mutiny Bill, and a further relaxation of the religious penal code. The Irish leaders were in a position to back their ultimatum by arms; and they meant to do so if necessary. The Rockingham Ministry on its advent to power had, therefore, to face the prospect of another America in Ireland.

Feb. 15, 1782

In India, after the withdrawal of Clive's strong hand, maladministration and political blunders brought about a collapse. The deposition of Mir Jafar by the Council, and the substitution of Mir Kasim as Nawab of Bengal, were followed by an open quarrel caused by the unrestrained depredations of the Company's servants. Mir Kasim was in turn deposed and Mir Jafar replaced; and the war

with the Emperor and the Nawab Wazir of Oudh, who supported
Mir Kasim, was signalised by Munro's great victory at Buxar, which
shattered the combination and completed the results of Plassey. Oct. 23,
But the continued financial and administrative mismanagement of 1764
the Council led to Clive's return in 1765, with plenary powers as
Commander-in-Chief and Governor of Bengal. Clive remained for
eighteen months, and with the aid of a select committee instituted
a series of valuable reforms. Oudh was restored to the Nawab
Wazir; the Nawab of Bengal was relieved of the burden of maintaining a native military force; the Emperor ceded the Diwani for
Bengal, Behar, and Orissa, *i.e.* the right to collect and administer
the revenue, which made the Company in form as well as in fact
the governors of the districts ceded. A mutiny in the army
was crushed, and both in the civil and military branches factious
opponents were removed. Private and illicit trade by the Company's servants was suppressed ; presents were forbidden and salaries
raised, in order to diminish the incentives to corruption. When Clive
returned to England he had rendered to India and Great Britain
services of great eminence, but the inherent difficulties of the problem remained.

India required not one but a series of Clives. The irreconcilable contradiction between the objects and organisation of the
Company as a commercial concern requiring large profits and
dividends on its capital, and its superadded and growing functions
as a Government entrusted with political administration, became
more pronounced, and could not be solved merely by tinkering
and patching the existing machinery. Directors and proprietors
of stock alike naturally expected the Company's agents to make
government pay, a view that was fostered by the general delusion
as to the inexhaustible wealth of India, and ignorance of the difficulties and conditions under which the Company as a sovereign
power was compelled to work. Clive's success and the defeat of
the French had, in short, created a complex problem in imperial
policy, administration and organisation, which called for as drastic
a reconstruction of machinery and as new an attitude of mind
as the American question. It was thoroughly characteristic of
English methods that the problem was not squarely faced and was
dealt with piecemeal, as one crisis after another thrust this or that
aspect into prominence.

Chatham certainly in 1767 contemplated treating the anomalous position of the Company on broad lines of imperial policy, but before he could think out or formulate his proposals he was struck down by gout.   All that was done was to reguarantee the charter, prohibit a dividend of more than 10 per cent., and exact from the Company, plunged in debt, a subsidy of £499,999 a year.   A famine in Bengal, the menace of Hyder Ali in the Carnatic, and increasing debt, led to North's Regulating Act of 1773, which enforced the right of Parliament to interfere, and was a step in the right direction, in that it partially reconstructed the administrative structure.   Under it the Governor of Bengal was transformed into the Governor-General with a Council of four, deciding by a majority.   A court of supreme jurisdiction, under a Chief Justice, was also set up, while other regulations dealt with the limitation of dividends, the control of the Crown over civil and military policy, the auditing of accounts and the prevention of financial and administrative abuses.   The blots in the Act were the right of a bare majority in the Council to override the Governor-General, the vagueness of the relations between the supreme judicial and the supreme administrative powers, and the lack of precision in defining the respective spheres of the Crown, the Directors at home, and the Governor-General in India.   The Company remained a huge commercial concern with a trading monopoly, to which vast political powers were entrusted.   The Governor-General, responsible for the political security of the territories held for the Crown, and for an adequate dividend to the proprietors of stock, would be certain to be judged at the India House by commercial, and in Parliament by conflicting political, tests.   The Act had been preceded by a parliamentary inquiry, in which Clive appeared as a witness.   " By God, Mr. Chairman," he had exclaimed, when he detailed the temptations that pressed on him, " at this moment I stand astonished at my own moderation "; and though Parliament voted that he had " rendered great and meritorious services to this country," the criticisms of the disinterested and the attacks of the interested preyed on his mind, and he committed suicide.

Fortunately for Great Britain she had already produced a successor of the like quality.   Warren Hastings, Governor of Bengal in 1772 and Governor-General in 1773, ranks with Clive, Wellesley, and Dalhousie in the first division of the first class of

1770

Nov. 22, 1774

rulers whose name is imperishably bound up with the consolidation
of British ascendency in India ; and Hastings was the greatest of
the four.   Like every master-builder, he recognised that the statesman who never makes mistakes never makes anything.   " My whole
time and all my thoughts, I may add, all my passions," he asserted
truly, "are devoted to the service of the Company."   He would do
—the words ring with the spirit of Danton—" what he knew to be
requisite to the public safety, though he should doom his life to
legal forfeiture or his name to infamy ".   And the severest critic of
his government must admit that in a position of unlimited power
for evil and self-enrichment he worked in honourable poverty, misunderstood, traduced, handcuffed by ignorance and jealousy, never
for himself but always for England and India.   The fifteen years of 1772-85
his rule coincided with the titanic battle for empire fought
no less plainly in the East than in the West.   It is the bare truth
that Hastings' iron will and insight saved British dominion in India ;
and the star of his genius in the years of the French, American, and
Mahratta wars, black with mediocrity and blunders, shines out with
a triumphant and lonely splendour.

Two grave dangers menaced the British settlements—the extensive Mahratta confederacy in Central and Northern India, and the
adventurer Haidar Ali of Mysore who was building up an empire
in the South.   The Company was in sore financial straits, and
apart from the difficulties in his Council, Hastings had to deal with
incompetent and vacillating governments at Madras and Bombay.
To save Allahabad from the Mahrattas, Hastings transferred it to
the Wazir of Oudh and lent a British brigade to crush the Rohillas,[1]
who were driven out with unnecessary harshness, for which the
Governor-General was not responsible.   The Wazir's cruelties were
much exaggerated, but Hastings, judged by modern standards, was
to blame for not securing adequate control over the soldiers thus
lent.   But both in this and other instances he acted on a principle
well understood in India, that a paramount Power must protect its
political dependents, and is entitled to contributions from them.
In the West the Bombay Council, on the death of the Peishwa, who
was the head of the Mahratta confederacy, made the Treaty of
Surat with " Ragoba," one of the claimants to his throne, by which
he ceded Salsette and Bassein for a cash payment ; but Hastings' 1775

---

[1] Afghan military settlers recently established in the region north of Oudh.

19

Council quashed the treaty and drew up another with a rival claimant. War with the Mahrattas followed, marked by military failures, and at this point France stepped in; French officers ap-
1778 peared at Poona, and were inspiring Haidar and the Nizam, who had been alienated by the incompetence of the Bombay authorities. A great alliance of the Mahrattas, the Deccan, and Haidar Ali, was coming together, whose object was to expel the British from India. The French fleet was expected, and Great Britain was not able to spare money, men, or the necessary ships. British rule had to be saved by the resources and brains on the spot, and British prestige had been lowered in the South and the West. "Acts," said Hastings, "which proclaim confidence and a determined spirit in the hour of adversity, are the surest means of retrieving it." He sent Goddard to aid the weak Bombay government. Ahmeda-bad was captured and Sindhia defeated. Popham captured the fortress of Gwalior. The Nizam and the Gaekwar were detached from the alliance. In the South Haidar, fully prepared, burst on the Carnatic and the unprepared Madras authorities, defeated their forces at Pollilur, took Arcot, and threatened Madras. Hastings suspended the Governor, and despatched the veteran Sir Eyre Coote,
July, 1781 who by a series of victories at Porto Novo, Pollilur, Solingarh,
Jan., 1782 and Vellore added to his reputation and restored the damaged credit of our arms. Pondicherry and Mahè had already in 1778 been seized, and the Dutch stations at Trincomalee and Negapatam captured; when in 1781 a superior French fleet under the Bailli de Suffren appeared, and fought five indecisive actions with the British commander Hughes. Cuddalore fell, and Trincomalee was recaptured. Suffren's skill had given the French the command
1782 of the sea. Peace was then made with the Mahrattas, which enabled our efforts to be concentrated on Haidar in the Carnatic. Tippu,
Dec., 1782 Haidar's son, succeeded to his father; and when the Treaty of Ver-sailles withdrew France from the war, he made peace with the
March 11, Madras Government on the basis of mutual surrender of conquests.
1784   In the terrible strain of this contest two episodes subsequently figured conspicuously in the impeachment of Hastings. In 1781 Cheyt Singh, the Rajah of Benares, one of our vassals who refused the demands made upon him, was heavily fined, himself reduced, and his estates confiscated. The Begums of Oudh, mother and widow of the late Nawab, refused to restore the treasure of the

State to the ruling Nawab-Wazir, who was thus unable to meet his obligations to the Company. In each of these cases the financial aid to the embarrassed treasury of the Company may have played a part in Hastings' policy. But far more than finance was at issue in the transaction. Hastings was determined, and entitled, to enforce the obligations of " protected " dependents to the paramount Power. In Oudh two grave issues were at stake. The treasure illegally seized by the Begums did not belong to them— but to the Nawab-Wazir, our ally and dependent. There was unimpeachable evidence (produced at Hastings' trial) that the Begums were concerned in a conspiracy with other rulers, the avowed object of which was to root out the English from India. So long as the Begums held the treasure good government in Oudh was impossible; and the State was a dangerous menace to British authority as well as to its neighbours. Hastings, on broad grounds, was determined to disarm the conspiracy and place the Nawab-Wazir in a position not merely to carry out his obligations, but to ensure that Oudh should be an efficient, well-governed, and " subsidiary " buffer State between Bengal and the turbulent North-west. The vindication of the Wazir's authority was therefore essential, and Hastings did not shrink from the measures necessary to achieve this. He rejected the counter-policy of the Opposition in Council—to leave Oudh impotent, misgoverned, the prey alike of the Company and its greedy and powerful native foes. Neither then nor since did he waver in his conviction that his policy was both politically expedient and morally right. And the subsequent examination of the evidence at the impeachment, confirmed by modern historical critics, ended in a verdict of acquittal from charges inspired by the fiendish animosity of Francis and the exuberant ignorance of Sheridan. In both cases British rule benefited by the result, and Hastings had to suffer the penalty. Similarly in the tragic fate of Nandu Kumar (Nuncomar), an unscrupulous and dangerous intriguer, impartial investigation has cleared Hastings of an unjust indictment. Nandu Kumar had charged Hastings with corruption, and the Governor-General had brought a counter-charge of conspiracy against him. On a private March, charge of forgery Nandu Kumar was tried, condemned, and executed. 1775 His death relieved Hastings of an opponent, formidable because he was supported by the Opposition in Council; but there is no proof that Hastings inspired the charge of forgery or thought Nandu

Kumar innocent, or made the law by which he was hanged, or in any way manipulated the trial. The judges were unanimous—a striking fact in Hastings' favour; and, still more striking, a bitterly hostile Council refused to intervene or prevent the sentence from being carried out.

During the most critical period of his rule Hastings was thwarted by his Council with inscrutable perversity. From 1774 to 1776 his opponents, led by Philip Francis, who has the best title to be regarded as "Junius," had a majority which they used to blacken the Governor-General's character and to reverse and nullify his policy. After the death of Monson, one of the Council, Hastings' supremacy until 1782 rested on his casting vote; and so bitter was the struggle that in 1780 he deliberately risked his life to fight a duel with Francis (who was guilty of a gross breach of faith), in order to end the opposition one way or another. After 1782, and until his retirement in 1785, he was much hampered by the directors at home. Nevertheless he worked to consolidate, by internal reforms, the dominions he had saved for the Crown. The administrative system that he organised in Bengal marked an epoch; "it remains essentially the system of the present day". Nor were his efforts confined to finance and administration. In 1764 he had attempted unsuccessfully to establish a Professorship of Persian at Oxford; he promoted topographical surveys, founded the Asiatic Society and the Calcutta Madrisa for encouraging Mohammedan culture. In foreign policy his insight and mastery of the facts stamped his measures with that quality of statesmanship which solves the problems of the day on principles that can be adapted to the needs of the future. His object, he said, "was to make the British nation paramount in India, and to accept the allegiance of such of our neighbours as shall sue to be enlisted among the friends and allies of the King of Great Britain". In other words, by inaugurating the system of "subsidiary alliances," through which the native rulers became allied and protected States of the para- mount power, he created the instrument by which political ascend- ency could march hand in hand with internal reform. And when he retired he could proudly plead that he left "the provinces of my immediate administration in a state of peace, plenty, and security". During his impeachment the numerous and spontaneous addresses from native communities testifying to the gratitude that his services and character had inspired, long after he had ceased to hold power, are the most telling evidence of his ideals and record. But both his difficulties, his mistakes, and his splendid achievements combined to point an unmistakable moral. A legislative reconstruction of the fabric of the government of India and a revision of the powers of the Chartered Company were matters that statesmen at home could no longer burke.[1]

§ 3. THE CROWN AND THE WHIGS. MARCH 20TH, 1782— MARCH 25TH, 1784.

The brief duration of the Rockingham Ministry illustrated the aims and zeal of the Whigs. In Fox's words they wished "to give a good stout blow to the influence of the Crown". The revenue officers, whose votes were reputed to turn seventy boroughs, were disfranchised; contractors were prevented from sitting in Parliament. Economic reform was promoted in a Bill which cut down secret-service money and the pension list, abolished various sinecures, and saved the public funds about £72,000. But for the strenuous objections of the King, who found two valuable allies in the Cabinet—Thurlow and Shelburne, Burke's Bill would have corresponded more exactly with the sweeping changes advocated by himself in Opposition. Burke himself set a noble example by the self-denying limitation that he imposed on the bloated emoluments hitherto enjoyed by the Paymaster-General; but the grant of pensions to the Chancellor, Dunning, and Col. Barrè did the Ministry no little harm. The dangerous and unconstitutional proceedings of the Commons in the Middlesex election were deliberately reversed. Wilkes, who since 1774 had taken his seat for Middlesex, had annually moved that the disqualifying resolution of February, 1769, be expunged from the Journals of the House; the motion was now carried and the record solemnly erased.[2] The wider question of parliamentary reform—of the franchise and the redistribution of seats—which went to the root of Crown influence and the relations of the Legislature to the over-represented and the non-represented, was raised by Pitt's motion for an inquiry into the existing system. Though cordially supported by Richmond in the

---

[1] See Appendices VIII and XXII.

[2] Wilkes died in 1797 in the odour of Toryism, "reconciled to every reputable opponent from the King downwards".

Cabinet and by Fox in the House, the Ministry treated it as an open matter and it was rejected by twenty votes (161-141).

Coerced by Grattan, the Cabinet conceded with considerable reluctance the demand for the legislative independence of Ireland. Resolutions, subsequently expressed in statutes, swept away Poynings' Law and the Declaratory Act (6 Geo. I.). A later Renunciation Act due to Flood reiterated "the exclusive right of the Parliament and courts of Ireland in matters of legislation and judicature," and restored the appellate jurisdiction of the Irish House of Lords. A limited Mutiny Act was also passed. This legislation completed the unconditional freedom of the Irish Parliament from the British Legislature and established a dual system of government. The Crown apparently was left the sole link between an independent Great Britain and an independent Ireland. Grattan's question "whether we shall be a Protestant settlement or an Irish nation," was not answered. The new *régime* started with a Parliament at Dublin, endowed with powers of taxation and legislation and uncontrolled by the formal fetters of the previous restricting statutes. But the gravest evils of Ireland—a corrupt and non-representative Legislature, political and religious disabilities, an unjust and complex agrarian economy—were as yet untouched. Burke's comparison of the Revolution of 1782 to that of 1688 was superficial and illusory. In 1783, Ireland, unlike the modern colony, was not dowered with responsible self-government. The heads of her Executive were not responsible to the Irish Parliament; they were appointed by and obeyed the British Cabinet and carried out the policy of the party with a majority in the British Parliament. This fundamental contradiction between a supreme Legislature and an irresponsible Executive could only be harmonised, either by further drastic changes, or by "influence," *i.e.* by permanently securing a parliamentary majority organised to accept without question the policy of that Executive. Hence the Revolution of 1782, so far from diminishing British "influence," of necessity intensified the motives and increased the sum of its degrading and sterilising efforts. Though futile under the circumstances, the reluctance of Shelburne and Fox to grant unconditionally the programme of the volunteers was intelligible. For in 1782 one of the golden opportunities rarely offered by Fate, and never twice, was let slip. Had a sane, liberal, and cleansing measure of

1783

parliamentary reform been made the necessary preliminary to the Repeal and Renunciation Acts, the record of "Grattan's Parliament" would not have been one of accumulated failures, culminating in the red ruin of 1798. The formative and healing forces of the new Ireland had grown up and attained maturity outside the walls of Parliament. At Dungannon, not at College Green, were most truly voiced the aspirations of a nation's new spirit. But "the Revolution of 1782" by the mockery of legislative independence shut the door on the life outside and imprisoned the future of Ireland in a Legislature, the corrupt control of which it was the interest and determination of the British Executive to maintain. The sequel showed how Pitt was driven by a logic he could not master to the extinction of the Irish Parliament, and to an incorporating union as the least disadvantageous remedy for an intolerable and apparently insoluble situation.

The making of peace was the most critical of the Ministry's tasks. The French conviction that at Yorktown the sun of British power had set had been rudely shaken by Rodney's victory; and the ambition of Spain to add the capture of Gibraltar to that of Minorca was again foiled by the skill and adamantine resolution of Eliott. De Crillon, the victor of Minorca, made a supreme effort to destroy the fortress by an overwhelming bombardment from the sea; but the attempt failed with great loss to the besiegers, and Howe's Sept. 8-25 masterly relief of the gallant garrison was the finishing touch to Oct. 12 Eliott's heroic defence. Negotiations were already being actively pushed. Had the Ministry taken full advantage of the distressed and disorganised condition of the Americans and the improvement in quality and number of our ships the diplomatic position might have been made more favourable; but the Whigs had come in to grant independence, and the Americans were pledged not to conclude a treaty without their allies. Two difficulties hampered the British Cabinet. Colonial Affairs belonged to Shelburne as Home Secretary, Foreign Affairs to Fox. At Paris, Oswald negotiated with Franklin, while Thomas Grenville represented Fox's dealings with Vergennes. Shelburne desired to make the concession of independence the condition of a concurrent settlement with France, in which he was supported by the King. Fox wished to separate America from the Bourbons by conceding independence at once, which would have left us free to concentrate on the European coalition and also transfer the whole negotiation to the Foreign Secretary. The difference as to method was aggravated by Fox's distrust of Shelburne's sincerity and ultimate aims—a distrust shared by every one who was brought into intimate political relations with the Home Secretary. Shelburne's ability, knowledge, and industry are unquestionable. He kept closely in touch with the best minds of the day; he was the first political leader to assimilate the ideas of Adam Smith; his patronage of Bentham, of learning and the fine arts, proved the breadth and variety of his intellectual interests; but his nickname of "Malagrida" and "the Jesuit of Berkeley Square" testified not merely to his general unpopularity, but to a conviction among politicians that as a colleague, for all his remarkable gifts, he was impossible. Pitt's marked omission of him from his Cabinet next year, after he had served under him, confirms a verdict first pronounced by Henry Fox in 1762. To Shelburne indeed might be applied Canning's remark about Sidmouth. He was like the measles. Every one had to have him once; no one would have him twice unless he could not help it.

Rockingham alone could keep the party together; and his death on July 1st brought the rupture between the two Secretaries of State and the divisions in the ranks of the Whigs to a head. Many of the Whigs, including Fox, held strongly the view laid down by Grafton in 1765, that it was for the Cabinet and the party to choose Rockingham's successor, and their principle was reinforced by their determination to pare down the influence of the Crown. But on the purely constitutional point they were clearly wrong. The selection of a Chief or Prime Minister belonged by right, usage, and convenience to the Crown, and the evolution of a true Cabinet system required that it should be retained as part of the royal prerogative. Fox had already quite correctly pointed out that Rockingham's Administration really consisted of two parts, "one belonging to the King and the other to the public"; and when George III. now invited Shelburne to form a Ministry he declined to serve under him. His decision was sound. Shelburne's views on prerogative and the influence of the Crown were diametrically opposed to his own; he had virtually quarrelled with him over the peace negotiations, and he had no confidence in the policy, aims, and sincerity of the new Premier—a title that Shelburne significantly repudiated. Even if he erred in his interpretation, it was his duty not to serve under a leader whom he thoroughly distrusted. Fox's resignation was followed by those of Portland, Lord John Cavendish, Burke, Sheridan, and later by Keppel and Grafton. Unfortunately, Fox's conduct had all the appearance of being inspired by factious personal jealousy ; it puzzled the public, angered the King, and alienated Pitt, who at the age of twenty-three now became Chancellor of the Exchequer. The political rivalry of Pitt and Fox, repeating the rivalry of their fathers forty years before, dated from that day. Pitt, though he had sided with the Whigs in their attacks on North, had to the full Chatham's ambition, pride, hatred of "faction and party connection," and already his views on public policy differed vitally from those of Fox. The separation of the two leaders was inevitable if regrettable. Henceforward every year only made the gulf between them wider.

Shelburne's Ministry pushed the peace negotiations with vigour and skill. The preliminaries with the Americans were settled by November 20, 1783. The Treaty of Versailles then definitely Sept. closed the war. A new epoch for the American continent, for Europe, and for Great Britain, opened with the frank recognition of the sovereignty and independence of the United States. The Mississippi was taken as the boundary of the West, and a line drawn through the Great Lakes separated Canada from the new Republic. The French obtained concessions, but not as many or as valuable as they had expected. Tobago in the West Indies, a redefinition of the right to the Newfoundland Fisheries with the islands of St. Pierre and Miquelon in sovereignty, Senegal and Goree in West Africa, the restoration of her commercial stations in India, the abandonment of our claim for the destruction of the fortifications at Dunkirk were her chief gains. Spain received from Great Britain Minorca and East Florida, but restored the Bahama Islands (already recovered), and admitted the right to cut logwood in the Bay of Honduras. But though the cession of Gibraltar was discussed in the Cabinet, and the King was not unwilling to barter it for some valuable compensation, the firmness of Pitt and Shelburne retained the key to the Mediterranean in our hands. With Holland a mutual restitution of conquests was arranged, save that England retained Negapatam. The prior recognition of American independence much assisted our diplomacy, thereby proving that Fox's plan had been the sound one. But while the grant of independence came

direct from Great Britain and not as a gift from France and Spain, the methods of the American diplomatists left much to be desired. Pledged not to make a treaty apart from their ally, France, to whose intervention in the war they owed so much, the Americans did not hesitate to arrange privately with Great Britain everything but the formal conclusion of the treaty; nor would they in the hour of triumph concede to the "Loyalists" more than a vague recommendation to Congress that their claims should be considered. The complete disregard of this futile reference, probably foreseen by Franklin and his colleagues, placed the supporters of Great Britain at the mercy of vindictive victors. To the honour of our Government, and the dishonour of the United States, British Ministers were obliged to provide for the many thousands of men and women to whom the defeat of their cause meant misery and ruin. The establishment of the United Empire Loyalists brought some ten thousand "Tory" settlers from the American colonies under the British flag, subsequently to become the backbone of the maritime provinces of Canada. It is remarkable also that the great colonial struggle produced singularly little change in the principles and practice, administrative and economic, of our colonial system. If any moral was drawn, it was not that drastic reform was needed, as that reform was useless. Colonies would, in Turgot's phrase, drop off like ripe fruit from the parent tree, and it was idle to try to avert what was inevitable in the nature of things. For the dawning of a new epoch and the adoption of new principles, we have to wait half a century for Papineau's rebellion and the epoch-
1840   making Report of Lord Durham, which appealed to a generation saturated with the economics and the political thought that took their rise in Adam Smith, and the victory of reform at home.

As a whole, the terms of peace were as satisfactory as could be expected; but the Opposition was determined to destroy the Ministry. Shelburne, aware of the weakness of the Government, desired to come to terms with North, but the Cabinet preferred through Pitt to sound Fox, who adhered to his refusal to serve with Shelburne. Fox then made the cardinal blunder of his life. He united with North, defeated the Administration in the Com-
Feb. 24,   mons, and Shelburne resigned. After six weeks spent in vain by
1783   the King in desperate efforts to escape the triumphant junction of the man whom he most hated with the ungrateful "deserter"

from the Crown, the famous Coalition Ministry of Fox and North, who became Foreign and Home Secretaries respectively, under the nominal leadership of the Duke of Portland, came into office. The April 2 other important members of the Cabinet were Lord John Cavendish (Chancellor of the Exchequer), Carlisle (Privy Seal), Stormont (Lord President), and Keppel (the Admiralty). It was significant that Thurlow, the King's most trusted representative, disappeared, and the Great Seal was put in commission.

The majority of the Administration in the Commons was irresistible, and Fox intended to use it to establish the supremacy of a responsible Cabinet and of Parliament, and to carry out a far-reaching programme in finance, Indian affairs, and foreign policy—to destroy piecemeal the system of personal government by an irresponsible Sovereign. Parliamentary reform was left an open question; but the composition and terms of the coalition confirmed the King's worst fears that he had fallen bound hand and foot to the mercies of Fox and the new Whiggism. It was North who had surrendered to Fox, not Fox to North.[1] But if the objects of the coalition are creditable to Fox's earnest sincerity and principles, the new Ministry was an unpardonable and incomprehensible blunder. No one had condemned North with more vehemence and effect than Fox. Unless ends justified means the coalition seemed to proclaim the determination of two unscrupulous opponents to seal an artificial union by office obtained by any methods and at any price. Fox had quarrelled with Shelburne and broken with Pitt. He now apparently obtained a personal revenge by turning them out and syndicating their offices between himself and the statesman whom he had threatened with impeachment. Fox, in fact, supplied chapter and verse to the critics who called him a dissipated gambler, to whom politics were a game the only purpose of which was to score the odd trick. He defied the public as well as the Crown. And the plain man had this in common with George III.—he neither wished for nor could understand an explanation of conduct that perhaps could be, but sorely needed to

[1] " If you mean there should not be a government by departments, I agree with you. I think it is a very bad system. There should be one man or a Cabinet to govern the whole and direct every measure. Government by departments was not brought in by me; I found it so . . . the appearance of power is all that a King of this country can have " (North in *Fox's Memoirs*, 2, 38).

be, explained.   Worst of all, Fox shattered the instrument—a united Whig party based on popular support—on which his sole hope, not of success in the narrow sense, but of enduring and beneficial reforms, rested.   In the spring of 1783 the trump cards were in his hands.   Shelburne was disliked by the King and unpopular with his colleagues.   Twelve months of the tactful neutrality of the candid friend would have rallied the forces of Whiggism within and without the Administration to Fox's leadership.   Like Mirabeau he had to purge the sins of his youth.   Unlike Mirabeau he would have been in a position before long to dictate his terms without sacrifice of consistency, principles, or popular approval.

Nothing now but success could justify so audacious and bewildering a shake of the party kaleidoscope.   And success was what George III. intended the Ministry should not have.   It was wittily said that when the new Ministers kissed hands the King put back his ears with the air of the vicious horse determined to throw a detested rider.   To the King Fox's industry in office, deference, and wonderful personal charm were only the devil's gifts to a political Iago.   And to destroy the "tyrants" George III. was ready to use every resource that the Crown could provide or devise.   The rejection of Pitt's motion for parliamentary reform, though supported by Fox, and the compromise over the allowance from the Civil List to the Prince of Wales, who followed the Hanoverian tradition in giving the warm support of the heir to the throne to the political opponents of the reigning Sovereign, were mere preliminaries.   Fox took his fortune in both hands when he brought forward his two India Bills to deal with the problem of Indian government.

Nov. 18

The way had been prepared by the reports of two Committees in 1781, by the deadlock created by the refusal of the proprietors to recall Warren Hastings at the request of the Secretary of State, and by the dropping of Dundas's private Bill to reform the government of India.   Fox's comprehensive measures were largely inspired by Burke, who since 1765 had taken the deepest interest in Indian affairs.   He proposed to transfer the political, administrative and patronage powers of the Company to seven Commissioners nominated in Parliament, holding office for four years, and controlling as trustees the property of the Company.   For commercial business and the management of the property a subordinate Council of Directors was to be created, acting under the control of the superior

Board and selected by Parliament from the proprietors of £2000 stock. Vacancies in this subordinate Board were to be filled up by the Court of Proprietors. After four years the superior Commissioners were to be nominated by the Crown, *i.e.* on the advice of its confidential servants. The second Bill dealt with the chief abuses of Indian administration—monopolies, presents, the employment of mercenary troops, and so forth. But criticism fastened at once on the first Bill, which vitally affected the vested interests of a powerful company with great financial and political influence. It seemed to shift a vast patronage, worth it was calculated £300,000 a year, not from the Company to the Crown, but to a political party who, it was asserted, would use it to debauch Parliament, and gild the chains of a new political slavery. The fact that the seven Commissioners nominated were all supporters of Fox's party lent plausible colour to the charge. Thurlow, Pitt, and Dundas saw their chance and at once made the measure a party question. Pitt voiced both the interested attacks of the Company and the unjust assertion of political opponents that Fox aimed at placing "the diadem on his own head". He ignored the object of the bill, which was to secure the resumption of imperial rights, to remedy on the sound principle of parliamentary control the antagonism between the accidentally-acquired political power of the Company and its commercial functions, the abuses to which this had led, and the necessity of co-ordinating policy in India with policy at home. There is no reason to suppose that the predicted abuses would have followed; there is every reason to suppose that the measure would have been beneficial to the government and peoples of India. The bill was a sincere and statesman-like effort to deal with a great problem on comprehensive lines; but George III., Pitt, Thurlow, and the East India Company did not consider nor apparently wish to consider it on its merits. Every effort to inflame popular feeling and the prejudices of the vested interests was employed. Fox, not the imperial problem, was made the issue. And, what was most regrettable, Pitt by lending himself to these unscrupulous tactics tied his own hands for the future treatment of imperial administration in India. Foiled in the Commons, where the Bill was carried by a large majority, the King stooped and stooped low to conquer. He authorised Lord Temple to influence votes in the Lords by informing waverers (truly enough) that any one voting for

the Bill " would be considered as a personal enemy to the Crown ".
Pitt was probably cognisant of this unconstitutional and dishonourable expedient.[1]   Sixteen years later in the matter of Roman
Catholic emancipation, George III. taught him as he taught Fox
now what mischief superstitions and fixed ideas could work ; and
unhappily the King succeeded now as he succeeded in 1800.   On
December 17th the Bill was thrown out in the Upper House by
nineteen votes.   The next day the King, with graceless haste, dismissed by a message the Secretaries of State ; and at the age of
twenty-four Pitt accepted the invitation to form a Ministry and
defy the Opposition.

The new Cabinet, with the exception of Pitt, who combined
the offices of First Lord of the Treasury and Chancellor of the
Exchequer, was drawn from the Upper House—Thurlow (Chancellor), Gower (Lord President), Rutland (Privy Seal), and Caermarthen
and Sydney (Secretaries of State).   Shelburne, as already noted,
was significantly passed over.   The Opposition, however, were confident of a speedy return to office, for their majority in the Commons
was overwhelming, and they affected to treat Pitt's experiment as a
boyish freak :

A sight to make surrounding nations stare,
A kingdom trusted to a schoolboy's care.

But under the mature leadership of Fox mistake was piled on
mistake.   Fox should have been content to place on record the
solemn protest of the House at the dangerous and unconstitutional
action of the Crown, and then given the new Minister a fair chance.
It was his duty and his interest to demand an appeal forthwith to
the nation, to convince every moderate man that he cared more for
principles than for office, to give time for the heated feelings aroused
by the India Bill to evaporate in the larger air of the constituencies,
to prove that he could be just and generous if his opponents could
not.   Instead, he showed that a dissolution was the one thing that
he feared, a return to office the one thing that he desired, and he
used his majority to throw out Pitt's first India Bill and to force
motion after motion, making all government impossible.   He forgot
that the King was fighting also for a principle—the prerogative to

[1] See the letter of Pitt to Rutland of December 6th (Rutland Correspondence,
p. 5) ; Fitzmaurice's *Shelburne*, 3, 393 ; Grafton's *Autobiography*, p. 383 ; and *cf.*
Salomon's *Pitt*, i., 124.

select and dismiss Ministers—and that the final verdict lay not with the Commons, nor with the Crown, but with electors and public opinion. Pitt's conduct was as faultless as his rival's was faulty. His serene courage on the Treasury Bench and his refusal of a rich sinecure, the Clerkship of the Pells, repeating his father's superb contempt for the material rewards of royal favour, inspired a growing admiration. He broadened the issue at stake into one which raised the rights and place of the Crown in government. By a stroke of rare intuition he claimed to be the champion of a sane Toryism against a coalition of renegade Whigs (under North) and factious Radicals (under Fox). He thus evaded the issues on which Fox might have fought with advantage and challenged battle on ground where Fox was compelled to fight with every disadvantage. The hostile majority leaked steadily away; public opinion rallied daily to the young Minister, and on March 25th, 1784, Parliament was dissolved, and with it was also dissolved Fox's party. The election cost the Opposition 160 seats—" Fox's Martyrs " they were not untruly called. It was not a defeat; it was a rout. But the nation voted not for the King's system as he understood it, but for Pitt against Fox, and also for what with sound instinct the nation divined were Pitt's principles and the use he would make of supremacy.[1]

The struggle between the Crown and the Whigs is not an edifying episode. During no other period of his reign was the King's behaviour so unworthy of his position and his duties. His personal conduct revealed the worst side of a narrow and bigoted nature. Nor in order to gain his ends was it necessary to sacrifice the grace, dignity, generosity, and sincerity that so easily would have won sympathetic admiration. His interpretation of his official duties is even less defensible. George III. invariably expected his Ministers to behave in their relations to the Crown like honourable gentlemen; while if he disliked either their character or their policy, however unreasonably, he considered himself entitled to a plenary absolution from the code that remained binding on them. Resentment at the methods or steps taken to prevent the public service being hampered by royal insincerity or intrigues he regarded as a personal affront and an additional reason for further loading the dice or queering the cards. Neither Rockingham, Shelburne, nor Fox expected the King's personal confidence; but so long as they

[1] See Appendix XXII.

were the confidential servants of the Crown, accepted by the Sovereign, the King abused his powers and failed in his duties if he
publicly assented to their policy and then behind their backs traduced their characters, thwarted their measures, and intrigued with
their opponents to overthrow them.   For two years this is what
George III. did, relying on the obvious inability of the Ministerial
victims of his royal code of ethics to retaliate with like methods.
If the King disliked the India Bills he was entitled to dismiss the
Ministers who insisted on introducing them.   If Parliament refused
its confidence to the new Ministers he was entitled to dissolve.   If the
nation placed that Ministry in a minority the Crown must give way.
Had George III. dismissed Fox and North in the autumn of 1783
and then dissolved, his conduct could not be criticised.   Instead he
assented to the introduction of the Bill and then fomented the
opposition to it secretly, invited the advice of irresponsible critics,
and finally—an act for which he was well aware he could not be
made responsible—consolidated the royal plot against his own
servants by the authorised use of the royal name.   Such conduct,
intrinsically dishonourable, was destructive of any sound system or
constitutional monarchy and parliamentary government.   It was a
menace to the Ministerial system from the consequences of which
the Crown was only saved by the tactical blunders of the Opposition
and the skilful leadership of Pitt.

The issue of the struggle brought out many points of great
historical interest.   We are still a long way from the Victorian
Cabinet system, and the Victorian conventions and customs with
regard to the place and functions of a constitutional Crown.   Pitt's
Parliamentary duel and the general election, when compared with
the action of William IV. and Peel in 1834, illustrate not merely
the astonishing power of the Crown in 1784, but the strong if
vague desire of the nation that the Sovereign should not be relegated to the position of the Peishwa.   How this position was to
be reconciled with parliamentary supremacy was left to the future.
Fox's crushing defeat conclusively proves how public opinion once
aroused could override all the limitations and defects of the franchise, and make even the unsatisfactory representative system of
1784 an organ of the nation's wishes.   Walpole's and Chatham's
careers had also shown the same result ; Pitt learned it again in
1791, and it was enforced up to the hilt after 1793.   It was facts

such as these which furnished the opponents of reform with their strongest arguments; whether their standpoint was like that of Burke, a reasoned and philosophic dissent from the principles and objects of the Reformers, or like that of the King and the King's Friends, hostility to change simply because it was change, and because reform would destroy the basis of their power and influence.

Yet the situation in 1784 was not a return to that of 1770. Pitt was not a North, nor had he any intention of playing North's part. If like Bismarck in 1862 he had rallied to the Crown and defied a Parliamentary majority, like Bismarck he desired to use the forces and resources of the Crown not to carry out the Crown's policy but his own. Like Strafford in 1628, he attacked from 1780-82 a weak, blundering and incompetent Monarchy, working through a vicious system as a public danger. With genius astonishing in a young man of twenty-four, he understood that he had in 1784 now received a mandate to go forward not to go back. His power would continue so long as he fitly interpreted national feeling. Territorial and aristocratic Whiggism was dead. Liberalism under Fox had its forty years of wandering in the wilderness to fulfil. With 1784 we cross the threshold into the Age of the new and constructive Toryism of which Pitt is the prophet. George III. had hunted with tears for another docile instrument, and he had found instead a master. A great place was now vacant and Pitt proved his greatness simply by filling it.

NOTE.—For the General Election of 1784 see Appendix XXII. On George III.: Hon. Sir J. W. Fortescue, *Correspondence of George III.* (1760-1783), 6 vols., 1928. This entirely replaces the earlier book by Donne. The editor's comments and interpretation can be separated from the letters. Dr. Holland Rose's *Life of Pitt* (1912) is the most recent and critical biography; vol. i. deals with Pitt down to 1789.

20

CHAPTER III

PITT AND THE NEW TORYISM (1784-1792).

THE nine years that precede the formation of the First Coalition against Revolutionary France have an interest and quality peculiarly their own.   They are years of unbroken peace for Great Britain, inserted between the seven years of war in which the empire was disintegrated and the twenty-two years of the Titanic struggle with the Revolution and Napoleon, in which the British State fought rather for existence than for supremacy.   It is the period in which the basis of the Industrial Revolution is laid ; of consolidating internal reform and successful foreign policy, ruthlessly cut short by the unforeseen revolution in the Europe of the *ancien régime*.   Above all the decade from the autumn of 1783 to March, 1793, is unified by the personality and achievements of the young Minister, heir to fulfilled renown.   Across the record is written in each session the name of William Pitt.

The need for a new departure, for a healing and constructive policy, was absolute.   Great Britain was without allies, and her prestige and place in the councils of Europe had sunk to a lower ebb than had been touched since the Hanoverian dynasty ascended the throne.   Abroad, it was commonly believed that our sun had at last begun to set, and that the British State was doomed to sink to the second rank.   Ireland and India called for legislative treatment.   Our national finance was demoralised and disorganised.   The balance sheet showed a deficit of £12,500,000 ; the 3 per cents. stood at 57 and the National Debt had risen to £224,000,000 of funded, and £20,000,000 of unfunded, obligations.   The gangrene of extravagance, maladministration, and corruption was corroding every organ of the body politic.   Economic reform had been proved by Burke to be not a controversial issue between warring parties, but an imperative political and financial necessity, a categorical precondition of any hope of restoring a sick and dispirited nation to a clean, healthy, and growing life. The parliamentary machine, clogged by the personal system of George III., had lost the national confidence. Commerce was strangled by an antiquated fiscal code that fostered smuggling and bred administrative incompetence and jobbery.

Great Britain needed a new way of life. The popular voice with unerring instinct repudiated by its votes in 1784 alike the King's Friends and the old orthodox Opposition; it expressed a conviction that the new ideals and the new methods would only come if at all from a new man, and it looked to the son of Chatham to be that man.

The career of William, the younger, Pitt is exceptional in every feature. On the boy, born in the year of victory, 1759, had been centred from the first his father's dearest affections and ambitions. Chatham's son naturally inherited a great name and a great tradition; he roused great expectations. And when he made his maiden speech in the House of Commons men pronounced with a thrill that this was not a chip from the old block, but the old block itself. In our political annals it is not easy to find a parallel for a father and son so unquestionably endowed with the genius that brought both into the first rank of statesmanship, while father and son alike stamped on their generation the same indefinable and ineffaceable impression of power. Pitt was born into the purple of the Premiership. Chancellor of the Exchequer at twenty-three, he was Prime Minister before he was twenty-five. When he died in 1806 he had been at the head of Government for a longer period than any statesman save Walpole. No political figure of the first rank before or since his day has spent so brief a period of his political life out of office. Charles Fox, also a remarkable case of hereditary ability, presents a dramatic contrast; for he passed a longer part of his career in Opposition than any other statesman save perhaps Bolingbroke, or Pym.

It is difficult to frame with confidence a sound comparative estimate of statesmen as of generals who have never had to conduct in the plenitude of their strength a retreat with broken forces against a victorious foe. But Pitt's intellectual qualities stand out in clear relief. He inherited from his father the gift of oratory, a patriotism that could burn white hot, the serene confidence in his capacity to

lead, the proud spirit that neither feared nor flattered flesh.
Events proved that if he was a great financier, he was neither a
great administrator nor a great War Minister.   But as the leader of
a party, as a parliamentary master in the eighteenth century, he is
equalled but not surpassed by Walpole alone.   His private life was
singularly pure.   He drank too often and too much ; but beyond an
incomprehensible and culpable extravagance in his personal expenditure he had no vices.   Even more conspicuously than Chatham
he despised the material and decorative rewards of success.   The
creator of the modern House of Lords, the lavish distributor of
peerages, ribands, and pensions, he was *bien distingué* in his generation by his haughty indifference to all such honours for himself.   His ambition was unlimited, and he loved power with the
same demonic passion that inspired his devotion to parliamentary
life.   From first to last he gave all that was best in his nature and
intellectual strength to the service of his country, and its interests as he conceived them.   We may quarrel with his reasons and
his conclusions, but it is impossible to impugn his motives.   Save
Dundas, Wilberforce, Wellesley, and perhaps George Rose, he had
few intimate friends ; from Canning he won and retained the affection and reverence of a son ; but Pitt dominated Parliament as he
dominated the Crown and country by that sheer force of character
and ability which placed him in a lonely class by himself on the
Treasury Bench.   The tears of human things, of pathos and tragedy,
haunt the career of this solitary man, dwelling apart on the heights
of great affairs ; who never knew the love of wife or child ; who
worked so hard in the golden premise of his political apprenticeship
for peace, retrenchment, and reform ; who in the maturity of his
powers constituted himself the champion of a cause that linked continuous war abroad with repression and reaction at home, with
swollen debt and bloated armaments ; who died in the bitter knowledge that popular liberties had been suspended, the National Debt
more than doubled, taxation strained to the breaking point, a
quarter of a million of human lives sacrificed, and that peace and
reform were further out of sight than ever ; bitterest of all, that
the old order in Europe had perished and that Napoleon, the
incarnate spirit of the principles of the French Revolution, was
triumphant over two-thirds of the Continent.

Pitt's first ten years have often been claimed as his Whig period, which precedes his desertion from Liberalism, or his conversion to a reactionary Toryism in 1793. In reality, as is the case with Burke, there was neither desertion nor conversion, but a simple and intelligible evolution. With each statesman the later development is implicit in, and the logical outcome of, the principles of his creed and the pressure of events. Pitt was never a Whig, as Fox or Burke or his father were Whigs. His premiership therefore emphasises a double departure—the re-creation of the Tory party, the slow evolution of a new Whiggism through puzzling and halting phases into modern Liberalism. If Fox is the founder of the party of Holland, Grey, Melbourne, and Palmerston, Pitt is the creator of the Toryism of Castlereagh, Canning, Wellington, and Peel. In 1783 Pitt deliberately came forward as the saviour of the Crown from the Whigs. It was his genius that extricated the monarchy from a *débâcle* and made its cause intelligible and attractive to the average man, who is by instinct conservative. Henceforward his policy set the battle in array between himself and the Opposition on strict and definable two-party lines. Fox, Burke, and Sheridan correctly opposed him, not because he had stolen their measures, but because both his principles and objects, if successfully realised, involved the final defeat of Whiggism. Pitt repeated in fact Bolingbroke's work. He re-created the Tory party by sloughing off the false tenets which had grown up round it; but, unlike Bolingbroke, he harmonised the claims of the Crown with the best and progressive ideas of the day, such as those of Adam Smith in economics. Whatever the problem may be—in home or foreign politics—it is not enough, in Pitt's eyes, to prove an abstract principle or a distinct grievance. It must be shown that the need is really felt, that public opinion is ripe, above all that legislative action will strengthen not dislocate the central organs of government, and that the remedy can be introduced in gradual doses. It is not a new order that is required but the progressive revivification of the old. In no single instance was Pitt the creator of great ideas or the unrequited pioneer of new causes. In finance and economic reform he applied the ideas of Adam Smith, Burke, Shelburne, Price; Chatham, Savile, Wilkes, Richmond, Fox, taught the nation the programme of electoral reform; the splendid failure of Fox and Burke was the basis of his India Bill; to the making of his Irish policy contributed many workers—Grattan, Cornwallis, Castlereagh; he learned the abominations of the slave trade from Wilberforce and Clarkson; his later foreign policy was profoundly influenced by Grenville; as a "War Minister" he was dominated, to England's cost, by Dundas. And this assimilative quality had its conspicuous disadvantages. It forced him into the dangerous fictions which disfigured his solution of the Regency question. Only once, in 1800, in his career did he sacrifice office for a principle; and it is significant that the abolition of the slave trade was advocated but not effected by the Minister who was in power for seventeen years, but carried by his rival who enjoyed office for half as many months. Similarly in 1791 Pitt abandoned the threat of war for a principle with Russia in a humiliating hurry, when he discovered that public opinion was with the Opposition not with the Ministry. But perhaps the gravest omission in the programme after 1783 was Pitt's continuous blindness to the need of financial, administrative, and professional reform in our military organisation. The starvation of army and navy, and the disregard of the lessons of the American war during the ten years of peace, cost the country many thousands of lives, many millions of public money, and contributed in a signal degree to the failure of the Minister's foreign policy after 1793.

But Pitt had correctly diagnosed one cause of mischief; the Monarchy quite as much as any branch of the constitutional machinery called for rehabilitation. In its own interest it required to be weaned from the worship of false gods and a false ritual; and from the first Pitt set quietly but decisively to cut down the groves and break the images that had been set up by the priests and idolaters of A Patriot King. A crop of legislative measures facilitated the work of purification. Crown and Court learned that the son of Chatham would not tolerate the treachery against which Rockingham and Fox had fought in vain. The thought of Fox in power, of Pitt alienated and in Opposition, was sufficient for the next ten years to keep the King on the path of a workable political sanity. The Cabinet as a Council of the Crown was restored; if the King's Friends did not wholly die out, they were reduced to submission; Ministerial responsibility was revived and the departmental system noiselessly put on the self. Pitt was a true Prime Minister. He led the Government in the Representative Chamber, which like Walpole, Peel, Palmerston, and Gladstone (but unlike Chatham and Beaconsfield), he steadily refused to leave. He was the mainspring of Governmental action. The dismissal of the traitor Thurlow in 1791, the recall of Fitzwilliam in 1795, clinch conclusions derivable from copious cumulative evidence. His personal relations with George III. are equally instructive. The note of affectionate intimacy which marks the royal intercourse with North and Addington is absent. Dignity we find on both sides; in George III. a growing confidence that deepens into genuine admiration. Pitt had his father's reverence for the Monarchy and a sincere sympathy with the wearer of the crown, but the King never penetrated or disarmed the Olympian reserve of his Prime Minister. It is the same with his colleagues. Even where there is friendship they write of and to him as of a power living apart in an austere atmosphere of his own. To his Cabinet as to the House of Commons he was always the Chief *sans phrase*. His personality, as of a Dantean angel, was something to be felt. How different the sunny human weaknesses and strength, the friendships of Fox, feared and hated as a politician, loved as a friend as no other character in our political record. Fox's passion for justice, liberty, and humanity, for the causes to which the future belonged, and the far-off mountain tops where dwelt the spirits of freedom and the dawn, were as unintelligible to Pitt as were Fox's love of gambling and of women, and his amazing blunders in the strategy and tactics of parliamentary life.

Curiously enough, Pitt's first action met with a smart rebuff. After a fiercely fought contest, Fox had been elected as the second member for the great borough of Westminster, but the High Bailiff, instead of making a proper return, granted a scrutiny, and thus deprived the electors of their representation. Fox, who had also been returned for Kirkwall, petitioned the House to order an immediate return, but the petition was opposed by Pitt, who used the Governmental majority to inflict a malicious humiliation on his rival. After eight months had been wasted Pitt, against the King's judgment, still persisted, only to find his majority turned into a minority, and the return was duly ordered. The defeat in no way affected the Minister's position. Pitt had mistaken the temper of the Commons, and the rebuke administered to his ungenerous chicanery was fully justified. Fox with all his faults was incapable of such childish spite to a defeated opponent.

The India Bill, revived from the previous Parliament, was passed with ease. Drafted after consultation with the Directors, it was avowedly a compromise. The political authority was handed over to a Board of Control, six members of which were appointed by the Crown. Patronage was retained by the Directors, but the Governor-General, the Governors and members of Councils and the Commander-in-Chief were chosen subject to the pleasure of, and could be dismissed by, the Crown. The supremacy of the Governor-General in Council over the presidencies of Madras and Bombay was assured. Various regulations checked administrative abuses; and a special court was provided for inquiry into such offences. The measure, in short, aimed at combining the vested rights of the Company with the prerogatives of the Monarchy ; it made no attempt to solve the problem of Indian government on scientific principles. The system of Dual Control which it set up lasted until the Act of 1858 resumed for the Crown the sovereign rights acquired by the Company. And the future showed that the Board of Control under Dundas could exemplify all the defects so freely urged against Fox's scheme. Scotland, his party, and himself, were the three passions of Dundas's life ; and under the protection of Pitt and his majority he exercised the powers permitted by the Act to indulge all these up to the hilt.[1]

In the session of 1785, Pitt made his last attempt to carry a measure of parliamentary reform. The leading features of his scheme were : (1) the disfranchisement of thirty-six rotten boroughs and the transfer of the seventy-two members they returned to the counties with London and Westminster ; (2) the extension of the franchise to copyholders in the counties and to householders in the boroughs ; (3) the compensation of the extinguished vested interests by a million of public money. The King, of course, was opposed to the proposal, and Pitt obtained with difficulty his consent to its discussion by the House. Leave to introduce the Bill, however, was refused by 284 to 174 votes, an illustration not merely of the temper of the representative Assembly, but of the difference between the constitutional conventions of that day and modern practice. The defeat of the head of the Government in no way affected his authority. But it is significant that Burke argued against the upsetting of the traditional balance of interests, and that Fox anticipated the principle of the Reformers in 1832, when he attacked the proposed compensation on the ground that electoral

[1] See Appendix VIII.

rights were a trust not a vested property. Pitt seems to have regarded the decision as final. He had salved his conscience and he
now left the cause to the Whigs. Yet it is difficult to believe that
a popular Minister could not have carried a moderate scheme in
the next eight years, had he really been in earnest and devoted
his authority to educating his party and to genuine co-operation
with the champions of reform inside and outside the House. Great
Ministers can always find time for causes they really have at heart;
and Pitt's speech was the best proof of the strength of the case
for reform, a statesmanlike instalment of which might have spared
Great Britain some of the worst features of the black years after
1793.

The main work of the sessions of 1784, 1785, 1786, and 1787
was financial. Here Pitt was thoroughly in earnest, and the varied
field was thoroughly congenial to a mind saturated with the ideas
of Adam Smith. "We," he had said to the great economist, "we,
are all your pupils." The chief characteristics of the Budget of
1784 were: the raising of revenue and the crippling of smuggling
(in which it was calculated 40,000 men and 300 vessels were employed) by a scientific rearrangement of the tariff; the duty on
tea was reduced from 119 per cent. to 12½ per cent.; the excise on
home produce was raised; the duty on imported brandy was lowered;
the deficit in revenue was met by a variety of new taxes—on windows, hats, raw silk, licences, and by grouping a variety of other
items under the Assessed Taxes which shifted the burden on to
richer classes; £6,500,000 of floating debt were funded, and a
new loan was put up to public competition at the lowest tender,
and not (as had been the practice under North) allotted amongst
the supporters of the Ministry to the degradation of Parliament
and the public loss. Next year the deficit had dropped to
£1,000,000, which Pitt met by a loan from the Bank of England
and by throwing the net of taxation still wider. Ten millions
more of floating debt were consolidated. These measures led up
to the famous Sinking Fund of 1786, which the nation was led to
believe would by an automatic magic extinguish the National
Debt in twenty-eight years. The idea was borrowed from Dr.
Price and consisted in the establishment of a Board of Commissioners, independent of Parliament and the Ministry, to whom
annually £1,000,000 was assigned for the purchase of stock. Each

million would thus accumulate at compound interest, and simple arithmetic seemed to prove that only a limited period of time was required to amortise the total deadweight of debt. The scheme certainly was effective when taxation could provide the annual £1,000,000 from surplus revenue; but when it became necessary to provide the £1,000,000 by borrowing, at a higher rate of interest, larger sums than the amount extinguished, the result was a dead loss and in principle pure financial quackery. The nation was cozened into the delusion that if the Sinking Fund were only kept up, it did not matter what reckless or high-priced additions were made by loans to the capital obligations of the country. The plain fallacy was not fully exposed until 1816; but it is probable that Pitt himself had discovered the truth, and maintained the Fund as a device for reconciling the taxpayer to the gigantic expenditure of the French wars. If the supposition be correct[1] it is creditable to his financial penetration, but leaves a grave slur on his reputation as a statesman. Neither doctors nor financiers are entitled to credit for dosing their patients with soporifics, cumulatively injurious and incapable of curing the disease for which they are prescribed.

Pitt's mastery of principles and details was exemplified to the full in his Budget for 1787. The Bill for the Consolidation of the Customs and Excise laid the basis of the Consolidated Fund which is the core of our modern financial system. The whole of the tariff, a labyrinth of antiquated, conflicting and injurious rates, was revised, and no less than 3000 articles dealt with on a reconstructed schedule. A single tax was laid on each item. Simplicity in incidence, efficiency and cheapness in collection were the features of the new rate-book. The whole of the revenue thus raised was then brought into a single (Consolidated) Fund on which all the public liabilities were secured, and any deficiency was to be met by special taxation. The result was not merely beneficial to commerce, and public economy (by reducing the cost of collection and abolishing sinecures and jobbery), but made possible a national balance sheet over the revenue and expenditure over which Treasury and Parliament could exercise an effective control. Specially blessed by Burke,

---

[1] It is noticeable, however, that as late as October 25th, 1797, Pitt believed in the Sinking Fund (see the Financial Minute, *Dropmore Papers*, iii., 382).

this masterpiece of detailed work set the seal on the financial fame of its author.

The session of 1785 witnessed Pitt's first effort to cope with the Irish problem. Apart from the constitutional and administrative difficulties created by the Settlement of 1783 the two most pressing problems of Ireland were the disabilities of the Roman Catholics and parliamentary reform—twin aspects of a single malady. The Irish Executive under the Duke of Portland was opposed to any serious concessions, and the defeat of Flood's proposals for reform on a Protestant basis and the dissolution of the Volunteer Convention under Charlemont and Flood administered a temporary quietus to the agitation. But as the violent conduct of the Bishop of Derry, Lord Bristol, showed, the forces of discontent were either being driven underground or passing under the control of demagogues very different in temper and aim from the leaders, Charlemont and Grattan, the creators of the patriotic Volunteers. In the democratic fanaticism of the Presbyterian north and the religious and agrarian grievances of the Catholic peasantry two storm centres were developing which, once united, might shake the whole fabric of Irish society and government to its foundation. The criminal folly of postponing a remedy for ills so patent and unjustifiable was eloquently expressed by Grattan, but the Irish Parliament, controlled by the Irish Executive, shut both its ears and eyes to the warning. As yet Pitt neither contemplated nor was convinced of the desirability of a legislative union, and it is characteristic that he first dealt with the economic relations of Great Britain and Ireland. The proposals of 1785 aimed at making the two islands, though under separate and independent Legislatures, a single fiscal unit. The Navigation Act was to be suspended and the colonial trade thrown open to Ireland, with the exception of the East India Company's monopoly. All goods were to be interchangeable, free, or at equal duties; woollen exports from England were forbidden, and Irish exports in raw produce might be prohibited. In return Ireland was to contribute half a million to the imperial navy. The eleven resolutions, embodying these proposals, accepted by the Irish Legislature, met with violent opposition from the strongly represented mercantile classes in the British Parliament. The Opposition snatched at the opportunity and fanned the agitation. The interests of English commerce were to be bartered for the slavery of the Irish Legislature. " That," said Fox, " is not the price I would pay, nor is this the thing I would purchase." Concessions to a vested and prejudiced mercantilism whittled away the terms of the bargain; and when the mutilated scheme was resubmitted to the Irish Parliament, Grattan made it clear it would be rejected, and it was promptly withdrawn. This lamentable miscarriage must have endorsed in Pitt's mind the political evil that can be wrought, not by " a nation of shop-keepers, but by a nation dominated by shopkeepers," as well as the difficulty of governing Ireland through an Executive in no way representative of, or responsible to, an independent Legislature. The proposals of 1785 were never revived. For some years Pitt put Ireland out of his mind, and when it forced itself again on his attention the hour for a great healing policy had all but passed. From 1785 to 1793 the opportunity lay at the door of Downing Street and was unheeded. And the gods had decided that Pitt, " the spoiled child of fame and fortune," should be called happy before the end had been seen.

The Commercial Treaty of 1786 with France provides a welcome contrast. In this connection it is not without interest to note that Adam Smith had recommended compensating for the lost American monopoly by developing our European and, above all, our French trade. The treaty of 1783 had provided for the future revision of the commercial relations of France and Great Britain; and Pitt, pressed by a French threat of the complete prohibition of English goods, threw himself in 1785 with ardour into the negotiations. In April, 1786, Eden, afterwards Lord Auckland, was sent as a special commissioner to Paris, and on September 26th the treaty was signed. On the British side the main object was to open fresh markets, strengthen the cause of peace by economic bonds, and by promoting industrial prosperity to increase taxable capacity at home. Pitt, from careful evidence collected at the Board of Trade, was convinced, as were our manufacturers, that given a reasonable tariff we could compete successfully in the French market. Thus armed with statis-tics furnished by our trade he negotiated for a revision of the duties. The difficulty presented by the Methuen Treaty was surmounted by an arrangement that French wines should not be taxed higher than Portuguese, the duty on which might be lowered by one-third. Fox attacked the treaty with the armament of the traditional

Whig political economics. France was our natural and eternal foe. To strengthen her power to injure us by increasing her trade was the blunder of a Utopian idealist. Pitt's reply met both arguments. National enmities were neither perpetual nor irremovable. We had the best of the economic bargain, but even without this the greater the exchange between two countries the greater the benefit to both. Through the speech of Pitt, dandled in the anti-Bourbon mercantilism of his father, ring the spirit and science of Adam Smith and the new Toryism ; and it was not his fault that the French Revolution wrecked the beneficent consequences he had a right to expect from the treaty. Arthur Young's *Travels in France* and the statistics of our commerce bear out Pitt's conviction that British manufacturers were on their way to capture the French market. The growing superiority that scientific inventions, new processes, and organised capitalistic production on the grand scale—the Industrial Revolution, in short—were conferring on our chief industries is already apparent.

The same session saw the initiation of the proceedings which culminated in the impeachment of Warren Hastings. Since Hastings' return from India his implacable foe, Francis, had aided Burke in collecting evidence, and in 1786 and 1787 the Opposition formally identified itself with a demand for a public prosecution. Three main charges were preferred in connection with the Rohilla War, the Raja of Benares, and the Begums of Oudh, moved respectively by Fox, Burke, and Sheridan.[1] The first was rejected, but the second, which to the consternation of his party was supported by Pitt, and the third were adopted ; and the impeachment was opened in Westminster Hall on February 13th, 1788—an event, it has been pithily said, which "occasioned more eloquence (including Macaulay's) than any event in history". The trial proved long, and financially ruinous to Hastings ; very soon the inflamed rhetoric of the prosecutors wore out the ephemeral interest of the audience of intellect and quality collected to witness not a judicial investigation but an exhibition of oratorical gladiators. Not until 1795 was judgment pronounced, acquitting Hastings on every count in the indictment. Modern research has fully endorsed the justice of the verdict and absolved the accused's character and rule from the charges, mostly untrue and needlessly envenomed by ignorance and

Feb., 1785

[1] See Appendix viii.

party prejudice. Hastings' trial was the last (for that of Melville in 1806 was unimportant) of the great impeachments, and enshrines the principle that in the High Court of Parliament exists the one tribunal from whose jurisdiction no servant of the State, however highly placed, is exempt. All such machinery must be judged not by individual instances of its working but by the cumulative effects and the bracing reaction on public opinion and public administrative morality as a whole over wide periods of time. In the creation and enforcement of severer standards in the financial and political administration of Indian government a trial such as that of Warren Hastings taught both an educational and deterrent lesson which went far beyond the individual or the transactions concerned. Nor did the inevitable disadvantages ever prevent our country from obtaining for India or elsewhere the services of the best of her sons. But it would be foolish to ignore the lack of charity and gratitude so conspicuous in the Opposition's and Directors' treatment of a great public official. The trial brought Hastings to the verge of bankruptcy and embittered beyond reparation the closing years of his life, not wholly compensated by the subsequent recognition in Parliament and at Oxford of his signal achievements. The quintessence of fortune's irony lit up the old man's later days. He lived to see his prediction fulfilled that his official enemy, Dundas, would himself be impeached ; and at the precise moment when the Court of Directors was voting a statue to Hastings, Wellesley, whom India had taught bitterly to regret his former vote for Hastings' impeachment, was returning to England, condemned by his masters and menaced by a similar public prosecution for services second only to those of Clive and Hastings himself.

1813

After an interval of a year and a half, in which the government was carried on provisionally by the senior member of Council, Macpherson, Lord Cornwallis was sent out as the first Governor-General under Pitt's Act. Cornwallis's ability and vigour made his tenure of power a fitting appendix to that of Hastings. Valuable reforms in administration, in the police, in the judiciary and code of procedure were carried through. And though Cornwallis was not the originator of the Permanent Settlement in Bengal, his name is rightly associated with its successful completion. Equally decisive were his dealings with Haidar's son, Tippu Sultan. In 1789 the danger from Mysore was anticipated by the formation of

1786-93

an alliance with the Mahrattas and the Nizam; and in 1791 Cornwallis took the field in person. The first campaign ended in a
retreat, but next year peace was made at the gates of Tippu's
capital, Seringapatam. One-third of his dominions was surrendered; an indemnity of £3,000,000 imposed, and Coorg was
brought under British rule. Tippu thus received an impressive
warning, but the problem of Mysore and other Native States was
necessarily left by Cornwallis (promoted on his resignation to a
marquisate) to his successors.

Pitt, in the meanwhile, had turned from domestic to foreign
affairs, which until 1787 had been left mainly to the Secretary of
State, Carmarthen. The Prime Minister's previous indifference to
foreign policy was probably deliberate, and can be largely explained
by his absorption in finance. Not that Pitt did not recognise that
the isolation of Great Britain was a serious danger, but with admirable self-restraint he saw that there were more important things
than alliances and the recovery of our prestige abroad. In a strong
Ministry, annual surpluses, a diminishing debt, restored credit and
confidence lay the surest basis of a successful foreign policy. He
was perfectly right. Great Britain found allies without difficulty
when her alliance was worth the having, and the door for a new
departure was opened by the success of the French Commercial
Treaty. Yet a spirited foreign policy was far from Pitt's wishes.
Peace was necessary to complete the convalescence into which Great
Britain by 1787 had been sedulously nursed, and the identification
of our interests with the preservation of European peace is the keynote of his action. The Prime Minister's suspicion and caution as
to all but the most carefully safeguarded engagements are enforced
in despatch after despatch. Our foreign relations are watched with
the eye of an anxious financier. Like Walpole, Pitt desired a
foreign policy that would prove a remunerative investment, an
aid to retrenchment, not a source of incalculable and unproductive
expenditure.

Three different systems—the Bourbon Family Compact, the Bourbon-Habsburg Alliance, the *entente* (since 1781) between the Emperor Joseph II. and the Tsarina Catherine—governed the European
situation; and outside them stood Frederick the Great, watching
the Emperor, determined to keep the line between Berlin and St.
Petersburg open, and coldly hostile to England. At London a

British system to counterbalance the formidable Bourbon alliances was regarded as absolutely necessary. One school of diplomatists would have created it by an understanding with Prussia, another by weaning Austria from France and a consequential agreement with Russia. In either case the Minor States—Holland, Sweden, Denmark—might be attracted into the new combination. Carmarthen at the Foreign Office shared to the full the traditional fear of ubiquitous French intrigues against Great Britain. In every European event he read the mysterious wire-pulling of relentless Bourbon hands. But up to 1786 Carmarthen's counter-efforts produced little. By making common cause with Russia and Denmark, French diplomacy in Sweden was checked, but the direct overtures to Russia, Prussia, and Austria were a failure. The attempt of Joseph II. to reverse the Barrier Treaty of 1715 and open the Scheldt to navigation—a policy that vitally affected British interests and threatened to involve Europe in war—was foiled curiously enough by the French at Versailles. Thanks to the Treaty of Fontainebleau, Nov., 1785 the Emperor renounced his demands, and an alliance between the Dutch and France, ominous for Great Britain, rewarded Vergennes' mediation. Another cardinal project of the Emperor's, the exchange of the Austrian Netherlands for the Electorate of Bavaria, was checkmated by the League of Princes (Fürstenbund), under the auspices of Prussia. George III., indeed, joined the League as Elector of Hanover, but his adhesion in no way committed Great Britain, and his first approval of the scheme was given without the knowledge of his British Ministers, a remarkable instance of the anomalous dual position of the English Crown. But the hopes that this step would lead to a renewal of an Anglo-Prussian understanding proved vain ; and further overtures to St. Petersburg only produced the insulting condition that in the interests of Catherine's ally, Austria, the Fürstenbund must first be given up, to which George III. very rightly refused to listen.

Aug. 17.
1786   The death of Frederick the Great and the rapid development of a crisis in the Netherlands ushered in a momentous change. The Republican party, "the Patriots," aided by French gold and diplomacy, were bent on compelling the Stadholder, William V., whose wife was the sister of the new Prussian King, Frederick William II., to resign his hereditary office. If they succeeded, Holland would become a province of France in all but name. The maintenance of

the Dutch constitution was, therefore, a prime principle in our diplomacy, and Harris, our representative at the Hague, an earnest advocate of an anti-Bourbon system, had long been striving to defeat the Republicans. Summoned to London where he explained May, 1787 his views, he was liberally provided with secret service funds. The arrest of the Princess Stadholder by a Republican free corps at the June 25 frontier fired her brother at Berlin to demand reparation and an apology, failing which he would intervene with armed force. Pitt, who had now taken over the direction in foreign policy, worked hard for a joint mediation, while his agents, Ewart at Berlin, Harris at the Hague, zealously strove for an Anglo-Prussian understanding. War loomed into sight, as the French announced their readiness to support the Dutch. The Court at Berlin vacillated; but after the outbreak of the war in the East which made Austrian aid to France impossible, the Prussian troops crossed the frontier and the Republicans collapsed. Harris succeeded in getting the Dutch demand for French aid rescinded, and Montmorin at Paris, hampered by bankrupt finances and pressed by British diplomacy, agreed to abandon his previous promise of aid to the Republicans. The Stadholdership was re-established, the Orange party was triumphant, and the Court of Versailles was so publicly discredited that Napoleon reckoned its humiliation as one of the causes of the Revolution. Very shortly the separate Treaties of England and Prussia with the Dutch were converted into a triple alliance which April 15, brought Great Britain into a powerful European combination and 1788 marked the end of her perilous isolation. The credit was not Aug. 13 wholly Pitt's. Harris had fully earned the peerage which made him Lord Malmesbury; but it was Pitt's first big international problem, and he had solved it with the first big diplomatic success that British statesmanship had won on the Continent since Chatham and the Seven Years' War.

Domestic events once more absorbed the Minister's energies. The proposals in 1787 and 1789 to repeal the Test and Corporation Acts were supported by Fox, but opposed by Pitt and two-thirds of the episcopal bench, and rejected. In 1787, and again in 1791 and 1792, the indefatigable Wilberforce, aided by Clarkson and Sharp, and the newly-founded Society for the Abolition of the Slave Trade, found eloquent support from Pitt, Fox, and Burke. But the opposition of the King, of powerful members of the

21

Cabinet, such as Thurlow and Dundas, and the strength of the mercantile interest in a lucrative traffic, prevailed.   Even Dundas's compromise, providing for gradual abolition, proved illusory, thanks to the obstructive tactics of the Upper House, aided by the Bishops and the Crown.   Though Pitt became lukewarm, Wilberforce and his allies kept pegging away, but it was not till 1807 that the dying Fox drove the business through.   A further instalment of relief to Roman Catholics, conceding freedom of worship and education, was passed in 1791, and here Pitt and Fox were at one, though Fox would have considerably extended the concessions.

But on the Regency question of 1788 the two leaders were set in the sharpest antagonism.   Unfortunately the exalted position of the heir to the throne and the influence exercised by his conduct and character make it impossible to omit altogether the unedifying chapter of his personal relations with his parents. George, Prince of Wales, born in 1762, unquestionably had considerable abilities and a singular personal charm that exercised a powerful spell on the men and women of his intimate circle.   The Phœbus Apollo of dandyism, he won for himself the strange title of the First Gentleman in Europe, one that in this case surely parodies to perfection the qualities required from gentle blood. Apart from his undoubted capacity to pose as a princely Turveydrop, it is difficult to detect in his character or conduct a single lovable trait or worthy feature.   A finished rake—his mistresses were as numerous and varied as those of Charles II.—a drunkard, a spendthrift and a gambler, he was also an undutiful and ungrateful son ; a traitor alike to his friends and to the women whom he dishonoured ; the vindictive and faithless husband of the unhappy girl, Princess Caroline of Brunswick, condemned in 1795 to be his wife. He posed as a Whig from perverse opposition to his father rather than from serious conviction, and his alliance with the Opposition was a serious stain on the Whigs and their leaders, Fox, Sheridan, and Moira.   As Regent, his championship of Toryism discredited the principles of the party to which he deserted in 1810, and he succeeded as a ruler in making himself, not unjustly, the most unpopular sovereign for two centuries, and in reducing the prestige of the monarchy to its nadir.   From first to last his career is an epitome of unsavoury scandal, and his personal influence wrought infinite moral mischief and conferred no compensating benefit on any class of society in the kingdom.

In 1787 he was deeply in debt; moreover, two years earlier Dec. 21 (December 21st, 1785) he had privately married a widow, Mrs. 1785 Fitzherbert. This marriage was a fraud on an honourable woman, for it was invalid under the Royal Marriage Act, and, even if valid, as his "wife" was a Roman Catholic it incapacitated the Prince from inheriting the throne. Fox, however, was deluded into denying publicly in the House of Commons that the marriage had taken place, and then Sheridan was instructed to contradict, unintelligibly enough, Fox. It is heartily to be wished that the rupture which this prevaricating trickery brought about between Fox and the Prince had been permanent. But it served its purpose. The royal debts were arranged for by Pitt and Dundas; nearly £200,000 were voted, and the King added £10,000 from the Civil List to his son's income. A temporary reconciliation followed, the Prince agreeing to a pledge in the royal message to Parliament that he would not get a second time into debt—a pledge which, of course, he had no intention of keeping; and in 1795 his debts amounted to £650,000.

The question of a regency became urgent when, on November 5th, 1788, George III., whose health had been failing, was prostrated by a serious attack of insanity. Pitt's policy in the crisis was governed by three main considerations: the certainty that the Prince of Wales would dismiss the Ministry and summon Fox to office; a belief, supported by the best physician, Dr. Willis, that the King would recover; the desirability of limiting the Regent's powers. Against Fox, who boldly asserted that the Prince of Wales had an inherent right to assume the prerogatives of the Crown, Pitt maintained that it was for Parliament to nominate the person and define the powers of the Regent. He thus "un-Whigged" his rival and appeared as the champion of the Legislature against the prerogative. But this position involved some grave constitutional difficulties. After much bitter controversy a Bill was brought in establishing the Prince of Wales as Regent with restricted powers, while the royal assent to the measure was to be provided by placing the Great Seal under Commission, with directions to affix it when the Bill had passed both Houses. This grotesque and clumsy fiction enabled a parliamentary majority to vamp up a puppet and phantom royalty, clothed with authority solely to obey the dictates of its creators. Fortunately the recovery of the King by March 10th, 1789, rendered the procedure unnecessary, though the fiction had necessarily been employed to open and validate the Parliament in which the Regency Bill was introduced. The Irish Legislature, with wiser judgment, avoided the mistakes made in England by adopting an address which simply invited the Prince to assume the Regency without restrictions; it thereby provided the requisite legal machinery for any subsequent and limiting legislation on the Regent's powers.

The parliamentary episode bristles with suggestive points. On the purely constitutional issue Fox certainly had the worst of it; and as usual his tactical blunders and verbal indiscretions, skilfully utilised by his rival, made him his own worst enemy. But if Pitt is not to be blamed for straining the machinery of the Constitution to retain power, it is difficult to condemn Fox for his eagerness to regain it. Burke's violence and lapses from taste in debate marred, but did not destroy, the strength of the Whig argument against Pitt's methods for providing the royal assent to the proposed legislation. The Ministerial lawyers had in fact shown how a disputable legal fiction could be extended to supersede the Crown, and had established a dangerous and unnecessary precedent, by which the monarchy itself could in the name, and by the process, of law be legislated out of existence by a Parliament determined to carry its point. Unquestionably, Whig society was bitterly disappointed at the King's recovery. Fox and his colleagues were so confident of their return to the Treasury Bench that the list of the new Ministry was already drawn up. And had the King remained insane the certainty of the transfer testifies to the extraordinary power of the Crown as late as 1788 in making and keeping a Minister in office.[1] An exchange of Fox for Pitt might have proved beneficial in many ways, but the country was mercifully spared the substitution of George, Prince of Wales, even for George III. Pitt's popularity was much enhanced by the firmness with

[1] A Private Paper of May 1st, 1788, gives an analysis of the Commons. " The Party of the Crown, *i.e.* all those who would probably support His Majesty's Government under any Minister not peculiarly unpopular," are placed at 185; "the independent or unconnected members " at 108; the Foxites, 138, and the Pittites at 52, of whom only 20 would be returned if Pitt resigned. Pitt's precarious parliamentary position if the support of the Crown were withdrawn is therefore intelligible.

which he fought for his Sovereign and the privileges of the Queen, and his conduct earned the deep gratitude of the King. After 1789 there comes into his relations with George III. a new note of cordial personal esteem. Pitt, too, had discovered the treachery of Thurlow. The Lord Chancellor arranged with the Prince and Sheridan to retain his post by ratting from his colleagues and betraying Cabinet secrets; and though Fox detested the compact, made in his absence, it was impossible to go back upon it. But with the King's recovery Thurlow re-ratted. His appeal to God to forget him if he forgot the King's favours drew from Wilkes the just retort: " Forget you! He will see you damned first!" But not until 1792 was Thurlow properly punished. The Chancellor's opposition in the Lords over two sessions to Fox's Libel Bill, which had been supported by Pitt, coupled with an attack on his chief's finance, caused Pitt to insist on his dismissal. The supremacy of the Prime Minister in the Cabinet and the principle of collective agreement on fundamental political issues were thus enforced by a salutary lesson. After six months' delay Thurlow's place was taken by Lord Loughborough (Wedderburn), who now definitely threw in his lot with the Tory party.

Foreign policy, disturbed by the Regency crisis, again became prominent. Pitt, profoundly convinced that war would shatter the results of years of patient work (from 1788-92 the budget showed an average surplus of half a million), was determined to use the Triple Alliance to maintain peace. It was a defensive not an offensive weapon, and Pitt resisted steadily the efforts of the restless and vacillating Court at Berlin, no longer guided by the selfish and lynx-eyed patriotism of Frederick the Great, to exploit the treaty of 1788 for the aggrandisement of the allies. The increasing and substantial divergence of aim between Berlin and London finally by 1792 drove England and Prussia apart. In the North, Sweden, allied with the Turks, had invaded Finland. Invaded in turn by Denmark, and repulsed by Russia, Gustavus III. was saved by the intervention of Prussia and Great Britain, who compelled Denmark to accept terms that maintained the balance of power in the Baltic. The failure of Joseph's Turkish War, and revolts in Bohemia, Hungary, and the Netherlands, caused by the Emperor's passion for precipitate and logical reform, offered Prussia a splendid opportunity. Frederick William caressed a comprehen-

sive scheme for recognising the insurgent Belgians, uniting them
with Holland, restoring Galicia to Poland and annexing the Polish
Danzig and Thorn to Prussia.   Pitt was willing to use the Triple
Alliance to impose a peace on the basis of the *status quo*, but refused
to commit England to offensive operations beyond her strict treaty
Feb. 20,   obligations.   The death of Joseph II. left the Austrian State in the
1790   most dangerous dilemma she had faced since the accession of Maria
Theresa.   Had Prussia, as Herzberg desired, broken from the Triple
Alliance and struck for her own hand, Pitt could not have prevented
a general conflagration.   But the new Emperor, Leopold II., was a
consummate diplomatist, and Frederick William II. could not make
up his mind.   British influence at Berlin was small ; Prussia was
out-manœuvred by the Emperor and sullenly agreed to the terms
July, 1790 agreed on at the Conference of Reichenbach.   The Austrian
1791   Netherlands were restored to Habsburg rule ; the Treaty of Sistova
made peace between Leopold and the Turks ; Catherine, fearing a
joint Anglo-Prussian intervention on behalf of Sweden, concluded
peace at Werela with Gustavus III.   Pitt's policy of peace had so
far prevailed.   It only remained to coerce Russia into the acceptance of a similar settlement.

Pitt's hands in these complicated transactions had been partly
tied by a short, sharp, and decisive dispute with Spain.   The Span-
April, 1789 iards had evicted a British settlement at Nootka Sound, hauled
down the British flag, and made the British settlers prisoners.[1]
Pitt peremptorily rejected the Spanish claim of previous discovery
on the ground that not discovery but settlement conferred a valid
title, and demanded an apology and adequate reparation.   Appeals
to our allies the Dutch and Prussia, the equipment of a big fleet
under Howe, and a vote of credit for a million proved that the
Prime Minister was in earnest.   Florida Blanca in turn appealed
to the hereditary ally, France.   But the Revolution had altered
the situation, and the National Assembly rejected the Family for a
National Compact and was both reluctant and unable to give adequate assistance.   Florida Blanca had no alternative but to submit ;
and the convention of October 28th, 1791, secured for England
complete reparation, the retention of Nootka Sound, and the separation of Spain from France.   The retention of the Sound secured for the Canada of the future a window, little valued at the
time, into the Pacific of profound importance to her national and

[1] See Appendix XVIII.

economic expansion. Contemporary opinion, indeed, prized more highly the dissolution of the Family Compact, so long a nightmare to our Foreign Office. But the laurels of this fresh triumph for Pitt were sadly tarnished by an unexpected rebuff in the East.

Catherine, successful in her Turkish War, was determined to extend her position along the northern littoral of the Black Sea, and to extort Ochakov and the line of the Dniester as the price of victory. Alike the suggested Anglo-Prussian mediation and a peace based on the *status quo* were rejected as inadmissible. Pitt, anxious to maintain the integrity of the Ottoman Empire against the menacing Russian expansion and to save Prussia from a second disappointment, convinced himself that coercion, so successful elsewhere, would be equally effective at St. Petersburg. An ulti- March 27 matum was sent to the Tsarina. But Pitt had seriously miscalcu- 1791 lated every element in the situation—the importance of Ochakov, the temper of Catherine and of public opinion at home. The Cabinet was sharply divided; Fox and Burke, supported by the mercantile classes, convincingly attacked the Minister's policy, and Catherine, well aware of English feeling, refused to give way. It must be either war or surrender to her demands, and Pitt surrendered. The ultimatum was hurriedly countermanded, and the April 16, definitive Peace of Jassy, made without the mediation of the 1791 allies, gave Russia the line of the Dniester. Jan., 1792

It was an important episode in every way for Pitt. The personal prestige of the Prime Minister was seriously shaken. The haste with which the surrender was made suggested truly enough that the Minister attached more importance to the retention of office than to the maintenance of his principles. The resignation of the Foreign Secretary, the Duke of Leeds (Carmarthen), whose place was taken by Lord Grenville,[1] revealed the rupture in the Cabinet. The Triple Alliance was silently broken up and buried. Frederick William, disgusted at the double "desertion" of his ally, at Reichenbach and in the East, turned to Russia and Austria— thereby embarking on the policy which led to the Second Partition of Poland and the War of the Three Monarchies against Revolutionary France. But the quarrel with Russia has a historic importance of its own. It ushered in the modern phase of the Near Eastern Question in our foreign policy. The development of

---

[1] H. Dundas succeeded Grenville as Home Secretary.

British power in India, and the expansion of Russia into Europe and Asia were already transforming the geographical, strategic, and political features of the eighteenth century Eastern problem. Between the principles at issue in 1791 and those of 1853-54 and of 1876-78 exists a striking identity, while the modernity of the arguments employed in the debates by Pitt, Fox, and Burke will strike every student. Burke in particular anticipated the language of Gladstone and the modern Liberals. He protested against war on behalf of an anti-Christian, barbarous and alien race, whose partition or expulsion "bag and baggage" would be a public benefit. Fox, too, desired a close understanding with Russia in the interests of peace, our trade, and as a counter-balance to the Bourbon system in the West. War with Russia on behalf of the Ottoman Empire, he argued, almost in the historic language of a great modern Foreign Minister, was "to put our money on the wrong horse". Pitt, on the other hand (unlike his father who was a Pro-Russ), opposed the Whig point of view. He desired to stand for the integrity of the Turkish Empire as a bulwark against the establishment of a Slav Power, dominating the Black Sea and aiming at Constantinople, which would place it on the flank of our Mediterranean route to the East.

But at this point the significance of these issues was abruptly obliterated. Pitt was now summoned to deal with problems of foreign and domestic policy far more vast and complex than any that had yet been thrust upon him. The meeting of the Estates-General at Versailles on May 4th, 1789, had inaugurated a new era. With the spring of 1792 France and Europe had already crossed the threshold of the baffling labyrinth that for lack of a better name history has agreed to call the French Revolution.

NOTE.—For additional authorities see the Supplement to the Bibliography, pp. 550-552.

CHAPTER IV

THE INDUSTRIAL REVOLUTION[1]

A BRIEF summary of the capital features of the inner dynamic
evolution in the social and economic organisation of the
British State since 1760 is a necessary preliminary to the prolonged
struggle with Revolutionary and Napoleonic France. For the Industrial Revolution is the true prologue to the European upheaval.
Even a superficial comparison of the economic structure and needs
of Great Britain in 1792 with those of 1760 lays bare an astonishing qualitative and quantitative difference. Ignorance or misinterpretation of this difference partly accounted for the prevalent
continental view that Great Britain in 1783 was a decadent Power ;
whereas the increasing supremacy and volume of our trade was the
result rather than the cause, as was commonly supposed, of a vitality whose roots lay deep in national character, organisation, and
resources. By 1793 England was already a generation in advance
of the Continent in the science, machinery, and processes of production, and of the distribution and organisation of industry, while the
coincident reaction affected the whole political and social fabric.
The forces that had brought a new Great Britain into existence
were continually operating in the ensuing epoch of unrelieved war,
nor were the inevitable evils of the transition from the commercial
to the industrial state as yet intolerable. Shifted and aggravated
by the absorbing strain of the struggle, they were only fully revealed
in the era of suffering, dislocation, and repression that would have
marched to revolution had it not been appeased by Reform in 1832.

Changes that affected the tenure and cultivation of the soil
came first. The continued advance of scientific farming and the
enclosures are partly connected, partly independent. The work
begun by Townshend and Jethro Tull was continued by numerous
public-spirited and progressive landlords, notable amongst whom

[1] See Appendix XIX.

were Coke of Holkham, Rockingham, Bedford, and the King himself. The cultivation of artificial grasses, of clover and rye, of seeds, beans, potatoes and roots, of horse-hoeing, scientific and economic ploughing, the study of soils and manures, and the rotation of crops (*e.g.* a five-course husbandry) advanced steadily. The introduction of leases with conditions as to the methods of farming, of improved machinery, and of the expanding market provided by the growth of population stimulated powerfully the application of capital and the increase of profits on its application. In another direction, the stock-breeding experiments at Dishley in Leicester-

1725-95 shire made "the Leicester long-horns" and "the new Leicesters" famous in Europe, and placed Robert Bakewell in the front of the agricultural pioneers. His object especially was to breed sheep as meat-producing rather than as wool-producing animals, and his success was astonishing. Competent experts have pronounced that his principles and example wrought a veritable revolution in the graziers' art and laid the foundation of the flocks and herds that brought wealth to their breeders and food to an expanding nation. Amongst the many writers and workers Arthur Young, himself

1741-1820 curiously enough a failure as a farmer, stands out *facile princeps* as the indefatigable missionary of the new age. His encyclopædic pen instructed his own generation and bequeathed to the historical student a series of pictures, *bien documentés*, as vivid as those of Defoe, and reinforced by the thirst for knowledge and saturated with the personality of a traveller, the rival of John Wesley in zeal and the faith that can move mountains. The establishment of the Board of Agriculture in 1793, under Sir John Sinclair and Young himself, is an event of economic and historic importance which fitly crowned the labours of three generations.

The enclosure movement, a topic of perplexing controversy at the time, is still complicated by disputes as to the interpretation of evidence not yet exhausted by the researcher. It was not a new feature. Much land had been enclosed in the sixteenth century, and the process had continued since the Tudor epoch with varying degrees of languor and activity. Hanoverian England witnessed a marked revival, accentuated in the last half of the eighteenth century to an astonishing extent, for which various causes may be held responsible. The consolidation of small into large farms and estates, due partly to social reasons, independent of the advance in agricultural science, appealed with special force to the progressive agriculturist anxious to reduce the cost of production and benefit by the law of increasing returns from scientific agriculture on the large scale. The wasteful farming and the very existence of the common fields system were the most serious obstacles to the illuminated empiricism of the new school. The demand of the new England in process of creation for a great increase in the quality and quantity of food absolutely necessitated the extension and improvement of cultivation and the introduction of new methods and new conditions. Even if there had been no greedy landlords and no new agricultural science it is tolerably certain that the industrial revolution would have in time swept away the common fields and the mediæval village community which they typified and perpetuated. In this historic change, two different kinds and three different processes of enclosure must be distinguished. The enclosure of commonable waste, implying the extension of cultivation, is distinct from the enclosure of arable common fields, which generally, but not necessarily, led to a more intensive and scientific tillage, or to the conversion of arable into pasture. The change could be effected either by the common consent of the co-owners, or by the buying out of commoners' rights by a single purchaser or group of purchasers, ratified in each case by the Court of Chancery or by royal licence, or brought about by Act of Parliament. The percentage of enclosures effected by the first two methods is one of the most difficult to determine, for the evidence and statistics are either not forthcoming, or incomplete, or open to various interpretations. The statistics of enclosures accomplished by legislation, however, are very impressive. Between 1702 and 1750 there were passed 112, between 1750 and 1810, 2921 such Acts, including the General Act of 1801, and affecting approximately about 2,500,000 acres of common fields, and 1,750,000 acres of waste. Nor do these figures, of course, include enclosures achieved by means other than legislation. Yet in 1794 it was calculated that the open field system still obtained in 4500 out of 8500 parishes. It has been pointed out that there is a rough but calculable connection between the price of wheat and the number of Enclosure Acts in the century. One or two other features are also worth noting. There are no Acts for Kent, only one for Essex. In Lancashire, Devon, and Cornwall only commonable waste is legislatively enclosed, and the process is virtually completed by 1793.   To a large extent in Durham, Cumberland, Westmoreland, Northumberland, the counties on the Welsh border and Hertfordshire, enclosure took place at different dates without recourse to Parliament.   Hence the " Parliamentary belt " broadly covers a band from north-east to south-west, *i.e.* a line drawn from Southampton to Norwich, from Bristol to Durham and from Bristol to Portland, in which the enclosure is mainly, but not wholly, an eighteenth century movement, continuing until 1845. While the magnitude of the change is not in dispute, the results cannot be summarised without many modifications in detail, and are still subject to the collation of future research with the older evidence.   That as a whole enclosure was inevitable, the indispensable condition and the result of more scientific and economic agriculture ; that in the long run it added enormously to the productive resources of the nation ; that without it the new population could not have been fed, the industrial revolution stimulated, and the strain of the great war endured, is generally accepted.   But unless we set aside the testimony of witnesses so competent as Young, Eden, and Marshall, corroborated by details from many sources and localities, the revolution was, perhaps inevitably, accompanied by much suffering, and no little injustice to the small, weak, and poor commoner.   The rapidity and area of the change gave an undue advantage to the strong and the rich, the capitalist, the big landowner, the scientific reformer, intolerant of ignorance, obscurantism, or vested interests that barred the road to an increased totality of national wealth and to scientific progress.   This inference is no doubt most applicable to the enclosure of arable common fields.   Enclosure of commonable waste, tantamount to reclamation, was for the most part beneficial, creative of employment and organised production, and more usually than not resulted in an increase of small holdings.   Yet it would be unfair to suggest that the suffering and injustice in most cases were the work of landlords, capitalists, lawyers, deliberately preying on the poor and helpless.   The pathos of the new hedges and the deserted village does not lie in the wickedness of the strong but in the passive and unrecorded misery of the many, evicted or maimed by the community in the cause of the community, in its remorseless march to a new life and a new order through the wreckage of the old.

In the industrial world three features are conspicuous : the number and variety of inventions, the substitution of machinery for human power, the transition to organised production on a large scale—*la grande industrie* of the modern epoch. These affected especially the textile trades, mining, iron and steel and hardware, and then reactively almost every form of manufacture. The second half of the century is the age of the inventors. Starting from the flying shuttle of John Kay, Paul and Wyatt's roller spinning, 1733 we pass to the spinning jenny of Hargreave, Arkwright's water 1738 1765 frame, Crompton's mule, Cartwright's power-loom, the wool- 1767 combing machines of Toplis, Hawskley and Wright, and Murray's im- 1788 proved spinning frame and carding engine, which are perhaps the 1790 1793 most striking in a long list ; while the application by Tennant of Glasgow of Scheele's and Berthollet's discovery of chlorine to the 1800 bleaching process, and Bell's machine for cylinder printing, contributed powerfully to the revolution in the cotton, linen, and, ultimately, the woollen manufactures. No less remarkable was the advance in metallurgy and mechanical engineering. The blast furnace of Smeaton at Roebuck's Carron Iron Works, the con- 1760 tinuous improvements made by three generations of Darbys at the famous Coalbrookdale Works, Huntsman's discovery for casting steel, are synchronous with the application by the brothers Cranage of the reverberatory furnace to smelting, and Henry Cort's patents for rolling iron, and for puddling, notable because a century's 1783 progress, if it has added much to our knowledge in metallurgical 1784 chemistry, has added little to the principles and methods of the inventors. Their discoveries, steadily improved by the brains and practical experience of numerous competitors, achieved one transcendant result. By enabling pit coal to be substituted for charcoal as the fuel of the furnace, they added at a stroke the extraordinary mineral resources of British coalfields to the productive wealth of the nation, and called into existence a new, if a black, world in South Wales, the Midlands and Northern Counties of England, and the southern basin of the Clyde. Coal mining, iron and steel, no less than the textiles, became the reinforced cement that bonded into a cohesive structure the new industrial empire of Great Britain.

In the china and earthenware trades Derby, Chelsea, Worcester, and Birmingham have the first place. Planché, Dunsbury, Wall,

Sadler created flourishing centres of activity; but the master of them all was the modest and indefatigable Josiah Wedgwood. His works at Burslem and then at Etruria are a red rubric in the history of pottery and porcelain. Great as a worker and organiser, he was greater in his artistic intuition for quality and design. A study of the Wedgwood collection in the Birmingham Museum only emphasises the debt due to his eye for form, and his determination always to combine the best material with the skill of the best workmen. It will be noticed too that in this wonderful epoch Great Britain owed little to foreign help. The most striking results are the products of British brains and energies; and in the long list the place of honour belongs to James Watt, one of the finest and most fertile scientific minds that our country has produced. The invention by which he transformed the atmospheric machine of Newcomen and others into the steam engine was theoretically completed in 1765. But it was not till Watt's partner-

1774

ship with Matthew Boulton, the founder of the Soho Works, that the discovery was turned to practical use. The alliance of a genius in mechanics with a genius in business inaugurated the age of steam. The consequences of the invention were as remarkable as the invention itself. Improved by Watt himself with the assistance of such able coadjutors as John Rennie, Pickard and Murdock, steam power was rapidly applied to, and finally conquered, the industrial world. Steam pumps and hammers were followed by steam mills for sawing, sugar, flour, silk, cotton and wool. By 1800 the new power had triumphed, and it was only a question of time when it would be applied with similar success to transport by land and water, and take a new form in the steam train and the steam ship. Nor is it uninteresting to remember that the steam engine and *The Wealth of Nations* were both gifts to the nation from Glasgow University. The grant of a laboratory for his experiments to the one genius, and the professorial chair of the other, enabled the two greatest Scotsmen of the eighteenth century to be the pioneers of a twin revolution in the world of mechanics and the world of thought.

For twenty years after 1760 the conditions of communication and transport were deplorably bad. Turnpikes had been authorised as early as 1663, but except in a few cases covered by special Acts the making and maintenance of roads were left to the parishes and grossly neglected. Arthur Young's vivid description of his

experiences appears incredible to modern readers; but with the
extension of the home and foreign markets the peremptory need of
replacing " what it would be a prostitution of language to call turnpikes" by efficient lines of communication brought about a steady
improvement. From 1760-1774, 452 Acts were passed, and in 1773
a general measure affecting the public highways came on to the
statute-book. Men like Blind Jack of Knaresborough, an uneducated but practical genius, were pioneers; but the application of
engineering science as distinct from a felicitous empiricism came
much later with Telford, Macadam, and their school. To commerce,
the cheap transport of goods in bulk was more important even than
sound roads—safe from highwaymen and smugglers. The need was
met by the making of canals. It is characteristic and discreditable
that until 1759 England, unlike France and Holland, had ignored
the value of artificial waterways. The famous Bridgewater Canal,
from Worsley to Manchester, however, constructed by James
Brindley for the Duke of Bridgewater, proved at once a commercial
success, and was promptly connected with an extension to Runcorn,
thus linking the growing Liverpool into the system. It is notice
able that the primary object of the canal was to bring coals to
manufacturing and distributing centres. Brindley, like Blind
Jack, was wholly uneducated, but in sheer ability he has seldom
been surpassed. His connection with the Duke of Bridgewater is
another striking example of the invaluable help given by enlightened members of the aristocracy to the application of science to
industry. Brindley planned in all some 350 miles of canals, including the Grand Trunk, which connected Runcorn with the
Humber and brought Birmingham and the Potteries into touch
with Northern, Eastern, and Southern England. From 1770 onwards the passion for canal making anticipated the feverish railway
mania of the next century; and by 1800 hundreds of miles had
been completed, with benefits to trade as difficult to estimate as to
gainsay.

The results of these extraordinary and many-sided activities
furnish material embarrassingly rich for analysis. Statistics are
valuable in this connection because they supply the numerical precision and graphic illustration necessary for grasping the significance
of the forces in operation. In 1720 our exports were valued at
£6,910,899; in 1760 at £14,694,970; in 1800 at £34,381,617; in

1815 at £58,624,550. At the same dates the imports are figured at £6,090,083, £9,832,802, £28,257,781, £32,987,396. In 1781, as compared with 1764, the imports of cotton show no increase, being under 4,000,000 lb. ; in 1800 they are 56,000,000 lb. ; in 1815 nearly 100,000,000 lb. In 1740, 17,350 tons of pig-iron were produced ; in 1788, 68,300 tons ; in 1796, 125,079 tons ; in 1806, 256,206 tons. In 1760, 471,241 tons of British shipping were cleared outwards ; in 1800, 1,269,329 tons. And the numerical tests for every one of our staple industries tell a similar marvellous tale. It is unfortunately impossible to measure with the same precision the volume of home and internal trade, but the evidence available suggests that its increase was even greater in percentage than that in the foreign trade proper. This gigantic advance in national wealth and productive power explains how the country raised and endured a National Debt which leaped from £130,000,000 in 1760 to £250,000,000 in 1783, and was swollen by more than £600,000,000 during the great war; while the permanent charge on the public revenue rose from £4,750,000 in 1763 to £30,500,000 at the peace of 1815. The statistics of population in England and Wales can only be given approximately before the census of 1801; but it has been calculated by experts that from 1720 to 1760 the increase was about 1,250,000, *i.e.* from 5,500,000 to 6,750,000. The figures for 1801 work out at just under 9,000,000, and by that time the full effect of the industrial changes is felt; and in 1811 we have census totals of 10,000,000, and in 1821 12,000,000, an addition of over 3,000,000 in twenty years compared with 2,250,000 and 1,250,000 in the two previous periods of forty years respectively. It is not surprising, therefore, that the views of thinkers exhibit a remarkable change also. To the previous fear of depopulation succeeded the fear of over-population. The Napoleonic era in England was not concerned with the deficiency of men ; the men were there ; and the problem was how to secure them for the service of the State ; but it was seriously concerned with the problem of food supply. The figures correlated to the statistics of food production enable us to understand how the famous essay of Malthus, first published in 1798 and republished in 1802, fermented in the brain of every economist and politician, and ultimately coloured till it warped the public mind.

But some further disengagement of the figures is necessary to

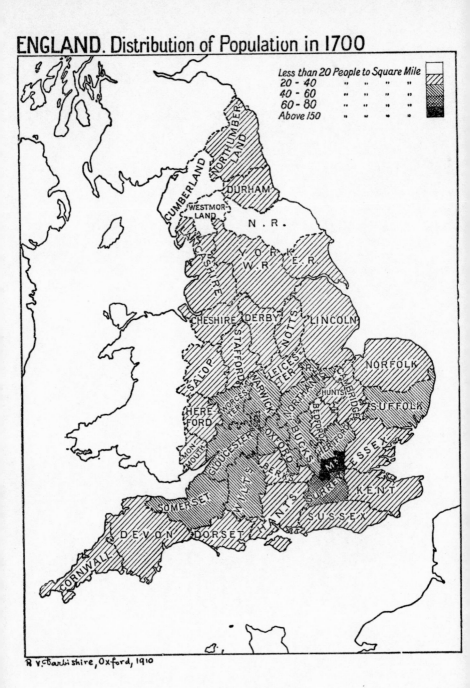

ENGLAND. Distribution of Population in 1700

Less than 20 People to Square Mile
20 – 40   ,,   ,,   ,,   ,,
40 – 60   ,,   ,,   ,,   ,,
60 – 80   ,,   ,,   ,,   ,,
Above 150   ,,   ,,   ,,   ,,

R V. Darbishire, Oxford, 1910

interpret the full significance of the growth in population. An
economic statistician, indeed, might have predicted *a priori* from
the industrial changes the geographical distribution and stratification of the movement in population. A comparison of a population map for 1700 with that of to-day reveals two wholly different
Englands. In 1700 no county outside Middlesex and Surrey has
on the average more than sixty inhabitants to the square mile ; and
the zone of chief density lies in a triangle, the apex of which is
the Wash and the base is the Bristol Channel. But in 1801, outside
the London area, Lancashire, the West Riding, and Staffordshire
are the most thickly populated, and the map as a whole reveals in
distribution and relative density the same features as that for 1901.
In both cases population has tended to concentrate in two areas;
the counties immediately affected by the monster growth of London
and the counties west and north of a line drawn from the mouth of
the Severn and the Humber, *i.e.* the districts directly affected by
the new industries. But while for 1801-1901 the distribution is
simply an accentuation of accomplished results, for the eighteenth
century it was a revolution. The change had not begun in 1701,
it is a faintly traceable tendency in 1751, it is completed by 1801.
The true commencement and the consummation lie in the thirty
years after 1770, rather than in the half-century after 1750. Quite
recent modern history provides an approximate parallel in the
internal evolution of the German Empire after 1870 ; but for the
eighteenth-century England the change was neither foreseen nor
could have been predicted in 1750. And both the character and
results of the transformation that Great Britain underwent in
little more than a single generation were and remain unprecedented and unique. The new population in its new distribution,
which upset the long-established balance of South as against North,
was also a different population in methods of life. In 1801 we are
already far from the economic picture pieced together with such
convincing and painstaking detail in Adam Smith's classical masterpiece. The influx from the country into the towns, the concentration of men and women in towns is all the more marked because
so many of the centres are new towns. London retains, it is true,
its marked ascendency, and remains the capital in every sense ; but
Norwich has sunk from the third to the tenth place by 1801, while
Liverpool, Manchester, Birmingham, Sheffield, Leeds, Oldham,

22

Stafford, Bradford, Burnley, are the creations of the industrial revolution as conspicuously as Glasgow and Lanarkshire.

The new England must be sought in Lancashire and the West Riding, in the coal-pits of Durham, Northumberland, and South Wales, in the Black Country and the Potteries. The industrial town partly creates, is partly created by, the industrial area. The division of labour, the concentration of population followed inevitably the localisation and distribution of the raw material of manufactures. Men and women, more and more penned into the towns, are dependent for their earnings not on the sun and rain, on the soil and seasons of the home-land as was the England of 1701, but on the brains of engineers, the commercial capacity of capitalists, on imports from East and West, on the bowels of the earth, and on specialised skill and mechanical powers. Three things they must have or perish—the raw material of their trade, food, and expanding markets. Every year the application of machinery and motor power, first water and then steam, stimulated enterprise on the large scale, and increased the profits of scientific organisation. The volume of the product outstripped the most sanguine estimates. Every new invention facilitated the rate at which the total output could be increased, while it demanded a corresponding organisation for distribution, exchange, and consumption. The object of the British manufacturer was not so much to win or maintain a superiority—that had already been achieved—as to create and control markets and make their consumptive capacity as elastic as his capacity to produce. England as "a workshop for the world" involves a world ready to absorb the products of the workshop, and the crux of the problem did not lie in the certainties of production but in the potentialities of exchange and consumption. Hence the new economic data necessitated the rewriting of old and the addition of new chapters to the theory of Political Economy, and the school of Ricardo is born out of the school of Adam Smith. The centre of political gravity slowly shifts with the shifting of the centre of economic gravity. The political and economic needs and interests of a vast class of industrial workers and consumers, divorced from the land and linked with the capitalist and manufacturing *entrepreneur*, become more and more opposed to the interests of the landowner, which were not essentially identifiable with those of his tenants and the

ENGLAND. Distribution of Population in 1801

20-40	People	to Square Mile			
40-60	"	"	"	"	
60-80	"	"	"	"	
80-100	"	"	"	"	
100-150	"	"	"	"	
Above 150	"	"	"	"	

B.V.Darbishire, Oxford, 1910

landowners, the steady disappearance of the mediæval village community as a co-operative organisation for the cultivation of the soil. These were a social and economic revolution, of which the establishment of capitalist farming, and the evolution of the " free-hand," the landless-labourer working for wages were the direct consequences. A new landed interest, differently graded, with a different outlook and social economy was in process of creation. Its chief function was to provide more and more food ; its chief object to reap the profits of its combined duty and interest. Goldsmith's *Deserted Village* written in 1770, the Corn Law of 1773, conveniently mark a point of departure. The Legislature controlled by the landed interest desires to make England self-sufficing, but the effort breaks down. The theory of economic rent based on the law of diminishing returns, first clearly stated by Malthus, West, and Ricardo in 1815, is exemplified with depressing automatism. As population increases, the margin of cultivation is forced down and prices go steadily up. The need of increasing supplies can only be met by increased cost of production. The rise in rents keeps pace with the rise in prices, to the landlord's gain ; but the problem of pauperism, rooted in low wages and high prices, yearly becomes more formidable. The plausible principle that the interest of the landed classes as a whole was identifiable with the interest of the nation, once a comfortable axiom, became first an arguable assumption and then an acutely controversial hypothesis. And by 1804 fundamental problems of government have been formulated. Can agricultural science aided by the Legislature provide the necessary supply of food from home resources ? In the economy of Great Britain which is the more important, agriculture or manufactures ? Which is the more beneficial to the nation, cheap food or a lowered margin of cultivation and high rents ? Was the landed interest or the industrial interest to have the deciding voice in determining the principles and methods of the food supply for the future ? Hard questions, indeed, anxiously discussed in the debates over the Corn Law of 1815, and handed over unsolved to the next epoch.

The new industrial interest was coming to rest more and more surely on a new social economy. Since 1750 there had been a vast increase of capital, to which every element in the British State contributed. The political expansion of the empire since 1713, the

new markets across the seas, and the development of colonial possessions and tropical dependencies precede the Industrial Revolution.
The stability of the Whig Government, and the freedom of the
country from invasion, meant that England, unlike the Continental
States, was spared the periodic devastation of fixed capital, its consequent necessary replacement, and the hindrances to accumulation
that invasion brought with it.   Alike scientific agriculture and
the industrial advance demanded more and more capital, while
they provided the means for producing it.   The unanalysable but
invincible commercial spirit and aptitude, as difficult to account
for in its waxing and waning as the efflorescence of artistic genius
in a nation, but which are a more potent cause than fiscal systems
of success in commerce, are conspicuous in eighteenth-century England, particularly in the latter fifty years.   The character of our
citizens and the conditions of the epoch combined to focus the
energies of our race on the creation of wealth, and the openings for
profitable investment put a premium on saving.   We can broadly
measure the increase in wealth by the plain fact that the financing
of the agricultural and industrial revolution, and of the colossal
cost of eighteenth century wars, was accomplished from British
resources alone.   The marvel is not that the effort entailed suffering
and a cruel strain, but that it was successfully achieved at all.

The " capitalist " in the strict economic sense was no new ap-
parition.   Nor was industry working on a capitalistic basis new.
What is new is, first, the capitalist *entrepreneur*, primarily a manufacturer, not a moneyed man engaged in commerce, as Petty, Swift,
Bolingbroke understood the term ; secondly, the growth of a class
or order of capitalist *entrepreneurs ;* thirdly, the gradual domination
of industry by that class ; and, fourthly, the type of industrial organisation that he creates and the scale on which he applies it.   Richard
Arkwright is the incarnation of the new order.   He exploits the
brains of inventors, devises and controls the framework of industry
that will enable machinery to produce on a large scale a specialised
product, aided by a specialised division of labour.   To Adam Smith a
"manufacturer" was still a workman, working with his own hands in
his own home or workshop, with his own tools.   The manufacturer
of the Industrial Revolution is the modern master who provides
capital, owns his mill or factory, together with the machinery and
tools provided for his " hands," pays these " hands " wages, and

creates and maintains a market. Matthew Boulton, Josiah Wedgwood, John Wilkinson, Roebuck of Carron, the Crawshays of
Merthyr Tydvil, are the precursors of the Peels, Horrockses, Rad-
cliffes, Fields, Strutts—the names of the *élite* that can be extended
at pleasure—who made wealth for themselves and fame for English products. Already there are iron and cotton " kings ". The
business capacity, the higher command are the distinguishing
features of these captains. To their commercial genius and system
the British Empire and British trade owed as much as to the
inventors.

About 1780 England enters on the era of the factory whose
chimneys and grimy windows proclaim the localisation of manufacture and of the mill hands—male and female, adults and children.
With the new capitalist is born the new industrial proletariat, that
ever-increasing army of men and women who are wage-earners and
are a new stratum in the economic world. England had long known
the *ascriptus glebæ*, the rural " serf " ; but the Revolution that dissolved the link between the peasant and the soil forged the bond
that chained the wage-earner to the town. The *ascripti et ascriptae
urbi*, the urban " serfs " of labour are a new and portentous appari-
tion. Swollen by the dislocated peasantry, by the dying yeomanry,
by their own power to reproduce themselves in obedience to the increasing demand of capital and science for human hands and bodies,
they have come to stay, and to create another England. The slow
establishment of a reserve of labour that can be called up into the
working line when trade requires it, and be thrust back when it is
slack, the problems of unemployment and of the unemployable, are
not the least of the formidable economic enigmas forced on Government and humanity by the wage-earner and the Industrial Revolution. The Sphinx-like Zeitgeist that presides over the destinies of
empires and races imposes on each generation its peculiar riddles and
mutilates or destroys the race that fails to answer them correctly.

But if we can broadly trace three stages in the evolution—the
first of inventions and new processes, the second of hydraulic power
where industry is dependent on water, so that trades and their
workers have to be brought to the power, the third of iron and
steam where power can be brought to the workers—it is no less
true that these stages are not chronologically separate, but are
blended and, frequently, synchronous. Any picture grouping the

features, already emphasised, in a clear-cut symmetry would be false to the facts. In different trades, in different areas, under varying conditions and degrees of pressure, an amazing diversity, not uniformity, is the prevailing note of the economic phenomena. The old order did not perish at a blow. The new was not introduced complete by a few remarkable inventions and a group of organisers. The wool trade, for example, was transformed long after the cotton trade. In 1800 the common fields and the manorial economy still survived in appreciable quantities; home industries still flourished in many districts; the peasant cottager was not universally divorced from industry nor the industrial population from rural employments and the soil. But in the stream of tendencies and the competition between old and new every year saw one more stone in the ancient fabric dislodged, one more stone in the new fabric clamped in and cemented. Experts may reasonably differ as to the definition and duration of dawn or the twilight, but they agree in distinguishing between night and day, and one day and another. And on the England of 1800 the facts leave no doubt that there had dawned another day.

The face of the country was being altered. Enclosure brought the hedges and hedgerows that transformed our rural scenery to the familiar aspect of to-day—a land no longer open, but a variegated mosaic of squares and oblongs, varying in size and pattern and product, that to the unfamiliar eye suggest an unending series of gardens, on which the towns stealthily encroach. The new roads and the canals are made not for the traveller on pleasure bent, but to bring the places where men produce into communication with the centres of exchange, where men buy and sell—"the markets" of the political economist. Mark, too, how the roads and canals more and more lead to and from the urban workshops to and from the sea. From the sea the bulk of the raw material must come—to the sea much of the finished product will go. Seventeenth century England had learned and exploited the unrivalled strategic advantages for commerce that the geographical position and configuration of Great Britain conferred. Potential harbours, created by nature, are set on her seaboard—Glasgow, Liverpool, Bristol, Plymouth, Southampton, Dover, the estuaries of the Thames, the Humber, the Tyne, the Forth, the Clyde, and the Tay. Great Britain looks east into the North Sea and the Baltic, west and south across the waters of the Atlantic; she is the terminus to, or lies astride of, all the oceanic routes of Europe. Commerce, like war, is an affair of positions to start with, and the trend of population is at first to the strategic and focal centres of a distributing, exchanging, bartering, and carrying trade. Thus far to 1760. Then comes the revelation of the internal resources. Geological formation underpins geographical configuration. From 1770 onwards a student with a geological map and some knowledge of the economic data of the new trades might predict *a priori* not where the industrial centres may be, but where they must be. Many of these tracts are laid by nature on the sea coast—in South Wales, in Lancashire, in Durham and Northumberland, Ayrshire, Fife, and the Lothians—but if they are not, as in the coal strata of Lanarkshire, Derby and Stafford and Central Yorkshire, the sea is at hand and can be speedily reached by canals and good roads. In the whole of this humid island so bitten and fretted is the coast line, that it is impossible to place a pin-point anywhere on the map which is more than sixty miles, as the crow flies, from salt-water and the pathways of the deep. What that means for exports and imports needs no laboured exposition. But by 1800 we are dependent on both exports and imports, are marching to the conditions summed up by the modern statistician when he tells us that in the Great Britain of to-day for every minute of the year two tons are being landed or taken from our shores. And mark a difference. Prior to the Industrial Revolution the seaborne and carrying trades, with their invisible exports, are an expanding source of wealth, but are not indispensable. But already by 1801 they are an absolute necessity of bare existence. The cessation of our maritime trade and commerce meant the starvation of the population, and the starvation of every factory and furnace in the United Kingdom. Hence the loss of the command of the sea in the struggle with Napoleon involved not merely, as before, the political collapse caused by invasion, but the destruction by starvation in raw materials of the industrial State over which the imperial Crown ruled.

The county town of the old England has still its functions—it is the centre of the new agriculture, but it is either transformed by industry or it slips into subordination to the new towns which are springing up. These are not places which men and women inhabit from choice, but to live in, to work in, to produce, to exchange, to breed in and to die. They are stamped with the feudalism of industry. The territorial feudalism had dominated its dependants from castles and manor-houses; the industrial feudalism is seated among its factory chimneys, its warehouses, the roar and glare of blast furnaces, the undying throb of its machinery drowning the tramp of the wearied feet of men and women born tired and condemned to toil. Over the new towns—Manchester, Leeds, Sheffield, Birmingham—are hung the banners and scutcheon of the industrial lords, whose indentures and service bind a host more numerous, and more dependent than were ever sworn to the bear and ragged staff of a Nevile. The dull monotony of brick and stone, sweat and grime and smoke, unceasing noise, the stress of a competition whose cessation means ruin—these are the new towns. Is it surprising that many who had known the old cities before steam, coal, iron and the machines scrapped the old home life and the home industries, who had seen "the doghole of St. Helens" and the underground life of the coalpits, were ready to call the new towns porches of Hell, to cry on the housetops that it was merry in England before the new industry came up?

The new urban race living under new conditions is a new people. Its pleasures, hopes, fears, needs will be different, alike from those of the old cities, the old mercantilism, the old agriculture. It will create a new type of character, frame new values, hammer out from the dirt and roar of the teeming hives ideals of life and government bound to clash fiercely with the ideals inherited from a different past. It will ask for new creeds; it will demand a new economics; it will need and make a new literature. The action and reaction of the forces of the Industrial Revolution, transformed by or colliding with those of the French Revolution, starting from "The Village" of Crabbe, "The Cottar's 1783 Saturday Night" and "Holy Willie's Prayer" of Burns, to the 1785 and age of Wordsworth, Coleridge, Southey, Shelley, Keats, Byron, 1786 Scott, and Jane Austen, furnish an instructive chapter that merits the closest study. The rearrangement also of the elements of society, and the regrading of classes, buried deeper and deeper each day the legal framework of the old order. Industrialism, as modern experts now insist, involved a new drink-question. The problems of national physique, motherhood, childhood, education, pauperism, citizenship, happiness were old; but restated in the terms of a growing industrial democracy they became new, and with every decade more complex, urgent, and formidable.

A new element, iron, had passed into industrial and social life. John Wilkinson, the first of the great ironmasters, significantly insisted on being buried in an iron coffin. He saw that the iron age had come at last. With Darby of Coalbrookdale he had made in 1779 the first iron bridge (over the Severn), and he launched in 1790 the first iron vessel. John Rennie substituted gears of iron for the wooden gears at first used for Watt's engines. The correct use of iron or steel was the condition of all advance in engineering; and in the science of the mechanical engineer lay the foundation and future of almost every trade. To an unprecedented extent spinner, weaver, potter, shipbuilder, miner became dependent on his tools. For whether it was pins or petticoats, the diaphanous muslins of Madame Récamier and Les Merveilleuses, the dimity of Charles Surface's little milliner, the shawl and bonnet of Miss Elizabeth Bennett, a Bramah lock or a steam hammer, the tool was indispensable. Henceforth the nation that can make the best tools and be trained how to use them to their utmost capacity will become the workers and workshop of the world.

And by 1800 this new England is ready to be the workshop of the world. She is the sole industrial State in existence at that time. Judged by the test of types and structure, the France of Danton and Napoleon is the France of the Grand Monarque. But the British State that grappled with Napoleon is of a different type and structure to the State that grappled with Louis XIV. The Roi Soleil fought, as he said truly enough, with a nation of shopkeepers; Napoleon repeated the remark because he failed to see that he fought not with a nation of shopkeepers—a commercial State—but with a nation of capitalists and artisans—an industrial State. The French had no reason to fear the gold of Pitt; they had every reason to fear the factories of an Arkwright or the machinery of a Watt.

The dependence of productive industry and successful agriculture on science is another striking feature, and the stimulus and reaction that the needs of industry and the brains of the scientific researcher mutually exerted provide pregnant lessons. Physics, chemistry, metallurgy, geology, contributed both to the founding, renovation, and triumphant extension of our staple industries. In this case it is not a matter of purely British achievement; but Joseph Black, Joseph Priestley, John Canton, William Cavendish, Humphrey Davy, John Hutton, William Wollaston, William Smith, Thomas Young have their assigned and honourable places in the records of the physical sciences. So closely interlaced are the departments of intellectual activity that results apparently as useless as Bradley's discovery of the nutation of the axis of the earth and of the aberration of light may be ultimately momentous. 1748 To a nation, also, whose present and future lay on the water, the famous *Nautical Almanac* of 1767 was worth many ships and men. How much of "useless" astronomy and "academic" mathematics was not squeezed into its tables and helped Jervis to win at St. Vincent and Nelson at Trafalgar? The *Naval Tactics* of an Edinburgh merchant, John Clerk of Eldin, the son of one distinguished Scottish judge and the father of another, an old gentleman with a strange passion for sailing toy boats on his pond and scribbling his thoughts thereupon, but who had never seen a shot fired in anger, reappeared in the victories of Rodney and of Duncan and in "the Nelson touch". Assuredly in the temple of the British Empire the niches do not belong only to the men of action.

But in every department of the national life the epoch from 1770 to the war with revolutionary France is singularly fertile in aspiration and achievement. The age of the Bill of Rights and of triumphant mercantilism had created the National Debt, the Bank of England, a new system of public finance, and new methods and principles of taxation, the incidence and effects of which were the subject matter of political and economic controversy. Similarly after 1770 old institutions were adapted, new ones established to meet the new needs. Lloyd's Coffee House, quartered at the Royal Exchange in 1774, testified to the growth of our mercantile marine, the indispensable basis of military sea power, and England's world-wide interest in marine traffic. "Lloyds" became the world-centre of shipping registration, and its rules the model of marine insurance. The London Stock Exchange made investment and speculation a 1773 national affair, for Great Britain is in the way to become the great creditor of Europe. The demand for capital in every direction, and the multifarious opportunities for its profitable employment, gave a vast impetus to the spread of banks, and the banking system riveted more tightly the grip of the capitalistic *régime*. Bills of exchange, discounting, the foreign exchanges—the ingenious devices of the higher finance for extending and improving credit—throve with the influx of continental financiers into London which became the money market of Europe, of which the Bank of England, more closely associated than ever with the Government under Pitt's Administration, was the brain and heart. The memorable report of the Bullion Committee in 1810 and the controversial literature which it provoked is not merely a classic contribution to the economics of currency, banking, and foreign trade ; it is a remarkable proof of the power, devotion, and knowledge with which the problems of Lombard Street were being studied by some of the best brains in the nation.

If modern political economy was created by one man and one book, that man was Adam Smith and the book was *The Wealth of Nations*. Smith remains the greatest of the British school; his masterpiece shares in the qualities both of the literature of knowledge and the literature of power. It owed its vogue to its penetrating analysis of economic phenomena, its cumulative criticism of accepted principles and methods, its constructive creed based on the fusion of economic principles with the ideals of national liberty. But the broad humanism of its pages, generous passion bitted by science, is as impressive as its *curiosa felicitas* in the phrases that stick, and its hunger for a true historical method. J. S. Mill observed with happy force that its finest characteristic is that the principles are invariably associated with their application. But the writer was no mere economic man, born and cradled in a professor's study, the pitiless analyst of economic men. He taught that freedom, justice, humanity were greater and more desirable qualities for nations as for individuals than opulence and trade. In its influence *The Wealth of Nations* is second only to *The Origin of Species*, and it is instructive to note how in the debates on the Corn Law of 1815 Adam Smith was cited on both sides of the House. To no other modern professor has it been granted in like measure to be the master not only of those who know but of those who govern. Not even Bentham made disciples so influential as the list from Pitt through Peel to Cobden and Gladstone, from Ricardo to Mill and Cairnes and Jevons.

Adam Smith's generation was one of notable and humanised intellectual activity, particularly in political science, of the renascence

of the passion for reform, the cry for a new way of life of which
John Wesley had been a pioneer. To it belongs the best work of
Edmund Burke, *clarum et venerabile nomen*, the rough-hewn figure
of Johnson, great by reason of his robust and characteristic Toryism,
his superb industry, his friendships " kept in such constant repair,"
greatest in his tenderness of heart. " About the things on which
the public thinks long," said Johnson, " it commonly attains to
think right." " It is prodigious," he also remarked, " the quantity
of good that may be done by one man if he will make a business
of it." These two sentences mirror the careers of four notable reformers. Johnson himself was one of the earliest and sturdiest
opponents of the slave trade. At the table of his friends met
Clarkson and Wilberforce, who determined, like Abraham Lincoln,
that if God granted them one day to hit the accursed thing they
would hit it as hard as they could. And between 1773 and 1784
a dissenting High Sheriff of Bunyan's county of Bedford, John
Howard, at great peril to himself, awakened the conscience of the
nation to the unspeakable horrors of our jails and bridewells,
manufactories of crime, disease, vice, and cruelty. That Howard,
essentially a practical philanthropist, did not achieve more was the
fault of the Executive and the Legislature; and what might have
been accomplished in 1780 was left to Elizabeth Fry and the reformers of the next generation. With Howard ranks the name of 1780
Robert Raikes, whose first Sunday School taught the Established
Church a neglected duty and laid the foundation of the modern
system. Raikes had indeed put his finger on one of the blots of
the age, the neglect of the child.

Amongst the more notable workers whose pens brought the new
Radicalism to the birth were John Cartwright; Richard Price, the
friend of Franklin; Granville Sharp, the strenuous colleague of
Clarkson; Sir William Jones, a distinguished Orientalist, the as-
sociate of Johnson and Gibbon; Joseph Priestley, the Unitarian
minister described by Cuvier as " the father of modern chemistry who
would not acknowledge his daughter ". From Priestley's *Essay on
Government* Bentham borrowed the magic phrase " the greatest
happiness of the greatest number;" and Priestley, like Bentham
and the young Romilly, belonged to the Shelburne circle which met
at Bowood and exchanged ideas with Mirabeau, the Abbé Morellet,
and Dumont. Reform in theology, the extirpation of abuses, the

removal of political and religious disabilities, the extension and alteration of the conditions of the franchise, were powerfully reinforced by the assaults on the colonial and fiscal policy of Lord North and the establishment of American Independence. The political disintegration of the empire was a triumphant vindication of the claims to freedom and liberty based on inalienable natural rights, and a sinister warning in the reformers' eyes of the consequences of defying them. The link between the movement in thought and the forces underlying the industrial expansion was thus completed. The great organisers of production demanded freedom from an antiquated mercantilism, subversive of economic freedom, in order that each producer might find the freest play for himself as a citizen endowed with a natural liberty, and that industry might cut for itself natural channels unimpeded by artificial barriers. *Laissez faire, laissez passer* became a watchword and an ideal. The function of Government as the Executive of a society born to freedom was to level the dykes and impose no obstacle by test or statute on the prerogative of the individual unit to decide and follow his own natural interest.

Thus the theory and policy of the new school came into sharp collision with the old Whiggism. In Pitt's reconstruction of Toryism, as far as 1793, they found a reserved but valuable champion. Their most formidable opponents came from their own camp. Burke's aversion from metaphysical speculations in politics, his peremptory refusal to confine the statesman to the logic of pure reason, unaided by experience, his vision of society as essentially a slow growth in an ordered evolution in which the spiritual and inexplicable were essential elements, his appeal to and reverence for the past—these qualities of intellect and temper, winged by a literary power that made him a master of English prose, constituted him the champion of the historical method, so fatal to any abstract theory of natural rights. On the other side the corrosive dialectic of Bentham, as passionate a reformer as the advocates whose defective history and logic he impeached, sapped the groundwork of an unadulterated naturalism. To Bentham *écrasez l'inâme* was a very misleading cry of battle. In morals as in political science not natural rights, the figment of idealogues, but utility was the sovereign principle. The function of Government was not merely to destroy everything that hindered trade or bred crime,

vice, and misery, but to base politics on a scientific ethics and focus
the forces of society on good government; in a word, to promote 1780
the greatest happiness of the greatest number.   Although *The* 1776
Introduction to the Principles of Morals and Legislation, carrying
to a constructive conclusion the *Fragment on Government*, and
containing the pith and marrow of his contribution to ethics and
jurisprudence, belongs to this epoch, Bentham had not yet captured
the mind of his generation.   Not until Napoleon had entered the
last phase at St. Helena did he come into the kingdom mapped out
the year before the disaster at Yorktown.

The extension of personal freedom secured by statutory law or
judicial interpretation was one of the main efforts of the Reformers.
The decision in *Somersett's Case*, pronounced by Mansfield with 1771-2
the greatest reluctance, and after a failure to arrange a compromise, finally laid it down that the law of England did not tolerate
slavery, and that rights claimed by slave owners would not be
enforced within the jurisdiction of the English Courts.   The prolonged struggle for freedom of political criticism was focused
round the law of libel and the respective functions of judge and
jury in libel trials.   Mansfield's judgment in *Woodfall's Case* that 1770
the jury could decide only the question of fact, *i.e.* of publication,
was savagely attacked by Junius and other writers in the Press,
and contested by the leaders of the Opposition in both Houses,
Chatham and Camden, Burke, Savile and Dowdeswell.   Camden
openly asserted that Mansfield's "doctrine was not the law of
England," and challenged Mansfield to a debate which was declined.
Apart from the black-letter legal controversy in which two such
high authorities so profoundly differed, the underlying political
issue was a vital one.   If a verdict on the criminality of a libel
were permanently withheld from the jury, the judges were established as a censorship by whose judicial imprimaturs the subject-
matter, scope, and character of public criticism would be rigidly
defined, and breaches of the judicial definition without appeal
made penal.   For twenty years after 1770 the Whig Opposition
fought against the principles of Mansfield which were reasserted by
him in the *Case of the Dean of St. Asaph*, in which one of the 1779
consummate advocates of the eighteenth century, Thomas, afterwards first Baron, Erskine, made his reputation.   Finally in 1792,
despite the obstructive tactics of Thurlow, Fox's Bill was passed,

reversing Mansfield's interpretation and empowering juries to give a general verdict, *i.e.* to decide whether an alleged libel was criminal or not. Pitt supported the Bill "as conformable to the spirit of the Constitution," but the main credit belongs to the unwearied opposition of twenty years, to Erskine and Fox in particular. Fox's argument on behalf of the Bill—one of his finest efforts—was a noble vindication of the wider issues at stake, whilst the subsequent history of the English Press is an adequate comment on Thurlow's recorded protest that the change would work "the confusion and destruction of the law of England". The Bill came in the nick of time. Erskine's deliberate opinion in 1810, that "if the alarms of the French Revolution had come on us before the press was established (*i.e.* by Fox's law), it would have been beat down for ever" was no exaggeration. For Erskine had lived through the trials of 1793-1810, and witnessed in the hurricane of reaction the manipulation of judicial machinery and the temper of the Bench. If freedom of criticism could not be safely left to the great intellect of Mansfield, how would it have fared at the hands of Thurlow, Loughborough, Braxfield, Kenyon, and Eldon, backed by the *ex officio* informations of the Attorney-General, and the coercive legislation of the Government?

The social changes wrought by the Industrial Revolution as yet founds canty expression in the legal framework of the Constitution and the political distribution of power. Pitt had, however, anticipated some of the results by his remodelling of the *personnel* of the House of Lords. On the accession of George III., the peers numbered 174, including thirteen minors and twelve Roman Catholics. Between 1760 and 1770 there were forty-two new creations or promotions. Between 1770 and 1782 North was responsible for thirty more, "a mob of nobility," as Horace Walpole, that strange combination of democratic opinions and fastidiously aristocratic temper, contemptuously described them. In the seventeen 1783-1801 years of his first premiership, Pitt doubled the generosity of his predecessors, creating or promoting no less than 140 peers. And the sixty years from 1760 to 1820 saw 388 creations or promotions compared with 111 from 1700 to 1760. Pitt's objects were clear enough—the reward of merit, lavish recognition of party services, the recruiting of the Upper House from the new wealth, and (most important) the independence of the Crown from "factious combina-

tions among existing peers," *i.e.* the provision of a permanent and
safe Governmental majority in the Upper House. By 1788 this
had been comfortably secured. But the proposed restriction on
the Regent's powers to create peers laid down in the Bill of 1788
was one of the weakest in the many weak points in that measure.
Pitt, no doubt, feared that a Whig Regent, advised by a Whig
Ministry, would undo the work achieved by a Tory Sovereign
advised by a Tory Minister, and with the zeal of a keen party
tactician was ready to prevent a rival from freely exercising a right
so freely exercised by himself. The restrictive clause, moreover,
encouraged the existing peers to believe that they were independent of the peer-making prerogative which would probably have
revived the dangerous pretensions defeated in the Peerage Bill of
1719. The sole justification lay in the assumption, happily verified,
that the regency would be short. But when in 1810 the terms
of a Regency Bill had to be reconsidered and the assumption was
no longer tenable, the restriction on the peer-making prerogative
of the Regent was wisely limited to twelve months only.

Pitt's sweeping additions to the peerage were one of the factors
in the alterations of the character and status of the Upper House.
After the rejection of Fox's India Bill in 1783 conflicts between the
two branches of the Legislature were rare : the preponderant Tory
majority in the House of Commons was faithfully mirrored in the
Lords. And so long as this was the case it was easy to carry on
the King's Government. But the more strongly entrenched that
Toryism became in the House of Lords the greater the danger of a
deadlock, which might bring the nation face to face with revolution,
if the representative House of Commons became Whig or Liberal.
The crisis of 1831-32 was made inevitable by the changes in the
House of Lords from 1783 to 1820. Nor did the preponderant Tory
majority exhibit that independence in political issues, that intuition into, and sympathy with, the interests of the nation as a whole,
which had characterized the previous Whig ascendency. The debates after 1783 steadily lose the illuminating touch, the indefinable political aptitude that were the prerogative of the aristocracy
of 1688. The Senate was transformed into a dignified political club
whose decisions, unaffected by debate, registered a foregone conclusion. The driving power, the great makers of policy—Pitt, Fox,
Castlereagh, Canning—were in another place, and the high per-

23

centage of peers in the Ministries did not correspond to the quality
of the individuals, nor did their presence as "the domestic furni-
ture of Pitt's (and other) Cabinets" redeem the chamber in which
they sat. The great struggles after 1783 were decided on the floor
of the House of Commons ; and from 1783 to 1815 it is not easy to
find examples of initiative in legislation by the House of Lords
which reveal the prevision of the statesman to meet national needs
or recognise patent grievances, though it would be easy to compile
a list of measures mutilated or rejected, and of beneficial reforms
postponed.   Tacitly and gradually the House of Lords lost or
abandoned the functions of a co-ordinate branch of the Legislature,
and perforce slipped into the *rôle* of a revising Chamber. This, not
unnaturally, perhaps, the peers under Eldon's sway interpreted as the
function of placing a permanent brake on the legislative machine,
of resisting all change, simply because it was change, unless the
pressure was irresistible, and of defending the interests of property
and the existing social order, of whose true creed they conceived
themselves to be the wisest and most authoritative exponents. No
student of the period would deny that these functions they per-
formed with regularity, zeal, and efficiency. But a student of
English history, limited to the records of the House of Lords,
would learn more of the forces and movements to which the future
of England belonged from the protests of an insignificant minority
in that House, and from what the majority refused to do, than
from the positive contribution of that majority to political and
social science and progress.

But in one and not the least important department of civic
life—the administration of the Poor Law—the policy and methods
of the epoch were disastrous. Since 1760 a reaction against the
stringent enforcement of the Elizabethan and Caroline system set
in, partly due to an awakened and scientific interest in the problems
of pauperism, partly to the humanitarian philanthropy which did
such noble service under Howard and the Abolitionists—"the
saints," as Wilberforce's party came to be called. Gilbert's Acts of
1782 are the watershed between the new policy and the old. The
intentions of the promoter were excellent ; the results proved
deplorable. The virtual abolition of "the workhouse test" (imposed in 1722), the power to provide for the able-bodied by work
in their homes, and by outdoor relief to supplement wages with

allowances, sterilised the optional reforms specified in the Acts (such as the grouping of workhouses into unions), and opened the door to a policy of lavish outdoor aid, more cruel and demoralising in the long-run to the classes it was intended to assist than to the classes who provided the funds.   The beneficial modification in 1795, of the law of settlement by which newcomers into a parish were protected from the tyranny of the overseers until they were actually chargeable, was destroyed by the action of the Justices, who met at the Pelican Inn, Speenhamland, Berkshire, and agreed to grant allowances to the families of the able-bodied on a definite scale calculated to bring a deficiency of wages up to a reasonable standard of subsistence.   This, in plain words, meant that inadequate remuneration by the employer was to be supplemented by a grant from the rates at the public cost.   Originally, perhaps, a temporary and local expedient in a period of acute distress, it was generally adopted by one county after another and erected into a permanent system.   "The Speenhamland Act of Parliament" made the green-room of Quarter Sessions and its members, the Justices, a new centre of arbitrary and irresponsible power, and a non-representative taxative authority.   The results of the deepening and wide-flung demoralisation are best studied in the classical Report of the Poor Law Commissioners of 1834.   The financial burden and waste were the least of the evils, though the figures are eloquent.   The average cost of the Poor Law, 1748-50, was £689,971, for 1776 £1,521,732, for 1783-85 £1,912,241, for 1803 £4,077,891, for 1812-13 £6,656,105.   The reconciliation of the landed interest to this gigantic increase was due to the rise in rents, which more than covered the rise in rates, and to the partial payment of wages out of other pockets than the landowner's.   Both landlord, farmer, and manufacturer were able to depress wages and supplement the hiatus between the living standard and the wage by outdoor relief, to which all ratepayers contributed.   Hence the conspiracy of falsely interpreted interests—the pauper, the wage-earner, the landlord, and the employer—which corrupted and stupefied each class and maimed the nation.

Yet it is only fair to remember that the problem imposed by the Industrial Revolution was new ; the Elizabethan system had been devised for a social and industrial economy which it served admirably, but the familiar economic stratification was now cracking

and crumbling under the feet of the governing class.   The dislocation of peasantry and yeomanry, the growth apace of the "free
hand," the operative and rural labourer, who was simply a wage-
earner, a series of bad harvests, the steady rise in prices, and the
tacit recognition by the State in 1782 of the right to work and the
right to exist, drove Justices along a fatally easy path.   Where
thinkers were puzzled the plain man, with poverty and misery at
his door, strove to act, and the whole nation paid for his ignorance
and class bias.   Then came the great war, the need of men, the
premium on breeding children who might be absorbed into industry
or required to die of fever in the West Indian expeditions—but who
could always be kept alive by a rate-aided pittance, still rising prices,
over-trading, over-speculation, crushing taxation, more bad harvests,
and bewildering spurts and depressions in commerce.   It was impossible to go back on accepted principles, and the critics of the system
quarrelled more with the social order it was intended to conserve
than with the evils it inflicted on that order.   Beside the spectre of
destitution and disease at the door had now stalked, at the nod of
the Legislature, into the drawing-rooms of the manors and the par-
lours of Quarter Sessions, the red and grey spectres of Jacobinism,
Atheism, and Revolution.   "A decent provision for the poor," had
said the Tory Johnson, "is the true test of civilisation."   He had
lived in an epoch when optimism could be challenged to stand and
deliver.   But the England which for twenty years before 1793 had
so freely plunged into the bracing and purifying stream of ideas
now refused to allow its civilisation to be tested or impeached.   It
built walls and more walls to prevent a drop from the toxic tides
surging without poisoning the paradise within.   And those who
protested that it was no paradise were Levellers, the enemies of God
and home.   To a free country the crushing of free criticism is the
crushing of science.   Unless it is daily fed by the freedom of speech
and freedom of thought, to which nothing is common and unclean,
nothing is dangerous save what in the open air has been proved to
be untrue, self-government only too easily shrivels into a parody
of autocracy—the ghost of aristocracy sitting crowned on the grave
of liberty.

NOTE.—See Supplement to Bibliography, pp. 550-552.

CHAPTER V

ENGLAND AND THE FRENCH REVOLUTION (1789-1802)

THE main stages in the French Revolution can be briefly summarised.   From May 4th, 1789, to September 3rd, 1791,
the internal reconstruction of France under the National Assembly
is the chief feature.   This is the period when Pitt was occupied July 27,
with the quarrel with Spain, the diplomacy of the Triple Alliance, 1791
the Convention of Reichenbach, and the dispute with Russia.   So
far French "reforms" interested but did not alarm our Foreign
Office.   But the virtual imprisonment of the monarchy after the
unsuccessful flight to Varennes, the dispute over "the dispossessed
princes" in Alsace, the decrees uniting Avignon to France, were
disquieting, and the social and economic changes roused obstinate
questionings.   More ominous was the *entente* between Austria and
Prussia, and the Declaration of Pillnitz, in which the rulers at Berlin July 25
and Vienna publicly invited the Powers of Europe to preserve Aug. 27
the French Monarchy.   But with the meeting of the Legislative
Assembly events began to march with uncomfortable rapidity. Oct. 1
The veto on the decrees against the *Emigrés* and the non-juring Nov. 12
priests was followed by an offensive and defensive alliance (Treaty Dec. 19
of Berlin) between Austria and Prussia.   The menace of interven- Feb. 7,
tion from without, stimulated by the invitation to intervene from 1792
within, the Counter-Revolution against the Revolution, brought
the extremists to the front at Paris.   The Feuillant Ministry fell.
Their successors, the Girondins, were bent on war.   The wise
Emperor, Leopold, had died, and war was declared on the empire. March 1
Prussia took the side of its imperial ally.   Then followed the in- April 20
vasion of the Tuileries, the Declaration that France was in danger, June 20
the Treaties between Austria and Russia, and between Russia and July 11

July 13
Aug. 7
Prussia. On July 27th Brunswick, commanding the Prussian army, issued his manifesto, inviting France to rise against its "oppressors," and threatening Paris with "exemplary and never-
Aug. 10 to-be-forgotten vengeance " if any further steps were taken against
Sept. 2-5 the monarchy. Paris replied with the attack on the Tuileries and the massacres in the prisons. The fall of Longwy and Verdun
Sept. 20 seemed to promise a military promenade to the invaders, but the cannonade of Valmy, which in Goethe's famous phrase heralded a new world, checked the Prussian advance. On September 21st the Convention met ; the Republic was proclaimed next day, and on October 14th the Prussians, disorganised and disillusioned, were in retreat. On October 20th the French seized Mainz. The three Monarchies were now at war with a Republic established on the wreck of the Bourbon system by the architects of the Revolution. It was certain that unless the French were checked they would assume the offensive. Victory promised one of the "natural" frontiers, the Rhine, an object of French ambition defined by Richelieu and Louis XIV.

Concurrently the three monarchies had been engineering a revolution of their own. The Russians had invaded Poland in
Jan., 1793 May, followed by the Prussians ; and the Second Partition Treaty paved the way for the extinction of a monarchy far older than the Prussian or Russian, and for the division of the spoil between the royal champions of public law, property, and the monarchical prin-
Oct., 1795 ciples and order in the West. The Third Partition Treaty consummated the process begun in 1772 and wiped an ancient kingdom from the map of Europe.

This iniquitous triumph of organised robbery Great Britain by sheer impotence was prevented alike from preventing or sharing. But her attitude to the European Coalition and to Republican France was now the supreme issue. So far Pitt had deliberately observed the strictest neutrality. The internal affairs of France were her own concern. If Frenchmen chose to paralyse their country, they conferred a positive benefit on Great Britain. The dissolution of the Family Compact, of the Austro-French Alliance, struck from the French Government the two potent instruments of French ascendency in Europe. The maintenance of peace was the prime object of Pitt's foreign policy, and the evidence that Pitt worked with sincerity and conviction to keep Great Britain at peace is conclusive. He rejected the overtures of the allies of Pillnitz, and snuffed out the idea of a loan desired by the "émigrés enragés" in order to further the counter-revolution. So little did he contemplate or desire British action that the Budget of 1792—for which he has been so severely criticised—reduced our naval force to 16,000 men, and the Budget speech held out hopes of a long era—fifteen years—of tranquillity and increasing prosperity. The Coalition was informed as late as September, 1792, that England remained and wished to remain neutral; a decision which exasperated the allied Courts as well as the party at home, burning to throw the forces of Great Britain on the side of the counter-revolution. But Pitt could not evade the logic of events. Would England, whose Ambassador had been recalled after the deposition of Louis XVI., recognise the Republic? Under the guidance of Nov. 6 Dumouriez and Danton the victory of Jemappes and the occupation Nov. 14 of Brussels menaced Holland, where there was a strong Republican party, friendly to France; and Holland by the Treaty of 1788 was our ally. Grenville had already assured the States-General that Nov. 13 England would observe her treaty obligations,[1] when the declaration Nov. 16 of the opening of the Scheldt, and the decrees of November 19th and December 15th, promising aid to nations struggling for freedom and the remodelling of their institutions on revolutionary lines, developed an acute crisis. England was a signatory to the treaties which had closed the Scheldt, and defiance of these in the name of natural rights provided a technical *casus belli*. More serious was the prospect of a French Belgium and Holland, which shattered a fixed principle of our policy, that the littoral from Helder to Brest should not be controlled by a single and possibly hostile Power. At present the attack on Holland was delayed, but the union of the revolutionary creed of 1789, militant and propagandist, with the national ambitions of the *ancien régime* might win for the Republic "the natural frontiers," Rhine, Alps, and Pyrenees, and plant the tricolour where the Bourbons had failed to plant the golden lilies.

In London, Chauvelin officially, Talleyrand unofficially, had striven to secure our neutrality and assent to the attack on Bel-

---

[1] The Government was much embarrassed by the refusal of the Dutch to ask officially for the help England was by treaty pledged to give on demand (*Dropmore Papers*, ii., 365).

gium. Pitt and Grenville coldly declined to commit themselves. Talleyrand returned to France; Chauvelin's conduct was meddlesome, provocative, and highly offensive to the large party in Great Britain, angry at the coercion of the monarchy, alarmed at the military failure of the Coalition. Grenville combined to perfection the pride of the aristocrat with the magisterial morality of the pulpit. He refused to accept Chauvelin's credentials as the representative of the Republic, and emphasised the worthlessness of French assurances as to Republican policy. Parliament was summoned for December 13th when the militia was already partly embodied,[1] army and navy were prepared for a war footing, while the Order in Council prohibiting the export of grain and the Aliens Bill drew protests from Chauvelin which only further incensed public opinion. Fox pleaded for recognition of the Republic and the despatch of an Ambassador to Paris, but was defeated by the significant majority of 290 to 50, many leading Whigs voting with the Government. The King, the Court, the Church, all the influential classes of society, and the professions were hostile to negotiation save by ultimatum. But Pitt revealed his extreme reluctance to war when he discussed the causes of the situation, the decree of November 19th, and the threatened invasion of Holland with an unofficial agent, Maret (afterwards Duc de Bassano).

Dec. 31

Chauvelin's memorandum of December 27th was answered by Grenville, who stiffly declined to admit the claim of the French to abrogate treaties, guaranteed by Great Britain, in order to gain an ascendency in Holland or to insult and disturb other Governments. A further reply on January 21st to a supplementary explanation by Chauvelin only italicised the temper and attitude of the Cabinet. The trial and execution of Louis XVI. stirred a storm of indignation in London; and Chauvelin, whose letters of

Jan. 21

---

[1] In order to call out the militia it was necessary to assert "that rebellion or insurrection" existed in England. Pitt (writing to Dundas (Stanhope's *Pitt*, ii., 177)) was aware that "present materials" would not give a "precise" proof. He therefore urged "what passed at Dundee" as "the specific ground". Elliot's comment on this (*Life and Letters*, ii., 80) : "This is certainly ridiculous to those who live in Scotland and know the truth"; and Elliot (Minto) was supporting the Government! Fox in Parliament demanded proof, and said, when he failed to get it, truly enough: "though this insurrection has existed for fourteen days they have given us no light whatever, no clue, no information where to find it . . . it is not the notoriety of the insurrections which prevents them from communicating to us the particulars, but their non-existence."

credence from the Republican Executive Grenville again refused
to accept, was ordered to leave the kingdom, one day after his Jan. 24
recall had been decided at Paris.   Maret, sent to take his place
and offer terms for peace and an alliance, arrived on January 30th,
having passed Chauvelin without knowing it.   He was too late.
The hour for recognising the French Republic or discussing French
concessions had slipped away.   It mattered little now from which
side the inevitable declaration of hostilities came.   At Paris the
arrival of Chauvelin was accepted as decisive, and on February 1st
war was declared on Great Britain and Holland—a challenge warmly
welcomed by George III. and an overwhelming majority of his
subjects.

The transition in public policy from neutrality to conflict was
matched by a similar change in sentiment at home, finely portrayed
in Wordsworth's verse.   The early stages of the Revolution were
hailed as the dawn of a new era.   Cultivated intellects, such as
those of Priestley, Price, Gilbert Wakefield, Erasmus Darwin,
Boulton, Watt, Parr, Robert Hall, and William Roscoe, agreed
with the spirit of Fox's comment on the fall of the Bastille : " How
much the greatest event that has happened in the world and how
much the best ".   In Nonconformist and Unitarian circles the
sympathy was strong, while ardent reformers welcomed the doctrines
of 1789 as a powerful ally to the progressive movement in England.
The more moderate and conservative average man was benevolently
patronising.   A revolution that gave to France a constitutional
monarchy and parliamentary government such as we had achieved
without bloodshed in 1688 was a sincere form of flattery, the more
acceptable because France had disarmed her formidable powers for
mischief.   Yet events soon suggested serious differences between
the principles, methods, and objects of the French and English
revolutions.   Burke's *Reflections on the French Revolution*, published in November, 1790, was a tocsin to a society, puzzled,
ignorant, and ill at ease, and unconsciously ready to be panic-
stricken.   The book was the manifesto of the counter-revolution ;
every "gentleman" followed the advice of George III. and read it ;
and what Burke said in November was soon in the heart and on the
lips of the governing classes in Great Britain and Europe.   Its
interpretation of the Revolution burnt itself into the minds of two
generations, and has not yet been obliterated by two generations

of French historical scholarship, from Tocqueville to Taine, Sorel and Aulard.   Defective as was Burke's analysis of the economic conditions of the old, and the political ideals of the new, France, which he damned with his eloquence, the capital thesis of his argument, that the doctrines of 1789 were applicable not merely to France but to Europe, that they were subversive of the foundations of existing political institutions and the social order, that unless they were stamped out religion, property, and the inherited civilisation of the past, as the ancient orders understood these terms, would be submerged in a welter of atheism and democracy, seemed to be confirmed by every subsequent stage in the Revolution.   The *Reflections* provoked many replies.   The best of these, Mackintosh's *Vindiciæ Galliccæ*, an acute, temperate, and academic criticism, produced little effect.   But *The Rights of Man* of Paine, notorious for his *Common Sense*, was more than an answer ; it was a brilliant if crude counter-manifesto of the extreme Radical and Republican school, which summed up an embittered democrat's hates and hopes.   The reckless bravado of its creed, aided by an enormous sale, sharpened the worst fears.   The riots at Birmingham on July 14th, 1791, in which Dissenting chapels and Priestley's house, with its scientific apparatus, library, and papers, were sacked, was a sinister illustration of how the hatred of French ideas and their sympathisers was shared in by the mob and could be exploited by reaction.   And when the second part of *Natural Rights* was published in the winter of 1792 nine educated Englishmen out of ten had convinced themselves that the Revolution meant the guillotine for Kings, the despoliation of the Church, the confiscation of property—a communistic Bedlam, misgoverned by cut-throats and bandits.

The difference of view revealed by Burke's *Reflections* led to an open rupture in the Whig Opposition.   In the debates on May, 1791 the Constitutional Act for Canada, which divided the colony into the two provinces of Upper and Lower Canada, Fox and Burke came into painful conflict.   Burke went so far as to declare that he had done his duty in warning the country and his party from the evils of the French Constitution, "at the price of my friend," and that the memorable intimacy with Fox "was at an end".   From that day the two leaders stood in bitterly opposed camps.   Burke's *Appeal from the New to the Old Whigs*, a powerful and dignified statement of the creed of the old Whiggism, was a further blow at the solidarity of the Opposition.   Led with profound reluctance by the Duke of Portland, the representatives of many of the historic Whig houses were wavering between personal loyalty to Fox and an increasing aversion from his principles.   In the autumn of 1792 Burke openly joined the Ministerialists, and Loughborough entered the Cabinet as Lord Chancellor, while Portland, Carlisle, Spencer, Jan. 28, Fitzwilliam, Windham, and Elliot paved the way for the future [1793] coalition by voting with the Government.   The Opposition was shattered.   Fox, with the help of Grey, Erskine, Sheridan, and Tierney, could number only fifty adherents in the Commons, and in the Lords only the Dukes of Norfolk and Bedford, Lansdowne (Shelburne), " Citizen " Stanhope, Derby, and Lauderdale.   The bitterness of party feeling and the inflamed atmosphere can only be judged by a study of the pamphlet literature, the memoirs, the State Trials, and the savage caricatures of Gillray.

The activity of the organisations—The Friends of the People, The Revolution Society (founded to commemorate that of 1688, not of 1789), The Society for Constitutional Information, The London Corresponding Society—was remarkable.   The Corresponding Society, in particular, founded by Hardy and Frost for artisans, aimed at linking up a network of local committees with a central directorate at London.   Focussing every element of discontent, it became conspicuous for its advocacy of drastic reform and its attacks on existing institutions, while the despatch of an address to the Convention at Paris convinced many of the identifi- Nov., 1792 cation of its programme with that of the Republican Revolutionists. To combat its efforts, John Reeves, the erudite author of *A History of English Law*, organised The Association for Preserving Liberty and Property, or Crown and Anchor Association, which met with strong support and no little success.   The effect of events on the public mind can be partly measured by the division in 1793 on Grey's motion for reform rejected by 232-41, as compared with 248-174 in 1785.   Pitt, still in principle a Reformer, declared " it was no time for hazardous experiments," though the Government promptly showed it was a time for stern repression.   The publication of the proclamation against seditious writings began the May 21 series of measures which accentuated the public panic and ushered in a black era of reaction and coercion.   Repeated on December 1st the proclamation and the King's Speech warned the Legislature of a widespread conspiracy to destroy the Constitution and subvert

law and order. The prosecution of Paine, who fled to France, was followed by the Aliens Act, placing foreign immigrants under severe restrictions and giving the Secretary of State a discretionary power of expulsion. This " temporary " measure was not repealed until 1826. In 1794 the Habeas Corpus Act was suspended and the suspension annually renewed until 1801, a procedure unprecedented in its duration, and arming the Executive with a formidable *droit administratif*. In 1795 came the Treasonable Practices Act, which created a new law of treason, dispensed with the proof of overt acts, and made any writing, printing, preaching, or speaking, inciting to hatred or contempt of the Sovereign, the established Government or Constitution, a high misdemeanour. In the same year the Seditious Meetings Act prohibited meetings of more than fifty persons without notice to a magistrate, who was to attend and empowered to break it up if he deemed it " tumultuous ". The stamp and advertisement duties were also increased in order to crush cheap newspapers, while stringent regulations on the responsibility of printers tightened the control on the Press. In 1799 the London Corresponding Society and the Society of United Englishmen, Scotsmen, and Irishmen were suppressed under a law which put unlicensed debating clubs and reading-rooms on the same footing as brothels. Another Act in the same year made trade combinations or unions illegal. "The popular Constitution," sums up Sir Erskine May, " was suspended."

Englishmen had now to learn that they must hold their tongues, and that to express an opinion that the Constitution was not perfect, or that there was corruption in the Government or Parliament might, probably would, be twisted into treason or seditious libel by the judges on the bench and by Crown lawyers scavenging in the reports of spies and *agents provocateurs*. A long list of trials sternly taught the lesson that reigns of terror were not the monopoly of revolutionary republics. Words held to be seditious in spite of contradictory evidence or satisfactory proof of seditious intent were sufficient in 1793 to procure the condemnation of John Frost, Winterbotham, a Baptist minister, Briellat, and Dr. Hudson. In Scotland, Muir and Fyshe Palmer, Skirving, Margarot, and Gerrald —commemorated to-day in the Martyrs' Memorial on Calton Hill

—were sentenced to long periods of transportation after trials which, in Lord Cockburn's words, "sank deep, not merely into the popular mind, but the minds of all who thought". In 1794 secret committees of the Upper and Lower Houses reported the existence of a traitorous and detestable conspiracy to subvert the Constitution; and armed with these reports and relying on the readiness of the judiciary to stretch the doctrine of constructive treason,[1] put Hardy, Horne Tooke, Thelwall, and nine others on trial before a Special Commission. But thanks to Erskine's superb efforts the evidence which had convinced with ease the Lords and Commons failed to convince a jury, and the prisoners were acquitted. Justice had not yet wholly disappeared; but the records of the case are deeply suggestive of the value of much of the material, unsifted by cross-examination, on which a panic-stricken Parliament and a reactionary Executive relied. The failure of the prosecution gave a fresh impetus to the various organisations, and the great public meetings at Copenhagen House and in Palace Yard illustrate the advance to 1795 modern methods of political agitation.

It is easy to account for the inflexible policy of the Cabinet and the Legislature. Pitt and his colleagues were confronted with problems of great difficulty and complexity at home and abroad, and they felt the ground crumbling under their feet. A terrible and unsuccessful war, the failure to arrest the collapse of the old order in Europe, the economic and social dislocation produced by the Industrial Revolution, Ireland on the verge of rebellion, were aggravated by the strain of taxation and bad harvests. Before the trumpets of a new nation created by a new civilisation the cankered citadels of the *ancien régime* were rocking and falling. Bread riots in the industrial centres at home in 1794, 1795; the attack on the King on his way to Parliament; the mutinies of the fleet, and the Oct. 29, hooting of Pitt by the mob in 1797; the schemes of foreign invasion 1795 to be aided, the French asserted, by revolutionary risings; the

---

[1] An instructive example, out of many, of the temper of the Bench will be found in the trial of Vint, Ross, and Perry in 1799, in which the conductors of the *Courier* were charged with a libel on the Emperor of Russia. The " libel " was a criticism of Russian tariff edicts as injurious to British trade. Lord Kenyon directed the jury that if this criticism " passed unreprobated by our Government and Courts of Justice " " this great Sovereign ' might ' call for satisfaction as a national affront ". (*St. Tr.*, xxvii., 627). If this were good law Burke and Gillray would have ended their days in the hulks.

violent utterances of some agitators; the loose talk of fools and babblers, and the demonstrable activity of the democratic associations, came like flashes of forked lightning across an inky sky and earth. The Executive was bombarded with proofs of sedition and treason — sermons, pamphlets, speeches, toasts, gibes, pikes and daggers (such as the one flung by Burke in a frenzy on the floor of the House of Commons)—unearthed by the bishops and parochial magistrates, spies and informers, and the voluntary agents organised by " The Crown and Anchor Association," who watched inns and taverns, the kitchens and stables of the gentry, and noted and exaggerated the whispers of sober chambermaids and drunken ostlers alike. From France swept over England and Europe the mysterious, irresistible gusts of new ideas, an intoxicating challenge, a corrosive dissolvent. Burke desired to be the Peter the Hermit of a new crusade. Fox said that he did not fear French principles, but that he had a very wholesome fear of French power. And both in a sense were right. The secret of French strength lay in the moral magic of French principles, pitted against the worn-out monarchies of the Continent and the Empire in its dotage, with no faith but in the divine right of dynastic selfishness. At home the Cabinet and the governing classes lashed themselves into a panic, the more intelligible because the *régime* of coercion was not unpopular in the sense that it was ruthlessly imposed by an oligarchical minority. Francis Place, in the heart of the democratic agitation, frankly tells us that in the mass of shopkeepers and working people "such was the terror of the French regicides and democrats" that they submitted to the harsh measures for fear of worse treatment. The coercion, under the inspiration of the Government, was the self-flagellation of a nation first cowed by its own responsible statesmen.

The danger of a revolutionary upheaval was grossly exaggerated. Demand for reform was deliberately for political and party purposes identified with demand for revolution. Yet the reform movement was deep-rooted in economic and social causes; it had been fed by ten years of copious discussion and widespread agitation ; it challenged abuses, denounced by Pitt himself, which the French Revolution did not remove but only made more patent. A programme of annual Parliaments, payment of members, equal electoral districts, a widely extended franchise and the extirpation of corrupt pocket-boroughs, may have been Utopian, but it was not revolutionary and treasonable. There were probably not as many genuine republicans in Great Britain as there were members of the House of Commons, and of these not half were willing or able to fight for their creed.[1] The propagandist decrees of the Convention, the invitations to rise and overthrow their tyrants, fell absolutely flat in England. Had Hoche or Napoleon landed on our shores it is questionable whether either would have been joined by ten adherents, while it is certain that ninety-nine Englishmen out of a hundred would have died in the last ditch in defence of their country.[2] It is inconceivable that the mutineers at Spithead and the Nore, crews filled with the victims of the press-gang and reinforced from the dregs of the population, driven into mutiny by undeniable grievances would not have deserted to the French had the lower classes been honeycombed with disaffection and treason. There was a good deal of loose talk, much violent criticism, and a certain amount of " seditious " writing confined to a small handful of unimportant agitators. It is surprising how few cases, such as those of Watt and Downie, were brought to light by the Government, and how insignificant, impotent, and incompetent such traitors invariably proved to be. Yet all the causes that make a proletariat go mad—crushing taxation, high prices, unemployment, misery and starvation—were operating after 1793, and the genuine cases in eight years of serious political crime, or overt action, would not have kept a Crown lawyer in bread and cheese. Half the prosecutions were for trumpery folly, which would not have been criminal if special legislation had not made freedom of speech a penal offence. The coercion by the Executive probably created more disaffection and provoked more violent utterances than it prevented. But it is not surprising that when a Government acts upon the principle of Lord Braxfield, that to preach the necessity of reform was seditious, discontent became disaffection, and was driven underground with baneful results. Violence in repression provoked violence in utterance. Ministers did not deny the existence of serious evils, but

[1] See particularly W. T. Laprade—*England and the French Revolution* (Johns Hopkins Univ. Studies, xxvii., nos. 8-12). 1909. See Appendix XXIII.

[2] When the much-dreaded Corresponding Society was suppressed in 1799 the subject for discussion was volunteering to resist a French invasion. Yet twenty-eight men were arrested and kept in prison for three years without trial—thanks to the suspension of the Habeas Corpus Act.

with the help of the judges they insisted, by law and administration, that the greater the grievances the greater the necessity of suffering in silence. " God help," was Fox's unanswerable comment, " God help the people who have such judges." The existence of a great conspiracy alone could justify such legislative methods and such a temper in the rulers, yet the conspiracy did not exist, and the situation, the peril from within, were not comparable to that in 1689 and 1698, when half our public men were in secret correspondence with St. Germain, and great nobles did not scruple to betray plans of campaign to the enemy.[1] The Ministerial indictment, in Fox's words, " was," and remains, " an intolerable calumny upon the people of Great Britain ".

If Pitt had only slept when the lawyers and spies saw a Phrygian cap on every workman's head, as he slept when he heard of the mutiny at Spithead, or had retained his father's bracing faith in the curative efficacy of free institutions, and the conviction so nobly expressed by Fox, that the free Constitution of England was not only good for sunshine and holidays but would prove its power in days of distress and difficulty, the red spectre would have vanished, and such disorder and sedition—a trifling quantity at the worst—as existed could have been dealt with effectually by the ordinary law and the existing machinery. But Pitt brooded over the fire, apparently convinced that " by to-morrow we may not have a hand to act or a tongue to utter," that if he resigned his head would be off in six months, pessimism as astonishing and difficult to justify as the optimism which thought that the war of 1793 would be a struggle of a few months.[2] The plea that Pitt's policy was justified by the need of devoting our whole energies to the war would be stronger if the energies of the Government

[1] Mr. Laprade, *op. cit.*, who has recently examined the evidence, concludes (p. 186): " There is no trace anywhere in England during these years of any considerable bodies of men who upheld or propagated either the republican principles of T. Paine or the extravagant doctrines of the French Revolution"; *cf.* Burges to Auckland, December 18th, 1792: " There appears to be but one sentiment throughout the country, that of loyalty to the King, affection to the existing Constitution, ardour to support it, and an earnest desire to go to war with France" (Auckland MSS. in British Museum, xxxiv., 85; cited by Laprade, p. 123).

[2] *Cf.* Grenville to Auckland at the Hague, December 3rd, 1792: " I have not expressed in my despatch all the security which we feel respecting the comparative state of our preparations with those of France . . . but to you privately I may say that our confidence on that head is very great indeed" (Auckland MSS., xxxv., 32).

had been given wholly to the prosecution of the war, and not to the
prosecution of every actual or possible critic of the Government's
mismanagement at home and abroad.   Evil as well as good unhappily lives on.   The last twelve years of Pitt's life saturated Toryism
with a paralysing fear of concession to popular liberties, with the
belief that the Constitution of 1793 was an ark of the covenant to
touch which was impious sacrilege, and with the theory that coercion was a permanent necessity.   Toryism ceased to be a movement
inspired by thought or thinkers ; and the illuminated political faith
which had widened the visions and quickened the pulses of the
generation from 1783-92 severed itself from the intellectual currents
and the economic needs of the new England.   The widening abyss
between the governed and the governors it declined to bridge.   It
slowly petrified into a cramping championship of privileged monopoly and of the prejudices and superstitions of the Crown and a
reactionary governing class.

Fox was the hero of the forlorn hope, finely supported by
Charles Grey and Erskine.   It is easy to emphasise vices—wine,
women, dice—which would have corrupted the soul and sterilised
the moral fibres of any other man.   But neither his vices nor the
vindictive enmity of the Crown, nor the desertion of his political
allies, nor the ferocious misrepresentation of his aims, soured his
mind or weakened his passionate hatred of cruelty, violence, and
capricious and brutal law, his advocacy of the oppressed, his unfaltering conviction that justice and liberty were stronger to save
than *ex officio* prosecutions, the suspension of the Habeas Corpus,
a gagged Press, the jails, and the constructive treason of panic-
stricken and reactionary judges.   "It was," as Sydney Smith said,
"an awful time for those who had the misfortune to entertain
liberal opinions."   In 1793 recantation would have given Fox office,
power, honours.   But he never wavered.   Instinctively as a plant
turns to light, his heart turned to the sun of freedom.   It was
no sentimental, arbitrary whim.   Fox's creed was rooted in strong
intellectual convictions.   "Liberty is order, liberty is strength"
was the essence of his faith, and he pleaded for the rights of a self-
governing nation to use freedom of thought, freedom of speech,
freedom of criticism as its most formidable weapons in defence of
its nationality and security.   And but for Fox and his colleagues
Liberalism as a living and growing political faith might have
24

perished. They established and handed on a great tradition which explains the homage of the revivified Whiggism after 1815, that centred at Holland House, to the leader of 1793-1806.

Yet the value of Fox's advocacy went far deeper than the pre-servation of a great party from degradation and disloyalty to its principles. He discerned from the outset that the essentials in the doctrines of 1789—nationality, the sovereignty of the people, democracy, equality before the law—would outlive the accidental excesses by which their execution was accomplished. Napoleon was beaten in the end by a Europe not of the old order but of the new, not by a war of Governments or Courts bolstered up by subsidies, but of peoples recreated by the reforms inspired by, or borrowed from, the doctrines of 1789. Fox foresaw that in the fight with the French Revolution bayonets would be useless unless they were backed by better ideas and more satisfying principles than those of the French. He strove to save his country from sacrificing the living elements in her own system and the ideals of her political life to the dead and rotten principles of the continental monarchies. He had an unquenchable faith in the true secrets of England's power—free government for and by a free people, against which Jacobins and Cæsars would dash themselves in vain; and events showed that he was right. He said harsh and violent things.[1] It was the painful duty of those to whom the trusteeship of truth and freedom had fallen to speak without fear and to defy. The theory that war must hush criticism and silence opposition is one which has never been accepted by the great leaders of great causes in our history, not by Pym or Shaftesbury, Swift and Bolingbroke, Chatham and Pitt himself in 1781 ; and, if ever unsparing criticism and unflinching protest were needed, the period from 1793-1801 imposed the task on public men who were not afraid of their duty.

Foreign policy and the war were the urgent issues in 1793.[2] Events had made neutrality impossible for Great Britain. Public opinion put an alliance with revolutionary France out of the question, and between alliance and overt opposition there was no middle way. "Security" was the keynote of Pitt's interpretation. But the tragedy of Pitt's foreign policy lay in the precision and

[1] See *Dropmore Papers*, ii., 372.   [2] See Appendix.

definition which the plans to achieve "security" involved. The
First Coalition came into existence with the treaties of alliance
shortly concluded with Prussia, Russia, the Emperor, Spain, Sardinia, and the Two Sicilies. It was to be a war of conquest and
plunder as well as of self-defence, "of plunder abroad," as Windham
said, "and patronage at home". The French colonies, the Belgian
frontier, Alsace and Lorraine (with a further partition of Poland)
were to cement the Grand League at the expense of France. The
avowed object was to impose on the French people a form of
government based on principles, repudiated by themselves, but acceptable to the allies—the counter-revolution at Paris, signed,
sealed, and delivered by the restored Bourbons and paid for by the
cession of French territory. An easy victory was anticipated.
How could a bankrupt nation, racked by internal divisions which
were to be studiously fanned into the most demoralising of all
forms of conflict, civil war, resist a coalition of three-fourths of
Europe?

Thus Great Britain was now pledged to interfere with the form
of the French government, and to invite Frenchmen to rise and
throw off their tyrants. The armed propaganda of the Monarchies
was to contend with the armed propaganda of the Revolution. It
would be a war of ideas as well as of shot and cold steel, and the
bayonets with the best ideas at their points would win. Presumably,
also, if the Coalition were entitled in the interests of "security" to
parcel out Poland and compel the French to accept a constitution
at their dictation, the French were equally entitled to plunge the
inhabitants of every hostile State into an internecine struggle with
their rulers, and force on them institutions suitable to French
"security". Great Britain was now committed to the system of
the continental monarchies. She was to pay the piper, but the piper
was to call the tune. Had the Coalition succeeded, the counter-
revolution would have been triumphant from one end of Europe to
the other. It is not difficult to conjecture what a Holy Alliance,
worked by Thugut and Lucchesini, Artois and Godoy, Frederick
William II. of Prussia and the Habsburgs, the Bourbons of Madrid
and Naples and Great Britain in the fetters of the reaction of 1793-
1801, would have wrought in a Europe that knew nothing of the
Spanish Rising, Stadion, Hofer, and Stein, and the Wars of Liberation. Fox and the Whig remnant realised the peril for England and

the world.[1] But happily such a catastrophe to civilisation and intellectual liberty was averted.

The war breaks into two well-marked halves, divided by the critical year 1797. In the first England fights as a member of the Coalition, but by 1796 the Coalition has dissolved and Napoleon has appeared on the scene. In the second the struggle is with the Directory and with Napoleon after the *coup d'état* of Brumaire, and is notable for the formation and collapse of the Second Coalition. It ends with the peace of Lunéville for Europe, of Amiens for Great Britain, which register the failure to achieve the objects for which we fought. If the Treaty of Amiens acknowledged the independence of Great Britain, the Treaty of Lunéville bore unimpeachable testimony to a stable revolutionary Government in power at Paris, in possession of the "natural frontiers," and to the military, political, and moral ascendency of revolutionary France in Europe. And so frail was the " security " obtained that in eighteen months the struggle must be renewed. Though Pitt was not in office when peace was made, the first eight years are controlled by his policy and methods.[2]

Broadly, these methods can be examined under four heads— diplomatic combinations, finance, naval power, and military expeditions. Great Britain started with conspicuous advantages, of which Pitt was one of the most conspicuous. As a leader he stands out in Europe in a class by himself. Until Napoleon appeared no other country had a statesman of the like quality. Not without reason Pitt to the Continent was England and England was Pitt. His inflexible spirit, national pride, and faith in his country, were an inspiration in the blackest hours of peril and disaster. He led a party with an overwhelming majority ; in 1794 the Ministry was reinforced by the Portland Whigs, Portland becoming Home Secretary, Earl Spencer First Lord of the Admiralty, Fitzwilliam Lord-Lieutenant, and Windham in the Cabinet as Secretary at War ; Pitt enjoyed the confidence of the governing classes and the confidence of the Crown. An Opposition of barely fifty could not amend much less reject a single measure or method on which the Government insisted.

---

[1] " My undisguised opinion is that, if the Coalition for the restoration of the Bourbons had succeeded, the consequences would have been amongst all the Kings of Europe a perpetual guarantee against all peoples who might be oppressed by them in any part of the world " (Fox, *Speeches*, 6, 459).

[2] See Appendix, *Dropmore Papers*.

But while Ireland and India (after 1798) severely strained our resources at critical epochs, we were matched for the first time since 1715 not against a decadent Bourbon monarchy but a rejuvenated French nation.   Europe was as little prepared for Danton, Carnot, and the Committee of Public Safety as it was for Napoleon.   It is worth noting, also, that it was not Napoleon who made the essential difference.   Europe was beaten and the First Coalition dissolved before the Italian campaign of 1796; and Great Britain was relatively more successful against the Consulate than against 1796-1801 the Revolutionary Republic.   1793-96

The causes of our failure lie in the grave mismanagement of the operations and the conditions under which we chose, or were compelled, to fight.   The early campaigns were vitiated by delusions as to the character of the war.   Once French trade was crippled, her West Indian Islands annexed, and a victory or two won in the Netherlands and the Rhine, the bankrupt Republic, it was thought, must succumb.   The error was as gross as the French belief that Great Britain was ripe for revolt, and far more disastrous to the strategy of the allies.   The unadulterated selfishness of those allies might have been foreseen by our Foreign Office, and was very soon revealed.   Even without Poland to wreck the campaign in the West, the divergent aims and sleepless jealousy of Prussia and Austria, were fatal to unity of purpose and effort.   Both now and in 1799 the allies spent more time in discussing and thwarting their own plans than those of the enemy.   Deficient in equipment, organisation, and leading, the monarchies of the old order betrayed their own cause and failed piteously.   Great Britain, too, entered the war unprepared, and paid a terrible price for ten years' neglect of the lessons taught by the previous war.   Once again she undertook a task calling for years of scientific organisation with machinery improvised and hastily braized together in the stress of crisis by amateurs.   Cheeseparing, neglect, and the absence of any system to supply the crews required (save by the press-gang and drafts from a depleted army) seriously weakened the first line of defence, the navy.   The mutinies of 1797 might easily have been prevented had grievances which affected the whole service been removed before another war came.   Fortunately the disorganisation of the French navy, by good luck and not good management, averted the consequences of a vicious economy and a blind optimism.

But the condition of the army was discreditable to the Government. In 1793 the starved, reduced, despised, and mismanaged military forces were incompetent to perform the functions now required of them, mainly because no attempt had been made to frame an idea of what the functions of an army for an empire at war might reasonably be supposed to be. The Admiralty knew, and the country vaguely agreed, that a fleet could not be created in a few weeks. But for fifteen years the Government and Parliament persisted in believing that an army could be created in time of war by a bundle of conflicting statutes, and many millions in bounties to colonels of regiments, recruiting crimps, parish officers, and what the navy left from the sweepings of the workhouse and the jails. The series of statutory enactments 1793-1801 creating on paper volunteers, fencibles, militia, supplementary militia, *levées en masse*, and of ballots, remains a pathetic monument of misguided zeal and perverse amateurism.[1] And in 1803 the process began all over again. Happily for Great Britain there was the fleet, and the military failures fell mainly on the sacrificed soldier, on the crushed taxpayer at home, and on our allies abroad. In 1795 the Duke of York, with Windham to help him, began reform in a small way. But what ten years' neglect in peace and eight years' blundering in war cost the country in millions of money and thousands of lives not even the indefatigable researches of Sir John Fortescue[1] can exactly calculate.

The organisation at headquarters was similarly defective. No efficiency of separate departmental administration can compensate for the absence of co-ordination of diplomatic policy and strategy, without which the higher policy of offence and defence, and the higher control are impossible. Conversely, the unified higher control, as Chatham's and Marlborough's record proves, exercises a bracing reactive stimulus on defective departmental organisation. Pitt was a bad War Minister, because he did not organise the higher control, and because he failed to recognise the necessity of organising it. The failures were obvious; the causes were not penetrated. The interpretation of true strategic values was vicious or neglected. The Government was cursed with a criminal fertility of ideas and plans and the absence of a system and a unified strategical scheme. The records exhibit a tragic monotony

---

[1] See Appendix x.   [2] J. W. Fortescue, *History of British Army*, vol. iv.

of inadequate resources dispersed in conflicting directions, expeditions dropped here and picked up again, and a series of half-hearted dabs at the enemy's coast-line ; the navy, disorganised to convoy them there, to stand by and take them away, and the army, badgered into believing its true function was to create futile and weak diversions—to land if it could—to fight and run away.   Not without reason our continental allies came to regard Great Britain as perfidious moneylenders and shopkeepers, unfit to fight on shore. The five years "of filching sugar islands," which we could not hold, cost a hundred thousand lives and made service in the army a more terrible penalty than slavery in the galleys of Algiers.   Lord Grenville complained that he could only find " some old woman in a red riband " to command ; but Abercromby, Charles Stuart, Cornwallis, Moira were first-rate officers.   The materials of Wellington's Peninsular army were in England long before 1808.   It was the " old women in red ribands " in the Cabinet and at the Horse Guards who failed to discover the fact or to employ the resources at their disposal.   The creation of a Secretary of State for War—a step in the right direction—was marred by Dundas, who held the office from 1794-1801, and whose record justifies the criticism that "he knew as much of war as a monthly nurse ".   Pitt appointed Dundas and kept him in office for seven years ; and it was Dundas, the tyrannical "satrap" of Scotland, who was matched against Carnot and Napoleon.

The navy fortunately fared better.   The Admiralty enjoyed a comparative administrative independence ; its action was not dissipated over half a dozen jealous departments ; it was far freer than the Horse Guards from the demoralising claims of the prerogative. The sailor chiefs were scientific students of strategy and tactics, with a great tradition behind them.   Ministers, too, were aware that an army failure meant at most a penitential confession, an unpleasant debate, and plenary absolution by a docile majority ; but a naval catastrophe would mean impeachment.   A rope round the neck, as the French Revolution proved, is a healthy stimulus to intellect in high quarters, and a fine deterrent to incompetence. Yet down to St. Valentine's Day, 1797, the Admiralty record was disappointing.   Howe, whom Nelson judged to be "the first and greatest sea officer the world had produced," was worn out by 1794 ; Hood did not justify his reputation and abilities.   Officers such as Bridport, Hotham, Mann, Colpoys, were guilty of culpable slackness, and of fumbling and hide-bound tactics. Lord Spencer, however, was a happy gift from the Whigs to Pitt, and his record at the Admiralty was a marked contrast to that of his Army colleague, Dundas. And shortly the patient study and work of the Howe-Kempenfelt school which had striven to combine the best of the French theorists with the experience and ideals of British seamanship, made itself felt. With 1797 began a new era, lit up by great names, Jervis, Duncan, Cornwallis, Nelson, and "the Nelson touch".

Finance was one of our chief weapons, and finance was Pitt's department. The cost of the war was tremendous. By 1801 £292,009,604 had been added to the National Debt. The actual sum borrowed was £334,500,000, but the Sinking Fund reduced it by some £42,000,000. Yet so strained was credit that Pitt, who operated mainly in 3 per cent. stock, only raised about £200,000,000 in actual cash. Subsidies to foreign Governments accounted for about £9,000,000, a poor investment compared with the return on the £2,500,000 that Frederick the Great made in the Seven Years' War. Nor did the loans represent the total cost of the war. Pitt showed fertility of resource in taxation. The assessed taxes were trebled; succession duties were introduced and increased; the stamp duties were doubled. In 1798 an income tax, novel and graduated, was imposed, and in 1798 and 1799 the Minister appealed for voluntary contributions, a dubious expedient which infringed the parliamentary control in finance. A more high-handed act and wholly inexcusable was the guarantee of £1,200,000 to the Emperor in 1796 without the previous assent of Parliament. By 1800 it was calculated that the charge on the National Debt absorbed 10 per cent. and taxation 20 per cent. of the total income of the nation. In 1797 the strain culminated in a grave crisis. The drain on the available specie made it impossible for the Bank of England to meet its note issue with coin. Cash payments, except in sums below £1, were promptly suspended, and Bank of England notes became an inconvertible paper currency.

Pitt's financial policy and measures have been criticised and defended by authoritative experts in currency and banking. Statistical computations make it very doubtful whether loans at a high rate of interest, and raising the ratio of cash received to the

nominal liability, would have proved less costly. The Sinking
Fund operated at an increasing loss, but the confidence it inspired
is not quantitatively comparable with the cost of maintaining it.
Pitt has been severely blamed : (a) for not raising more by taxation
and less by loans ; (b) for not imposing the Income Tax as early
as 1793. Pitt's conception of the war probably affected his
Budgets in the first four years, but questions of taxation cannot
be decided by pure economics. Subsequent criticism is often more
successful in the exposition of principles and the analysis of incidence than in re-creating the political conditions and atmosphere
of a period of terrible strain. And the due weight assignable to
Pitt's deliberate judgment and decision is not easily determined.
The best expert opinion, however, agrees that the suspension of
cash payments until 1819 was wholly unjustifiable. But Pitt's
responsibility for this ends in 1806, and the worst effects were felt
after 1808. It is probable, too, that Pitt would have grasped, as
Canning did, the arguments of Horner, Ricardo, and the Bullion
Committee of 1810 more intelligently than did Castlereagh, unversed
in economics, and the woolly-headed Vansittart.

At the outset the war was popular, but the operations in
1793 were badly planned and feebly executed. Disorganised France
offered a fine opportunity for a vigorous blow at the heart, but our
Government chose to scatter its inadequate resources in four areas,
linked by no single strategic scheme. (1) In Belgium the British
and Hanoverian army, under the Duke of York, co-operated with
the Austrians under Coburg. Condé and Valenciennes were taken ; July 13
but instead of a united march on Paris the Duke besieged Dunkirk, and 28
while the Austrians pottered over frontier fortresses. Houchard's
victory at Hondschoote, and Jourdan's at Wattignies caused the Sept. 8
siege of Dunkirk to be abandoned. Carnot's reorganisation of the Oct. 16
Revolution armies had saved the north-eastern frontier. Hoche,
too, on the Upper Rhine, had driven the Imperialists across the
river and seized the Palatinate. (2) The expedition sent out under
Moira to aid the revolted Vendeans sailed too late, and returned Dec. 1
without any results. (3) The 12,000 men thus uselessly employed
might have proved invaluable to Hood, despatched to Toulon Aug. 26
to aid the Royalists there. Soldiers were badly wanted, and after
the fall of Lyons the Republicans pressed the siege in which the
young Napoleon Bonaparte made a brilliant début. Hood was

Dec. 19   obliged to abandon the harbour. Nine French vessels were burnt, but the arsenal was not destroyed and fifteen of the Toulon fleet remained intact to form the nucleus of a serious squadron. (4) Small successes elsewhere were the sole comfort of the Government. Pondicherry, St. Pierre, Miquelon, and Tobago were captured with ease, although the attack on Martinique was foiled. The Cabinet now planned operations on a large scale in the West Indies, which for the next four years absorbed half our effective force in a pestilential climate and handcuffed our efforts in the European sphere.

April 19   To keep Prussia in the Coalition, Malmesbury was sent to Berlin with the bribe of a heavy subsidy. But the sequel showed that the money paid to maintain 62,000 Prussian troops in the field was diverted to maintain the Prussian forces in crushing an insurrection in Poland, while the Austrian Court, with its eyes too on Poland, and disgusted that our gold had flown to Berlin, not Vienna, was ready to throw up the game in the Netherlands.

The British forces in the Netherlands were terribly deficient in

April 30   numbers, training, and equipment. After the capture of Landrécies

May 17   the allies united at Tournai, but were defeated at Turcoing, where the Austrian failure to support the overwhelmed British troops was a fresh cause of mutual recriminations. The French now

June 20   turned both flanks. Coburg, defeated at Fleurus, fell back on Maestricht. The Duke of York, evacuating Ostend and abandoning Antwerp, was driven from the Maas to the Waal, and sur-

Nov. 27   rendered the command to Harcourt and Walmoden. A hard frost made all the Dutch water and marsh defences useless. The French

Dec. 27   crossed the Maas, and our demoralised army, cut off from the Austrians, who had retired across the Rhine, made a disastrous retreat to the Yssel and the Ems. " Your army," wrote Walmoden, " is destroyed. The officers, their carriages, and a large train are safe." In April, 1795, the shattered remnants were shipped home from Bremen. The French had overrun Holland, sent the Stadholder helter-skelter to England, and captured the Dutch fleet frozen up in the Texel. A Batavian Republic, dependent on Paris,

May 16   was shortly declared. The insurrection in Corsica under Paoli was

May 20   aided by Hood's fleet and the capture of Bastia (where Nelson, previously marked out by Hood as an officer to be consulted on

Aug. 10   tactical questions, lost his right eye) and of Calvi, effected the conquest of the island. In the Atlantic, west of Ushant, Howe's

famous victory of "The First of June" was the culminating point
of four days' exhausting manœuvres against the fleet of Villaret-
Joyeuse. Howe endeavoured to break the enemy's line, ship by
ship, and by engaging to leeward make the action decisive. But
this daring conception was imperfectly executed, and the battle
resulted in the capture of six ships only. The bulk of the enemy's
fleet made good their escape, and the important convoy which
Howe had desired to cut off escaped also. Across the ocean
Jervis and Grey, working together admirably, captured Martinique, March 23
St. Lucia, Guadeloupe, with Marie Galante. More serious for the April 2
future was the seizure of harbours in St. Domingo, which com- May 21
mitted us deeply to that centre of malaria and negro revolutions.
And the slackness of observation in Europe enabled French reinforcements to reach the West Indies and recover Guadeloupe. The Dec. 10
mastery of the sea, the destruction of French trade, the defeat of
the French armies, were not to be achieved by eccentric raids and
isolated expeditions, but by a superiority of force properly employed at the strategic centres.

The break-up of the First Coalition was the outstanding feature
of 1795. Tuscany and Spain deserted the alliance. Prussia, deservedly deprived of our misused subsidy, capitulated (Treaty of Basle) to
the Revolution and surrendered its territories west of the Rhine. It April 5
was then able to complete the Third Partition of Poland. Gorged Oct.
with the spoil, and financially bankrupt, the Hohenzollern State em-
braced the policy of nullity, miscalled neutrality, which in ten years
brought it to Jena and dismemberment. Catherine at St. Petersburg astutely confined herself to good wishes, doles to Vienna, and the
lion's share of Poland. Pitt and Grenville proceeded to bolster up
the Emperor by guaranteeing a loan of £4,500,000, raised at 7 per
cent. Pitt's speeches illustrated his persistent belief that the French
were too exhausted to continue much longer their efforts, but the
successful establishment of the Directory in the autumn ushered in
a new phase of the Revolution. And slackness before Brest enabled
the Toulon fleet to be reinforced from their Atlantic squadron,
while Hotham threw away two chances of destroying the enemy in March 13
the Mediterranean. His immortal "We have done very well," July 13
which stirred Nelson's wrath because only two ships were captured,
has passed into history. The failure to secure the command of the
sea, more than the Austrian defeat at Loano, made Bonaparte's Nov. 23
epoch-making campaign next year possible.

In the Atlantic, too, Bridport showed how things should not be done. With superior force he engaged the Brest fleet off the Île-de-Groix, and instead of wiping it out, was content with taking three prizes. Earlier in the year, however, Cornwallis—" Blue Billy," as the sailors called him—had signalised himself by the capture of a French convoy and the safe-conduct of it to Plymouth before superior numbers. Another expedition to the Brittany coast, composed of French *émigré* regiments, joined later by the Comte d'Artois, was despatched, too late, as usual, to co-operate with the Royalists, and the Quiberon expedition collapsed in shame and ruin. Quarrels broke out between the *émigré* leaders and the Chouans on shore; the scanty British naval force, reduced to impotence on the rocky island it had seized, could only take away some 4000 from the peninsula and leave the remainder to be shot down by the victorious army of Hoche. To save the Dutch colonies from

Sept. 15
Feb. 15

falling into the hands of the French the Cape was successfully seized, and next year Ceylon, Malacca, Amboyna, and Banda in the East, Demerara in the West, fell into our hands. In the West Indies insurrections in Grenada, St. Vincent, St. Lucia, and Jamaica aided the deadly climate in sapping the *moral* of the decimated troops. St. Lucia was evacuated, Grenada all-but lost. Undeterred and impenitent, Dundas despatched in 1796 a big expedition under Abercromby which crushed the rising in Grenada and St. Vincent and recovered St. Lucia, but at a terrible cost. These three years killed or disabled 80,000 troops, " exceeding the total cost of Wellington's army from the beginning to the end of the Peninsular War". The superstition that ports commanded the sea was still nourished both by the French and ourselves. Had the men and ships wasted in the West Indies been employed in Europe, in the Netherlands, and off Brest and Toulon, the results might have been far different. Hotham, whose squandered opportunities had wrought irreparable mischief, was strangely rewarded by an Irish peerage, and gave way to Sir John Jervis, who inaugurated a new era of strenuous discipline and vigilance. But Bonaparte's campaign in North Italy crushed Sardinia out of the coalition, shut the Austrians up in Mantua, and drove Naples and the Papacy

Aug. 19

into neutrality, while Spain concluded an alliance with the Directory. The closing of the Italian ports and the threatened addition of the Spanish to the French fleets necessitated the order to evacuate the Mediterranean. Corsica was abandoned, and for eighteen months the French were left masters of the inland sea.

The war was no longer popular at home.[1] Repeated failures, the strain of taxation, and the prospect of the Emperor's desertion coerced the Cabinet into the repellent task of negotiating with the revolutionary Government. Overtures in the spring were rejected, but despite the opposition of the King, the extremists in the Cabinet, and of Burke, whose *Letters on a Regicide Peace* breathed fresh fire and slaughter, Malmesbury was sent to Paris. Instead of a France ruined by the Revolution he found unwelcome signs of prosperity and growing confidence. The desire for peace in both the English and French people was genuine, but the negotiations broke down over the proposed restoration of the Austrian Nether- Dec. 19 lands, and Malmesbury was ordered out of France by the Directory.

The ensuing eighteen months were the blackest that a British Government has yet had to face. Spain and Holland were in alliance with France; Bonaparte forced our ally, Austria, to accept the Preliminaries of Léoben subsequently converted into the Treaty April 18 of Campo Formio, by which Venice was suppressed and handed to Oct. 17 the Emperor, the French securing the Netherlands, the left bank of the Rhine, and the Ionian islands. Portugal made peace with France. Aug. 10 Ireland was marching to the Rebellion of '98, and a double invasion was planned—of Ireland from Brest, of England by the Dutch fleet in the Texel—the wings to a central stroke to be delivered by the united French and Spanish fleets in the Atlantic. There were fierce dissensions in the Cabinet, general discontent bred by high prices, scanty food, and severe taxation. The suspension of cash payments witnessed to the financial exhaustion, and the loan of £18,000,000 was only raised by an appeal to the unexhausted loyalty of the nation. At a critical period our naval power was crippled by the mutinies at Spithead and the Nore. It is not surprising that Pitt's health never recovered from the cruel strain of these terrible months, but the haughtily serene courage with which

---

[1] *Cf.* Sheffield to Auckland, September 12th, 1793 : "If something very extraordinary does not happen, he (Pitt) and the war will be in a damned hobble" (Auckland MSS., xli., 68). Again, January 5th, 1794 : "You would all be kicked out before the end of the session if there was a suitable man to put in the place of Pitt" (Auckland, *Correspondence*, iii., 168). Sheffield had written, January 23rd, 1793 : "I like it much (Grenville's reply to Chauvelin) ; it seems to show that war is inevitable" (Prothero, *Private Letters of Gibbon*, ii., 362).

the Prime Minister confronted the situation made him a worthy incarnation of the national spirit.

Hoche's expedition to Ireland was a serious affair. Some forty ships with 15,000 troops were shipped out of Brest, the greater part of which reached Bantry Bay. There was no effective force to dispute their landing, but luckily Hoche had been separated from the main body and Grouchy trifled with time and a fair wind. A heavy gale blew the armada from the coast, and, after losing five vessels in the storm and seven to British warships, reached Brest again, on January 17th. Bridport's slackness made this daring stroke of invasion by evasion memorable. "The grand fleet" was at Spithead, instead of lying off Brest; Bridport was not at sea till January 3rd, and he failed to intercept the returning expedition. Though the French had not secured the command of the sea, 15,000 men under a leader of Hoche's genius, in the Ireland of 1797, denuded of troops and ripe for rebellion, and with the mutinies in our squadrons imminent, might easily have put the British Executive in a dangerous dilemma. The moral of a tighter grip on the hostile harbours was obvious. The subsequent landing from two French frigates of 1200 ruffians, mostly liberated convicts, at Fishguard, who surrendered at the first summons, was an incident of no importance except in further alarming public opinion. To Jervis fell the honour of restoring our nerve. On St. Valentine's Day, with fifteen sail of the line, he came up with the Spanish fleet, twenty-seven strong, off Cape St. Vincent. England, as he said, needed a victory. The junction of the Spanish fleet with the French squadron at Brest must be stopped, no matter what it cost. It was quality against numbers, and quality won. Better still the battle brought Commodore Nelson at a bound to the front. The enemy had been cut into two divisions, and at the critical moment Nelson, disobeying an order, wore his ship *The Captain* out of the line, and, gallantly supported, prevented the divisions from uniting. Four prizes were taken, two of which were boarded and captured by Nelson himself. Jervis was content to let things stand at that, and the Spaniards escaped into Cadiz, where they were closely watched. Jervis was made Earl St. Vincent, and Nelson a Knight of the Bath. A new epoch had dawned. The self-confident commodore had begun to teach the lesson that he rammed home in Aboukir Bay, that "not victory but annihilation" must henceforward be the ideal.

The right wing of the invasion scheme, the Dutch fleet in the

Dec. 21

Feb.

Feb. 14

Texel, watched by Duncan, still remained intact, and at this point occurred the mutinies in the fleet. The Spithead division was the first affected ; a revolt precipitated by the undeniable grievances April 15 of the sailors—scandalously low pay, bad food, degrading punishments, no proper medical service, administrative injustices. After a short struggle the Admiralty conceded the main demands of the crews. But delay in voting the increase of pay and proclaiming the royal pardon caused the mutiny to break out again ; and not till May 7 Howe had been specially despatched to convince that there was no breach of faith was discipline restored. The outbreak at the Nore May 12 was more serious, and under Parker's leadership spread to Duncan's fleet at Yarmouth. The mutineers demanded revision of the Articles of War and virtual control over the officers. When these were peremptorily refused the crews endeavoured to terrorise Admiralty and country into submission. Yet the mutineers behaved more as strikers than as traitors. No attempt was made to desert *en bloc* to the enemy. The Spithead fleet refused its sympathy, and the resolute steps taken by the Admiralty broke up the revolt. By June 14th the last ship, Parker's, surrendered, and Parker with eighteen others was hanged. Symptoms of a similar spirit at the Cape and off Cadiz were sternly repressed by Macartney and St. Vincent. And shortly the navy splendidly vindicated its character.

Neither French nor Dutch utilised the crisis to strike. The French were partly handicapped by the renewal of peace negotiations, for Pitt had again sent Malmesbury to treat at Lille. Pitt's desire for peace was proved by the concessions offered—recognition of French conquests in the Netherlands, Luxemburg, and Savoy, the restoration of our colonial captures, save the Cape. Carnot and his party were anxious to accept these terms, but the *coup d'état* of 18 Fructidor put the war party in power, and Malmesbury for the second time was ordered to leave France. But the hopes of the reorganised Directory were now frustrated by the skill and iron will of Duncan. During the crisis of the mutiny the Admiral watched the Texel with two vessels only, resolved, if need be, to fight and sink with his flag flying. But the Dutch did not come out till October 6th; and on October 11th Duncan, with sixteen battleships to fifteen against him, after a general chase, signalled, without waiting to form a line, to break the enemy's line and engage to leeward — a daring order, for the Dutch ships were in shallow water only five miles off the land.   But Duncan was of the stuff of Hawke ; he wanted a smashing victory and saw how it could be won ; and he was rewarded by a greater success than Jervis had obtained at St. Vincent.   A pell-mell engagement, concentration on the Dutch rear, and ding-dong fighting on both sides resulted in nine Dutch ships being taken.   The invasion project was ruined.   No admiral better deserved his viscountship, and the handling of the fleet at Camperdown, which gave him his title, put "Keppel's Duncan" into the first class of our great sea officers. The secondary naval operations were not uniformly successful.   In

Feb.   the West Indies Abercromby and Harvey captured Trinidad,
July   but an attack on Puerto Rico failed.   Jervis detached Nelson to attack Santa Cruz de Tenerife.   But two attempts to carry the
July 22-25 town and harbour failed disastrously, and Nelson, having lost his right arm and nearly his life, was obliged to r turn.

With 1798 the war entered a new phase.   The determination of the Directory to make the issue one between a France victorious on the Continent and an isolated Great Britain, rallied the national forces on the side of our Government.   Although Pitt still clung to his idea that the revolutionary power at Paris might be upset, the main purpose of our policy now was to maintain intact our national independence.   It was a struggle in 1798 essentially between a great land and a great sea power, and for Great Britain the result would be settled on the water.   Bonaparte, appointed to the command of " the army of England," recognised that the project of flinging a force across an uncommanded Channel was too hazardous ; yet the expedition to Egypt was a subtle and gigantic development of the scheme of invasion.   Since the abandonment of the Mediterranean in 1796 that sea had been a French lake, but

May 2   Nelson was now sent to reconnoitre Toulon where a formidable armada was known to be in preparation.   Nelson missed the great armament of Bonaparte and Brueys, which sailed on May 19th,
June 13 captured Malta and then left for Alexandria.   Reinforced with the pick of Jervis's ships, Nelson, hot in pursuit, again missed his enemy
June 22 by some sixty miles and reached Alexandria two days in advance of the French.   Convinced that their destination was Syria, he sailed off; Napoleon slipped in behind him, landed, and was able to conquer Lower Egypt.   But Nelson was presently back again, to be rewarded with the welcome sight of Brueys' thirteen battleships

in Aboukir Bay. The battle of the summer night of August 1st was a masterpiece of decision, tactics, and seamanship, and deservedly set the seal on Nelson's fame. The wind was blowing down the French line and both fleets learned that they had to deal with a man who trifled neither with time nor wind, and whose favourite signal was " Engage more closely ". By doubling on the French van and containing the centre Nelson showed that annihilation was his object, and, had not a serious wound in the forehead prevented his controlling the action to the bitter end, it is probable that not a single French ship would have escaped. As it was, only two battleships and two frigates got away. The rest were either captured or destroyed. Nelson's peerage was the fit recognition of the most decisive victory as yet recorded in our naval annals. Bonaparte, who had narrowly escaped being destroyed at sea, was now shut up in Egypt.

At home the foolish secession of the bulk of the Opposition from Parliament, which marked the session of 1797, left the Government with a comparatively free hand. Fox, however, continued to agitate outside Parliament, and the repetition at the Whig Club of a toast, " To the sovereignty of the people," provided George III. with the pleasure of striking the Opposition leader's name from the roll of the Privy Council. In the Commons, Tierney had taken Fox's place. Accused by Pitt of obstruction he sent him a challenge, and the two statesmen satisfied their honour by exchanging harmless shots on Putney Heath. But Pitt's task was more seriously aggravated May 27 by the prolonged crisis in Irish affairs.

The constitutional and political difficulties inherent in the settlement of 1783, exemplified in the failure of the commercial proposals of 1785, had been re-exemplified in 1788 when the Irish Parliament proceeded in the Regency Question by methods in sharp contradiction to those adopted by the Ministry in London. The determination to maintain an unbroken control over the Irish Legislature involved in practice the concentration of power in the hands of the Lord-Lieutenant and the Castle Junto, *i.e.* the Executive group controlled by the English Cabinet. Hence the worst feature of the existing situation was to place the English Cabinet necessarily at the mercy of the small official circle, bent on preserving by every corrupt method the bigoted and reactionary Protestant ascendency. The two ablest representatives of this system were Fitzgibbon, who became Lord Chancellor in 1789 and Lord Clare in 1795, and John

Beresford, First Commissioner of Revenue; both were strenuous opponents of Catholic emancipation, and their advice and influence fatally dominated the Irish Government and the British Cabinet. The eleven years from 1782-93 offered golden opportunities. Had the problems of religious disabilities, of tithes, of the endowment of the Roman Catholic priesthood, of places and pensions, of an extended franchise and a redistribution of seats, and of the land system, been handled with sympathy and constructive statesmanship, the deep-rooted causes of agrarian disorder and political discontent might have been effectually extirpated. The remarkable decline in sectarian fanaticism, the increase in material prosperity dating from 1783, traceable to the awakened national spirit, the removal of trade restrictions and the encouragement of industry, pointed the plain moral that Ireland was ripe for, and would profit immensely by, reform. But in vain Grattan and the Whig party pleaded for a removal of the most patent evils. Under the corrupt and unjust representative system the majority of the Legislature could be controlled by the Castle; the Castle opposed reform, and the Cabinet at London took its policy from the Castle. The duty of converting a Protestant settlement into a prosperous and loyal Irish nation was burked or denied to be a duty at all. Outside the Legislature three well-marked sections can be broadly traced—the Catholic nobility and gentry, the Catholic democracy, and the Presbyterian north. But Catholic and Presbyterian had in the Legislature neither direct representation nor direct political influence. They could only proclaim and press their grievances through associations outside Parliament, in whose action the transition from agitation to disaffection, from a programme of drastic reform to revolution, was easy. The chronic lawlessness was seriously aggravated by three potent causes — the weakness of the Executive, the absence of respect for the unjust laws of a minority, the vices of the agrarian system. The success of the Volunteer movement had impressed Irishmen with the dangerous conviction that the Government would not yield to argument, but to organised force alone. By 1789 many thinking Irishmen argued that, until the Castle Junto had been broken up, there was no future for reform. "If," said Sir John Moore in 1798, "I were an Irishman, I should be a rebel." Such a sentence explains the careers of Wolfe Tone, Arthur O'Connor, and Edward Fitzgerald.

The French Revolution altered the whole situation. The sovereignty of the people, the principle of nationality, the abolition of tithes, the removal of religious disabilities, equality in civic and political rights before the law, the destruction of a privileged land system—these and other features corresponded to a nicety with the programme of ardent Reformers in Ireland. The Roman Catholic had long demanded emancipation, the Presbyterian urged political reconstruction with annual Parliaments, manhood suffrage, abolition of tests, and equal electoral districts. The Catholic as yet was not disaffected. He could be controlled through the priesthood, the prelates and the gentry, classes to whom much in the French Revolution was hateful. And with Canada before their eyes British statesmen, could they have thrown off the fettering superstitions of Fitzgibbon's faction, might by justice, sympathy, and toleration have reconciled the Roman Catholic population, at least three-fourths of Ireland, to British rule. The danger of uniting Roman Catholic and Presbyterian in a common hostility had long existed and been emphasised by keen-sighted observers of Irish conditions. And now in 1791 the pamphlet of *A Northern Whig* (Wolfe Tone) advocated strenuous co-operation between Presbyterian and Catholic, in order to force through a common programme. Its popularity was significant. Equally significant were the writer's open contempt for the settlement of 1782, and for the Irish Parliament, his plain hint that salvation would be found in political separation and democratic independence. The foundation of the Society of United 1791 Irishmen laid the basis of a revolutionary organisation. Next year the Catholic Convention began a fresh lease of vigorous life. The alienation of the Catholic from British ascendency had begun.

In 1793 pressure from London forced the Irish Executive to pass a large measure of relief. The disabilities on property were removed ; Dublin University and commissions in the army and navy were thrown open ; the franchise was conceded on terms of equality with the Protestant. But this long-delayed act of justice was fatally marred. Parliament was not thrown open to the Catholic, and the leadership of the enfranchised Catholic vote was deliberately withheld from the loyal Catholic nobles and gentry. Nothing was done to remedy the rotten borough system through which the Government maintained its reactionary majority. The deciding voice lay with the Castle Executive as before, and religious relief without Parliamentary reform, and the abolition of tests were an aggravation rather than a mitigation of Irish grievances.   But it is clear that when the Cabinet at London was determined on a measure it could compel the Irish Executive to give way.   The ultimate responsibility both in 1793 and later must and can only lie on Pitt and his colleagues at Whitehall.

By 1793 Great Britain was at war, and the creeping paralysis of panic had smitten the directors of policy at London.   Grattan, detesting republicanism and revolution, supported the war, but Grattan had lost much of his influence.   And the leaders of the United Irishmen, having broken away from constitutional Whiggism, were contemplating the overthrow of the Government with the help of France.   Defenderism, secret organisations for the abolition of tithes, and the Peep of Day Boys, a counter Protestant organisation, showed how on both sides the elements of a terrible civil war between races and creeds were being steadily piled up. And the successful landing of a French force might at any moment precipitate the crisis.   The last chance of averting disaster came with the viceroyalty of Fitzwilliam, whose appointment was due to the junction of the Portland Whigs with Pitt in 1794.   Fitzwilliam, convinced that the completion of Catholic emancipation was urgent, dismissed Beresford and negotiated with Grattan. The Viceroy thus clearly foreshadowed a change both of policy and system, which had the enthusiastic support of Catholic and Whig, but was a menacing challenge to the party entrenched in the Castle.   But the hopes that he had raised were speedily dashed. Disavowed by the British Cabinet, and recalled, Fitzwilliam left Dublin, lamented as no other Viceroy in the century.   His place was taken by Lord Camden, a weak and colourless puppet ; the Catholic Emancipation Bill was shelved, Beresford was restored and Fitzgibbon made Earl of Clare.   The Castle Junto was thus re-endowed with its old supremacy.

Jan. 4, 1795

Feb. 23
March 25

The evidence in a matter bitterly controverted then and since supports the conclusion that Fitzwilliam misinterpreted his powers and his mission.   He made the fatal mistake of acting with premature haste and not on explicit written instructions, but on a verbal understanding.   He was not authorised to dismiss Beresford ; he gave pledges precipitately which went beyond the policy contemplated by the British Cabinet, which was not prepared for a change

of system. His recall, concurred in by his Whig colleagues, was
therefore justified on the narrow merits of the case.[1] But both
Pitt and Portland shared the responsibility for the initial misunderstanding. Their neglect of urgent messages from the Viceroy, and
their failure to appreciate the gravity of the crisis were inexcusable,
and contributed in no small degree to the wrecking of Pitt's later
policy. On the broader issue, it is at least arguable that Fitzwilliam's scheme of reform by a reformed Administration, resolutely
supported from London, could have been carried, and that it alone
at the eleventh hour could have kept the Roman Catholics loyal
and have saved Ireland three years of horror and degradation, and
a century of memories that no subsequent statesmanship could
obliterate.

It was not to be. Camden's viceroyalty inaugurated a period
of lawlessness, disorder, outrage, flaming finally into the inferno of
religious and racial civil war. Haunted by the fear of invasion, of
armed Jacobinism within, reinforced by armed Jacobinism from
without, obsessed by spies and informers, the Irish Government, in
the absence of regular troops sufficient to defend the country and
maintain peace, had recourse to yeomanry and militia raised locally.
At the Diamond in Armagh, Defenders and Peep of Day Boys Sept.
came to open conflict. The Orange Society was founded, and
Ulster was ravaged by Protestants bent on driving the Catholics
"to hell or Connaught". The United Irishmen attempted to
organise a counter-resistance. But the Insurrection Act of 1796
provided the Executive with unlimited powers, and "martial law"
was virtually proclaimed and enforced up to the hilt. After Ulster
the midland and southern counties were taken in hand, and the
yeomanry and militia, aided by the magistrates, let loose on the
Catholics. During 1796 and 1797 the licence of the undisciplined
and uncontrolled "troops," the tortures, burnings, floggings,
shootings in cold blood, in which women and girls were
not spared, make a sickening record. In the name of law,
security, and religion the anti-Jacobin government of Ireland and
its agents showed that it could match the excesses of a Committee of Public Safety or the Revolutionary Tribunal at Paris. Feb.-May
In 1798 the United Irish movement was broken by the arrest of

---

[1] See especially the correspondence in *Dropmore Papers*, vols. ii. and iii.,
and references in Introduction, iii., xxxv.

390 ENGLAND AND THE FRENCH REVOLUTION [1789-

its leaders—Arthur O'Connor, Robert Emmet and McNeven, Edward Fitzgerald (who died from the wounds received in an attempt to resist arrest), Henry and John Sheares. A rising had been planned for the summer, but the rebels were now leaderless. Ulster gave little trouble; Munster and Connaught were quiet; in Leinster alone was there serious civil war. In Meath, Kildare, and Carlow the insurrection was easily suppressed. But in Wexford a force formidable in numbers was mustered. It swept the country-side, headed by fighting priests as generals, won some successes and signalised its temporary triumph by the murder of a good many Protestants, notably at the massacre on Wexford Bridge. The failure to take Waterford, a severe repulse at Arklow, and the final defeat of the main body and the capture of their camp at Vinegar Hill by General Lake shattered the rebellion. The smouldering embers were then quenched in a final orgie of exultant vengeance which sought its excuse in the recent excesses of the rebels. The leaders of the United Irish movement planned to overthrow the Government with the aid of France, and the French made serious efforts to provide assistance. The checkmating of the schemes of invasion was more the sailors' than the soldiers' affair, and after the failure of Hoche, French help proved futile. Humbert reached Killala Bay, landed with a small force, and routed part of Lake's force at Castlebar (The Race of Castlebar), the militia and yeomanry running away in a panic, but was obliged to surrender at Ballina-muck. Hardy's expedition was effectively blocked at Brest until September, when it slipped out and reached Lough Swilly, only to be cut up by a British squadron. Wolfe Tone, on board one of the French ships, was captured, but he preferred to cut his throat before sentence of death could be executed. A third attempt by Savary brought his ships to Killala Bay, whence they promptly returned, not without difficulty, to Rochelle. In fact, unless the French could land in adequate numbers the troops, and probably the ships, were a gift to their enemies; a formidable armada made evasion more difficult, and was threatened by disaster at sea unless the fleet prepared to dispute its passage was first disposed of. Nor did suc-cessful evasion confer the command of the sea. The repeated efforts to prove the contrary from 1795-1801, provided by Ireland and Egypt, taught our Admiralty valuable lessons for the later war with Napoleon.

Wolfe Tone's scheme of a united Irish insurrection was wrecked when Protestant turned on Catholic. The Catholics who rose in 1798 did not fight for an Ireland of both religions, united on a democratic basis, but rather to save themselves from extermination. No civilised Government can palter with conspiracy and treason, overt or concealed. It is claimed that the barbarities, euphemistically termed "severity," during the two and a half years that preceded the rebellion proper broke the back of a gigantic scheme; that the rebels, particularly in 1798, were guilty of indefensible excesses. Literally, both claims are true. But the first argument would absolve Alva and the authors of the September massacres. The true indictment against the Irish Executive is that it employed methods calculated, perhaps deliberately, to provoke the innocent into resistance, and such as no civilised Administration can ever be entitled to employ. The enforcement of obedience to law and order by butchery and torture is a crime as well as a blunder. The Irish Executive forgot the first duty of a Government, that it is responsible for the future no less than the present. And the weight of the evidence supports the conclusion that the barbarities of the rebels were trifling compared with those of the victors, and were largely reprisals when Catholic Ireland had been maddened by the fanatic savagery of magistrates and yeomanry. The encouragement and protection of those who did the worst things remain a blacker stain on the men in authority than even the ghastly cruelties perpetrated. A Government, for example, that rewarded the ruffianly official, Thomas Fitzgerald, the High Sheriff of Tipperary, with a baronetcy is beyond defence. Abercromby and Moira were soldiers who knew the horrors of war; the former was compelled to resign because he told the truth in a proclamation; the latter was voted down in the British House of Lords because he had the courage and the humanity publicly to protest. Cornwallis, also a soldier and experienced administrator, who succeeded Camden, was horrified at the state in which he found Jure, 1798 Ireland and at the tone of bloodthirsty bigotry prevailing in Dublin. But after Abercromby's resignation not till Cornwallis's arrival was a serious attempt made at headquarters to discountenance and check the atrocities committed in the name of law. Nor did Pitt think fit to intervene, though a few lines from the Prime Minister might have done much. Yet on Pitt the doctrine that

the end, the legislative union, justified the means took a stern
revenge, and a still sterner retribution on Protestant Ireland and
England.

The formation of the Second Coalition against France was the
indirect result of the victory in Aboukir Bay. Great Britain's
resources were further strengthened by the courage of Colonel
Maitland, who evacuated St. Domingo on his own responsibility
and left Toussaint L'Ouverture the master of a black republic
which for five years had crippled our military power in Europe.
The seizure of Minorca by Stuart imposed a fresh strain on our
depleted army and overworked navy. Nelson, too, in an evil hour
for his fame, had sailed for Naples, where he fell under the demoralising influence of Lady Hamilton, the bosom friend of the debased
Queen of a debased Court. For the next eighteen months his genius
was in eclipse. Yet the omens were favourable for a renewal of
the European struggle with France. Napoleon was shut up in
Egypt. The corrupt Directory was unpopular. Its aggressive
action in attacking Switzerland and Piedmont, substituting a republic at Rome in the seat of the aged Pontiff, Pius VI., driven
into exile, and its domineering claims in the settlement of German
affairs had roused the fears and indignation of Europe. Pressed
by Russia, the Sultan had declared war on France, and the half-
mad Tsar Paul, who had succeeded the Tsarina Catherine in 1797,
deeply mortified at the French capture of Malta, now allied with the
Turks, and was ready to co-operate with Great Britain and Austria.
A vigorous league, which had struck hard in the autumn of 1798,
might have extinguished the Directory. But delays and the damning lack of unity of purpose ruined the cause of the dynasties.
Prussia refused to abandon its neutrality. Austria was more
jealous of Prussia than of France, suspicious of Russia, and at
loggerheads with England over money and military plans. Naples,
as Nelson said, was a Court of fiddlers and harlots. The Anglo-
Russian Treaty was not concluded until December 29th, and Austria
did not declare war until March 12th, 1799. Six months earlier,
Naples, with Nelson's consent, foolishly attacked the French. Ferdinand entered Rome but was promptly driven out; his army under the
Austrian Mack was routed and the Bourbon Court under Nelson's

Nov.

escort fled to Palermo. On the mainland the French established the Parthenopean Republic. In the north the House of Savoy took refuge in Sardinia, and Piedmont was overrun. Against these French successes the allies could only place the capture of Minorca, Dec. 9, the blockade of Malta by British forces, and the seizure of the Ionian 1798 Islands by a Russian squadron.

The terms of the Second repeated those of the First Coalition. The main military operations in North Italy, Switzerland, and the Rhine were allotted to Russian and Austrian armies, subsidised by Great Britain. Our naval supremacy in the Mediterranean was to be employed in assisting the Italian campaign. The avowed object of the allies was to crush the Revolutionary Government at Paris and reduce France to the limits of 1792. Pitt laid down the restoration of the Bourbons as the unalterable object of British policy; nor so long as he was in power was this object abandoned; and he still cherished the idea that the resources of the Revolution were nearing exhaustion. Pitt's British courage, tenacity, and singleness of aim might have saved the League of which England was the heart and soul; but our allies, the Courts, had not changed their character nor improved their methods; Bonaparte, by a stroke of luck, returned to France and revealed a genius in statesmanship and administration as formidable as his genius in war; and the military direction in Great Britain showed that it had forgotten and learned nothing.

The initial successes of the allies were remarkable. Jourdan was driven across the Rhine by the Archduke Charles; Suvorov in command of the Russo-Austrian forces won the victories of Cassano, the Trebbia, and Novi. The Cisalpine and Roman Republics dissolved and the French in North Italy now only held Genoa. April 29 Contrary to Russian wishes, but in agreement with England, the June 19 Austrians refused to restore the House of Savoy and proposed to Aug. 15 annex Piedmont. In the South, Cardinal Ruffo organised a rising on behalf of the Bourbons; the French withdrew northwards and Naples was re-occupied. The Republicans, however, held out in June 13 two forts, and Ruffo arranged for their capitulation. Nelson, June 19 arriving from Palermo, set the capitulation aside. None the less, the garrison came out. Their leaders were seized and on Ferdinand's arrival executed. Nelson went further. Carraciolo, a Republican formerly in the royal service, had escaped prior to the capitulation but was subsequently arrested. Nelson insisted on his being tried by a court-martial of Neapolitan officers on his own flag-ship; and when he was found guilty of treason had him hanged the same **June 29** evening. It seems established that Ruffo exceeded his instructions and that Nelson acted on Ferdinand's authority and in accordance with his wishes. But no legal or technical justification can exonerate him from the charge that he forgot he was, not the agent of a vindictive Court, but a British admiral and the representative at Naples of the British nation. The honour of his country was in the keeping of the victor of Aboukir Bay, and, to his lasting discredit, he betrayed the trust.[1]

With the summer the star of the Coalition paled. A joint Anglo-Russian expedition was despatched under Abercromby, who disapproved of the scheme but was overruled, to the Helder, and the Dutch fleet in the Texel was successfully seized. Delays **Aug. 27** in the arrival of the Russian contingent enabled the French and the Dutch to organise their defence. The Duke of York, appointed to the command of the allied forces, was then defeated in an attack on Bergen and the troops were pinned down to their entrenchments. The expected aid from the Orange party came to nothing; and on October 18th the Duke made the Convention of Alkmaar, by which he evacuated Holland and surrendered his prisoners but retained the captured fleet—a humiliating conclusion to a badly planned, badly equipped and executed enterprise. The campaign in Switzerland also completely miscarried. Masséna **Sept. 26** defeated the Russians under Korsakov at Zürich, and Suvorov was compelled to make a calamitous if heroic retreat into Tyrol. Worse still, Bonaparte had escaped from the East. Earlier in **Feb. 15** the year he had attacked Syria, taken El Arish and stormed Jaffa. But at Acre the sea power that had shut him up in Egypt again baffled him. He could only invest it by land, while British ships under Sir Sidney Smith intercepted the French stores, kept the garrison supplied, and helped the Turks to repel every attempt to storm their lines. Acre stood between Bonaparte and his plan of taking Europe in the rear. On May 20th the siege was raised and the French returned to Egypt. The news from Paris convinced Bonaparte that " the pear was ripe ". He deserted **Aug. 23** the army, slipped through the British cruisers and landed in France.

[1] See Appendix xi.

The *coup d'état* of Brumaire overthrew the Directory.   France craved Oct. 9
a Cæsar, and the Cæsar was there in the person of the military Nov. 9
chief, the incarnation of the triumphant Revolution.   The Consulate, with Bonaparte as First Consul, and a new constitution were
set up.   He fully understood that a victorious peace would make
him Dictator of France, and that he might still be master of the
world.

Our Admiralty was being taught some useful lessons in the
disposition and control of their forces.   Bonaparte's unmolested
escape to Fréjus was not creditable.   More striking still was
Bruix's famous cruise.   He slipped out of Brest, passed into the April 25
Mediterranean, reached Toulon, convoyed transports to Genoa,
picked up Spanish ships at Carthagena, and another squadron at
Cadiz, and got safely back into Brest without being brought to Aug.
action by Bridport, Jervis, Keith, or Nelson.   Bridport's grip on
Brest was culpably slack, but Jervis's disposition of the Mediterranean fleet and Nelson's devotion to the Neapolitan court of fiddlers
and harlots are open to grave censure.   Good luck and Bruix's lack
of initiative, not good management, saved us from sharp retribution.

The final break up of the coalition was preceded by a letter
from the First Consul to George III., expressing his desire for
peace.   Grenville answered it by a lecture in the shape of a
despatch, to the effect that the restoration of the Bourbons would
be the best guarantee of pacific dispositions.   Even George III.
thought this gratuitous advice as to the most suitable form of
French government " much too strong," but Pitt allowed it to go ;
and the Ministerial principle that, as Fox said, " we must keep
Bonaparte in a state of probation " was duly approved by a large
majority in both Houses of Parliament.   The state of probation
proved a process of disillusionment, short, sharp, and decisive.
The Tsar Paul, angry with both his allies, withdrew from the
League.   Moreau drove the Austrians back on the Upper Danube ;
Masséna held out in Genoa until Bonaparte could cross the Alps
and deliver at Marengo the *coup de grace* to Austrian ambitions June 14
in Lombardy ; and then Moreau's crushing blow at Hohenlinden
completed the business which was neatly wound up by Macdonald Dec. 3
and Brune on the Mincio and the Adige.   The Emperor was in
fact smashed out of the Coalition.   The peace of Lunéville conceded to France the line of the Rhine, and of the Adige, while Feb. 9,
                                                              1801

the revolutionary Republics in Holland, Switzerland, and North Italy were formally recognised as independent. Murat had cowed Ferdinand of Naples into submission. By the Treaty of Florence the Neapolitan ports were closed to Great Britain and Taranto handed to a French garrison, an arrangement with one advantage. It freed Nelson for better work than the protection of Lady Hamilton and her Bourbon patrons.

Our military operations had been singularly inept. June and July were wasted in sending troops to Brittany, where it was discovered nothing could be done. Reinforced, they sailed south, inspected Ferrol and reimbarked, repeated the inspection at Vigo, and went on to Gibraltar. Co-operation with the Austrians in Piedmont had been promised, but Abercromby was not able to leave Minorca until June 22nd, when Marengo had been won, and he was now sent to Gibraltar with the idea of a stroke at Cadiz. But the sailors declined to guarantee a re-embarkation, so the force proceeded to Malta, which, after a two years' blockade, had at last been captured. Dundas then decided Abercromby should try what he could do in Egypt, which he reached February 8th, 1801. No proper preparations for a desert campaign had been made, but Abercromby's brilliant disembarkation in Aboukir Bay and victory at Alexandria saved headquarters from another failure. Abercromby himself was mortally wounded. Bonaparte's reinforcements gave Jervis (who had replaced Bridport) the slip, but were hunted back to Toulon ; Cairo was taken before a force under Baird, sent from India, arrived, and the capitulation of Alexandria provided for the evacuation of Egypt by the French. It was the first success on land won in nine years of war, and if sea-power alone made it possible the gallant Abercromby had more than his share in the result.

It came at the right time. To Pitt's expressed willingness to join in a general peace, Napoleon had replied by insisting on including the sea in the necessary armistice, for he desired to reinforce the French garrisons in Malta and Egypt. But this, with good reason, our Government refused. Napoleon then concentrated on isolating Great Britain. The Tsar Paul, whose admiration for the First Consul was strengthened by his resentment at the retention of Malta by England, was negotiating to revive the Armed Neutrality of 1780. Prussia, Sweden, and Denmark joined Russia in a league to enforce the principles laid down twenty years earlier, and Dec. 18, an embargo was laid on British vessels. Our Government replied [1800] with a counter-embargo, and despatched a fleet under Sir Hyde Jan. 14, Parker, with Nelson as second in command, to the Baltic. Parker [1801] was a pedantic and cautious leader, but the genius of Nelson, freed from the atmosphere which had "Sicilified" his brain and conscience, never shone out more brilliantly. Entrusted by Parker with the attack on the Danish fleet at Copenhagen, supported by the batteries of the King's Deep, he carried it through with a superb combination of nerve and judgment. Parker's signal to discontinue the action (which if it had been obeyed would probably have entailed a disaster), was answered by keeping the signal "Engage the enemy more closely" flying; and an armistice with the Danes ended a contest remarkable for the tenacity with which both sides had fought. Parker was recalled, Nelson rewarded with a viscountship and the supreme command. But the assassination of the Tsar Paul, and the accession of Alexander I., who came to March 24 terms with Great Britain, broke up the league. Napoleon was June 19 not unnaturally furious. Portugal had agreed to close her ports June to England. The mysterious power of the sea, at Malta, in Egypt, and in the Baltic was robbing him of every advantage. And another check followed. Linois with three battleships was successfully sent from Toulon to raise the blockade of Cadiz, unite with the Spaniards and sail for Egypt. Saumarez attacked him in Algeçiras Bay with six battleships, was severely handled by the shore batteries, lost one of his ships, and retired to Gibraltar. The Spaniards came to Linois' aid, but Saumarez had refitted, chased the allies, who lost two vessels, into Cadiz, and sealed the squadron up in the harbour. His skill and obstinacy had, in St. Vincent's phrase, "put us on velvet". Outside Europe, Surinam had been July 3-8, occupied in 1799, Curaçoa in 1800, the Dutch and Swedish islands [1801] in the West Indies captured, and Madeira taken from the Portuguese in 1801—the fruits of British supremacy on the seas.

In India operations of great importance had effectually frustrated serious dangers to British rule. The master-hand in this critical period had been that of Richard Colley Wellesley, Earl of Mornington, the head of a remarkable family which gave four distinguished servants to the public service, the most famous of whom was Arthur, afterwards Duke of Wellington. Lord Mornington, who became Marquess Wellesley in 1799, was a polished scholar, a keen disciple of Adam Smith, an ambitious man of the world, the friend of Wilberforce, Grattan, and Canning, and one of the few intimates of Pitt, who selected him for the Governor-Generalship in 1797. When Wellesley arrived in India in 1798 he had already decided that the policy of non-intervention pursued by his predecessor, Sir John Shore (Lord Teignmouth, Viceroy, 1792-98) was no longer suitable. In the North, Oudh, badly administered, was threatened by invasion from Afghan, Sikhs or Mahrattas. The death in 1794 of the great Mahrattan prince, Madhaji Rao Sindhia, "who had made himself," in Malcolm's phrase, "the sovereign of an empire by calling himself the headman of a village," had temporarily shaken the solidarity of Mahratta supremacy, but in the dissolving combinations, ineradicable ambitions and fighting power of the Mahratta chiefs—Sindhia's successor, Holkar, the Bhonsla of Berar, the Gaikwar of Baroda—always capable of uniting under the formal primacy of a puppet Peishwa at Poona, lay a perpetual challenge to the East India Company and the peace of Hindostan. Haidarabad was another centre of danger. A union of the Nizam with the Mahrattas would be serious for Bombay and Madras, and in the Carnatic the slackness of the Madras Government and the incompetence of the Nawab had brought about chaos. Most serious of all, at Mysore was Tippu, burning to avenge the check administered by Cornwallis. These dangers were aggravated by the intrigues of the French. Mauritius provided the Republic with a valuable base for operations. Bonaparte's expedition to Egypt was a step in a far-reaching scheme, the avowed purpose of which was to undermine the foundations of the British Empire. French soldiers had helped Sindhia to organise his power; French officers were assisting the Nizam to "create a French State in the peninsula," while the Mahometan ruler of Hindu Mysore professed sympathy with the principles of 1789, with his tongue in his cheek could call himself "Citizen Tippoo," and was in active communication with Mauritius.

Wellesley's period of rule is a chapter in the world-wide struggle of Great Britain with France, as well as a chapter in the consolidation of British ascendency in India. The new Viceroy, as member of the Board of Control, had previously studied Indian affairs, and he arrived with a clear conception of the task before

him and a no less clear confidence that he was the man successfully
to carry it through. The first phase of his administration covers
the years 1798-1801. Mysore was the pressing danger. It was
necessary to isolate Tippu. By a judicious combination of diplomacy and pressure the Nizam was induced to disband his French
contingent and replace it by a force officered by the British. John
Malcolm remained as Resident at Haidarabad, and the offer to
mediate between the Nizam and the Mahrattas ripened into the
defensive alliance of 1800, by which the territories of the Deccan
State were guaranteed and the Nizam entered the subsidiary system
with its correlative consequence of British control. Overtures to
Tippu for a similar arrangement failed. Between refusal of and
submission to our terms there was no middle way, and Napoleon's
Egyptian expedition made it necessary to strike hard and promptly.
The experience gained in Cornwallis's campaign was of great value,
and Wellesley came down to Madras to control and direct opera-
tions. War was declared on February 22nd, 1799 ; on May 4th
Seringapatam was carried by an assault, in which Tippu fell.
Part of Mysore was then allotted to the Nizam, part annexed to
direct British rule. The remainder was reserved as a compact
State, to which the Hindoo dynasty displaced by Hyder Ali was
restored under British protection. A similar policy was followed in
Surat and Tanjore ; and in the Carnatic, on the death of the
Nawab, whose disloyalty had been proved by documentary evidence,
the new Nawab was restricted in revenue, and steps were taken to
clear up the financial chaos and bring the administration under the
Company's control. Oudh in the North presented similar features
—a buffer State, an incompetent ruler, no adequate guarantee for
security from without or satisfactory government within. Wellesley has been blamed for coercing the Nawab into acceptance of the
terms he thought necessary, viz. the cession of a frontier district to
pay for the increased contingent of British troops, and the reform of
the military and financial administration. To the wrath of the
directors at home, to whom patronage was a valuable perquisite, the
Governor-General had placed his brother Henry, afterwards Lord
Cowley, a very competent officer, in charge of the ceded district.
But Wellesley conceived that the situation in Oudh left him no
option. Oudh was on the British border ; its condition was a peril
to British rule ; its present administration was a burden to its in-

habitants ; its weakness was a temptation to Sikh, Afghan and Mahratta. It has even been argued by competent judges that Wellesley would have been justified in annexation, subsequently effected by Dalhousie in 1856, and that Oudh would have gained by such a policy. Be that as it may, the vigorous policy of the Governor-General had shown by 1801 that Pitt had sent no un- worthy successor to Warren Hastings to Calcutta in 1797.

Peace, much needed, was at hand, but the negotiations fell to a new Prime Minister. Ireland, the treachery of his colleagues and the obstinate superstition of the King had driven Pitt to resign. The rebellion of 1798 and the deplorable conditions of swollen debt and envenomed fanaticism which its suppression had entailed had clinched the conclusion, growing in Pitt's mind since 1785, that a legislative union between Great Britain and Ireland was now in- evitable. The incorporation of the Irish into the Imperial legis- lature offered a practical solution of the difficulties and anomalies in the administrative and constitutional relations inherent in the settlement of 1782. Healing measures for Ireland were now a matter of equity and urgency, and Pitt was convinced by Lord Clare that it was dangerous, if not impossible, in 1798 to combine the Protestant political ascendency with justice to the Catholic, and reform for Ireland save through and by a Parliament of the United Kingdom of Great Britain and Ireland. In Pitt's policy, therefore, the legislative union came first as an essential preliminary ; but it was vitally bound up with Roman Catholic emancipation, the commutation of tithe, the provision of endowment for the Catholic priesthood and the Dissenters, and free trade between the two countries to be legislatively united. The union, in brief, was only an element and not the most important element in a compre- hensive scheme which, by large and generous concessions, was to eradicate deep-seated grievances and stanch wounds inflicted by three years of barbarous civil war. Pitt, at least in 1798, was not guilty of the superficial assumption that a compulsory incorporation of two legislatures, involving the sacrifice of the symbols and organs of Irish nationality and self-government, but unaccompanied by far reaching reform, would by itself solve the complicated Irish problem. Nor in 1798 was he blind to the fact that to deprive Ireland of its Legislature in order to bolster up every feature of the existing system would aggravate rather than diminish the grievances of every class, save the official Castle Junto, in the country. But his policy as he framed it was never tried. Pitt lived long enough to suffer the humiliation of defeat. He was spared the long-drawn bitterness of seeing his mutilated scheme whittled down to the Legislative union alone, and erected into an instrument for refusing the reforms and perpetuating the abuses which it was the main object of his plan to extirpate.

Although the proposals for a union were not formally made in the Irish Parliament of 1799, the Address was generally recognised to raise the principle. Successful in the Lords, the Government Jan. 23 was defeated in the Commons by five votes. Concurrently Pitt April carried with ease in both Chambers of the British Legislature resolutions in favour of a Union. Yet had the Irish Executive been responsible to the Irish Legislature the Ministry must have resigned or a general election followed; and it is tolerably certain that in 1799, so strong was anti-Unionist feeling in Ireland, the Opposition would have increased their majority. But Pitt dared not risk an appeal even to the limited and corrupt Irish electorate. The Union must be carried in the existing Parliament or it would not be carried at all. A majority, therefore, had to be created. The young Lord Castlereagh, specially selected by Pitt to be Chief Secretary to the Viceroy in 1799, a strong Unionist and supporter of Roman Catholic emancipation, convinced the British Cabinet that unless Roman Catholic support was secured the Government scheme would be wrecked. He returned to Ireland authorised to secure the support required. No definite pledge was given; but Cornwallis, the Viceroy, explicitly stated that so long as the Irish Legislature existed the Government would resist concessions to the Catholics. It was generally understood in Catholic quarters that the British Cabinet was in favour of relief and the Viceroy was officially informed of the Cabinet's views and permitted to utilise the information. Castlereagh accordingly secured, on this general understanding, a large measure of Catholic help. Assurances alone, however, would not create a majority in the Legislature. The Viceroy and the Chief Secretary, therefore, set to work to haggle and job with " the most corrupt people under heaven," the members ; Cornwallis's letters remain as a proof of how repulsive and dirty the task was, but it was carried through with a thoroughness that would have made Henry Fox envious. The borough owners, condemned

26

under the scheme to lose their patronage, were compensated on the scale of £15,000 apiece ; forty-one peerages were created or advanced a step, and a brisk trade in honours, places, and pensions went on ; the British Secret Service Fund was heavily drawn on. The result was seen in the Parliament of 1800 when an amendment to the Address was rejected by forty-two votes. By March 28th the articles of Union were carried, then approved by the British Parliament and embodied in a Bill passed by the Irish Legislature. On August 1st the measure received the royal assent and the first meeting of the Parliament of the United Kingdom of Great Britain and Ireland met at Westminster, January 22nd, 1801.

Resembling in form the Legislative union of England and Scotland in 1707 the statute incorporating the Irish Parliament was necessarily different in various details. A new Great Seal, an amended Royal Standard, and a redrafting of the title and designation of the Crown symbolised the amalgamation. The succession to the throne as defined by the Act of Settlement was confirmed. Twenty-eight peers elected for life represented the Irish House of Lords, a hundred members the House of Commons ; but restrictions were placed on the prerogative to create Irish peerages, while an Irish peer was permitted to sit for a British constituency in the Commons of the United Parliament. Castlereagh himself and Palmerston were prominent examples of this privilege. The Protestant Episcopal Church of Ireland was united, " in discipline, doctrine, and government," with the Established Church of England, and the maintenance of this union declared to be a fundamental article of the " treaty ". Four spiritual peers represented the Irish branch of the Church in the House of Lords, which was also made the final Court of Appeal from the Irish Courts. Economic equality and freedom of trade on the lines of the scheme of 1785 were laid down, and the financial relations of the two countries were regulated by complicated clauses, the interpretation of which has provoked a century of insoluble controversy. In the articles of Union as originally carried, the absence of any prohibition of Catholics from sitting in the future Parliament of the United Kingdom is noticeable, and is a striking indication of Pitt's policy. It is also characteristic of the transaction as a whole that its terms were so arranged, and the procedure carefully planned, not merely to avoid a reference of the measure to the Irish electorate, but to prevent

the Opposition in Dublin or at Westminster raising the question of
Parliamentary reform in either country.　No one understood better
than Pitt or Castlereagh the vulnerability of the representative
system in Ireland to unanswerable criticism.　An unreformed
system in Ireland was therefore taken over untouched in order that
an unreformed system might continue unquestioned in Great Britain.
The Union was not, as was the treaty of 1707, a union of two free
and independent nations, arranged by plenipotentiaries, in which
every sacrifice compatible with imperial unity was made to the
national sentiment of the party surrendering the symbols and
organs of its independence.　The Irish Union was a legal instrument arranged by the British Cabinet on the advice of Irish
officials responsible to that Cabinet alone, and carried by corruption in a Parliament which did not represent the Protestants, and
to which three-fourths of Ireland were by statute prevented from
sending representatives of their own religion.　It could not have
been carried by any other means than corruption and a vague but
authorised expectation of Catholic relief.　The end, such as it was,
has been held to have justified the means.　No other justification
has been or can be suggested.

The transactions of 1799 and 1800 also re-emphasise the conclusion that when a British Cabinet had made up its mind it could
force any policy or measure it thought necessary through the Irish
Parliament.　In 1790 that Irish Parliament might have been remodelled as easily and by the same methods as those by which it was
extinguished in 1800.　The " unbribed intellect of Ireland," voiced
by Grattan, Foster, Parsons, Charlemont, opposed the Union ; but a
viceroy in 1790, armed with the mandate and resources of Cornwallis and Castlereagh, would have had the unbribed intellect on
his side, the whole-hearted aid of the Roman Catholics and no small
help from the northern Nonconformists.　The purchase in 1790 of
the fee simple of Irish corruption would have led in a reformed
Parliament to measures that would have prevented the rebellion of
1798, and might well have led to a union as national in essence and
as richly blessed in its results for the uniting nations as that of
1707.　But the driving power of 1799 was not applied in 1790.
Pitt nibbled at the Irish problem in 1785 ; he did not grapple
with it until 1798.　It was then too late.　Cornwallis pithily
summed up the situation.　Ireland could not be saved without

the Union; but "you must not take it for granted that it will be saved by it".

Pitt at least was not guilty of so foolish a delusion. The Union completed, he submitted to the Cabinet a draft of the healing measures—provision for the Catholic priesthood and the Dissenting clergy, commutation of tithe, and a political instead of a sacramental test for office by which Roman Catholics would be able to enter the Legislature and hold offices at present locked against them by "the symbols of atoning grace". Loughborough, the Lord Chancellor, aware of the King's conviction that he would violate his Coronation oath if he assented to Roman Catholic Relief, betrayed the Prime Minister's confidential communication to his royal master; and with the help of Auckland, who owed his political career and peerage to Pitt,[1] and the Archbishops of Canterbury and Armagh, stiffened, if that were possible, the bigotry of George III. Once more the King asserted that he would consider any man a personal enemy who proposed such a measure; and the Cabinet that had previously agreed to emancipation now turned against it. Pitt could only tender his resignation, which was accepted. The King's mind gave way and Pitt promised not to raise the question in his lifetime. Fox gave a similar pledge in 1806. Neither statesman, in strict constitutional theory, had the right so to bind themselves. But there was no question of the King yielding. Pitt, Fox, and Ireland had therefore to wait either for the King's permanent madness or his death. The arch-wrecker of Pitt's Irish policy was George III. He enjoyed a fivefold triumph without the concessions that hurt his "principles". He got the Union; he drove Pitt, when he resisted, from office; he exacted a pledge from the two leading statesmen of the day; he outlived both Pitt and Fox; and he did not go permanently mad until he had inoculated his son and successor with his own bigotry.

The healing measures were postponed, some for thirty years, some for ever. After 1801 the Tory policy was not Pitt's Irish policy, but it was a policy made possible and doubly pernicious by the Union. Pitt subsequently blamed himself for his delay, which enabled treacherous colleagues to mine the ground in advance, in submitting his healing measures to George III. But

Feb.

---

[1] It is significant that Auckland was excluded from Pitt's second Administration in 1804.

haste or delay after the Union was safely on the Statute Book mattered little. King and Cabinet then had Pitt in a vice of his own making. Pitt in 1798 could have insisted on a preliminary pledge from Sovereign and colleagues that the complementary relief measures were to follow the Union ; and that in or out of office he would oppose Union unaccompanied by reforms ; he was, as his action proved, prepared to resign to keep his moral pledges to the Catholics, and to enforce the necessity of those healing measures. A threat of resignation before the Union was carried, to be followed by the certainty of opposition, would have placed Pitt in a position impregnable to misconstruction, and would have defined an issue of momentous import to the future both of Ireland and Great Britain.

The new Ministry was formed by the Speaker, Henry Addington, a dull, decorous, well meaning and vain mediocrity, thoroughly congenial to the King. Of the old Cabinet, Grenville, Spencer, Dundas, Windham and Cornwallis, together with the subordinates Castlereagh and Canning, both advocates of Roman Catholic relief, resigned with their chief. Portland, Chatham, Auckland, and Westmoreland remained. New recruits were found in Lord Hawkesbury (Foreign Secretary) and Lord Hobart (Secretary for War), to whose office Colonial affairs were transferred. Loughborough was properly punished by exclusion from the new Ministry. In his place Lord Eldon began that memorable tenure of the Lord Chancellorship which, with one brief interlude, lasted until 1827. The Government was admittedly weak in *personnel* and experience. Next year it was strengthened by the adhesion of Castlereagh, who, at Pitt's request, became President of the Board of Control.

Overtures for peace were made by our Foreign Office in March, 1801, and the next twelve months were spent in prolonged and wearisome negotiations. Popular opinion demanded a serious effort to end an exhausting war. Napoleon's power on the Continent was as indisputable as was our command of the sea ; and Napoleon recognised that he needed time for the internal reorganisation of France and the consolidation of his supremacy in the territories adjoining the French frontier. The signing of the preliminaries Oct. 1 gave great satisfaction both in France and Great Britain, and Cornwallis was sent as Special Envoy to Amiens to meet Napoleon's brother, Joseph. The definitive treaty, in which Spain and Holland joined, was finally signed on March 27, 1802. Of her conquests Great Britain retained only Ceylon and Trinidad, the rest being restored to France or her allies. Malta was to be given back to the Knights of St. John within three months of the ratification of the treaty, and to remain under the guarantee of the Great Powers. The French undertook to evacuate Taranto and the States of the Church. French and British troops were withdrawn from Egypt, which was restored to Turkey, whose integrity was established. Compensation to the Prince of Orange was promised by Napoleon.

The discussion in Parliament revealed both anxiety about, and opposition to, the one-sided nature of the settlement. Ministerial argument could not conceal that England had conceded much, Napoleon little or nothing. Joseph Bonaparte had been peremptorily instructed " to rule completely outside our deliberations with England" the affairs of Switzerland, Germany, and Italy, and our Government had reluctantly been compelled to accept this haughty limitation. The refusal to discuss a commercial treaty was a grievous disappointment to our manufacturers, hard hit by the war and prohibitive tariffs. Grenville and the leading Old Whigs— Spencer, Fitzwilliam, Windham—therefore attacked the terms as dishonourable, giving us nothing but a frail and deceptive truce. But Pitt decisively pronounced against our claim " to settle the affairs of the Continent," a notable surrender of his point of view in 1793, and Fox supported the Government. England demanded peace ; it was even ready to thank Ministers who had the courage or the weakness to pay a heavy price for obtaining it. The first epoch of the great war had ended.

It is not surprising that the treaties of Lunéville and Amiens gave unbounded satisfaction in France. The First Consul, the heir to the Revolution, had achieved more solid and brilliant results than a century of Bourbon rule. "Look," said Sheridan a year later, " at the map of Europe. You will see nothing but France." The Revolutionary Government established at Paris on the destruction of the old monarchy and *régime* had annexed the left bank of the Rhine. Belgium had disappeared. Terms had been dictated to Spain, Portugal, the Hohenzollerns, and the Habsburgs. Holland was now the washpot of France, and over Switzerland and Piedmont she had thrown her shoe. Great Britain had undertaken to withdraw from every port east of Gibraltar in the Mediterranean—Elba, Malta, Minorca, Corfu. The recasting of Germany, culminating in the dissolution of the Holy Roman Empire and the establishment of the Confederation of the Rhine that followed Lunéville, were a telling witness to the dictator- ship claimed at Paris, to the helplessness, disunion, and short-sighted greed of the German States, and to the exclusion of Great Britain, accepted at Amiens, from the affairs of the Continent. And behind these tremendous territorial changes lay the moral, intellectual, and spiritual forces of French ideas and French civilisation. The ascendency of France rested on an ascendency of mind and of French genius, more subtle, pervasive, and irresistible than the strength of material power. But if Great Britain had signally failed to stem or extirpate the French Revolution, or to set limits to French ambition and power, expressing under the conditions of the Revolutionary era and through the men of the Revolution the imperishable ideals of the historic France, France had no less failed to shake the character or undermine the security of Great Britain. Alone amongst the European States, England had withstood and repulsed the assault both of French arms and French ideas. If our commerce had been hard pressed the French commercial marine had been practically extinguished. The seaborne trade of neutrals was passing into our hands or being compelled to work under conditions imposed in our interests. Our credit was not exhausted. Despite an unparalleled increase of the National Debt and crushing taxation, exports and imports continued to expand. In 1800 they totalled over £12,000,000 more than in 1796. Population was rapidly going up. The Treaty of Amiens registered the surrender of an impressive list of colonial acquisitions ; it did not register the sur- render of the strength and means by which they had been acquired. In a word, Great Britain, an essentially national State, retained in 1802 every feature unimpaired which had enabled her to maintain successfully her independence. It was reserved for the second period of the war to reveal the full scope and potency of British sea-power and nationality as weapons of offence and defence against the Napoleonic Empire determined to destroy both.

NOTE.—For the newer authorities see the supplement to the Bibliography, pp. 550-552.

CHAPTER VI

THE STRUGGLE WITH NAPOLEON (1802-1815)

THE prophecy of the critics that the Peace of Amiens would prove a short and delusive truce was fully borne out by the sequel which in fifteen months led to a rupture and the renewal of war. The desire of the commercial classes for peace had been largely due to the dislocation of trade and the loss of valuable markets, and the necessity of a restoration of normal relations with the Continent. But Napoleon's refusal to crown the boon of peace by a commercial treaty was a bitter disappointment which greatly strengthened the widespread and deep suspicions of Napoleon's ambitions and the political future. The whole basis of the relations of France and Great Britain was, in fact, thoroughly false. Napoleon had consented to come to terms because he wished to consolidate his power in France by a series of healing measures for which peace was essential. But, as the treaty showed, he was determined to exclude Great Britain from the affairs of the Continent, and both at Amiens and subsequently he argued and acted on the principle that her intervention was inadmissible and must be prevented. Addington's Ministry had tacitly accepted the assumption in order to secure peace ; but they also assumed that the *status quo* defined at Lunéville and Amiens would remain unaltered. Neither their own views nor an alarmed and disillusioned public opinion would tolerate radical changes in the European situation which could only permit Napoleon to renew his attacks on Great Britain with a maximum of advantage on his side, when he chose to throw off the mask. It was impossible that any settlement could be durable which explicitly required that Great Britain was to ignore or meekly acquiesce in acts of aggression which destroyed whatever value the Treaty of Amiens had originally possessed. Andréossy's despatches prove conclusively that Great Britain sincerely desired to have and to keep peace; that it was not this or that particular stroke, but the sum total, which caused acute anxiety, and (which Napoleon could not grasp) that a Ministry responsible to Parliament could not, even if it wished, withstand the pressure of public opinion and the exigencies of our national future.

Diplomatic relations were very soon sorely strained.   A French expedition sent to San Domingo had wasted away, and a fresh ex- Dec., 1801 pedition in preparation was interpreted as really directed against Great Britain.   Napoleon became President of the reorganised Italian (Cisalpine) Republic; the Ligurian Republic was reorganised under Jan. 25, 1802 French control and Piedmont practically incorporated with France. June 29 Intervention in Switzerland led to the "Act of Mediation," which Sept. 21 recast the Helvetic Republic, brought it under French domination, Feb. 19, and gave Napoleon a strategic base of first-rate importance.   The 1803 occupation of Flushing and Utrecht and the French influence in the Dutch Republic were a further direct menace to British security. The ubiquity of French agents in Ireland and the examination of British harbours such as Hull were not adequately explained away by assertions that they were for commercial purposes only; while the publication of Sebastiani's report on Egypt in the official *Moniteur*, Jan. 29, drawing attention to the ease with which the country could be re- 1803 conquered by France, was an inexcusable piece of bravado.   Decaen, sent to India to take over the French stations ceded by the Treaty, March, had instructions to intrigue with the native States against the British 1803 power.   Under these threatening circumstances the Ministry, finding that repeated protests were brushed aside on the ground that Great Britian had no diplomatic *locus standi*, refused to evacuate Malta. They also demanded compensation for the gains that Napoleon had made since the Treaty.   The retention of Malta was a false step, as well as a clear violation of the Treaty.   We were strong enough at sea to prevent Napoleon capturing it; and if war came we could occupy it again with ease.   Napoleon was able to point to broken pledges and to argue with arbitrary plausibility that the subject-matter of our protests was wholly outside the scope and articles of our Treaty rights.   The embittered feeling in England was not improved by Napoleon's demands for the suppression of virulent attacks in the Press on his character, for which French *emigrés* were largely responsible.   The trial and conviction of Peltier for a libel on the

First Consul was a wholesome proof that the courts would protect
if our hospitality to political exiles were abused, but national pride
resented the claim of a foreign ruler to prescribe the terms of that
hospitality. The conviction that war was inevitable steadily gained
Nov., 1802 strength, and the request of the Ministers in Parliament for large
additions to the peace strength of army and navy was regarded as
a justifiable precaution. Whitworth had been sent as special am-
Sept. bassador to Paris, but no agreement on the proposals submitted
could be reached. Napoleon regarded his policy in Piedmont,
Switzerland, and Holland as justified by French needs, and pointedly
declared that he would as soon see the English in the Faubourg
Feb. 15, St. Antoine as at Malta. After two theatrical scenes with Whit-
March 13 worth at the Tuileries our ambassador left Paris on May 12th and
war was declared on May 18th. Exactly twelve months later the First
Consul was proclaimed Emperor of the French.

The Maltese question was perhaps the occasion, but it certainly
was not the cause, of the final rupture. Peace could only have been
preserved by one of two methods—the acceptance by Great Britain
of whatever Napoleon chose to do on the Continent, or the limitation by Napoleon himself of his ambitions to the gains of France
laid down at Lunéville and Amiens. In the nature of things
neither was possible in 1803. And the inevitable result was a trial
of strength which would necessarily be a fight to a decisive finish.
Great Britain must be either broken into submission or she must
succeed in imposing terms on Napoleon which would shatter not a
French ascendency in, but a French dictatorship of, Europe. The
French Empire as Napoleon conceived it, and the British Empire as
the British people conceived it, could not co-exist in the same world.

The weakness of the Addington Ministry and Pitt's pledge on
the Roman Catholics question made Pitt's exclusion from office
unnecessary and undesirable. Pitt's friends, indeed, ever since his
resignation had been striving to bring him back to power. Grenville openly attacked the Government, and the mordant wit of
George Canning (already shown in the *Anti-Jacobin*), and his
political and personal devotion (exemplified in the famous verses
to "The Pilot that Weathered the Storm," written for the celebration of his chief's birthday) were liberally employed in pouring
ridicule on "Doctor" Addington. Pitt himself, however, until
war came, treated the Ministry as one formed under his protection.

He could and would only return to the Treasury Bench as Prime Minister, and loyalty to Grenville required that he should return with him. Grenville, however, positively refused to serve with Addington, who, strong in the confidence and support of the King, was willing to reconstruct but not dissolve his Administration. Pitt came to be more and more dissatisfied with Ministerial measures, while public opinion insisted that war required his immediate return to the Prime Ministership. On the recovery of the King March, from a short mental collapse, the parliamentary attack was pressed 1804 and the Government majority sank rapidly. Finally hard pressed by the combined Opposition, Addington resigned and Pitt was April 25 somewhat reluctantly invited by the King to frame a Ministry.

It is highly creditable to him that he at once urged the formation of a united Administration, which would include both Fox and Grenville. The latter George III. consented to accept, but to the former his hostility was invincible. Only at the cost of civil war would he submit. Fox, with the chivalrous generosity that justified the devotion of those who knew him best, quietly accepted the royal veto, and advised both Grenville and his own friends to join Pitt. It was, as has been happily said, the finest moment in his life. But Grenville, who had a year before wrecked Pitt's schemes, now wrecked them again. He declined to serve with his former chief, and prevented Fox's friends from following their leader's desire to make the new Ministry truly national. The Cabinet, therefore, had May 12 to be patched up out of the Addington group, and the remnants of Pitt's party. Lord Harrowby (Foreign Secretary, vice Hawkesbury transferred to the Home Office), Melville (Dundas) at the Admiralty, Eldon as Lord Chancellor, and Castlereagh at the Board of Control, were its chief members. Addington, as Lord Sidmouth, joined in January, 1805, but retired in a huff in July. Canning, not in the Cabinet, was rewarded with the Treasurership of the Navy. The wits pronounced with truth that the Administration was composed of William and Pitt, while of its eleven members nine were in the House of Lords. What, Pitt remarked, can you do with skim-milk like that? But that he had to deal with skim-milk on this occasion was due to the obstinacy of George III. and the pride that was the curse of Grenville. Nor was the chief the Pitt even of 1793. He resumed office and the power that he so dearly loved, broken in health; and in eighteen months he died

broken in hope.   Fortunately for Great Britain, the work of the
moment was the sailors' affair, and these months so tragic for Pitt
were the ἀριστεῖα of Nelson.

The war of 1803 resembled that of 1793 in one feature alone—
the unbroken continuity of the struggle for the two main combatants, France and Great Britain.   The other States of the Continent, as in the previous war, fought now on the British, now on
the French side, but for no single one of them in either war was the
contest continuous.   But in every other feature that distinguishes
the struggle the difference is vital.   In 1793 Great Britain wrestled
with France as the architect of the Revolution.   In 1803 the contest is with Napoleon and the Napoleonic Empire, rather than with
France.   And the issue emphasised the difference.   Great Britain
failed to destroy and ended by accepting the main political results
of the Revolution, both for France and for Europe.   But she was
the main instrument in shattering the Napoleonic Empire.   This
difference was already recognised in 1803.   In 1793, we went
exultantly into war.   But its popularity soon ebbed.   The war had
its political, social, and military aspects ; the thermometer of our
temper rose and fell with success and defeat, but the heart of the
nation was never unitedly in it, and peace even on humiliating
terms was welcome.   In 1803 it is apparent that the nation was reluctant to fight.   Yet when the issues were understood the struggle
became truly national.   And there dawned slowly and surely into
the mind of the British people the conviction that in fighting to
the death for their own nationhood they were also fighting for the
nationhood and liberty of the different peoples and States of
Europe.   It is this ennobling aspiration that enhances our cruel
sacrifices, and sharpened our weapons with a moral momentum lacking in the first war.   The ideas and ideals of the future fought
with, and not against, us.   For we had as our ally not the exhausted civilisation of a perishing social order, but the cause of
which Great Britain was the champion—the right of every national
State to work out its own salvation, and to decide for itself what its
civilisation should be and how it should achieve it.   And we closed
the struggle with peremptory pleading for a great moral principle
—the abolition of the slave trade—and with voluntary concessions
from our conquests more numerous than have ever been made by a
victor in the hour of victory.

Napoleon aimed first at breaking British power by invasion, and then of combining Europe against us. The first clear phase of the war lasts till 1805—the development and frustration of the scheme of invasion reinforced by a counter-stroke—the Third Coalition. The second ends with the overthrow of the Third Coalition and the Treaty of Tilsit in 1807; the third is covered by the Continental system proper, and its breakdown with the Russian campaign of 1812; and finally come the War of Liberation, Napoleon's abdication and return, the Hundred Days, and the European Settlement at Vienna. Cutting across these phases are the Spanish Rising of 1808, and, inspired by it, the Austrian War of 1809, which only seemed to end in a fresh triumph for Napoleon and a reconsolidation of his Empire by the Habsburg marriage. For Great Britain the decisive dates are 1805, 1808, 1812. After Trafalgar these islands are practically safe, but the scale of the continental blockade and the Treaty of Tilsit seemed to make the contest a desperate one for England. The Spanish Rising as by a miracle revolutionised the situation, political and military and intellectual. Down to 1809 our military direction shows the familiar half-hearted and scurried picnics on the rim of the strategic theatre, the familiar scattered and conflicting objectives, and officers handcuffed by inadequate forces, impossible or immature instructions, and defective organisation. But the Peninsular War was a national one for national ends, it was continuously maintained and it used the assured command of the sea for the military penetration of the enemy's strategical lines. It was organised and led by a military genius second only to Napoleon himself. War, as Napoleon said, is an affair of a man, not of men ; but for Wellington, Moore's great march on Napoleon's communications and retreat might have been the tragic prologue to a drama that was never begun. Had Chatham in 1809 been sent to Lisbon and Wellington to Walcheren the result is not difficult to conjecture. And after 1812 Napoleon knew that, whatever the issue in Central Europe might be, the failures of his marshals in the Peninsula now necessitated war on two fronts, and that Wellington's strategical objective was not the Pyrenees but Paris.

The first phase was decided on the water. For every student of war and every British citizen the stategy and operations which culminated at Trafalgar are packed with imperishable lessons.

Nor does the popular imagination err seriously in figuring the struggle as a tremendous duel between two supreme masters, Nelson and Napoleon. The sailors of 1803 started with greater advantages and utilised them more skilfully than those of 1793. The higher command at the Admiralty had a closer grip on science, and in the navy an instrument quantitatively and qualitatively superior. To our sailors the Channel was not, as apparently it was to Napoleon, simply a big river which the French army must cross in the face of a hostile but inferior force on the opposite bank. Napoleon asked his admirals to give him the Channel free for three days or even for twenty-four hours, and the business would be done. But if "free" only meant temporarily clear of hostile fleets whose striking power remained intact, the gift would scarcely begin the business. And our Admiralty was determined that the Channel should not be free in any sense for three hours. Hence the task correctly interpreted was how to prevent the command not of the Channel but of the sea, of which the Channel was only an important strategic area, passing from our hands. If that command were retained, invasion in the Napoleonic sense was impossible. Accordingly our strategic dispositions were based on the principles of naval science adapted to the geographical and maritime conditions. We had the interior lines. Effective observation of the enemy's main posts would divide the hostile forces and enable them to be followed or defeated in detail. The chiefs at sea, Nelson in particular, understood that their function was to neglect no opportunity to bring the enemy's effective force at sea to decisive action. An independent force was also kept in home waters adequate to impeach invasion unsupported by a large fleet. But as evasion by the enemy, and mistakes by ourselves, might shift the stategic dispositions, the main forces were ready to fall back and counter-concentrate on the threatened vital centre, the Channel. Napoleon underrated the quality of the British navy and the genius of its greatest commander. His elaborate and shifting combinations, whose object was to unseal the blocked ports in a series, and mass a superiority of forces at the Western end of the Channel, were necessarily carried out by fleets inferior in *personnel*, training, and initiative, and they rested on the arbitrary dovetailing of links in a chain which allowed no proper margin for accident, misinterpretation, or failure of nerve at the critical moment or for direct interference by a determined adversary. The "decoying" away of our main striking forces did not obliterate either their power or their intention to return and fight. And until they had been crushed by action into impotence the Grand Army could not be escorted across the Channel by any fleet, however strong numerically, unless Napoleon wished to repeat in the Downs his own and Brueys' experience in the Bay of Aboukir. The true problem of invasion was for Napoleon, therefore, not how to transport 100,000 men, but how to secure unimpeded possession of the only road by which they could cross—the sea. If that were secured there was no problem at all, either for him or for us. If it were not secured the Grand Army was condemned to wait and pick up pebbles on the shores of France—or go elsewhere by roads that it could use unimpeded. The sequel showed that accidents due to the fog of war inevitably happened, but they did not alter the decision; they only transferred it from Ushant or Cape Finisterre to Cape Trafalgar.[1]

When war broke out Nelson was given the command in the

[1] The leading authority on the invasion schemes is Desbrière, *Projets et Tentatives de debarquement aux Îles Britanniques*, vols. iv. and v. The two most recent writers: J. Corbett, *The Campaign of Trafalgar*, 1910 (p. 12 *et seq.*), and J. W. Fortescue, *Hist. of the British Army* (1910), vol. v., agree in regarding Napoleon's scheme as a genuine plan, whose failure caused him to represent it later as a mere feint—"clumsy lying, designed to cover the Emperor's own blunders". Sir John Fortescue points out the hopeless inadequacy of the organisation of our home land defences under the Addington ministry, and how Pitt met the situation by fresh legislation—the Volunteer Consolidation Act, the Army of Reserve Act, the Permanent Additional Force Bill and the Supplementary Militia Bill which were not successful. More effective than the Martello towers, the Sandgate Canal, the entrenched camps, were the organisation of the transport and the brigading of volunteers and yeomanry for which the Duke of York and Sir John Moore, then carrying out his reforms at Shorncliffe, were responsible. The real defence lay in the measures of the Admiralty, which under Lord Barham, "may be taken as the highest expression of the living strategical tradition . . . and reveal how little the Board regarded the invasion as a serious danger". Mr. Corbett points out that Napoleon never had 150,000 men ready at Boulogne; the numbers did not exceed 93,000; and both Fortescue and Corbett agree that Napoleon's organisation for transporting this force, across even a free channel, was quite inadequate. "No great master of war ever so fatally miscalculated the possibilities and limitations of invasion . . . nothing, not even the army, was ready" (Corbett, *op. cit.*, p. 15). "The boasted organisation of the army and flotilla of invasion existed only on paper, being when reduced to practice a very chaos" (Fortescue, *op. cit.*, p. 251). "Upon the whole," sums up Sir John Fortescue, "if the French army had managed to get into England it could never have got out again" (p. 265). How the Admiralty and our sailors took care that the "if" should not be realised can be read in detail in Sir Julian Corbett's pages.

Mediterranean, and Cornwallis ("Blue Billy") in the Atlantic, and both admirals were determined that the Toulon and Brest fleets should not come out without being compelled to fight as soon as

Oct. 5
Dec.

they were found. An attack on the Spanish treasure ships was the prelude to war with Spain. But this, while adding to our responsibilities, did not alter the main lines of our strategy—vigilant observation, and counter-concentration at the Western end of the Channel, if required. Subsidiary squadrons were detached to watch the Texel, Ferrol, Cadiz, and Carthagena. The national spirit was also braced up by organisation of the land defences at home, which, in St. Vincent's phrase, soothed the nerves of the old women of both sexes. Pitt, however, fully recognised that the fleet could frustrate Napoleon's schemes, but neither it nor the Martello towers could

May 26
June

defeat him. Our diplomacy, therefore, aimed at forming a new and Third Coalition. The coronation of Napoleon as King of Italy, the annexation of the Ligurian Republic, and other violations of the Treaty of Lunéville made Austrian hostility a certainty. The ruthless military murder of the Duc d'Enghien caused a rupture with Russia. But there were endless delays which once again fatally marred the chances of success. Not till April 11th, 1805, were the treaty with Russia concluded and Austria and Sweden

Aug. 9

brought into line by separate negotiations. Prussia, with Hanover dangled before her as a bait by Napoleon, refused to join, and united, as Fox said, all that was rapacious in robbery with all that was hateful in slavery. Her selfish and vacillating policy not merely ruined the coalition but recoiled shortly with terrible effect upon herself. But the objects of this Third Coalition showed a marked difference in our policy. The repudiation of interference with the form of the French Government, the expulsion of the French from North Germany, the independence of Piedmont, Switzerland, and Holland made its aim an effort to enforce little more than the Treaty of Lunéville, while the proposed settlement of the public law of Europe by a concert of the European States anticipated the ideas of 1814 and 1815. The coalition, therefore, is the transition stage between the previous anti-revolutionary alliances of the dynastic States and the later national risings. Its subsequent failure had a salutary effect on our diplomacy and methods, as well as on the continental Powers. But while Napoleon was preparing to meet it the interest was shifted to the sea.

For nearly two years Nelson and Cornwallis had battled with
the gales of the Mediterranean and the Atlantic. Finally Missiessy Jan. 11
slipped out from Rochefort and reached the West Indies, where he
failed on Martinique. Villeneuve, after a false start, got away from March 30
Toulon, passed Gibraltar, picked up six Spaniards at Cadiz and April 9
arrived at Martinique to unite with Missiessy. But the junction May 16
failed, for he had returned to Rochefort. Nelson, after seeking Ville- May 20
neuve in the direction of Egypt, was now "decoyed" into hunting May 10
him in earnest. But Villeneuve had no desire to meet him in the
West Indies and turned back, followed by Nelson. Villeneuve made June 10
for Cape Finistère, Nelson for Cadiz, where he came into touch with June 12
Collingwood, and then sailed north. The Admiralty, warned by June 18
Nelson from the West Indies, had, thanks to Lord Barham, ordered
their counter-concentration, and Calder, sent south, with fifteen
vessels to twenty of the enemy, crossed Villeneuve's path at Cape
Finistere. But Calder contented himself with an indecisive action July 22
(for which he was subsequently court-martialled) and captured only
two ships, while Villeneuve got into Corunna and united with
fourteen Spanish ships there. Cornwallis, who was watching Ganteaume's twenty-one ships in Brest, was then joined by Nelson on
August 15th. Thence Nelson passed on to England, setting foot
on land for the first time after two years. But Villeneuve, instead Aug. 18
of striking north, uniting with Missiessy, who had put to sea, and
endeavouring to set Ganteaume free, which would have given Cornwallis the honour of a decisive battle, turned south into Cadiz, Aug. 15
outside which the imperturbable Collingwood waited like a terrier
at a rat-hole. August 15th decided Napoleon's scheme of invasion.
Even if Villeneuve had united with Missiessy and Ganteaume and
driven off Cornwallis, manœuvring for the position did not by
itself confer the command of the sea. The British fleets had still
to be reckoned with, and until they were disposed of Napoleon
might abuse his admirals but he could not move. But before he
heard that Villeneuve had gone to Cadiz he recognised that his
combinations had broken down; and the first detachments of the Aug. 26
Grand Army were moving to the Rhine and the Upper Danube.

To Nelson was fitly reserved the right to administer the *coup de
grace*.[1] To the great joy of officers and men he rejoined Collingwood's reinforced fleet on September 29th. The famous memorandum of October 9th—" the Nelson touch"—which embodied

27   [1] See Appendix XII.

his latest tactical conceptions for realising the Nelsonic ideal of annihilation not victory, was a masterly combination of Duncan's attack at Camperdown and his own in Aboukir Bay. The order of *sailing* in two columns as the order of attack, concentration on the rear with a superior force in one column under the second in command, for whom complete freedom of action was to be secured, the cutting off of the van by the Commander-in-Chief in the other column and throwing it out of action, together with the containing and crushing the centre until the second in command had "completed his business," and the confusion of the enemy by the concealment until the last moment of the Commander-in-Chief's function of securing a superiority of forces at the vital points—these were its leading ideas. On October 21st, off Cape Trafalgar, Nelson to windward found his foe. He had twenty-seven ships to Villeneuve's thirty-three, but the enemy's fleet had to be destroyed, the wind was dropping, the October day was short and a storm was coming on. And Nelson was the last man to trifle with wind or opportunity. The plan of the memorandum was substantially carried out, with such minor modifications as the special circumstances required. And the *mêlée* that the memorandum was designed to force on the enemy then became the affair of his captains. The issue bore out Nelson's assertion that he had no fear as to the result; while officers and men showed that the famous signal, "England expects every man to do his duty," was an exhilarating anticipation of their resolve. Collingwood, in command of the leeward right-hand column, broke the line at the twelfth (really the fifteenth) ship from the rear, Nelson, after feinting at the van, turned to starboard, passed down the enemy line and broke it at the selected point so as to crush the centre. Wounded mortally, he lived long enough to learn that the victory he sought was his. Eighteen prizes were taken, and though Collingwood's refusal to anchor was perhaps responsible for some of the captured ships being wrecked, Trafalgar was the last great fleet action of the war. But not even the universal relief that invasion was no longer to be feared compensated for the loss of the Commander in Chief. To England there was and could be only one Nelson. No other commander, before or since, by sea or land, has won and kept the affections and homage of our people to a like degree, for "the Nelson touch" inspired the national spirit by the same indefinable magic that it wielded over the fleets he commanded.

Napoleon took a swift and masterly revenge on land. The day

before Trafalgar he had out-manœuvred the Austrian commander
Mack into a humiliating surrender at Ulm; Vienna was shortly
occupied, and at Austerlitz he won, over Austrians and Russians, the Dec. 2
most classic of his victories. The Treaty of Pressburg then struck Dec. 26
Austria out of the coalition. As against this we had made two
futile military efforts. An Anglo-Russian force landed at Naples, Oct. 8
effected nothing, and Cathcart's expedition to North Germany to
co-operate with Russians and Swedes was withdrawn at Prussia's
request, having also achieved nothing.

In India, however, events of great importance were registered.
Wellesley's relations with the Court of Directors were already 1802
severely strained. With dividends as their ideal and non-intervention as a maxim of policy the activity of this ambitious
Viceroy filled the masters of the India House with alarm; and
Wellesley's autocratic temper, independent and judicious exercise
of patronage, and deplorable ideas of freedom of trade, aggravated
their resentment. Undeterred, the Governor-General was bent on
extending the subsidiary system to the Mahratta chiefs, the formidable power whose rivalries and depredations made Central and
North-Western Hindustan an area of French intrigue, disturbance,
and danger. Holkar's defeat of the Peishwa and Sindhia at Poona Oct., 1802
offered an opportunity not to be missed. By the Treaty of Bassein Dec. 31
the Peishwa agreed to accept a subsidiary British force, to employ
no Europeans from a nation at war with Great Britain, and to make
war only with British approval. He was then reinstated at Poona. May, 1803
Holkar and the Gaekwar for the moment took no action. But
Sindhia and the Bhonsla plunged us into war. The first campaign
was singularly decisive. Arthur Wellesley, already notable in the
Mysore War, laid the basis of his military reputation by his victories at
Assaye and Argaon, which, with the capture of Gawilgarh, struck Sept. 23
down the Bhonsla. Lake, in the north, captured Delhi and Agra and Nov.
crushed Sindhia's army at Laswari. Both chiefs thereupon agreed to Oct. 31
dismiss the French officers in their service and accept British mediation with the Nizam. A slice of Berar was added to that Prince's
dominion; Cuttack in the east and Doab in the north-west were made
British territory, while the capture of Delhi had given the Company
the control of the Mogul, an aged, blind, and helpless sovereign,
the phantom heir of the long-lost empire of Akbar and Aurangzib.
Holkar now drew the sword, but Lake mismanaged the operations.

Colonel Monson, sent forward to join hands with a force striking from Gujarat, was driven back in a disastrous retreat, and the victorious Holkar laid siege to Delhi. The blow to British prestige resounded through Hindustan, and the Directors in a panic recalled Wellesley and persuaded Cornwallis to go out and reverse his policy.

Before he could arrive Holkar had been repulsed from Delhi, beaten at Dig, and driven from the Doab, though Lake had failed in a costly effort to take Bhartpur. Cornwallis's instructions were to carry out a policy of scuttle and return to non-intervention, and Sir G. Barlow, who acted as Governor-General on Cornwallis's death, obeyed the Directors. Holkar, hunted beyond the Sutlej and disavowed by Ranjit Singh, the genius who founded the Sikh power, was to his surprise allowed to resume possession of his territories. Sindhia was appeased by the restoration of Gwalior, and the Rajput princes, deserted by their British allies, were left to the tender mercies of the Mahrattas. Barlow, however, annoyed the Directors by persisting in maintaining the Treaty of Bassein. The settlement was a sorry ending to Wellesley's plans; weak because it lowered unnecessarily our prestige; wrong because it surrendered allies and Central Hindostan to rapine and disorder; short-sighted because the work had to be done all over again by Hastings a dozen years later, when Wellesley's policy was fully justified.

Nevertheless, Wellesley's tenure of power marks an interesting and important epoch in the dynamic evolution of British power. In 1798 he found the Company established as a Sovereign State, whose political duty and functions had grown to be far more important than the trade and commerce of a joint-stock chartered enterprise. From the first the Governor-General insisted on the logic of the situation and the frank assertion of British ascendency as desirable on its own merits and in any case inevitable. Neutrality, based on non-intervention, and deliberately blind to events and developments beyond the frontiers of our direct administration, would prove more dangerous and costly in the long run than a courageous acceptance of the obligations that British ascendency involved—unless we were prepared to lapse again into a purely trading organisation and permit the French or some other European Power gradually to annex the work of Clive, Hastings, and Cornwallis, and finally thrust the commercial company from India altogether. Such an alternative meant suicide in India and political

disaster in Europe. To prevent this Wellesley used the great
instrument of subsidiary alliances which he inherited from Warren
Hastings. By it he extirpated the French danger, crushed the
internal rivalries, oppression, and maladministration of the native
States—no small boon to their subjects—and laid down the principle
that the British power had an interest which it was determined
to enforce in every development of Indian rule and policy. In administration he gave opportunity to a school of workers, of whom
Malcolm, Metcalfe, Mountstuart Elphinstone, and Munro won
permanent fame. By his foundation of Wellesley College he desired to carry out an idea of Warren Hastings and provide for the
young and raw staff of the Company a scientific and liberal training
in the subject matter and problems of Indian government, but
the jealousy and short-sightedness of the Directors mutilated the
scheme. Had he also not been prevented he would have destroyed
the French base at Mauritius and incorporated Ceylon under the
Company's rule. It is eminently characteristic of the man and his
policy that he strenuously insisted on centralising the higher direction
and control in the hands of the Governor-General. Unification
and centralisation, as Warren Hastings had foreseen, not only
gave the big men full scope but made for efficiency and an effective
responsibility. It was a necessary step if British policy in the East
was to be adequately correlated to the authority—the Cabinet at
home—responsible for imperial policy as a whole.

Violently as the directors disapproved of Wellesley, the attempt
to attack particularly his Oudh policy in Parliament failed. Politicians and the public understood Indian affairs better than in the
days of Burke and Warren Hastings, and the idea of impeachment
fell still-born to the ground. But it was a sad home-coming in
every way for Wellesley, who found his friend Pitt at the gates of
death. Early in 1805 a Parliamentary Commission had reported Jan. 14,
that Lord Melville, then H. Dundas, as Treasurer of the Navy in 1806
Pitt's former Administration, had been guilty of illegal and culpable
laxity in the administration of public funds. Whitbread moved a
resolution of censure, which was carried by the casting vote of the April 8
Speaker, to the exultation of the Opposition. Melville resigned
next day, and was formally impeached, but Pitt did not live to
hear the verdict of acquittal. It was a cruel mortification to a shattered man. The House had disregarded Pitt's suggestion for a select

committee of investigation ; Dundas was one of his oldest personal and political friends, and the blow was made heavier by the vote against him of another tried friend, Wilberforce, the leader of " The Saints". The scene in the House when the numbers were announced is perhaps the most vivid illustration on record of the bitterness of party feeling at the time. And Sidmouth's retirement from the Cabinet with Buckinghamshire further weakened the Ministry. Pitt's failure to win the King's consent to his renewed application to unite with Fox and Grenville was a further disappointment, though it shows how close the idea of a coalition was to his heart. Then came the news of Ulm, the significance of which Trafalgar could not obliterate, and, after Ulm, Austerlitz. " Roll up that map" (of Europe), he said, "it will not be wanted these ten years "—a remark memorable for its accidental but singular accuracy of prediction. But the unquenchable spirit of Chatham had flashed out in an imperishable sentence of the last and shortest

Nov. 9 of his speeches—at the Guildhall. " Europe is not to be saved by any single man. England has saved herself by her exertions, and will, as I trust, save Europe by her example "—a noble epilogue to Nelson's words to Hardy: "Thank God, I have done my duty". On January 23, at Putney, Pitt died, and was buried in the Abbey by his father's side.

Fox, who had felt it his painful duty to oppose the motion for a public funeral and a public monument, voted with generous satisfaction for the payment by the State of Pitt's debts; and when the Administration, bereft of its greatest figure, fell to pieces, even George III. recognised that Fox could no longer be ostracised. The new Ministry was a coalition of "all the talents," under Grenville as First Lord of the Treasury. Fox was Foreign Secretary, and other offices were held by Sidmouth, Charles Grey, Spencer, Windham, Fitzwilliam, Moira, Erskine, and Lord Henry Petty. For the last time a Lord Chief Justice, Ellenborough, had a seat in the Cabinet. The Catholic question was by agreement shelved, and the King, on whom the irresistible magnetism of Fox's personality was not without its effect, treated the Foreign Secretary with dignified courtesy. Fox knew that his days were numbered ; but he still hoped to live long enough to carry one great reform, the abolition of the slave trade, and to make a sincere and earnest effort for peace. In the first he was successful. Before he died, on

September 13th, the resolutions for which Wilberforce, Clarkson, Fowell Buxton, and Fox himself had pleaded for nearly twenty years had passed both Houses; and on March 25th, 1807, the bill, founded on the resolutions, became law. The slave trade from and after January 1st, 1808, was prohibited, and a great advance made towards the abolition of slavery altogether in the dominions of the Crown.

The Ministry was also troubled by the first public mutterings of a painful and repulsive scandal. The heir to the Throne had, in order to please his father, consented to marry Princess Caroline of Brunswick-Wolfenbüttel, and the marriage had been celebrated in 1795. The Prince of Wales was not fitted to be the husband of any woman, and unfortunately his bride, a kind-hearted, untidy, eccentric and reckless girl, had neither the beauty nor the tact to gain even for a time the worthless affections of her bridegroom. From the outset the "first gentleman in Europe" showed his intention to violate his marriage vows, and after the birth of her daughter, the ill-fated Princess Charlotte, he openly deserted his wife. Left to herself, the Princess retired to Blackheath, where, April, 1796 embittered by neglect and the knowledge of her husband's dissipation and infidelities, she permitted herself to speak and act with deplorable indiscretion. In 1806 she was acquitted of the more serious accusations brought against her, but the King, on the advice of his Ministers, was compelled to administer a censure on conduct unbecoming the Princess of Wales.

Peace Fox was not able to gain. Napoleon, aware that negotiations could do him no harm, had no intention of limiting his Continental schemes. Prussia had swallowed the bait of Hanover Feb. and agreed to close her ports; the same month King Ferdinand, Feb. 15 driven from Naples, had taken refuge in Palermo, and his kingdom on the mainland was assigned to Joseph Bonaparte. In June the Republic of Holland became a kingdom under another imperial brother, Louis; and in August the final dissolution of the Holy Roman Empire and the formation of the Confederation of the Rhine under Napoleon's guardianship proclaimed the new "Grand Empire Français," in which the imperial France of the natural frontiers replaced the tributary bastion republics of the Directory system by tributary kingdoms and duchies, with Napoleon's kinsmen and marshals at their head—*les rois préfets*. Lord Yarmouth and then Lord Lauderdale had been sent to Paris to negotiate. Talleyrand, under Napoleon's directions, listened, made counter-proposals and temporised. Fox proved less pliable than Napoleon had expected. He offered an arrangement based on the principle of *uti possidetis*, but he refused to surrender Sicily or the Cape (which had just been retaken) without adequate compensation and guarantees, and he declined to be separated from our ally Russia.

July 21 The Russian envoy was cozened into a separate treaty, and had the Tsar ratified it Napoleon would probably have thrown off the mask and sent Lauderdale home. But on the Tsar's refusal he

Oct. 1 was bent on smashing the Coalition. Prussia had at last awaked to the value of Napoleon's pledges, and now single-handed challenged the victor of Austerlitz. Rosbach was signally avenged at the twin

Oct. 14 battles of Jena and Auerstädt. The military bankruptcy of the Hohenzollern State was revealed; Napoleon entered Berlin in triumph and the edifice of Frederick the Great toppled over with a crash.

In contrast with this dazzling success our efforts appeared unusually puerile.. Stuart, landing in Calabria, astonished Europe by winning a battle over superior numbers, blasting the French

July 4 columns by the deadly fire of the British line, at Maida—and then (as usual) withdrew. From the captured Cape Sir Home Popham, unauthorised, entangled the Government in an expedition to South

June America, which seized Buenos Ayres and lost it soon after. Re-

Feb., 1807 inforced, the troops stormed Monte Video, but Whitelocke, after much slaughter, failed signally on Buenos Ayres, surrendered Monte Video, and withdrew. Court-martialled on his return, this incompetent general, nicknamed "Whitefeather," was dismissed the service. Two further failures strengthened Napoleon's contempt for our

Feb., 1807 power to strike. Duckworth, despatched with a naval force to Constantinople, in order to compel the Sultan to break with France, wasted precious time in futile negotiations, and finally with much loss had to fight his way back through the Dardanelles, fortified by batteries thrown up under expert French guidance. Fraser,

March 30 flung at Egypt, captured Alexandria, was repulsed at Rosetta and finally driven into a humiliating convention, by which we agreed to evacuate the country.

If the Coalition Ministry thus proved that it could not make war, the responsibility for the failure to make peace rests not with

Fox nor the Cabinet, but with Napoleon. Fox and Howick his successor were sincere and straightforward; they offered concessions which were genuine and liberal, but they were not prepared to sacrifice the essentials of a durable settlement; and, as Fox freely admitted, they were defeated by Napoleon's refusal to meet them in a reasonable or honest spirit. The revelation of Napoleon's character, objects, and methods was a tragic disappointment to Fox, who had hoped against hope, and now died crushed by the same Sept. 13 terrible conviction as Pitt, that his country was committed to a struggle from which she could not retire and of which no man could see the end. But both Pitt and Fox also recognised that Napoleon could not be beaten by England alone, and that coalitions of the old type were useless. To Fox this had long been clear. And he had laid it down as a principle of our action for the future that Great Britain, while strenuously maintaining her own independence, would no longer create or purchase a futile Continental opposition, and no longer build artificial alliances to carry out schemes of dynastic or anti-revolutionary aggression. But that spontaneous opposition for national interests and independence would find in England an earnest ally.[1] It was the same idea that underlay Pitt's famous prophecy that the one hope for Europe lay in national risings and national wars against the imperial dictatorship of France.[2] After 1807 our Foreign Office under Canning, Wellesley and Castlereagh virtually accepted this principle as the basis of our action.

The disappearance in the same year from the scene of the two protagonists whose duel had been prolonged for more than twenty years made a profound impression on public opinion. Every competent contemporary put Pitt and Fox in a class by themselves, nor has the verdict been altered by posterity. Pitt's character, career, and record, however they may be interpreted and judged, must always remain an inspiring example of the single-hearted devotion of wonderful powers to the service of State and country. But time with its gift of tears has done justice to Fox,

[1] " The system of forcing and persuading foreign Powers by means of subsidies to enter into wars against their own conception of their interests . . . was now effectually renounced . . . we were not the less determined to assist her (Austria) in a defensive war." (Fox's instructions to Adair at Vienna in 1806).

[2] On this question see articles by A. V. Dicey and H. Hall—" Was Pitt a Prophet ? " *Contemporary Review*, Sept. and Oct., 1896 ; *The Athenæum*, May 12th, 1900 ; April 19th, July 12th, 1902.

the statesman, without doing injustice to Pitt. Yet it is not Fox's personal character and private conduct, but his public career and the principles of which he was the most eloquent, courageous, and far-sighted champion where the perspective has been markedly corrected and the scheme of values readjusted. Fox, the man, remains to-day as for his contemporaries a singular blend—a gambler, a *roué*, a passionate lover of letters and literature, a friend whose charm was irresistible, an orator and debater in some respects *hors concours*. But if he had been nothing but these things, he would never have stamped himself as an intellectual force on the politics of his own day or bequeathed to his successors a political ideal which they rightly cherished as of greater value than the personality and friendship of the leader they had lost. When he had shaken himself free (and he was only nineteen when he entered Parliament) of the demoralising environment of his father and his school, the consistency of the principles that he advocated in all the great political issues from 1774-1806 is remarkable. The American colonies, India, the Cabinet system, the power of the Crown and "the King's Friends," economic reform, the slave trade, parliamentary reform, the removal of religious disabilities, the French Revolution, the freedom of the Press, and the restoration of the Bourbons, coercion and administration by suspension of the *Habeas Corpus Act* and *ex officio* indictments. No less remarkable are the spirit and ideals of self-government and liberty which illuminated and elevated his political teaching. England would have been the poorer morally, the lamp of liberty would have flickered with a dimmer light, but for the public career of Fox; and his truest justification came to be that, what Fox thought on most of these things an England exorcised from the anti-Jacobin superstitions came to think too.

Though weakened by the death of Fox and the retirement of Fitzwilliam, the Ministry provoked a collision with the Crown on the Roman Catholic question and was signally worsted. The Cabinet desired to bring in a Bill opening all commissions in the army and navy to Roman Catholics. The King refused his consent and the Bill was withdrawn, but the Cabinet in a formal minute insisted on retaining their right as the confidential servants of the Crown to advise the King to proceed with measures of relief. Strengthened by Sidmouth, who resigned, and by the staunch

janissaries of the prerogative led by Eldon, George III. required
his Ministers to repudiate by a pledge their intention to propose
at any future date such legislation. This the Ministers rightly
refused to do, and resigned. The Cabinet unquestionably mismanaged the matter. They were not united on the desirability of
further relief, and Palmerston's criticism that they desired to retain
both their places and their opinions was not without point. But
on the question of a collective pledge they were wholly in the
right, and though resolutions affirming the sound constitutional
doctrine (subsequently accepted by Peel in 1835 and Stanley and
Russell in 1851), were submitted to the House, the Commons burked
the issue by passing to the order of the day (268 to 242 votes). April 9
The controversy brought out very clearly the dangerous interpretation of the royal prerogative by the King, his continued reliance
on advice outside the Cabinet, and hostile to his confidential servants, the reconstitution under Eldon and the Tory highfliers of a
party of "King's Friends," and the undiminished power of the
Crown to transfer a solid block of votes in the House of Commons
—all of which nothing but parliamentary reform could alter.
Dunning's famous motion in 1780, in fact, was as applicable in
1807 as in the struggle with the Monarchy during the American
War.

The death of Pitt and Fox broke up the old party divisions, and
from 1806 till 1820, when the Whigs made the franchise and redistribution of seats the main articles of their programme, and thus
once more provided a true and fundamental line of division which
restored the two-party system, the political situation resembled
that which followed Walpole's death, save that in 1807 for Whig
we must read Tory. The historic names were retained, but the
ideas they conveyed were usually traditional and more arbitrary
than real, more concerned with methods than with ends. In the
place of parties there are groups, "connections," clustered round
prominent but not dominant public figures. Liverpool, who was
Prime Minister from 1812 to 1827, owed his position not to his
leadership, but to his tact, to his capacity to make colleagues work
under a chief who would not work together without him, and to
his anticipation of Melbourne's maxim of letting everything alone
that any group in his Cabinet was strong enough to demand should
be let alone. Every Ministry after 1805 was a coalition of two or

more of these groups, with the disastrous consequences that all attempts to work Parliamentary Government on the group system seem inevitably to involve. Ministries could be upset as easily as they were made. A dexterous politician outside the Cabinet could by a shake of the parliamentary kaleidoscope turn an artificial majority into an artificial and temporary minority ; leadership in the Cabinet or against it becomes an affair of the tactics of the whip and of the *salon* and club rather than the political strategy of the generals. Worse, the group system offered sinister opportunities to the personal, divorced from the public, motive, to the saturation of the atmosphere of public life with the miserable and paltry wraths that, unchecked by collective solidarity on great issues, are the curse of ambition and ability. These "dreadful personal animosities" (Wellesley's phrase) were conspicuous after 1806. The careers of Canning, Castlereagh, Wellesley, Grey, Grenville, Moira—the copious memoirs and correspondence now at our disposal—illustrate with painful iteration how deeply the acid of intrigue, jealousy, and suspicion had bitten into the Treasury and Opposition Benches. And the evil was aggravated by the personal interpretation of his prerogative and royal duties that was the congenial inheritance of the Regent.

Grenville, in Canning's eyes, was "the direct and lawful inheritor" of Pitt's party, but Grenville, obstinate as ever, refused to separate from Sidmouth, and Canning from his small connection. "The jarring interests" declined to combine, and the new Ministry under Portland therefore brought back the Pittite rump led by Eldon, the uncrowned king of the House of Lords, and Perceval, in the Commons, whom Pitt had marked out as his successor as early as 1801. But its two ablest members were Castlereagh (Secretary for War and the Colonies) and Canning, who as Foreign Secretary now entered the Cabinet for the first time. Unfortunately both for England and themselves these two devoted followers of their master, Pitt, were separated by a personal antipathy which their agreement on the necessity of prosecuting the war *à outrance* with Napoleon, on Catholic emancipation, and opposition to parliamentary reform, only seemed to strengthen. Both were proud and sensitive men with marked gifts for administration, solid industry, tenacity of purpose, desire for power, and lofty ambition. Both were deservedly loved by the intimate friends who saw the best of their characters.

Castlereagh was a wretched speaker, but Canning's polished rhetoric and wit gave a lustre of their own to his achievements in office now and later. Canning, as Lady Malmesbury had already noted in 1801, " had more enemies than anybody living ". Castlereagh's unpopularity is at least intelligible, but Canning's reputation, like Shelburne's, remains somewhat of a puzzle. Croker asserted that " nobody will believe he can take his tea without a stratagem "; and in the superheated atmosphere of the narrow political circles of 1806-15, Canning's rapid rise, ambitions, vanity, and petulant flippancy, his intellectual powers, barbed by a bitter tongue, combined to convict him of a Machiavellian aptitude for intrigue. And after 1809 he was in eclipse until his rival Castlereagh's death left him without an equal in the sphere of foreign policy.

The course of the European war shortly developed into an unexpected *dénoûment*. Napoleon wiped out the check the Prusso-Russian forces had administered at Eylau by a crushing victory at Friedland. The Tsar, angered by the paltry financial aid that our Feb. 8 Ministry offered, and by the despatch of troops, as usual, too late to June 14 the Baltic, calmly threw over his ally, Prussia, and made peace with Napoleon at Tilsit. The Prussian State was dismembered, its July 7 western provinces incorporated into the new kingdom of Westphalia (under Jerome Bonaparte), her Polish territory turned into a Duchy of Warsaw, and a heavy indemnity imposed on the diminished remainder. More serious for Great Britain, the Tsar agreed to close his ports to our trade and to join in compelling Denmark, Sweden, and Portugal to follow his example. The Danish and Portuguese fleets would then be at the disposal of their master and ally, Napoleon. The secret articles of this treaty were betrayed to Canning,[1] and with dramatic promptness he prepared to foil the conspiracy. An expedition was at once despatched to Copenhagen to offer our alliance to Denmark, and to insist on her fleet being deposited with Great Britain on satisfactory terms of hire. The Danes refused ; Copenhagen was bombarded and the fleet carried Sept. 2 off by force. This high-handed act stirred great indignation in Europe, and was bitterly attacked by the Opposition in Parliament. Canning and his colleagues justified it as a war measure, the sole ground of which was necessity. And no other defence is possible. The alliance of France and Russia, and the abject humiliation of

---

[1] See Appendix xiii.

Prussia, had created for England the most menacing crisis she had faced since 1797. Every day was important, and to wait until Napoleon had coerced Denmark was treachery to our right to exist as an independent State. The accuracy of Canning's brilliant penetration of Napoleon's aims has been substantiated up to the hilt by modern research. And Napoleon's fury at the success of Canning's counter-stroke to the plot against Great Britain hatched on the raft in the Niemen revealed how clean and hard the home-thrust was. But Canning only partially achieved his policy. The " capitulation " of September 7 reduced the expedition to a stroke simply at the Danish fleet, and Canning's scheme of an alliance between England and the united Scandinavian States to keep the Baltic open and frustrate the Continental system broke down.   Nor was Nov., 1807 Napoleon's rage diminished when Junot, despatched with a Franco-Spanish army to compel Portugal to a rupture with Great Britain, seized Lisbon, but was forced to witness the royal family embark for Brazil under the escort of British ships.   The deposition of the House of Braganza, following on this military *coup de main*, was an object lesson in the value of Napoleon's denunciations of our " international outrage " at Copenhagen, and a conclusive proof of his intentions so selfishly acquiesced in by the Tsar at Tilsit.

That astonishing alliance (which remains one of the many paradoxes that the character and career of Alexander I. provide) was the starting point of a new era in the war for Great Britain, in the history of Napoleon and of Europe.   The Emperor had now definitely embarked on the plan of " conquering the sea by the land ; " and his " Continental system " was formulated in a series of formidable decrees (Berlin, Nov. 21, 1806 ; Milan, Dec. 17, 1807 ; the Trianon Tariff of Aug. 5, 1810 ; Fontainebleau, Oct. 18 and 25, 1810).   The British Isles were declared to be in perpetual blockade.   British ships were excluded from French or allied harbours ; all trade with Great Britain or in British goods were prohibited.   Subsequently, neutral vessels complying with our regulations were "denationalised " and constituted lawful prize.   And in 1810 a high tariff was placed on Colonial imports as being virtually in British hands, and British goods wherever found were to be confiscated and burnt.   Neither the idea nor the methods of this policy of isolating Great Britain and coercing her by the destruction of her trade into surrender at discretion was new.   Napoleon here as elsewhere adopted the

economic theory of the *ancien régime* and the Revolution as developed by the Directory, and erected it into a vast system which he
bound up with the political organisation of his "Grand Empire
Français". Acceptance of the Decrees became the condition of
French friendship, refusal provided a plausible *casus belli*. By 1808
the leading States with a seaboard had agreed to close their ports
—Spain, Naples, Holland, Prussia, Russia, Denmark, Portugal,
Austria. Success, as Napoleon saw, depended on two conditions—
the whole coast-line of Europe must be sealed up, and the Decrees vigorously enforced. After 1806 Imperial policy was largely
governed by these two objects. Intervention in Spain and Portugal
was necessary to close patent gaps ; the Russian campaign of 1812
was to administer condign chastisement for Alexander's defection
from the system. And with every year Napoleon was driven to
extend the boundaries of the Empire in order to control effectively
a longer coast-line. When "Les rois préfets" tended to become
national and to relax the rigour of the code, deposition and annexation were the only alternative, as happened with his brother Louis
and Holland in 1810. Nor could Napoleon, once committed to the
struggle, draw back without a damaging confession of political impotence, and direct encouragement to other submissive allies to
revolt. Politically and commercially, the Continental system was
all or nothing. Its success might be gigantic ; its failure was certain to be so. Yet what other way was there after Trafalgar and
Tilsit of reducing Great Britain to acquiescence in the Napoleonic
Empire ?

The British Government replied by a counter series of Orders in
Council,[1] which laid down that ports from which British ships or
goods were excluded were to be regarded as effectively blockaded,
forbade neutrals to trade between such ports, and pronounced as un-
lawful and subject to confiscation trade in articles produced by the
excluding countries or their colonies. Under these Orders various
portions of the Continental coast were effectively blockaded, and
the British navy exercised a rigorous right of search over all neutrals
which naturally caused widespread resentment. The object of the
Orders in Council was, first, to extirpate the French seaborne trade ;
secondly, to compel neutrals to trade with Great Britain, and, thirdly,

---

[1] It is noticeable that the first of these was promulgated in January 7th, 1807,
by the Whig Ministry of "all the talents".

to make the Continental system so odious to Europe that it would revolt against it. The text of the Orders, and the facilities granted to neutrals whose inability to resist Napoleon was recognised, prove that, whatever the indirect result may have been, it was not our intention to extinguish neutral trade and absorb it into a vast British monopoly. But precisely because we were in a position to assert our regulations at sea the neutral felt most severely the burden of our maritime supremacy. Moreover the Continental system and the Orders powerfully influenced our policy. Outlets for our exports had to be found. Isolated and militarily ineffective expeditions pierced temporarily the sealed coast-line. The capture and control of colonial centres of trade or production became doubly desirable as a measure for coercing Europe through the regulation of the supply of all colonial raw material or products.

Neither Napoleon's system nor our counter-system was completely enforced. Napoleon was obliged to permit certificated evasions in necessary articles (*e.g.* cloth, machinery, raw material, etc., which only Great Britain could supply), and British " licences" were issued on a large scale which narrowed considerably the area of operation and incidentally penalised the British manufacturer and shipowner.

The Orders in Council were arbitrary and novel in principle, harshly executed, and only defensible as acts of war due to sheer military necessity against a relentless adversary. They ultimately embroiled us in a collision with the United States at a highly critical phase of the European struggle ; and as measures of commercial policy they were very unpopular with the manufacturing and trading interests which they were framed to defend. To Brougham's searching indictment in 1810 no adequate reply was made by the Government, and after the death of Perceval, their chief advocate, they were practically dropped. But they had the merit of defining the issue for England as one of existence, while they reduced it to a desperate match in the resources of the combatants. In 1806 Napoleon's correspondence shows that he anticipated a speedy and decisive victory; and he was certainly disappointed by the unexpected stubbornness of our resistance. He had misjudged the commercial capacity of Great Britain, and his crude economics ignored vital elements in the problems of international trade. The superb tenacity of our Government and the national spirit of our people, assisted by the adaptation of our commerce as organised by the industrial revolution to the new conditions, and the impotence of Napoleon to prevent our trade by sea with East and West outside Europe, rather than the Orders themselves, combined to foil his plan. But the damage and suffering involved were immense, though it is not easy to decide whether the Continent or ourselves in the struggle suffered the more severely. British trade was undeniably hard hit. The loss of markets, the depredations of privateers, the artificial diversion of traffic, the gluts in production, the overspeculation caused by violent fluctuation in prices, accentuated the havoc wrought by the maintenance of an inconvertible paper currency, grinding taxation, bad harvests, and the wastage of capital by the war. In 1810 a grave commercial crisis supervened. Fortunately, Napoleon's economic theory limited his efforts to strangling our exports. Had he cut off, as he might have done, the imports of grain from 1809-12, when prices [1] were rising to famine point, we might have been starved into surrender. But by 1812 the blockade in the Baltic had broken down, and in 1813 the Continental system virtually collapsed. The burden of loss fell mainly on the neutrals and Napoleon's allies. The French seaborne trade was wiped out, although France lived at the expense largely of her tributary States. Most important of all, Napoleon failed to foresee the immense indirect political effect of his gigantic scheme. The renaissance of nationalism — Napoleon's most deadly foe, because it was a spiritual and not a material force, and could only be combated by spiritual forces—was fostered powerfully by the fear and hatred bred by the Continental system. Commerce, denationalised by, and sacrificed to, the ambitions of a despotic dictator, became the badge of political denationalisation. Our statesmen continuously proclaimed that any people in revolt would not only have our political aid to recover a lost independence, but would at once be freed from the degradation of our commercial coercion. In brief, our quarrel was not with Europe but with Napoleon, and between Great Britain and every nation fighting for its nationality it was

---

[1] The average price of corn from 1804-12 was 88s. 11d.; in 1810, 106s. 2d.; in 1811, 94s. 6d.; in 1812, 125s. 2d.; in 1813 (to August), 116s. In 1810, 1,250,000 qrs. (value more than £7,000,000) were imported. In 1801, when the Baltic trade was cut off, the price went up to 155s. and dropped in 1804 to 49s. 6d. By December 1814, it had fallen to 73s. 6d.

28

our duty to prove a complete identity of economic, political, and intellectual interests, and a common end, the restoration of a European system based on independent and sovereign national States. And the indispensable preliminary to this was resistance to, and the overthrowal of, the Napoleonic Empire of 1810.

The year 1808, however, was chiefly remarkable for the intervention of Great Britain in the affairs of the Iberian Peninsula, which led to the Peninsular War. This was due to a singular combination of events. Napoleon was determined to enforce the Continental system in Spain and Portugal and thus close an enormous line of seaboard to British goods and shipping, sever England from her historic ally at Lisbon and control the colonial possessions of the House of Braganza. The secret Treaty of Fontainebleau forced on Godoy, the incompetent and unprincipled lover of the Queen of Charles IV. of Spain, had provided for the expulsion of the Portuguese reigning family and the partition of the kingdom. It is probable that as early as 1807 Napoleon had also decided to overthrow the Bourbon dynasty at Madrid; as Bourbons they were offensive to his imperial dynastic policy, and Godoy was marked in Napoleon's memory for chastisement with his worthless master and mistress. But on the face of it the Fontainebleau Treaty was no more than the system of Tilsit enforced in a new sphere. Junot already in 1807 had invaded Portugal; the Royal Family fled to Brazil under British escort, and Junot, in the spring of 1808, made Lisbon his headquarters, suppressed the Council of Regency, and took the government into his own hands. The Portuguese business gave Napoleon an excuse for pouring troops into Spain and seizing some of the important fortresses and strategic points. Spaniards and King played into his hands. A popular rising in Aranjuez frightened Charles IV. into abdicating, and his treacherous and worthless son was proclaimed as Ferdinand VII. Murat, the Emperor's brother-in-law, entered Madrid. Force and fraud, as Wellesley said, were alike to Napoleon. Murat and his agents played off father against son, lover against the heir, mother and wife against husband and son. Charles and Ferdinand were cozened or coerced into a journey to Bayonne, where Napoleon threw off the mask. The father was induced to abdicate, the son, terrified by threats of death, into following his example. The Crown of Spain was then conferred by the grace of the Emperor

Oct., 1807

March, 1808

THE PENINSULAR WAR

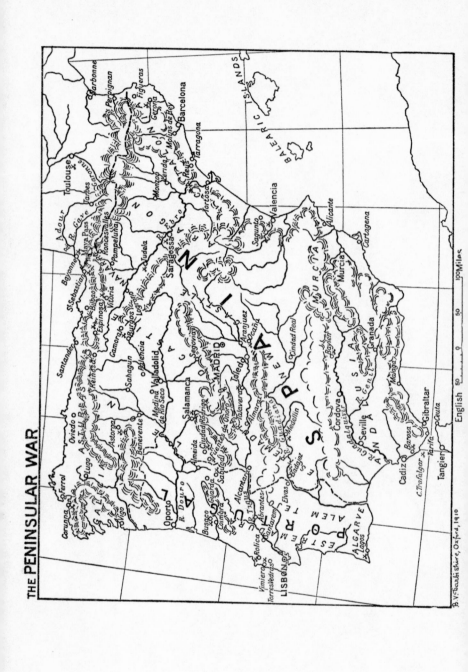

English 50   0   50   100 Miles

B.V. Darbishire, Oxford, 1910

on his brother Joseph, transferred from Naples to Madrid, while
Murat was sent to Naples vice Joseph, seconded to the Spanish
throne. So far the episode had been a wonderfully successful
example of Napoleon's methods, and a dramatic illustration of his
dynastic ambitions and continental policy. Napoleon had bullied
and tricked the Spanish dynasty. He had forgotten the Spanish
people.

To the surprise both of the Emperor and Europe spontaneous
insurrections—the memorable Dos de Mayo (Second of May)—at
Madrid and throughout the peninsula, which cost the French
troops hundreds of lives, proclaimed a passionate protest against
the degrading sale of a kingdom at Bayonne. A thrill ran through
Germany, inflaming the hearts of Stein and the Prussian patriots
already burning to avenge Tilsit. For here was a nation rising on
behalf of a worthless dynasty, because even the miserable Fer
dinand VII. symbolised nationality and independence. Valencia
Saragossa, and Gerona withstood the French attacks ; Barcelona
treacherously occupied by the French, was assaulted from the sea
with British help under Collingwood. Napoleon saw himself committed to a campaign of conquest, which he estimated would be
easy. At Medina de Rio Seco, Cuesta and Blake were defeated by July 14
Bessières, but Dupont was surrounded and compelled to surrender
at Baylen the day that the new King reached Madrid. Proclaimed July 20
King of Spain and the Indies, he now fell back behind the Ebro.

Great Britain at this point despatched 12,000 men under Sir
Arthur Wellesley to aid the Spaniards and Portuguese in throwing
off the yoke of France. Landing at the mouth of the Mondego he Aug. 13
defeated a small French force at Roliça, and advancing thence
towards Lisbon, met Junot at Vimiero. Wellesley had the advan- Aug. 21
tage both in numbers and position. The French attacked with
skill and determination, but were driven back in confusion, and the
victory might have been converted into a crushing disaster by a
stern pursuit. Unfortunately, Wellesley was superseded by Burrard
on the day of the battle, to be superseded next day by Dalrymple,
and these successive commanders most culpably let the opportunity
slip. Instead, by the Convention of Cintra (finally arranged
at Lisbon), Junot was permitted to hand over Lisbon and other
Portuguese fortresses, while his army and himself were to be sent
back to France. At the same time, by another convention, the

Russian fleet, blockaded in the Tagus, surrendered. Portugal was
thus evacuated by the French. The Convention of Cintra was
justifiably condemned at home. Popular sentiment was deeply
stirred over the Spanish rising, and the easy terms granted to
Junot provoked great indignation and a pamphlet from Wordsworth, significant of the poet's and the nation's feelings. A military court of inquiry exonerated the generals, but it was clearly
recognised that Wellesley alone came out of the transaction with
honour. He had justified the military reputation won at Assaye,
he had twice defeated the French, and the failure to crush Junot
after Vimiero was due to his mediocre superiors. Canning wisely
marked him out for further employment if events offered the opportunity, though as yet neither Napoleon nor Canning perceived that
in Wellesley Ireland had produced a military genius of the first order.

Oct. 7   Sir John Moore had assumed the chief command in Portugal.
He had recently returned from an expedition to aid Gustavus IV.
of Sweden, at war with Russia, Napoleon's ally, but the Swedish
king made co-operation impossible. Shortly afterwards he was
obliged to abdicate in favour of his uncle, Charles XIII., and the
adoption of Marshal Bernadotte (the founder of the present royal
line in Sweden) as Crown Prince brought about a reconciliation
with Russia and France. Moore was an officer of great ability,
with a deservedly high reputation, but his Whig views and ill-
concealed scepticism about the military prospects in the Peninsula
did not commend him to Canning, who profoundly mistrusted his
colleague at the War Office, Castlereagh ; and Moore's task of
co-operating with the Spanish armies was made more difficult by
lack of local information, the exaggerated estimate of the Spanish
troops, our defective military organisation, and the immense efforts
now made by Napoleon. Baylen and Vimiero had been a serious
blow to French prestige ; Austria, inspired by the Spanish rising,
was arming ; Prussia and North Germany were honeycombed by
patriotic plans of a similar national rising. Napoleon, freed by
Oct. 12   the Convention of Erfurt with the Tsar, who promised aid against
Austria and recognised Joseph as King of Spain, had planned an
elaborate and masterly campaign to crush Spanish resistance. The
Nov. 11   Spanish armies were successively routed at Espinosa, Gamonal,
Nov. 10   and Tudela. On December 4th Napoleon was in Madrid. The
Nov. 23   same day Moore, who had reached Salamanca, was joined there by

his cavalry and artillery.   But Baird, sent with reinforcements, dis- Nov. 13
embarked at Corunna, had only reached Astorga on November 22nd. Oct. 26.
Nov. 4
Moore's position was critical.   He knew of the Spanish defeats, but
not that Napoleon was already in Madrid.   After some days of delay
and indecision he determined to advance, strike at the Emperor's
communications " bridle in hand," but ready to retreat if necessary.
He would thus draw on himself the full weight of the French force,
might ruin their plan of campaign, and give the routed Spaniards
some months of breathing time to reorganise.   It was a fine and
courageous design which might succeed.   And it did.   Baird's retreat from Astorga was cancelled, and Moore left Salamanca knowing Dec. 11
that Madrid had fallen.   On December 13th he turned aside for
a stroke at Soult; on December 20th he was joined by Baird; on
December 23rd he reached Sahagun.   Four days earlier Napoleon
had at last discovered Moore's movements, and now with demonic
energy hurled every man at his disposal to exterminate the British
force.   But Moore too had learned what was in store for him, and
promptly retreated.   Pursuer and pursued drove their men by forced Dec. 24
marches through cruel winter weather.   At Benavente the French Dec. 29
were brilliantly checked.   On January 1st Napoleon, seeing that
his prey would probably escape, handed the command to Soult at
Astorga.   Moore reached Corunna on January 12th with an army
terribly demoralised by the strain of the retreat, but before he
could embark he turned to bay, and the worn-out troops completed
their commander's task by repulsing at every point the French
attack.   Moore himself fell in the action, which was a brilliant Dec. 16
close to the operations which had foiled Napoleon and shattered
his plan of campaign.   The army, leaving the body of its chief in
its honourable grave at Corunna, was quickly embarked next day.
If Moore had thus failed to keep the field in Spain, it is only fair
to remember that, with the Spaniards routed, no man could have
done more against 250,000 victorious French directed by the
Emperor himself.   And if Moore drove his men too hard in the
retreat he knew not merely that the capture of his force would
probably seal the fate of the Spanish rising, but that he was in
command not of *a* British force but of *the* British army.   As it was
he drew on himself " the whole disposable force of the French,"
saved his own army, and proved that when French and British met
on equal terms Vimiero had not been a lucky accident.

A new phase of the war opened in the spring of 1809. Great Britain made a treaty of alliance with the Spanish Junta, the central organisation formed to control the national resistance; Beresford was sent out to work up the Portuguese army; and Arthur Wellesley was appointed to the chief command. His famous memorandum, drawn up before he left England, embodied his views and foreshadowed his conception and conduct of the war. Assured of the command of the seas, Wellesley (as against Moore) held that Portugal could be defended irrespective of the contest in Spain; that we could secure a foothold there from which we could not be driven; that the French would require at least 100,000 men to overrun Portugal, and that such an effort would vitally affect their operations in Spain. In a word, an adequate British force in Portugal with reorganised local support might in time achieve the liberation of the whole Peninsula from the French. Such a result could not but shake Napoleon's position in Central Europe.

The first step was to clear Portugal of the invaders. March-
May 5   ing from Lisbon, Wellesley by masterly manœuvres crossed the
May 14   Douro in the face of the French at Oporto, and compelled Soult
to retreat in disorder to Galicia. Combining with the Spaniards
July 27-28 under Cuesta he advanced east into Spain, and at Talavera was
attacked by the French under Joseph, Jourdan, and Victor. The Spaniards proved of little value, but the British troops signally repulsed the French assaults, and the victory, which cost our army 6268 casualties and the French some 9000, turned Wellesley into Viscount Wellington. But Soult had thrust himself between the British and their base, and Wellington was compelled to make a circuitous retreat *via* Badajoz to the Portuguese frontier. The army suffered severely, and critics in England not unnaturally saw in the campaign of 1809 only a discouraging repetition of Moore's operations—a risky advance, a bloody battle, called a victory, and a demoralised retreat.

Elsewhere Great Britain appeared to singularly little advantage. At sea there were gleams of success. Cochrane's brilliant
April 11 cutting-out expedition in the Basque Roads was prevented from
being a complete success by his chief's, Lord Gambier's, negligence Collingwood in the Mediterranean captured the Ionian Islands and destroyed a French squadron in the Bay of Genoa

Meanwhile Napoleon from Spain had decreed exile for the Nov. 16 great Prussian statesman, Vom Stein, but despite Prussia's refusal to join her, Austria, under Stadion and the Archduke Charles, proclaimed a national war.   Napoleon had hurried from Astorga to April 9 Paris and then took the field.   Victories at Regensburg and Eckmühl seemed to proclaim the invincibility of the Emperor, who entered Vienna.   But the attempt to cross the Danube resulted in May 13 a serious repulse at Aspern, and for six weeks the French army was May 18 virtually imprisoned in the island of Lobau.   Extricated from his perilous position, Napoleon, after heavy loss, defeated the Austrians on the northern bank at Wagram, and though the struggle might July 6 have been continued, an armistice at Znaim converted into the July 14 Treaty of Vienna ended the war from which so much had been Oct. 14 hoped.   Stadion was replaced by Metternich, and the national policy of Austria flickered out in an inglorious peace.

During this critical phase the worst aspects of our political and military direction were painfully exemplified.   We were still nomin- Jan., 1809 ally at war with Austria, and until correct relations had been established our Government, whom a long and bitter experience had made hostile to Austrian plans, declined effective assistance.   True to its traditions, headquarters divided its efforts and despatched 15,000 June men from Palermo against Naples, which captured two rocky islands and then retired.   Had a large force been despatched in April, as the Austrians demanded, to the Elbe, a serious diversion might have been effected and Prussia brought into the struggle.   But the Peninsular War, the military folly of the Ministry of all the Talents, and the lack of organisation at home, had drained England of men, and not till July 28th when the Austrian campaign was over did the armament of thirty-five ships of the line and 40,000 men leave the Downs.   The conception was sound—to strike at Antwerp and destroy the docks and fleet—but the Walcheren expedition was ruined by its independence of the Continental operations, by the long delay which advertised its despatch, by the incompetence of the commander, who justified his nickname of "the late Lord Chatham," and by the absence of medical equipment for a force dumped on to malarious swamps.   The French fleet was allowed to escape ; Antwerp, that might easily have been rushed, was let alone till it could defend itself ; Flushing, of no importance, was taken ; and then the army, unable to advance, mouldered away Aug. 16

in malarial fever. The shattered remnant was finally withdrawn on December 24th. Never had there been a more complete fiasco. Walcheren deservedly made us the laughing stock of Europe, and embittered a disillusioned public opinion against every future military stroke at Napoleon. Worse even than the disaster and the loss of life and the waste of money—when men and money were so sorely needed in Portugal—was the condonation of those concerned. Sailors and soldiers freely threw the blame on each other, yet it was not this disgraceful catastrophe that broke up the Ministry, but a personal quarrel between the two ablest members of the Cabinet, Canning and Castlereagh.

For two years the Ministry had been hampered by internal dissensions, aggravated by a domestic scandal which excited more public interest than the events that were making history on the Continent. Furnished with information by a vindictive and disreputable woman, Mrs. Clarke, who had been the Duke of York's mistress, one Colonel Wardle, M.P., accused the Duke of corruption in the exercise of his patronage as Commander-in-Chief. The corruption was in reality practised by Mrs. Clarke herself, and a Committee of the House of Commons acquitted the Duke of the charges. But opinion was so deeply stirred that the Duke felt it necessary to resign. His resignation was a real loss to the army, for at the Horse Guards the Commander-in-Chief had done valuable work as an administrator. With a genuine interest in military organisation the Duke had instituted a series of reforms which bore fruit later, and the future required that they should be carried much further. The true nature of the case brought against him was brought to light later in a lawsuit, in which it appeared that Mrs. Clarke had become the mistress of Colonel Wardle himself, who had rewarded her services by furnishing a house for her, the payment for which had to be extracted by the machinery of the law. The revelation of this sordid conspiracy to levy blackmail in the name of public purity helped to reinstate the Duke in public favour.

The quarrel between Canning and Castlereagh was no less fertile in envenomed recrimination. Both were unpopular with the public, and Canning was so dissatisfied with Castlereagh as a colleague that he pressed for his removal from the War Office. The Cabinet agreed to a scheme by which the Marquis Wellesley was

April
July

to succeed Castlereagh, transferred to the Lord Presidentship of the Council, to be vacated by Camden's resignation.   But the change was postponed while the Walcheren expedition was in progress. Canning understood that Castlereagh was to be informed, but the Prime Minister, Portland, from sheer slackness or reluctance to be disagreeable, kept silence ; and when ill-health compelled him to Sept. 6 declare his intention to resign, Canning, to his indignant surprise, learned that the change had not been communicated to Castlereagh, and at once resigned.   Castlereagh followed suit, and then demanded satisfaction for what appeared to be a base intrigue on Canning's part.   In the duel, Canning was slightly wounded.   It Sept. 21 is fairly clear now that the affair was the result of a misunderstanding for which neither Canning nor Castlereagh was to blame. Curiously enough the issue made Castlereagh less unpopular and Canning more unpopular than before.[1]   And for Canning the result was disastrous.   Portland's retirement finally broke up the admini- Oct. 29 stration.   No pleading or proofs could prevent the political world from concluding that while Canning's conduct could be explained it eminently needed explanation.   Castlereagh came back to high office in 1812, but Canning was excluded from real power until Castlereagh's death in 1822.   Had Canning been Foreign Secretary in the place of Castlereagh in the critical years after 1812 his record after 1822 shows that Great Britain and Europe would have been the gainers.   And, as Canning himself bitterly reflected later, two years of power in 1812 would have been worth twenty years in 1822.   In 1809, Great Britain lost a statesman of genius and the one Tory who, in spite of defects of character and temperament, really believed in a liberal foreign policy, and was able and willing to resist on principle the insidious reactionary legitimism and crafty opportunism incarnated in the new Chancellor, Metternich, at Vienna.

After wearisome negotiations in which the personal element was disagreeably predominant, a new coalition Administration was patched up under Perceval as Prime Minister and Chancellor of

[1] See Holland, *Further Memoirs of the Whig Party* (1807-21 ; Murray, 1905): "He sunk in the same proportion as his rival rose in public estimation, and particularly in the House of Commons" (p. 36).   And on the whole affair see *Canning and His Friends* (ed. Bagot), vol. i. ; Walpole's *Perceval*, I., ix., II. i. ; Phipps, *Memoir of Ward*, pp. 210, *et seq.;* Twiss, *Eldon*, ii., 88 ; Colchester, *Diary*, 2, 209; *Creevey Papers*, i., 96 ; and the *Annual Register* for 1809 (vol. 51).

the Exchequer, whose two most important colleagues were Lord
Liverpool, who replaced Castlereagh, and the Marquis Wellesley,
who replaced Canning.   Canning, Castlereagh, and Sidmouth remained outside the Ministry.   The Whig leaders, Grenville and
Grey, declined the overtures made to them.   The Whig party was,
in fact, thoroughly disintegrated.   The Clarke-Wardle scandal had
keenly stimulated the movement for purity and efficiency in the
public administration ; and the public accounts, which revealed a
million and a half spent on useless sinecures, provided ample material
for agitation.   The left wing of the party, represented by the eccentric Burdett, Cochrane, the naval hero of numerous daring exploits, Viscount Folkestone and Whitbread, had taken up again
the cause of parliamentary reform, and they were aided outside by
"demagogue" Hunt and Cobbett, whose power as an unwearied
pioneer begins with 1809.   But official Whiggism fastidiously dis-
owned alike the programme and the alliance.   The party was rent
by divisions.   A great impetus, indeed a new life, had been given
to Whig principles by the foundation in 1802 (the year also of
Cobbett's *Weekly Political Register*) of the *Edinburgh Review*
under Jeffrey, within whose buff and blue covers were concentrated
the best brains of the day.   It was a veritable "pillar of fire," "the
effect of which," Cockburn said truly, "was electrical," and it marked
an epoch in our periodical literature as well as in our political
history.   To its white and scorching flames contributed Cockburn,
Sydney Smith, Francis Horner, and the marvellously versatile talents
of Brougham.   Sir Walter Scott also wrote for it until his rugged
and healthy Toryism revolted and found more congenial outlet in
the rival *Quarterly Review*, started in 1809 by John Murray and
edited by Gifford.   From 1808-17 the titular Whig leader in the
Commons was Ponsonby ; but within the Whigs were many groups
who followed their clan leaders with a perverse and personal fidelity.
Lords Grey and Grenville represented the aristocratic tradition of
the eighteenth century ; Moira and Sheridan were the confidential
intimates and advisers of the Prince of Wales, who still deluded
himself with the idea that he was a Whig ; and outside there was
the cluster who "followed the principles of Mr. Fox," led by Henry
Vassall, third Lord Holland, husband of the autocratic lady, weaned
by divorce and re-marriage from Toryism, who made Holland House
the social centre of the new Whiggism, and the shrine for two

generations of all who acknowledged the master, Charles James Fox. The abolition of slavery and the slave trade, a free Press, religious toleration, Roman Catholic emancipation, the reform of our criminal and civil law—for these Holland and his group pressed unceasingly ; and yeoman service in the cause was rendered by Horner, Baring, Romilly, whose knowledge of law and equity was unrivalled, and who, had he lived beyond 1818, might have been one of the greatest of nineteenth century Chancellors, and Brougham, as well as by Lord Lauderdale and "citizen" Lord Stanhope. The Regency Bill was a fresh cause of division to the Whigs, and they were fatally split by the Peninsular War.

It is difficult for the generation of to-day to understand how responsible public men could so bitterly oppose our continued intervention in the Peninsula ; how so cool-headed a statesman as Grey felt it his duty to enter a protest in the Lords' Journals[1] against Wellesley's viscountship for the victory at Talavera. It is only fair to remember the conviction of Napoleon's invincibility universal in Europe at the time, which not even Moscow and Leipzig (three years ahead and wholly unforeseen) dissipated. In 1809 Napoleon was the victor of Marengo, Austerlitz, Jena, Friedland, Eckmühl, and Wagram : the ally of the Tsar, the master of the "banks of kings and princes" of the Erfurt Congress. Since 1793 our military efforts were a record of monotonous and humiliating failure. Walcheren was one more addition to a black list. Men had come to believe that the stars in their courses blessed Napoleon and cursed the puny politicians who fought with heaven's decrees. Talavera had been "followed by the necessity of a precipitate retreat" ; it was the inevitable prelude to another Corunna. Our War Office could not organise victory ; it never had and it never would. And until 1812 the Peninsular War seemed to bear the critics out—advances, "victories," retreats to the base in Portugal and the sheltering guns and decks of our fleet. We were so little accustomed to military genius that the greatness of Wellington was not recognised, still less that the hard, cold, reserved leader who mastered his staff and men because he had mastered himself, who never won their love because he did not love them, was month by month forging the instrument which cleared the Pyrenees passes in 1813, and in their general's opinion (and Welling-

[1] Rogers, *Protests of the Lords*, 2, 424.

ton measured his words) would have made Waterloo an affair of three hours. Canning had detected Wellington's genius; and if the Marquis Wellesley and Castlereagh adhered through evil report to Wellington there were many sceptics in Perceval's and Liverpool's Cabinets—stout Tories who shared in secret the outspoken disbelief of "unpatriotic" Whigs. But Holland and Horner, to their honour, believed in the Peninsular War. To them it was more than a campaign; it was the struggle of a nation to be free, and the assertion of nationality based on freedom was more important even than the overthrow of Napoleon.[1] They believed with justice that had Fox been living in 1809 he would have thought and said the same.

Perceval, as Grattan said, was not a first-rate line of battle ship, but he was a first-class cruiser out in all weathers. His Administration was framed on the principle of maintaining the Orders in Council, and resisting the demand for Roman Catholic emancipation. In home affairs the two most important events were the famous Report of the Bullion Committee and the Settlement of the Regency. The commercial crisis of 1809 and the scarcity of specie had resulted in the appointment of a Committee under Horner to examine the state of the currency. The report (the work of Horner, Baring, Thornton, and Huskisson) showed that the suspension of cash payments since 1797 had removed "the natural and true control" over the circulating medium; that the prices of gold bullion had risen, involving a general rise in prices and the depression of the exchanges; that these results were the outcome of a non-convertible paper currency, the over-issue of which, particularly since 1806, had been stimulated by its inconvertibility, with the inevitable consequence of an appreciation of gold and a depreciation of the paper money. Confirming the analysis of the report of 1804, the committee recommended the

[1] See Holland's *Further Memoirs of the Whig Party*, *passim*, and Horner's *Memoirs*. " I cannot hesitate now in believing . . . that the Whigs ought to adopt the war system, upon the very same principle which prompted them to stigmatise it as unjust in 1793 and as premature in 1803. The crisis of Spanish politics in May, 1808, seemed to me the first turn of things in a contrary direction; and I have never ceased to lament that our party took a course so inconsistent with the true Whig principles of Continental policy, so revolting to the popular feelings of the country, and to every true feeling for the liberties and independence of mankind " (Letter in 1813, *op. cit.*, 2, 158).

resumption of cash payments in two years. The weight of economic experts was wholly on the side of the Bullionists, and Ricardo's pamphlet was a crushing exposure of the adverse critics. Canning, with wit and grasp of the theory, defended the Committee; but Castlereagh and Vansittart, by misrepresenting the Bullionist economics, which they were incapable of understanding, persuaded the House of Commons to postpone the restoration of cash payments and a convertible paper currency until "the conclusion of a definite treaty of peace". Ministers had convinced themselves that the suspension of cash payments, like the Orders in Council, was a weapon of war. They did not see that it was a weapon which every year inflicted far more damage on ourselves than the enemy against whom it was employed.

In the same year the King, oppressed by the death of the Princess Amelia, the outcry against the Duke of York, and the collapse of the Walcheren Expedition, permanently lost both his sight and his reason. It was necessary to provide for a Regency, and Ministers adhered to the dangerous and unhappy precedent of 1788. The Regency Bill appointed the Prince of Wales Regent with Feb. 4, restricted powers, while the personal care of the King was vested in 1811 the Queen and a Council. The legislative limitations and the legal fictions by which the resolutions were carried into law were violently debated. The Prince and his royal brothers bitterly resented the restrictions on the Regent's powers. (After 1812, when it was clear that the King's derangement was incurable, these restrictions were withdrawn or modified.) Lord Holland ably represented the Whig constitutional view, and restated the formidable objections advanced in 1788; but Grenville was hampered by his former support to Pitt's proposals and the breach between Moira and Sheridan, the Prince's confidential advisers, and Grey and Grenville the official Whig leaders in the Lords. And the Bill which made the Prince of Wales virtually King did not, as it would have done in 1788, cause any change in the Ministry. Since 1807 the Prince Regent had really ceased to be a Whig. Whiggism had been with him probably but a skin-deep creed; the alliance with Fox had been an effective instrument for carrying on the hereditary opposition of his royal house between the heir to, and the occupant of, the throne. And since Fox's death George, who disliked Grey and Grenville, who with good reason disliked the conduct of the Prince of Wales, had gravitated steadily towards the Eldonian Toryism of maintaining the *status quo*. In and after 1810 there was much correspondence, many interviews and discussions which kept the Tapers and Tadpoles very busy, and occupy a vast deal of unnecessary space in the memoirs and letters of the day, but they came to nothing. And by 1812 the rupture between the Regent and the Whigs was complete. The Prince believed (as he later believed that he had taken an effective share in the battle of Waterloo) that he had been deserted and betrayed by the Whigs. The Whigs with more truth regarded their quondam royal patron as a renegade to reaction, who offered to place them in power on terms which made the Regent the *ex throno* Pontiff of the Whig faith. In fact by 1810 the Prince Regent had nothing in common with the Whigs, save the sentimental bond of having loved and lost in their company. Once he had easily overcome his personal aversion from Eldon and his colleagues, he was wholly in agreement with their political principles. And with the facility of a self-centred character for which imaginary personal grievances were the mainsprings of political action, the Prince Regent henceforward made it his main object to keep the Whigs out of office.

The Peninsular War was the one all-important issue until 1812. The peace with Austria after Wagram enabled Napoleon to pour copious reinforcements into Spain, to rout the Spanish armies and prepare for driving the British leopards into the sea. Barcelona Dec., 1809 was relieved and Gerona taken ; Suchet made himself master of Aragon, while the efforts organised by the Spanish Junta to take the offensive again with Madrid as the objective ended in disaster Nov. 19 at Ocana, where Joseph and Mortier wrecked the main Spanish army. Jan.-Feb., Soult was flung into Andalusia which he overran, Cadiz alone hold-1810 ing out. Aragon, Castile, and Andalusia were thus in French hands ; it remained to complete the conquest of Valencia and Catalonia, and clear Portugal, for which latter Masséna, probably the ablest of Napoleon's marshals, was specially selected by the Emperor. Wellington with less than 30,000 British troops had to face the certain prospect of invasion by a field army of 70,000 under Masséna, and the likelihood of a co-operating movement south of the Tagus by Soult from Andalusia. Left practically to his own resources, for neither men nor money in any adequate degree were sent from home (another consequence of Walcheren), Wellington had planned the campaign on a novel defensive, which was carried out with unflinching courage, skill, and consistency. Unknown to Masséna the triple lines of Torres Vedras across the neck of the Peninsula on which Lisbon stood were constructed by the engineers, and these converted the capital into a vast and unassailable fortress. Behind these lines Wellington intended to retire with all his forces, British and Portuguese, while—equally surprising to Masséna—the country was systematically denuded of all supplies by the peasantry, who were withdrawn from their homes. Masséna for his part intended to make Lisbon a second Corunna, and to punish the British so severely that they would fall back on their fleet and leave Portugal to its fate. Astorga was taken, April 22, Ciudad Rodrigo on July 10, Almeida on August 27. At Busaco, Wellington, to hearten Sept. 27 his men and test the Portuguese re-organised under British direction, stood up to the invaders and repulsed the French assaults, Masséna having 4400 casualties to the Anglo-Portuguese 1300. The Portuguese—again to Masséna's surprise—showed that they could fight and fight well, and Wellington fell back behind the lines of Torres Vedras, which Masséna now discovered, and which his trained eye revealed could not be forced. And in and about Santarem, from November 15 to March 5, 1811, Masséna remained impotent, his flanks and communications unceasingly harassed by the Portuguese militia, his army perishing from hunger and disease. He had intended to eat up the British. Instead the inflexible Wellington was remorselessly using the stripped land to eat up the French invaders. Soult contented himself with defeating a Spanish army at the Gebora Feb. 19 and capturing Badajoz. Driven by starvation, Masséna, followed by March 10 Wellington, led the wreck of his army from Santarem to Ciudad Rodrigo, and at Sabugal, in Wellington's opinion "one of the most April 4 glorious actions British troops were ever engaged in," the invasion April 3 of Portugal of 1810 ended in a brilliant defeat of Regnier's corps by the Light Division. A month earlier Graham at Barrosa, outside Cadiz, inflicted a sharp repulse on the French, but, unsupported by March 5 the Spaniards, retired to the city. In the East, Suchet however captured Tortosa and isolated Catalonia for a time, following the Jan. 1, 1811, stroke by storming Tarragona, the centre of Catalan strength. June 28

Wellington meanwhile laid siege to Almeida, which Masséna May 3 endeavoured to relieve, attacking the British twice at Fuentes and 5 d'Onoro. The battle of the second day was a critical one—"there was not," Napier records, "during the war a more perilous hour"—as the English divisions were separated and their right wing turned, which necessitated a new line being taken on new ground, while the struggle in the village of Fuentes d'Onoro was very severe. But in the end, thanks to the superb resistance of our men and Wellington's unshakeable nerve, Masséna was beaten off (with some 3000 casualties to our 2000). The French garrison in Almeida cut its way out, but the fortress fell to Wellington. Beresford concurrently had

May 16 invested Badajoz when Soult marched to its relief. At Albuera, south of the city, after a bloody engagement, in which French and British infantry fought with terrible determination, Soult was finally repulsed. The French lost 6000 men out of 23,000 engaged, but of the 10,500 British more than 4000, or 37 per cent. of "unconquerable British soldiers" had fallen "on the fatal hill". Compared with this the Spanish and Portuguese loss was trifling (not more than 2000, including prisoners). Soult retired, and Wellington, hurrying from the north, joined hands with Beresford and invested the fortress. Assaults failed. Marmont, who had replaced Masséna, united with Soult, and Wellington had to abandon the siege. Had the two marshals used their superior forces to compel a decisive action, Wellington might have been very roughly handled, and the safety of Portugal imperilled. But Soult broke away to safeguard Seville, and Wellington struck north at Ciudad Rodrigo. Marmont promptly returned, reinforced, from the valley of the Tagus, and Wellington was obliged to leave Ciudad Rodrigo and fall back on to the Portuguese frontier where he offered battle, that was refused, and the opposing armies went into winter quarters in October.

The autumn of 1811 marked the turn of the tide. Talavera, Busaco, Fuentes d'Onoro, Barrosa, and Albuera had proved the fighting quality of the British troops, but they had been victories strictly defensive in character. Yet, foiled as he had been at Badajoz and Ciudad Rodrigo, Wellington had kept his word. Portugal had not been overwhelmed; and if the French retained the two great fortresses—Ciudad Rodrigo and Badajoz—which barred the main lines of advance into Spain, Masséna's mighty effort in 1810 had ended in failure, and the summer of 1811 had seen the operations of the Anglo-Portuguese forces transferred to the frontiers. In 1810 and 1811 the French had employed some 350,000 and 300,000 men respectively in the peninsula, and Napoleon's best marshals had been in command. Every day that Wellington kept the field against them stiffened the ubiquitous local Spanish resistance east of the frontier, from Galicia to Andalusia, Castile, Leon, Valencia, and Catalonia. The national war, in which they were now so inextricably involved, involved the French generals in a critical dilemma. Until the hydra-headed local resistance—a war of guerrillas which cut the lengthy communications, absorbed thousands of troops, and imperilled the grand operations against the Anglo-Portuguese army—was finally crushed out, it was impossible to use their vast superiority of force against Wellington and pin him down to the neck of the isthmus at Lisbon. And until Wellington was pinned down the Anglo-Portuguese army was " in being," strong enough to hold its own against any main body of the French of equal numbers ; and the Spaniards were encouraged and enabled to continue their local efforts over the whole theatre of war, from the Pyrenees to the Portuguese frontier. The French marshals had discovered they were pitted against a commander as skilful at least as themselves, of infinite nerve and resource and singularly determined. Every month improved the quality of the Anglo-Portuguese army, an instrument forged in the best of schools, experience, and led by a chief whose long nose the British soldier had learned was worth one if not two divisions.

The marshals indeed had a cruelly difficult task. The Spanish War was not a campaign like that of Austerlitz, Jena, Friedland, or Wagram. Victory only secured the ground on which the victors stood. They were disunited amongst themselves, and they were directed, counter-directed, and abused by their imperial master. Spain in 1811 demanded Napoleon's presence in person and every man he could spare. But in 1811 the Time-spirit had reversed the hour-glass. For Napoleon the European situation had steadily worsened. If the divorce of Josephine, the marriage with the Archduchess Marie Louise, the birth of an heir to the empire, the April 10 King of Rome, had strengthened his dynastic position, Austria March 20, under Metternich was a dangerous ally, moved by self-interest 1811 alone. France under the pressure of the " blood tax " had lost its enthusiasm ; the Continental system was a second ulcer which, like the Spanish one, steadily sapped the moral and material resources

29

of the empire.   Prussia was being recast by the successors of Stein
—Scharnhorst, Hardenberg, Von Humboldt—and the unquenchable fire of the Spanish patriots inspired every German nationalist
to pray that the hour for Germany would soon come to rise and do
likewise.   Most serious of all, the system of Tilsit had broken down.
Aug., 1811 The Tsar was alienated, and Napoleon plainly contemplated an open
rupture and war with Russia, to seal up the Baltic to British ships
and goods.   The autumn saw the preparations for an overwhelming
Russian campaign pushed forward ; and just at the moment when
a supreme effort was urgent in the Peninsula, Napoleon began to
recall troops from Spain.   By the spring of 1812 30,000 men had
been withdrawn.   It is as easy as it is futile to be wise after the
event.   Contemporaries in the winter of 1811-12 could not foresee
that the περιπέτεια of the Napoleonic tragedy was at hand.   But
in the " might have beens" of history there is no more fascinating
subject than to speculate on what might have happened had
Napoleon, in October, 1811, postponed the quarrel with Alexander,
poured 250,000 men into Spain, and fought the campaign of 1812
in person with Lisbon and not Moscow as his objective.

The Emperor underrated Wellington and the Tsar.   He was
misled by gleams of success in Spain, the conditions of which he
never understood.   Suchet defeated Blake and his Spanish army
Oct. 25 decisively outside Sagunto and the fortress fell ; Blake was driven
into Valencia, and his force, 16,000 strong, surrendered with the
Jan. 9, capital of the province.   Wellington, seizing the chance for which
1812 he had quietly been waiting, replied by a quick concentration ;
Jan. 8 pounced on Ciudad Rodrigo, and carried the fortress by a brilliant
Jan. 13 assault before Marmont could move.   Marmont again dispersed
his army into its winter quarters, and Wellington struck with speed
March 16 and determination at the southern barrier—Badajoz ; and " against
time " the place was stormed by a desperate and bloody assault, in
which 5000 of the assailants fell.   Both at Ciudad Rodrigo and
Badajoz our troops committed deplorable excesses, but the storming
of the latter in particular, immortalised in Napier's narrative,
was a signal proof of what their commander owed to his officers
and men.   These decisive opening moves were rammed home in a
brilliant campaign.   By a masterly stroke, finely executed by Hill,
the pontoons at Almaraz on the Tagus—the sole line of direct
communication between Soult in the south and the army of Por-

tugal in the north—were destroyed; and Wellington then marched north, determined to force an issue with the isolated Marmont. After some weeks of manœuvring, Marmont gave him his chance at the Arapiles, where Wellington won the most finished tactical success of his career at the battle of Salamanca. The French left wing was July 22 rolled up and routed; the main body pushed off the field. Eight thousand French casualties and 7000 prisoners testified to the completeness of the victory. King Joseph fled to Suchet in Valencia, who was also joined by Soult from Andalusia, which Salamanca had compelled him to abandon; and on August 12th Wellington entered Madrid amidst the delirious enthusiasm of the Spaniards. The autumn did not quite bear out this triumphant advance. Wellington struck north at Burgos, which he besieged but failed to take; and then, faced by a triple French reconcentration (Souham Sept.-Oct. from the north, Soult and King Joseph from Valencia) fell back on Salamanca, where Hill, abandoning Madrid, joined him. Soult, united now with Souham, pressed the advance in superior force, and Wellington made a costly retreat to Ciudad Rodrigo. The troops Nov. again got out of hand, but Portugal was safe, French prestige had received an irretrievable blow, and Southern Spain was free of the French. The prospects for 1813 were far more promising than in any previous period of the war.

The summer of 1812 witnessed a reconstruction of the Ministry. The Prime Minister, Perceval, was assassinated by one Bellingham. May 11 Lord Liverpool, whose chief gift lay in reconciling to his leadership the leading members of his party, formed an Administration which was a loosely jointed Tory coalition, and the most remarkable feature of which was his continuance as First Lord of the Treasury for fifteen years. Canning and the Whigs were not given office. The former 1812-27 was still distrusted, but alike with Grey and Grenville might have joined the Ministry had he been willing to give up principles and connections. Eldon retained the Great Seal; Sidmouth became Home Secretary; Lord Bathurst, Secretary for War and the Colonies; Vansittart, Chancellor of the Exchequer. But the most important member of the Administration was Castlereagh, who had succeeded Wellesley as Foreign Secretary two months before Perceval's assassination. Wellesley, like Castlereagh, was an advocate of Roman Catholic emancipation, which was now left an open question in Liverpool's Cabinet; he had strongly complained of the lack of

support to his brother in the Peninsula ; but Castlereagh was determined to make the Spanish war as complete a success as British resources would permit.   And in this task our War Office was much
assisted by the development of the organisation originally laid down
1807   by Castlereagh himself when he was Secretary for War.[1]   The main
features of this system consisted in (*a*) the formation of a permanent
local militia on a territorial basis, as a third line behind the regular
army and the militia proper, which was largely raised by a compulsory ballot ; and (*b*) supplementing enlistment for the regular army
by drafts from the regular militia, which thus really ceased to be
a militia proper and became almost a linked battalion system for
filling up the corps of the depleted regiments of the regular army.
Athough this did not completely solve the problem of numbers,
training, and recruitment, and was not a voluntary system at all, it
seems certain that without it the army from 1811 to the end of the
war could not have been maintained.   It is noteworthy that from
1805 onwards more than 100,000 men were in this way supplied
from the militia to the regular army.

   The first three years of Liverpool's Government were crowded
with events of supreme importance.   No modern British Cabinet
has been called on to deal with problems of greater magnitude
than those presented by European affairs from the spring of 1812
to the battle of Waterloo and the settlement of peace after
Napoleon's downfall ; or to determine the principles and ends of
British policy under a more continuous strain of epoch-making
events and a more complex tangle of conflicting elements.   British
action, in fact, is merged in the general history of Europe.   Castlereagh, as the chief representative of the British nation in foreign
affairs, was vested with an authority in the Councils of the Powers
which he owed to the military prestige of Wellington and to the
naval, military, and financial resources of the British Empire.
Finance indeed and British credit were two of the most potent
weapons with which Great Britain had fought throughout, and
never were they more potent than in the years 1812-15.   Had the
British Government and Treasury not been willing and able to
bear, at a tremendous cost to the generation after 1815, the
gigantic burden of financing the efforts of the coalition as well

<hr />

[1] See Appendix x.

as their own, that coalition must have broken down. And the bare figures justify the epithet heroic for the British share.[1]

This tremendous strain was imposed on a population of not more than 15,000,000, demoralised by the system of Poor Law Relief which in 1812 cost £6,500,000, for whom the price of corn in 1812 and 1813 averaged 120s. a quarter, and who in 1810 had suffered a series of commercial crises consequent on feverish speculation in our export trade, and been hard hit by the Non-intercourse Act of the United States that preceded the American War. The suffering and misery of the agricultural and artisan classes were intense, and were mainly responsible for the epidemic of "frame-breaking" riots that spread in 1811 and 1812 from Nottingham to the chief industrial centres of the North and Midlands. True to its reactionary creed the Ministry, armed with the customary alarmist report of a Secret Committee of the House of Lords, treated an economic disease, aggravated by very intelligible ignorance, as a dangerous Jacobin demonstration. Sidmouth, anticipating the Six Acts of 1819, and reviving Pitt's principle that force was the only remedy for popular discontent in a time of war, armed the magistrates with despotic statutory powers, and added "frame-breaking" to the long list of capital offences which disgraced our criminal code, and which Romilly in vain endeavoured to modify. Sixteen unhappy "Luddite" frame-breakers were accordingly executed by special commission in 1812. Is it surprising that the Prince Regent, Castlereagh, and Sidmouth, who inspired this policy, earned for themselves that deep and widespread unpopularity which every year after 1812 only made more indelible?

[1] In 1812 the amount raised by taxation was £67,497,807; in 1813, £64,671,787; in 1814, £72,807,991; in 1815, £74,289,368. For the same years respectively the amounts of debt (funded and unfunded) raised were £64,973,000, £80,700,925, £105,300,609, £88,892,390. In the same years the military and naval expenditure was £49,952,488, £55,267,544, £70,647,786, £69,183,301. Observe the proportion of military and naval expenditure to revenue raised by taxation. From 1793-1815, £57,153,819 were paid in subsidies to foreign Powers. In 1812 the amounts were £3,748,981; in 1813, £6,785,982; in 1814, £8,442,578; in 1815, £10,101,728. In 1812 we had 145,000 troops beyond the seas, 30,000 foreigners and 30,000 Portuguese in our pay (exclusive of subsidies), and 250,000 militia at home; in 1813, 203,000 regulars, 52,000 foreign and colonial troops, 71,000 regular militia and 193,000 local militia; the numbers borne for the navy (including marines) were in addition (1812) 144,844, (1813) 147,047, (1814) 126,414, (1815) 78,891. The charge for the maintenance of the National Debt rose to £32,500,000 in 1815, representing about 45 per cent. of the revenue raised by taxation.

A month before Salamanca, Great Britain was plunged into war with the United States, the origin of which lay in the maritime military measures pursued by our Government since 1803, the Orders in Council and the necessities of the Republican party under Jefferson and Madison.   Since the rupture of the Peace of Amiens and the successful assertion of her supremacy at sea, Great Britain had vigorously exercised the right of search.   Based on the British doctrine by which British-born subjects were held to retain their nationality unless formally freed from it by their own country, the claim had been regarded as implying the right to search for and impress British deserters serving on American ships, even though under American law they had been converted from aliens into American citizens.   In 1807 the memorable *Chesapeake* affair occurred in which a British ship of war, the *Leopard*, compelled by force the American frigate of war, the *Chesapeake*, to submit to a search for deserters from another British ship, the *Halifax*, in which three other deserters from H.M.S. *Melampus*, Americans by birth, were arrested and removed.   The British Government disavowed this high-handed act and the claim to search vessels of war ; but it refused to abandon the right of search of commercial vessels or the doctrine of allegiance and nationality which was maintained by eminent jurists in this country.   The embittered feeling aroused by the *Chesapeake* affair and our naval practice were seriously aggravated by Napoleon's Continental system and our counter-system of the Orders in Council, which hit the American shippers and traders with great severity.   The United States desired to remain neutral in the tremendous European struggle, but neither Great Britain nor Napoleon was prepared to tolerate a neutrality which undermined the measures adopted.   Each desired by grinding pressure to drive the United States into an alliance, and Great Britain as the supreme sea-power was able to make its pressure consistently more effective.   Had the United States been strong enough at sea to protect its commerce and repel French and British coercion it might have extorted satisfactory terms from either or both of the belligerents ; but it had not the strength to do this, and Jefferson, the Republican President, rejecting the Federalist counter-policy of allying with Great Britain and obtaining "most favoured nation" terms, clove to neutrality and passive resistance. In 1807 a prohibition was laid on all foreign trade by the United

States; and in 1809 "the Non-intercourse Act" empowered the President to raise the embargo on France or Great Britain if either suspended its treatment of neutrals. The "Non-intercourse Act," which expired in 1810, was disastrous to American trade, and was revived against Great Britain in 1811, President Madison erroneously Feb. believing that Napoleon had cancelled his decrees against American trade. Lord Liverpool's Administration withdrew the Orders in June 23, Council applying to the United States, but it was too late. The 1812 United States had declared war on June 18th.

At a critical moment, therefore, our country was embroiled with a new adversary. And the war of 1812 was most unfortunate in every way; worst of all in the terrible legacy of resentment and injury which, following so soon after the War of Independence, poisoned the relations of the two English-speaking States for more than two generations to come. If it be granted that our claim of search was exercised in a high-handed way, that our diplomacy after 1807 was stupid, clumsy, and arrogant, and that Perceval, in particular, was mistaken in refusing all concessions on the Orders in Council, a proud nation engaged in a desperate struggle for bare existence against the Napoleonic Empire could not obliterate at dictation its legal doctrines or abandon military measures which American critics have recognised were an essential element in our strategy and tactics.[1] English feeling was embittered by American privateers utilising French harbours, by the strong sympathy with Napoleon in the Southern States, and by Madison's forcing on a war at so grave a crisis in our struggle with France. The President's acquiescence in Napoleon's treacherous seizure of American vessels and cargoes, and assertion that the decrees had been with- March, drawn, which was not true, made it doubly difficult for Great 1810 Britain to withdraw her Orders while the decrees were still operative. Madison's ultimatum was undoubtedly influenced by the determination to purchase for the forthcoming Presidential election the support of the Republicans, who hoped to conquer Canada.

The events of the war were a sharp disappointment to both belligerents, and both on the high seas and the Great Lakes furnished instructive lessons in the value and methods of sea-power. The invasion of Canada of 1812 proved a failure. Hull was sur-

[1] See particularly Mahan, *Sea-Power in Its Relation to the War of* 1812 (2 vols., 1905).

Aug. 16   rounded, and surrendered at Detroit; Wadsworth surrendered at
Niagara, and Smyth was repulsed at Chippewa. At sea, to our
bitter surprise, the American frigates, superior in gun-power and
gunnery, obtained a series of successes over British vessels whose
inferior armament was due to excessive attention to "spit and
polish" discipline, bred of a long undisputed naval mastery.[1]

Far more important in the autumn came the colossal catastrophe
of Napoleon's Russian campaign. Prussia had been forced into a
Feb. 24   humiliating alliance, and Austria nominally supported the Emperor.
March 16   The vast Grand Army crossed the Niemen, fought the terrible
June 24
Sept. 7   battle of Borodino and reached Moscow. Alexander refused to
Sept. 14   negotiate and Moscow was evacuated. Closely pursued, with an
Oct. 18
army already decimated by disease and exhaustion, Napoleon only
Nov. 26-29 saved himself from surrender by forcing the passage of the Beresina
with frightful loss, and then deserted the most appalling retreat on
Dec. 5   record, which he left to Murat to complete. The Grand Army of
June lost 100,000 prisoners, 400,000 men, and 1000 guns. The
Emperor had been ruined by his overweening ambition, and the
blunders of the campaign. The army was destroyed before the
winter frost finally extinguished it.

The next year, 1813, was the critical period alike for Napoleon
and Great Britain. Previously to the campaign of 1812 Sweden
April 5,   had allied with Russia, and Great Britain virtually acceded to the
extended   alliance, with promises of financial aid. The basis of a fourth
Aug. 28
great European coalition was thus laid. By the Convention of
Dec. 30   Tauroggen the Prussian army was coerced into neutrality; national
feeling in Prussia forced the hand of the vacillating Prussian King;
a Prusso-Russian alliance was made at Kalisch, and Prussia declared
Feb.   war. Great Britain was not formally a party to this alliance,
March 17   though she warmly supported it; and a further step towards a
complete understanding was taken by Prussia's renunciation of
claims on Hanover. There remained Austria. British diplomacy
aimed at securing her adhesion. But Austria, under Metternich,
preferred neutrality. Metternich feared Russian predominance,

Aug. 16,   [1] The chief of these were the capture of H.M.S. *Guerrière* by the U.S.A. *Con-*
1812   *stitution*, H.M.S. *Frolic* by the *Wasp*, H.M.S. *Macedonian* by the *United States*,
Oct. 18   H.M.S. *Java* by the *Constitution*; and in 1814 H.M.S. *Penguin* by the *Hornet*,
Oct. 25   remarkable because the *Penguin* "failed to hit her opponent once with her great
Dec. 29   guns".

distrusted Prussia, and was thoroughly opposed in principle and
in Austrian interests to the rising tidal wave of nationalist feeling
in Prussia, and the reconstitution of a liberated Germany on a
unitary system. British distrust of Austria, the sediment of
Anglo-Austrian relations since 1793, was also strong, and the
supreme effort made by England during 1813 was most effectively
concentrated on the Peninsula.

Wellington's campaign — breaking naturally into two well-
marked sections—had a decisive influence on the European War.
Public opinion was now enthusiastic in his favour. He had spent
the winter in reorganising the Spanish and Portuguese military and
civil administration and in preparing for a decisive advance. Soult,
with many picked troops, had been recalled to Germany, and the
supreme command fell to Jourdan and King Joseph. The French
could control some 200,000 troops, but they were scattered and
not easily concentrated. Wellington, disposing of some 90,000
men, had conceived " a grand design "—a rapid frontal advance in
force with continuous flanking and turning movements by the left
wing. Graham was secretly pushed into the mountainous province
of Tras-os-Montes, thence debouching into the plains of Leon, overlapping the French right. It was "grandly executed". From his
base at Ciudad Rodrigo, Wellington crossed the Coa, " the glories May 22
of twelve victories playing about the bayonets " of his veterans,
" rose in his stirrups and, waving his hand, cried, ' Adieu, Portugal ! ' "
Thus outmanœuvred the French evacuated Madrid and Toledo and
fell back on Burgos. Overlapped again by Graham and the left
wing, they blew up its citadel and retreated to the Ebro. Over- June 13
lapped again, they abandoned the line of the Ebro and offered battle
at Vittoria. The battle was disastrous to the French. Graham, June 21
turning the enemies' right, cut off the direct retreat to San Sebastian
and Bayonne ; our centre and right drove the French in on the
town, and the retreat by the one line left open, mountain tracks to
Salvatierra and Pampeluna, became a disorderly rout. Our loss
was some 5000, the French 6000 and 1000 prisoners, but the French
abandoned artillery, stores, plunder, and a million of money in the
military chest. The French army was a broken mob, driven across
the frontier to rally at Bayonne ; Suchet was compelled to evacuate
Valencia and confine his operations to Catalonia, north of Tarragona, which was captured and held by the allies. On July 1st

Wellington ended the first phase by laying siege to Pampeluna and San Sebastian. The memorable "forty days" from May 22nd left the French with the prospect of an English invasion across the Pyrenees.

Napoleon, by exerting all the strength of his genius, had created an army of 200,000 to withstand the coalition, but his efforts were cruelly handicapped by the rawness of the recruits, the lack of cavalry, the absence of thousands of seasoned troops locked up in the fortresses east of the Elbe, and the altered character of the Prussian soldiers. Had he been able to bring up the 200,000 men absorbed by Spain the campaign in Central Europe might have

May 2

May 21
June 4

ended very differently. After winning the victories of Lützen and Bautzen, and occupying Breslau he consented to an armistice which was to last until August 1st. The news of Vittoria greatly strengthened the allies' determination, and Napoleon was obliged to organise against his base in France being threatened by an Anglo-Spanish invasion. Great Britain was sparing nothing to complete the over-

March 3

throwal of the French Empire. She had come to terms with Sweden and Bernadotte, and promised a subsidy of one million and the an-

June 14, 15

nexation of Norway; had made treaties with Russia and Prussia (Reichenbach), with subsidies of £1,250,000 and £650,000 respectively, and promised to Austria the guarantee of a loan. With Austria lay the decisive word in these six weeks. Napoleon's failure to concede satisfactory terms brought the armistice to an end

Aug. 12

Twelve days later Austria joined the Coalition and declared war

Aug. 26

Victorious in person at Dresden, Napoleon found that his lieutenants

Aug. 23
Sept. 6
Aug. 26
Aug. 28
Oct. 16-18

were no match for the allies. Their defeats at Grossbeeren, Dennewitz, the Katzbach, Kulm, compelled the Emperor to retreat on Leipzig; and there in the awful three days' "battle of the nations," the *coup de grace*, costing 50,000 on each side, was given to the Napoleonic "Grand Empire Français". Napoleon fell back behind

Oct. 8

the Rhine. Bavaria had deserted him (Treaty of Ried); Holland expelled the French and proclaimed the Prince of Orange; Switzer-

Nov. 9

land dissolved the French constitution. Russia, Austria, and Great Britain united to offer peace on the basis of the "natural frontiers" —Rhine, Alps, and Pyrenees for France—and Napoleon would have done well to accept these terms. But the date of the ultimatum ran out, and the Prussians, with Jena in their hearts, crossed the Rhine. Unless a miracle intervened peace would be made at Paris

And the tide of invasion was swelled now by the English in the south.

Soult had been despatched to take the offensive across the Pyrenees; and though Soult's campaign justified his reputation as a commander of skill and resource, and the French fought superbly, he was matched against a greater master than himself and an army whose fighting power and divisional leading made it probably the finest instrument ever directed by a British general. Soult, who had more than 100,000 men at his disposal, aimed first at relieving Pampeluna. By a rapid concentration he flung himself on the British right, forced against Hill and Picton the passes of Ronces- July 25-26 valles and Maya, but, despite desperate fighting, was rolled back at Sauroren, having lost 10,000 casualties. Turning westwards, he next July 27-28 endeavoured to relieve San Sebastian, but was frustrated by Hill and the Spaniards at the battle of St. Marcial, and after his failure the besiegers stormed the town with terrible loss, and the castle Aug. 31 surrendered. Pampeluna was starved out. The French offensive Sept. 9 by "the battles of the Pyrenees" had thus been checked with severe Oct. 31 punishment. Before Pampeluna fell Wellington, urged by the home Government, now struck back at Soult, who had taken up a strongly fortified defensive position on the Nivelle. The Bidassoa was crossed and the French lines behind the Nivelle were penetrated Oct. 8 after heroic efforts on both sides, and Soult fell back on his third Nov. 10 line on the Nive. Once again Wellington forced the passage, and Dec. 9 after four days of fighting, in which Hope's and Hill's divisions sur- Dec. 10-13 passed themselves, repulsed every effort to dislodge the victors. Weakened by withdrawals to Napoleon's army, Soult left Bayonne to its fate and retired eastwards to threaten Wellington's flank if he advanced on Bordeaux, where the Bourbons were now proclaimed. At Orthez the French, driven from their position after a stubborn Feb. 27, engagement, fell back on Toulouse, where with heavy loss Welling- 1814 ton stormed the entrenchments, and Soult evacuated the town. It April 10 was the last pitched battle of the Peninsular War. A costly sally from Bayonne, involving 800 casualties on both sides, ended the April 14 struggle which had begun at Roliça in 1808. Toulouse was a use- less slaughter. Unknown to the commanders, Napoleon had abdi- cated on April 6. Napier's conclusion to his immortal epic is the fitting epitaph: "Those veterans had won nineteen pitched battles and innumerable combats; had made or sustained ten sieges and

taken four great fortresses; had twice expelled the French from
Portugal, once from Spain ; had penetrated France and killed,
wounded, or captured 200,000 enemies—leaving of their own number 40,000 dead, whose bones whiten the plains and mountains of
the Peninsula ".

While Soult in the South had lost all but honour, Napoleon,
with a handful of an army, had fought a striking campaign in
Champagne against the triple army of the allies. The Emperor's
March 1   efforts to detach Austria were met by the Treaty of Chaumont,
which pledged Great Britain, Russia, Prussia, and Austria to continue the war and make no separate peace until France had been
reduced to her ancient frontiers. While Napoleon was making a
fruitless dash against his adversaries' communications their armies
March 30   marched straight in and occupied Paris. The Senate deposed the
April 6   Emperor and proclaimed Louis XVIII. Napoleon abdicated, renounced by treaty the Crowns of France and Italy, and was assigned
the island of Elba, while his wife, Maria Louise, was provided with
the Duchy of Parma. The task of settling Europe now devolved
on the four Great Powers, whose coalition had been sealed by the
Treaty of Chaumont.

Great Britain was still at war with the United States. In 1813
Proctor defeated the Americans at Frenchtown, but advancing
farther was obliged to retreat. Commodore Perry on Lake Erie
Sept. 10   obliterated the British squadron, and Proctor's force retiring to-
Oct. 5   wards York was practically annihilated at Moraviantown. The
Americans secured the mastery on Lake Ontario, a British attack
on Sackett's Harbour, badly managed, being a failure. The Ameri-
can invasion, however, of Lower Canada was successfully repulsed ;
Oct. 26   the southern Army was defeated at the Chateaugay River; an
Dec. 7   Eastern division was also roughly handled at Chrystler's Farm—in
both cases the Canadian militia proved their loyalty and their fighting quality. On the open sea the memorable combat between the
British *Shannon* and the American *Chesapeake* was the most re-
June 1   markable event, in which Captain Broke vindicated British gunnery,
and in fifteen minutes compelled his opponent, of the same strength,
to surrender. British commerce suffered severely from American
privateers, but the American commercial marine was practically
swept off the seas. Nor was the next year decisive. A drawn
July 25   battle on the Niagara frontier at Lundy's Lane, ending in the

retirement of the Americans, frustrated the renewed invasion of
Canada. A counter-invasion of New York State was foiled at
Plattsburg, and Prevost in command retired into Canada. Farther
south, General Ross landing in Chesapeake Bay, defeated the local
militia at Bladensburg, and then occupied Washington, the public
buildings of which he burnt as a reprisal for similar American Aug. 24
acts at York and Newark. Re-embarking, Ross made a stroke
at Baltimore, which failed and in which he was killed. Peace
was finally made at Ghent; but before the news reached America Dec. 24
Pakenham, reinforced by seasoned troops from Wellington's army,
badly bungled an attack on New Orleans, which ended in his death, Jan. 8,
after a mad attempt to storm impregnable entrenchments. We 1815
lost 2000 men to the Americans' 300. The Treaty of Ghent deliberately omitted to deal with the questions which had caused the
war. It provided for a delimitation of frontiers and for the suppression of the slave trade. Had Madison held his hand for six
months in 1812, and the British Government shown a juster appreciation of the American case against the Orders in Council, two
and a half years of stupid warfare, mismanaged on both sides, might
have been avoided. As it was, against the continuous and costly
inroads on our commerce, and the sharp lessons taught our navy,
we could only place as counter-assets severe material damage to
American trade and the fine loyalty of the Canadians, French and
British, to whom the safety of Canada was mainly due.

Minor events elsewhere increased the difficulties of the future
territorial redistribution of Europe. Trieste had been captured Oct., 1813
by a joint Austro-British force, and the British reduction of Cattaro Jan., 1814
completed the efforts of the Montenegrins to wrest Dalmatia from
the French Empire. King Joachim of Naples (Murat) came to
terms with Metternich, which left him in possession of his kingdom,
to the disgust of the Bourbon Court at Palermo ; and to hasten
the expulsion of the French from Italy Lord William Bentinck
landed at Leghorn and seized Genoa. The capture of Java,
Mauritius, and the Ile de Bourbon had swept the last of the French
colonial possessions into British occupation. The allies were thus
in a position to deal with a France and a Europe of which, if they
remained united, they were absolutely masters. But there can be
no greater mistake than to assume that the map of Europe in 1814
was or could be regarded as a clean sheet on which an Areopagus of

four great nations could draw lines and demarcate divisions at their
arbitrary pleasure or on principles irrespective of facts.   From the
first the diplomatists' hands were tied by engagements made with the
minor States in the course of the struggle of 1813 and 1814, *e.g.*
that concluded by Austria with Bavaria, which guaranteed the
independence of the South German Kingdom ; with Joachim of
Naples, to which Great Britain was not a party; the conventions

Jan. 14,
1814

with Sweden (Kiel), which assured the annexation of Norway from
Denmark ; and that with Denmark, by which Great Britain undertook to restore British conquests, save Heligoland.   Still more
important were the pledges which had brought Prussia, Austria,
and Russia into the coalition—a general undertaking that these
kingdoms respectively were by the future settlement to be restored
to a status equal in geographical area and population to that en-

1807

joyed previously to Tilsit.   The exact form of the " compensation "
that this would assume was not predetermined, and its definition
was bound to involve a conflict of views, arising from a conflict
of incompatible interests.   The compensation of Prussia touched
Austria as deeply as Prussia itself.   The delimitation of Russia's
western frontier (involving the settlement of Poland) raised an
inexhaustible crop of unsolved, perhaps insoluble, problems.

Moreover, Europe was not a *tabula rasa.*   The Bourbons alike
at Paris, Madrid, Palermo, and the Pontiff at Rome, might show
that they had learned or forgotten nothing, and might cling to the
grotesque assumption that in 1814 Europe, exorcised at last from
the incomprehensible insanity which had smitten it on May 4th,
1789, was now able to re-enter on its dynastic inheritance, swept and
garnished for the restoration of the ancient order; but the moving
finger of the Revolutionary and Napoleonic Time-spirit had written,
and having written still moved on ; and the Congress of Vienna
proved that "not all your piety and wit could lure it back to cancel
half a line, nor all your tears wash out a word of it."   The master
diplomatists were only too obsessed with the fear that " Jacobinism,"
in its widest sense, was not dead in 1814 ; and throughout their
work runs a consistent purpose.   The settlement must above all
provide against to-morrow and for peace.   It should foster the anti-
septic and the prophylactic elements that within the political organism of a corporate Europe would automatically expel or sterilise
the germs of the disease from which that organism had for the

moment been saved. To the revolutionary principle must be opposed a counter-principle. And the Congress found its salvation
not in nationalism, as Vom Stein desired, but in the ex-revolutionist
Talleyrand's gospel of legitimism, translated into the language of
compromise by Metternich.

Nor can the personal characteristics of the leading figures be
ignored. Talleyrand showed that against genius, when diabolically
unscrupulous, brute force fights a losing battle. Two others stand
out prominent—the Tsar Alexander I. and Metternich—and the
Congress of Vienna was the battle-ground of the ill-concealed duel
between these two which began in 1813 and ended in 1819, when
Alexander surrendered to the Austrian's policy of the Carlsbad
Decrees. Their strength and their weakness lay in the plethora of
ideas in the one and the absence of ideas in the other. Alexander
was in love with his ideas as a libertine is in love with his mistresses
—chronic infidelity broken by paroxysms of a sincere but fleeting
devotion. Metternich was the unconscious victim of the pathetic
diplomatic fallacy that tact and a knowledge of the world could
be an efficient substitute for convictions and ideals. It was unfortunate both for Europe and Great Britain that the supple
Hardenberg, and not the stern but imaginative Vom Stein, inspired
and represented the policy of Prussia; that Castlereagh, our leading political statesman, was denied by temperament, principles, and
environment the clear and steady vision and judgment of the liberal
ideas whose secret force had stiffened our national resistance and
swept the allies from the Niemen and the Mondego to Paris; that
Wellington, whose personal prestige was second to none in Europe,
only lacked (but that lack was damning) love of his fellow-men to
be as great a statesman as he was a general; and that Canning,
on whom alone the mantle of his master, Pitt, had fallen, was
condemned to the cruellest fate of ambitious ability, the cross-
benches.

In British policy certain fixed ideas are conspicuous. Castlereagh and the Cabinet were acutely sensible of their responsibility
to Parliament; they were aware that public opinion in Great
Britain was a real force; and that, however much this or that line
of action was intrinsically reasonable, they could only be a party to
acts which could be explained to, defended in, and were likely to be
approved by, the House of Commons. The continuous insistence

on the suppression and abolition of the slave trade is a memorable instance of this indirect pressure.   And there is some truth in the aphorism that the slave trade was the one thing about which the moral conscience of the nation as a whole was in grim earnest.   The Cabinet, too, was, with the consent of the nation, quite ready to retain only the barest minimum of our conquests compatible with the security of the empire.   Napoleon's criticism that our spontaneous cessions revealed our failure to utilise the gifts of fate and of sea-power and make ourselves masters of the world, was one more proof of how little he understood the British nation.   Great Britain in 1814 desired not supremacy but peace and stability.   The restoration of the conquests of war, if it was generosity, was generosity inspired by conscience and principles.   And Englishmen have some right to-day to be proud of the pride that inspired it.

Two other principles are apparent—our policy towards France and the Netherlands.   In siding with the Tsar in 1814, as against Metternich, when France was reduced to the limits of 1792, we stood for the principles that underlay the policy of Pitt from 1792 to 1801, inherited from the principles of 1689.   A France " of the natural frontiers" was a menace to the balance of power and the independence of the central European States.   Correlatively, also, British statesmen (Wellington in particular) insisted that the Bourbons must be restored to a historic, not a mutilated, France ; and resisted the Prussian demand for the annexation of Alsace and Lorraine.   The German nationalism that voiced the demand for this annexation was countered by the concession to the French nationalism that opposed it.   Eight centuries, and an unbroken tradition of our foreign policy, gave renewed strength to the Cabinet's insistence on an effective barrier to French extension across the land frontier from Calais to Luxemburg.   Belgium (the former Austrian Netherlands), not strong enough in itself, must be artificially stiffened, and the requisite " buffer State " was created by uniting Holland and Belgium into a single kingdom under the friendly and allied House of Orange—the realisation of an idea never out of the minds of our Foreign Office since 1689 and 1713. No principle indeed of British policy was more tenacious in its grip on Whig and Tory alike than that the littoral opposite our shores from the Helder to Ushant must not be in the occupation of a single, and possibly hostile, Power.   The sea frontier, broken at

Calais, must be coloured differently to the east from its colouring to the west of that arbitrary point.

The Treaty of Paris, 1814, defined for the restored constitutional May 30 monarchy of Louis XVIII. the limits of France as those of 1792, together with a slight but advantageous rectification of frontier on the East and the absorption of Western Savoy (an addition of 150 square miles in all and 450,000 inhabitants) ; the French colonies, with the exception of Mauritius, St. Lucia, and Tobago, were given back. A European Congress was arranged to meet in September at Vienna; and the Four Great Powers—Great Britain, Russia, Austria, and Prussia—agreed (as arranged at Chaumont) by secret articles to reserve the control of the settlement in their exclusive but joint control. Prior to the Congress the King of Prussia and the Tsar visited England on the invitation of the Prince Regent, and were received with lavish hospitality and unbounded enthusiasm. The Congress at Vienna in every sense marked an epoch, not least in the new system of European deliberation that it inaugurated and the explicit claim of the great Powers to a right of protection over the collective interests and peace of Europe. Castlereagh was the chief British representative until February, when he was re-placed by Wellington, created a duke. The first serious step was May, 1814 taken when Talleyrand, representing France, broke down the assumption that an alliance against France existed, and triumphantly forced the Four Great Powers to recognise the participation of the French State in the Concert of Europe.

The Saxon and Polish questions very soon brought the fundamental differences of the leading States to a critical issue. The Prussian proposal (whose real author was Vom Stein) to annex the whole of Saxony (which involved the disinheritance of its King, Napoleon's one faithful ally) was supported by the Tsar, and at first by Castlereagh. The British minister apparently hoped that, despite the rejection of the principle of " legitimism," Prussia would then unite with Austria to resist Russian demands for a kingdom of Poland, revived under the supremacy of the Tsar (which earlier in the autumn he had been disposed to favour). Castlereagh's suspicion of Alexander's objects, his fear of Russian power, and his aversion from the deep taint of " Jacobinism " in the Tsar's present liberal and nationalist phase, were almost as acute as Metternich's rooted distrust of Prussia and fear of a Russian hegemony. Alex-

30

ander distrusted and disliked Metternich ; he was devoted to the King of Prussia. His support of the Prussian proposal was repaid by Prussian support of the Russian scheme of a constitutional monarchy for a Poland created by extending the Napoleonic Duchy of War-saw to the limits of the Poland dismembered in 1795. Castlereagh's arctic reserve and brittle resolution fitted him singularly ill for the part of honest or dishonest broker. His mediation was a failure ; and, angered at Prussian and Russian obstinacy, while Talleyrand acted as Mephistopheles, he lost his head, joined Metternich, and agreed to the Triple Defensive Alliance of January 3rd, 1815. This amazing document pledged Great Britain and Austria and France to place 150,000 men apiece in the field, in the event of attack on account of proposals to which they had jointly agreed for carrying out "the principles of the Peace of Paris". War, in fact, was contemplated, in which it was certain that the prisoner at Elba would be let loose by the allies or their opponents, even if that prisoner, well informed of the proceedings at Vienna, had not (which is more probable) promptly joined in on his own accord.[1] The treaty was kept a profound secret, but Napoleon anticipated the modern researcher, and communicated the French copy during the Hundred Days to Alexander, hoping, but failing, thereby to divide his enemies. Fortunately so terrible a catastrophe as a vast European war, wantonly provoked by the Powers assembled to make peace, was averted by Metternich's passion for compromise ; and when Castlereagh left for England the lines of a settlement were
Feb. 8   already laid down.   More decisive still was the news that Napoleon
Feb. 25   had left Elba and landed not in Italy, where his brother-in-law,
March 8   Joachim Murat, was ready to strike on his behalf, but at Cannes.
"*Le Congrès est dissous,*" Napoleon remarked truly enough. Ney set out to bring him in an iron cage back to Paris, but joined him
March 14   instead. To France the spell of his genius was irresistible. The
Bourbon monarchy rocked on its paper foundation of the Charter and toppled over. Louis XVIII. fled on March 19th, and that night Napoleon slept at the Tuileries.
March 13   Six days earlier a declaration, signed by the representatives of

[1] On Napoleon's relations at Elba with the Powers, see: Comm. Weil, *Le Revirement de la Politique Autrichienne,* Turin, 1908 ; G. Galavresi, *La Rivolu-zione Lombarda e la Politica Inglese* (Archivio Storico, 1909) ; *Quarterly Review.* January, 1910.

eight Powers, pronounced him an outlaw, "the enemy and disturber of the peace of the world". Austria, Prussia, Russia, and Great Britain pledged themselves to place 150,000 men each in the field; Napoleon's overtures to Austria and Great Britain were rejected; and the House of Commons defeated Whitbread's protest against war by 273-72 votes, and voted subsidies of more than 5,000,000 April 2l to the allies by 160-17. By that day Napoleon had lost his one May 26 ally. Joachim I. appealed precipitately to Italian nationalism, proclaimed a national war against Austria, and marched to the Po. At Tolentino the worthless Neapolitan army was routed, the King May 3 fled from Naples, occupied by an Anglo-Austrian force, to Toulon; May 9 where, a king without a crown, a general without an army, he found his brother-in-law furious at his folly in ruining the campaign that was now inevitable against the allies.

Wellington had been at once ordered to Brussels, where the British Government was feverishly endeavouring to create an army for him. Unhappily the American War had drawn the bulk of the Peninsular battalions across the Atlantic. A motley force was patched up of British corps (with many raw recruits), the German Legion (of Peninsular fame), Hanoverian, Brunswick, and Nassau contingents, and Dutch-Belgians, and was extended on the line from Mons to Ghent. To the east the Prussians, more than 120,000 strong, under Blücher, tolerably homogeneous and more seasoned troops, with Liége as their base, were stretched out on the line from Liége to Charleroi. Napoleon by superb energy had collected a fine force of 125,000 men, most of whom were tried veterans, on the line Valenciennes to Thionville. Soult replaced Berthier as chief of the staff, and Ney commanded the left wing. But the Emperor was without the other famous marshals, and events proved that he would have done better to have given Soult the command on the left. Napoleon had decided to strike at once at the allies, penetrate between them before they could concentrate, and crush them separately. Two victories over Blücher and Wellington would recover Belgium, consolidate his rule in France, be a shattering blow at the solidarity of the coalition, and give him time to complete his organisation and deal with the Austrians and Russians in the late summer and autumn.

The opening moves in their rapidity and strategic conception were worthy of Napoleon at his best. He left Paris, June 12th;

the army had been swiftly and secretly concentrated ; on the 15th it was over the frontier, drove back Ziethen's corps in confusion and seized Charleroi. His left was in touch with the British outposts at Quatre Bras. Wellington as well as Blücher had been surprised at the swiftness of the stroke ; and the duke, badly served by his scouts and staff, and doubtful whether Napoleon would advance by the Mons or the Charleroi roads, had only 4000 men at Quatre Bras, while the rest of his force was deliberately extended for subsequent concentration on either line. Not till the night of the 15th did the concentration begin—the night of the Duchess of Richmond's ball, which Wellington attended. Blücher, hurrying westwards, had brought up 90,000 men to Ligny and St. Amand, and Napoleon turned on him the next day. Wellington visited Blücher and promised help if he were not himself attacked. And Blücher needed such help, for at Ligny he got the "damnable mauling" which Wellington had foretold when he saw his exposed position. The French lost more than 10,000 men, but the Prussians lost 20,000, and might have been wiped out but for Ney's mistakes and the stubborn resistance at Quatre Bras. Ney, whose instructions were to brush away the enemy on his front and then turn and roll up the Prussian right, deferred his attack until 2 P.M. This enabled Wellington to bring up division after division, pressed as they hurried up into the firing line. It was a pell-mell business of hard fighting, in which each side lost more than 4000 men and divided the honours. But by nightfall Wellington had a marked superiority in numbers on the field. Had Ney attacked at 10 A.M. the superiority in numbers would have been decisively his. Worse than this, D'Erlon's corps, Ney's reserve, had been ordered by Napoleon to fall on and crush the Prussian right ; it was recalled by Ney when he found himself outnumbered, to aid him at Quatre Bras, with the result that it marched first east and then west, and took no part in either battle. Had D'Erlon disregarded Ney's counter-command, and flung himself on Blücher's right at the critical phase of the action, the Prussians might have been so overwhelmed as to be incapable of rallying. As it was, with iron determination and unmolested in their retreat they fell back, not on Liége, but northwards to Wavre, in order to keep in touch with Wellington. Napoleon, however, had won a victory, and prevented the British commander from giving any aid to his allies at Ligny. At the same time had Wellington concentrated twelve hours earlier he could have crushed Ney at Quatre Bras.

Napoleon then threw away precious hours. Grouchy was detached with 33,000 men to follow the Prussians, whom his master vainly imagined to be retreating on Liége, but detached so late that the cavalry failed to get into touch or (far more important) discover the real line of Blücher's march. On the night of the 17th Grouchy was at Gembloux, while the Prussians were at Wavre. Wellington fell back early from Quatre Bras, but Napoleon did not follow him until 2 P.M., when the advance was pressed, but delayed by heavy rain. By nightfall Wellington stood at bay across the two high roads from Nivelles and Charleroi to Brussels. Napoleon confronted him on the ridge opposite Mont St. Jean. The duke had decided to fight the battle that Napoleon desired ; he had been assured by Blücher, despite the objections of Gneisenau, his chief of the staff (who distrusted Wellington most unjustifiably), that he would march on the 18th against Napoleon's flank, and Blücher, old Marshal *Vorwärts*, meant business. Wellington had some 67,000 men, of which 24,000 were British and 14,000 Dutch-Belgians (the weakest section of his composite force) ; in addition a day's march away at Hal, to the west, was a detachment of 14,000 men, and it is difficult for a layman to understand why the duke left them there—possibly he did not wish to have any more Netherlanders in line, for this force was mainly formed of troops of that nationality. Napoleon, and Wellington knew it, had made no sign of attempting to turn the British right flank. Napoleon, at La Belle Alliance, had about 74,000 men. Confident that Blücher was either falling back on his base, or would be intercepted by Grouchy, he delayed the attack till noon of Sunday, June 18th. It was to be a direct frontal onslaught, the column against the line—the crumpling up of the two-deep formation by sledge-hammer impact. Soult and Reillé, who had fought against the line as used by Wellington in the Peninsular War, and against British and Hanoverian infantry, which Napoleon had not, had serious doubts of these tactics. And they were right.

The battle had four distinct phases. D'Erlon's assault in massed columns was preceded by a failure against Hougomont (on the British right) and by the unwelcome appearance of Prussians six miles to the east. The infantry assault ended in a bloody re-

pulse, consummated by a charge of the brigade of heavy cavalry.
Phase two was under Ney's supervision—great cavalry charges,
avalanche upon avalanche of horse, met by the British forming
square. It was deathly work on both sides, but the mauled squares
stood firm, though it needed all Wellington's wonderful nerve and
all his infantry reserve to hold his position. Blücher, thanks to
Gneisenau's doubts and bad staff work, was not in touch with the
French until the cavalry charges began ; Napoleon detached Lobau
with 10,000 men to contain them at Planchenoit. Lobau fought
heroically, and, reinforced by the Young Guard at 6 P.M., held his
own. Phase three was signalised by Ney's final effort (about 6 P.M.)
to break the British line with infantry, and D'Erlon's corps at last
carried La Haye Sainte (about 6.30 P.M.). This was the critical
moment. Had Napoleon flung his last reserve, the Old Guard,
there and then into the gap, before Wellington could pull the shattered battalions together and rearrange his line, the effort might
have succeeded. But Napoleon waited until Planchenoit was again
cleared against Blücher's third onslaught ; and Wellington's nerve
did not fail him nor his men either. The gap was closed by a
supreme effort, and when, after 7 P.M.—the last phase—Napoleon
launched the Old Guard in columns, en échelon, the line, under
Wellington's direction, asserted its fire-discipline and blasted the
attack. The British cavalry reserve was hurled on the recoiling
battalions, and the French centre shivered and dissolved. Simultaneously the Prussians, reinforced by their last corps, had broken
down the French flank. Wellington's decimated and exhausted army
advanced to the crest of the French position ; and when the duke
met Blücher at La Belle Alliance, Napoleon had left the field and
the French force was a disorganised mass of fugitives. For the
Emperor it was not defeat, but ruin, completed by the relentless
pursuit of the Prussian cavalry. The French lost 30,000 in killed
and wounded, some thousands of prisoners, and all their artillery.
The remainder, in disunited bands, crossed the Sambre and the
frontier next day. The Prussians owned to 6000 casualties, 1000
less than the purely British loss ; Wellington's army in all had
more than 13,000 killed and wounded. Differ as the experts may
on the many disputable points in the campaign from June 13th to
18th, it seems clear that Grouchy was not responsible for Napoleon's
disaster. He carried out his chief's orders; and because, like

Napoleon, he failed to perceive Blücher's flank march, or because on
the 17th he was detached too late to discover the Prussian line of
retreat after Ligny and was so placed that it was physically impossible either to intercept Blücher or rejoin Napoleon in time to fight
at Waterloo, it is unjust to make him the scapegoat. What might
have happened had Napoleon never detached Grouchy at all, or
ordered him at the first to march on Wavre and secure his right
flank, neither expert nor amateur can decide now. But on the
facts as history presents them what most impresses the layman is
probably, first, the astonishing nerve of Wellington, and, secondly,
the heroic resistance of his infantry, German as well as British. It
was their commander's nerve that drew the last ounce from his men.
Tactically, Wellington fought a superb battle. But it was not
tactics that won or lost the day. The moral gift of the great commander was Wellington's ; never was it more needed, never was it
more conspicuous than in the awful hours from 4 to 7 P.M. And it
is this quality, too, that rightly made Blücher the co-hero of Waterloo. He kept his word ; he made his march to the flank of a genius
who had soundly beaten him thirty-six hours before ; the Prussians
did not win Waterloo, but they co-operated to make it an irretrievable catastrophe for their foes.

Napoleon made a second abdication ; Waterloo had ruined the June 22
brief Empire of the Hundred Days. Louis XVIII. crossed the
frontier from Ghent, proclaimed the restoration of the Bourbon June 25
Monarchy and the re-enactment of the Charter. The Anglo-
Prussian armies under Wellington and Blücher met with some
resistance, but Paris capitulated on terms which explicitly recognised the replacement of the Bourbon Monarchy. On July 7th July 3
the allies made their second triumphant entrance into the capital.
Napoleon, who had fled to Rochefort, found that British cruisers
made escape to America impossible. The Prussian cavalry on his
track were prepared to seize him, and the Emperor surrendered to
Captain Maitland of the *Bellerophon*. He claimed the protection
of the Prince Regent, but he was clearly warned that he surrendered at discretion. The British Government, pursuant to the
declaration of March 13th, treated him as a prisoner of war ; and
on August 8th he was sent to St. Helena, to be kept under the
custody of Great Britain. And at St. Helena the last phase of the
most astonishing career and the most richly gifted personality in

modern history ended in 1821, after six years of captivity spent in petty quarrels with the tactless governor Sir Hudson Lowe, and in the compiling of much garbled military history.

The Second Treaty of Paris redefined the status and conditions of the restored Bourbons, and the relations of France to the Allied Powers. The Prussian demand for the chastisement of France by the cession of Alsace and Lorraine, at first supported by the Liverpool Ministry, was wisely negatived, thanks to the pressure of the Tsar and Wellington, supported by Castlereagh ; and when Metternich changed his mind, Prussia was obliged to bow to the decision of Russia, Austria, and Great Britain. But the allies insisted that : (1) the rectification of frontier previously granted should be withdrawn ; (2) an indemnity of £40,000,000 should be paid, and the occupation of the northern fortresses maintained until this was done ; (3) the treasures of art taken by Napoleon to Paris from the Europe he had conquered should be restored to their former public owners. And the allies solemnly renewed the engagements made in previous treaties to regard a disturbance of the *status quo* in France as a case for concerted action, and to continue the European Concert by congresses. The way was thus paved for the epoch of "the Holy Alliance," and of counter-revolutionary reaction.

The final settlement of Europe was consummated at the resumed Congress of Vienna, where indeed the diplomatists had not ceased their labours during the Waterloo Campaign. It must suffice to summarise the main features of complex arrangements embodied in a sheaf of treaties which belong to European rather than British history. Belgium and Holland were united under the House of Orange into a single kingdom, to which the old bishopric of Liége was added, together with the Dutch colonies restored by Great Britain. Norway was annexed to Sweden, which definitely abandoned its claims to Finland and Vor-Pommern (Swedish Pomerania). This latter, assigned by the Treaty of Kiel to Denmark, was reassigned to Prussia for a money payment. And Denmark was obliged to remain content with another money compensation for the loss of Norway, and with part of the petty Duchy of Lauenburg. Prussia received her Polish acquisitions of 1772, together with Thorn and portions of the Department of Posen, her former possessions on the Elbe and Weser, and a solid block of territory in the Middle Rhine, which made her the guardian of that river from Wesel to Mainz; Austria took her main compensation in Italy, where she acquired Lombardy and Venetia, and in Central Europe recovered Galicia, Illyria, Dalmatia, the Quarter of the Inn, Tyrol and Vorarlberg—in all, an increase of nearly 5,000,000 inhabitants on the Habsburg dominions of 1792. To Russia went Finland, and the bulk of the Napoleonic Duchy of Warsaw, constituted as a constitutional kingdom perpetually annexed to Russia. Italy was parcelled out in a series of principalities which broadly resembled the political mosaic of 1792. Ferdinand IV. recovered the Two Sicilies (Murat had made an effort to return, but was captured and shot); the Papal States recovered their former Oct. limits as far as the mouth of the Po; Parma, Piacenza, and Guastalla were assigned to the ex-Empress Marie Louise; Tuscany to the Grand Duke Ferdinand (a Habsburg); Modena to the House of Habsburg-Este, heirs to the last Italian duke; Lucca to Marie Louise (the Bourbon "ex-Queen of Etruria"); the Republic of Genoa was suppressed and thrown, together with Nice and Savoy, into the Kingdom of Sardinia. The House of Braganza returned to rule in Portugal (with which Brazil was incorporated), and Spain fell back under the clerical and reactionary rule of its worthless, treacherous, vindictive, and "national" sovereign, Ferdinand VII. The Swiss Constitution was remodelled on the basis of a loosely jointed Federal State of twenty-two cantons; more important was the joint recognition by the Four Allied Powers of the perpetual neutrality of the Helvetic Confederation, and the inviolability of its territory.

The harmonisation of the claims of the German States and the establishment of a system of government raised more difficult questions than any other problem. The State in which Great Britain was most directly interested, Hanover, received a considerable accession of territory, notably East Frisia, which excluded Prussia from a direct frontier on the German Ocean. The Federal Act of the Congress created a Germanic Confederation of thirty-nine States in which the sovereign powers of the component members were very imperfectly readjusted to the machinery of the Federal Diet presided over by Austria. The dream of the German Nationalists of a single German State—based on Gneisenau's memorable conception, "the triple supremacy of German science, a German army, and

a (representative) Constitution "—was completely shattered; and
Germany, like Italy after 1815, a "geographical expression," had
to wait for the recreation of the Second Napoleonic Empire, on
whose destruction by German arms and German science was erected
the unified Germany of 1871. The first German Emperor was a boy
of ten when the first Napoleon entered Berlin in 1807, he could
remember Tilsit and actually served in the War of Liberation.
Moltke, the military hero of 1870, was a lad of fifteen when
Waterloo was fought.

Great Britain retained of her conquests Heligoland, Malta, the
Cape of Good Hope, Mauritius, Ceylon, Demerara, Essequibo,
Beatrice, Trinidad, St. Lucia, and Tobago. The rest were, as
already noted, spontaneously restored to their former owners. She
was also assigned the Protectorate of the seven Ionian Isles. But
these permanent acquisitions, moderate as they were, were due more
to military or naval considerations than to desire for an imperial
colonial empire. And despite the efforts of Castlereagh, pressed by
Wilberforce and the party of "The Saints," Great Britain was
unable to procure the immediate abolition of the Slave Trade. She
had to remain content with the Declaration of February 8th, 1815,
signed by eight Powers, pledging the signatories to its extirpation,
which, however, left the date and the means to the choice of the
country concerned. But unquestionably the decree of abolition for
July 30 France, enacted by Napoleon on his return from Elba, and its
adoption by Louis XVIII., was a great step forward, while the
printing of the Declaration in an annexe to the Final Act of the
Congress of Vienna gave to it a quasi-international sanction. One
other matter—the opening of the River Scheldt—in which Great
Britain was principally interested, and which had a historical connection with the great war, was provided for, and a similar code
was laid down for the principal waterway of Western Europe,
the Rhine.

In the broad features and principles of this settlement, unprecedented alike in its scale and complexity, British diplomacy had its
full share, and cannot be acquitted of responsibility. The points
most vulnerable to criticism—the rejection of the principle of nationality, the absence of any consistent policy (for the doctrine of
legitimism was very partially applied), the adoption of the Napoleonic system of compensation, the artificiality of many of the arrange-

ments—were either initiated by or concurred in by Castlereagh and his colleagues. The failure to make good the iniquitous Partitions of Poland of 1793 and 1795; the forced union of Norway and Sweden, of Belgium and Holland; the restoration of the demoralised Bourbons in South Italy and of Ferdinand to Spain under conditions which later left England only able to register ineffective protests; the riveting of a denationalised and denationalising Austria on an Italy quickened to a new life, betrayed in our diplomatic leaders not a lack of ability but impoverished imagination, limited vision, and a deplorable ignorance or distrust of the moral and spiritual springs of action in national life. Not the absence of convictions or principles, but their sterilising character and the consequent rejection of principles of illimitable spiritual and intellectual potency, and with a richer future of development, are written indelibly on British action in 1814 and 1815. The true meaning of what Castlereagh and his colleagues did and meant to do cannot be fully grasped by a study of the Congress; it has to be interpreted by their conception of British duty and of British interests at home and abroad in the next eight years. Foreign policy, like charity, begins at home; unlike charity, it also ends at home. A Chatham or a Canning in our foreign relations started from, and returned to, the axiomatic principle that Great Britain stood irrevocably for free self-government; and that for her to concur in any departure from that principle, or assent to any arrangement which avowedly blocked its gradual realisation, was treason to the interests of Europe and treason to the historic mission of Great Britain itself, for which both Europe and Great Britain would assuredly pay the penalty. Castlereagh and his colleagues failed in 1814 and subsequently to grasp the vital difference between thrusting British principles on foreign States and a refusal to approve settlements which locked, barred, and bolted the national aspirations for assimilating British principles in the Europe that had liberated itself from the denationalising and military empire of Napoleon. They did worse. They made "the Holy Alliance" inevitable; and the reaction of that reactionary epoch is written in the internal history of our country. What an emancipated Toryism could have accomplished alike at home and abroad was shown by Canning and Peel after 1822. And a British statesman in 1814, whose spirit had really been finely touched to the fine issues of the colossal struggle from 1802 onwards, whose imagination had been truly fired by the living coal from the altars of God and freedom, might conceivably have failed to make as neat and finished a settlement as the historic one, but would have stamped the contribution of Great Britain with an irresistible power. The Congress of Vienna closed an epoch. The opening of the new epoch came not from the men who made it, but from those who deliberately undid their work. That is the fate of statesmen who have never risen to the *credo quia impossibile* of a Bismarck or a Cavour. The Present, if it will have the Future accomplish, shall itself commence. But the Toryism of Castlereagh and Eldon was cursed by the superstition of the *status quo ;* it did not hope for but feared a future different from the present. And by denying reform it defeated its most cherished aim. It testified to the efficacy of Revolution in the past ; it proclaimed the necessity of Revolution in the future.

It is no less regrettable that the British Cabinet neglected to grapple with the Eastern Question, with the relations of Spanish and Portuguese South America to Spain and Portugal—both problems of vital importance to the British State. The root of the Turkish question lay in the refusal of the Sublime Porte to reform its administration, or to remedy the admitted grievances of its subject populations (the Greeks, in particular). Greece, the Danubian Principalities, Egypt, were not new phenomena in the diplomatic world. But an assertion of the right of the European Concert to coerce the Sultan into a wholesome respect for treaty obligations, and a precise definition of the attitude of Great Britain, might have saved much avoidable trouble in the future. Castlereagh, no less than Canning, was aware that the old *régime*, restored at Lisbon and Madrid, could not be restored in South America ; as early as 1807[1] there are clear indications that Great Britain would not tolerate the extension of the Continental System across the Atlantic, or the perpetuation of dynastic tyranny and commercial selfishness. Nothing but the Peninsular War and the national rising against Napoleon probably prevented in 1807-9 the recognition of the independence of Spanish and Portuguese America —an anticipation of the famous calling into existence of the New World to redress the balance so grievously upset in the Old. But

[1] See Bagot, *Canning and His Friends*, ii., 126, 172-204, 229, 237-241.

in 1815 nothing was done save to permit an impossible *status quo* to be restored, which British diplomacy from 1815-24 was primarily occupied in sweeping away. And in 1814 Great Britain had both the coercive power and the moral mandate to enforce her principles in the Councils of "The Pentarchy". The Secret Treaty—the Triple Defensive Alliance of January 3rd, 1815—showed that she was ready to fight to prevent Saxony from being absorbed into a nationalist Prussia, or Poland being reconstituted as a national kingdom ; she was the paymaster of Europe, whose subsidies and credit were indispensable ; she was the undisputed mistress of the seas ; and the free and aristocratic Government of Great Britain alone of all the European Powers since 1802 had peremptorily re-fused, dire as had been her need and cruel as had been her suffering, to bow the knee to Napoleon, to purchase peace, territories, or rule by surrendering her independence or her moral right to represent national freedom in and for itself. It is the barest justice to the aristocracy that ruled our land to point out that they were incapable of the Treaty of Tilsit or of sealing the Napoleonic Empire by the gift of a British Marie Louise. And they did not palter with the birthright of the nation they governed. Nothing is more impressive in 1815 than the acceptance by Europe of our maritime supremacy, which we had acquired, indeed, at a great price; but no less im-pressive is the homage of Europe to the value of our system of government. The freedom of Great Britain from the revolutions that had convulsed Europe, the stability of our institutions, the relentless continuity of our policy, and the moral strength that representative institutions gave to the Executive of the Crown, sank deep into the minds of foreign thinkers and statesmen confronted with the problem, why had Great Britain succeeded where other States, greater in area and numbers and the apparent power of the Executive to command the finances and lives of their subjects, had collapsed ? And foreign historians looking back to-day to the epoch that dates from 1814 have emphasised its characteristic as the age in which the constitutional ideals and practice of Great Britain most pro-foundly influenced the intellectual and political life of Europe. Certainly in 1814 Great Britain had no reason to regret the Revolution of 1688. The test of a long and varied experience had placed her flexible system of a Constitutional Monarchy, rul-ing through Ministers responsible to a representative Parliament,

amongst the accomplished contributions to the science of government and the progress of the world.

The struggle with France that began in 1689 and closed in
1815 ended in a marked extension of the empire.   Yet in its last
Napoleonic phase it was not primarily nor deliberately a struggle
for imperial extension, for colonial expansion, for imperial consolidation.   This partly explains why our statesmen so readily restored
the colonial conquests made since 1802—even such rich and tempting
possessions as the Dutch East Indies.   The retentions were made on
military or naval grounds ; for security, not as the nuclei of a desired
and foreseen colonial development.   Hence the criticism of two
generations later that we threw away conquests invaluable to the
colonial future of Great Britain.   But the statesmen of 1815 were
imbued with what they conceived to be the true moral of 1783.
Naval bases—the Cape, Malta, Mauritius—were essential to the
protection of a world-wide commerce and the policing of the seas
and the trade routes ; an island like Ceylon was necessary for the
protection of the British possessions in India ; others such as Trinidad or Tobago could not be permitted to pass into hands that
would use them as nurseries of privateers in a future war ; Heligoland was a guardship to Hanover.   But naval bases were one thing ;
colonies, like the Parliaments of Charles I., became cursed with age.
They were costly in infancy, troublesome in youth, and they rebelled in manhood.   The need of a Britain beyond the seas to
which superfluous population could emigrate was not felt, for the
home country could under her industrial expansion absorb the
multiplying proletariat with profit and comfort.   New markets
would be provided in Europe, in South America, in the United
States, in inhabited and developed States, not in puny settlements
wrestling for existence with Nature and natives, absorbing capital
and paying no dividend on the investment.   And a generation
staggering under a gigantic debt, crippled by taxation and military
armaments, exhausted by twenty years of war, justifiably regarded
disarmament and reduction as the crying need of the day.   Colonies
were an expensive luxury.   Nations on the verge of bankruptcy
must reduce their expenditure or perish.   The portentous gravity
of the financial situation in 1815 cannot be exaggerated.   And, as is
always the case with a long war and a supreme effort, the full effects
of the strain since 1802 asserted themselves for more than a decade.

Hence Australia was not regarded as the gift of Providence and British explorers to compensate for the loss of the United States. Pitt's Government in 1788 viewed it as a convenient outlet, now that America was lost, for transportation, copiously fed by the comprehensive criminal code of the day. New South Wales started as a colony for convicts, though Captain and Governor Phillip was convinced "it would prove the most valuable acquisition Great Britain ever made," and repudiated the idea (not held by a sceptical Government) that "convicts could lay the foundation of an empire". As usual the colony owed more to the independent Englishman than to the men in office. The energy and faith of the individual Briton were as conspicuous and fruitful as the collective scepticism and apathy of "Downing Street". By 1815 little more than the bases were laid of the future Commonwealth of Australia. Phillip selected Port Jackson and started Sydney; MacArthur brought sheep from the Cape and began the breeding of pure merino; the Blue Mountains were crossed and Bathurst opened up; Macquarrie's governorship practically created New South Wales; Bass in 1798 discovered that Van Diemen's Land 1813 was an island; Collins started the settlement at Hobart; Port 1809-21 Phillip was discovered in 1802, and Flinders surveyed the southern coast.

The burden of Empire was nowhere more acutely appreciated than at Calcutta and the East India House. After Wellesley left India the duty imposed on the administration was to defend what we had won, not to add to responsibilities already onerous enough. Minto's Governor-Generalship was a period of consolidation and 1807-13 administrative reform; the annexation of Amboyna, the Moluccas, and Java were, like the seizure of the Mauritius, acts of war imposed by European not Indian policy, and their restoration was decided at London, not Calcutta. Moira (the Marquess of Hastings), who succeeded Minto, however, found that the British power could not stand on the *status quo;* and the war with the Ghurkas of Nepal, 1814-16 the reduction of the Pindari freebooters, and the final dissolution of the Mahratta confederacy at Poona (which fell after 1815), reluctantly undertaken, were the necessary completion of Wellesley's work. Sir Thomas Munro's series of administrative and financial reforms in the Madras Presidency furnishes another aspect of the obligations, faithfully interpreted, of empire. In 1813 the renewal of the Charter to the East India Company was closely debated at home. That in the critical years of the European War time could be found for such a discussion exemplifies not merely the wide public interest in Indian affairs, but how parliamentary government, which is "government by public meeting," provides opportunity and the machinery for ventilating important but subsidiary issues in the stress of a crisis. The opening of Indian trade to all vessels of less than 400 tons—a breach in the Company's monopoly strenuously but unsuccessfully resisted—was a distinct advance towards separating the decaying commercial functions of the Company from its delegated imperial and political task.

The whole situation had been profoundly modified by Wellesley's policy and achievements. The dissolution of the Napoleonic Empire, and our undisputed supremacy at sea, had dispelled the danger of French invasion across the water, aided by native assistance from within. The annexation of Ceylon, the retention of Mauritius and the Cape, secured the main route from Gibraltar and the British ports, while Malta and the Ionian Isles guarded the alternative line of communication through the Mediterranean, the Isthmus of Suez, and the Red Sea. But this latter, it will be observed, passed Aden (not yet British) and the mouth of the Persian Gulf, a superb lair for pirates bent on toll or blackmail. But on the whole, the menace of the sea routes was now replaced by the menace of the land routes—invasion through the mountains to the west and northwest, by which the Mogul conquerors had once reached Delhi. This was both an Indian and a European problem. The Sultan at Constantinople was the head of the Mohammedan world; the Government at Calcutta was responsible for, and to, Mohammedan chiefs and races. The advance of Russia to the Caucasus and the Caspian and beyond, to the mouth of the Danube and beyond, could not be overlooked. A European Power of the first rank at Constantinople threatened the Eastern Mediterranean and Egypt. And the same logic that drove the British in India was driving the Russian rulers.

A safe and "scientific" frontier was a necessity to British India. Where was the line to be drawn? Policy, geography, military considerations entered into the problem. But wherever the line was drawn Government House at Calcutta could not remain blind and deaf to events on the other side of it. Mountstuart Elphinstone's mission to the Amir of Afghanistan, Malcolm's two missions to

Persia, Metcalfe's mission to Ranjít Singh, the creator of the Sikh 1807 and military state, and one of the most remarkable in the long list of 1810 native statesmen and rulers in Hindostan, illustrate the inexorable pressure of the situation. Metcalfe came to an agreement with the Sikh, and the Sutlej was faithfully maintained during Ranjít Singh's lifetime as the frontier beyond which neither British nor Sikh should d. 1839 pass. The foresight of Warren Hastings had predicted that the Persian Gulf would thrust itself upon us, if we did not wisely anticipate the day.[1] And the frontier question pressed, not at our choice, into the framework of the picture that every Governor-General found awaiting his study at Calcutta. Directors at the East India House might renounce ambition in italics, and Governors-General who thought they had mastered the Indian problem at the Board of Control in foggy London came out determined to seek peace and ensue it. But the East India House could not extirpate ambition in native chiefs, nor suppress the appeal of the oppressed to the Lât Sahib at Calcutta. The Jumna Sikhs in 1809 were responsible for Metcalfe's mission. Before now the whispers of the Brahmins at Poona had set Central India in a blaze. Governors-General could not sleep soundly simply because the Maidan at the door of Government House was quiet. Delhi, the tomb of Akbar, the Moti Musjid, and the Taj Mahal enshrined the spell of the Mogul Empire—the day when India had acknowledged a single imperial dynasty whose place the British had taken. The sceptre of Akbar and Aurungzíb could be wielded now by none but a British Sovereign or his delegate. Dull indeed of soul had that ruler been who could step into the chair of Clive, Warren Hastings, and Wellesley and not be fascinated and absorbed by the problems of this vast India—its millions of inhabitants, its races, religions, languages, civilisation, and aspirations—be stung by the splendour of the unfolding dreams which set a polished imperial jewel in the imperial crown of the United Kingdom of Great Britain and Ireland ; be fired by the passion to achieve by administration, legislation, institutions, new reforms for the millions committed to his charge.

[1] " That the Persian Gulf is the most important position in Asia, one of the most important in the world . . . If I were the War Minister of the Czar . . . I should endeavour to occupy Persia and to establish myself at the head of the Persian Gulf . . . I could strike at India with the one hand and at Asia Minor with the other ; I should take Constantinople in the rear." (A remark of Hastings quoted from G. W. Hastings' *A Vindication of Warren Hastings*, p. 202.)

31

The Popes, borne in the curule chair of Roman consuls and empe-
rors, fanned by the imperial peacock of the Cæsars, entrenched at
the Vatican in the heart of the mistress city of the world, could
resist the undying appeal of imperial traditions for temporal sovereignty as little as the gifted aristocrats sent in succession to the
East to govern on behalf of the democracy of Great Britain.   It
was India that converted the critic Wellesley into an admirer of
Warren Hastings.   Minto and Hastings, the critics of Wellesley,
found it impossible to refute the arguments that convinced their
misunderstood predecessor, or to be untrue to the mission thrust
upon them by the obstinate facts of the case and by the genius of
their race.

Canada was not yet able to refute sceptical or disillusioned imperialists.   The Constitutional Act of 1791, which divided the
colony into Upper and Lower Canada, had not solved the difficulties of government nor bridged the rift between the autocracy of
the Governor and Executive and the democratic ideals of the
governed.   Dorchester's resignation in 1795 removed the most experienced and far-sighted of Canadian empire-builders.   The best
feature of the situation was the loyalty of the French Canadians in
the war of 1812, under the Governor, Sir George Prevost, and their
independent readiness to repel the American invaders.   But the
colony grew very slowly.   In 1815 the population was not yet
300,000 in Lower, nor more than 80,000 in Upper, Canada.   Great
Britain had neither the means nor the will to send what was needed
most—men and women.   And the great fur-trading Companies,
the Hudson Bay and the North-West, jealously resisted expansion
westwards into their monopoly.   Nor was Canada self-supporting
Its scanty revenue until 1818 was necessarily supplemented from
the burdened Imperial Treasury.   Imperial authorities construed
the lesson of 1783 as teaching that self-government ended in
separation.   The commercial system of mercantilism was not relaxed.   The Imperial Legislature could legislate for, and tax
Canada.   The new epoch came a generation later, and as the
result of rebellion.   It was preceded by, and the outcome of, reform
or, rather, revolution in the heart of the imperial organism,
the mother country.

Thus, the Toryism of 1815 was a political creed, an interpretation of life, formally expressed in, and working through, the legal

machinery of government. But its strength did not lie in the venerable and hoary battlements of the historic Constitution. It drew its vitality from the catena of conventions, the customs and usage which determined the application of the legal machinery, the prestige of the Crown, the accepted predominance of the aristocracy and the landed classes in both Chambers of the Legislature, and in local government through Quarter and Petty Sessions, in the alliance of squire and parson, and the union of the spiritual hierarchy with the temporal peerage in the House of Lords. It was entrenched in the social and economic organisation of society, whose subtle, all-pervading atmosphere, breathed alike in palaces and country seats, manor-houses, rectories, cotton-mills, and cottages, coloured unconsciously the ideas of man, woman, and child. Reform would come when, and not until, the new ideas with their new atmosphere—in 1815 the monopoly of a handful of "Jacobin" speculators and agitators outside, and the Radical left wing in, the House of Commons—had mastered the educated, the moderate, the average sensual man and woman. Before ideas and a creed of life held by a majority, organised and determined, in any country, institutions are helpless. They fall as the walls of Jericho. But in a State already provided with the apparatus of self-government revolution is not necessary ; for the difference between revolution and reform does not lie in the result but in the method. The reformer finds to his hand the instruments that the revolutionist has first to invent and then to apply. The lessons of 1688 were being relearned in 1815 ; and, assisted by Peel and Canning after 1822, the new ideas were triumphantly driven home in 1832, and gave Great Britain a new life, resting on new values.

That reform was needed in 1815 scarcely requires proof. The great wars left Great Britain sick, suffering, despondent. It was not the inevitable reaction in a healthy body politic after a prolonged and exceptional effort, which would be cured by a year or two of repose. Wounds and bruises and festering sores testified to organic disease and functional dislocation. The Crown was steadily losing its command on the allegiance and respect of its subjects. A monarchy is indeed marching to a parlous pass when stout-hearted Tories, such as Eldon and Wellington, found it difficult to reconcile their veneration for the Crown with their healthy and growing contempt for the Prince Regent. It is significant that when, Great

Britain, intoxicated in 1814 with the victories over, and the downfall of, Napoleon, was cheering to the echo Alexander I. and Frederick William III., the Regent was hooted in London.[1] For the poor blind and mad King there was universal pity; but his heir and representative, by the scandals of his family life, his cynical immorality and excesses, and his self-centred identification of public duty with personal passion, was destined to depress the Crown that he inherited in 1820 to the nadir of its moral and political influence. The House of Lords[2] resisted, or mutilated when it could not reject, every movement towards reform. A barbarous, inhuman and ineffective criminal code,[3] which punished with death every offence that could be swept within its net, and meted out the same penalty to the sheep-stealer or the shop-lifter as to the murderer, a procedure that in the common law courts made justice the expensive luxury of the rich and in Chancery rendered it impossible for a suitor with a determined adversary to obtain a decision in his lifetime, savage game laws, a system of land law that was a baffling labyrinth of conflicting feudal relics, and an effete jurisprudence placed Great Britain half a century behind the countries of the Napoleonic codes.

Yet to Eldon and Ellenborough, Romilly's efforts to modify some of the most flagrant and demoralising features were Jacobinical attacks on property, aggravated by a milksop humanitarianism, while the merciless exposure by Bentham was simply the despicable dialectic of a reason-besotted leveller. The police in the modern sense had not been created. In the metropolis the watchmen were a corps of Bumbles or of Jonathan Wilds. The local government was fortunate if it was gifted with a stupid, lazy, but honest Dog-

---

[1] See Holland, *Further Memorials of Whig Party*, p. 197.

[2] "Nobody," said Wellington, "cares a damn for the House of Lords; the House of Commons is everything in England," *Journal*, 1817-18.

[3] In 1800 more than 200 crimes were punishable by death, and two-thirds of these had been added in the eighteenth century. An offender could be hanged for falsely pretending to be a Greenwich pensioner, for injuring a county bridge, for cutting down a young tree, forging a banknote, being a fraudulent bankrupt, stealing property value 5s., or more than 1s. from the person, stealing anything from a bleaching-ground, and, if a soldier or sailor, for begging without a pass. In 1816 a boy of ten was sentenced to death. Not till 1820 was the flogging of women abolished. Not till 1836 could a prisoner's counsel in a charge of felony address the jury on his behalf. Eldon successfully opposed the alteration of the law in the case of bleaching-grounds and property worth more than 5s. In 1815 no married woman could make a contract, or acquire personal property, while all her earnings belonged to her husband.

berry. The flogging of women was still a legal penalty; public elementary education by the State did not exist; our jails and the treatment of prisoners, when Elizabeth Fry in 1817 took up the arrested work of John Howard, would have caused King Bomba some twinges of conscience, and were a disgrace to a Christian country, as well as a breeding-ground of crime, disease, and vice; the sponging-house to which Rawdon Crawley was conveniently relegated was a familiar institution. The country under its system of poor law relief, which relieved only the landowner and the employer, paid nearly £7,000,000 annually to lower wages, discourage thrift, penalise the industrious, soften the lot of the dissolute, the loafer, and the vagrant, and to breed bastards. The Grand Inquisition of the nation, the House of Commons, with the exception of a few great constituencies, such as Westminster, was largely filled by the nominees to the Treasury boroughs, or the nominees of the landowners and the borough-mongers. A seat could be bought at a known price as easily as a ticket for the opera or the lottery, or the stock of the National Debt. The electoral law for the boroughs was a tangle in which no two boroughs were alike; in the counties the richest leaseholders or copyholders had no qualification for a vote. Property, that summed up the Decalogue of Toryism, was only useful for buying what did not rest on property. A farmer cultivating 2000 acres on a long lease was disfranchised; but a faggot freeholder of 40s. made by the landowner was on the suffrage roll. An Arkwright who had created an industry that employed thousands, and who could buy up a hundred squires or a dozen peers, had to acquire, if he could, a trumpery but limited qualification in a borough to be on a level with men who voted in virtue of a disused doorway, their sole possession. Great towns created by the Industrial Revolution had no representation at all save through the county in which they lay, and then only through a few freehold votes.

The House of Commons, unmanipulated, was as imperfect a representation of the classes with " a stake in the country " as the House of Lords. The system gave a direct representation to one category of one class of property, ownership of land, persistently regarded in defiance of facts as identical with the agricultural interest. Ownership of seats was apparently considered as equivalent to ownership of land. Other classes of property and other interests could only secure indirect representation by corrupting and manipulating the system.   Peerages could be bullied or bribed out of Ministers by wealth ; seats could be purchased from a borough-monger by Indian nabobs, rich *entrepreneurs*, by all who wished to recoup themselves from the perquisites of patronage. The Whigs cynically acquiesced in the system because reform was impossible, and because Providence created Whig as well as Tory landowners, and these co-operated with Providence by creating a Whig Opposition.   The democracy was wholly excluded ; a mere fraction of the middle class had votes.   Neither had the wealth nor the opportunities to pervert the system, and so secure an in-direct representation.   Hence the gross financial abuses which, in a country bled white by taxation and the reckless creation of debt, aggravated the gravity of the financial situation.   The public ser-vice from top to bottom and in every department was clogged and demoralised by pensions, sinecures, and payments by fees enjoyed by functionless drones who absorbed public funds and were a per-petual bar to efficiency.   Two millions at least were doubly wasted in this way—they produced no service and every recipient was a vested interest opposed to reform.   And the Front Opposition Bench connived at defeating reform, partly because it hoped to return to office and would need the system, not less because the Whigs of the ruling class had their full share of pensions and sine-cures.   The Radicals alone were in earnest, and the day of the Radicals with their terrible utilitarian creed and catechism—the Tribunal and Guillotine of political philosophy for every public person and institution that could not prove their utility and con-tribute to promoting the greatest happiness of the greatest number —had not yet come.   But it was coming, and faster than Bumble dreamed.

Most serious was the dislocation of the new economic organisa-tion of society from the political and legal framework of society, and one fraught with national peril.   The glories of the Great War coincided with the mounting misery and degradation of the wage-earners.   The agricultural labourer and the artisan, unrepresented and credited with an incurable Jacobinism, had one duty alone—to suffer in silence and breed sons for the army and militia, daughters for the service of the gentry, hands of both sexes for factory and workshop.   In the villages they were at the mercy of squire, parson, and farmer, aided by the surveyor of the Poor ; in the industrial towns they were exploited by the capitalist *entrepreneur*. Trades unions, combinations to raise wages, were illegal, and the anti-Luddite legislation of 1812 showed that if the law was not strong enough it would be strengthened ; but combinations in Parliament to depress wages and keep up the price of food (with the aid of the statute book) were legitimate and in the public interest. Gilbert's Act of 1782 recognised practically the right to work and the right to exist ; but outside the workhouses the reign of *laissez faire* and the theory of free contract was now dominant. The dawn of a new epoch dates strictly from the Act of 1802 due to Sir R. Peel, the father of the statesman, which attempted to regulate through State intervention the hours and conditions of labour in factories. Unfortunately, it was a complete dead letter.[1] But in principle it was the parent of the "Factory legislation" of the nineteenth century. Effective control by the State in the interests of the community was as yet far away. The hours and conditions of labour endured by the industrial proletariat were far worse than low wages. And above all, for the women and children economic slavery and degradation as always were dogged by physical degradation, by disease, vice, and crime. The Industrial Revolution brought Great Britain wealth, an addition to her intellectual capital, and the commercial supremacy of the world; but these gifts were purchased at a heavy price. The fear of revolution that haunted the ruling class was one of the many pernicious superstitions that needed extirpation. What the working classes required in 1815 was not charity but justice, not a fostered ignorance but knowledge. British statesmen had yet to learn that there is only one safe system of insurance against revolution—the conviction in the heart of every citizen, however humble, that he is really a partner in the best life which his State exists to promote.

That Great Britain with these and many other fundamental defects could accomplish what she did from 1793-1815 is not the least remarkable feature of a remarkable epoch. But nations, like individuals, are capable of astonishing efforts when it is a fight for life and independence. And after 1802 Great Britain fought for bare existence. Any and every internal evil, any and every sacrifice was preferable in the national mind to the surrender of the right to

---

[1] Robert Blencoe, a worker, first learned of the law twelve years after it became law. It is omitted in the *Parliamentary History* by Cobbett.

exist as a free people, masters of their own fate, captains of their own souls.   And there is no more bracing or instructive example of the vitality and sustaining power of political conceptions and ideals than this refusal, through disaster, disillusionment, and blunders, to make peace except upon terms that left Great Britain free to define her civilisation and future in accordance with a free nation's will.   The aristocratic government of our country is entitled to its full credit for its proud and inflexible leadership.   But there is no reason to suppose that if Great Britain had been governed through manhood suffrage and equal electoral districts the decision would have been different, the obstinacy less stiff, the courage less proud and heroic. In the ends of our foreign policy Pitt, Fox, Canning, Wellesley, Castlereagh correctly interpreted national sentiment, and were supported by the national will.   The political aptitude, the inherited political instinct, the intuition of a race trained by centuries of struggle, wrested from defective machinery illegitimate benefits. Nations that can defy their maladies and blunder into success are the despair of the political theorist.   The truest hope for the future of Great Britain in 1815 lay in a simple quality.   She had been strong enough to endure and survive her vices and her diseases ; she was therefore strong enough—and the nineteenth century is one long proof—to devise and endure the drastic but effective remedies.

NOTE.—For additional authorities see the Supplement to the Bibliography, pp. 550-552.   There is an admirable and objective survey of the development of Whigs, Tories, Radicals and their political creeds and acts in H. W. C. Davis, *The Age of Grey and Peel* (1929).   The best account of England in 1814-15 is in E. Halévy's *Histoire du Peuple anglais au XIXe siècle* (vol. i., Eng. transl.)

APPENDICES

I. THE PRISONER OF AHLDEN

THE fate of Sophia Dorothea of Celle, the wife of George I., who might have been Queen of Great Britain, is beyond question. But her relations with her lover, Count Philip Christopher von Königsmarck, are still a matter of controversy. Nor, so far, is there certain evidence as to how he met his death, though both Stepney, the contemporary English resident at Dresden, and Cressett, at Celle, had no doubt he had been murdered. It seems very unlikely that any fresh material will come to light, either to acquit or convict George I. of being the instigator of, or privy to, his sudden and inexplicable disappearance. It seems not unreasonable to conclude that the count met with a violent end, and that the Hanoverian Court, which "issued a lying report" and shrouded the whole affair in impenetrable mystery, both knew and had good cause to conceal the truth. The romantic version of the tragedy, which has persisted till to-day, rests chiefly on the *Römische Octavia* of Duke Antony Ulric of Brunswick-Wolfenbüttel, published in 1711, and obviously a semi-fictitious, semi-historical *roman à clef*. A new development was given to the critical discussion of the relations of Sophia Dorothea to Count Philip Königsmarck by Kramer in his *Denkwürdigkeiten von Aurora von Königsmarck* (1843), and some supplementary evidence was published by R. F. Williams in his *Memoirs of Sophia Dorothea* (1845). The most recent discussion of the problems involved will be found in A. D. Greenwood, *Lives of the Hanoverian Queens of England*, vol. i., and A. W. Ward, *The Electress Sophia and the Hanoverian Succession* (2nd ed.). Dr. Ward has supplemented the series of letters in French and cipher, preserved at Lund, between Sophia Dorothea and Königsmarck, by printing thirty-four additional letters preserved in the Geheimes Staatsarchiv at Berlin, which clearly belong to the same correspondence (see *Eng. Hist. Rev.*, April, 1910, pp. 314-15, for proof of this). Dr. Ward thinks that no further letters are in existence. The student will find in the two modern works cited above a full bibliography of the literature on the subject. A translation of the Lund letters was published by W. H. Wilkins, *The Love of an Uncrowned Queen* (2 vols., 2nd ed., 1900), and a transcript, with annotations, by Mrs. Everett Green is in Brit. Mus., Add. MSS. 28259. The interpretation of these letters is almost as various as that of the Casket Letters, with the exception that their authorship is not disputed. Lord Acton (*Lectures on Mod. History*, p. 267) pronounced that "nobody doubted that Königsmarck had been made away, and that the

489

author of the crime was the King of England, whose proper destination therefore should have been not St. James but Newgate, and indeed not Newgate but Tyburn ". But without adopting so extreme a view it is difficult to understand Miss Greenwood's scepticism (*op. cit. supra*) as to the guilty relations between Königsmarck and Sophia Dorothea, which, given the character of the lover and of the princess, and the unhappiness of her marriage, the letters leave in little doubt. And the princess's father, it is noteworthy, believed in his daughter's guilt. Lord Acton's words (*op. cit.*, p. 152) on Mary's share in the murder of Darnley sum up the case against George I. : " The case is highly suspicious and compromising ; but more than that is required for a verdict of guilty in a matter of life and death ". The ethical question raised by his divorce and imprisonment of Sophia Dorothea cannot be discussed satisfactorily in an appendix. But his conduct was eminently characteristic of the man.

II. WALTON'S DESPATCH

In connection with the operations of Byng (Lord Torrington) in the Mediterranean in 1718 allusion is generally made to the famous brevity of a despatch by Captain (afterwards Admiral) Sir G. Walton, and the allusion generally consists in misquoting its supposed contents (*e.g.* Stanhope, *History of England*, 1-474 ; Lang, *History of Scotland*, iv., 262). The received version first appeared in *The Gentleman's Magazine* for 1739, p. 606, and has been repeated without verification by many writers since. The author of this garbled version was T. Corbett, who in 1718 was Byng's secretary, and in 1739 was Secretary to the Admiralty. Sir J. K. Laughton, who had already exposed the error in his article on Walton (*Dict. of Nat. Biography*, lix., published in 1899), printed the correct text of the despatch (dated August 5th, 1718) in *The Times*, December 29th, 1905, p. 5, and pointed out (1) that the despatch was not limited to a single sentence, the exact wording of which usually runs, " We have taken and destroyed all the Spanish ships and vessels that were upon the coast, the number as in the margin," but to a letter running to fourteen lines of small print ; (2) the popular version " is thus not simply erroneous, but a lie " ; (3) that the "lie" gave Walton " a sort of distinction which he never merited " ; (4) that Walton's force was " overwhelmingly superior " to that of the Spaniards.

III. THE WAR OF JENKINS' EAR, 1739

Although Burke, Horace Walpole, and others doubted whether Jenkins lost an ear, as he stated to the House of Commons on March 17th, 1738, the fact has been substantiated from official records. It was suggested, indeed, later by Jenkins' critics that he lost his ear in the pillory, or that he had both his ears when he appeared to give evidence. Sir J. K. Laughton published in *The English Historical Review* for 1889 (vol. iv., pp. 741-49) the text of various letters discovered by him in the Admiralty Records bearing on the complaints arising in the West Indies. One of these, from Rear-Admiral C.

Sept. 12, 1731

Stewart to the Governor of Havana, is a protest against "cruel, piratical outrages" committed by the Guarda Costas, and refers explicitly to Jenkins : " About April 20th last . . . after using the captain in a most barbarous, inhuman manner, taking all his money, *cutting off one of his ears* . . .". A return also in 1737 mentions in a list of vessels "taken or plundered " the " *Rebecca*, Robert Jenkins, Jamaica to London, boarded and plundered near Havana, 9th April, 1731 (*i.e.* 20th April, n.s.) ". The Spanish captain, a letter of June 16th, 1742, further states, one Fondino, who " took Jenkins, when his ears was (*sic*) cut off," had been captured, and the captor on this occasion was a great-great-grandson of Oliver Cromwell, Admiral Sir T. Oct. 12, Frankland. It is significant that Rear-Admiral Stewart, writing to Newcastle, 1731 has much to say unfavourable to British conduct, *e.g.* " Give me leave to say that you only hear one side of the question . . . the sloops manned and armed on that illicit trade has (*sic*) more than once bragged to me of their having murdered 7 or 8 Spaniards on their own shore . . . but villainy is inherent to this climate . . . a parcel of men who call themselves merchants, but except two or three . . . they are no better than pedlars, and one of them formerly in jail for piracy". The origin of the war of 1739 has recently been examined by Mr. Temperley (*Royal Hist. Soc. Transactions*, third ser., vol. 3 (1909), pp. 197-236), who has collated fresh documentary information from the Record Office with the evidence from Spanish archives utilised by Baudrillart and Armstrong. Mr. Temperley, in brief, shows very clearly (1) that there is much to be said for Stewart's view : " The question will be whether we, by carrying on the clandestine trade, are not ourselves the authors of our complaints " ; (2) the Convention of the Pardo was a sincere effort of both Governments to establish a preliminary basis for a complete and satisfactory understanding ; (3) the complication caused by the affairs of the South Sea Company being introduced into the diplomatic negotiations, and the refusal of the Company to produce their accounts or pay what they owed to the King of Spain ; (4) Newcastle's extreme sensitiveness to public opinion and the clamours of the Opposition (a singular anticipation of his conduct in 1756-57) ; (5) the fear in the Cabinet, aware of the Pacte de Famille of 1733, that in 1738 a Franco-Spanish alliance was on foot ; (6) the disastrous effect of the Opposition attacks on the Ministry and the Convention in inflaming an ignorant and prejudiced public in England ; (7) " the counter-orders " to our fleet in the Mediterranean on March 10th, 1739, for which Newcastle was primarily responsible, and the issue of which Newcastle instructed Keene to deny. Spain was then convinced that England meant war, broke the Convention by refusing to pay the £95,000 agreed to, and thus made war inevitable. Mr. Temperley proves that Walpole's Ministry had " not truckled to Spain, and were not prepared to sacrifice our trade and navigation," and concludes " that popular and parliamentary agitation was the main factor in causing the war ". April 12, Montijo, President of the Council of the Indies, summed up the quarrel fairly : 1738 " There were faults on both sides ; our (English) contrabandists ought to be punished, and some of their (Spanish) Governors hanged ". The extent of the illicit trade was enormous. The return of 1737, alluded to above, specifies 52 British vessels taken by the Spaniards, and Rear-Admiral Stewart mentions that we had " 50 ships to one Spaniard in those seas ". See, also, Hertz, *British Imperialism in the Eighteenth Century*, p. 15 *seq.*, where the pamphlet literature is carefully analysed.

IV. " THE DOUBLE-MARRIAGE PROJECT "

Carlyle's phrase describing the tortuous and wearisome negotiations for a double dynastic connection between the British Royal House and the Royal House of Prussia by a marriage of Frederick, Prince of Wales, to Princess Wilhelmina, afterwards Margräfin of Baireuth, and of Frederick, the Crown Prince, the Frederick the Great of 1740-1786, to the Princess Amelia, has passed into history. (See Carlyle's *Frederick*, vol. ii., Bks. vi. and vii.) Since Carlyle wrote the negotiations have been documentarily investigated, particularly by Oncken (*Forschungen zur Brand. und Preuss. Geschichte*, vol. vii., 1894) and Berneck (*Denkwürdigkeiten der Margräfin und die Eng.-Preuss. Heirath's Verhandlung*, 1894). (See also *Wilhelmina, Margravin of Baireuth*, by Edith Cuthell, vol. i., London, 1905.) From these sources it seems established that (1) the double marriage was ardently desired by the Queen of Prussia, but opposed by her husband ; (2) that Sir C. Hotham practically secured the Prussian Court's consent to the single marriage of Wilhelmina and Prince Frederick ; (3) that the English Court learned nothing of this definite settlement because they preferred not to learn ; (4) that the proposal for a double marriage was a project to detach Prussia from Austria ; (5) that the plan to destroy the influence of Grumbkow and Seckendorff over King Frederick William I. failed ; and on the failure the marriage of Wilhelmina to the Prince of Wales was then abandoned for good by the British Court.

V. PITT'S RESIGNATION IN 1761 AND THE PEACE OF 1763

The circumstances under which Pitt resigned in October, 1761, have been the subject of considerable controversy. A writer in *The Quarterly Review* (Mr. H. Hall) (Oct., 1899) maintained (1) that Pitt had "positive knowledge" of the Family Compact of 1761 ; (2) that "the secret of the Family Compact was probably divulged to Pitt from a wholly unexpected quarter " ; (3) "that there can be little doubt . . . that Dutens informed Pitt secretly, through his friend, Robert Wood, of the nature of the correspondence which Tanucci (Neapolitan Foreign Minister) carried on with Madrid under the nose of Sir J. Gray (our envoy at Naples). There can be still less doubt that this intelligence was amongst the papers which Pitt brought down 'in his bag' to the Council Board on that memorable October day " ; (4) that Pitt's " pride forbade him to disclose " his " proofs " to " an incredulous audience " ; (5) " a conjecture " that " Pitt had in his possession a copy of the secret treaty of August 15th, 1761 ". The same writer asserts that a copy of the treaty exists amongst the miscellaneous papers of 1761 in the Newcastle Collection ; and argues that " the writing, the paper, and especially the water-mark, clearly indicate that it came from Pitt's office in Cleveland Row ". Hence the inference that Newcastle "received this copy of the Treaty from Pitt himself ".

Aug. 15, 1761

Oct. 2

Two distinct points are here brought into the discussion : (1) On what evidence did Pitt rely in his demand for instant war with Spain ? (2) Did he in forming his own conclusions rely on evidence, however obtained, which "pride" or any other motive "forbade him to disclose" ? In other words, did Pitt withhold from his colleagues proofs which it was in his power to bring forward ? It is difficult to understand à priori why pride should have commanded this secrecy. The issue was very critical, and Pitt clearly desired to convince his colleagues that he was right in his interpretation of Spain's action. Why should he withhold categorical information which would have clinched his argument ? If he already had a copy of the Treaty of August 15th revealing its real terms, his failure to produce it and confound the sceptics who doubted those terms is quite inexplicable. Pride or any other motive at least did not forbid him to lay before the Cabinet the intercepted correspondence of Fuentes and Grimaldi. (2) As to the copy in the Newcastle Collections we have no evidence (beyond a doubtful argument from a water-mark) that Pitt had seen it, that Newcastle received it from Pitt, or that it was in British hands before October 2nd, 1761. The mere fact that it is included in the Newcastle Papers for 1761 is no proof that it was received by Newcastle in 1761, particularly before October 2nd of that year. And if Newcastle before October 2nd had seen a copy of the terms of the Treaty of August 15th, why did he write when explicitly informed on December 1st of the treaty by the Portuguese ambassador, " I think Mello's account can't be true " (B. M. Add. MS. 32931 f. 425)—a wholly inexplicable comment if Pitt previous to his resignation had already communicated to him the terms of the treaty ?

The Newcastle Papers (B. M. Add. MS., 32923, ff. 63-8) and the Hardwicke Papers (B. M. Add. MS., 35870, ff. 297, 301, 303, 310) supply detailed information as to what took place in the numerous Cabinet meetings between August 5th and October 2nd, 1761. On September 18th Pitt and Temple in a written memorandum to the King (printed in *Grenville Corr.*, 1, 336) demanded that Bristol, our ambassador, should be withdrawn from Madrid after delivering an ultimatum to the Spanish Court. The final decision was taken at a Cabinet meeting on October 2nd. On August 31st Wall, the Spanish ambassador, had presented to Bristol a paper declaring that the memorial on the Spanish grievances had been submitted by Bussy, the French plenipotentiary, on July 15th, " with the full consent, approbation and pleasure of his Catholic Majesty " (*i.e.* of Spain)—clear proof that the two Bourbon Courts were acting in conjunction and on explicit orders from Madrid. An intercepted letter from Grimaldi to Fuentes of August 31st (printed in *Chatham Corr.*, 2, 139) contained these sentences : " The fear of our (Spanish) Court, which is not badly grounded, is for the fleet (*i.e.* the flota of silver galleons). They want to gain time there (*i.e.* at Madrid) till she is arrived at Cadiz, and are privately sending twelve ships by way of convoy . . . they have remained here entirely bound by the Family Agreement and the Convention . . . now there is no room for this fear, since both instruments were signed on the 15th, and I expect shortly the ratification ". On September 2nd Stanley wrote from Paris to Pitt : " I have secretly seen an article, drawn up between

France and Spain, in which the former engages to support the interests of the latter equally with her own in the negotiations of the peace with England ; it was entitled Article 10. *I am as yet a stranger to the other nine."* On September 13th another intercepted letter from Grimaldi to Fuentes contains this passage : " It would be sufficient to repeat to Bussy the order of the 10th of August, not to sign anything without the accommodation of matters with Spain likewise, according to the stipulation of the Treaty between the two Courts, which is already ratified ". We know from the Hardwicke and Newcastle Memoranda that these documents in full were submitted to Pitt's colleagues in the Cabinet. It is clear, therefore, that every one in the Cabinet by October 2nd knew that : (1) Spain was acting in conjunction with France ; (2) an instrument or treaty between the two Courts had been signed on August 15th, and was already ratified. On this evidence Pitt based his demand for war with Spain (already made in the written memorandum of September 18th) before Spain, as he argued, made war on us. He practically made two points : (*a*) an inference that the Treaty of August 15th was offensive and not purely defensive or merely for joint diplomatic action in the negotiations for peace ; (*b*) a measure of policy, that it was better to anticipate and not wait for the inevitable blow. The Cabinet had therefore to decide : (1) What was the correct interpretation of the Treaty of August 15th ; (2) what, as a measure of policy, was the best action to take. Newcastle's note on Pitt's speech runs : " That the papers he (Pitt) had in his bag (meaning my Lord Bristol's letter and Mr. Wall's paper) fixed an eternal stain on the Crown of England if proper measures were not taken upon it ". Hardwicke's note on Granville's speech runs : " 1. Whether the memorial of Mr. Wall, together with the intercepted letters, are a sufficient foundation for your lordships to form a fixed opinion that Spain means to make war against England, and to warrant you to make war or to come to an open rupture with them ? " Hardwicke also notes that the intercepted letter of September 13th was produced "and the translation read ". The conclusion, therefore, seems clear ; first, that no other evidence was submitted by Pitt except Wall's memorial of August 31st and the intercepted letters of August 31st and September 13th, and that these and these alone were in Pitt's " bag " ; secondly, that Pitt did not produce any other evidence, because on October 2nd he had no other evidence to produce. The supposition that he suppressed or withheld other information must, therefore, be dismissed. And this supposition is further disproved by the vote of the Cabinet which decided that (1) Pitt's interpretation of the treaty of August 15th as offensive was not borne out by the evidence, and " neither founded in justice nor expediency " ; (2) as a measure of policy it was dangerous to provoke a war with Spain, in which the military experts, Anson and Ligonier, concurred. It is inconceivable that if Pitt could on October 2nd have revealed the actual terms of the Family Compact he would not have done so. Such a document, if in existence, would have blown out of the water the interpretation of the majority in the Cabinet that the treaty of August 15th did not necessarily bring Spain into the war. That Pitt was correct in his inferential interpretation events subsequently proved. But on October 2nd it was an inference which he could not prove, and which even so experienced a diplomatist as Granville (Carteret), the Lord President, decided against Pitt's hypothetical interpretation. The argument on policy does not affect the question as to the evidence submitted by Pitt: though the course of events showed that Pitt, and not the military experts, were right in this also. The student will consult with advantage, in addition to the authorities cited above: *Memoir*, by H. Fox, prefixed to vol. i. of the *Letters of Lady Sarah Lennox*; *Eng. Hist. Review* (Jan. and April, 1906), in which the text of the important passages from the Newcastle and Hardwicke Papers is printed; W. D. Green, *William Pitt*, App., 383-85; Ruville, *The Earl of Chatham*, II., part iv., chap. xvi. ; J. S. Corbett, *England in the Seven Years' War*, II., chap. vi. ; Waddington, *La Guerre de Sept Ans*, vol. iv.

On the peace of Paris and the negotiations leading up to it see especially *Royal Hist. Soc. Trans.*, 3rd series, vol. 2 (1908) (article based on documentary study by Miss K. Hotblack); W. L. Grant, *Mission de M. Bussy à Londres* (1761); G. L. Beer, *British Colonial Policy*, 1754-65; *American Hist. Review* (article by Mr. Hubert Hall), July, 1900.

(Note 1929): The standard life of Pitt is, since 1914, the biography in 2 vols. by Prof. Basil Williams. The student should read his narrative (ii., pp. 103-25) of the events which led to Pitt's resignation. Prof. B. Williams accepts the view expressed in this Appendix (written in 1910), *i.e.* that Pitt's policy and demands were based, not on a copy of the Treaty, but on the intercepted correspondence of Grimaldi, particularly the letters of August 13th and September 13th, referred to above.

VI. THE AUTHORSHIP OF JUNIUS

The student will find the arguments for and against the Franciscan authorship of Junius summarised and criticised in the article by Sir L. Stephen on Sir P. Francis in *Dict. of Nat. Biogr.*, vol. xx., with a bibliography of the chief literature of the controversy (see also article by the same writer—"Chatham, Francis and Junius"—*Eng. Hist. Rev.*, iii., 233). Macaulay (*Essay on Warren Hastings*) for five reasons "had a firm belief" that Francis was the author. Sir W. R. Anson (Introd. to *Autobiography of Grafton*, pp. xxxi, xxxii) notes that "it is remarkable that throughout the autobiography no allusion is made to the letters of Junius "; and while not prepared to dispute the Franciscan authorship, maintains that the letters "suggest an intimacy with the higher walks of political life and a knowledge of the persons concerned " which could not have been acquired by Francis alone ; and that Francis's career does not "explain the savage ferocity of the attacks made by Junius upon the Duke of Grafton and Bedford". Sir W. Anson finds the clue in Temple who, for reasons advanced *op. cit.*, may be supposed to be "the guiding spirit of Junius," and expresses "a conviction that whatever part Francis may have played in the composition of these letters, Temple directed their policy, supplied much of their information, and may conceivably have polished their invective ". Shelburne (*Life*, by Fitzmaurice, i., p. viii) apparently not only asserted that he knew who Junius was, but that it was a person wholly different from any one suspected on various grounds of being the author by contemporary opinion; and he intended to write a pamphlet revealing the secret. The pamphlet was never written, and the statement seems at variance with that recorded of Shelburne's views elsewhere (*op. cit.*, iii., 466). Sir W. Anson's suspicion that the Grenvilles were concerned in the publication and writings of Junius is curiously borne out by *The Further Memorials of the Whig Party*, by Lord Holland (ed. Stavordale, J. Murray, 1905, App. D, p. 404). Lord Holland records his own "impressions of Francis's conversations, inasmuch as he always seemed to me to know or imply something about Junius, but to *deny* strictly his being the author," and relates a story according to which Charles Lloyd (private secretary to George Grenville, and suspected by Lord North of being the author of " Junius ") on Francis's admission, " wrote the letters and Francis corrected the press". Shelburne's authorship is stated in " Junius " by C. W. Everett (1927).

VII. GRAVES'S ACTION WITH DE GRASSE (SEPT. 5TH, 1781) AND RODNEY'S ACTIONS OF APRIL 17TH, 1780, AND APRIL 12TH, 1782

1776-94

"New light" (to quote the editor) "of the most startling kind" has recently been thrown on the tactical history of the period from 1776-1794 by the publication in 1909 of *Signals and Instructions*, edited by Mr. J. S. Corbett (Navy Records Society, vol. xxxv.). This volume contains the collection of Signal Books and Instructions made by Admiral Sir T. Graves, K.B. (Nelson's second in command at Copenhagen) and "embodies for us a practically complete history of the transition" in tactics, laid down in the old system of instructions (see *Fighting Instructions*, 1530-1616, vol. xxix., Navy Records Society, ed. J. S. Corbett), which was superseded by the Signal Book System. Previously to the discovery in 1908 at the United Service Institution of the Graves Collection the gap from 1776-1794, pointed out by the editor, had remained unfilled; and the principles and methods of the transition from the old system to the new, so long discussed by naval historians, were necessarily a field simply of inference, conjecture from scanty facts, and, as it proves, erroneous interpretation of these facts. The fortunate discovery of the new material has now provided documentary material which fully explains the critical period of development in naval tactics from 1776-1794. The problems and their solution are discussed at length by Mr. Corbett in his lengthy introduction to the documents (pp. 1-81) to which the student can safely be referred. A layman naturally will not attempt to pronounce on matters that belong to the province of a few naval experts and are still under discussion. It must suffice here to point out that Mr. Corbett places the leading sailors of the time—Howe, Rodney, Hood, Kempenfelt, and the lesser lights in an entirely new setting —and to note some of his most striking conclusions, *e.g.* : (1) the influence of French theoretical writers, *e.g.*, Morogues, in particular, on British naval theory and practice ; (2) the " invaluable work " of Clerk of Eldin, " many of whose ideas must have been perfectly familiar to the leading spirits in

in 1782

the Navy," "can only be regarded as one expression of a deep and wide-spread movement"; (3) the existence of a great school of naval tacticians and reformers, of which Howe and Kempenfelt were the leading spirits, the great object of whose labours was to free commanders from the fetters of an obsolete system, and which was quite distinct from the conservative school of Rodney, that sought improvement in the established system. The debt of our Navy to Kempenfelt and Howe and their followers is convincingly set forth by the editor. Mr. Corbett shows at length that in the manœuvre of "breaking the line," which for so long has been in our history text-books Rodney's chief title to immortality : (*a*) in April 17th, 1780, and April 12, 1782, "the idea of the manœuvre was familiar to both the French and the English services"; (*b*) "all the evidence points to the conclusion that so far from Rodney being the parent of the manœuvre," he belonged to the school which "condemned it as a dangerous and unsound form of attack"; (*c*) that the signal for the manœuvre had been introduced into the Channel Fleet, 1779-1780, was continued by Kempenfelt, and that Sir C. Douglas, Rodney's first captain, and Affleck, who made the manœuvre independently on April 12th, were "Channel Fleet men who had been serving under Kempenfelt's system". Equally striking are the considerations advanced by Mr. Corbett as to the real nature of the action fought by Graves with De Grasse on September 5th, for which Graves was so severely criticised by Hood and Rodney, and by all historians since. Here Mr. Corbett suggests that the *fiasco* was due, not, as generally supposed, to Graves's incompetence, but to the fact that Hood and his squadron "hide-bound in the stereotyped tradition of the old Fighting Instructions" failed to interpret intelligently and to carry out the signals of Graves (who belonged to the school of Kempenfelt and Howe). See particularly Introd., pp. 52-56. Hood, there-fore, on this reading of the action was really responsible for the result, which, by crippling Graves's fleet, enabled De Grasse to get back to the Chesapeake, and which led directly to the epoch-making disaster at Yorktown; and Hood "as a tactician must be placed in the school of Rodney," "the fanatical devotee of the letter of the law". Mr. Corbett goes on to point how "the golden period" of development which culminated with Trafalgar "must be associated chiefly with Howe's name, whose work from 1790-1794 laid the basis of the matured variation, on the "glorious First of 1794 June," of the manœuvre of breaking the line "which the French parry would not meet," finally consummated in "the Nelson touch," the Memoran-dum of October 10th, 1805, and the action of October 21st at Trafalgar. App. E. to Mr. Corbett's volume provides a complete bibliography of English works on Naval Tactics, 1750-1850, and much other supplementary and in-structive material.

VIII. WARREN HASTINGS

The interpretation and verdicts of Macaulay on Warren Hastings' career in his famous essay have been shattered by modern critical research. It is one of the most astonishing things in our modern government of India that

32

this essay is still used under governmental authority as a text-book for the education of Indian boys and university students.

The best short life of Hastings still remains that by Sir A. C. Lyall (English Men of Action Series, 1902). Hastings' administration is reviewed by P. E. Roberts (Introduction in one volume (*viz.* vii., pts. i.-ii.) of the *Historical Geography of the Dominions*, ed. Lucas: Oxford University Press, 1923), who examines the evidence for and against Hastings (pp. 167-219). Mr. Roberts holds that the least defensible of Hastings' acts were the measures taken against (i) Chait Singh, (ii) the Begums of Oudh, but also condemns in unmeasured terms the conduct of the impeachment by the Managers and the failure of the House of Commons in 1785 to recognise the exceptional difficulties under which Hastings laboured or his long and splendid services to Great Britain in the East, and adds the case for the recognition of those services by some high honour from the Crown. The student will do well to consult (a) G. W. Hastings, *A Vindication of Warren Hastings* (1909), (b) *The Selection of Letters and Despatches*, 1772-85 (3 vols., 1890), and *Selection of the State Papers* (Warren Hastings) with introduction by Sir G. W. Forrest, 2 vols., 1910.

There is a useful summary and review of the present position by Prof. J. W. Neill in *History*, April, 1918, pp. 36-47.

Hastings had to work under the Regulating Act of 1773; Hastings' successors worked under the Act of 1784, on which the opinion of a great Viceroy, the Marquess Curzon, is worth quoting: "Such (the machinery as 'reorganised' by Pitt) was the form of Government that was invented by the wisdom of our ancestors. . . . Had a Committee been assembled from the padded chambers of Bedlam, they could hardly have devised anything more extravagant in its madness or more mischievous in its operation. To it must be attributed many of the astounding errors and contradictions that characterised our Indian policy at that time" (*British Government in India*, ii., 69), coinciding with Hastings' judgment that "fifty Burkes, Foxes and Francises" could not have planned a worse measure.

IX. THE DROPMORE PAPERS

The syncopated treatment of foreign policy, particularly after 1793, required by the exigencies of space in the text offers no opportunity for discussing in detail the many difficult problems that arose between 1785 and 1801. On these *The Dropmore Papers* (Hist. MSS. Commission Reports, MSS. of J. B. Fortescue) throw the most valuable light, and are a mine of information which has not yet been fully worked out by students. Six volumes of these papers have so far been published from the archives at Dropmore, and apart from the Pitt correspondence, utilised by Dr. Ruville in his *Life of Chatham*, which occupies half of the first volume, the material consists of letters to or from William, first Lord Grenville, particularly bearing on his period at the Foreign Office in Pitt's Cabinet. This rich material was not used by the Duke of Buckingham in his *Memoirs of the Courts and Cabinets of George III.*, nor by Lord Stanhope in his *Life of Pitt*, though it has been used by Professor Salomon in his *William Pitt, der Jüngere*, which, however, has only reached the year 1792. The information is as varied as it is important. The student's attention may be directed here to a few of the many points on which new light has been shed : (1) The correspondence on Irish affairs from 1782-1801, and the Legislative Union ; chiefly letters from Grenville's brother, the Marquis of Buckingham. The working of the Castle system, the Regency question in 1788, Fitzwilliam's recall, the Rebellion of 1798, the attitude of the Protestant Ascendency party, the dead set against " Clemency " Cornwallis are here fully illustrated. (2) Pitt's strong hostility in 1782 and 1783 to the system of personal government by the King, the unconstitutional influence of the Crown and the need of electoral reform are exemplified (see particularly i., 212 *et seq.*). (3) Thurlow's opposition to Pitt in the Cabinet, which makes it more surprising that he was not dismissed earlier than 1792. (4) Dundas's political system in Scotland. " My secession from all political life at this time would be a very fatal step to the strength and hold Government has of Scotland " (i., 534). (5) British relations with Holland from 1787 onwards (see particularly Introd. to vol. vi. and references there given). (6) The rupture of the Triple Alliance of 1788 and the collision with Russia in 1790-91. The editor notes (iii., p. viii): " It appears probable from Mr. Whitworth's letter to Grenville dated June 17th, that the story of Fox having sent Adair to the Russian Court to thwart Fawkener and bring Pitt's Administration into discredit in England was the suggestion of a mortified diplomatist ". (7) Confirmatory evidence of Pitt's determination to remain strictly neutral after the French Revolution broke out (see particularly vol. ii.). (8) The rapid change in public opinion in the autumn of 1792, reflected in the Cabinet. (9) The reports from secret agents on the Committee of Public Safety. After 1793, when the war had come, a brief analysis of the material is impossible, so rich and suggestive are its contents. The cumulative evidence the more it is studied the more it strengthens the opinion of the incapacity of the Cabinet in its military measures and foreign policy. From first to last there were fierce dissensions (Dundas was in continual collision with Grenville) which handicapped continuity and vigour of effort. As the editor notes, our military plans and operations throughout are " a strange exhibition of miscalculations, wavering purpose, and ineffectual action ". " Probably at no other period of its history did the military reputation of England, in all respects except bravery in the field, fall so low as during Pitt's first Ministry." The absence of any organisation of the Higher Direction is conspicuous. Pitt and the Cabinet veered backwards and forwards from week to week between rival plans and policies. Home and foreign strategists drew up plans and quarrelled over their merits ; they were hung up, amended, mutilated, and invariably executed too late and with inadequate means. Melancholy confirmation of the disorganisation and divided councils is apparent in vols. ii.-vi. (see particularly the Introductions to vols. iv. and vi. and specific references there given). The incapacity of our officers is another constant theme (vi., 89 and 183, are good examples), but no officers could have achieved anything remarkable under so defective a system. Dundas's share is discreditable. Pitt down to 1798 seems to have placed himself in his hands; yet Pitt remarked (vi. 89): "Dundas's geography, you will observe, is as accurate as his language" (Dundas's grammar being notoriously defective). No less striking is the evidence as to the phases and difficulties of our foreign policy, the rotten organisation of the European monarchies, the selfish and divergent aims of the members of the alliances which ruined the First and Second Coalitions. The information as to Prussia (see particularly vi., 492, and Elgin's confidential despatches for 1796 and 1797 in vol. iii.) explains the conduct of that Power; our relations with Austria throughout constitute a remarkable chapter in diplomatic history, very similar to the relations that prevailed from 1741-48. The recriminations, jealousy, suspicion, conflicting policies, financial quarrels, charges of bad faith, military dissensions are copiously illustrated (see particularly ii., 614-36; iii., 47, and vols. iv. and vi. *passim*). Nor was our co-operation with Russia in the Second Coalition more satisfactory, ending in a rupture and military collapse (vol. vi.). The phases through which our foreign policy passed are instructive. In 1792 Dundas seems to have imposed the policy of "indemnity and security," and of dismembering France on the Cabinet, as the only policy which would reconcile public opinion to the war. On the complete failure of this, Grenville's plan of restoring the French monarchy with the boundaries of 1792 was adopted. This too had broken down by 1796. Pitt and Grenville's plan of securing peace, or purchasing Prussian help by cutting up Germany and aggrandising Prussia and Austria by the Austrian Netherlands and Bavaria, and slicing up the small and helpless German States, was condemned by George III. as "Italian politics" (iii., 227 and 330), "immoral and unjustifiable" (iii., 173, 278, 311), to which he gave a very reluctant consent. Napoleon's cynical principle of compensation—blessed are the strong for they shall prey upon the weak—was in fact anticipated by the monarchies of the old order, which professed to be the bulwarks against Jacobin revolution. In the Second Coalition the British principle of restoring the Bourbon monarchy was wholly opposed to Austrian views. Austria had frankly abandoned the aim of expelling the French from the Netherlands or restoring the French monarchy. And the collapse of the Coalition caused its abandonment by the British Cabinet, which quite failed to understand the strength of Napoleon's hold on France and the healing effect of his reconstructive measures after Brumaire. Grenville's blindness to Napoleon's greatness is extraordinary, and was shared apparently by the whole Cabinet. Vol. vi. is full of this attitude towards "His very Corsican Majesty" which was responsible for the failures of 1799 and 1800. Napoleon apparently to Grenville and his colleagues was a somewhat mediocre adventurer, of little merit as a statesman, and not the equal of "famous" Austrian stategists. We are reminded of the Prussian belief in 1806 "that your Majesty has several generals superior to M. de Bonaparte". It is not surprising that in each case Marengo and Jena were a rude awakening, or that politicians who made such imaginary and comfortable pictures brought disaster on themselves.

Equally pathetic throughout is the confidence year after year that France must shortly succumb. In 1792 (ii., 282 and 314) it was held at London that the Republic could not resist the Duke of Brunswick; in 1793 Grenville thought that "the Toulon business" would "be decisive of the whole war". (His brother thought, and for good reasons, very differently, ii., 424-29.) In 1795 and in 1798 he was no less confident (iv., 334). Ministers throughout were buoyed up by their convictions, inspired by the reports of secret agents (a good example in iii., 80), that financial exhaustion and a royalist counter-revolution would destroy the Republic. But see the disagreeable counter-evidence in vi., 289. Our secret service and representatives, Wickham particularly in Switzerland (see vols. ii. and iii., 67-133), were employed lavishly to subsidise and organise insurrections in France, with singularly little success, while the aid in Brittany and elsewhere, hopelessly mismanaged, ended in a series of disasters. It is not surprising to find in 1793, 1795, 1800 much evidence of deep popular discontent at home with the war, and no little discouragement amongst Ministers themselves. The subsidy system was dis trusted and very unpopular. Fox's criticism had sunk deep. Dundas wrote to Pitt (vol. v., 434): "The Government of this country dare not venture to revolt Dec., 1798 the feeling of the public" by reviving the subsidy system. No less interesting and disagreeable is Carysfort's candid evidence from Berlin (confidential letters in vol. vi., 104-174) showing that our maritime policy and claims and implacable attitude as regards peace (contrasted with Napoleon's apparent moderation) had turned continental opinion completely against us (vi., 334-402). Great Britain was regarded as the incarnation of insidious treachery, of insular and commercial selfishness, and pursuing the war with reference to her own ends entirely. And it was not till long after 1802 that this opinion, prevalent in educated circles in Europe, was removed. It is instructive, lastly, to note the early expression of the fixed ideas in European affairs, which finally were realised in 1815. In 1793 and in 1799 the reduction of France to the limits of 1792, with the implied restoration of the monarchy, was put forward by England, and adopted as ground for common action by Russia and by Thugut for Austria; the union of the Dutch and Austrian Netherlands and their permanent separation from France under the House of Orange was the fixed policy of Great Britain and adopted by Russia in 1799; the Memorandum (vi., 122) sent by Keith to Dundas shows how in 1799 and 1800 the Austrian Government, anticipating the policy of Metternich, was de-termined to bring the Italian States—Sardinia ("there must be no Genoese"), Modena, Tuscany, the Papacy, and Naples entirely into the possession of, or in complete dependence on, the Habsburg Emperor. "The English have no right to interfere in this arrangement; and if they do, they cannot prevent it." Throughout the six volumes the student can analyse the personal characteristics of Lord Grenville, which he did not shake off in 1801 when he resigned, and after 1794 the permanent and deep influence of his views on Pitt, which Malmesbury and the young George Canning thought as detri-mental as the influence of Dundas, though this had waned considerably by 1798. From 1793-1801 these three—Pitt, Dundas, and Grenville—constituted a Triumvirate within the Cabinet, whose deliberations and material were not always communicated to their colleagues, and generally only when a decision had been taken. In connection with the Dropmore Papers the student may

1789-97
consult with advantage Mr. Laprade's monograph, *England and the French Revolution* (Johns Hopkins University Studies, series xxvii., Nos. 8-12), which analyses the internal movement in Great Britain and is based on an examination of the contemporary pamphlet and journalistic literature.

X. MILITARY MEASURES, 1793-1801

1793-1802
The first period of the war shows that the Government was continuously faced with four main difficulties : (1) Of manning the fleet ; (2) of manning the regular army ; (3) of providing a force for home defence ; (4) of welding the military forces as a whole into a coherent, efficient, and organised system. And these had to be solved under the strain of war. Adequate machinery had to be improvised under the pressure of events, for it did not exist in 1793. It must be remembered also that in 1793 no less than five different departments, whose functions and jurisdictions were not strictly defined, overlapped and conflicted, were responsible for the army, *viz.* the Horse Guards, the Secretary of State for the Home Department, the Ordnance Board, the Treasury, which dealt with finance, transport and supply, and the Admiralty (where joint operations on the transport of troops in connection with the naval forces were planned). In 1794 the office of Secretary for War and Colonies (a third Secretary of State) was created, but the office did not abolish the existing and conflicting functions of the other departments ; in 1795 the creation of a Field-Marshal Commanding-in-Chief (H.R.H. the Duke of York) gave the army a single military head, but he was a purely executive officer. He was not a chief of a general staff and the first military adviser and expert of the Government ; nor was any general staff created which could act as a military brain to the Government, provide, criticise, and work out military plans of campaign, and operations required by the policy of the civil and supreme Cabinet. The need of a direct and efficient hyphen between the Cabinet as the politically responsible director of policy and the army as the instrument of execution was never met. The Government did not devise or attempt to devise machinery to utilise in organised form the brains of the army in the planning of strategy and the tactical execution of its schemes. The unification and utilisation of the higher control—the union of policy and war—of the political and military brains working in co-operation, are damningly conspicuous in their absence from all Governmental measures down to 1809. And this lack of system, of a definite and thought-out plan, was equally evident in the measures for providing a military force. Roughly these measures were : (1) As regards the regular army to enlist recruits by bounties, by raising new regiments (offering commissions to an individual or individuals who would furnish a body of men), or by raising men for rank, *i.e.* promotion to officers, or a commission to civilians who would provide a defined number of recruits. The main instruments of these last two methods were the army-brokers and the crimps. A special Act in 1796 authorised the levying of 15,000 men from parish to parish, with bounties, the maritime counties supplying the navy, the inland counties the army. But the Act was a failure ; (2) the militia—increasing the number of embodied militia under the Act of

1757 (Additional Militia). In 1796 a Supp'ementary Militia Act authorised the raising of 60,000 men with a fixed quota for each county. In 1798 and 1799 Acts were passed to enable militiamen to enlist in the Line, the total not to exceed 10,000. In 1793 a militia was created for Ireland, in 1797 for Scotland ; (3) the creation of fencibles, *i.e.* regulars limited to service at home, and thus free the regular army for service abroad ; (4) the creation of volunteer corps, infantry, yeomanry and artillery ; (5) in 1796 provisional cavalry were created ; (6) the enlistment of foreigners into corps, as distinct from and supplemental to the hiring of regular foreign troops (Hanoverians and Hessians) ; (7) to feed the navy from the army. " In 1795 no less than fifteen regiments were serving in the fleet."

These measures were framed on no single plan or system. They did not distinguish between the formation and the maintenance of an army, *i.e.* providing for supplying the wastage of war in the depleted cadres. They did not distinguish between the supply for the regular and that for the auxiliary forces. By allowing substitutes in the militia ballot, and by permitting a volunteer to escape the militia ballot, the Government ruined the militia and put a premium on an inefficient, badly armed and disciplined body. The recruit market was swept dry by the crimps competing for recruits for the regulars, substitutes for the militia, recruits for the fencibles, while evasion from all was the basis of the volunteer corps. Foreign enlistment was a bounty to " the foreign crimps competing for the refuse of the recruits of the Continent". No attempt was made to affiliate the volunteers, yeomanry, and fencibles to the militia. Hence by 1801 the problem of providing Great Britain with a permanent and efficient regular force and a co-ordinated auxiliary organisation was quite unsolved. Had the Government (1) kept the recruiting market, by voluntary enlistment, as a strict monopoly for the regular army required for service abroad ; (2) dropped all bounties, raising men for rank, etc., and materially enhanced the soldier's career by increasing his pay and perquisites ; (3) abstained from encouraging volunteers who were costly and useless ; (4) strenuously enforced the Militia Act by a ballot in which personal service for home defence was required and no substitutes allowed, the policy would have been cheaper and more efficient in the end, and a better class of men provided for both services ; a link between the auxiliary or home defence and the regular force could have been made by permitting militiamen (as was partially done) to enlist, and filling up their places in the home reserve by the compulsory ballot. The way would thus have been paved for a compulsory training for home defence of all males capable of bearing arms, leaving the regular army (for service out of the United Kingdom) to be fed by voluntary enlistment.

From 1803-15 the measures were no less various, and for many years the absence of system and the retention of the previous vicious defects equally conspicuous. In 1803 the militia was embodied, substitutes being permitted; the volunteers reconstituted (providing exemption from the militia ballot) and an army of reserves created (43 Geo. III., c. 82). These methods only led to a gigantic rise in bounties and the starvation of the regular forces. In 1804 came Pitt's Permanent Additional Force Act (44 Geo. III., c. 56), which made the parish officers responsible for producing a definite quota; the Volunteer Consolidation Act (44 Geo. III., c. 54) and an Act permitting the supplementary militia to enlist in the regular army. These measures were a failure.

In 1806 Windham endeavoured to (1) introduce short service and better terms of pay; (2) suppress the volunteers, who were only to exist at their own expense; (3) suspend the ballot and create a militia by a limited bounty; (4) provide a short training for a balloted force (46 Geo. III., c. 90). But these measures were only partially successful; and in 1808 Castlereagh made a great step forward by (1) authorising the enlistment of men from the militia into the regulars; (2) creating a permanent local militia (48 Geo. III., c. 111) with a training of twenty-eight days, and forbidding substitutes or bounties to the balloted men. This local militia was supplemental to the regular militia, and was the basis of a national force for home defence resting on a national liability to service. Had it been extended and completely enforced it would have brought about in time a universal training in arms for the whole male population. As it was, with the consolidation of the Militia Acts (52 Geo. III., c. 58) the nation after 1809 provided for the war on these lines: voluntary enlistment for the regular army, supplemented by continuous drafts from the regular militia; the regular militia embodied under the amended Act of 1757; the local militia utilised as a third line behind the regular militia; and the enlistment or hiring of foreign corps. It is noticeable that after 1807 the volunteers were gradually squeezed out of existence, and that after 1809 the popularity of the war and service in it steadily increased. In 1813 Castlereagh obtained powers to employ the militia in any part of the United Kingdom and the local militia outside their counties. But the strain of providing men for the regulars and the regular militia was making itself increasingly felt, while the partial application of the local militia system and the aversion in many parts of the country to the military measures were sources of weakness. The creation of an adequate military organisation, capable of expansion to meet a sudden or continuous demand, had not been effected by 1815, and after that date the nation abandoned the attempt with disastrous results experienced in 1854.

This note is mainly based on the wealth of material to be found in J. W. Fortescue, *History of the British Army*, vol. iv., pts. i. and ii., and the same writer's *The County Lieutenancies and the Army* (1803-14), which are indispensable to every student.

XI. NELSON AT NAPLES

The most recent discussion of the questions arising out of Nelson's conduct at Naples and the execution of Caracciolo will be found in Mr Gutteridge's volume, *Nelson and the Neapolitan Jacobins* (Navy Records Society, 1903), in which the documents are printed, and a complete bibliography of the literature and a critical introduction by the editor are provided. Mr. Gutteridge points out that the documentary evidence is not yet complete. The letters written by Lady Hamilton to Queen Caroline, between the

24th and the 30th June, and the *pièces justificatives* sent by Micheroux with the *Compendio*, have not yet come to light, though it seems probable that these and other documents are in existence, though not available to the historian. After reviewing the evidence at length Mr. Gutteridge (p. xcii) concludes that "there is not the slightest proof at present of any foul play on Nelson's part; and if the garrisons were deceived, it was only because Ruffo was willing that they should be". As regards Caracciolo, he sums up : "Technically, at all events, this sentence cannot be impeached, but the haste with which he was executed is more open to criticism . . . it must be judged by the standards and according to the exigencies of the times" (p. xciii). Mr. Gutteridge substantially concurs in the view taken by Captain Mahan, *Life of Nelson* (2nd ed., 1899), ch. xiii., and in his replies to Mr. Badham in the *English Historical Review* (July, 1899, and October, 1900). From the considered verdicts of Sir J. K. Laughton every student who knows what our naval history owes to his researches, unrivalled erudition, and discriminating judgment will dissent only with hesitation, but it is difficult to concur in his opinion : "on a careful examination it is difficult to see that Nelson could have acted otherwise. . . . He had no further responsibility than that of restoring and maintaining the civil power" (*Dict. Nat. Biogr.*, xl., art. "Nelson"). And still more strongly : "Nelson's conduct at this period, far from being judged blamable, disgraceful, 'a stain upon his memory,' will appear rather most honourable and meritorious" (*Nelson*, by J. K. Laughton, Macmillan & Co., 1895, p. 139). But it is only fair to remember that these opinions were expressed before much of the recent evidence in the Neapolitan archives and elsewhere was available. Nor is it possible on that evidence (still more so as the letters of Lady Hamilton alluded to above are not before us) to assent unreservedly to Sir J. K. Laughton's view : "it is well attested that with the annulling of the capitulation, and with the death of Caracciolo, Lady Hamilton had nothing to do" (*Dict. Nat. Biogr.* art. *cit.*). On Lady Hamilton's relations with Nelson see Laughton's article on "Emma, Lady Hamilton," in vol. xxiv. of *Dictionary of National Biography*. The student should also consult on the whole question *Archivio Storico per le provincie Napol.*, vol. xxiv., and the *Revue Historique*, September, 1903, and January, 1904 (articles by Dr. Hueffer).

XII. THE BATTLE OF TRAFALGAR

The brief account given in the text, pp. 417, 418, is practically that of the first edition of 1911 ; it rejected the traditional narrative generally accepted at that date, which represented Nelson as abandoning on October 21st, the famous memorandum of October 9th, and attacking the Franco-Spanish fleet in two columns parallel to each other and at right angles to the enemy line. In this traditional account no explanation was offered why Nelson should draw up on October 9th an elaborate memorandum, communicate it to his officers and then abandon it—for a tactical scheme, open to grave objections—on the day of battle—without any explicit counter orders to that effect.

The history of this "legend" is a characteristic example of how uncritical interpretations develop and become embedded in the text-books.   The myth apparently started with Southey, whose *Life of Nelson* (1813) had a great vogue, and whose description of the battle was supported by a picture, illustrating the attack, which was assumed to be evidence for the interpretation, whereas the picture simply translated into a diagram what the biographer had written.   Southey's narrative (and picture) were faithfully copied and reproduced for seventy years without question by numerous writers who never attempted to ascertain on what evidence, if any, Southey had based his narrative.   Writers, as usual, were too lazy or too ignorant of naval matters to consult the sources ; and "the legend" became history by dint of sheer repetition.   It was even embodied in the relief-plan shown at the United Service Institution—a further "proof" to the lay mind of its accuracy.   Even so "scientific" a naval historian as Admiral Mahan adopted it in his *Life of Nelson* (1897)—so potent is a tradition.   The decadence in the scientific study of naval strategy and tactics between 1820 and 1890 was no doubt largely responsible for the prevalence of the "Southey" interpretation : for if naval "authorities" accepted it without question, laymen cannot be blamed for concurring.   But with the rise of a new school of naval strategists, led by Admirals Sir Cyprian Bridge and Colomb, the original authorities for naval history, strategy and tactics as a whole, *i.e.* the documents and ships' logs in the archives of the Admiralty and the Public Record Office, began to be racked.   In 1905 and 1907 two writers attacked the traditional view and argued that Nelson, so far from throwing over on October 21st his memorandum of October 9th, had really carried it out—these were J. R. Thursfield (a layman) in his *Trafalgar and other Naval Studies* (1909), and E. Desbrière (a French Staff officer) in his *Trafalgar, La Campagne Maritime de* 1805 (Paris, 1907).   A hot controversy at once was kindled.   J. S. (later Sir Julian) Corbett, a naval historian of distinction, published in 1911 his *Campaign of Trafalgar* in which he rejected Thursfield's and Desbrière's view and concluded for "an unprecedented vertical attack in line a-head"—a slightly modified version of the Southey narrative.   Corbett's book was at once severely criticised by Capt. (now Admiral Sir) Mark Kerr in *The Nineteenth Century* for October, 1911, in which he agreed with Thursfield and Desbrière that the battle was fought in accordance with the memorandum of October 9th, "the Nelson touch," and not in two columns perpendicular to the enemy's fleet, "the worst possible tactical scheme that could have been devised".   Kerr's two main points were : (*a*) all the original evidence in the ships' logs, correctly plotted out, proved the case ; and (*b*) there was no evidence that Nelson issued either after October 9th or in the battle any order or signals countermanding the previous instructions given in the famous memorandum.   In a word, the fleet knew what Nelson intended to do when they met the enemy— and did it.   The controversy between the specialists became so strong that the Admiralty instructed a special Commission of Admirals Sir Cyprian Bridge and Sir Reginald Custance with Prof. Sir Charles Firth to examine the evidence afresh.   Their Report (an official Blue Book—Cd. 7210) issued in

1913 rejected "Southey" or Mahan's view without qualification and concluded that Nelson fought Trafalgar in accordance with the Memorandum of October 9th, and did not at the last moment abandon it for some other unspecified tactical scheme, for which there was no evidence and which would have been wholly contrary to all his tactical principles and insight. This Report, therefore, remains the conclusive authority for the strategic situation leading up to the battle and for the tactical course of the battle itself, and based on an exhaustive examination by experts of all the evidence available was illustrated by specially drawn diagrams to show exactly what happened and how. It confirmed (a small matter) my conclusion of two years previously (before Corbett and Kerr intervened) and definitively exploded the Southey "legend". More, it placed the famous Memorandum of October 9th in its correct light as the culmination of Nelson's genius and prolonged reflection on naval tactics. Trafalgar, in fact, justified his famous confidence in "the Nelson touch". But legends die very hard and since 1913 some books still repeat the unwarrantable libel on Nelson's genius, which Southey's narrative really implies. It is worth noting that as early as 1895 in his admirable short *Life of Nelson*, which remains the best short life of Nelson in print, that accomplished naval scholar and historian Sir J. K. Laughton simply stated that, apart from unimportant details, the Memorandum was carried out on October 21st (p. 215); but Laughton's verdict was ignored—or rather the importance of his verdict (quietly dismissing without discussion the traditional Southey view) was completely missed or misunderstood.

Those who simply want to have a general idea of the *Campaign* of Trafalgar should read Corbett, *op. cit.*, and replace his account of the battle by the Admiralty Report, referred to above. Mahan's *Life* remains still the standard large-scale authority. A short biography by Sir G. Aston (Benn's Sixpenny Series) is well worth reading. The specialist literature is indicated in the Bibliography, pp. 528-29.

XIII. CANNING, TILSIT AND THE EXPEDITION TO COPEN-HAGEN

The information on which Canning and the Cabinet acted in sending the expedition to Copenhagen, and the sources from which the information was derived, have recently been investigated in great detail. (The student should consult the following: Stapleton, *Canning and His Times*, 123-38 ; J. H. Rose, *Napoleonic Studies*, 133-56 ; *Royal Historical Society's Transactions.* 1906 ; Bagot, *Canning and His Friends*, i., 232 *et seq.*; *The Life of Sir R. Wilson*, ii., 283 ; *Diaries and Letters of Sir G. Jackson*, ii., 162 *et seq.*; Malmesbury, *Letters and Diary*, 4, 391 ; *Edinburgh Review*, April, 1906 (internal evidence clearly points to Dr. J. H. Rose as the author) ; the *Athenæum*, Sept. 27th, 1902). A brief summary can only be attempted here. Napoleon met the Tsar on the famous raft on the Niemen on June 24th, 1807. The Treaty of Tilsit was signed on July 7th. On July 16th Canning had sent instructions to Brooke Taylor at Copenhagen telling him to reassure the Danish Minister that the presence of the British fleet in the Baltic was not intended as a menace to Denmark. On the same day important despatches from Mackenzie (of June 23rd), from Garlike (of June 26th), and from Garlike (of July 4th) reached the Foreign Office, the purport of which was that Napoleon had come to terms with the Tsar. On July 22nd, Canning wrote "most secret" to Brooke Taylor: "Intelligence reached me yesterday (*i.e.* July 21st), *directly from Tilsit*, that at an interview between the Emperor of Russia and Bonaparte on the 24th and 25th of last month the latter brought forward a proposal for a maritime league against Great Britain, to which the accession of Denmark was represented by Bonaparte to be as certain as it was essential". On July 28th the expedition under Gambier, with the ultimatum to Denmark, drawn up on the same day and conveyed by Jackson, set out. It is clear that (1) between July 16th and July 22nd the Cabinet, inspired by the Foreign Secretary, came to a momentous decision, based on important information; (2) on July 22nd, Canning did not know of the existence of a treaty. On August 4th he was inquiring what the terms of the treaty were, whether there were secret articles, etc. On December 4th he wrote: "The Peace of Tilsit is come out". Canning, therefore, clearly acted, not on a betrayal of the specific terms of the Treaty, but on general information from some person who, in Stapleton's words, "gave such proofs of the accuracy of his intelligence as left no doubt of its truth in Mr. Canning's mind". Dr. Rose has shown that no despatches from the Baltic States were received at the Foreign Office on July 21st. He has also proved from the Admiralty Records that on July 18th there was "an order of phenomenal importance, directing the immediate preparations of no fewer than fifty-one warships for 'a particular service' under Admiral Gambier"; and that on the same day "31 warships at sea were assigned to the same duty," and that July 21st-25th brought no new developments. Castlereagh stated (*Hansard* for 1808, p. 169) that July 19th was the day on which "Ministers took his Majesty's pleasure as to the propriety of the expedition;" and that July 18th was a day of strain for the Admiralty is confirmed from other evidence (*Edin. Rev., art. cit.*, p. 356). It is also confirmed by remarkable evidence in a contemporary MS. by Jackson, peremptorily summoned to the Foreign Office on July 18th to undertake a mission, "*the object*" of which "*was to get possession of the Danish fleet*". Hence the now almost certain conclusion that the despatches received on July 16th prompted the new and momentous departure. That it was not Mackenzie who came direct from Memel who orally conveyed the information on which Canning first acted is made certain by (*a*) the facts cited above; (*b*) the proof in the *Athenæum* (*art. cit.*) that Mackenzie did not arrive with his despatches until July 23rd. Canning's phrase in his letter of July 22nd that his information "came direct from Tilsit" and reached him "yesterday" (July 21st) has raised many theories that the information was betrayed from a foreign source, *e.g.* Bennigsen or Talleyrand, or from a British agent whom long-established tradition (Stapleton's story) asserted "was concealed behind a curtain of the tent, and was a secret witness of that most curious conversation". The "man on (or under) the raft" figures in the romance of diplomacy much as the famous "No. 101" who betrayed the Family Compact of 1733 and other Bourbon secrets. Mr. Oscar Browning (*Eng. Hist. Rev.*, Jan., 1902) stated that he had been assured by General R. Mackenzie that his grandfather was concealed on the raft at Tilsit and brought the news to London. Captain Bagot (*George Canning*, p. 233) explicitly states "that the Secret Service Accounts for 1807-9," in his possession, show "during that time an expenditure of some £80,000, but throw no light on the supposition of any one who was at Tilsit getting a large reward". And Canning himself (*Hansard* for 1808, p. 66) asserted in the House of Commons "that this information came from a British Minister". The difficulties of identifying the supposed informer are fully discussed in the authorities cited. On the whole it seems safe to conclude that : (1) the despatches received on July 16th were the basis of the Cabinet's decision ; (2) that the information at the Cabinet's disposal was serious but very meagre ; (3) Canning, with brilliant intuition, surmised the nature and scope of Napoleon's plans and alliance with the Tsar and determined to frustrate them at all costs ; (4) every piece of information subsequent to July 16th confirmed the accuracy of the hypothesis and the gravity of the impending crisis. The evidence was limited and circumstantial but cumulative ; (5) " Portugal never entered into Canning's calculations in the months June-July, 1807 " (Rose). It is now beyond question that Canning's guess as to Napoleon's plans was correct. The secret articles of the Treaty of Tilsit and the mass of evidence now available for their interpretation leave no doubt on this point. Whether the Cabinet was justified in anticipating Napoleon by despatching the expedition and coercing Denmark is a wholly different question. The arguments for and against Ministerial policy are fully stated in the great debate on January 21st, 1808 (see *Hansard*, " Parl. Debates," for that year).

Dr. Holland Rose (*Cambridge Hist. of Foreign Policy*, i., 360 *et seq.*), thinks that " the secrets leaked out through Bennigsen or some other malcontent officer ". He dismisses, and I concur, as " fantastic " the picturesque story of a British spy concealed on the raft. How such a spy got there, heard the conversation of Napoleon and Alexander and got away in time to be in London or convey his information by July 16th no one has ever explained.

Canning, in fact, was in the same position as Chatham in 1761 (see App. V., p. 494). He had certain information (from Memel, Copenhagen and Altona) which, pieced together, pointed to a certain conclusion. Like Chatham in 1761 he was correct in his interpretation of the evidence at his disposal ; unlike Chatham, he was in a position to have decisive action based on his conclusion.

XIV. THE CABINET

The origin and development of the Cabinet have been the subject of specialist articles, based on MS. material, *e.g. Eng. Hist. Review*, Oct., 1912, by Dr. H. V. Temperley ; Jan. and April, 1914, by Sir W. R. Anson ; Prof. E. R. Turner, April, 1917 and April, 1923 ; July, 1919, by R. R. Sedgwick, and Jan., 1922, by G. Davies; *American Hist. Review*, July and Oct., 1913, by Prof. E. R. Turner.   The detail in these articles is naturally considerable, and the writers are not always in agreement as to the interpretation.   Careful study of the material sifted and collected leaves me with certain conclusions, which do not, however, substantially modify the text, pp. 183-90: (1) The Cabinet did not originate in any committee or group of committees of the legal organ, the Privy Council; and that while it is easy to confuse known committees with the nascent Cabinet, and natural to ascribe parentage to the legal organ, more careful analysis separates the Cabinet protoplasm from any of the specific committees which can be traced and marked off as definite *ad hoc* bodies; (2) contemporary statesmen and ministers from whose letters, diaries, memoranda, etc., copious references are available were not always precise in their wording and did not anticipate the modern historian's diligence, interest and desire to arrange an ordered evolution in scientifically defined divisions and functions; like primitive man, who did not live his life merely to oblige a modern scientific anthropologist, so the men who worked the government machine between 1690 and 1783 were more concerned with getting their work done than in seeing that the various organs through which they administered would subsequently fit into a logical genealogical tree; and as Stubbs pointed out of the working of the *Curia Regis* the same men habitually met each other at different times in different rooms or places and did not always ask " Are we a committee, and if so, of what"? or " Are we *a* Cabinet, or *the* Cabinet, and "are we all here who ought to be here, and if not, who is away and if so, why"?   Most historians (Anson and Bryce were notable exceptions) have never had to carry on the King's business or make policy or correlate the position of a Privy Councillor with the position of a Minister of State and membership either in the House of Lords or House of Commons, and therefore do not ask, "How are or can things be done"? Maitland warned us repeatedly that primitive man was not simple or logical; simplicity and logic are the virtues (or vices) of civilisation and that it is, therefore, unhistorical to force simplicity on what was, in the nature of things, neither simple nor logical.   That important decisions will be taken by a group of important persons, holding office or perhaps merely Privy Councillors, meeting by accident or design, happened alike in the days of Tutankhamen, Queen Anne and King George V.; but the meeting of an important group does not make a Cabinet, even if all its members are "Cabinet Councillors," any more than a dinner party of Cabinet Ministers makes a meeting of the Cabinet, even if the decisions taken after dinner are far more important than those taken at the subsequent meeting of " His Majesty's confidential servants"; (3) by 1714 there was in existence a "Cabinet," *i.e.* a group of ministers who habitually, but not regularly, met, but not in the Sovereign's presence, to decide policy, much of whose business probably was prepared for it by one or more properly constituted committees of the Privy Council, and which tendered advice to the Sovereign because roughly it represented the party with a majority in the House of Commons; which advice was ratified, so far as was required either by law or for executive action, by the Privy Council; (4) From 1714-60 we find this

Cabinet recognised, not in the formal law or custom of the Constitution, but by all who were at the centre, and developing into two bodies—a larger group of all the chief ministers and officers—and a smaller, known as the " conciliabulum," and these can be distinguished as the "Outer" or "Inner," or as the "nominal" and "efficient" Cabinet. Efficiency, convenience, personality decided that the real power lay with the " Inner" Cabinet, which might vary from ten to five or six persons. Two points arise here : (a) When did this effective distinction begin? No exact date can be given at present but while some writers pronounce for Henry Pelham's system, i.e., from 1744 onwards, others see clear evidence of its existence in the later years of Walpole's régime. The interest in a specific date is antiquarian rather than important. But it seems clear that " The Inner" Cabinet was recognised and working by 1754 ; (b) this " Inner" Cabinet must not be identified with a group of three or four all-important persons. A real Cabinet is not those who make important decisions but that body of the King's confidential servants who habitually tender advice as a Cabinet to the Sovereign, which advice, so long as they are ministers, he is practically obliged to accept ; (5) By 1760 the parentage of the modern Cabinet is clear—it is the " Conciliabulum". George III.'s attempts to break it, to fuse "Outer" and " Inner," to work a system of " double Cabinets " (as stated by Burke), to get back to departmental government with an efficient King as the real Prime Minister, and to extirpate collective responsibility, etc., etc., belong to general constitutional history, and the Cabinet by 1784 emerged all the stronger and more definite from these royal efforts and failures.

Briefly, then, four stages can be distinguished : (1) The gradual dissolution of government by the Crown in (Privy) Council ; (2) the slow formation of a substitutive organ, which comes to be called the Cabinet, in the process of dissolution ; (3) the articulation of this organ, which develops a structure necessary for its function ; and (4) the co-ordination of structure and function into the organ called the "Cabinet," which can then become the central instrument in a system of Parliamentary Government, unique because it has created the Cabinet and the Cabinet has created it.

The essence of the whole evolution is really contained in a memorable sentence of Queen Victoria : " I expect my Ministers to recommend to me a policy or measures which they can explain, defend and carry in the House of Commons". The Cabinet originated and grew because the growth of the power of the House of Commons required a group of confidential servants of the Crown who could explain, defend and carry the advice tendered to the Sovereign.

Dr. Temperley (The Times, Dec. 18th, 1928) points out that there is no proved instance of George I. attending the Cabinet; but that there is clear evidence that George II., as Prince of Wales and Regent, attended, probably regularly, because he could speak English and his father could not; that Queen Caroline, as Regent, attended in 1729 and 1735, and that George II. attended (e g. on Dec. 6th, 1745) and on two other occasions (perhaps more. if the records were complete).

Some very interesting evidence as to the relations of the Cabinet with George III. will be found in *Report on MSS. in Various Collections* (Hist. MS. Commission), vol. vi., 1909; *MSS. of Captain H. V. Knox.* The King's idea of the departmental system is succinctly stated by Lord Hillsborough (p. 263): "His (Hillsborough's) object was to fall in with what he knew to be the King's plan, that each of his Ministers should hold of him and not of one another or of the first". It is a commonplace of our constitutional text-books that after 1714 the Crown ceased to attend or preside over meetings of the Cabinet. Yet we find two specific instances of a Cabinet meeting summoned by the King and presided over by him. The language used in Knox's memorandum makes it perfectly clear that these meetings were not meetings of the Privy Council. The first is on June 21st, 1779 (p. 263): "This morning all the members of the Cabinet were summoned by a message in the King's own handwriting to meet him at the Queen's House at one o'clock. They assembled accordingly. He desired them to walk into the library. He sat down at the head of his library table, and desired, for the first time since he became King, all the Ministers to sit down. He then began by saying Lord North had desired to know why they were summoned, but he had not thought fit to tell him, as he meant to tell it to them all together." George III. then made a "discourse" which "took up near an hour in delivering". The second occasion was on January 19th, 1781 (p. 272): "Despatches," writes Knox, "having come from Sir James Harris giving an account of a conversation with the Empress on the subject of the Armed Neutrality . . . the King summoned Ministers to the Queen's House on the 19th, when, being come, he ordered them to be seated round a table, himself at the head, opened the business, and desired their opinions separately. One asked who His Majesty would choose to speak first. The King said he should not point to any one. Lord Sandwich . . . said the usual way [was] for the youngest to begin, which being acquiesced in, Lord North . . . began without rising . . .". That this was a meeting of the Cabinet may be inferred from (*a*) the absence of the Privy Council officials; (*b*) the ignorance of the Ministers present as to the procedure to be followed if the King were present.

Two further quotations are instructive : When Burgoyne's failure at Saratoga "threatened to come under discussion," Thurlow, then Attorney-General, asked Knox for information. Knox showed him "*a précis* of the whole correspondence of the preceding year". Thurlow remarked : "Why, this is the very thing I wanted . . . pray, do Ministers know of this?" "Yes, sir, they have all had copies of it." "Then, by God," said Thurlow, "they have never read it, for there is not one of them knows a tittle of the matter" (p. 270). In 1782 Lord North desired to get rid of Lord George Germain, "because of his avowed principle of resisting treaty with America upon any footing but preservation of sovereignty. 'If you mean by his going out,' said the King, 'to relinquish that principle, you must make other removes.' 'No,' replies Lord North, 'for no one else has declared that principle.' 'Yes,' says the King, 'you must go further; you must remove ME'" (p. 276).

XV. LORD GEORGE GERMAIN, SIR W. HOWE, AND GENERAL BURGOYNE

That Burgoyne's disaster at Saratoga was due to carelessness on the part of Lord George Germain in transmitting the orders for a strict co-operation between Sir W. Howe and General Burgoyne is asserted in the MS. autobiography of Shelburne (Fitzmaurice, *Life of Shelburne*, i., 358). Shelburne probably derived his information from William Knox, Under-Secretary for the Colonies from 1770-82 ; and a comparison of the passage in the *Knox MSS.* (Hist. MSS. Comm. Repts., vol. vi. (1909), p. 277) shows that Shelburne's statement is a general paraphrase of Knox's detailed memorandum. Knox explicitly asserts that Germain would not wait to write " to Howe to acquaint him with the plan or what was expected of him in consequence " ; that D'Oyly wrote, " but he neither showed it to me nor gave a copy of it for the office, and if Howe had not acknowledged the receipt of it, with the copy of the instructions to Burgoyne, we could not have proved that he ever saw them ". It is clear that Burgoyne regarded his instructions as positive, and that he expected to have the co-operation of Howe. He wrote to Germain on July 30th : " I have spared no pains to open a correspondence with Sir W. Howe. . . . I am in total ignorance of the situation or intentions of that general " (*Life of Burgoyne* by E. B. de Fonblanque, p. 270) ; and again on August 20th " my orders being positive to 'force a junction with Sir W. Howe' " (*op. cit.*, p. 275). And the recently published *Stopford-Sackville MSS.* (Hist. MSS. Comm. Repts., vol. ii. (1910)) seem to confirm the inference that Germain was responsible for Howe's failure to understand the importance of co-operation by himself, if Burgoyne's operations were to be successful. On April 2nd, Howe wrote to Sir Guy Carleton (*op. cit.*, p. 65) that he would be able to offer very small assistance to a force advancing from Ticonderoga, " as I shall probably be in Pennsylvania ". " The officer in command therefore must pursue such measures as may from circumstances be judged most conducive." On May 18th Germain wrote to Howe : " As you must from your situation and military skill be a competent judge of the propriety of every plan, his Majesty does not hesitate to approve the alterations which you propose (*i.e.* the march into Pennsylvania) trusting, however, that, whatever you may meditate, it will be executed in time for you to co-operate with the army ordered to proceed from Canada and put itself under your command " (*op. cit.*, p. 67). This letter was received by Howe on his passage, August 16th, up Chesapeake Bay. Burgoyne had taken Ticonderoga on July 6th, and on August 16th was endeavouring to reach the Hudson River, where he had been led to expect Howe had been ordered to co-operate with him from Albany. His letters cited above show that he was anxiously expecting news from Howe, whose movements, unknown to Burgoyne but sanctioned by Germain, made a junction impossible. That Howe interpreted Germain's letter, not unreasonably, in the sense of giving him complete discretionary powers is shown in his letter to Germain of October 22nd after the

33

disaster. "I was surprised," he writes, "to find the General's (Burgoyne's) declaration in his message to Sir H. Clinton by Captain Campbell 'that he would not have given up his communications with Ticonderoga had he not expected a co-operating army at Albany,' since in my letter to Sir Guy Carleton, a copy of which was transmitted to your lordship in my despatch of 2nd April, 1777, no. 47, and of which his Majesty was pleased to approve, I positively mentioned that no direct assistance could be given by the southern army. This letter I was assured was received by Sir Guy Carleton and carried by him to Montreal before General Burgoyne's departure from thence" (*op. cit.*, p. 81). Germain, in short, ordered Burgoyne to carry out operations, of which a junction with and by Howe was an essential part, but failed to order Howe to make the junction, or to acquaint him clearly with the character and scheme of the parts assigned to Burgoyne and himself. The vague and confusing discretionary authority allowed to Howe and the approval of the stroke on Pennsylvania which made co-operation impossible permitted Howe to infer that the junction with Burgoyne was a matter of "trust" not an explicit command. Knox's memorandum, the accuracy of which may be accepted, shows how Germain in a matter of vital importance preferred not to "keep his horses waiting in the street" and himself late for a country visit, rather than spend half an hour in writing an authoritative letter to the commander-in-chief acquainting him with the plan. "There certainly," writes Knox, "was a weak place in Lord Sackville's defence, which was the want of an official communication to Howe of the plan and Burgoyne's instructions, with order for his co-operation, of which I was not only innocent, but it was owing to my interference that Howe had any knowledge of the business" (*Knox MSS.*, p. 277). Nor is it surprising that subsequently the Secretary of State endeavoured in every way to burke inquiry; he refused to grant a court martial of investigation to Burgoyne; and when (in 1778) a Committee of the House of Commons examined the affair, a sudden prorogation of Parliament prevented it from reporting its verdict, which would probably have been very adverse to Germain, or from making public the evidence. Burgoyne published in 1780 a vindication of his conduct (*State of the Expedition to Canada*), but the complete revelation of Germain's criminal carelessness was reserved for Knox. Thurlow's coarse comment is not amiss. "So, says he (Thurlow), because one damned blockhead did a foolish thing, the other blockhead must follow his example" (*Knox MSS.*, p. 271).

Since writing the above I observe that Professor Egerton has (*Eng. Hist. Rev.*, Oct., 1910), drawn attention to the passages in the *Stopford-Sackville MSS.* cited above.

XVI. BYNG AND THE LOSS OF MINORCA

Byng's failure and the loss of Minorca raise two quite distinct issues: (1) The strategical dispositions of the Admiralty and the measures of the Government: (2) Byng's personal conduct, trial and execution. A recent book, *Admiral Byng and the Loss of Minorca* by B. Tunstall (1928), reopens both issues.

The report of the court martial was published by the Admiralty in 1757 ; the relevant original document on the strategical and political issues (not on the trial itself) were edited for the *Navy Records Society*, vol. 42 (1913), by Capt. (now Vice-Admiral Sir) H. W. Richmond, a high expert authority. The following points are worth noting on both issues.

(1) Sir H. W. Richmond conclusively shows that the dispositions taken were either inadequate or faulty, or too late. Minorca could have been saved had the right dispositions been made in time : the old, old story in fact ; (2) the fall of Minorca caused great excitement and indignation at home. Byng was recalled, Hawke was sent out to replace him, and the court martial and execution followed. Every student who examines the evidence will concur in Sir H. W. Richmond's conclusion on issue no. (1) : " Byng was made the scapegoat to cover the sins of omission of the Administration whose blunders he had failed to retrieve " ; (3) Such a conclusion does not necessarily exculpate Byng from "negligence". Clearly, he was not the man for a difficult job. "He had resigned himself," says Sir H. W. Richmond, "to the loss of Minorca before ever his anchor was off the bottom of Gibraltar Bay." His action off Minorca was badly handled and he found himself 600 miles from his base (Gibraltar) with the French fleet less damaged than his own, operating from their advanced bases, near at hand. The Council of War on the flagship in answer to Byng's " leading questions" endorsed the withdrawal. Hawke or Nelson would not, I am convinced, have withdrawn, but then Hawke or Nelson would not have fought the indecisive and badly handled action which placed Byng in his dilemma ! (4) I can see no evidence that Byng did not have a perfectly fair trial—a much fairer trial than laymen got in a criminal court in the eighteenth century ; (5) Byng was not tried, as has constantly been stated and repeated, for "an error of judgment" but under Art. 13 of the Articles of War for having failed to do his utmost to carry out his instructions "through cowardice, negligence or disaffection". The Court acquitted him of cowardice or disaffection but found him guilty of "negligence". Having found him guilty, the Court had no discretionary power as to the penalty. The Articles of War had been revised after 1748 to meet abuses revealed in the war of 1739-48 and had removed from a court martial under this Article and charge a discretionary power hitherto allowed. Byng did not plead "an error of judgment" but that he had done the utmost possible ; the Court decided that he had not. Unless, therefore, we conclude that the Court was wrong (*i.e.* decided against the weight of the evidence) or was influenced by political pressure, its verdict must be accepted. The officers who composed it presumably could judge technical questions and were aware that each one of them might, if in command, subsequently be arraigned on a similar charge under Article 13. Of political pressure on the court martial I can find no evidence.

Ought George II. to have exercised his prerogative and commuted the sentence? This is a wholly different matter. Severe pressure was exerted both ways. The King refused to intervene and the sentence was carried out.

Boscawen and the naval disciplinarians in particular are charged with insisting on Byng being shot. Boscawen had signed the original Instructions, he was Commander-in-Chief at Portsmouth and he signed readily enough the order for execution on March 14th, 1757. "Old Dreadnought," "Wry-necked Dick," as Boscawen was called, was no doubt a rather brutal, rough and tyrannical "Sea-dog"; but he was a born and competent fighter and well acquainted with the dry-rot in the higher command; he knew Byng's record as of a man "prone to find difficulties" and that (*e.g.* in 1747 on the coast of Provence) he "neglected" (or "funked") going through with a difficult job. He had probably convinced himself that the country and the Navy in 1757 had no use for "Byng's" and that a very terrible lesson was necessary to convince the Navy of that fact. Boscawen would probably have signed with still greater pleasure an order to put some of the "politicians" alongside of Byng and in front of the firing party on the deck of *The Monarque* on March 14th, 1757. Whether he was inspired by personal bias against Byng I do not know—nor does anyone else to-day. But the layman must remember that "negligence" in the higher command in War is wholly different from "negligence" in civil life, and that 1739-48 had revealed unpleasant episodes. Boscawen, I infer, would not have dissented from Voltaire's famous comment —that the execution was carried out "to encourage"—and it certainly had that effect. The years 1757-63 are very different from 1739-48. Boscawen's character is exemplified by the (legendary) story. "Sir," asked the night officer of the watch in alarm, "there are two large French vessels bearing down on us. What are we to do?" Boscawen had tumbled up on deck in his night-shirt. "Do?" he replied. "Do? damn 'em! Fight 'em!"

Byng was unfortunate in being the first officer to be tried under the Revised Articles of War. He was the wrong man for the Minorca job; and he paid a terrible penalty for being that wrong man. Probably most students would agree that had George II. commuted the death-sentence and dismissed Byng, "the Crown having no further use for his services," substantial justice would have been done. But unquestionably ministers were rightly afraid that, if Byng was not shot, a lamp post and a halter might have been used by the mob in Whitehall on some prominent civilian. In addition to the authorities cited above consult articles on Byng and Boscawen (*Dict. Nat. Biog.*, by a high naval authority, Sir J. K. Laughton).

XVII. JOHN WILKES

A new biography of Wilkes by H. Bleackley (1917), based largely on the copious MS. material in the British Museum and elsewhere, collects and restates the facts of his life and gives a detailed account of the political struggles between 1762 and 1780 in which Wilkes was engaged, as well as of the personal and unedifying vicissitudes through which this impenitent libertine passed.

It is difficult to understand why Mr. Bleackley dismisses (p. 139) the issue of General Warrants so summarily and with the astonishing reason: "Since a police constable enjoys the same power of arbitrary arrest as was then exercised by a Secretary of State," which would surprise Lord Camden's successor Lord Hewart to-day as much as it would have surprised Lord Camden himself. Mr. Bleackley points out that there is more to be said for Lord Sandwich than is generally allowed : Sandwich was not responsible for securing the copy of "The Essay on Woman," which was managed by Philip Webb, the Solicitor to the Treasury, and on becoming Secretary of State in Egremont's place endeavoured to get the unsavoury business patched up, but failed because Wilkes refused all terms of compromise. Sandwich also discovered a ribald lampoon on himself, in Wilkes' handwriting, which he considered dissolved the previous friendship. The question whether Wilkes was really the author of "The Essay on Woman" and not one of his former Medmenham "brothers" Thomas Potter (a son of the Archbishop of Canterbury and a well known social and political figure of his day) was answered in the negative by C. W. Dilke (*Papers of a Critic*, ii., 229-79) and Potter's sole authorship was accepted by Mr. Rigg (art. in *Dict. Nat. Biog.* on Wilkes). The problem was re-examined by E. R. Watson, *Notes and Queries*, 11th Series, ix., 121 *et seq.*, who on convincing evidence proves that the real poem (not the version printed and *published* in Wilkes' life-time, which is unquestionably spurious), of which there is a copy in the Dyce Library at the Victoria and Albert Museum, was probably written by Potter and Wilkes in collaboration and brought up to date by Wilkes later. Potter, who died in 1759, could not make allusions subsequent to that year. Mr. Bleackley accepts Mr. Watson's conclusions. On the constitutional issue raised by No. 45 of *The North Briton* it is worth noting that the opening sentence runs: "The King's speech has always been considered by the Legislature, and by the public at large, as the speech of the minister". To George III. this was doubly offensive : it asserted a doctrine of ministerial responsibility which he wished to extirpate ; and it was a personal attack on himself by a person, notoriously immoral—for the article asserted that "the honour of the Crown was sunk even to prostitution".

The articles, in fact, illustrated Wilkes' witty reply to the question what are the limits on the liberty of the Press? "That is precisely what I am trying to find out".

XVIII. JAMES COOK

The standard life is by J. C. Kitson (1907), and is based on a critical study of the original sources, particularly the documents and official records at the Admiralty. It corrects many mistakes and misinterpretations in the popular lives. Some interesting and personal data, collected in Yorkshire and elsewhere by Sir Walter Besant, are embodied in his short *Life* (English Men of Action Series).

James Cook's remarkable career in rising from a position before the mast to high commissioned rank in the Royal Navy—a very exceptional fact in the eighteenth century—and his scientific attainments give him, by universal consent, the first place amongst the explorers by sea, which can best be appreciated by comparing a map of the Pacific in 1760 with the map as he left it in 1780. For if one man brought the Pacific into the world politics of the nineteenth century, that man was James Cook.

The famous voyages that began in 1768 had as much a political as a scientific object. The Secret Instructions of the Admiralty of July 30th, 1768, make clear that the observation of the transit of Venus at Tahiti (discovered and annexed by Wallis, 1766-67) was not the chief object of the voyage, but a determination to counter the Spanish occupation and fortification of the Island of Juan Fernandez by further British annexations and to clear up the mystery of the alleged Southern Continent, which many held might be a new mineral Eldorado. Cook, therefore, was instructed to secure for Great Britain prior rights and the valuable ports. The Admiralty were influenced by the traditional fear that in 1768 the Spaniards aimed at reviving the policy of Spain in the sixteenth and seventeenth century and at sealing up the Pacific as an exclusively Spanish sea.

The Secret Instructions were repeated and extended (June 25th) in 1772— *i.e.* to complete the exploration of Antarctica (now that his previous voyage had proved that Tasmania and New Zealand, annexed to Great Britain, were great islands separated from the Southern Continent) and to discover a passage from the North Pacific to the North Atlantic. Cook's last voyages demonstrated the true character of the Antarctic Continent (*i.e.* there were no natives and no areas of fabled mineral or other wealth but only impenetrable ice) and the impossibility of finding a navigable passage to the West of Alaska via the Behring Straits owing, again, to the currents and ice-flow. But the result of his push northwards was the charting of the coast of " British Columbia " and the establishment of a fur-trading station in " King George's Sound " at Nootka. It was the Spanish attack on this and the desire to remove the British Settlement and assert a complete Spanish sovereignty which led to the conflict with Spain, briefly described on pp. 326-27, and to the recognition of the British right to settle, navigate, fish and trade on the coasts and in the seas to the north of the Spanish dominions in South America and Mexico. The modern Province of British Columbia in the Dominion o. Canada really owes its origin to James Cook. And it was Cook's exploration, discoveries and annexations, which by exploding the myth of a great Southern Continent which might be another America, made the Pacific a free sea and concentrated European trade and colonisation on the great islands—Australia, Tasmania, New Zealand—and on the northern half of the Ocean with its western littoral of the United States and of Canada. These discoveries were bound to be made in time (Bougainville was at work for France) ; but it was important that they should be made by a British sailor and scientist between 1769 and 1790. Cook's seamanship, iron will and scientific attainments (seen in his conquest of scurvy and the accuracy of his charts and observations) combined to produce one of the great figures of the eighteenth century—well worthy of the celebration of the bicentenary of his birth in 1928. Cook, in short, at sea ranks with David Livingstone on land in bringing, by exploration, a wholly new world into the sphere of European and world-politics.

XIX. THE INDUSTRIAL REVOLUTION

In the last twenty years no field of the eighteenth century has been more fruitfully or more industriously explored by able economists, economic historians and sociologists than "The Industrial Revolution". It is impossible here to summarise adequately or fairly the results of this extensive and intensive investigation. "The House was still sitting while we went to Press"; and many of these results belong not so much to general or political history as to the special sphere of economics, economic history proper, and the history of particular industries. Some broad comments, however, will be helpful.

1. The phrase "Industrial Revolution" was invented by Arnold Toynbee in 1882 and has so far held the field; but the modern economic historian is more and more disposed to question its accuracy, on the ground that (a) it covers a period far too long to justify a single label, e.g. from some date about 1740 to some date about 1850, and (b) that "Revolution" is a misleading term for describing a complicated series of forces, processes and discoveries which, unlike political or constitutional "revolutions," worked very slowly, very gradually created a new economic organisation, and never at any time culminated in a single decisive crisis or cataclysm. Whether the economic historians will succeed in replacing the title "Industrial Revolution" by some such phrase as "The Transition of Industrialism" ("transition" itself implying more than a century :, remains to be seen; but so long as students and teachers clearly understand that "The Industrial Revolution" was industrial but not a revolution, the phrase will be as useful and as accurate as that of "The Augustan Age of Anne" (in literature) which was not "Augustan" and was not limited to Queen Anne's reign from 1702 to 1714.

2. "The Industrial Revolution" covers a combination of inter-related but separable phases and factors, e.g., the origins in the pre-existing economic organisation, the growth, migration and distribution of population, the specific features of change in industry, particularly in manufacture, the "great inventions" and the great inventors, the changes in transport and communications, the concurrent "Enclosure" movement, the principles and new sciences of economics, currency and finance, wages and the movement in prices, the rise of a new capitalism and of an industrial proletariat and the origins of "labour organisations," the Poor Law, old and new, and the policy and principles of central and local government. On each and all of these separate "research" work has been done and is still proceeding.

3. Modern research tends to push the origins of the new Industrialism farther and farther back and the terminus in the nineteenth century farther and farther forward—to decline, in a word, to fence off "The Industrial Revolution" within precise and agreed chronological dates in the eighteenth century.

4. Less emphasis is placed on the *decisive* character of the "great inventions," or, more accurately, the desire is to limit their revolutionary effect to specific industries. The social, as distinct from the individualist, aspects of invention are stressed.

But, broadly, two essential points seem to remain more and more true:

(1) the creation of the factory system with all that it involved; and (2) if a qualitative and a quantitative comparison be made between Great Britain in 1750 and Great Britain in 1815 (beyond which my book does not go) and making all allowance for light and shade, differences of development in different areas and different industries, a new Great Britain had come into existence. The *totality* of the changes, measured against the preceding or succeeding definable epochs, amounted to a "revolution". The Great Britain of 1750 could not have fought successfully Revolutionary and Napoleonic France; and "The Industrial Revolution," or whatever term we agree to use, made this decisive difference. And if we could sum up this difference by a scientific picture of Great Britain in 1816 compared with a similar picture in 1749 the *"revolutionary"* character of the change would be convincingly revealed. For the student of political history too much emphasis on detail or minute and qualifying conclusions may really mislead either by concealing or by minimising the gravity, extent and consequences of a totality of change. What the student needs to appreciate is first the stages through which the "transition" passed, then the forces at work and the broad results of the "transition" when it has been accomplished. For help in the literature of the subject consult *The Industrial Revolution*, 1750-1850 (a select Bibliography) by Eileen Power (published by The Economic History Society) and two "Historical Revisions" in *History* for July, 1927, and July, 1929, with their full references. The most helpful approach seems to me to start in reading Mantoux' classical work, *La Revolution Industrielle*, and follow it up by Prof. Clapham's *Economic History of Modern Britain*, J. L. and B. Hammond's *The Rise of Modern Industry*, and L. Moffitt, *England on the Eve of the Industrial Revolution*. After that, teacher or student can pursue the literature so fully described in Dr. Eileen Power's valuable Bibliography, referred to above, according to taste and needs.

XX. THE WAR OF AMERICAN INDEPENDENCE

Since 1911 the historical literature on the British Empire, the American Colonies, the causes of the American Revolution and the conduct of the war has steadily increased in volume and in the intensive study of detail. So far as I have been able to master this literature, the results have not materially modified the statements in the text. At the end of this note I select a few books that will help, I hope, the reader to appreciate the trend of modern research and of thought. British writers to-day are now fairly well agreed to accept Mr. Zimmern's distinction of three (in time) British Empires, *viz.*: (1) The old colonial empire from the end of the sixteenth century down to 1783; (2) The middle empire from 1783 to 1926; and (3) "The third British Empire" (see A. E. Zimmern's book with that title) which can be roughly dated from the epoch-making conclusions embodied in the decisions of the Imperial Conference of that year. On the old colonial empire of the eighteenth century American scholars naturally have been more, though not exclusively, interested in the history of the American colonies, British scholars in the colonial or imperial system as a whole; but American historical scholarship has been singularly fruitful and decisive in its criticism of the traditional American interpretation, as set out *e.g.* in Bancroft's *History of the United States*, in its indictment of the "legends" embalmed in the ordinary textbooks used in American schools, and in writing textbooks more in accordance with historical accuracy and impartial interpretation—not without incurring from compatriots savage criticism and denunciation of their unpatriotic "treason" against "the Fathers of the Revolution". Hagiology is always more popular than true history—alike in monarchies and republics. British students are apt to forget in concentrating their attention on the American colonies down to 1783, that for the eighteenth-century politician and citizen these colonies were only a part of the Empire, that Jamaica or Tobago might and did frequently seem more important than Canada, that India like Ireland and the poor was always with them and that a drastic reorganisation of one part of the system, inevitably and uncomfortably reacted on the parts left untouched—in a word that principles of imperial government are like the ether of the modern physicist, something very difficult to define, at times provoking a blank denial of its existence, and always impossible to localise and segregate for a specific purpose. Modern research, therefore, has tended to concentrate on different aspects of the problem, *viz.* : How far was there a recognisable "old colonial system"? How did it work? What were its organs? What were its economic principles and aims? What were its political theory and ideas? How was it affected by the wars, above all the great struggle with France culminating in the Seven Years' War which wrested Canada from France and roughly put the whole North American Continent into British hands?

Two American scholars (G. L. Beer, and H. L. Osgood) seem to me to be the true begetters of much of the best work that has been done on both sides of the Atlantic. The three volumes on *The Old Colonial System from* 1578-1765 (largely based on British MS. material) like Tocqueville's *Ancien Régime* both anticipated and originated a mass of fine research work, confirming, qualifying, supplementing, and correcting the main ideas that underlay Beer's pioneer research and conclusions ; Osgood's seven volumes (three on the American Colonies in the seventeenth, four on those of the eighteenth century) constitute, as far as I can judge, the best, most comprehensive and fair description by a single author of the American Colonies from their origin to the final rupture—and these seven volumes have been supplemented or preceded by a library of specialist works and study which steadily increases in quantity and quality. Anyone who has carefully read Beer and Osgood will be adequately prepared to judge the meaning of the collision that began in 1765 and ended in 1783 both for Great Britain and the American Colonist— and to enter the dense jungle of controversy, that even a limited bibliography necessarily offers, with a map, a hatchet and a compass in his hand. The American colonist had " rebellion and revolution " in his blood ; his English forefathers had largely been voluntary exiles in revolt against the England that they proceeded to transplant and reproduce in America ; he came of a stock which had dealt faithfully with the Kings that his race disliked from Edward II. and Richard III. to Charles I. and James II., and which had fought one Civil

War, and only avoided a second because the other side ran away or declined to fight, and which above all was morbidly sensitive on the subject of taxation. When Prof. MacIlwain tells us that the cause of the Revolution was "a collision between two mutually incompatible interpretations of the British constitution," and Prof. Pollard that "the American Revolution of 1776 is the second volume of the English Revolution of 1688," and the economists pronounce that Mercantilism only existed because of the evasions of the system, and the military and naval experts are convinced that we ought to have won the war of 1775 with ease, if the government at home had known its business, and the political philosophers prove that the authors of the Declaration of Independence did not understand what they were saying or what they were imposing on the would-be Independents (as shown by the subsequent careers of Hamilton and Jefferson), we are still left with two permanent historical conundrums : How do minorities (and it is agreed that the " independent rebels " were a minority) make successful revolutions? what is the flash-point at which criticism and opposition flare up into rebellion ? one is almost tempted to conclude that lawyers are always the real makers of Revolution.   Once the lawyers in Great Britain had laid it down with impeccable logic that the Crown in Parliament was a sovereign with power to legislate for, and tax, all subjects of the Crown whether in London, Old Sarum, New York, Goree or the Falkland Islands, and the lawyers in the American Colonies had laid it down that there was in logic, reason and practice a clear distinction between the sovereignty of the Crown in Council whose subjects the colonists admitted they were and the sovereignty of the Crown in Parliament which was limited to Great Britain—the antithesis between the laws of nature and of God (which transcended the principle of a sovereign Parliament) and the legal sovereignty of the Imperial Crown in a purely British Parliament could only be resolved either by disruption or abject submission, in either case only to be obtained by force.   What would or could have been done had Great Britain smashed the American rebels before the French intervened in 1777, no one, so far, has seriously endeavoured to make clear.   The "might have beens" of history are only important as throwing indispensable light on what actually was in issue and happened.

One further point is also clear.   From the *Mayflower* to the Boston Tea-Party the English settlers were unconsciously engaged in the mysterious process of creating a national consciousness ; by 1749 they had passed the first stage—the achievement of a state or province consciousness, *e.g.* the Virginian mind was recognisably different from the Massachusetts mind and repeatedly came into conflict with it.   The Declaration of Independence of 1776 was a premature anticipation of an American mind, the elements of which came on to the anvil and very nearly broke into fragments under the hammer of civil war ; how far the formation of a national consciousness had got and how far it was still incomplete when Independence was secured can only be judged by a study of American history from 1783 onwards, and particularly of the struggle over the making of the Constitution—issues with which my book is not concerned.   But the controversies that raged from 1763 to 1776 are only intelligible if we are aware that the psychological factor was, perhaps, the most important element in the struggle—on both sides of the Atlantic. It was as difficult for the British citizen in Great Britain to understand that in the Colonies these English-speaking fellow-citizens, blood of his blood and bone of his bone, really differed in mentality from himself, as it was for the American colonist to understand that over there in the Mother Country the same language could and did mean different things to minds that ought to be the same but as a fact were not. The British visitor coming from an American Washington to-day to Washington's house at Mount Vernon suddenly feels that he is back in England with a typical English manor before him ; and then as his eye travels from the superb sweep of the Potomac back to the house itself he realises that this, for all its "home" memories, is *not* an English manor, but it is not, yet, an *American* country house. It is an English manor which is subtly passing into and becoming American ; and just because it is kept to-day as George Washington left it, for all time we have before us the subtle but unfinished transition, arrested and embodied in a material presentation. George Washington was not, despite the hagiologists, an American ; he was not English. What he was, neither he could precisely define, nor can we. But his house and himself mirror for us a consciousness that has passed the stage of the Colonial "state mind" and has not yet reached the American national mind, as it was to be.

Students will find in vol. i. of *The Cambridge History of the British Empire* (1929) a summary of the present historical position ; very helpful beside Beer's and Osgood's books are : R. G. Adams, *Political Ideas of the American Revolution* (1922), A. F. Pollard, *Factors in American History* (1925), C. H. MacIlwain, *The American Revolution* (1923), S. E. Morison, *Sources and Documents illustrating the American Revolution* (1923), H. E. Egerton, *Causes of the American Revolution*, C. H. Van Tyne, *Causes of the War of Independence* (1922).

XXI. THE WHIG POLITY

Mr. Namier's book, *The Structure of Politics at the Accession of George III.* (2 vols., 1928), is an important and illuminating study, based largely, but not exclusively, on the material in the vast Newcastle Papers in the British Museum. But there has been a tendency to exaggerate the extent and novelty of Mr. Namier's conclusions. For example, nearly thirty years ago that accomplished scholar, Miss Mary Bateson (*Eng. Hist. Rev.*, vol. v.), in a finished and amusing article, "Clerical Preferment under the Duke of Newcastle," based on the Newcastle MSS., gave chapter and verse in one sphere, the ecclesiastical, for much that Mr. Namier now brings out in full detail for the more purely political side of things. And the Rev. N. Sykes in his recent biography of Bishop Gibson (1669-1748) exemplifies fully the relations between "Church" and "State" on similar lines in the early Hanoverian period. Still more relevant to Mr. Namier's main issue are the Robinson Papers, printed and edited for the Royal Historical Society by Prof. W. T. Laprade (1922). John Robinson was Senior Secretary of the Treasury Board, and in this volume we have his *Secret and Special Service*

Accounts from 1761-82, which reveal precisely the same structure of administration, method and working as that which Mr. Namier gives us for the earlier period.   Prof. Laprade's Introduction, based on the accounts, anticipates for George III. much of Mr. Namier's conclusions for the Newcastle epoch. Clearly, to any thorough student of the eighteenth century, the "system" which Robinson worked so efficiently was not the creation of George III.   It was already in existence; its conventions were well known; its atmosphere was familiar; its applications were the product of a polity that had slowly grown.   To the Newcastle politician the charge of "corruption" would have been as meaningless as a similar charge against farmers and landowners who under the Speenhamland system of 1795 supplemented the "economic" wage of the labourer out of the rates.

As Prof. Laprade observes : "The truth is, the parliaments just previous to 1832, *like those in the next succeeding generation and in fact like those of to-day* (my italics) were representative of the ruling group of the time . . . the ruling class in Robinson's day was actually represented in the House of Commons of the period . . . the moderateness of the sums involved rather than the amount impresses us most.   These papers by no means give evidence that George III. and his ministers indulged in the practice of bribery and corruption in the degree that has sometimes been alleged."   "The political nation" of the eighteenth century was, of course, a very limited one; it regarded itself as entitled to share in the "perquisites" of the government of the nation, and these were managed and distributed on principles which may offend the twentieth century conscience, but which were accepted in the prevailing code of ethics.   "The King's Government" had to be carried on, through a representative system, and things were so managed as to secure that it was carried on broadly in accord with the wishes of the majority of the then political nation.   Certainly, at its worst, England never exhibited the state of things prevalent in Ireland (see *The Irish Parliament of* 1775 (1907) edited by the Rev. W. Hunt) simply because the political nation in Ireland was a mere handful of the Irish people and its "system" was devised to maintain this small Anglican minority in control, not as an Irish political nation, but as an affiliated bureau of the British Government.   Ireland to the managers did not mean the Irish nation, but the English Government in Ireland.

As to the working of the electoral system under George II. Mr. Namier confirms with much patient detail and in the language and idiom of contemporaries—not posing for the historian's camera—what had hitherto rested on guesses or generalisations from second-hand evidence, *e.g.* in such standard treatises as that of Porritt, *The Unreformed House of Commons*, and similar works.   In some quarters some surprise, with corresponding reflections, has been expressed at the parasitical character of certain sections of the Whig "political nation" and the shameless begging revealed.   "Parasitism" exists in all forms of society and under all forms of government ; *e.g.* Lavisse showed the amazing extent to which certain sections of the French nobility in 1680, simply lived on the royal bounty, *i.e.* on money obtained by national taxation. The truth is that national funds are always, and have always been, regarded as employable justifiably on and by the political nation, as it may be constituted.

for its own self-preservation. Mr. Namier shows that much of the so-called "corruption" was really charity (Old Age Pensions and the like) to the indigent or unemployable of the eighteenth century political nation. To-day the political nation is very differently constituted. But have the conventions and principles and applications really altered?

Again, was "Whig Society" more importunate and more shameless in its begging for place, honours, sinecures, titles (national or local), etc? If in Victorian, Edwardian, or Georgian England we could have access to a Newcastle or a Robinson—if we could cross-examine Prime Ministers, and above all Private Secretaries and Whips in the ante-chambers to Prime Ministers—should we discover that those who desired these things were less importunate, less shameless, less explicit? The beggars would no doubt be different and the things asked for in some cases be different; but the plain truth would probably emerge that so long as society is so constructed and social conventions are based on certain scales of values and so long as "the State" is a vast reservoir of what human nature covets, human beings will not hesitate to importune those who have the power to grant their wishes and to give what to the recipient is socially valuable or has a monetary value. The smug conclusion that Whig Society was parasitic in a sense in which Stuart Society or Regency or Victorian Society was not lacks both historical, philosophical and psychological perspective. Nor does the Whig assumption that the interest of "the Publick" coincided with the interest of the individual beggar differ essentially from the assumptions that preceded or followed the Whig regime. Bolingbroke was just as "corrupt" as Newcastle or as Dundas.

Not the least convincing of Mr. Namier's investigations is the *coup de grâce* that he administers to the legends as to "corruption" (in the narrower sense) and the uses of the secret service money. In the text eighteen years ago I expressed my complete scepticism as to the ordinary charge of "corruption" against Walpole, which at that time rested on the unverified but continuous accusations of political opponents and fragments of tittle-tattle diligently collected from stray and unverified assertions by biased or uncritical persons in memoirs, letters, etc.—the kind of evidence on which the ordinary "ghost story" passes muster with those who want to believe in the ordinary ghost story. Mr. Namier brings the matter to the test of figures—the only trustworthy test, and he demolishes the "Tory" legend. The analysis in vol. i., ch. iv., pp. 214-90, *Secret Service Money under the Duke of Newcastle* with its facts and figures is conclusive: "the vast engine of Parliamentary corruption called "Secret Service money" when measured has proved surprisingly small in size; a mere supplement to places and other open favours, and on further inquiry it was found that there was more jobbery, stupidity and human charity about it than history"; and again, "the ill-famed, subterranean stream of corruption when uncovered and measured, proves to have been after all not nearly so dirty as generally supposed; it was the last resort of political beggars in distress and of opposition leaders in search of a topic."

Two clear points seem to emerge: (i) the traditional indictment of "corruption" on a large scale has mainly come from the partisan statement of political opponents, *e.g.* "The Bolingbroke" coterie and *The Craftsman* in Walpole's day, "The Leicester House and Dowager Princess of Wales party" in Newcastle's day, who convinced themselves (if they did !) first and the writers of history subsequently, that nothing but bribery could have kept Walpole in office for twenty years or the Whigs in power from 1742-60; (ii) a plain confusion between "secret service money" proper, *i.e.* money used for obtaining foreign intelligence or special services and the like, and unappropriated sums in the Civil List, alleged to have been spent on "corruption" (for on what else could they have been spent?). Neither the critics nor the later historians mastered or understood the financial system of the eighteenth century, which requires elaborate analysis and patient unravelling to make intelligible. Two quotations will make this point clear : Newcastle noted in 1756 "that the King had for special service, which was sent to Hanover for the payment of troops, etc., £90,000 *which we did not think it advisable to lay before Parliament (e.g.* because there would have been an anti-Hanoverian 'patriotic' debate). I know the (Dowager) Princess of Wales said that these great sums drawn that year on account of the Civil List were employed for bribing the House of Commons to approve the Russian Treaty"; in 1771 George III. wrote to Lord North : "as there is no publick mode of obtaining the money that is expended in that corruption (*i.e.* influencing the Court of Sweden) it must be taken from my Civil List, consequently new debts incurred ; and when I apply to Parliament for relieving me, an odium cast on myself and Ministry, *as if the money had been expended in bribing Parliament.*" Obviously, a minister could not come to the House of Commons to ask for £50,000 to "influence" the Court of Sweden, or to pay for spies, stolen documents, intercepted letters or the like : still more obviously, receipts for such payments could not be exhibited to Parliamentary or other auditors— hence the argument—£90,000 unaccounted for, a certain defeat of the Ministry unaccountably warded off; conclusion, the requisite majority must have been bought out of the Secret Service Fund.

Mr. Namier completes his demolition of the legend, not merely by showing exactly how Newcastle spent "the Secret Service" Fund, but the wider implications involved.

This becomes clearer when we consider how the "system" broke up. Three forces ultimately broke the "Whig System" which became the Tory Citadel after 1783 : (i) The growth in the wealth of the country made the totality of patronage infinitely more valuable ; "the original" and ordinary shareholders had a larger cake to divide and a larger ordinary dividend to distribute. Hence the "ins" were relatively better off than the "outs" and a seat in Parliament became more and more valuable, because it made the possessor an "in"; (ii) the great growth in population from 1780 onwards made the existing political nation relatively smaller and smaller and the unrepresented larger and larger ; (iii) the growth of a powerful and unrepresented industrial middle class, paying a larger and larger share of taxation ; this class did not so much want a share in the "perquisites" as a voice in determining national policy. We are apt to forget that from 1688 onwards the Whigs maintained certain fundamental constitutional principles—above all that taxation and representation went hand in hand and that the Crown must govern through ministers responsible to Parliament. The experienced "managers" behind the screen who worked the system startle the student from time to time by

naïve comments, almost humorous to-day, to the effect that the King's
ministry has a majority but it has no one to lead them and, as a leader in open
debate, "manage," *i.e.* persuade the House of Commons. The real secret of
Walpole, of Pitt the elder, and of Pitt the younger, lies in their gift of leadership. These three anticipated by their genius and their personality the position of Peel "who played on the House of Commons as a fiddler on his fiddle,"
of Gladstone and of Lord Asquith in his prime. The Whigs and the Crown
required leaders, *i.e.* men who could conduct "the King's business" in
a debating assembly. The combination of gifts that make a leader is unanalysable and unpredictable—but we know them when they are seen daily at
work. Walpole, Henry Pelham, Chatham, Charles Fox, the younger Pitt, in
different degrees were Parliamentary leaders. Carteret, Newcastle, Henry
Fox, North, Burke (for all his oratory) were not. Hence the principles that
the Whigs laid down in 1688 were the principles which made Reform both
constitutional and inevitable. Since 1832 "corruption," in the only correct
sense in which the term is applicable to the Whig regime, was not abolished,
it only changed its form. The Old Age Pensions Act of modern democracy
is the democratic form of the Civil List and the Secret Service Funds of the
Whigs: and if to-day a twentieth century Newcastle or John Robinson is piling
up the requisite material for the twenty-second century to discuss, the Party
Funds and the Honour Lists may prove to have as close a connection as the
evidence set out in all its nakedness by Mr. Namier and Prof. Laprade. And
the historian of the twenty-second century may have to explode the legends of
the political pamphleteers and show that what is suprising is not the extent of
the "corruption" but the vehemence of the indictment as compared with the
slenderness of the evidence in its favour.

A useful commentary on Mr. Napier's instructive two volumes are: Prof.
Turberville's *English Men and Manners in the Eighteenth Century* (1926),
and *The House of Lords in the Eighteenth Century* (1927).

XXII. THE GENERAL ELECTION OF 1784

The sentence at the end of the first paragraph on p. 303 has been left as
it was originally written, but Prof. Laprade has convinced me that, as it stands,
it requires very serious modification. This note is based on an article in *Eng.
Hist. Review*, "Public Opinion and the General Election of 1784" (April, 1916),
supplemented by *Parliamentary Papers* of John Robinson, edited for the Royal
Hist. Society by Prof. Laprade (1922), together with an article in the *American
Hist. Review*, XVIII., 254, which should be studied carefully by all interested in
the eighteenth century. John Robinson, in fact, who "managed" the election
of 1784 for the King and Pitt is in the witness box and we have before us his
calculations, his statistics and his results—and John Robinson had "managed"
the elections of 1774 and 1780. Briefly the story is: in March, 1783, Pitt
refused to form an administration; the Fox-North Coalition came into power;
Fox's East India Bills stirred intense fear and antagonism in the powerful
commercial and vested interests of the East India Company; the Bills *must* be
defeated; coalition of these interests with the King; the Bill passes the
Commons; can it be defeated in the Lords? the King intervenes and the Bill

is defeated; Pitt comes in; Robinson (Dec. 15) instructed to make his calculations as to how a favourable election can be "made"; he makes his calculations for secret meetings of Dundas and Pitt and promises if the requisite measures are taken an adequate ministerial majority in the next Parliament; General Election three months later and majority secured; verdict of historians since that "the nation in its wrath put Pitt and purity into power as against Fox and North and a venal coalition".

Robinson's calculations and analysis are illuminating and complete; every seat and member were discussed and tabulated; 42 seats are ticked off as "close or under decisive influence" and favourable; 69 are "partly accessible in one way and partly in other ways"; 38 are laconically labelled "money," i.e. if the funds are available they can be bought either privately or in the open market; 27 are grouped "No money," i.e. the patron must have his compensation in some other form than money; 17 are "open Boroughs where seats may probably be obtained with expense". In a word, if £200,000 are available, at least 137 seats can be transferred to the (Pitt) ministerial party. Robinson showed that, when Pitt took office, of 558 members 231 were pledged to Fox and North with 74 doubtful supporters, and that if the election were properly managed Pitt could rely on 255 certain, with only 123 definitely in opposition, and that the Ministry could count on 116 additional probables, while the Opposition might have 64 additional probables—i.e. 255 + 116 versus 123 + 64, and the election confirmed his estimate; the requisite measures were taken for "things were in the hands of men of resolution". Prof. Laprade produces evidence to show that the bill was met (a) by 17 peerages or promotions in the peerage, following the General Election; (b) by a redistribution of patronage and offices; (c) by large subscriptions from the vested interests in the East India Co.; (d) by private subscriptions from friends and political supporters; (e) by clearing out what was available in the Treasury and the King's private funds—as was done in 1780. He quotes from a contemporary pamphlet: "Sir Robert Walpole himself was a simpleton to this wonderful young man (Pitt)"; he shows that in all his calculations Robinson never refers to the supposed unpopularity of the Coalition or the national disgust at the Fox-North combination as influences to be employed in deciding the results; the men or the seats to be dealt with were calculable factors to be handled by methods familiar to the manager, provided that that manager was in office working for a ministry in office with the Crown at its back, which could, in vulgar phrase, promise and "deliver the goods". The essential preliminary was (a) to get Fox and North out of office and the Treasury into "the right" hands; (b) to prevent the Coalition fighting a General Election *while they controlled the Treasury. patronage*, etc.

George III. managed the preliminaries by dismissing Fox and North; Pitt, who had refused office twelve months previously, now came in because with Dundas he had met Robinson secretly, seen his calculations and was prepared to go through with the business. Hence Prof. Laprade's final conclusion: that to see in the General Election of 1784 the spontaneous expression of an overwhelming public opinion is to ignore the evidence in the Robinson papers, the carefully riveted links in the sequence of events and completely to misunderstand the nature of the eighteenth century Parliamentary system.

But the General Election of 1784 does explain very clearly (*a*) why Pitt could not produce an India Bill that would have dealt faithfully with the deficiencies of the East India Co. ; and (*b*) why his subsequent attempts at Parliamentary Reform were so lukewarm and such complete failures. Pitt could not throw over the East India men who had helped to put him into office and partly paid the election bill of 1784, or reform by "confiscatory" legislation a system to which he and his ministerial supporters owed their own Parliamentary existence.

Robinson provides the final comment : "Parliamentary State of Boroughs . . . and a wild wide calculate of the money wanted for seats but which I always disapproved and thought very wrong".   Delicious.

XXIII. REFORM AND THE FRENCH REVOLUTION.

Nothing is more difficult to judge sanely than reform movements in a great war, particularly when those movements have been inspired from a country which is a belligerent. The present generation is better able to understand the effects of a "war-complex" and a "spy-complex" after its experiences of 1914-18 and to appreciate more accurately the war-mentality of a period such as 1790-1815, very largely similar to that of 1689-1714 with Jacobitism rampant at home. All such periods will always be judged politically (even by trained historians), rather than scientifically, and the political principles of a later generation will be read into the political controversies of the earlier, *i.e.* writer and reader will consciously or unconsciously start from an assumption that Pitt must broadly have been right and Fox wrong, or *vice versa* : and the evidence will be interpreted from that angle. The French savant who remarked that the flaw in all research was that the researcher usually found what he was looking for, and added that the best of all proofs of a proposition was a simple assertion, because you cannot discuss the value of a proof that is not given, was nearer the truth in periods of war-mentality than in other spheres of human affairs.

The general course of the Reform movement from 1789-1830 is fully discussed in G. S. Veitch, *The Genesis of Parliamentary Reform* (1913), J. R. M. Butler, *The Passing of the Great Reform Bill* (1914), G. M. Trevelyan, *Life of Charles, 2nd Earl Grey* (1920), G. D. H. Cole, *Life of W. Cobbett* (1924), Graham Wallas, *Life of Place* (1918), J. L. and B. Hammond, *The Village Labourer*, 1760-1832 (1920), and the student can safely be referred to these works, with the authorities that are cited in them, together with the books given on pp. 523 and 531, and the masterly survey by E. Halévy in his *Histoire du Peuple Anglais au 19e Siecle*, 3 vols. (1923).

"The revolutionary" movement from 1789-98 has been examined besides Laprade's monograph, in particular by Veitch, *op. cit.*, Graham Wallas, *op. cit.*, and by J. Holland Rose, *Life of Pitt*, vol. ii. (1911), pp. 164-94 ; by P. A. Brown, *The French Revolution in English History* (1924), and the results of their researches only confirm the view taken in the text. In short, the attempt to show that there was a widespread conspiracy amongst the "British Jacobins" ("Jacobin" being a term equivalent to the modern "Bolshevist") breaks down at every point; yet the existence of such a widespread conspiracy could be the only justification for the action of the Government, for the repressive legislation and the savage prosecutions.   The argument that the repression extirpated the alleged conspiracy is doubly vicious: (*a*) it is not borne out by the MS. evidence; and (*b*) it perverts the ministerial argument that the conspiracy was the cause of the legislation.   Prof. C. Gill in *The Naval Mutinies of* 1797 (1913) which so terrified ministers shows conclusively that none of the political or "seditious" societies formed plans, or were responsible for, a general mutiny; and that in the genuine grievances of the naval mutineers there was incomparable material for a general treason, yet the mutinous fleet saved England from revolutionary France.   It is impossible to avoid the conclusion that Pitt, Dundas, the ministers and the "society" in which they moved did not know and did not trouble to ascertain the facts, and that the ministerial legislation and executive measures were the product of a war and panic complex, which was shared by three-fourths of the nation in every class.   As Prof. Veitch, *op. cit.*, p. 342, puts it: "It was, as if a nation of self-appointed policemen had turned out in force to keep guard over a handful of suspected pickpockets".   Even if all the British "Jacobins" had risen *en masse* in red caps and with pikes and muskets (which they had not got), they could probably have been dispersed by a squadron of yeomanry; but the British "Jacobins" had no such intention of rising, and no evidence has so far been adduced to prove any such intention or that they were subsidised by French gold.   The French contention that every "traitor" to the Revolution was corrupted by Pitt and English gold had—in view of our active support of the *Émigrés*—far more plausibility than the allegation that French gold (of which the Revolutionary Government had very little) was pouring into England to complete the demoralisation of a treasonable nation.   But just as in 1914-18 even to know German was almost a proof of "Pro-German" treachery, so in 1795 Burke and the British nation saw "republican daggers" not only in the air but considered they had proved their case by flinging a handful on the floor of the House of Commons. Pitt's argument in 1794 remains on record; he solemnly depicted to the House of Commons "an enormous torrent of insurrection, which would sweep away all the barriers of government, law and religion, and leave our country a naked waste for usurped authority to range in, uncontrolled and unresisted" (*Parl. Hist.*, xxxi., 497-500).   Dr. Holland Rose's comment is relevant: "So far as I have found, not one life was taken by the people in the course of this agitation. . . . The hero of the year 1794 is not William Pitt, but the British nation" (*op. cit.*, ii., 194).

The attempt to defend the Scottish Judges, Braxfield in particular, has long been abandoned.   But Pitt "upheld the Scottish Court of Justiciary in what was perhaps the worst speech of his career" (Rose, *op. cit.*, ii., 180).

The trials for "treason" in both countries, in fact, make a soiled chapter in the history of the British Judiciary, which distinguished lawyers since are only too glad either to scourge or to forget.

The student can refer to the *Quarterly Review*, Oct. 1912, and Oct. 1913, for two articles in which the present writer reviews the more recent evidences on Pitt, Shelburne, and Windham.

TABLE I

THE HANOVERIAN SUCCESSION

JAMES I.

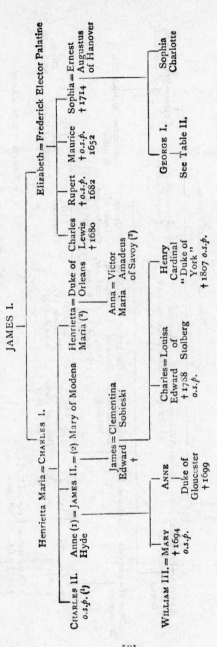

(¹) Charles II. had no legitimate children.

(²) The only child of Charles I. from whom there is issue surviving to-day. On strict hereditary principles the children of Charles I. and their issue had prior rights to those of the daughter of James I. and her issue.

(³) On the death of Henry Cardinal "Duke of York" the strict hereditary claim passed to the issue of Henrietta Maria. Their claim is on this principle vested to-day in Maria Teresa (b. 1849), married to Louis, son of Liutpold (Regent of Bavaria), whose son Rupert (b. 1869) is heir to the Bavarian throne.

TABLE II

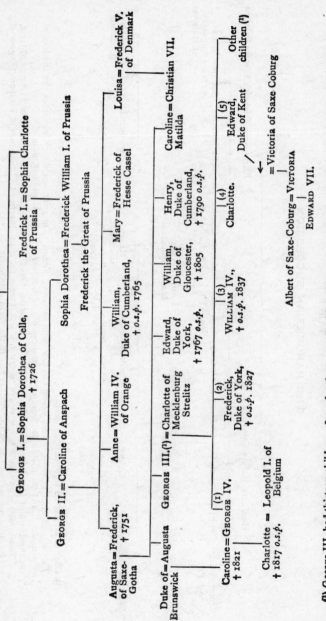

(*) George III. had thirteen children. In order they were (besides those given in the above table): (6) Augusta; (12) Sophia; (13) Amelia, who died unmarried; (7) Elizabeth, wife of Frederick of Hesse Homburg; (8) Ernest, Duke of Cumberland and King of Hanover; (9) Augustus, Duke of Sussex, † *o.s.p.*; (10) Adolphus, Duke of Cambridge: (11) Mary, married to Duke of Gloucester, son of William Henry, Duke of Gloucester, grandson of George II.

TABLE III

THE NATIONAL DEBT

Year.	Funded.		Unfunded.	Total.	Interest and Annuities.
		£	£	£	£
1714		27,820,321	8,355,139	36,175,640	3,063,135
1727	G.B.	47,665,052	4,249,371	52,523,923	2,360,934
	Ireland	46,153	—	—	—
1739	G.B.	42,740,024	3,651,397	46,613,883	2,030,884
	I.	222,462	—	—	—
1748	G.B.	68,056,824	7,391,985	75,812,132	3,165,765
	I.	363,323	—	—	—
1756	G.B.	73,751,255	815,555	74,575,025	2,753,566
	I.	8,215	—	—	—
1763	G.B.	128,564,808	4,705,990	132,716,049	5,032,733
	I.	507,692	—	—	—
1775	G.B.	122,963,255	3,079,802	126,842,811	4,703,519
	I.	799,754	—	—	—
1783	G.B.	211,363,255	18,513,114	231,843,631	9,065,585
	I.	1,410,092	557,170	—	—
1793	G.B.	232,064,743	12,656,233	247,874,434	9,711,238
	I.	1,625,297	1,183,485	—	—
1802	G.B.	508,924,557	14,349,500	537,653,008	20,268,551
	I.	13,307,229	1,071,722	—	—
1815	G.B.	792,033,426	42,229,300	861,039,049	32,645,618
	I.	24,278,515	2,497,808	—	—

N.B.—These figures are taken from the official return in a Parliamentary Paper, printed by order of the House of Commons, July 29th, 1869, generally cited as "Public Income and Expenditure, 1688-1869" (1869).

TABLE IV

THE COST OF WARS FROM 1714-1815

Years.	Paid from Revenue.	Paid by Loans (Debt).	Total War Expenditure.
	£	£	£
1718-21	3,545,122	1,022,202	4,547,324
1739-48	13,930,997	29,724,195	43,655,192
1756-63	22,605,495	60,018,243	82,623,738
1776-85	3,039,427	94,560,069	97,599,496
1793-1815	391,148,370	440,298,079	831,446,449

Note in this table the extraordinary proportion of expenditure met by creation of debt, to expenditure met by taxation in the American War (1776-83)—characteristic of the spendthrift and reckless finance of Lord North's Administration and the King's system during those years.

BIBLIOGRAPHY

(This bibliography does not profess to be exhaustive. It is intended to provide the student with the requisite aids to advanced or detailed study of the various aspects of eighteenth century British history. Contemporary or original authorities are marked with an asterisk.)

General Aids for the Whole Period, 1714-1815

S. R. Gardiner and J. B. Mullinger.—*Introduction to English History* (4th ed.), 1903.

The Cambridge Modern History. Bibliographies to vols. vi., viii., ix. (referred to as *C. M. H.*).

Dictionary of National Biography (D. N. B.).

G. K. Fortescue.—*Subject Index of Modern Works added to the Library of the British Museum*, 1881-1906.

S. R. Scargill-Bird.—*A Guide to the Various Classes of Documents in the Public Record Office*, 1908.

M. Livingstone.—*A Guide to the Public Records of Scotland*, 1905 ; *Catalogues of the Additions to the MSS. in the British Museum* (arranged in years) ; and particularly *Index of the Catalogues of Additions to the MSS.*, 1880.

Atlases : *The Clarendon Press Historical Atlas.* Spruner-Menke.—*Hand. Atlas für die Geschichte* (3rd ed.). Droysen.—*Historischer Atlas.* C. G. Robertson and J. G. Bartholomew.—*Historical and Modern Atlas of the British Empire.* S. R. Gardiner.—*Student's Atlas of English History.*

*Treaties : G. F. and C. de Martens.—*Recueil des principaux Traités* (avec supplément), 1761-1808, 8 vols. F. de Martens.—*Recueil des Traités Conclus par la Russie*, vol. x., England, 1710-1801 (introduction and notes based on Russian archives). C. G. de Koch and M. S. F. Schoell. —*Histoire abregée des Traités de Paix* (2nd ed.), 15 vols. ; new ed., continued to 1815, 4 vols. A. F. Pribram.—*Oesterreichische Staats Verträge*, England, vol. i. (1526-1748 ; introduction based on original Austrian and British sources).

*A. Boyer.—*Political State of Great Britain* (from vol. viii., 1714).

The Gentleman's Magazine (from 1738).

The Annual Register (from 1758).

H. B. George.—*Genealogical Tables Illustrative of Modern History* (4th ed.).

F. Lorenz.—*Genealogisches Handbuch.*

535

PART I.—1714-60

The chief original MSS. authorities in the British Museum are: The *Stowe MSS.* (see *Catalogue of the Stowe MSS.*, London, 1895), the *Newcastle MSS.* (Add. MS. 32, 679-33, 201), the *Hardwicke MSS.* (Add. MS. 35, 349-36, 278), *Carteret Papers* (Add. MS. 22511-19, 22523-24), *Gualterio Papers* (20241-20583), *Melcombe Papers* (Egerton MS. 2170-75), *Norris Papers* (Add. MS. 28128-29, 28135, 28143-47, 28154-56), *Coxe Papers* (9128-97), *Whitworth Papers* (37361-97).

For the State Papers in the Public Record Office see *Special List*, xix. (a catalogue of State Papers down to 1782, and invaluable), published in 1904; and information in *C. M. H.*, Bibliographies. The *Pitt-Pringle (Chatham) Papers* (partly published in *The Chatham Correspondence*) are in the Record Office.

A. Foreign Policy

For bibliographies consult: G. Monod.—*Bibliographie de l'histoire de France.* Dahlmann-Waitz. — *Quellenkunde der Deutschen Geschichte* (ed. Brandenburg, 7th ed.). V. Loewe.—*Bibliographie der Hannoverschen und Braunschweig Geschichte*, 1908.

The following for the chief European States will be invaluable to the student:—

E. Armstrong.—*Elizabeth Farnese*, 1892.

E. Bourgeois.—*La Diplomatie Secréte au XVIIIe Siècle*, vol. i., 1909 (deals with Dubois).

G. de Flassan.—*Histoire de la Diplomatie Française*, vols. iv.-vi.

E. Lavisse.—*Histoire de France*, vol. viii., pt. 2.

L. Wiesener.—*Le Regent, l'abbé Dubois et les Anglais*, 3 vols.

J. E. Droysen.—*Geschichte der Preussischen Politik.*

B. Erdmannsdörffer.—*Deutsche Geschichte* (Oncken's series), from 1648-1740, vol. 2.

C. T. Atkinson.—*A History of Germany*, 1713-1815.

R. Koser.—*König Friedrich der Grosse*, 2 vols.

E. Bourgeois.—*Manuel de politique étrangère*, 2 vols.

A. Baudrillart.—*Philippe V. et la Cour de France*, vols. iii.-iv*
Cambridge Modern History, vol. vi.

British History (Foreign and Political).—*(For Bibliographies, Memoirs and Hist. MSS. Com. Reports, see special Sections)*

M. Brosch.—*Geschichte von England*, vols. viii. and ix.

J. F. Chance.—*George I. and the Great Northern War.*

    „   *List of Diplomatic Representatives and Agents, England and N. Germany*, 1907.

    „   *John de Robethon and the Robethon Papers, Eng. Hist. Rev.*, vol. xiii.

J. S. Corbett.—*England in the Seven Years' War*, 2 vols.

G. B. Hertz.—*British Imperialism in the Eighteenth Century.*
A. D. Innes.—*Great Britain and Her Rivals.*
J. S. Leadam.—*Political History of England,* vol. ix., 1702-60.
L. G. Wickham-Legg.—*List of Diplomatic Representatives, England and France,* 1689-1733.
W. E. H. Lecky.—*History of England in the Eighteenth Century,* 7 vols.
A. T. Mahan.—*The Influence of Sea Power upon History,* 1660-1783.
W. Michael.—*Englische Geschichte im XVIIIten Jahrhundert.*
L. von Ranke.—*English History* (Eng. ed.), vols. v. and vi.
J. R. Seeley.—*The Expansion of England.*
    ,,   *The House of Bourbon,* Eng. Hist. Rev., vol. i.
Earl Stanhope.—*History of England from the Peace of Utrecht,* 7 vols.
R. Waddington.—*La Guerre de Sept Ans,* 5 vols.
A. W. Ward.—*The Electress Sophia and the Hanoverian Succession* (2nd revised edition, 1909).
    ,,   *Great Britain and Hanover.*
B. Williams.—*The Foreign Policy of England under Walpole,* Eng. Hist Rev., vols. xv. and xvi.

Biographies, Memoirs, Letters, etc.

These are very numerous; the following are amongst the most important :—

A. Ballantyne.—*Lord Carteret.*
Bedford, Correspondence of Fourth Duke of, ed. Lord J. Russell, 4 vols.
Chatham Correspondence, ed. Taylor and Pringle, 4 vols.
Cowper, Earl.—Private Diary (Roxburghe Club).
* ,,   Countess of.—Diary,* ed. S. Cowper.
W. Coxe.—Memoirs of H. Pelham, 2 vols.
* ,,   Memoirs of Horatio Lord Walpole,* 2 vols.
* ,,   Memoirs of Sir R. Walpole,* 3 vols.
W. D. Green.—*William Pitt, Earl of Chatham.*
A. Greenwood.—*Lives of the Hanoverian Queens of England,* vol. i.
Grenville Papers, ed. W. J. Smith, 4 vols.
Hardwicke, Earl of.—Miscellaneous State Papers, 2 vols.
G. Harris.—*Life of the Earl of Hardwicke,* 3 vols.
F. Harrison.—*William Pitt, Earl of Chatham.*
John Hervey, Lord.—Memories of Reign of George II., 2 vols.
Marchmont, Earl of.—Papers, 3 vols.
A. Mitchell, Sir.—Memoirs and Papers, 2 vols.
J. Morley (Viscount).—*Sir R. Walpole.*
E. S. Roscoe.—*Robert Harley, Earl of Oxford.*
A. von Ruville.—*William Pitt, Earl of Chatham* (English translation), 3 vols.
W. Sichel.—*Bolingbroke and His Times,* 2 vols. (vol. ii. deals with the period after 1714).
Suffolk (Countess of).—Letters (1712-1767), 2 vols.
Waldegrave, Earl of.—Memoirs, 1 vol.

*Horace Walpole.—*Complete Letters*, ed. Mrs. Paget Toynbee, 16 vols.
*   ,,   *Memoirs of the Reign of George II.*, ed. Lord Holland,
   3 vols.
Wentworth Papers, ed. Cartwright.
C. Whitefoord, Papers of, ed. Hewins.

The *Reports of the Historical MSS. Commission contain very valuable
information. The following reports are important (Roman figures give the
Report, numerals the Appendix referred to) :—

Westmoreland MSS., x., 4 ; *Bath MSS.*, xv., vols. 1-3 ; *Buccleuch MSS.*,
xv., 8 ; *Carlisle MSS.*, xv., 6 ; *Dropmore Papers*, xiii., vol. 1 ; *Kenyon MSS.*,
xiv., 4 ; *Lonsdale MSS.*, xiii., 7 ; *Onslow MSS.*, xiv., 9 ; *Portland MSS.*, xiii.,
vols. 2, 5, 6, 7 ; *Townshend MSS.*, xi., 4 ; *Weston-Underwood MSS.*, x., 1 ;
Buckinghamshire MSS., xiv., 9 ; *Hare MSS.*, xiv., 9 ; *The Stuart Papers*,
vols. 1, 2, 3, 4 (largely Jacobite material).

Constitutional and Parliamentary History

The Register of the Privy Council is kept at the Privy Council Office,
and can, by permission, be consulted there. Classified details of the Home
Office Papers are given in Scargill-Bird, *op. cit.*, pp. 367-69. The MSS. of the
House of Lords dealt with by the Hist. MS. Com. only reach 1708. The
following are official or semi-official :—

The Statutes at Large. 1st series to 1801 ; 2nd series from 1801-62.
Journals of the House of Lords, vols. xx.-li. *Index to the Journals*, 3rd
   part, 1714-79 ; 4th part, 1780-1820.
Journals of the House of Commons, vols. xviii.-lxx. *Index to the Journals.*
   2nd part, 1714-73 ; 3rd part, 1774-1800 ; 4th part, 1801-20.
Catalogue of Parliamentary Reports, with a breviate of their contents, 1696-
   1837 (1837).
Reports from Committees of House of Commons, 1715-1801, 16 vols. (1803).
Official Return of Members of Parliament, 2nd part 1705-98 ; 3rd part,
   1801-74.

For Reports of Debates consult *The Gentleman's Magazine, The London
Magazine*, and—

The Parliamentary History of England, 1066-1803, ed. Cobbett and Wright,
   36 vols.
Collection of Parliamentary Debates in England, 1668-1741, 21 vols. (index in
   vol. 21).
The Parliamentary Register (1743-1802), 88 vols. (compiled from newspapers and magazines, and supplements many gaps in Cobbett).
A. Mantoux.—*Notes sur les Comptes Rendus des Séances du Parl. Anglais*,
   1906.

Other useful printed authorities on Constitutional History are :—

W. R. Anson, Sir.—*The Law and Custom of the Constitution*, 2 vols., vol. ii.,
   in 2 parts.

R. Beatson.—*Chronological Register of both Houses of Parliament* (1807).

W. Blackstone, Sir.—*Commentaries on the Laws of England.*

M. T. Blauvelt.—*Development of Cabinet Government.*

Campbell, Lord.—*Lives of the Lord Chancellors.*

W. Cobbett and T. B. Howell.—*State Trials,* 33 vols.

G. E. C.—*Complete Peerage.*

De Lolme.—*La Constitution de l'Angleterre.*

R. Gneist.—*English Constitutional History* (English translation).

H. Hallam.—*The Constitutional History of England,* vol. iii.

J. Hatsell.—*Precedents and Proceedings in the House of Commons,* 4 vols.

D. J. Medley.—*English Constitutional History.*

Montesquieu, Baron.—*L'Esprit des Lois,* vol. i. (English translation), bk. xi.

L. O. Pike.—*Constitutional History of the House of Lords.*

E. and A. G. Porritt.—*The Unreformed House of Commons,* 2 vols.

J. Redlich.—*Procedure of the House of Commons* (English translation), 3 vols.

* C. G. Robertson.—*Select Statutes, Cases, and Documents,* 1660-1832 (Fifth
    Rev. Ed., 1925).

* Th. Rogers.—*Protests of the House of Lords,* 3 vols.

A. Todd.—*Parliamentary Government,* 2 vols.

W. M. Torrens.—*A History of Cabinets,* 2 vols.

*W. W. Wilkins.—*Political Ballads of Seventeenth and Eighteenth Century,*
    2 vols.

Irish History, 1714-1815

Consult especially the bibliographies in *C. M. H.,* vol. vi., ch. xiv. ; vol.
ix., ch. xxii. ; vol. x., ch. xxii., which give an exhaustive analysis of the MSS.
sources, the pamphlets, etc., and the printed literature. A select critical
bibliography will be found in O'Connor Morris, *Ireland,* 1494-1905 (Camb.
Hist. Series, 2nd ed., by R. Dunlop, 1909). As an Introduction to Irish
History the best authority is W. E. H. Lecky, *History of Ireland in the Eight-
enth Century to 1801* (4 vols., published separately, but originally part of the
author's great *English History in the Eighteenth Century*). The text-books
and histories for the most part are controversial and very numerous. The
following represent various points of view :—

R. Dunlop.—*Life of H. Grattan.*

J. A. Froude.—*The English in Ireland,* 3 vols.

W. E. H. Lecky.—*Leaders of Public Opinion in Ireland,* 2 vols.

R. R. Madden.—*History of the Penal Laws.*

Studies in Irish History.—Ed. R. B. O'Brien.

Two Centuries of Irish History, 1691-1870 (2nd ed.), 1907.

For the period of Grattan's Parliament, the Rebellion of '98, and the
Union, consult especially : **The Irish Parliament* (MS. edited by W. Hunt),
the **Charlemont MSS.* (Hist. MS. Com., Rept., 12, x. ; 13, viii.), the **Castlereagh Correspondence,* the **Cornwallis Correspondence* (cited below, part ii.),
and the **Dropmore Papers,* vols. i. and v. ; also the following selected books :—

*J. Beresford.—*Correspondence,* vol. ii.

*E. Cooke.—*Arguments for and against a Union,* Dublin, 1798.

*R. L. Edgeworth.—*Memoirs,* 2 vols.
*H. Grattan.—*Speeches,* vols. ii.-iv.
T. D. Ingram.—*A Critical Examination of Irish History,* vol. ii.
    „   *History of the Irish Union.*
J. S. Macneill.—*How the Union Was Carried.*
*T. Wolfe Tone.—*Autobiography,* ed. R. B. O'Brien, 2 vols.

Scottish History, 1714-1815

For the literature of Jacobitism consult the full bibliography in C. S. Terry, *The Rising of 1745* (ed. 1903), and *C. M. H.,* vi. (pp. 858-63) by the same author, which gives a full account of MS. and printed material ; also by the same author *Index to Papers Relating to Scotland in the Hist. MS. Commission* (a most useful analysis). A select critical bibliography for the period will be found in P. Hume Brown, *History of Scotland* (Camb. Hist. Series), vol. iii. The student should also examine the publications of the Scottish History Society, the New Spalding, Abbotsford, Maitland, Roxburghe and Wodrow Clubs, which have printed, under competent editors, a great mass of MS. material ; also the volumes of *The Scottish Historical Review.*

As an introduction consult :—

Argyll, Duke of.—*Scotland as It Was and as It Is,* 2 vols.
P. Hume Brown.—*History of Scotland,* vol. iii.
J. Hill Burton.—*History of Scotland,* vol. viii.
*Cockburn, Lord.—*Memorials of His Times.*
H. Craik, Sir.—*A Century of Scottish History,* 2 vols.
H. G. Graham.—*Social Life in Scotland in the 18th Century,* 2 vols.
A. Lang.—*History of Scotland,* vol. iv.
W. L. Mathieson.—*Scotland and the Union,* 1695-1747, 2 vols.
G. W. T. Omond.—*The Lord Advocates of Scotland,* 2 vols.

Military and Naval History, 1714-1760

For naval material consult Scargill-Bird, *op. cit.,* pp. 370-76, and *Select Index,* xviii. (Public Rec. Off.), on *The Admiralty Records.* A bibliography will be found in *C. M. H.,* vi., pp. 885, 910. The student should consult the articles in *D. N. B.,* by J. K. Laughton, on naval commanders. Besides the works of Corbett and Mahan, cited above, the following are useful :—

M. Burrows.—*Life of Lord Hawke* (2nd ed.).
G. Chevalier.—*Histoire de la Marine Française* (to 1763).
*J. S. Corbett.—*Fighting Instructions,* 1530-1816 (Navy Rec. Soc.).
W. James.—*The Naval History of Great Britain,* 6 vols. (with index by Toogood (Navy Rec. Soc.), vol. iv.).
W. Laird Clowes.—*History of the Royal Navy,* vol. iii.

For military history, see classification of documents in Scargill-Bird, pp. 388-90 ; and the introductions and appendices to J. W. Fortescue, *History of the British Army,* vol. ii. (based on MS. and printed material and very stimulating reading), which is the best narrative both of military operations and the inner history of the army. For the operations 1740-48 and 1756-63 consult also C. T. Atkinson, *History of Germany*, 1713-1815 ; F. H. Skrine, *Fontenoy ;* and for colonial operations, A. G. Bradley, *Wolfe and the Fight with France for North America ;* A. Doughty and G. W. Parmelee, *The Siege of Quebec*, 6 vols. ; F. Parkman, *Montcalm and Wolfe.* [See also section below on Colonial History.]

Colonial History, 1714-1760

A full bibliography of MS. and printed material will be found in *C. M. H.*, vol. vii., to chapters ii., iii., iv. ; also supplementary in *C. M. H.*, vi., pp. 874-77. The standard work is : J. A. Doyle, *The American Colonies*, 1714-60 ; which the student can supplement first by—

*W. L. Grant and J. Munro.—*Acts of the Privy Council of England*, Colonial Series, vol. ii. (to 1720).

W. J. Ashley.—*Surveys : Historic and Economic.*

G. L. Beer.—*Commercial Policy of England towards the American Colonies.*
    ,,   *British Colonial Policy*, 1754-65.

H. Egerton.—*History of Colonial Policy* (2nd ed.).

H. Hall.—*Chatham's Colonial Policy (Amer. Hist. Rev.*, July, 1900).

G. B. Hertz.—*The Old Colonial System.*

G. Kimball.—*Correspondence of W. Pitt with Colonial Governors*, 2 vols.

C. Lucas, Sir.—*Historical Geography of the British Colonies* (with useful Select Critical Bibliographies) : West Indies, vol. ii. ; West Africa, vol. iii. ; S. and E. Africa, vol. iv. (2 pts.) ; Canada, vol. v. (pt. i.).

F. Parkman.—*La Salle and the Discovery of the Great West.*
    ,,   *The Old Régime in Canada.*

Indian History

Consult the bibliography in *C. M. H.*, vi., pp. 925-32. A general history of the East India Company based on modern critical research is much needed. The student may refer to :—

A. J. Arbuthnot, Sir.—*Lord Clive.*

P. Cultru.—*Dupleix.*

*G. W. Forrest.—*Selections from State Papers* (Bombay).

*   ,,   *Selections from State Papers* (Mahratta Series).

A. D. Innes.—*A Short History of the British in India.*

A. C. Lyall.—*The Rise and Expansion of the British Dominions in India.*

G. B. Malleson.—*The History of the French in India.*

J. Mill.—*The History of British India*, ed. H. Wilson, 10 vols.

H. Weber.—*La Compagnie Française des Indes.*

Economic and Social History, 1714-1760

Useful bibliographies in *C. M. H.*, vi., pp. 850, 855, 874, 875. Cunningham.—*Growth of English Industry and Commerce, Modern Times*, 2 vols.—P. Mantoux.—*La Révolution Industrielle.* The statistics and explanatory matter in *Public Income and Expenditure*, 1688-1869 (Cd. 1869, Parliamentary

Paper, over 1000 pages) are indispensable. Consult also : J. P. Anderson. —*Classified Catalogue of the Topographical Works in Library of British Museum Relating to Great Britain and Ireland* (1881); *Calendar of Treasury Papers*, 1714-28, 2 vols. ; *Calendar of Treasury Books and Papers*, 1728-45, 5 vols. Consult also :—

A. Anderson.—*Historical and Chronological Deduction of the Origin of Commerce*, 4 vols.

J. Andreades.—*History of the Bank of England* (English translation).

N. A. Brisco.—*The Economic Policy of R. Walpole.*

*J. Brown.—*Estimate of the Manners and Principles of the Times.*

*D. Defoe.—*Tour through the Whole Island of Great Britain.*

*F. M. Eden.—*The State of the Poor*, 3 vols.

F. G. Price.—*A Handbook of London Bankers*, 1677-1876.

R. E. Prothero.—*Pioneers of Agriculture and Farming.*

Th. Rogers.—*Six Centuries of Work and Wages.*

,,   *A History of Agriculture and Prices*, vol. vii.

*C. de Saussure.—*A Foreign View of England under George I. and II.* (English translation).

G. Schmoller.—*The Mercantile System* (English translation).

*J. Sinclair.—*History of the Public Revenue*, 3 vols.

*A. Smith.—*The Wealth of Nations* (2nd vol., ed. E. Cannon).

S. and B. Webb.—*English Local Government* (1688-1834), 3 vols.

T. Wright.—*Caricature History of the Georges.*

Religion : The Established Church and Dissent

Useful bibliographies will be found in *C. M. H.*, vi., pp. 851-57. Leslie Stephen.—*History of English Thought in the Eighteenth Century*, 2 vols. J. H. Overton and F. Ralton.—*The English Church* (1714-1800) (the most convenient text-book on this subject). For Wesley and Wesleyanism consult : R. Green.—*Bibliography of Works of John and Charles Wesley* (new ed., 1906); *Anti-Methodist Publications during the Eighteenth Century* (1902). The *Wesley Historical Society (from 1896) has published valuable material. **John Wesley's Works* (15 vols., London, 1856) have been published. A new edition of his **Journal* in 6 vols. (4 published) is being brought out, and is the best material for understanding the man. Useful general works (besides those mentioned above) are :—

C. J. Abbey and J. H. Overton.—*The English Church and Its Bishops*, 1700-1800, 2 vols.

R. W. Dale.—*History of Congregationalism in England.*

T. Lathbury.—*History of the Non-Jurors.*

J. H. Overton.—*The English Church in the Eighteenth Century*, 2 vols.

L. Tyerman.—*J. Wesley's Life and Times*, 3 vols.

,,   *The Oxford Methodists*, 2 vols.

,,   *Life of George Whitefield*, 2 vols.

The works of * Berkeley (ed. Fraser, 4 vols.), * Butler (ed. Bernard, 2 vols.), * Hoadly (3 vols.), * Law (9 vols.), * Warburton, are available in collected editions.

PART II. (1760-1815)

Many of the authorities specified in Part I. belong also to Part II. They are not repeated in the several sections below, which are strictly additional. The student should, therefore, refer back to the corresponding section in Part I. for general information or particular books.

MSS.—In the British Museum the chief MSS. are : Nelson MS. (Egerton 1614-1623, add. 18, 676) ; Wellesley (Egerton 12, 564-13, 915 and add. 29, 238-239) ; Warren Hastings (add. 28, 973-29, 236) ; Wilkes (add. 30, 865-30, 896) ; Sir R. Wilson (30, 095-30, 144) ; Hutchinson (Egerton 2659-2666) ; Sir W. Hamilton (Egerton 2634-2641) ; Mackintosh (add. 34, 487-34, 526) ; Auckland (add. 34, 412-34, 471 and 34, 435-34, 453) ; Bute (36, 801-36, 813, 37, 080-37, 085) ; Place MSS. (add. 27, 789-27, 859) ; Leeds MSS. (27, 918, 28, 570, 28, 064-28, 067) ; Reeves MSS. (16, 919-16, 929).

In the Record Office the special printed Catalogue, List XIX, of State Papers only goes as far as 1782. Valuable indications as to particular volumes and particular countries bearing on specific problems and periods will be found in the bibliographies in *C. M. H.*, vols. viii. and ix. ; F. Salomon, *William Pitt der Jüngere*, vol. i. (to 1793) ; J. H. Rose, *Life of Napoleon*, 2 vols. ; W. H. V. Temperley, *Life of Canning*. The following articles by J. H. Rose in the *Eng. Hist. Review* should also be consulted : *Napoleon and English Commerce* (viii, 704) ; *Canning and Denmark* (xi, 82) ; *The Secret Articles of the Treaty of Amiens* (xv, 331) ; *France and the First Coalition* (xviii, 287) ; *The Commercial Treaty of* 1786 (xxiii, 709) ; *William Grenville's Mission to the Hague and Versailles* (xxiv, 278) ; *Pitt and the Campaign of* 1793 (xxiv, 744). A very useful list of the pamphlet literature 1789-1897 will be found in W. T. Laprade, *England and the French Revolution* (Johns Hopkins Studies, Ser. xxvii, Nos. 8-12).

I. *Home and Foreign Policy*

[The general history of the European States in their relations to Great Britain will be most usefully studied in : C. A. Fyffe, *A History of Modern Europe* (3 vols.) ; W. Oncken, *Das Zeitalter der Revolution, des Kaissereichs und der Befreiungskriege* (2 vols.) ; A. Sorel, *L'Europe et la Révolution Française* (8 vols.), and the various chapters on the European States in *C. M. H.*, vols. vi. (1714-89) ; viii. (1789-1801) ; ix. (1801-15).]

Consult, also, *J. Debrett, *A Collection of State Papers Relative to the War against France*, 11 vols., 1794-1802 ; *Rose, *Despatches relating to the Third Coalition* (Roy. Hist. Soc., 1904). The **State Papers (Domestic)*, 1760-75 (4 vols.), have been calendared. Useful secondary authorities are :—

J. Adolphus, *History of England* (1760-1820), 7 vols.

**The Annual Register*, 1760 *et seqq.*

G. C. Brodrick and J. K. Fotheringham.—*Political History of England,* vol. xi.

P. Coquelle.—*Napoléon et l'Angleterre*, 1803-15.

M. Dorman.—*History of the British Empire.*

W. Hunt.—*Political History of England*, vol. x. (1760-1801).

H. Jephson.—*The Platform : Its Rise and Progress.*

W. T. Laprade.—*England and the French Revolution* (Johns Hopkins Studies, Aug.-Dec., 1909).

J. McCarthy.—*History of the Four Georges.*

H. Martineau.—*History of England* (1800-15).

E. Smith.—*The Story of the English Jacobins.*

W. Massey.—*History of England in the Reign of George III.*

From the numerous Biographies, Memoirs, Correspondence, etc., the following may be chosen :—

*Addington (Lord Sidmouth).—*Life and Corresp.*, ed. G. Pellew, 3 vols.

The Anti-Jacobin, 36 nos., 1797-98.

*Auckland.—*Journal and Correspondence*, 4 vols.

*M. Bateson.—*Changes in the Ministry*, Camden Series, 1898.

*Bland-Burges.—*Letters and Life*, Ed. J. Hutton.

*Buckingham.—*Memoirs of the Courts and Cabinets of George III.*, 4 vols.

Buckinghamshire : Papers (1762-65) of the Earl of.   Royal Hist. Soc., 1900.

*Brougham.—*Life and Times*, by himself, vols. i. and ii.

*E. Burke.—*Works*, 6 vols. (London, 1826).

*   „   *Correspondence.*   Ed. Lord Fitzwilliam, 4 vols.

      „   *Memoir*, by T. MacKnight, 3 vols.

      „   *A Political Study*, by J. Morley.

G. Canning.—*Political Life*, by A. G. Stapleton, 3 vols.

*   „   *Correspondence.*   Ed. Stapleton, 2 vols.

*   „   *Speeches.*   Ed. Therry, 6 vols.

G. Canning and His Friends, ed. Bagot, 2 vols.

      „   *Lives of*, by J. A. R. Marriott and H. W. T. Temperley.

*Castlereagh (Viscount).—*Memoirs and Correspondence*, 12 vols.

Castlereagh (Viscount) : Life of, by Sir A. Alison, 3 vols.

Castlereagh (Viscount).—*A Study*, by Marchioness of Londonderry.

W. Cobbett : *Life of*, by E. I. Carlyle.

Coke (Earl of Leicester) : Life of, by A. M. Stirling, 2 vols.

*Colchester.—*Diary*, 2 vols.

*Cornwallis (Marquis of).—*Correspondence*, 3 vols.

The Creevey Papers, ed. Sir H. Maxwell, 2 vols.

*G. B. Doddington (Lord Melcombe).—*Diary.*

*Eldon.—*Life and Letters*, by H. Twiss, 3 vols.

*Elliot (Earl of Minto).—*Memoir*, by Countess of Minto, 3 vols.

*Erskine (Lord).—*Speeches*, 4 vols.

C. J. Fox : *Early Life of*, by Sir G. O. Trevelyan.

*C. J. Fox.—*Memorials and Correspondence*, ed. Ld. J. Russell, 4 vols.

C. J. Fox : *Life of*, by Ld. J. Russell, 3 vols.

*C. J. Fox.—*Speeches*, 6 vols.

C. J. Fox : *A Study of*, by J. L. D. Hammond.

*George III.—*Correspondence with Lord North*, ed. Donne, 2 vols.

George III. : *Memoirs of the Life and Reign of*, by J. H. Jesse, 3 vols.

George IV. and Mrs. Fitzherbert, by W. H. Wilkins, 2 vols.

*Gower.—*Despatches of the Earl*, ed. O. B. Browning.

*Grafton (Duke of).—*Autobiography*, ed. W. R. Anson.

*Holland (Lord).—*Memoirs of the Whig Party*, 2 vols.
*   „   *Further Memoirs*, ed. Lord Stavordale.
*Holland (Lady).—*Diary*, 2 vols.
*Jackson (*Sir G.*) : *Letters and Papers of*, 2 vols.
*Junius.—*Letters*, 2 vols. ; London, 1904.
*Leeds (*Duke of*) : *Political Memoranda of*, ed. O. B. Browning.
*Lennox (*Lady Sarah*) : *Letters of*, ed. Lord Stavordale, 2 vols.
*Mackintosh (Sir J.).—*Memoirs*, 2 vols.
*Malmesbury (Earl of).—*Diaries and Correspondence*, 4 vols.
W. Pitt : *Life of*, by Earl Stanhope, 4 vols.
     „   „   by F. Salomon (to 1793), vol. i. (In German, not translated.)
*W. Pitt.—*Correspondence with Duke of Rutland*.
*   „   *Speeches*, 4 vols.
     „   *Some Chapters of His Life*, by Ld. Ashbourne.
W. Pitt : *Life of*, by Lord Rosebery.
F. Place : *Life of*, by Graham Wallas.
*Rockingham (Marquis of).—*Memoirs*, ed. Lord Albemarle, 2 vols.
*Romilly (Sir S.).—*Memoirs*, 3 vols.
*G. Rose.—*Diaries and Correspondence*, ed. Harcourt, 2 vols.
G. Selwyn and His Contemporaries, by J. H. Jesse, 4 vols.
*G. Selwyn.—*Letters and Life,* ed. Roscoe and Clergue.
     „   *Title and Letters*, 2 vols.
Shelburne (*Lord, Marquis of Lansdowne*), *Life of*, by Lord E. Fitzmaurice, 3 vols.
*R. B. Sheridan.—*Speeches*, 5 vols.
R. B. Sheridan, *Life of*, by W. F. Rae, 2 vols.
     „   „   by W. Sichel, 2 vols.
*H. Walpole.—*Memoirs of the Reign of George III.*, ed. Le Marchant, 4 vols.
*W. Wilberforce.—*Correspondence*, 2 vols.
W. Wilberforce, *Life of*, by R. and S. Wilberforce, 5 vols.
*   „   *Private Papers of*, ed. A. M. Wilberforce.
*W. Windham.—*Diary*, ed. Mrs. Baring.
*   „   *Speeches*, ed. Amyot, 3 vols.
*N. W. Wraxall (Sir).—*Historical Memoirs of His Own Time*, 4 vols.

Historical MSS. Commission Reports (No. of Report in Roman figures, of the Appendices in numerals).—*Dropmore Papers*, 6 vols. *Dartmouth MSS.*, xi., 5; xiii., 4; xiv., 10; xv., vol. i. *Rutland MSS.*, xii., 4 and 5; xiv., vol. 3. *Kenyon MSS.*, xiv., 4. *Carlisle MSS.*, xv., 6. *Stopford-Sackville MSS.*, ix., 3; xvi., 2 vols. *Ailesbury MSS.*, xv., 7. *Bagot MSS.*, x., 4. *Bath MSS.*, xvi., xvii., 2 vols. *Ancaster MSS.*, xvii., 1 vol. *Charlemont MSS.*, xii., 10; xiii., 8. *Lansdowne*, ii., iii., iv., v., vi., with respective appendices. *Leeds MSS.*, xi., 7. *Townshend MSS.*, xi., 4. *Round MSS.*, xiv., 9. *Weston-Underwood MSS.*, x., i. *Du Cane MSS.*, xvi., 2. *Savile-Foljambe MSS.*, xv., 5. *Lothian MSS.*, xvi., vol. i. *Abergavenny MSS.*, x. 6. *Ketton MSS.*, xii. 9.

Constitutional and Parliamentary History.

For the Parliament of 1768-71 consult : *H. Cavendish.—*Debates in the Unreported Parliament* (with *Journal of Fourth Duke of Bedford*), ed. by J.
35

Wright. These shorthand notes were continued to 1774, but for 1771-74 have never been printed from B. M. MS. Egerton, 215-62. For general and other works see :—

*J. Almon.—*Political Register* (1767-72), 11 vols.
*   „   *History of the Late Minority.*
A. V. Dicey.—*The Law of the Constitution.*
H. R. Fox-Bourne.—*English Newspapers,* vol. i.
C. B. Kent.—*The English Radicals.*
G. C. Lewis (Sir).—*Essays on the Administration of Great Britain* (1783-1830).
T. E. May.—*Constitutional History of England from 1760,* 3 vols.
Revolution Society, The Correspondence of, London.
S. and B. Webb.—*English Local Government from the Revolution to the Municipal Corporation Acts,* 3 vols. (Invaluable and indispensable.)
*J. Wilkes.—*Complete Collection of Genuine Papers and Letters,* London, 1767.
*   „   *Correspondence and Memoirs,* ed. J. Almon, 5 vols.
*C. Wyvill.—*Political Papers,* 3 vols.

Military History

The most useful general book is the Hon. Sir J. W. Fortescue, *History of the British Army,* vols. 3-5, which gives valuable information on authorities, MS. and printed. For the Peninsular War : Sir W. Napier, *History of the War in the Peninsula* (6 vols.), and C. W. C. Oman, *History of the Peninsular War,* are indispensable. Consult also . * *The Diary of Sir J. Moore,* ed. J. F. Maurice, 2 vols. A good bibliography of the extensive literature will be found in *C. M. H.,* ix., pp. 851-53, by Professor Oman. For the Waterloo campaign (bibliography in *C. M. H.,* ix., pp. 876-77) consult especially : G. Chesney, *Waterloo Lectures;* F. von Clausewitz, *Der Feldzug von 1815* (works, vol. 8); H. Houssaye, *Waterloo;* J. C. Ropes, *The Campaign of Waterloo;* and J. H. Rose, *Life of Napoleon,* vol. ii. The Dispatches of Wellington have been published : *Dispatches,* ed. Col. Gurwood, 8 vols. ; *Supplementary Dispatches,* ed. by his son, 15 vols. Consult also : J. W. Fortescue, *The County Lieutenancies and the Army.*

Naval History

Consult the full bibliographies in *C. M. H.,* vii., pp. 782; viii., pp. 821-26; ix., pp. 816-23. The following * volumes of the *Navy Records Society* are particularly useful : J. K. Laughton, *Official Documents on Social Life;* T. S. Jackson, *Logs of the Great Sea Fights,* 1794-1805 ; J. S. Corbett, *Signals and Instructions,* 1776-94 ; Lord Barham, *Letters and Papers,* 1758-1813 ; J. Leyland, *Dispatches and Letters Relating to the Blockade of Brest.* Nelson's *Dispatches and Letters* have been published and edited by Sir H. Nicholas (7 vols.).

Good general works are :—
P. Coquelle.—*La descente en Angleterre.*
E. Desbrière.—*Projets et Tentatives de débarquement aux Îles Britanniques* (1793-1805), 5 vols.
      „   *La Campagne de Trafalgar.*

A. T. Mahan.—*The Influence of Sea Power during the Wars of the Revolutionary and Napoleonic Epoch*, 2 vols.
	„	*Life of Nelson* (2nd ed.), 2 vols.
J. K. Laughton.—*Nelson.*	(See also article in *D. N. B.*)
H. Newbolt.—*The Year of Trafalgar.*
J. R. Thursfield.—*Trafalgar and Other Naval Studies.*

Colonial History

A. *The American Colonies to 1783.*—A full bibliography of the extensive literature will be found in *C. M. H.*, vii., pp. 753-88.	No less valuable and indispensable are : J. Winsor, *Narrative and Critical History of America*, vols. 5, 6, 7 ; *The Reader's Handbook of the American Revolution;* J. Larned, *The Literature of American History* (a bibliographical guide, with supplement for 1900 and 1901 by Walls) ; J. N. James, *The Literature of American History;* M. C. Tyler, *The Literary History of the American Revolution.*	In the Hist. MSS. Comm., the *Dartmouth MSS.*, xi., 5 ; xiv., 10 ; the *Shelburne MSS.*, v. ; the *Stopford-Sackville MSS.*, xvi., vol. ii. ; and the *Dorchester MSS.* (*Report on the American MSS.* in the Royal Institution, 3 vols.) bear particularly on America.

The most useful general works are :—
G. Bancroft.—*History of the United States*, 6 vols. (the old view).
E. Channing.—*The United States of America*, 1765-1865 (Camb. Hist. Series).
J. Fiske.—*The American Revolution*, 2 vols.
A. B. Hart.—*American History told by Contemporaries*, 4 vols.
G. O. Trevelyan.—*The American Revolution*, 3 vols. (an English Pro-American view).
F. S. Oliver.—*Alexander Hamilton.*
C. H. Van Tyne.—*The Loyalists in the American Revolution.*

The following biographies in the American Statesmen Series are very useful : *Samuel Adams* (J. K. Hormer), *Alex. Hamilton* (H. C. Lodge), *Washington* (H. C. Lodge), *Jefferson* (J. T. Moore), *Franklin* (J. T. Moore), *Patrick Henry* (M. C. Tyler), together with F. S. Oliver, *Alexander Hamilton* ; F. V. Greene, *General Greene*, and the standard *Life of Washington*, in 5 vols., by J. Marshall.

B. *The British Colonies and Dependencies.*
[Consult the bibliographies in *C. M. H.*, ix., pp. 883-91, and x., pp. 871-78, and the select list in H. E. Egerton, *op. cit. infra.*]
The most useful general works are :—
J. Bourinot.—*Canada under British Rule*, 1760-1900.
	„	*Manual of the Constitutional History of Canada.*
Brougham (Lord).—*The Colonial Policy of European Powers*, 2 vols.
G. Bryce.—*History of the Hudson's Bay Company.*
*A. G. Doughty.—*Constitutional Documents of Canada* (1760-1791).
B. Edwards.—*History of British Colonies in the West Indies*, 3 vols.
H. E. Egerton.—*A Short History of British Colonial Policy*, 2nd ed.
*H. E. Egerton and W. L. Grant.—*Canadian Constitutional Development* (selected original documents)

E. Jenks.—*A History of the Australian Colonies.*
H. H. Johnston.—*A History of the Colonisation of Africa.*
W. Kingsford.—*History of Canada,* 10 vols.
P. Leroy Beaulieu.—*De la Colonisation chez les Peuples Modernes,* 2 vols.
C. Lucas.—*The War of 1812,* 2 vols.
A. T. Mahan.—*The War of 1812 in Its Relation to Sea-Power,* 2 vols.
G. M. Theal.—*History of South Africa,* 5 vols.
G. Zimmermann.—*Die Europaischen Kolonien,* 5 vols.

India

[For works on Warren Hastings see Appendix.]
The *Rulers of India* Series supplies useful short biographies (with select bibliographies): *Sir T. Munro,* by J. Bradshaw ; *Haidar Ali and Tipu Sultan,* by L. C. Bowring ; *Mountstuart Elphinstone,* by J. S. Cotton ; *Ranjit Singh,* by Sir Lepel Griffin ; *Wellesley,* by W. H. Hutton ; *Sindhia,* by H. G. Keene ; *Marquess of Hastings,* by Major Ross. See also the bibliography in *C. M. H.,* ix., 883-86. The following are useful authorities :—
*Cornwallis (Marquis).—*Correspondence,* 3 vols.
Fifth Report of Select Committee of House of Commons on the East India Company, 1812.
G. B. Malleson.—*Final French Struggles in India.*
J. Malcolm, Sir.—*The Political History of India,* 1784-1823, 2 vols.
*Teignmouth (Lord).—*Life and Correspondence,* 2 vols.
*Wellington *(Indian) Dispatches,* ed. Gurwood, 5 vols.

Economics and Finance

For the Industrial Revolution consult the bibliographies in *C. M. H.,* x., pp. 883-92, Cunningham and Mantoux, *op. cit. supra;* also articles in Palgrave, *Dictionary of Political Economy,* 3 vols., and for the Labour Movement S. and B. Webb, *History of Trade Unionism.* The Webb MSS., collected by these last two authors, a very valuable collection of transcripts, pamphlets, etc., are in the British Library of Political Science, London School of Economics. J. R. Macculloch, *The Literature of Political Economy* (a classified catalogue, London, 1845), is a valuable help. Of contemporary works the following will probably be most useful to the student :—
*W. Cobbett.—*Rural Rides* (new ed., 1853).
*F. M. Eden.—*The State of the Poor,* 1797.
*T. R. Malthus.—*An Essay on the Principle of Population* (1798 ; second edition, 1803).
*W. Marshall.—*The Rural Economy of Norfolk* (1787), *Midland Counties* (1790), *Southern Counties* (1798).
J. S. Nicholson.—*A Project of Empire* (a valuable exposition of Adam Smith).
*D. Ricardo.—*The High Price of Bullion, a Proof of Depreciation of Bank-notes* (1809).
Report on the High Price of Gold, Parlt. Reports, 1810.
W. A. Shaw.—*The History of Currency* (1252-94).
*A. Smith.—*Lectures on Justice, Police, Revenue, and Arms* (1763), ed. by E. Cannan (1896).

*J. Steuart.—*An Inquiry into the Principles of Political Economy*, 2 vols., 1767.

*A. Young.—*Tours in England*, 5 vols., *in Ireland*, 2 vols.

Of Secondary Authorities consult :—

J. B. Bonar.—*Malthus and His Work.*

E. Cannan.—*A History of the Theories of Production and Distribution in English Political Economy from 1776-1848.*

L. Faucher.—*Études sur l'Angleterre*, 2 vols.

A. Held.—*Zwei Bücher zur Socialen Geschichte Englands.*

W. Hasbach.—*Die Englischen Landarbeiter in den Letzten hundert Jahren und die Einhägungen.*

A. H. Johnson.—*The Disappearance of the Small Landowner.*

H. Levy.—*Enstehung und Rückgang der Landwirthschaftlichen Grossbetuites.*

G. R. Porter.—*Progress of the Nation.*

G. Slater.—*The English Peasantry and the Enclosure of Common Fields.*

W. Tooke.—*A History of Prices and of the State of the Currency.*

A. Toynbee.—*Lectures on the Industrial Revolution.*

Abstract of the Answers and Returns to the Population Act, 41 Geo. III., 2 vols., London, 1802.

Political Thought, 1714-1815

The most useful general works are Leslie Stephen : *A History of Thought in the Eighteenth Century*, 2 vols.; and the same writer's *The English Utilitarians*, 3 vols. (particularly vols. 1 and 2). But the student can most profitably refer to the following * contemporary writers :—

B. Beccaria.—*Dei Delitte et delle Pene* (1764, English translation), 2 vols., 1769.

J. Bentham.—*Works*, ed. J. Bowring, 11 vols. (particularly, *A Fragment on Government*, ed. F. C. Montague ; *The Introduction to Principles of Morals and Legislation ; Théorie des Peines et des Recompenses*).

G. Berkeley.—*Works*, ed. A. C. Fraser, 4 vols.

W. Blackstone.—*Commentaries on the Laws of England*, 1765.

Bolingbroke (Viscount).—*Works*, 9 vols. (particularly *Dissertation upon Parties, The Idea of a Patriot King, Letters on the Study and Use of History*).

E. Burke.—16 vols., 1826-27 (particularly *Thoughts on the Present Discontents, Speeches on America, Reflections on the French Revolution, Appeal from the New to the Old Whigs*).

J. Cartwright.—*Legislative Rights of the Commonalty Vindicated*, 1777.

De Lolme.—*Constitution de l'Angleterre*, 1785.

A. Ferguson.—*Essay on the History of Civil Society*, 1783.

,,　　　 *Principles of Moral and Political Science*, 1792.

G. Filangieri.—*La Scienza della Legislazione*, 1780.

Mary Godwin.—*Vindication of the Rights of Woman*, 1792.

W. Godwin.—*Enquiry Concerning Political Justice*, 1796.

D. Hume.—*Essays and Treatises* (1758), ed. T. H. Green and T. H. Grose, 2 vols., 1875.

W. Jones.—*The Principles of Government* (2nd ed.), 1797.

J. Mackintosh.—*Vindiciae Gallicae*, 1791.
   „   *Discourse on the Law of Nature and Nations*, 1799.
T. R. Malthus.—*Essay on the Principle of Population*, 1798.
C. de Montesquieu.—*Esprit des Lois*, 1748.
T. Paine.—*Common Sense*, 1776 (*Works*, ed. by M. D. Conway, 4 vols., 1896).
   „   *The Rights of Man*, 1791.
W. Paley.—*The Principles of Moral and Political Philosophy*, 2 vols., 1790.
R. Price.—*The Nature of Civil Liberty and the Principles of Government*, 1776.
J. Priestley.—*Essay on the First Principles of Government*, 1768.
   „   *Letters to Burke*, 1791.
   „   *View of the Principles and Conduct of Dissenters*, 1769.
S. Romilly.—*Memoirs*, 3 vols., 1840.
   „   *Speeches*, 2 vols., 1820.
S. Romilly on the Criminal Law, 1811.
T. Spence.—*The Nationalization of the Land*, 1775.
J. Swift.—*Works*, ed. Sir W. Scott, 19 vols.

SUPPLEMENT

Note.—This supplement deals with books or articles since 1911, *i.e.* from 1911 to 1929, and therefore is additional in each section to the relevant section in the Bibliography that precedes. It is *not* a list of *all* books, documents, etc., on the eighteenth century which have appeared between 1911 and 1929, but of those which, in the writer's judgment, will be particularly helpful or bear on points dealt with in the text. Books or articles specified in the notes to the text or in the Appendices are *not* repeated here. Most of the books mentioned below have separate bibliographies of great value.

ATLASES

C. G. Robertson and J. G. Bartholomew.—*Historical Atlas of Modern Europe*, 1789-1922. (With historical Introduction.)
Ramsay Muir and G. Philip.—*Historical Atlas, Medieval and Modern*. (With historical Introduction 1928.)
Vol. XII. *of the Cambridge Modern History* (1911) contains useful genealogical tables, lists of officers, etc., and a general Index.
The Catalogue issued by H.M. Stationery Office gives complete information about Govt. Publications, *e.g.* Hist. MSS. Commission Reports, etc.
The two vols. of *The Subject Catalogue of the London Library* ought to be in every working Library.

CONSTITUTIONAL HISTORY AND POLITICAL THOUGHT

Consult : *A Short Bibliography of English Constitutional History* by Helen M. Camm and A. S. Turberville (Hist. Association, 1929).

D. J. Medley.—*English Constitutional History* (Revised ed. 1925).
C. E. Vaughan.—*Studies in History of Political Philosophy* (2 vols. 1925).
E. R. Turner—*Privy Council and Cabinet in the XVIIth and XVIIIth Centuries* (1928).

J. A. Farrer.—*The Monarchy in Politics,* 1760-1901 (1917).

J. B. Scott.—*The Armed Neutralities of* 1780 and 1800 (1919).

D. A. Winstanley.—*Personal and Party Government* (1913).

K. G. Feiling.—*A History of the Tory Party,* 1640-1714.

F. K. Brown.—*Life of William Godwin.*

E. Halévy.—*The Growth of Philosophic Radicalism* (Engl. trans.), 1776-1815.

C. G. Robertson.—*Select Documents on Constitutional History,* 1660-1832. Fifth Rev. ed. 1928.

BIOGRAPHIES, MEMOIRS, LETTERS, ETC.

The Windham Papers (1750-1810).

Countess Granville.—*Correspondence of First Earl Granville,* 1781-1821, 2 vols., 1916.

M. Percival.—*Political Ballads illustrating the Administration of Sir R. Walpole* (1917).

J. M. Robertson.—*Bolingbroke and Walpole* (1920).

T. W. Riker.—*Henry Fox,* 1st Lord Holland (2 vols., 1913).

Earl of Ilchester.—*Henry Fox,* 2 vols. (1920).

Earl of Rosebery.—*Chatham, his Early Life and Connections* (1912).

A. Greenwood.—*Lives of the Hanoverian Queens of England,* vol. ii. (completes the work mentioned in previous bibliography).

Joseph Farrington's Diary, ed. J. Greig, 1792-1821, 8 vols.

Memoirs of William Hickey, ed. A. Spencer, 1749-1809, 4 vols.

C. Charteris.—*Life of Duke of Cumberland* (1925).

P. Yvon.—*Vie d'Horace Walpole* (1925).

R. Coupland.—*Wilberforce* (1924).

Winifred Duke.—*Lord George Murray and the Forty-Five* (1927).

Earl of Ilchester.—*Life of Sir Ch. Hanbury-Williams* (1928).

G. M. Trevelyan.—*Life of Charles, Second Earl Grey* (Grey of the Reform Bill), 1920.

British Diplomatic Instructions

Sweden, 1689-1727 ; France, 1689-1721 and 1721-27 ; Denmark, 1689-1789 : (vols. 32, 35, 36, 38 of Camden Series in Royal Hist. Soc. Publications.

H. W. C. Davis.—*The Age of Grey and Peel* (1929, Oxford Ford Lectures).

FOREIGN AND POLITICAL HISTORY

Consult Bibliography in *Cambridge History of British Foreign Policy,* vol. i., and relevant articles in that volume ; R. A. Roberts, *Guide to the Hist. MSS. Comm. Reports* (1920) and the notes to the various chapters in the text.

C. K. Webster.—*The Congress of Vienna* (1918).

   ,,   *British Diplomacy* 1813-15.

Select Documents (1922).

Military and Naval History

G. E. Manwaring.—*A Bibliography of British Naval History* (1929).
(This bibliography is indispensable to all students of naval history.)
Hon. Sir. J. W. Fortescue.—*History of the British Army*, vols. 8, 9 and 10
        (1913-20). (The other volumes of this
        great work deal with events after 1815.
     ,,   *Wellington*, 1925. (A study by an expert.)
Sir C. Oman.—*History of the Peninsular War* (completing the history).
   ,,   *Wellington's Army*, 1913. (Indispensable.)
   ,,   *Studies in the Napoleonic Wars*, 1929.
H. Belcher.—*The First American Civil War.* 2 vols. (1913).
Navy Records Society (for details see Manwaring, *op. cit.*, above).
G. Callender.—*The Naval Side of British History* (1925).

Imperial and Colonial History

   Consult the Bibliography in *Cambridge History of the British Empire*,
vol. i., 1929, particularly p. 839 for the references to Miss Davenport, *Hist.
MSS. Commission Report*, xviii., pp. 357-97.

K. Hotblack.—*Chatham's Colonial Policy* (1917).
M. E. Monckton-Jones.—*Warren Hastings in Bengal* (1918).
L. Knowles.—*Economic Development of the British Overseas Empire* (1925).
R. Coupland.—*The Quebec Act—A Study in Statesmanship* (1925).
G. W. Forrest.—*Lord Cornwallis*, Introduction and Documents, 2 vols. (1926).
Cambridge History of the British Empire, vol. 5 (devoted to India), 1929.

   The American Colonies are dealt with in Appendix XX.

Economic and Social History

G. O'Brien.—*Economic History of Ireland in the Eighteenth Century* (1918).
M. Beer.—*History of British Socialism*, vol. i. (1919).
W. L. Mathieson.—*England in Transition*, 1789-1832 (1921).
    ,,   *The Awakening of Scotland*, 1747-97 (1913).
W. Smart.—*Economic Annals*, 1801-20 (1914).
E. C. K. Gonner.—*Common Lands and Enclosures* (1913).
H. W. Dickinson and Rhys Jenkins.—*James Watt* (Centenary Volume).

   The standard classical authority is now : B. and S. Webb, *English Local
Government from* 1688-1835—*e.g.* 1. The Parish and County ; 2. The Manor
and the Borough ; 3. The King's Highway ; 4. Statutory Authorities ;
5. Prisons ; 6. Poor Law History (1913-27).

SCOTLAND DURING JACOBITE RISINGS OF 1715 AND 1745

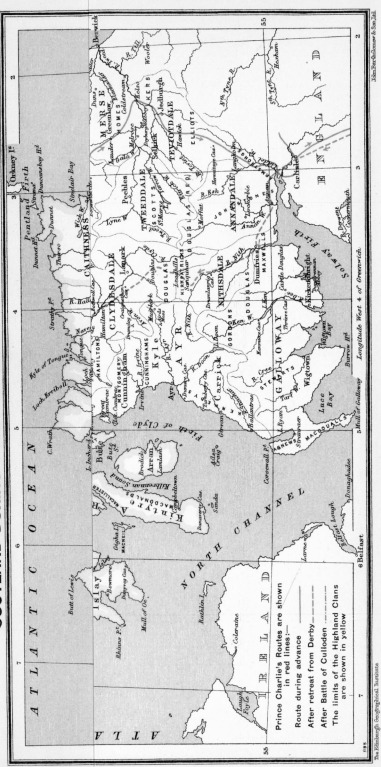

Prince Charlie's Routes are shown
in red lines:—
Route during advance
After retreat from Derby
After Battle of Culloden
The limits of the Highland Clans
are shown in yellow

The Edinburgh Geographical Institute

John Bartholomew & Son, Ltd.

Methuen & Co. Ltd. 36 Essex Street. London. W.C. 2.

Longitude West 4° of Greenwich

NORTH AMERICAN COLONIES, 1755-1763

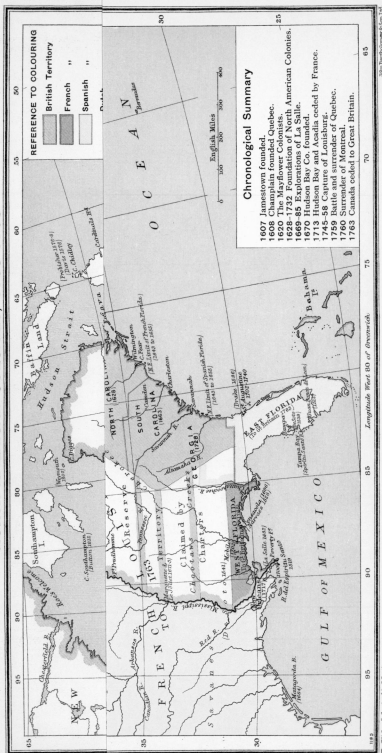

REFERENCE TO COLOURING

British Territory
French "
Spanish "
Dutch "

Chronological Summary

1607 Jamestown founded.
1608 Champlain founded Quebec.
1620 The Mayflower Colonists.
1628-1732 Foundation of North American Colonies.
1669-85 Explorations of La Salle.
1670 Hudson Bay Co. founded.
1713 Hudson Bay and Acadia ceded by France.
1745-58 Capture of Louisburg.
1759 Battle and surrender of Quebec.
1760 Surrender of Montreal.
1763 Canada ceded to Great Britain.

English Miles

0   100   200   300   400

Longitude West 80 of Greenwich

The Edinburgh Geographical Institute

John Bartholomew & Son,Ltd.

Methuen & Co.Ltd...36 Essex Street.London.W.C.2.

NORTH AMERICA, 1783

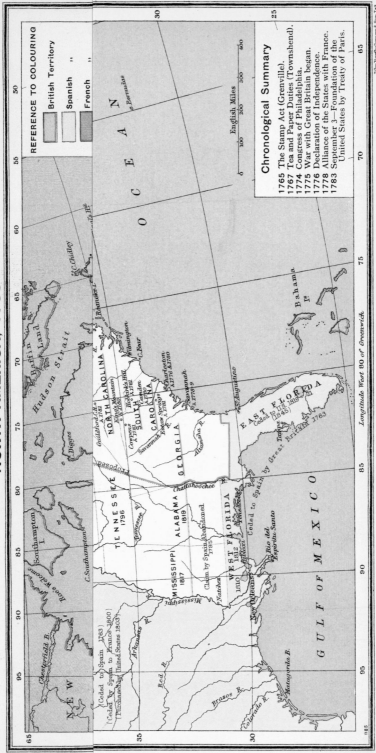

REFERENCE TO COLOURING

British Territory
Spanish   "
French   "

Chronological Summary

1765 The Stamp Act (Grenville).
1767 Tea and Paper Duties (Townshend).
1774 Congress of Philadelphia.
1775 War with Great Britain began.
1776 Declaration of Independence.
1778 Alliance of the States with France.
1783 September 3—Foundation of the
       United States by Treaty of Paris.

English Miles
0   100 200 300 400

OCEAN

Bermudas

Bahama Is.

GULF OF MEXICO

NEW

Baffin Land

Hudson Strait

Chesterfield B.

Southampton I.

Roes Welcome

C. Southampton

Digges

Chidley

Nelson R.

Matagorda B.

Colorado R.

Brazos R.

Red R.

Arkansas R.

Mississippi R.

New Orleans

Rio del Espiritu Santo

Natchez

Pensacola

Mobile

WEST FLORIDA
1810 1812

Claim by Spain abandoned
1795

Chattahoochee R.

EAST FLORIDA
Ceded to U.S. 1819-21

St. Augustine

Ceded to Spain by Great Britain 1783

ALABAMA
1819

MISSISSIPPI
1817

TENNESSEE
1796

Tennessee R.

GEORGIA

Savannah R.

SOUTH CAROLINA

Camden

Eutaw Springs
X 1781

Cowpens
X 1781

Kings Mountain
X 1780

Hobkirk's Hill
X 1781

Savannah
X 1779

Charleston
X 1776 & 1780

Alatamaha R.

NORTH CAROLINA

Guildford C.H.
X 1781

Wilmington

C. Fear

Roanoke I.

Proposed

(Ceded to Spain 1763)
(Ceded to France 1800)
(Purchased by United States 1803)

Longitude West 80 of Greenwich

The Edinburgh Geographical Institute

Methuen & Co.Ltd.36 Essex Street.London.W.C.2.

John Bartholomew & Son.Ltd.

INDEX

PRINTED IN GREAT BRITAIN AT THE UNIVERSITY PRESS, ABERDEEN